A Cinema
of Loneliness

WITHDRAWN

A Cinema
of Loneliness

Penn
Stone
Kubrick
Scorsese
Spielberg
Altman

Third Edition

WITHDRAWN

ROBERT KOLKER

OXFORD
UNIVERSITY PRESS

2000

OXFORD
UNIVERSITY PRESS

Oxford   New York
Athens   Auckland   Bangkok   Bogotá   Buenos Aires   Calcutta
Cape Town   Chennai   Dar es Salaam   Delhi   Florence   Hong Kong   Istanbul
Karachi   Kuala Lumpur   Madrid   Melbourne   Mexico City   Mumbai
Nairobi   Paris   São Paulo   Singapore   Taipei   Tokyo   Toronto   Warsaw

and associated companies in
Berlin   Ibadan

Copyright © 1980, 1988, 2000 by Oxford University Press, Inc.

Published by Oxford University Press, Inc.
198 Madison Avenue, New York, New York 10016

Oxford is a registered trademark of Oxford University Press

Library of Congress Cataloging-in-Publication Data
Kolker, Robert.
A cinema of loneliness: Penn, Stone, Kubrick, Scorsese, Spielberg, Altman/
Robert Kolker.—3rd ed.
p.   cm.
Filmography: p.
Includes bibliographical references and index.
ISBN 0-19-512350-6 (pbk.).—ISBN 0-19-512349-2 (cloth)
1. Motion pictures—United States.   2. Motion picture plays—History and
criticism.   I. Title.
PN1993.5.U6K57   2000
791.43'75'0973—dc21   99-43296

Book design by Adam B. Bohannon
Layout by Jack Donner

9 8 7 6 5 4 3 2 1
Printed in the United States of America
on acid-free paper

FOR DAVID WYATT
AND ANN POROTTI

CONTENTS

Illustrations follow page 420

PREFACE TO THE FIRST EDITION

American film begs us to leave it alone. From its beginnings, it has presented itself as an entertainment, as an escape; it is made to give pleasure to excite, to offer us a surrogate reality. On occasion it offers examination of a social or political problem. But rarely has it taken itself very seriously, and it has not, until quite recently, been taken very seriously by its critics. In recent years many people have stopped leaving it alone. As critical scrutiny continues, it becomes more and more clear that, despite what most producers would like, film is not temporary, not fleeting; it has had—particularly in those years from the early twenties to the middle fifties, when movies were the most popular form of entertainment—a cumulative effect, giving the culture a way of looking at itself, articulating its ideology, reflecting and creating its physical appearance and gestures, teaching and confirming its shared myths. The questions that continue to need asking are "Why?" and "How?" The deeper we probe, the more we discover about the ingenuity and the disingenuousness of American cinema, the ways it has used the intricacies of its formal structure to hide that structure and present itself as an unmediated presentation of reality, even when it was offering itself as an escape from reality. The more we look and the more we discover about American film, the more we discover about the methods of looking, about the ways film works on an audience and the audience on it.

The growth of serious critical inquiry into American cinema began as that cinema went into a decline. Beginning in the late fifties, production dropped, the studios collapsed, and the economic system of filmmaking degenerated into chaos. Television took over as the cultural image-maker, inheriting many of the attitudes, and few of the successes, of the major period of American filmmaking. These events permitted a space for inquiry, a convenient cleavage in cinema history. They also provided opportunities for some filmmakers to break out of the old production methods, the old assumptions of cinematic form and content, and to begin looking, along

x   with some critics, at the nature of their medium, its history, its methods and effects. Their works began to move in more than one direction. Their films were, and are still, primarily entertainments, and the concern for making a profit determines all phases of their work. But despite, or even in the face of, this overriding and often crippling concern, some filmmakers have seriously attempted to confront and examine the form and content of what they do. They make detours into their cinematic past, they reflect on the films that preceded them, they self-consciously call on the formal elements at their disposal to build a narrative and control audience participation with it. There has been no direct joining of forces of critic and filmmaker, but there has been an occasional paralleling of inquiry and an acknowledgment on both sides that film is a serious business, financially, formally, culturally.

Six of these filmmakers—Arthur Penn, Stanley Kubrick, Martin Scorsese, Steven Spielberg, Robert Altman, and, in the current edition, Oliver Stone—are the subjects of this study. They are part of a group that were referred to as "the new Hollywood," "the Hollywood Renaissance," the "American New Wave," phrases that suggest that they and others somehow changed or revitalized our cinema. Would that were the case. The ability of these filmmakers to function more independently than those who came before them, and their effect on filmmaking in general, have been rather compromised. What follows is an attempt to reach an understanding of the work, the independence, the compromise, and the effect of these filmmakers on American film, and the effect of that film on the culture at large.

PREFACE TO THE THIRD EDITION

In the second edition of *A Cinema of Loneliness*, in 1987, I suggested that American cinema was moribund as a creative force. However, just to cover myself—and aware that American film has a considerable talent for cyclical self-renewal—I pointed out that moribund is not the same as dead. There was unquestionably a falling-off in cinematic energy during the eighties. The inventiveness that flowed from Europe to Hollywood during the sixties and seventies was over. The recent newcomers who were the original subjects of this book were either finding their way into the mainstream of filmmaking, maintaining their inquisitive, experimental imaginations, like Martin Scorsese, removing themselves from Hollywood, like Robert Altman, or from filmmaking entirely, like Arthur Penn. Stanley Kubrick released two films during the decade before withdrawing into twelve years of silence, and then making *Eyes Wide Shut* before he died. Steven Spielberg was ensconced in his dominant position as the biggest moneymaker in American film. Oliver Stone and Spike Lee were just beginning their directing careers. Otherwise, there was not much indication that new directorial talent was emerging.

The filmmaking business itself was undergoing transformation, with more and more of the once independent studios becoming part of multinational corporations. That process has continued through the nineties until even the last holdouts are now corporate units. Twentieth Century-Fox is part of Rupert Murdoch's News Corporation and Universal is owned by Edgar Bronfman, a member of the family of whiskey distillers. Sony runs Columbia and Tri-Star; Paramount is part of the cable television enterprise, Viacom. MGM, which merged with United Artists in the eighties, was sold by Kirk Kerkorian to the French company, Pathé, in the late eighties, who then put it into receivership at Credit Lyonnais until Kerkorian bought it back. Disney runs a studio, a television network, an entertainment empire. Warner Brothers has merged with Time Inc. and bought out Turner Broadcasting. Early in 2000, America Online bought

Time Warner, signaling a radical shift in the structure and the delivery systems of the entertainment business.

All these entities are busy with many things in addition to movies, which are sometimes seen by them as source material for interactive computer games and licensing potentials for burgers and clothes. Computers have themselves been a major drive toward new studio endeavors. Every new film comes with a web site and, if it is an action film, may end as a CD-ROM game. Digital technology has changed filmmaking itself in profound ways, enabling action and special effects films to represent the most amazing stunts and in general replacing matte painting, process shots, and all the other tricks of visual economy that the studios have always used to allow shots to be inexpensively put together. Almost every film made now uses computer graphics in some aspect of its production and this has changed its very aesthetics.

Economies of production are nothing new in filmmaking; incorporation of filmmaking into large corporate structures is. But the result is not exactly what we might expect. Incorporation has not resulted in homogenization. Given the ever-growing appetite for visual narratives, increasing audiences for film in theaters, on videocassette, DVD and cable, and the total saturation of foreign markets by American product, the studios are attempting some diversity. Many of them have spawned or bought distribution units for "smaller" films. Sony Classics, Fox Searchlight, Disney's Miramax, along with a number of small, somewhat independent production houses, are busy attempting to define films for smaller than mass audiences. These films are rarely experimental in any radical way— that is, any way that questions the old formal rules or tries to discover a new path. Alhough rare films, like Ang Lee's *The Ice Storm* (1997) or Todd Solondz's *Happiness* (1998), can capture a meditation on characters in a cultural, political, and moral landscape that is otherwise hard to find. Otherwise, one thing that the retrenchment of the eighties seems to have done is to imprint on every director a set of norms that are either not very different from, or at the most extensions of, the classic studio style of the forties and fifties. In fact, the proliferation of film noir during the eighties and nineties has purposely evoked the studio style.

But despite all these strictures, and because of the recognition of new audiences and the proliferation of outlets for film (increased foreign markets, videotape, laserdisc, DVD, cable), there has been some interesting work done and a few interesting new filmmakers emerging during the past decade. As in the studio days, the very quantity of output seems to allow some diverse material to get through. There are no new schools of film-making or new genres developing, but there has been innovative work. Some of the directors originally discussed in *A Cinema of Loneliness* have gone on to become important influences on a new generation of filmmakers. For example, Martin Scorsese's style is an important influence on Spike Lee, a major figure in the creation of contemporary African-American cinema. Quentin Tarantino's first two films—*Reservoir Dogs* (1992) and *Pulp Fiction* (1994)—both play variations on Scorsese's *Mean Streets* (1973) and Stanley Kubrick's *The Killing* (1956). In fact, *Mean Streets* seems to be the most important film in a young male director's mind (think of Bryan Singer's *The Usual Suspects*, 1995; Kevin Spacey's *Albino Alligator*, 1996; Salvatore Stabile's low-budget film, *Gravesend*, 1997). To be fair, *Mean Streets* is itself a rethinking of the fifties gangster heist film—which is exactly what *The Killing* is—as well as a response to Coppola's *The Godfather*. Scorsese reconfigures the gangster genre into an ethnic male bonding film whose visual and narrative energy is appealing to viewers and potential filmmakers alike.

This imaginative energy, rethinking the old and reconfiguring the new, was a key to the filmmakers in the original edition of this book. They cared and thought deeply about film: reacted, emulated, alluded, parodied, embraced, and learned from it. Film was a way of articulating the world and their responses to it. The work they did was an important part of the modernist response that had occurred throughout the other arts many years earlier, in which the images and structures of one's craft and discipline become the defining and saving guidepost in an otherwise despairing historic and moral landscape.

The modernist movement in film, which began with the Italian neo-realists after World War II, flowered in the work of the French New Wave in the early sixties, and moved through Europe and into America, defined a view of the world within the structures of cinema, revitalizing those structures in the process. That movement ran its course by the eighties, even though Martin Scorsese, Robert Altman, and Stanley Kubrick maintained strong ties to it and continued to experiment with the expressive potentials of the medium. There were few others. Those who have since attempted some new explorations move mostly through postmodern territory where film became less a means of exploring the self and the world than of deflating both within images that either lack self-consciousness or mock it by turning inquiry into a sometimes indiscriminate embrace of pop-cultural images. Many recent filmmakers seem to have less a view of the world than simply a view of film. More accurately, they are filled with film, and they seem sometimes inclined to dump out their images with no driving idea, no articulation of what they or we should be seeing and why. Postmodern absurdity replaces modernist angst; cynicism edges out irony.

This creates a difficult situation for a summary view. Overall, American film in the nineties has become livelier and more varied. Digital composition has rearticulated cinematic space. But this is tempered by the fact that, formally, film has either fallen back into the standard patterns of the Hollywood continuity style, with foregrounded plots and invisible editing, or adopted a postmodern style of universal reference to other films and a constricted moral position and denial of meaning. A way out of the difficulty is to understand that, as always, film is a kind of cultural and ideological barometer. Film's conservatism echoes a broader and more disturbing conservatism in the culture as a whole. The postmodern urge to deny seriousness, meaning, and point of view hooks into that conservatism, translating it into a larger cultural cynicism, a belief that individual agency has been lost, worldviews are pointless, history is finished, and that the pleasures or terrors of the moment are all that can provide solace or excitement.

If we keep our eye on the inevitable interactions between film and the culture it is part of, and understand that the very structure of film (which creates plot and generates story) is an ideological event, determined by any number of economic and cultural forces, then we can see more clearly the trends that emerge and the films that are responsible for them. Coupling this with filmmakers who help create and drive the trends will offer a summary of what has happened to film since the eighties. I am very aware that auteurism—the idea that the director is the creative engine that drives a film—is somewhat out of fashion. It always was a convenient and very powerful myth because no film, especially no American studio film, is the result of one intelligence. It may indicate a counterproductive romanticism to argue otherwise. At the same time, it remains true that a strong and consistent director marks his or her films with a style and point of view that, through its coherence and repetitions, articulate a line of development easier to trace and analyze than the scatter-shot products of anonymous production.

Auteurism has perhaps always been a matter of convenience, and I find it still the most convenient tool to work through the complex, sometimes overwhelming, output of Hollywood. It is also a useful guide to the limits of the permissible. I noted earlier that most filmmakers respect, willingly or not, the basic conventions of the Hollywood continuity style. Those who do not are getting away with something and for a reason. That reason is almost always because the films they make are providing their producers with a reasonable return on investment. If profits are made, then people are seeing their films and responding to them positively. And if, as in the case of Scorsese, other filmmakers are also being influenced by their work, then their styles are being passed along across generations. The director provides, as Andrew Sarris pointed out many years ago, an entry into the history of film. One should always be careful not to allow history to turn into personality or vice versa. But if coherence and influence can be pinned on one figure, then it seems reasonable to let that figure and the work be set as the object of study.

Arthur Penn, Stanley Kubrick, Martin Scorsese, Francis Ford Coppola, and Robert Altman represented the best American film had to offer in the sixties and seventies and were the subjects of the first edition of *A Cinema of Loneliness*. Coppola lost his creativity by the late seventies while Steven Spielberg emerged as a major force in the eighties. He replaced Coppola in the second edition. At the end of the nineties, he, Scorsese, and Altman remain active forces in American filmmaking. They continue to probe and experiment, to refine their styles and explore the culture. Altman, now in his seventies, long past the age when most filmmakers have left the creative scene, continually attempts to reinvent himself with each film he makes. Scorsese restlessly moves from gangster film to costume drama to orientalist epic, refining his style and reperceiving the world. Unlike Altman, Kubrick entered his old age with relative inactivity. *Eyes Wide Shut* (1999) was his first film since *Full Metal Jacket* (1987) and his last. But Kubrick's films have become part of the culture's memory and help articulate its past and future history. He will remain a filmmaker who must be addressed, whose work bears reading and rereading. In his young age, Steven Spielberg has moved into the status of Hollywood financial and creative institution. As studio head, producer, and director, he is a one-person representative of the whole filmmaking apparatus. He is in the forefront of technological advances in the filmmaking process and once in a while attempts films of such enormous intended seriousness—*Schindler's List* (1993), *Amistad* (1997), *Saving Private Ryan* (1998)—that he must still be attended to. Because he is such an avatar of contemporary film, the chapter devoted to him will be used to sum up some themes and predicaments in Hollywood filmmaking during the nineties.

Penn would seem to be the one filmmaker of the original group who has left the scene. His two nineties films, *Portrait* (1993) and *Inside* (1996), were made for cable. Like John Frankenheimer, who also began his career in television before moving to theatrical features, Penn seems to have found a safe haven in the medium where he began. Frankenheimer has returned to filmmaking as a terrific action director (*Ronin*, 1998), while Penn went on to become head of the Actor's Studio. But however inactive, Penn is still an important part of the equation. His sixties and early seventies films define the modernist movement in American cinema and his influence is continual and inescapable. Oliver Stone has become his most important successor. Stone in the nineties was doing work akin to what Penn did in the sixties: addressing American history and culture, often in violent, unsettling images, making political cinema (as political as it gets in commercial film). In one instance, Stone has paid direct homage to Penn: *Natural Born Killers* (1994) is an update of *Bonnie and Clyde* (1967). Stone's Vietnam films—*Platoon* (1986), *Born on the Fourth of July* (1989, a film that can be roughly aligned with Arthur Penn's *Four Friends*, 1981), *Heaven and Earth* (1993)—and his political-historical grand works—*JFK* (1991) and *Nixon* (1995)—attempt to address contemporaneity and generational conflict as Penn did in almost all his sixties films.

Like Penn, Stone has become a controversial figure. In fact, he has become a more controversial, written about, admired, and despised figure than any filmmaker in recent memory. For this book, which attempts to contextualize film in its cultural and ideological complexities, this would make him important enough. But beyond Stone's place as a kind of ideological lightening rod is the fact of his filmmaking itself. Like Scorsese, Kubrick, and Altman—perhaps with them as his only company—Stone is exploring the formal properties of his medium. He attempts to make the creation and viewing of film an exciting, sometimes transgressive, interrogation of the medium's and the audience's boundaries. He is carrying on the modernist imperative that form be recognized as the creator of meaning and that meaning must be attended to in all its historical, political, and moral complexity.

Stone's films, along with Scorsese's, Kubrick's, and Altman's, are textually and texturally rich. Analysis becomes them and they become even richer with analysis. Spielberg's work and everything that his and his contemporaries' movies stand for are also rich with meaning and emotion for our culture. Their imagery and stories are ours. There is good reason that we respond to them and good reason to pay them attention.

What follows, then, is an updating and more. Except for *Eyes Wide Shut*,

I have not tacked recent films onto the various chapters, but gone directly into the chapters to weave in the relationship of the new work to the old. I've attempted to bring into the discussion some of the many new strains in film and cultural criticism while maintaining the close, textual analysis that I believe to be the heart of good critical analysis. What deserves attention yields richness under detailed scrutiny.

August 1999   R.P.K.
Silver Spring, Maryland

ACKNOWLEDGMENTS

I wish to thank the following individuals and organizations who helped me over the three editions of *A Cinema of Loneliness* with their time and conversation, their offers of prints and tapes to view, of research materials and permissions, and of help in reading or preparing the manuscript:

Gary Arnold, Josh Astrachan, Dick Atlee, Joellyn Ausanka, Joe Balian, Stephen Bernstein, Leona Capeless, Curtis Church, Eddie Cockrell, Wally Dauler, Linda Duchin, Don Elliott, Beth English, Charles Feiner, Marieke Gartner, Donna Gigliotti, Jamie Glauber, Stephanie Golden, Marsha Gordon, Emily Green, Judith Hancock, Myra Hoffman, Barbara Humphrys, Margot Kernan, John Kersting, Kathy Loughney, Mike Mashon, Sheldon Meyer, Dan Miller, Joe Miller, Clyde Norton, Devin Orgeron, J. Douglas Ousley, John Pacy, David Parker, Roberta Penn Buckberg, Stephen Prince, Gene Robinson, Elda Rotor, Mary Louise Rubacky, Martin Scorsese, Robert Self, John Sery, Nick Spitzer, Mike Swank, Frank P. Tomasulo, Harry Ufland, Joseph Weill, Rosemary Wellner, Fred Whitehead, Robin Wood, David Wyatt, and Justin Wyatt.

The American Film Institute, Cinecom International Films, Corinth Films, Films Incorporated, *The Journal of Popular Film*, The Library of Congress Motion Picture Division, The Museum of Modern Art Film Stills Archives, October Films, Sandcastle 5, *Sight and Sound*, Swank Motion Pictures, Oxford University Press, Twyman Films, the University of Maryland English Department.

My many students whose ideas and insights have slipped silently into my own.

And Linda.

A Cinema
of Loneliness

INTRODUCTION

When the studios, as independent corporate bodies, fell apart in the late fifties and early sixties, assembly-line film production ended. Previously each of the major studios was a self-contained filmmaking factory with its own labor pool of producers, directors, writers, players, and technicians, turning out many films a month during the years of peak production. This self-containment and mass production created mediocrity to be sure, as well as an arrogance that comes with security of product and market. But out of the arrogance and the mediocrity came also a body of work of formal skill and contextual complexity unmatched by the cinema of any other country. If the films produced were not intended to be taken seriously as enduring examples of individual artistic worth, they often enough overcame the intent of their makers to stand as enduring examples of *filmmaking* and all the collective energy that implies. They came as well to stand for the collectivity of film viewers; they created the images in which a culture consented to see itself and, as audiences responded favorably, the continuation of genres, plots, players, themes, and world views promoted by the studios were perpetuated in film after film.

The studios were places where support and security were offered to those who could work within their restraints, and, when they fell, that security and assuredness fell with them. The reasons for their fall were many and varied. Television, of course, was a major cause. In the late forties and early fifties, population patterns shifted. People moved to the suburbs and watched television rather than going out to the movies once or twice a week. Indeed, television has now overtaken film with the task of producing narratives for the culture, and cable television occasionally reaches for experimentation (or novelty) that commercial filmmaking will not attempt. But even before the impact of television was fully felt, movie attendance began falling from its 1946 peak. Studio executives met this falling-off by tightening budgets, firing production staff (mainly in their

4   story and publicity departments), and in general lessening the production values of their films. An attitude of self-defeat seemed to be in operation, an attitude that was reinforced by two other events that occurred between 1947 and 1949, which in fact initiated the studios' change and ultimate collapse. The hearings of the House Committee on Un-American Activities (HUAC) made production heads fearful and timid, uncertain as to what kind of content might be branded as subversive, what kind of creative person—director, writer, player—would be frowned on as un-American. HUAC and Hollywood's self-imposed blacklist managed to irrevocably damage any courage the old studios might have had. The courts managed to damage their economic power. The divestiture rulings of the late forties separated the studios from the theaters they had previously owned. They could no longer count on a guaranteed market for their films and had to seek out exhibition outlets on an individual basis. On top of this, foreign markets began placing quotas on American film. The confidence and self-sufficiency that had supported the studios since the twenties fell apart.

Uncertain as to what they could say in their films, uncertain as to whom they could say it, the studios floundered. They squandered their efforts on technical experiments—Cinerama, CinemaScope, 3D—and on overblown biblical and Roman epics. This is not to say that important films were not made in the fifties—they were, and it is a decade of complex films as rich in ideological contradictions as the eighties and nineties—only that the focal point of Hollywood filmmaking became diffuse. By the end of the decade the "product," once controlled by a studio from inception to exhibition, was controlled and executed by different hands, from different sources, and for ends that while they are not different from the studio days—films then as now are made to make a profit—lead to higher stakes, bigger egos, and an audience analyzed, compartmentalized, and continually tested for its response.

The studios still exist, of course, but the physical means of production are no longer as centralized as they were during the decades from the twenties to the early fifties. The studios do not have their own in-house players and technicians, nor do they have strong individual identities (during the thirties and forties, each of the studios had developed a style and approach, a stock company of players, and even typical story subjects that made their films quickly recognizable). On the contrary, they are without identity and homogeneous. Whereas individuals such as Louis B. Mayer at Metro-Goldwyn-Mayer, Darryl F. Zanuck at Twentieth Century-Fox, Jack L. Warner at Warner Brothers, Harry Cohn at Columbia guided their studios with dictatorial power for years, now production executives cycle from one studio to another, trading past successes on recent failures and the promise of future blockbusters.

The studios through which these individuals move are very powerful, if no longer independent entities (perhaps "independence" is a relative term, for in their original incarnation the studios were quite dependent on their financial officers on the East Coast and the banks who backed their films). Now they are either part of some larger, diversified corporation or owned by individuals whose function—and this is the major point of difference— is not making film, but amassing media outlets for various ideological reasons, the most important of which is the production of profit from the dissemination of news and fiction. The "product," more than before, is a means to this end. From assembly-line production made to service the mass entertainment market, film (and its reincarnation on videotape, laserdisc, and DVD) is now part of a large structure of ownership and distribution. The studios of the past appear to be small businesses by comparison.

The effect of all this on the films that are made is less than positive. Homogeneity of production results in homogeneity of product. Film-makers of imagination no longer have a centralized community of admini-strators and craftsmen who can be drawn upon to support them from production to production. Each project has first to be accepted by a corporate administrator or manager, developed, financed, and produced as part of a major "deal." To be accepted and secured, it must satisfy require-ments, stated and unstated, of conventionality, easy legibility, senti-mentality or brutality. Instead of the studio producer reigning over a production, the corporate executive, accountant, talent broker, and actor have powerful control. The deal and the contract loom over the production, affecting it perhaps more perniciously than any boorish old studio head ever could.[1]

Huge amounts of money are spent (or promised) in hopes of making huge amounts of money. The shaky independence originally gained by some filmmakers when the old studio structure fell has been thoroughly compromised. Many films are made as part of a complex economic structure that is created with the expectation that the individual film and its eventual appearance abroad and on electronic media will spawn not only large financial returns, but offspring that will further those returns even more. The phantom promise of "artistic freedom" offered when the old Hollywood structure collapsed has turned into something of an

■
6

economic nightmare where costs, salaries, profits, and reputations are juggled and manipulated, with the film itself all but disappearing in a mass of contracts and bookkeeping.

The small group of filmmakers who emerged in the late sixties and early seventies and were able to take brief advantage of the transitional state of the studios, using their talents in critical, self-conscious ways, examining the assumptions and forms of commercial narrative cinema, had a difficult task. They were without community or security. The corporate community that rapidly re-formed around them limited and compromised their small efforts, and they must now more than ever deal with the fact that without profitable returns on their work, they could not work at all. "Studio inter-ference" has merely changed its complexion and complexity, incorporating not only economic pressures, but the individual filmmaker's own judg-ment and fears.

Those filmmakers have survived or succumbed to the changes in pro-duction in various ways. Robert Altman and Stanley Kubrick accom-modated themselves to the situation, largely by ignoring or fighting it. During the seventies, Altman created his own mini-studio within which he could work with a minimum of interference. He seemed able to get backing for his films on his own terms, even though he had not had a commercial hit since *M.A.S.H.* in 1970. In 1980, after a number of his films failed commercially, Twentieth Century-Fox refused to distribute *Health*. Even though the enormous production of *Popeye* did do well, Altman decided to withdraw completely from mainstream filmmaking and sold his studio. In the eighties he continued his career with inexpensively filmed versions of works originally written and produced for theater and then returned to Hollywood, reviving his reputation with *The Player* and then continuing with a vengeance his adversarial stature, finally ending the decade with a relatively mild-mannered and rather conventional film, *Cookie's Fortune* (1999). Kubrick divorced himself from the chaos of contemporary American production in the early sixties. He worked in England, and his films have been successful enough so that he commanded both money and independence. He followed his demanding and uncommercial film *Barry Lyndon* with the commercially oriented adaptation of a Stephen King novel, *The Shining*, thereby reestablishing his financial viability. However, isolation and age seemed to have taken their toll. Seven years passed between *The Shining* and *Full Metal Jacket*, twelve between that film and *Eyes Wide Shut*.

Arthur Penn seemed able to work happily within the confusing bounds of post-studio production in the mid- and late sixties. His films were popular, though their popularity derived from an inherent sense of defeat that seems to have undone their creator. As a filmmaker, Penn barely survived into the eighties, and that survival came with a decline in formal control and an increase in reactionary content. His place as a political filmmaker, committed to examining the culture and its ideological contradictions, has been taken, in the nineties, by Oliver Stone. Martin Scorsese has survived well by making films for modest amounts of money and modest returns. He has gained enough power to attempt a number of genres and approaches and his best films remain thoughtfully constructed, inquiring deeply into the nature of cinematic and cultural perception. Unlike Scorsese, Spielberg has rapidly become the master of the enormous budget and enormous project; he has formed his own production company and oversees the work of other directors. He has managed to learn from Francis Ford Coppola how not to substitute ego for imagination, and flourishes at the heart of the Hollywood machine. But it is a peculiar kind of flourishing, in which imagination is put at the service of placation and manipulation. Spielberg's energy and ability to accommodate his audience make him, for the moment, the most significant figure of the "new" Hollywood and its economic contrivances.

But we must be careful. Dwelling on economic realities works only to a point, after which the critic runs the risk of getting caught up in a self-defeating cycle in which the film's existence as a commodity makes serious discussion of its form and content impossible. Other realities must be attended to. In American filmmaking (and not only in American filmmaking) the economic situation is only one of many factors that determine what a film will be. The sense of defeat alluded to in regard to Arthur Penn's work is not only a problem of film finance, but of the way Penn views, and communicates his view of, American culture. The fact that his later films moved to the right may be the result of a confluence of personal, ideological, and economic pressure, but it is not a move dictated only by that last item. That Stone was able to execute large, adventurous explorations of the sixties and seventies in films that pushed generic and structural boundaries is a sign that, sometimes, Hollywood will support experiments, as long as they return profits. That Scorsese is content to remain with smaller, more experimental works is as much a matter of personal inclination and emotional response as anything else and again reflects a less monolithic view of the Hollywood money machine. Spielberg has thrived on the big-budget, special effects film; but he is able to spend huge sums because the narrative structure and ideological energy of his films bring large audiences who are moved by them. Ideological assent generates money, not the other way around. What Spielberg has to say in *E.T.*, *Schindler's List*, or *Saving Private Ryan* and Scorsese in *Taxi Driver* or *Casino* is indeed determined by the economic necessities of filmmaking, but it is determined as well by the very different ways these filmmakers perceive and respond to the culture, the ways film has delineated that culture, and the response of the culture to film.

To understand this more clearly, let me repeat that the initial period of transition during the late fifties and early sixties permitted a certain freedom of inquiry, which, no matter how compromised, continues to leave a small mark on most of the filmmakers who concern us here. Most of them remain, despite economic pressures, delighted with film and its formal properties, curious about what they can do with their medium. Their roots go back to the burst of cinematic enthusiasm and creative energy in Europe in the late fifties, where young filmmakers reexamined traditions and conventions in ways that had an enormous influence on the Americans who followed them. Many of them went to film school, where they learned the history of cinematic form.

The French, and Europeans in general, never had a studio system comparable to America's. At the same time, they never had an intellectual condescension toward film comparable to America's. Unlike their American counterparts, French intellectuals have not considered film a substandard form of entertainment, but rather a form of expression to be taken seriously. They have loved film, and American film in particular, both intellectually and emotionally. In the fifties, a particularly obsessed group of Frenchmen, among them Jean-Luc Godard, François Truffaut, Claude Chabrol, Eric Rohmer, and Jacques Rivette, formed a group around Henri Langlois's Paris Cinémathèque and André Bazin's journal *Cahiers du Cinéma*. They glorified American film to the detriment of French film; they perceived the ability of the individual filmmaker to rise above studio uniformity. They recognized the visual strength of American film (partly because, knowing little English and seeing unsubtitled prints, they were unencumbered by dialogue), and they recognized the strength of American film's generic patterns. They used their understanding to fashion an approach both to their own and to American cinema in a concerted critical effort. They reevaluated the role of the screenwriter and the director, they explored film genres; in short, they celebrated and analyzed film as a special narrative form with a voice, a text, and an audience deeply interrelated.[2] Their critical perceptions were passed on to American film scholars. They themselves turned to filmmaking, with an organized knowledge of what they wished to do. Their films were small, personal, and inexpensive. Early on they worked together (for *Breathless*, Truffaut supplied the story, Chabrol the technical assistance, and Godard the direction), and at least briefly after they went their own ways a sense of communal origins, and certainly a sense of commitment to cinema, continued.[3]

The influence of the French New Wave on both American film criticism and filmmaking is important and sometimes still visible, if now somewhat perfunctory (Truffaut appeared as the scientist Lacombe in Spielberg's *Close Encounters of the Third Kind,* and his film *Wild Child* is alluded to in *The Color Purple*; a sign in a Paris café that reads "Don't Shoot the Piano Player Anymore" is visible in Penn's *Target*; Scorsese uses music from Godard's *Contempt* in *Casino* and makes visual reference to Godard's films throughout his work). Despite the influence, no "new wave" in America occurred, no movement. That brief freedom I mentioned was really a freedom to be alone within a structure that momentarily entertained some experimentation. The experiments that were undertaken, based on some things the New Wave was doing, were very much on an individual basis and made within the tradition of Hollywood film. The filmmakers discussed here used those traditions and the basic patterns of American filmmaking as a point of interrogation, foregrounding them, bringing them to con-sciousness, attempting to determine their further usefulness as narrative tools. They tried in various ways to come to terms with narrative itself, the story and its telling, and to realize the possibilities inherent in refusing the classical American approach to film, which is to make the formal structure of a work erase itself as it creates its content. These directors, especially in their late sixties and seventies work, delighted in making the viewer aware of the act of watching a film, revealing it as an artifice, something made in special ways, to be perceived in special ways. Even Steven Spielberg, younger than the others and deeply committed to commercial narrative con-ventions, continues the New Wave tradition of playful allusiveness to other films within his own work.

The paradoxes and the contradictions inherent in all this are painful. Influenced by a group of French intellectuals, some American filmmakers became thoughtful about their films. But, unlike their French colleagues, the films they made only rarely explored ideas or the larger cultural contexts of their existence. As delighted as they were (and in many instances still are) in the formal possibilities of their medium, as conscious as they were of the genres they emulated or attacked, most only stepped slightly in front of the conventional stylistics of classical American film (in Spielberg's films, especially, the knowledge of form and structure is used to reinforce traditional response and wholehearted assent). Although their films sometimes carry on an ideological debate with the culture that breeds them, they never confront that culture with another ideology, with other ways of seeing itself, with social and political possibilities that are new or challenging. If they do, as in the case of Oliver Stone's nineties films, initial acceptance may be followed by revulsion against the very attempt of a filmmaker to question the conventional wisdom of the culture's history. The films by the directors examined here rarely challenge the ideology many of them find abhorrent; too many of them only perpetuate the passivity and aloneness that has become their central image.

A critical approach to these films gets caught up in the conflicts and contradictions. These filmmakers have created a body of exciting work, formally adventurous, carefully thought out, and often structurally challenging. But for all the challenge and adventure, their films speak to a continual impotence in the world, an inability to change and to create change. When they do depict action, it is invariably performed by lone heroes in an enormously destructive and antisocial manner, further affirming that actual change, collectively undertaken, is impossible. When they preach harmony, it is through the useless conventions of domestic containment and male redemption. The only way to deal with them, therefore, is by examining the contradictions, keeping them present, in the foreground, confronting the films formally and contextually, aware that, no matter how much separation is made for the sake of discussion, form and content are inseparable.

To this end, this study will attempt to address the filmmakers and their works from a variety of perspectives. It will not constitute a complete history of recent American film, nor an economic survey, though both history and economics will support the discussions. There will not be a film-by-film analysis of each director's output. Not all films are of equal interest or of equal worth, and where a filmmaker's output is large it is impractical to give every film equal attention. I have attempted to avoid, wherever possible, the director's own analysis of his work. The interview, while a useful tool in film studies, seems to me too often to serve as a means of getting closer to the creator of a work rather than to the creation. My preference is to concentrate on the film itself—that organized series of images and sounds that have meaning, that exist in a carefully delimited time and space that is created when they are projected on a screen and perceived by a viewer. Films are initiated by individuals, who put the images and sounds together in specific ways, and who are influenced by their own perceptions of the world and by previous films. The films are perceived (and it is the act of perceiving that completes them) by individuals who are also influenced by their perceptions of the world and by previous films. This complex of relationships is my major subject.

The process of discussing these films will be, partly, a process of demystification (and demythification as well). There are no assumptions that what constitutes a film is merely a story with interesting and well-motivated characters that either succeeds or fails to entertain us for a few hours. On the contrary, the "story" is constituted by the formal structure of the film, which is in turn constituted by other films and the history of responses to them. Given the fact that the filmmakers under discussion already know this, one of my tasks will be to extend that knowledge further, to explain how they put it to use and how the spectator then uses it or is used by it. For this reason there will be digressions along the way, detours into the past of American cinema, discussions of its genres, some of its major directors and their influences, some of the formal attributes of film that the directors under discussion perpetuate, reflect upon, or change.

The major questions to be raised and, I hope, answered in this book are "How?" and "Why?" How and why do filmmakers construct their works the way they do? How and why does a viewer react to them? In answering these questions I must reaffirm the fact that film, by virtue of the popularity and the immediacy of its fictions, by the nature of its means of production and consumption, is profoundly tied up with the cultural, social, and political being of the viewer. In other words, the examination of a film cannot be restricted only to the formal and thematic elements of its text or genre. Films are seen and understood (in various ways) by a great many people. They have an effect, calculated or uncalculated; the conventions and myths they have built and continue to build go beyond them and are deeply embedded in the culture.

Film is a major carrier of our ideology. To define more precisely what I mean by this, it is necessary to back up and recover some ground. American film, from its beginnings, has attempted to hide itself, to make invisible the telling of its stories, and to downplay or deny the ways in which it supports, reinforces, and even sometimes subverts the major cultural, political, and social attitudes that surround and penetrate it. Film is "only" entertainment. Film is "realistic," true to life. These contradictory statements have supported American film throughout its history, hiding some basic facts about its existence. American film, like all fiction, is a carefully crafted lie: make-believe. Film processes "reality" into the forms of fiction (or, more accurately, uses its forms to create cinematic realities) that allude to, evoke, substitute for, and alter external "reality." Film is a representation, a mediation.

This processing or representation involves the active creation of ideas, feelings, attitudes, points of view, fears, and aspirations that are formed by images, gestures, and events that the viewer either assents to or opposes. Any given film is an organization, on the level of fictional narrative, of aspects of the self and the world. That narrative substitutes for ordinary experience characters and action in a cinematically determined space and time. This organization is not innocent (not since the early part of the century, at least). Choices are made as to subject and the way that subject will be realized, manifested—created, ultimately—in the forms of cinema. When it becomes a convention that those forms are to be invisible, that the act of substitution or representation will not appear to be an act of substitution or representation, that the form of the fiction will recede behind the fiction itself and therefore create the illusion that the fiction is somehow "real" and unmediated, then a very specific relationship is set up with the audience. This relationship is based on the assumption and assertion that what is seen is real and cannot be questioned.[4] There are enormous implications to this phenomenon, implications that some of the filmmakers discussed here are aware of and respond to in their own work. As indicated, they have begun to take cognizance of the cinematic forms at their disposal and make that cognizance apparent. Some even question the ideology, both formal and contextual, of their cinematic heritage and make their questions visible.

Yet I imagine many of them would hesitate if they were told they were involved in an explicit ideological endeavor, for the term itself is fraught with connotations of manipulation, of single-mindedness, of unyielding adherence to a political point of view. In our culture, it is often demanded by critics and artists alike that art be free of any specific political attitudes. Oliver Stone has learned this painfully. But film, of any period, by any filmmaker, speaks to an audience about specific things in specific ways. Its form and content, its fictional mode and the ways in which it is read, are part of and reflect the larger social, cultural, psychological, and political structure. That structure is itself determined by the way individuals alone or collectively perceive themselves and their existence in the world. This is what I mean by "ideology": the complex of images and ideas individuals have of themselves, the ways they assent to or deny their time, place, class, the political structure of their society. "Ideology is not a slogan under which political and economic interest of a class presents itself," write Rosalind Coward and John Ellis. "It is the way in which the individual actively lives his or her role within the social totality; it therefore participates in the construction of that individual so that he or she can act." The authors quote the French philosopher Louis Althusser, who offers a definition remarkable for its use of a cinematic metaphor: "*ideologies* are complex formations of montages of notions—representations—images on the one hand, and of montages of behaviours—conducts—attitudes—gestures on the other." Elsewhere, Althusser defines ideology as "the 'lived' relation between men [and women] and their world, or a reflected form of this unconscious relation."[5] Expanding on this, Terry Eagleton writes that ideology "is the very medium in which I 'live out' my relation to society, the realm of signs and social practices which binds me to the social structure and lends me a sense of coherent purpose and identity." He goes on to point out that ideology is "the link or nexus between discourses and power," the way an individual is represented in and to the world and the way the world represents itself to an individual. Ideology constructs the very image of the individual and his or her potency or impotence in the world.[6]

Every culture has a dominant ideology, and, as far as individuals assent to it, that ideology becomes part of the means of interpreting the self in the world and is seen reflected continually in the popular media, in politics, religion, education. But an ideology is never, anywhere, monolithic. It is full of contradictions, perpetually shifting and modifying itself as struggles within the culture continue and as contradictions and conflicts develop. American film is both the carrier of the dominant ideology and a reflector, occasionally even an arbitrator, of the changes and shifts within it.[7] Film tends to support the dominant ideology when it presents itself as un-mediated reality, entertaining the viewer while reinforcing accepted notions of love, heroism, domesticity, class structure, sexuality, history. During the late sixties and early seventies, some film questioned assumptions, as some directors became more independent and more in control of their work. In the eighties, American film once again became a great affirming force and, in some instances, went beyond affirmation to the active creation of ideological images and attitudes, forming discourses of power for the powerless. During the nineties, many films became either parodic or attempted a forced redemption for bad male behavior. The postmodern desire to evade seriousness collided with the old conventions of confirmation of "family values." In the discussions that follow, I will attempt to define and account for these events.

The essential point for the analysis that follows is that narrative film is fiction, not reality. It substitutes images and sounds for "real" experience, and with those images and sounds communicates to us and manipulates particular feelings, ideas, and perspectives on reality. Film is not innocent, not merely entertainment, and, most especially, not divorced from the culture out of which it comes and into which it feeds. This is why I find it impossible to talk about the events and the characters of films as if they had an existence separate from the formal apparatus that creates the fiction they inhabit. I will discuss conventional notions of motivation and character psychology, yet these discussions should always be seen in the context of the various structures and conventions of the cinematic fiction and the viewer's perception of them. The nature of conventional fiction is to present a clean and concentrated view of life. Even if this view is made to include ambiguities and questions, it is always neater than anything perceived in the loose and open narratives that constitute daily life. Modernism in literature tried to rectify this by foregrounding narrative processes and making reading as complex as the reading of ordinary experience. Some of the filmmakers under discussion here do the same. To understand what they are up to, I want to return cinematic fiction to its proper place as artifice, as something made, and to reduce the emotional aura that most American film narratives create in the viewer, in an attempt to understand the sources of that aura.

A few further things by way of methodology. Most of the films discussed here have been viewed, closely, on an editing table, a VCR, or on laserdisc or DVD. In some instances, I have had the film up on the computer screen, looking, analyzing, and writing with the object of study immediately in front of me. I have therefore been able to look at the films somewhat in the manner of reading a book, stopping, starting, going back and forth at will. This is, of course, not the way the films are generally seen by an audience. One of the many powers the film narrative exercises over the viewer is the inexorability of its telling. But because of magnetic and digital media, more and more viewers are able to counter this power and recreate the privileged viewing situation once the reserve of filmmakers or critics. To give one's self over to the controlling spell of a film narrative is now more an expression of desire than of necessity. Some readers may wish to use this new access along with the book in order to discover the mechanisms of the films.

Unfortunately, despite the greater availability of the image, the ability to create an accurate verbal rendering of it remains elusive. At best, the descriptions may recall or allude to what exists in the film for the purposes of analysis; they may occasionally evoke; they will never take the place of the images themselves. The verbal description is always tenuous and subject to correction.

There are two textual components of film that do not receive here the attention they should. One is music; the other is film acting. The reason for their slight treatment is, frankly, a feeling of inadequacy on my part to deal with them in any but a cursory way. Film criticism is slow to develop an analytic vocabulary appropriate to the complexity of music's interaction with the narrative, or its function in helping to create the narrative. (Eisenstein made a start many years ago, but certainly the difficulties involved in learning music theory have prevented film critics from carrying his work forward.)[8] Although it is difficult to analyze the relationships between music and narrative within a particular film, one can comment on larger trends in film music: especially the return of the symphonic score in the late seventies and the continuing practice of tying in sales of sound track CDs. There is a slowly developing vocabulary adequate to an accurate and objective discussion about film acting: what it is and how it affects the film and its audience, how an individual creates a presence on the screen, what that presence is, and what the viewer's relationship is to it. This new work is attempting to overcome the Hollywood cult of personality. The serious critic may talk about the director, but the publicist and reviewer still sell the picture by the star. This phenomenon tends to pull attention away from the film itself and focus attention on the individual—who, more often than not, is a person built up by the accretion of his or her roles and publicity (Humphrey Bogart, John Wayne, Marilyn Monroe are examples)—rather than look closely at what is being created within the particular film under discussion. When critical examination is given to character in the particular film, the tendency is to fall into the trap of psychological realism I noted earlier and begin discussing the character as if he or she had an existence rather than a function within the total narrative structure. Between these extremes fall the adjectives: such and such a player gave an "edgy" or "nervous" performance, was "brilliant," was "absorbed" in the role. And, that final refuge of unexamined assumptions, was "believable."[9]

As alternatives to these problems I would emphasize the fact that performance is one part of the film's structure and most interesting when integrated within the film's total design. I will be examining a few actors who move through more than one film under discussion, especially Robert De Niro in Martin Scorsese's films, and recent discussions of the construction of gender in film will help clarify how the actor's work in creating a fictional persona is determined by expectations of gender and recent responses to those expectations.

16

Finally, with the exception of Arthur Penn and Stanley Kubrick, all the filmmakers given major attention in this study are still working. Their careers are in progress and their future films will continue to prove or deny what is said about their work to date. Because of this I have avoided anything like a grand summary or an overall evaluation of what they have done. This book is deeply opinionated, but hardly final.

ONE

BODY'S MONTAGE; HISTORY'S MISE-EN-SCÈNE
Arthur Penn and Oliver Stone

Firsts are difficult to find in film history. There are so many films and so many lost films that one is put in danger suggesting that one film or another is the first of anything. The problem is compounded when one searches for the first film that demonstrates a cinematic movement and a critical theory. Modernism is a theory, as well as an artistic practice, based as any other theory on the empirical evidence of a number of films read against the culture and ideologies of a historical period. The first films that demonstrated the self-consciousness and foregrounding of form that are an important part of the modernism occurred early in American film. We can turn to Buster Keaton's *Sherlock Jr.* (1924), in which Buster plays a projectionist who walks into the film he is showing and gets caught in its montage. In the USSR, both Sergei Eisenstein and Dziga Vertov played against the already institutionalized classical form of film to bring the viewer into active participation with the meaning-making process.[1] Both filmmakers took the Russian Revolution as their theme and structure, and both thought deeply about the language native to their art. Eisenstein concentrated on montage, the building of structure through the arrangement of shots. Vertov, especially in *The Man with a Movie Camera* (1929), gave a kind of anthropomorphic life to the movie camera as a cyborgian extension of the filmmaker.[2]

When we add the thematics of modernism to our quest—the expression of lost order, a vision of a diminished human subjectivity and agency, a sense of history as loss and melancholia—we need to start with German Expressionism and, in American film, the work that retransmitted Expressionism into American film culture, *Citizen Kane* (1941). *Kane* represents a major break with the realist conventions and the seamless narrative construction that dominated film in the thirties. To fully comprehend its narrative, the viewer must be attentive to the ways the film plays on conventions of narrative and mise-en-scène, on what the viewer sees and how she sees it. Out of *Kane* and German Expressionism came film noir, which, like its predecessors, played on the visual to emphasize narratives that reversed thirties and forties givens of domesticity and placidity, of active male and passive women characters.

But it is Alfred Hitchcock's *Psycho* (1960) that marks the passage of American film from its classical to its modernist stage. Its grim, grayscale images of a barren Southwest and California landscape develops the mise-en-scène of so many low-budget fifties science-fiction films into a painful statement of the moral vacuum and incipient violence of postwar America. The film's unattractive characters, living diminished lives that come to violent ends, speak to the anxieties of fifties life—which Hitchcock had already addressed in *Vertigo* (1958). Both films address the failing of human community and positive moral action, a collapse not merely of faith, but of individual capability, action, and perception. They express a breakdown in meaning itself, while celebrating the ability of cinematic form to communicate this despair with the irony of its own knowledge. *Vertigo* indulges in a lushness of mise-en-scène, whereas the visual space of *Psycho* is so bare and brutal that even the jokiness of its narrative form—the fact that it often gives itself away at the very points where it seems to be building its mysteries—cannot mitigate its view that the violence of human life lies just below a banal surface and that the smiling face hides a deadly assault.

In its nameless and inexplicable horror, *Psycho* looks backward to America's wartime experience of Nazi Germany, which the culture has never been able to understand, absorb, or adequately represent, and forward to a new history of film violence, which it has never been able to have represented too much. The film's acute self-consciousness of its formal devices and its ironic stance toward its audience and its own narrative offer another challenge to the Hollywood style of invisible continuity, foregrounded story, and satisfying closure. It becomes an influence on many films to come.

Both *Citizen Kane* and *Psycho* are major influences on the directors who are the subjects of this study. *Psycho* in particular is the source not only of many formal strategies but of the blood that has flowed in so much recent film. Yet they are influences rather than initiators, and they will be referred to as such throughout. What needs to be located is a contemporary filmmaker who moves out of the mainstream of American production and looks at it, even for a moment, with foreign eyes—because it is, finally, the foreign perspective on American film, the French perspective in particular, that, along with economic changes in production, influenced the major changes in sixties and seventies films. Welles, Hitchcock—perhaps even John Ford, who also figures as a major influence on the filmmakers discussed here—might have gone unnoticed by American filmmakers and film critics alike, were it not for their recognition by the French. I am not exactly suggesting that American film in the sixties and seventies was a direct result of the French New Wave of the late fifties. But the French were responsible for recognizing the complexities of American film and, by their example, enabling some filmmakers to create work that reflected on itself and its context. They offered the intellectual means, through their criticism, and the practical means, through their films, for some Americans to stand back from their own tradition in order to reenter it with different points of view.

With this in mind, it is still incumbent to find a place of entry, a figure who offers an example of this standing back and whose films offer a reexamination of the conventions of American cinema. John Cassavetes comes to mind as a filmmaker who very early on recognized some things that could be done in American film in response to the New Wave. In *Shadows* (1960) he attempted to create a narrative structure that parallels the improvisatory nature of early Godard. He takes a direction away from the tidily plotted narrative of heroic endeavor and melodramatic longings, so much the core of American film, toward a more loosely observed structure in which the director, his players, and his mise-en-scène create a process where the telling of a story becomes subordinate to the moment-to-moment insights into character and situation. Almost to the end of his career, Cassavetes followed this direction unflinchingly in most of his work, sacrificing consistent and planned narrative development to microscopic observation of his characters' attempts to articulate their despair. Precisely because of this sacrifice, I find Cassavetes's work difficult to watch and even more difficult to talk about. In a book dedicated to the study of formal strategies and the realization of expression through the structure of expression, a detailed examination of Cassavetes's films would run the risk of being more judgmental than critical. But, because the work of Scorsese and Altman would be different without his influence, and because his films so defy the dimensions of commercial American cinema, he may lurk as something of a bad conscience over what is written here.[3]

I turn to Arthur Penn as an initiating figure, but with some ambivalence. Penn came to film in the fifties from television, as did many of his colleagues (though, unlike many of his colleagues, from the theater as well). His first work, *The Left-Handed Gun* (1958), was part of the cycle of fifties westerns that began reexamining and shifting some of the accepted conventions of the genre, psychologizing its hero and scrutinizing the myth of the hero itself. After that Penn moved in and out of various genres and various means of production, filming *The Miracle Worker* (1962), which he had originally directed on the stage; producing and directing *Mickey One* (1964); working for Sam Spiegel in an old-style studio production, *The Chase* (1966); finally achieving a major formal and financial success with *Bonnie and Clyde* (1967), which, indicative of the changing patterns of Hollywood production at the time, was produced by its star, Warren Beatty. These and the films that followed—*Alice's Restaurant* (1969), *Little Big Man* (1970), *Night Moves* (1975), *The Missouri Breaks* (1976), *Four Friends* (1981), *Target* (1985), and *Dead of Winter* (1987)—make up a patchwork of generic experiments, ideological reflections, guides to the culture's malaise, its best and worst fantasies, ending with a veer toward a conservatism in both style and content. Penn's sixties films, particularly *Little Big Man* and *Alice's Restaurant*, are so acutely barometers of the moment that, the moment gone, the films have receded, becoming not so much filmic as cultural artifacts.

Among his seventies films, *The Missouri Breaks* fell victim to its stars, Jack Nicholson and Marlon Brando, and it appears to have had five directors: the two actors, scriptwriter Thomas McGuane, and the United Artists production accountant, as well as Penn. Although the film carries through some favorite Penn oppositions—particularly that of the individual who lives on the fringes of the legal order and confronts the guardians of that order—and Penn introduces, for the first time and without much success, a woman of some strength and independence, it is a fairly lifeless work, unable to locate itself within a point of view or a consistent method of telling its tale. This lack of controlling point of view and consistency of structure continues to undo the succeeding films. *Four Friends*, despite its extraordinary syncretic images, is harmed by an inability to deal with the contradictions of nostalgia and bitterness, though it remains one of the most interesting films about the sixties—made by one of the filmmakers who helped invent the sixties. *Target* signifies nothing less than an exhausted liberal filmmaker surrendering to the reigning neoconservatism of the eighties. *Dead of Winter* is merely an exercise in gothic horror, indulging itself in the dreadful convention that proposes a woman free herself from the brutalities visited on her by enacting even greater brutality.

Night Moves was Penn's point of turning, his last carefully structured work, a strong and bitter film, whose bitterness emerges from its anxiety and from a loneliness that exists as a given, rather than a loneliness fought against, a fight that marks most of Penn's best work. *Night Moves* is a film of impotence and despair, and it marks the end of a cycle of films. For Penn, it stands as a declaration that the ideological struggles of the sixties are over and an announcement of the withdrawal and paranoia of the seventies, which he seemed to have overcome only by yielding to the conservatism of the eighties.

This is of necessity an elegy. Penn's decline appears permanent. *Penn and Teller Get Killed* (1989), written by and starring the magic act, Penn and Teller, is a cute trick. Penn's 1996 made-for-cable film, *Inside*, about a white man held in a South African jail during apartheid, has some of the gut-wrenching violence of the sixties work, but little of its political immediacy and none of its formal daring. Clearly Penn has been unable to survive the transition out of the sixties. The cultural conflicts and cinematic experimentation that marked the decade gave a strength and urgency to his work that diminished as those conflicts diminished. The final judgment on his work may be that he is not a great filmmaker, but rather an important indicator of what was happening in film, particularly in its response to immediate cultural situations. If popular enthusiasm for his work has diminished along with its own diminished structure (although *Night Moves* deserves more attention than it has received), the best of that work—particularly *Mickey One, Bonnie and Clyde, Night Moves*—retains its importance as a guide to the changes in American cinema in the sixties and seventies. These films remain major influences on contemporary film-makers.

Mickey One marks the first major guidepost. If my initial premise is valid—that French criticism and filmmaking of the late fifties and early sixties produced a visible influence on some American film—then *Mickey One* stands out, even more than *Shadows,* as being the film most influenced by the work of the New Wave, so much so that Robin Wood condemned Penn for denying his American heritage.[4] Penn himself dismissed the film as a work made in anger and in a spirit of obscurity. (He had just been fired by Burt Lancaster from *The Train* and replaced by John Frankenheimer, who, like Penn, had started his career directing live television.) Fortunately, the film cannot be so dismissed, even though it is largely unseen. In the mid-nineties, the UCLA Film Archives helped make available a fine laserdisc copy, which may save it from total obscurity. Not only is it a work of great energy and visual imagination, but it performs those operations on narrative structure that Godard and Truffaut were themselves performing in their early sixties work.

Mickey One undoes the closed and stable storytelling devices that American film depends on, suppressing direct statement, clear transitions, an objective, neutral point of view, making its central character almost inaccessible. In the course of this, the film does not attempt to hide its formal devices, but rejoices in them. In sum it writes, as Alexandre Astruc instructed his French colleagues to do, with the *caméra-stylo*, inscribing the director's imagination into the film and allowing the audience to meet it actively and inquisitively.[5]

Mickey One is also inquisitive about genre, and questioning the conventions of a genre, its assumptions and points of view, expanding its boundaries, revitalizing its form and content is a major activity of the modernist enterprise. *Mickey One* is a film of paranoia, of a man trapped and isolated by fear, who perceives his world in the perspective of that fear. The film of entrapment, of individuals caught in a dark and foreboding world that echoes their vulnerable state of being, began in the early forties and expanded into the major dramatic style of the decade. The prevalence of its style was matched only by a lack of consciousness of that very prevalence, for it seems no one making these films in the forties, and no one viewing them, was aware precisely of what was going on. The French, seeing forties American films in concentrated viewings after the war, recognized the change in form and content and brought it to critical attention, calling it film noir, based on the *Serie noire* crime stories.[6] Not until the late sixties, when American film critics began looking at the phenomenon in a concentrated way, and not until the early seventies, when American filmmakers began seriously to consider the applicability of noir to their own work, did the form come fully to the consciousness of the culture that developed it. Film noir has multiple origins: the original films were made without filmmakers being conscious that they were creating a new form based on German Expressionism and *Citizen Kane*. The form was named by French and then American critics. It was rediscovered by American filmmakers in the sixties and has been continually rediscovered ever since. Finally, film noir is perhaps the only concept born out of film studies that has suffused itself into popular consciousness. In short, almost everyone now knows what a noir film is.

The move to darkness in the forties—both a visual darkness in mise-en-scène (the coherent articulation of space in a film, including framing,

22

movement, lighting, production design, the use of color or grayscale) and a darkness in the narrative itself—was a result of cultural and technological forces operating simultaneously. At the end of the thirties, a faster film stock was developed, which meant lower light levels could be used and a greater contrast of light and dark achieved within a shot. As a result of this and other technological factors, Orson Welles and Gregg Toland could create the deeply shadowed and deeply focused space in *Citizen Kane* that became the basis of the noir style. They not only availed themselves of the new lighting possibilities of the time but reached back before the thirties to employ the largely dormant forms of German Expressionism and its chiaroscuro.* The result was that a decade of a particular lighting style was put to rest. The bright, even illumination and shallow focus that had prevailed in the thirties (with some major exceptions, such as the Universal horror films, which were heirs to the German style, and the films of Josef von Sternberg) gave way to a deeper focus and a deeper sense of the effect of light and shadow, just as the heroic male of the thirties gave way to a more vulnerable, anxiety-ridden character.

The formal qualities of Welles's mise-en-scène exist as profound manifestations of the film's narrative thrust. *Citizen Kane* is an attempt to grasp the personality of an enigma and prove the impossibility of such an attempt. The combination of depth of field, in which many details throughout the shot, from foreground to background, are visible, and the intense darkness that encloses these details, creates a tension. The viewer sees a great deal, but wishes to see more; the surrogates for the viewer within the film each offer partial information about the central character, and the viewer wishes to see more still. The effect is, finally, to leave the viewer and characters within the fiction rather alone and unfulfilled, or filled with the sense of Kane's mystery and isolation.

Citizen Kane altered the visual and narrative conventions of American film. In the years immediately following it, the darkness of its mise-en-scène began to inform much of Hollywood's output, particularly those films involving detectives, gangsters, and lower-middle-class men oppressed

---

* The history of film is never simple. Toland photographed *The Grapes of Wrath* and *The Long Voyage Home* for John Ford in 1940. Many of the visual strategies that would be further developed in *Kane* can be seen in them, particularly in *The Long Voyage Home*, though they stand very much apart from the content. It took Welles to integrate technology and narrative.

by lust and the sexuality of destructive women. The key year was 1944. Edward Dmytryk's *Murder My Sweet* (made at RKO, the studio of *Citizen Kane*) and Billy Wilder's *Double Indemnity* (at Paramount), the first from Raymond Chandler's *Farewell My Lovely*, the second scripted by Chandler from a James M. Cain novel, introduced the major subjects and formal structures of noir, beginning its first cycle that would continue through Robert Aldrich's *Kiss Me Deadly* (1956) and achieve a self-conscious conclusion, most fittingly by the man who started it, in Orson Welles's *Touch of Evil* (1958).

Throughout the forties and into the fifties, film noir played on basic themes of aloneness, oppression, claustrophobia, and emotional and physical brutality, manifested in weak men, various gangsters and detectives, and devouring women who lived—or cringed—in an urban landscape that defied clear perception and safe habitation. The appearance of these figures and their landscape became so insistent that they must have been responses to some profound, if unconscious, shifts in the way the culture was seeing itself. Was noir merely reflecting, as many critics have suggested, a postwar depression so prevalent that the audience merely assented quietly and passively to images of its own fear? Perhaps it was a response to the deep trauma of fascism, a brutality so profound that the culture had to deal with it, in part, through representations of lesser, more knowable and contained brutalities and helplessness. Perhaps the vicious noir woman was somehow a response to the fears of returning soldiers that the sweethearts they left at home were busy betraying them—or, even more terrifying, successfully working at their jobs? (*The Blue Dahlia*, 1946, directly addresses the fears of returning soldiers and their girlfriends.) Perhaps she was a more general representation of the misogyny particularly rampant in the culture and its films after the war, or a dialectic response to this misogyny in the figure of women who would free themselves from the restraints of the domesticity portrayed as normal in so many films.

Few of noir's forms of expression or character traits were new. The dark, brooding lighting of noir is present in German Expressionism. The dangerous woman has her origins in the twenties vamp and in the persona created for Marlene Dietrich by Josef von Sternberg in the thirties. The noir male has his origins in the Peter Lorre character of Fritz Lang's *M* (1931), Professor Rathaus in Sternberg's *The Blue Angel* (1930), Jean Gabin's François in Carné and Prévert's *Le Jour se lève* (1939), as well as in the gangster films of the early thirties. The fact that these figures of the dark appear so strongly in the forties and were so readily accepted speaks to the ideological shift mentioned earlier; but that shift was a temporary one. The noir style and themes slowly disappeared by the mid-fifties. The two most self-conscious examples of the form, *Kiss Me Deadly* and *Touch of Evil*, indicate the decline by their very self-consciousness. They recognize the formal properties of noir in a way its earlier practitioners did not, creating brutal, exaggerated worlds that, originating in actual locations rather than studio sets, go beyond the accepted conventions of cinematic realism and become subjective visions of entrapment and threat. Their characters are bizarre to the point of madness and realize to an extraordinary pitch the hysteria inherent in most inhabitants of the noir universe. They are the climax of the genre, or perhaps its first coda.

The suggestion has been made that the decline of black-and-white cinematography contributed to the decline of noir, but more likely the viability of its conventions had worn down, and further shifts in ideology demanded a change in the films that embodied it. Rather than the bourgeois man undone, a favorite theme of forties noir, the fifties were fond of portraying the bourgeois man at bay, threatened but often finding a way out of danger by accepting his diminished state. The fifties male was vulnerable in a different way than his forties forebears. Anxious, sensitive, often taking on aspects of character that might have been considered feminine by earlier film standards, he was less likely to become sexual prey than prey to his own doubts. The anxieties of the fifties needed a different expression than those of the forties; reassurance and affirmation, even self-examination, became more important than reinforcement of fears and uncertainties.[7]

Containment was the order of the decade on the geopolitical and the personal-political level. Tough guys still existed and could be placed within an anticommunist setting, as in Samuel Fuller's deeply noir *Pickup on South Street* (1953). Even here, the girlfriend-bashing gangster turns out to be misunderstood, a commie dupe despite himself. Generally, anti-communism and other overt cold war subjects came to be more comfortably treated in science fiction, where technology, the army, or heroic initiative could repel alien threats, and fifties noir began to address working-class fears of male economic potency, with characters who turn to crime to feed their families, as in the remake of Hemingway's *To Have and Have Not*, *The Breaking Point* (Michael Curtiz, 1950). Male anxiety, despair, and isolation became major themes in a variety of other genres. The juvenile delinquent film, such as the Marlon Brando vehicle, *The Wild*

One (Laszlo Benedek, 1954), or James Dean in *Rebel Without a Cause* (Nicholas Ray, 1955), or the film of high middle-aged angst, like Ray's *Bigger Than Life* (1956) and Hitchcock's *Vertigo*, provided a cinematic space for introspection about contained lives and repressed emotional and sexual expression. Even westerns, like Arthur Penn's first film, *The Left-Handed Gun*, would become containers for sensitive male angst. Noir, for the moment, had lost one of its causes, and would return only in the seventies, when the form was rediscovered by filmmakers who, having studied film in school, were anxious to revive the one form that appeared to them available for formal experiment and a vehicle for personal anxieties.

Coming as it does after the major period of film noir, but before the noir revival (of which his own *Night Moves* is a major part), Penn's *Mickey One* stands in a sort of generic limbo, carrying over the figure of the frightened and withdrawn male from the fifties and foreshadowing the paranoia films of the early seventies, reevaluating the narrative structure of the noir films that preceded it. Forties noir focused on a world of entrapment, isolation, and moral chaos, often by observing this world from the perspective of one character. Yet despite the attempts at first-person narrative, and despite the inherent isolation of the noir universe and its dark mise-en-scène, the storytelling structures of the films were traditional. The plots may have been complex (it is still difficult to figure out who committed one of the murders in Hawks's 1946 film, *The Big Sleep*), but their narrative form followed a basic expository style, directing the viewer through a causal series of events. Later filmmakers marveled at the way noir interrogated visual and narrative conventions. Noir's contemporaries were quite aware of just how far their studios would allow them to go. *Mickey One* tests the limits. It fractures causality, suppresses motivations, and not merely draws the viewer into an observation of the central character but forces one to share his perception, a perception that is confused, paranoid in the extreme, and unable to comprehend the world in anything but a jagged, fragmented manner. The noir world is internalized, and is seen the way the character sees it—not through his eyes, but with his sensibility.

The story told by the narrative is in fact simpler than that of most forties noir. Mickey (Warren Beatty) is a second-rate nightclub comic who gets involved with the mob in Detroit. He runs away in terror and comes to Chicago, living like a bum. He meets a girl, impresses a local nightclub impresario (Hurd Hatfield in a very bizarre role, obviously gay, friendly and menacing at the same time; his club, in obvious homage to Welles's *Citizen Kane*, is called Xanadu), who auditions him. He attempts again to flee, gets viciously beaten in a fight in Chicago's tenderloin, and, unable to clarify for himself who, if anyone, is pursuing him, assumes his paranoia as a permanent condition and takes again to the stage, open, vulnerable, yet with a sense of liberation.

The telling of the narrative presents this information obliquely, withholding so much in the way of discursive information and giving so much in the way of disconnected and grotesque images (photographed in a sharp-edged black and gray by Ghislain Cloquet and edited by Aram Avakian) that the spectator may be as affected with an opaque and fractured perception, and an attendant anxiety, as is the character in the fiction. This is not to say that the viewer identifies with the character in the sense of giving over emotions to that character, an experience that sometimes occurs while watching a conventional narrative. Rather, the sense of distance and confusion experienced by the viewer makes her perceptions somewhat analogous to the inhabitant of the fiction. The credit sequence, for example, is a seemingly disconnected series of surreal images. Mickey sits in a steam bath in a derby and overcoat with turned-up collar; behind him a group of fat men in towels looks on and laughs (one wears a gun). Mickey and a girl swim underwater in a pool. A girl is draped on the hood of a car, face pressed to the window as the wipers turn back and forth. (The image recalls Fellini's 1960 film, *La Dolce Vita*.) Mickey and a girl make love while, in deep focus behind them, a man is beaten up. The sequence comes to a close as Mickey runs in the dark from a man yelling at him, "There's no place you can hide from them. You'll have to be an animal." There follow quick shots of Mickey burning his identification papers and sleeping on a coffin in a railroad car.

Midway through the film, in what almost amounts to a failure of nerve on Penn's part, this sequence is explained, given a context, in a flashback. Mickey tells his lover about his past; the flashback shows his former employer, Ruby Lapp (an old and puffy Franchot Tone), who explains to him his obligations to the mob. Mickey runs in panic, and there is a repeat of Ruby yelling after him, "You'll have to be an animal." This is a moment of reversion to conventional narrative procedure, in which the character's past is explained and his present—his love affair—offered in melodramatic terms (although the images in the flashback do retain a bizarre and menacing presence—Ruby's warning to Mickey is given in a meat locker, slabs of beef on hooks providing a background). Perhaps it is unfair to criticize a film that does take so many chances just because it hedges at one point. Penn, after all, is a melodramatist, a creator of large emotions through dramatic excess, and in this he is firmly within the great tradition of American film. In *Mickey One*, he attempts to counter the melodramatic comfort of easy emotions, slips back into them, and then pulls away again.[8] The romantic interlude comes almost as a relief to the jarring world that otherwise surrounds and reflects the character (and is intended precisely as such a sanctuary for the character himself), a world in which Mickey is implicated but also detached from what he sees.

The body of the film retains this perspective. Mickey's wanderings in Chicago are marked by threat and provocation: in an automobile graveyard (a favorite image of Penn, occurring again in *The Chase* and in *Bonnie and Clyde*) he is pursued by a crane as the police demonstrate death by car crusher. The high- and low-angle shots of the crane turn it into a palpable and purposive menace and a reflection of Mickey's fears. A strange Asian figure beckons to him from the junkyard, a figure who reappears through-out the film, finally revealing himself as an artist who creates, out of junk, a self-destroying machine (symbolism that would be heavy-handed in a literary form, but effective in a visual one and based on an actual artist's work). Mickey goes to a derelicts' mission for shelter. The man who runs the place can barely speak and painfully stutters words that occur over and over throughout the film: "Is there any word from the Lord?" The words connote a fashionable (for the mid-sixties) religious angst, yet their irony and, finally, their poignancy in relation to Mickey's loneliness and fear are undeniable.

Loneliness and fear become manifest to Mickey in images of himself throughout the film. One sequence in particular indicates how clearly the world perceived by Mickey enfolds and reflects him. He flees the automobile graveyard and, as he flees, turns to watch a car that is bursting into flames. The camera is positioned behind him, and as he moves to screen left away from the fire, the shot begins to dissolve to another shot of Mickey, now on screen right and to the rear of the frame, walking as if through the fire, down a street toward the camera, drinking from a bottle. These images are held together briefly so that it appears as if Mickey were observing himself in flames. As both superimposed shots begin to dissolve out, a third is dissolved in under them, showing Mickey walking along a row of storefronts, his image reflected in the windows. For a brief moment there are three—actually four—images of Mickey on the screen at once. The entire sequence lasts only about thirteen seconds, but long enough to indicate the fragmented and inward nature of the character. Such cinematic bravura and directorial self-indulgence reveal how cinematic conventions can be exploited and invigorated, renewed as elements of increased perception. The dissolve is conventionally used to indicate a change in place and/or time. But in this sequence simple transition is made subordinate to an ability to signify an entrapment of the character by himself and to make manifest to the spectator the extent to which the images of the film reflect the character's state of mind. Narrative time and space are subordinated to perception.

Mickey One is a self-indulgent film, and self-indulgence is not looked on kindly in American cinema, where self-effacement is a traditional value. The breaking of the tradition has a liberating effect, on the film, on its viewers, on Penn himself. As a fiction, *Mickey One* celebrates a frightened individual who finally overcomes his fear (trite enough as a narrative premise, powerfully created through the visual structure Penn gives it) and is able to exist in a threatening and incoherent world. This is a central modernist premise. At the end of the film, a beaten and still paranoid Mickey goes before an audience. As he sits down at the piano to do his act, the camera pulls back to reveal him in the middle of Chicago's lakefront, exposed, vulnerable, but performing nonetheless. This is the most liberating moment in Penn's films, a rare instance when his central character does not die, become helpless, or is returned to a safe domestic enclave. And I suspect there is something allegorical in it, a reflection of the American filmmaker's allowing himself to become vulnerable and perform counter to the cinematic conventions of the moment. Penn survived the film by abjuring it, absorbing what he learned from it, and fairly quickly realigned himself within the commercial cinema, going on in three years to create the most influential film of the decade.

The films that follow *Mickey One* owe very little to it directly. The jagged and abrupt editing of Aram Avakian is replaced by the more cohesive, though sometimes arhythmic style of Dede Allen, which depends on rapid and dynamic associations of image and movement within the image, as opposed to the dissociations that mark the editing in *Mickey One*. The subjective intensity of *Mickey One*, the projection of an inner fear onto the outer world that is so much responsible for the uneasy disparities of the film, is replaced in the later films by more tangible quasi-historical and political forces: southern reactionism in *The Chase*, rebellion versus societal order in *Bonnie and Clyde*, threats to middle-class order in *Alice's Restaurant*, white brutality toward the Indians in *Little Big Man*. But

Mickey One remains an intriguing and exciting film as well as an important document. The narrative experiments of the French were inimical to traditional American cinema and for critic and audience to accept them had to be realized more quietly, more unobtrusively than they were in Penn's film. But they were realized, and *Mickey One* acts as a kind of pointer, a direction sign for Penn and other American filmmakers to follow.

Penn's films are all marked by a tension between vitality and oppression, by a desperate need for the self to extend itself into the world, to assume a measure of control and direction, no matter how illusory and how temporary that control is. *Mickey One* expresses this tension in an oblique and suggestive form, as well as expressing a way for the tension to be resolved and the individual to endure. But in his major films, at least until *Four Friends*, Penn refuses to allow resolution or compromise, or even endurance. Throughout his work, he assumes the conventions of the "realist" (or perhaps pessimist) too thoroughly to allow alternatives, to allow liberation to survive, to indicate that there are possibilities other than the repressive order he seems to see as inevitable. This tension exists in the form of his films as well. Even though he turns away from open, experimental narrative forms after *Mickey One*, he cannot entirely forget the opportunities they offer, so that the conventional melodramatic structures of his films are often altered by a distancing, an attention to their existence as film and as responses to existing film genres. Like the characters in Penn's fictional worlds, the filmic construction of these worlds threatens to free itself from the conventions and authority of accepted narrative procedures, only to yield to those procedures in the end, just as his characters are forced to yield to the social order.

Bonnie and Clyde is the film in which all these tensions and contradictions are played out fully and to great advantage. It attempts, with varying degrees of success, to achieve a structural integrity and becomes a social phenomenon and a major influence on many films and filmmakers who follow. Using a narrative form that appears straightforward and "realistic" in its detail but is in fact highly manipulative, it carefully forges a relationship between viewer and central characters without hiding the fact that it is doing this. All Hollywood cinema aspires to the former; few films combine that aspiration with a foregrounding of their own methods of construction. *Bonnie and Clyde* is also a conscious act of myth-making and extends this consciousness within the fiction and outside it simultaneously. The viewer is asked to feel a sympathy with and an admiration for its central characters, a joy in their lives and a fear for their survival, and at the same time realize they are larger than life—fictional beings in a fictional realm. The film creates a desire for emulation; the characters themselves attempt to create a version of themselves to be emulated. Like the figures of a traditional gangster film, a genre that *Bonnie and Clyde* reflects upon and updates—Rico in *Little Caesar* (1930), Tony Camonte in *Scarface* (1932)—Bonnie and Clyde are concerned about their image, about how they look to the world. They photograph each other and send the pictures to the newspapers. Bonnie's doggerel verse about their exploits so thrills Clyde that his potency returns (the impotence motif in the film, the substitution of gun for penis, is an obvious element, which still manages to work as a significant cultural image of substitution, the establishment of sexuality as violent domination).

31

The attempts of the early film gangsters to boost themselves, to create their own legends, were observed coolly and disparagingly as another sign of their pride, which the spectator knew, even that early in the life of the genre, would lead to their fall. But in *Bonnie and Clyde* the viewer is not permitted to observe coolly and is rather asked to share the characters' joy in their exploits and their notoriety. Many years of gangster films have modified that joy with the knowledge that it will lead to their fall. Penn therefore plays with convention and revision, with expectation and desire, leading the viewer to enjoy a world he knows is fantastic, enviable, and doomed—a desire that has kept the gangster genre vital over the life of cinema.

The myth-making that occurs within the narrative is doubled by the myth-making that is carried on by the narrative itself. The audience is privileged to both processes as well as its own reactions to them, a phenomenon Penn takes cognizance of in the film. After they commit their first murder, Bonnie and Clyde go to the movies to hide. The film they see is *Golddiggers of* 1933, and the particular sequence—in ironic parallel to their first successful bank robbery—is the number "We're in the Money." In the film they watch, people are in the audience watching the song and dance number. The audience for *Bonnie and Clyde* is therefore placed in the situation of watching a movie in which the characters watch a movie in which other people watch a song and dance number. The song and dance number comments on events in *Bonnie and Clyde* and was itself filmed at the time when the events in *Bonnie and Clyde* are meant to be taking place. Penn does not permit a lingering over this distancing device, for nowhere is it his intention to force his audience away from the fiction to a speculation on the nature of film images and narratives, in the manner of Godard. Yet the levels of involvement are clearly marked and there to be observed. The viewer is forced, on some level, to be aware of the fact that she is watching a film at the same time that the film cancels that potentially distancing device by demanding the viewer's emotional participation. The participation is countered by a warning not to participate, climaxed by the brutal rending of the emotional attachment at the end of the film. Finally, the viewer is forced into an observation of his or her own emotions.[9] The complexity of points of view within the film creates conflicts in the perception of the film and in the relationship created between the film and the viewer.

The use of a cinematic allusion and quotation within a film did not originate with *Bonnie and Clyde*, but it has since become quite commonplace. In the modernist context, allusion acts as a place marker in a film, anchoring it to the body of cinema of which it is a part and by so doing foregrounding its existence as a film, an artifact with a history. In recent films, as in most postmodern practice, such direct or indirect allusions proliferate not so much to make a narrative or structural point, but to affirm a community of popular culture, a web of works and fans, a bond of shared knowledge. The quotation from *Golddiggers* in *Bonnie and Clyde* is part of the film's unbinding, part of the cat-and-mouse game it plays with viewer sympathies, drawing them in and then rejecting them, confusing the viewer's point of view. In Oliver Stone's *Natural Born Killers* (1994), *Bonnie and Clyde* itself will be alluded to throughout, existing as a prolonged and invisible quotation and homage, as well as a discussion, reminder, and re-vision of Penn's own ironic play of distance and identification, of violence and attraction.

The opening sequences of *Bonnie and Clyde* immediately provide the conflicting points of view. The credit sequence, with its old photographs and printed biographies of the characters, creates a distance, a provocation of curiosity, enforced by the sound of a camera shutter and the graphics of the titles themselves. The letters turn to red on the screen, a premonition of the violence the viewer knows is coming. (The effect of foreknowledge that was brought to the film cannot be underestimated. *Bonnie and Clyde* was a matter of such controversy on its release that there could have been few people who went to see it without knowing, and therefore expecting, the outcome. Even without that foreknowledge, red is a fairly universal sign of danger, and a dissolving of the titles to it from a neutral color disrupts the continuity and creates discomfort.)[10] The titles set up a conflict, which is aggravated by the first shot of the film that follows: an enormous closeup of Bonnie's lips. Normally the first shot of a film is an establishing shot, situating the audience in a defined space that the characters inhabit, so that the filmmaker can begin his cutting pattern within that space. Here, as in the fragmented opening of *Mickey One*, no spatial coordinates are offered, no secure situating of the character, and, indeed, no character at all.

The closeup of Bonnie's lips (which is dissolved in over a photograph of Warren Beatty as Clyde) moves out to encompass her at her mirror. There follows a succession of abrupt shots, in which she lies on her bed, pounding on the frame, and flounces about her room. The cutting is swift and arrhythmical; many of the shots are terminated before the physical action contained within them is finished. In a brief time, the viewer is offered an unlocalized place and a barely determined figure. John Cawelti, in his excellent visual analysis of the film, states that the opening gives a sense of Bonnie's imprisoned sensuality, and certainly Bonnie's abrupt movements indicate frustration, a feeling of being trapped.[11] Even more, they give the viewer a sense of immediate, if confused, attachment to the character. In *Bonnie and Clyde* no time is lost and no space between viewer and characters is allowed. For, just as the viewer attempts to make sense of who and what Bonnie is, Clyde is introduced. He is seen first—by the viewer—in the street, by means of a shot inserted amid Bonnie's moving about and dressing. She immediately notices him from her window, and the next shot of him is from her point of view. When he responds to her question, "Hey, boy, what you doin' with my mama's car?" he makes eye contact with her. His glance up at the window provides the shot that responds to her observation of him in a variation of a cutting format that is the basic structuring principle of American film. So basic that it deserves some comment.

Two reasons for the firm establishment of the shot/reverse shot technique have been assumed: first, it is an easy and controllable production method. The best performances of each actor can be selected and cut in; both actors need not be present for the entire filming of the sequence. Second, there was the belief that rapid cutting of a dialogue sequence (indeed, of any sequence in American film from the early sound period through the fifties, when few shots are much longer than nine to fifteen seconds) and rapid changes in point of view would prevent viewer boredom. Other interpretations of this basic cutting pattern reveal profound ideological currents. The rapid cutting of numerous separate shots into a pattern that creates an illusion of smooth continuity and links the gaze of one character to another is a way of avoiding viewer objectivity. The illusion of wholeness that is obtained in the classical cutting style (as opposed to the fragmentation created by the cutting in a film like *Mickey One*) renders it invisible. The viewer is forced to attend to the events occurring within the narrative. The gaze is directed beyond the formal structure of the film and into the story, the surrogate reality of the characters and events on the screen. The shot/reverse shot sequence in particular does not permit the viewer to move beyond, or outside, the closed space of the characters. Their gaze is never directed outward to the camera/audience (of all conventions in fimmaking this is the strongest: no character within a film may make eye contact with the camera and with that contact announce the existence of a medium, a mechanical, optical, aesthetic structure that stands between the viewer and the people and events it creates). The viewer, therefore, is ignored but may not ignore what is seen—a fully inhabited, articulated, closed world. Furthermore, the constant opening and closing of that world—one character looks and in the next shot the other character answers the direction of his or her gaze—seal the viewer within it. The editing structure of American film is therefore based upon an extraordinary contradiction. Many images, rapidly linked, create a wholeness and completeness; the complexity of parts produces the illusion of an absence of parts, indeed, an absence of form. The viewer sees through the screen into a completely realized world offered as complete and valid.[12]

Bonnie and Clyde makes full use of the shot/reverse shot technique while simultaneously reflecting on it. The abrupt editing of the opening sequence seems at first to deny the convention. The linking of the characters' gaze when Bonnie sees Clyde out the window embraces it fully. The film is deeply concerned with the relationship of its characters and the relationship of the viewer to those characters, while at the same time it keeps questioning those relationships, making the viewer, on some level, aware of the act of gazing. At the moment in the film when the characters make eye contact, they are immediately linked and are not separated for the rest of the film. The viewer is immediately linked to them and rarely allowed to separate from them for the rest of the film, until violently wrenched away by their slaughter, as if being punished for being so close.

Bonnie trundles downstairs to meet Clyde, in a startling low shot that allows the viewer to look up her dress, at the same time presenting the figure in a distorting tilt. Once she is on the street, they are photographed in a two shot, and they talk and proceed to walk down a sunlit, deserted street, the camera tracking along with them, keeping them together in the shot. The camera remains close as they walk into an apparently abandoned town (the only other figure to be seen is a black man sitting in a chair, and throughout the film Penn will continually link Bonnie and Clyde to the marginalized and disenfranchised). They talk, drink Cokes, Clyde does his engaging trick with a matchstick in his mouth and boasts of his outlaw prowess. The first glimmer of violence appears as he tells her that he cut off his big toe with an axe to get out of jail. Bonnie caresses his gun and urges him to "use it," pressing the connection between repressed sexuality and the need for some physical action in which to sublimate it. At this point, Penn finally offers a more or less conventional establishing shot by cutting to a long shot of the street as Clyde enters a store to rob it. This occurs a good ten to fifteen minutes into the film, and it is the first time since the credit sequence that some distance is placed between viewer and charac-ters. But it is a contradictory distance. There is a spatial separation, but the bond between viewer and character is now so strong, curiosity as to whether Clyde will pull off the robbery so piqued, that the separation is unwanted. The bravura and bantering of the two and their complete isola-tion have allowed the viewer no emotional room. When the camera does finally offer visual space, it comes as an intrusion. Penn, as if realizing that this new distance is unwanted, cuts immediately to Bonnie's point of view, with a shot from behind her, looking at the store Clyde has entered. He cuts from this to a closeup of her looking concerned, mirroring the emotions that all members of the audience should be feeling, and thereby reestab-lishing the characters' link with each other and the viewer's with them.

From this point the bond between characters and spectator is not allowed to diminish. Occasionally one or the other character becomes more sympathetic. But Bonnie and Clyde's attachment to each other assures the viewer's attachment to them equally. As the violence of the film increases—and it does in a very measured progression—as the threats to their well-being become greater, they become increasingly isolated from their world. And it is exactly the combination of audience attachment to them and their own growing isolation that helps the film's myth-making mechanism to operate. Their need to be free of their society's restrictions, its economic and emotional poverty, the pleasure they take in their freedom, its tenuous-ness and the sympathies and fears it has created, generate a complex of

35

emotions that makes the characters, finally, surrogates for some basic psychological, social, and cultural desires and anxieties.

But herein lies the flaw of the film. The manipulation is too easily managed, viewer response too easily gotten. The reflexive qualities, Penn's ability to make the viewer consider his or her response, is insufficiently worked out. The myth-making process, apparent as it is, is directionless; the voice that speaks the discourse of the film is unclear. Too many questions are raised. Why should the viewer invest emotions in these two fictional characters and make of them surrogates for his or her own fears and desires? Why is the viewer given pleasure in their exploits, in their vitality, only to have that pleasure brutally attacked? Who are the enemies in the film? Why do they win? Why must the audience lose by seeing the characters violently destroyed?

Heroism in American film conventionally displays an individual who can conquer oppressive odds and adversity; if the hero loses, the struggle of his fight (and with the exception of some romantic melodramas it is usually a man who struggles heroically) transcends the victory of his adversaries. This pattern remains true even in the nineties mock-heroic melodramas spawned by *Die Hard* (John McTiernan, 1988) and *Terminator 2* (James Cameron, 1991). The Hollywood heroic melodrama is, of course, naive and reductive, but in attempting to overcome it Penn and screenwriters Robert Benton and David Newman sacrifice dialectical clarity for emotional entanglement. The adversary in *Bonnie and Clyde* is intangible. "Society," oppressive and denying, but without detailed articulation, is offered as the opposing force. A few details signify what this society is—barren landscapes, the empty, dusty towns, one failed bank and one dispossessed farmer, some Roosevelt posters signifying the Depression. But this historical moment is not fleshed out. The connotations of dearth and poverty are present but unaccounted for. (One need only recall the sequence in Ford's *The Grapes of Wrath* (1940), where Muley rages against the injustice of losing his farm, to understand how direct a definition of Depression politics and economics can be rendered, even within the Hollywood convention of personalizing the political.)

The people with whom Bonnie, Clyde, and their gang come in contact are defined only as scared, compliant, or mean. And they are usually silly or ugly. The man in the store who takes a meat cleaver to Clyde, who is only trying to steal a few groceries, is enormous and grossly unattractive. His violence is too great a response to Clyde's robbery. He scares not only Clyde but the viewer as well, who is asked to approve Clyde's pistol-whipping him. When the teller of the Mineola bank leaps onto the window of the escaping car and gets his face shot, it is an appalling sight (such bloodied flesh had never been seen in an American film), but the implicit comment is that, like the fat man with the cleaver, he didn't have to attack. These people who emerge from the empty, sunbaked, Depression-ridden Midwest to attack Bonnie, Clyde, Buck, Blanche, and C. W. are the ones trying to be heroes. The gang is only trying to rob banks, and banks rob the people. Bonnie and Clyde don't want to hurt anyone; they are lonely people trying to escape their loneliness, their sexual dysfunction, their economic oppression. They become heroes almost despite themselves. They take pleasure in their exploits, they take part in the making of their own legend. Their stature grows from the success they have in the face of these unattractive opponents, a success that continues until these single attackers begin to join into groups and become represented by the police. This is a successful maneuver on the part of the filmmaker, for it keeps the film focused on the main characters and the point of view steady. Social and political realities are present by suggestion only. Clearly something is amiss in the world, but exactly what remains unclear. The only certainty is that the film's heroes make the world come alive. The individuals who try to stop them are foolish and misdirected. When the police appear, they are as abstract and uncomprehending as the landscape.[13]

The police—seen briefly when they show Clyde's picture to the man who attacked him with the meat cleaver—first appear en masse as a faceless group of Keystone Kops. The initial shootout is presented as slapstick. The gang bulldoze their way out, Blanche is hysterical (which annoys not only the rest of the gang but the viewer as well, for no real threat or upset is desired, no realization that this is a desperate situation); the gang retain their control. The police are harmless until they themselves become concentrated in a single person, Texas Ranger Frank Hamer, who is humiliated by the gang. The sequence with Hamer tests and confirms devotion to the main characters. The scene is again one of isolation. The gang's car is shown in a far shot by a lake. Another car quietly glides into the frame in front of it. The policeman, serpent-like, insinuates himself into the gang's place of rest. They jump him, they take his picture, and he is roundly taunted. The group seems to be in control, but once again Blanche's hysteria threatens the mood of triumph, provoking a reconsideration of the consequences of their actions and the viewer's own reactions. When C. W. suggests, half-seriously, that they shoot Hamer, Blanche screams a very serious "No!" And on that scream there is a quick cut to Hamer looking over at her, sizing up her weakness and her future usefulness in trapping the gang.

Even though, after the Hamer episode, the gang go on to rob successfully and with even greater pleasure and confidence, the memory of Hamer's unblinking seriousness during his captivity, the ferocity with which he spits in Bonnie's face when she teases him, lingers and provides a troubling foreshadowing for all that follows. Opposition to Bonnie and Clyde is beginning to consolidate itself into something more serious than the Keystone Kops. The world surrounding them is not as receptive to the gang's exploits as one had thought; it is certainly not as receptive as is the spectator. When they are attacked again (an attack in which, significantly, the first bullet hits a mirror, shattering Bonnie and Clyde's reflected image, their closeness, their inviolability, and their protective isolation), blood flows: Blanche is blinded and Buck is shot in the head. The gang, in wretched shape, escape and huddle by their car. The scene dissolves to morning, and they are surrounded by a posse. The people, who with a few exceptions were friendly to Bonnie and Clyde when alone, are violent toward them when in a crowd and under the aegis of the police. But their violence is strangely impotent. The police do the serious shooting. Buck dies horribly. Bonnie and Clyde are wounded. The bystanders shoot the gang's car to pieces, whooping around it like Indians.

This is a particularly awful moment for the audience. Obviously the viewer is guaranteed a strong reaction to the violence committed on the people to whom he or she has grown attached; but, added to this, the impotent destructiveness of the crowd is a curious punctuation. Throughout the film the relation of Bonnie and Clyde to the people surrounding them is tentatively good. They are attacked only twice by ordinary people (the grocery man with the cleaver and the bank teller); otherwise "folks" maintain a respectful, even cynical, distance from them. After their last robbery, Penn inserts two "interviews" with people involved, contrasting a melodramatic policeman—"There I was, staring square into the face of death"—and a bystander who prophesies their end: "They did right with me, I'm bringin' me a mess of flowers to their funeral." The people touched by Bonnie and Clyde understand them within the fiction better than the audience does outside it. Within the fiction, people are clearheaded about the gang's mythological status and do not seem to embrace them as liberated surrogates for their repressed lives. The viewer's reaction, however, is split among desire for the gang's success, the fear generated by the crowd's response, and the knowledge, enforced by other films, that the

38

police will eventually get them. Penn, not missing a chance to play further with viewer response and the emotional dependency he has built for his heroes, shocks the spectator with the frustrated and maddening violence of the crowd at the ambush but then turns to give the viewer almost what had been hoped for all along. In their painful escape from the ambush, Bonnie, Clyde, and C. W. find a white car, which will ultimately be the place of their death. They drive all night, coming to rest in an Okie camp. The crowd of poor people huddle around the car, whispering, "They famous? . . . Is that really Bonnie Parker?" A man touches Clyde. A bowl of soup is offered. The scene ends on a long shot of the car, isolated, surrounded by a group of curious, wondering people.

Like most of the bystanders with whom Bonnie and Clyde come into contact, the Okies are distant. They cannot join with the robbers; they cannot really help them, for the key to Bonnie and Clyde's success and fame is their isolation from the world in which everyone else is caught up—the people in poverty, the police in the poverty of law and order. Bonnie and Clyde are not revolutionaries, for they cannot give the people anything, save some money at a bank robbery; they offer no opportunity for people to join them. The Okies' reaction demonstrates Bonnie and Clyde's success and their failure. They gain fame, even a recognition of sorts, but they fail because people are merely in awe of them. The result of that awe is isolation. The far shot that ends the Okie sequence sums up their situation within the film; they are alone and wounded, trapped in the car, surrounded by people with a distant and wondering attitude toward them but ultimately unconcerned, for the heroes do not touch their lives. The only ones still connected to them with concern are the members of the audience, and they are forced to share the characters' isolation. Bonnie and Clyde are constructed images of vitality and escape. Ungrounded in any reality, save the contemporary viewer's own counter-cultural fantasies, that imagery is doomed to dissolve.

Note must be taken of one of the central images of the characters' isolation. The car is the place of Bonnie and Clyde's existence, their freedom, and their entrapment. The car functions often as part of a double frame: it encloses the characters as it itself is enclosed within the screen. Penn makes a special point of this. In the first murder, the bank teller leaps at the car, pressing his face against the window. The spectator's point of view is inside, looking through the window with the characters, and therefore the viewer is made to share the act of violence against this man. But the feeling of intrusion is shared as well. The man is attempting to violate the car, the safe place. Clyde shoots him in response to this violation. In the Frank Hamer episode there is a particularly pointed repetition of this. Clyde grabs Hamer, pins his arms, and throws him down on the back of the car, against the rear window. As he hits the glass, there is a cut to inside the car looking out the rear window as Hamer hits it. But Dede Allen, Penn's editor, chooses to break continuity slightly. Hamer hits the window in the exterior shot, hits it again when the cut is made to the interior of the car.[14] The continuity break happens quickly and is easy to miss but nonetheless has a definite function. It emphasizes the action, of course, but emphasizes as well the outside/inside structure that the car creates. There is no one in the car when Hamer is seen from its interior. The gang is outside and in control of the intruding Texas Ranger (who Clyde, ever the good populist, insists should be looking after poor people and not chasing them). The sudden shift to a point of view from inside the car reveals a heretofore unexpected vulnerability, of which the gang themselves are as yet unaware.

The Hamer episode is the turning point of the Barrow gang's fortune. After this, the car will become a target, as in the ambush discussed earlier, which begins as the gang is huddled by the car, proceeds as they attempt an escape, driving in circles, and ends with the car being shot to pieces, and the place of their isolation, as in the Okie episode.[15] Like the film itself, which is the vehicle for the viewer's emotions, the security offered by the automobile is tenuous and it becomes the place of Bonnie and Clyde's failure. They are essentially alone; their vitality and their pleasures are attractive but tentative, and the link drawn between them and the spectator puts the latter at risk of also being isolated and alone.

The risk becomes realized at the end of the film, when the connection to and relationship with the characters are violently shattered. Again the car plays an important role. As Frank Hamer teases information out of the blind Blanche (whom he has captured), Bonnie and Clyde sit in their white car in the rain. Bonnie reads Clyde her doggerel on their life and death, and their faces reflect the rain on the car windshield. The car is again their refuge, their place of protection, and now, at the same time, their trap. There is a cut to the outside of the car and a dissolve to Hamer, reading the poem Bonnie has sent to the papers. There follows a dissolve back to Bonnie and Clyde, sitting by their car in a sunlit field. Bonnie reads the end of her poem, its celebration of their life giving Clyde a shot of potency. As they make love, the newspapers blow across the field (significantly, and perhaps heavy-handedly, two sheets of newspaper blow apart and separate). At this point an abrupt change in the visual form of the film occurs. By means of a panning telephoto shot C. W.'s father is observed, simultaneously at a distance and in proximity, walking down a street to rendezvous with Frank Hamer and betray the heroes. Penn has placed the spectator first in the most intimate proximity with the central characters and their newfound intimacy. He then moves as far as possible from that intimacy with a shot whose focal length disrupts perspective and proximity with something analogous to the point of view of a spy. The viewer knows clearly at this point that the end is near and knows also, finally, that as close as he has been allowed to come to the characters, permission has been granted only to act as observer, helpless to avert the destruction to come.

Bonnie and Clyde's deaths occur as their car is blocked in the road by C. W.'s daddy. Clyde is outside, Bonnie in the car. Their safe place is violated. Before the bullets fly, and as the two of them realize what is occurring, there is a rapid series of shots in which each looks at the other. Since the time they first meet, Penn has attempted to keep Bonnie and Clyde closely together in the frame. Now that they are to die, he separates them physically but at the same time associates them by the glances they exchange, glances that indicate their affection for each other and their resignation and which climax and end the play of their gaze at the beginning of the film.[16] Bonnie is ripped apart by bullets as she sits helplessly behind the wheel. Clyde is killed just outside the car. The very last shot of the film is from behind the car, observing through its window the police moving about the scene of carnage in quiet and awe. The camera almost cowers in reaction to what has happened. And what has happened is not merely the death of the characters in the film but the destruction of the point of view that has been so carefully forged. The car violated, its inhabitants dead, the audience has no one to look at and look with; no secure and mobile isolation. The viewer is alone and lost. The bad guys have won, and the film has nothing more to tell us about the heroes. Since there is, as far as Penn is concerned, nothing more to see, the screen unceremoniously and anticlimactically goes black.

With *Bonnie and Clyde* Penn created an extreme inversion of the structure and iconography of early gangster films. There the car functioned as an instrument of protection, aggression, and ostentation, entering the mainstream of American film narrative thereafter. How many dramatic films do not contain at least one major dialogue sequence in a car? The car, the road, the couple on the run have become among the most enduring images in American film, a semiology of escape, security, isolation, and violent death.[17] But no gangster used the car as a surrogate world the way Bonnie and Clyde do. Penn has changed the gangster environment. The genre, in its beginnings and through its metamorphosis into film noir in the forties, was radically urban in its setting. Gangsters were creatures of the city, which provided them with protection for as long as possible.[18] Bonnie and Clyde are country gangsters (a type that offers relatively little cinematic tradition— Nicholas Ray's *They Live by Night* and Joseph H. Lewis's *Gun Crazy*, both 1949; perhaps also Fritz Lang's *You Only Live Once*, 1937) and as such they require the mobility of a car and, more important, protection from the openness, the vulnerability that is paradoxically created by the sunlight. With *Bonnie and Clyde* Penn is, in a way, extending the investigation of film noir that he began in *Mickey One*. But it is an extension by contrast, placing the hunted characters in the open daylight rather than in an enclosing urban darkness. They are as vulnerable and ultimately as trapped as their noir relatives, but it is a vulnerability and entrapment countered by an openness and innocence signified by the country. In American film, as in the classical pastoral poem, the country is conventionally a place whose inhabitants are untouched by corruption, a place that offers security and comfort.*

42

This is of course another of the film's paradoxes. I have pointed out that the world Bonnie and Clyde inhabit is insecure, barren, and lifeless; they give it life by their activity. Unlike their thirties and forties progenitors, these two gangsters have nothing mean-spirited about them. They do not share the attractive repulsiveness of their thirties ancestors nor the depressed paranoia of their noir cousins, and the audience does not share the mixed feelings toward them that are experienced toward Rico in *Little Caesar* or Tony Camonte in *Scarface* or even Tommy Powers in *Public Enemy*. The morality of the thirties gangster films does not permit a wholehearted endorsement of their heroes. The brutality and stupidity of the early gangsters and their environment always stand in the way of an

---

* Noir gangster films such as Jacques Tourneur's *Out of the Past* (1947) and John Huston's *The Asphalt Jungle* (1950) clearly present the conventional contrast of city and country and the frustrated desire of their gangster heroes to find comfort in the pastoral world. Edgar Ulmer's *Detour* (1945), with its grotesque drive west, moves from the urban to the suburban. In the wake of *Bonnie and Clyde*, Ridley Scott's *Thelma and Louise* (1991) and Stone's *Natural Born Killers* confine the road to the suburban and desert Southwest, further south than their predecessor, but still in an uninviting, noncity landscape.

unmodified admiration of these small men who make it big. The viewer must actively separate the gross charm of these characters from their sordid urban background, their viciousness, the ugly people who surround them, and the morally platitudinous police who always look for a way to get them. When the gangster film was transformed into film noir, the characters became even more unreachable; they became small, mean figures scurrying about in the dark. Nicholas Ray attempted to redeem the gangster in *They Live by Night* but only managed to create a passive couple trapped by circumstance and their own innocence. The attraction of Bonnie and Clyde is that they are neither passive nor innocent. They are active and know perfectly what they are doing. They are attractive to us—as are their thirties forebears—precisely because of their energy and the way they give life to their barren world.

Bonnie and Clyde are self-made crooks. This is a basic trait of movie gangsters, to be sure. Admiration of them is rooted in the ideology of the individual who succeeds by dint of personal effort, the man who distinguishes himself by energetically circumventing normal societal patterns. Only a man—whether a gangster or in other business, the figure of admiration is male; if a woman circumvents normal patterns, she is looked on as strange or threatening. Few films have caused such gender-driven revulsion as *Thelma and Louise*, in which the outlaws—very much emulating Bonnie and Clyde, seizing a few moments of power—are women. The thirties movie gangster embodied this ideology to curious ends. He started as a member of the lumpenproletariat, an economically disenfranchised individual who began working his way up in an urban "business" organization. As he did so, he gathered to himself the tangible properties of a man of means: a fancy lady, clothes, cars, a penthouse, hangers-on, and a reputation. The gangster is a parody of the bourgeois on the make, every working man's dream of leaving his class and getting to the top. The working man had, after all, always been told he could get there—at least that he had the opportunity to. But obstacles such as class, education, and economic situation were never recognized, and so it was never quite apparent how that opportunity could be realized. The myth of the gangster provided a reasonable surrogate (all myths are surrogates) for his own desires. It also provided a built-in caution. If a poor man violently works his way to the top and remains unregenerate when he gets there, he will be destroyed.

Bonnie and Clyde reworks this ideology for the sixties. It generalizes it and depoliticizes it even more than did the early gangster films, appealing

43

to the cultural discomfort growing at the time, the ripening of a rebelliousness that was just beginning to find the Vietnam war an escapable object for rebellion. Penn sketches in a world that is unhappy and repressive, just enough to make the spectator uncomfortable with it, but not enough to provide the details of that repression. The viewer is therefore left free to generalize, to make it analogous to the repression many people were experiencing in the sixties. He makes his heroes young, appealing, and oddly classless (though, in the traditional style of Hollywood heroes, very classy, for Warren Beatty takes on the appearance of Robert Kennedy more than once in the film, and Faye Dunaway's Bonnie looks more like a woman's magazine model than a poor southwestern bank robber; in fact the film did create some fashion fads for a brief time). Officially, the characters, like their ancestors, are "lower class"—Bonnie is a waitress, Clyde a petty thief. But they have no essential class accouterments and do not seem to want them. Only a bit of glamour and recognition. Their robberies seem to advance their status not one whit; they gain no power, and they gain no things. What they do gain is a certain tentative freedom and happiness, self-esteem, and each other's love, qualities more immediately attractive to a young mid-sixties audience.

Romantic love plays almost no part in the early gangster genre, whereas *Bonnie and Clyde* can be read, on one level, as a love story. Clyde is a powerful and dominating figure. He tells Bonnie how to wear her hair; he offers her an exciting life. He can't make love, but somehow that is made to appear more Bonnie's fault than Clyde's. Early in the film she is portrayed as being too demanding and too insulting of Clyde's impotence. Clyde's self-deprecating acceptance of his problem makes the audience sympathize with him. Besides, clearly he is a man, because of his gun and his readiness to use it. Clyde's substitute phallus serves for Bonnie until the end of the film, at which point they have reached a closeness with each other that gives Clyde back his sexual potency. That they die soon after this gives the film a perfect melodramatic structure. Try as he may, Penn cannot bring himself to reverse certain fundamental cultural themes that are embedded in American cinema and the ideology that informs it. One of the most fundamental of these is that love triumphs only by great sacrifice. Sacrifice is the key element of melodrama, and Penn makes it a structural principle of this film and most of the films that follow it.

Love is never free. Neither, Penn would lead us to believe, is freedom. Bonnie and Clyde are shot down, as was every gangster in every film before them and most films after. Very rarely can American filmmakers break the convention of the criminal paying for his crimes. Even if he does not die, he suffers morally and spiritually (the figure of Michael in the second *Godfather* film is the perfect example). The very mythologizing process of *Bonnie and Clyde* demands that the characters, whose point of view is so closely shared by the viewer, be sacrificed so that they may transcend themselves. In that sense, Penn moves far from his generic starting point. The death of the thirties gangster had, of course, a moral necessity.[19] If such an individual survived, societal order would have little meaning; and, according to Hollywood, everyone must suffer for his or her sins. But Penn is not merely creating gangsters who go against the social order—all gangsters, by generic definition, do—he is using them to make the viewer uncomfortable with that order. By their ability to enjoy their criminal life, by their camaraderie, by the ease with which the viewer is permitted to share their point of view and therefore share their momentary triumph over the desolation that surrounds them, Penn allows Bonnie and Clyde to generate themselves as figures of freedom. As they proceed, they suffer loneliness and an awareness of their fate, and fear for them grows. But they are unyielding; they do not wish to change, nor does the viewer wish them to. At the same time, the understanding is that they will not prevail, and this makes the spectator angry with the society that she knows will undo them.

Finally, the subjectivity of the viewer must come to terms with the subjectivity of the characters and the relationship between viewer and character that is fostered and denied by the film. For the first part of the film that relationship seems sound, as the viewer is asked to support and enjoy Bonnie and Clyde's activities. When their fortune changes and it is clear that they will die, the relationship is strengthened; the viewer wishes their survival but begins to fear for his or her own reactions if they do not survive. When they are destroyed, the relationship is cut off, the inter-subjectivity so carefully fostered is broken, and the viewer is left, as it were, alone. The structure of the film is ruptured, and there is nowhere to turn except back inward. The crucial element of *Bonnie and Clyde* is its final sequence. The punishment the viewer receives by watching the grotesque, slow-motion, bullet-punctured destruction of the two characters is immense. Immediate and unanswerable questions are raised. Do these terrible images deny the admiration the preceding body of the text has insisted on? Is the narrative suddenly proclaiming its heroes were wrong? If they were wrong, if these fictional characters are to be disapproved of, then surely such pains to create the admiration for them should not have been taken.

Were they too free? Were they having too much fun? Is Penn assuming the melodramatic directive that everyone must pay for his or her pleasures? Is the viewer being asked to share the death agonies? If he or she has been asked, indeed commanded, to share the main characters' perspectives and, by sharing, to admire them and feel for them, then perhaps the demand is also made to share the agonies of their deaths.

But of course a screen death cannot be shared. And, as the attack begins, a great distance is created between viewer and characters, not only by means of camera placement, but because of the use of slow motion and the very horror of the sequence. Agony and dying are represented; the viewer must contend with reactions to the representations—a situation basic to most movie viewing. The representation of violent death stimulates a complex response of fear, revulsion, attraction, and desire, to see that which ordinarily cannot be seen, in the safe context of knowing that what is seen is not really seen. But in this particular instance, no such representation is desired; the viewer simply wants the characters alive and the conflict is therefore all the more intense. Benton and Newman's original script called for Bonnie and Clyde's death to be swift and indeed only alluded to, using stills to replace action. But Penn felt that a drawnout, slow-motion death would enlarge the characters, seal them in the viewer's memories, enforce their mythic dimensions.[20] That intention is successful. I do not think the film would have entered our mythology or have had the influence on American film it had without the characters dying the way they do. It is an interesting sign of differing directorial temperaments, if not times, to see what the two major *Bonnie and Clyde* spin-offs in the nineties, *Thelma and Louise* and *Natural Born Killers*, do with their characters. Thelma and Louise die, though their deaths are less immediate, not visible, and more transcendental than Bonnie and Clyde's; closer to the ends of an earlier, and oppositely gendered, pair of *Bonnie and Clyde* spin-offs, the title characters of *Butch Cassidy and the Sundance Kid* (George Roy Hill, 1969). Mickey and Mallory, the central characters of Stone's film, survive, thrive, and reproduce; but then Stone is, as we will see, standing on their heads all the conventions triggered by *Bonnie and Clyde*.

The end of the film makes manifest its inherent contradictions. In order to mythologize his characters, Penn makes the audience love them, share the intimacy of their gaze, and then severs the tie violently. The result is that the film leaves the viewer desolate, shattered, and alone, as if witness to the assassination of a public figure. The viewer is punished for enjoying the characters and their exploits too much. As I said, it is the nature of melodrama to deny unalloyed pleasure and freedom; the form regards them as attractive sins for which penance must be paid. *Bonnie and Clyde* merely extends this pleasure-pain, profit-and-loss phenomenon further than it had been extended before. The real changes it makes in the conventions of melodrama involve the extent of the suffering the viewing subject must endure and the extent of the violence that provokes that suffering, both the viewer's and the characters'.

With *Bonnie and Clyde* Penn breaks a major cinematic contract between viewer and filmmaker that held that violent death on the screen would be swift and relatively clean. A bloodstain was permissible, a recoil from the force of the bullet, perhaps, but little more. He solidifies the convention begun in *Psycho*. Violent death is now to have an immediacy and to create a physical reverberation; it is to have a sense of anatomical detail. No doubt this new element resulted from certain historical anxieties. The Kennedy assassination (which Penn alludes to not only in *Bonnie and Clyde*, but in *The Chase* and *Four Friends*) and the Vietnam war, two of the American traumas of the sixties, made the culture acutely aware of the details of physical suffering and placed those details within a profoundly emotional, not to mention political, context.

Penn is concerned in all his films with examining that context and the complex responses to violence and its representations. He begins the examination early in his career. In *The Chase* (written by Lillian Hellman), a liberal sheriff (Marlon Brando) of a Texas town is beaten to a pulp by the bored, bigoted, frightened petit bourgeoisie of the town because of their resentment of him. This same awful bunch, a kind of liberal's nightmare of contemporary southern reactionary degeneracy, assassinate the town's free spirit (Robert Redford), who has escaped from prison and whose return aggravates their repression and frustration. The film is a sort of miniaturized and overheated allegory of the Kennedy assassination, speaking of a violence born of hate, jealousy, ennui, and emotional impotence. No one is ennobled in the film. The middle class is seen as vulgar and destructive, its opponents—the sheriff and the escaped convict—capable only of helpless rebellion. The entire situation is repeated in a somewhat different register in *Four Friends*. Again the violence explodes out of repression and anger. The main character of the film, Danilo, plans to marry the daughter of a rich man; there is the suggestion of incest between daughter and father. At the wedding, the father shoots his daughter and himself in a sequence so structured and so carefully placed within the film—which is, among other things, a history of the sixties—

that it becomes, like the violence in *The Chase*, disturbingly analogous to the political assassinations of the decade.

The only possible response to the violence in these films is helplessness, for the massiveness of the perpetrators' bigotry in *The Chase* and their madness in *Four Friends* seems insuperable. Earlier, in *The Left-Handed Gun*, Penn attempted a different balance. Billy the Kid kills out of revenge, a sense of loyalty to a man who befriended him and was, in turn, shot down. But Billy is larger than his revenge. He is portrayed as a force, as the young vitality of the West; his high spirits puzzle him as much as they threaten the society around him. Penn deals differently with viewer attitudes toward Billy than with those developed toward Bonnie and Clyde. Billy is a creature, ironically, of the fifties, rather than of the old West, just as Bonnie and Clyde are of the sixties, rather than the Depression thirties. He is the misunderstood, misunderstanding adolescent, and Paul Newman's portrayal is closely related to James Dean's in *Rebel Without a Cause*, here an orphan with two surrogate fathers. One is murdered; the other is Pat Garrett, who murders Billy because he believes the anarchic force must be contained. The distortion of oedipal relationships, two fathers demanding two opposing kinds of action and order, finally destroys the suffering subject.

When Billy kills, it is out of a sense of righteousness and occasionally regret. The violence has an extraordinary (for the fifties) deliberateness. If violence in *The Chase* is overwhelming and revolting, in *The Left-Handed Gun* it is stylized and exaggerated. Measured images of violence are offered, more detailed and analytic than had usually been presented in American film, and intended to demonstrate both the suffering and the banality of the violence up to then taken so much for granted. Sequences of violence in the film foreshadow the ritualized violence that the Italian westerns of the late sixties (particularly those of Sergio Leone) would develop almost as a parodic response to the intensity of violence by that time rampant in American film. There is a sense of pain in these sequences, of suffering. Penn is inquiring into the physicality of shootings and beatings and the ways that physicality can be expressed on the screen, experienced by his characters, and understood by his audience.

The violence increases throughout Penn's films as the oppressive forces and those attempting to liberate themselves from them become stronger; and it begins to get out of hand. The *Left-Handed Gun* inquires into the ways violence is depicted. *The Chase* portrays the cruelty of violence blindly and fearfully directed at those who only want to avoid it. (Between

48

these two films, *The Miracle Worker* deals with violence as a therapeutic instrument, as a way of demonstrating how, by emotional and physical strength, a determined woman deals with the primitive, blind child she attempts to civilize; the violence of *Mickey One*—in particular the vicious beating of Mickey—grows out of the bizarre and perceptually distorted world in which the character dwells.) In *Bonnie and Clyde*, Penn begins to show signs of enjoying the presentation of violent events for their own sake and playing with the attraction–repulsion the audience feels with respect to these events, leading them to bloodshed and then punishing them when they get there. This is another contradiction that emerges from the film. The violent activities committed by Bonnie and Clyde have a liberating effect; the violence done to them disrupts viewer pleasure, creating a shocking and brutalizing effect. This violent play on emotions begins to reveal a certain amount of cynicism, culminating in his made-for-cable film, *Inside*. Here, as in his earlier work, violence emerges from oppression, very literally from the oppression enacted by a racist prison guard during the apartheid regime in South Africa. Surely, Penn meant for the film to represent the intensity of cruelty under that regime, but the effect is to make the film somewhat unreachable, even unwatchable. The intensity of the violence disallows the viewer to assume the point of view of a badly treated prisoner in an oedipal dance with his captor and instead turn away in horror. Comprehension of politics and racism is made difficult.

The sometimes cynical employment of film violence that developed in the films of Penn and other filmmakers in the sixties did not go undetected and unexploited. Violence is an easy way to command emotional response under the pretense of "realism." Penn showed the way. *Bonnie and Clyde* opened the bloodgates, and our cinema has barely stopped bleeding since. The intensity and detail of the violence in *Bonnie and Clyde*, though tame in retrospect, were at the time unlike anything that had been done before. The various and conflicting messages Penn had hoped to generate—the radical fracture of audience point of view; the massive overreaction of authority to individuals who try to defy it; the impossibility of vitality and freedom succeeding in an oppressive culture; the glorification in death of two martyrs to that vitality and freedom—are lost in the spectacle of characters who, having earned affection and admiration, are slowly shot to pieces. Form took precedence over meaning, and the formal trend of violence started by *Bonnie and Clyde* has been irresistible. American filmmakers have been ready to leap for the veins more quickly and easily than for the intellect.

The general bloodletting in American film, whether caused by repressive authority or by an individual seeking revenge or righting great wrongs, speaks not only to the desire to gaze at the forbidden, transgressive scene, but to some immediate needs and fantasies that grow out of fear or a desire to see enemies easily disposed of. Some filmmakers take pains to ratchet up the violence committed on their hero in order to defend the violence used in return (consider the sadomasochistic heights reached by Paul Verhoeven in *Robocop*, 1987). Fantasy and desire are what drive film audiences and filmmakers. Cynicism turns into convention and finally into parody. What was appalling in the late sixties has become an aesthetic and cultural imperative. Violence is so much a part of the popular discourse of the culture that it has become a way of speaking about ourselves, of thinking and representing the way we are—even if, in our daily lives, most of us are not especially violent or in a violent environment. Film, along with all mass media, speaks to the way we represent ourselves to ourselves, and every indication is that we see ourselves and our world as violent. But, at the same time, violence and violent action are dynamics that American cinema does with clarity, grace, and precision; it is adept at it. Following *Bonnie and Clyde*, Sam Peckinpah turned shattering death into a breathtaking spectacle of the end of an era, of the diminishment of masculine certainty and political innocence in *The Wild Bunch* (1969). From then on, aesthetics, prosthetics, cinematic ritual, and cultural consent sutured violence into the very structure of cinema. Once the heroes of eighties action films began surviving the most horrendous acts of violence to their bodies, or showed their bodies to be cyborg instruments, violence turned from convention to display.[21] It has become a kind of joke and spectacle, curiously, perhaps shockingly, a kind of pleasure.

Representations of violence constitute the integral structure of the films of all the directors discussed in this book. Sometimes violence functions as a means of demonstrating or analyzing important cinematic or cultural phenomena; sometimes it is there for the hell of it; sometimes it occurs as a simple, cinematic reflex. Often, it is the display of virtuosity at the service of narrative ingenuity or its utter lack; always it is there to achieve a response, earned or not.

After *Bonnie and Clyde* and until *Inside*, Penn toned down the violence in his own films. It still appears, but briefly and pointedly, until *Target* and *Dead of Winter*, where it has no point at all. All of Penn's themes surface in

Inside, whose particular historical base is far from his usual concerns. The overlay of the old thematics and the eruptions of violence on a distant, but pressing history of another country don't quite match up. The political is, finally, not enlightened by the personal, and the attempt to universalize the struggle of a young man jailed by a vicious supporter of the status quo turns out to finally miss history and shifts the realities of racial oppression onto the struggle of two white men.

The fact is that Penn's creative period extended only briefly into the seventies. He made two influential films—*Alice's Restaurant* and *Little Big Man*—that, like *Bonnie and Clyde*, addressed the cultural moment of the late sixties. *Night Moves*, in 1975, began a reflection back on the sixties and spoke to the growing sense of alienation and despair that grew from the decade. *Night Moves* returns to the noir world of *Mickey One*, yet without that film's delight in its cinematic exploits and its offer of liberation in the face of anxiety. To situate it properly, it is necessary to go back to our discussion of film noir. In 1964, the original noir cycle over, Penn could elaborate on it, reinvestigate its milieu and characters and its relationship to the audience. By the mid-seventies, a noir revival began that has now become a full-fledged return to generic prominence. From Altman's *The Long Goodbye*, Scorsese's *Mean Streets* and *Taxi Driver*, to Roman Polanski's and Robert Towne's *Chinatown* (1974), up through Bryan Singer's *The Usual Suspects* and Curtis Hanson's *L.A. Confidential* (1997), filmmakers are investigating again the dark, barren, angst-ridden urban world that had enveloped crooks, detectives, and lower-middle-class simple men in the forties. Noir has even infiltrated science fiction, with Ridley Scott's *Blade Runner* (1982) assuming the mise-en-scène of the dark city of noir and Alex Proyas's *Dark City* (1998) naming its mise-en-scène in its very title.

The reassertion of the noir spirit is not strange, given new filmmakers' consciousness of cinematic history, coupled with the historical and cultural events of the sixties and after. The first appearance of noir in the mid-forties can be explained, as I mentioned, by the war and an almost dialectic response to victory. The genre reflected an anxiety attendant on the expansion of power away from home, the separation of families, the new economic status of women, and, perhaps, a knowledge that the culture (and the country) was not as secure and as innocent as had been thought. Indeed, with the memory of fascism and the knowledge of nuclear power, it seems obvious that images of strength would be countered and even conquered by images of anxiety and fear. The fifties shifted the anxiety, making it a response to the communist myth. By convincing the culture that communism was the root source of evil and terror and that its dis-course could and should be expunged, a tentative feeling of control returned, along with a reactionary and protective innocence about the world at large. Representations of the domestic scene, of women sub-ordinated to male domination, of alien visitors destroyed, countered the anxiety that continued to appear in film from time to time, but was less and less expressed in noir formulations. In the sixties, domestic upheaval, assassinations, an unexplained and inexplicable war, a rebellion within the middle class of its children, the collapse of that rebellion; in the seventies, some understanding of how corrupt the political and economic institu-tions that went unquestioned in the fifties were, changed cultural repre-sentations once again. The culture went into something like a depressive reaction, a helpless withdrawal from political and social difficulties even as they pressed more urgently. Before the conservative regrouping of the eighties, when depression turned into an aggressive denial of social and political realities needing attention, the feelings of powerlessness became realized in film images and themes of paranoia and isolation stronger than forties film noir could have managed.

These images and themes took various forms. In the seventies, there were Peckinpah's male death songs, as well as his own revenge and vigilante films, like *Straw Dogs* (1971). Michael Winner's *Death Wish* (1974), Phil Karlson's *Walking Tall* (1973), Don Siegel's *Dirty Harry* (1971) and its sequels, and a long list of black exploitation films employed the Hollywood convention of the lone hero who takes on himself the task of cleansing corruption. The revenge film implies potency, an ability to act and correct oppressive situations, but it implies it on a local level only; the society is unchanged when the hero is finished destroying a few villains. As this genre moved into the eighties, the lone hero began working on a more global level. Rambo begins his imitation of life destroying a small town because the local sheriff doesn't like him (a potentially interesting point that his first act of revenge is self-protection rather than protection of others, and that the future protector of American interests is, like Arlo in *Alice's Restaurant*, told to get a bath and haircut by the constabulary). In his sequel, Rambo takes on Vietnam and the Russians. Victory unattainable by organized warfare is won by a determined loner. This figure is further exploited and expanded in a reconfiguration of the male hero who moves from Stallone to Schwarzenegger to Bruce Willis, each one mixing some manner of vulnerability and self-awareness (often self-parody) with an unbeatable strength.

The reverse side of the heroic venture manifested itself in the paranoia film, such as Sidney Pollack's *Three Days of the Condor* (1975), Alan J. Pakula's *The Parallax View* (1974) and *All the President's Men* (1976), Stanley Kramer's *The Domino Principle* (1977), Paul Schrader's *Blue Collar* (1978), Coppola's *The Conversation* (1974), films spawned by assassinations, the Vietnam war, and Watergate, whose images reinforced fears of lost control over political and economic institutions, whose discourse insisted that no matter what efforts are made, an unknowable presence—governmental, corporate, both—will have its way and exert its ineluctable power. These films exemplified impotence and despair and signaled disaster, a breakdown of community and trust so thorough that it left the viewer with images of lonely individuals, trapped, in the dark, completely isolated. But, in fact, whether the films offered the myth of a violent hero or spoke of no heroes available to conquer the threat, they affirmed passivity and by reiteration soothed and comforted it. The eighties revenge films, the films in which lone heroes once again conquered, or groups of children (child-like heroes in the case of Indiana Jones) asserted control via supernatural or extraterrestrial means, did not change the basic ideological position. Neither do the group-action films of the nineties, such as the producer Jerry Bruckheimer's *The Rock* (Michael Bay, 1996), *Con Air* (Simon West, 1997), and *Armageddon* (Michael Bay, 1998), many of the eighties and early nineties Vietnam war films, and some nineties science fiction, especially Roland Emmerich and Dean Devlin's *Independence Day* (1996). They shift the discourse a bit, adding some images of group action—usually based upon conventions of the World War II battle film—and suggest an idea of a victory for the common good. But even when such films offer a space for victory, their fantasies of power emerge from collective fears rather than the politics of decision making. They respond to terrors manufactured largely by film and other media. Their heroes are sometimes as repulsive as the villains; and they are quite self-aware of their status as heroes manqué. The seriousness of the characters and the viewers' relationship to them in the sixties films of Penn and Peckinpah are in these later films transferred entirely to the spectacle.

This has moved us far afield from noir. In all its distant and recent configurations, from Lang's *Scarlet Street* in the forties to *Red Rock West* (John Dahl, 1992) or *U-Turn* (Oliver Stone, 1997), it remains the genre of male despair and loss, incurring more often than not a tremendous sense of desolation. *Night Moves* is one of the great desolation films. Like many of its forties predecessors, it has as its subject a detective, a film figure who has continually responded to changing cultural attitudes about control and authority, potency, and success. During the Depression the urbane William Powell held the *Thin Man* series together, operating with the ease of the alcoholic dilettante, detached and disinterested, so much in control that detection became another upper-class amusement, a pursuit only momentarily dangerous and barely serious. There was little sense, in these films, of being in touch with the danger they hinted at, and it took the entrance into film of Dashiell Hammett and Raymond Chandler's darker fiction, and the development of the noir genre itself, to establish the detective as a lower-middle-class working man, morally committed to his work, willing to enter a dark, amoral world to find reasons and answers. Humphrey Bogart, as Sam Spade in *The Maltese Falcon* and as Philip Marlowe in *The Big Sleep*, became the archetype against whom all succeeding film detectives were measured. The sense of assurance, the willingness to descend into the dark world and return, sullied perhaps but with morality intact and order seemingly restored, turned the Bogart persona into the image of calm strength and persistence that would yield success. (The fact that this persona also manifested the opposite qualities—a dis-ease and insecurity, a control that was always tenuous at best and nonexistent at worst—is something I will examine further when we discuss Altman and *The Long Goodbye*.)

Night Moves consciously plays against the idea of the forties Bogart detective by retaining the world he inhabited, brought up-to-date in the seventies but still filled with the streets (more suburban than city), the fancy homes, and the labyrinthine plotting that marked the noir world of Spade and Marlowe. The difference lies in the detective himself. Gene Hackman's Harry Moseby is a figure of contemporary anxiety, with none of the wit and bluff that Bogart brought to his roles, none of the security in self-preservation—indeed, none of the sense of self and its endurance that allowed the forties detective to survive. I said he was the subject of the film, but in fact his subjectivity is on the point of dissolution. Harry is not the self-protective neurasthenic that Elliott Gould's Marlowe is in Altman's *The Long Goodbye*; quite the contrary, he feels very deeply and sees the world around him in a limited way. What he does see, however, fills him with an almost paralyzing unhappiness, an inability to move in a way that will make things clear and give them order. "Who's winning?" asks Harry's wife as he watches a football game on television. "Nobody," he answers. "One side's just losing slower than the other."

Detective films are about seeing, about perceiving and discerning. The success of the detection depends on how clearly things are seen and how secure the point of view of the perceiver is. Harry sees, but he has no point of view, no moral position from which to act on what he sees. Images in the film are continually reflected, often by distorting surfaces; Harry is observed, or observes, through screens and windows. Much of the central part of the film, Harry's visit to Florida, where he attempts to find and return his client's runaway daughter, Delly, and discovers a complex smuggling operation, is filmed in darkness and empty spaces. The cutting of the film does not permit sequences to complete themselves. A new scene may be entered with the dialogue of the previous one carried over, so that no comfortable continuity between narrative units is allowed. The viewer is given no more security of structure, no fuller sense of subjective certainty, no more certain sense of clear perception than is the character (a strategy similar to what Penn does in *Mickey One*).

However, the form does not function merely to make the viewer share Harry's darkness and despair, but to indicate the difficulties of seeing and knowing clearly anything about anyone. This perceptual murkiness extends to the character's insights about himself and the viewer's understanding of him. At one point a psychological explanation for Harry's anomie seems to be offered. His father ran away when Harry was young and Harry felt the need to find him. He tells his wife that he tracked his father down once, found him on a park bench in Baltimore, and walked away. This information could offer a touching bit of understanding for the character and a typical screenwriting ploy—when in doubt, explain the character's personality by giving him or her an unhappy upbringing. But here it serves a different function. What appears to be psychological motivation is not. No explanation is given for Harry's refusal to greet his long-sought-for father. It is offered as the expression of one more emotional dead end, one more provocation of anxiety and hopelessness. The oedipal structure is itself repressed, offering no promise for the subject to emerge into knowledge and order. In *Night Moves,* interior and exterior states are the same: fearful and insoluble. The act of detection creates an anxiety in Harry that does not permit him to bring the act to an end. Or perhaps the ending and the possibility of revelation that endings bring are too painful, or simply impossible. The question, and it saturates the film, is this: if the end of the search is painful, how much more so can it be than the search itself, which proceeds as a series of stumblings and humiliations, deaths and personal agonies? Penn raises this question again in *Four Friends*, and although that film ends with an affirmation of community—however small and delimited—the journey of its hero, like that of Harry, is lonely and despairing.

Impotent anger, impotent actions, impotent anxiety permeate *Night Moves*. Sexuality, as so often in modernist film and literature, is a thing of loathing and a weapon. Harry follows his wife and discovers his own cuckolding. When he confronts the man, a physical cripple (complementing Harry's emotional state), he is insulted with his own movie origins. "C'mon, take a swing at me, Harry, the way Sam Spade would." And when he confronts his wife, he can only let out his rage by grinding a glass down the disposal. The child Delly, one of the objects of Harry's search, is promiscuous to the point of destruction of herself and others. She sleeps with everyone, including her stepfather. "She's pretty liberated, isn't she?" asks Harry. "When we all get liberated like Delly," he is told, "there'll be fighting in the streets." The reorganization of sexual politics—one of the few major cultural achievements of the seventies—is here turned to another dismaying, oppressive image. Paula, the woman Harry meets during his Florida quest and who joylessly makes love to him, and betrays him, is saddened by her sexuality. In *Bonnie and Clyde*, sexuality is displaced into violence, and its momentary triumph over that violence becomes a prelude to death. In *Alice's Restaurant* it is a source of jealousy and conflict. In *Little Big Man* it is reduced to sniggering chauvinism. In *Four Friends* it is a major cause of Danilo's pain and Georgia's self-destructive activities. Penn is never very comfortable with it (but then none of the filmmakers discussed here are), and in *Night Moves* it is manifested as one more weight on his characters' spirits, a depressing activity good only for betrayal and further anxiety.

The emotional paralysis and moral corruption that permeate the film suppress any clear manifestation of plot and render any attention to it useless. Harry's job becomes not so much detecting as confirming the existence of a moral swamp, an unclear, liquid state of feelings and relations in which the drowning of the spirit is perpetual. Paula tells Harry how the films of the Kennedy assassination appear to have been taken underwater, and this metaphor for the opaqueness of the general political and cultural condition spreads over the film, literally—in the vague, swimming quality of the films Harry views showing Delly's death, of the scene of the discovery in Florida of an airplane underwater, its pilot's corpse eaten by fish, and of the climactic sequence of the film.[22]

At the end of his quest Harry goes out on a boat named, with perfect irony, the *Point of View*. As Paula dives in an attempt to discover the contra-band that is the source of everyone's machinations, we see Harry from her point of view, looking through the glass bottom of the boat, out of reach and out of touch. A plane buzzes Harry and shoots him in the leg. A Mexican antique surfaces on the water, an ugly statue similar to one Harry was looking at in a friend's office earlier in the film. Paula comes up, only to be hit by the plane, which goes under in its attempt to destroy them all. Through the glass bottom, Harry sees the drowning pilot, a friend from L.A., a stuntman whose only implication heretofore was his involvement in the "accident" that killed Delly. Each looks helplessly at the other through the water. Finally the camera withdraws, dissociating itself from anybody's point of view. It assumes the high, downward angle that Hitchcock loves to take when a character is in moral or physical danger. The spectator, removed from any certain understanding of events, left only with a response of shock, helplessly observes Harry, crippled in the *Point of View*, going around and around in the water.

Night Moves seems almost inevitable in Penn's career. In film after film he had attempted to maneuver the spirit of life against the repressive order and laws of society that bring death or diminishment to those who move against them. He had contented himself not with an attempt to understand the peculiarly American variety of the politics of repression and the attempts to struggle against it, but with the emotional power of the struggle itself, and reaped from his audience the emotional profit that seems always to come from being witness to the death of vitality, from the reaffirmation that we are lost and helpless. But in *Night Moves* the profit of loss seems to have run out. Harry Moseby is emotionally dead from the beginning. He does not so much entangle himself in the oppression of others as merely sink deeper into his own and their moral vacuum. There is not even the external force of authority to fight against as there is in the earlier films. As in *Mickey One*, the outside is a reflection of the inside, but in *Night Moves* there is no triumph, and both interior and exterior worlds remain squalid and empty. The destroyers seem to have won; they have become us.

In retrospect, *Night Moves* marked not only the end of Penn's creative period, but the dead end of the modernist movement in contemporary American film. Along with Coppola's *The Conversation*, made a few years earlier (a film that also starred Gene Hackman as a character named Harry), *Night Moves* takes a major element of modernism, its bleakness and desolation, its conviction that failure and isolation are the only ends available to a male character, as far as anyone wished them to go. Although other filmmakers returned to this state of fragmented and depressed subjectivity—most notably Robert Altman in *Short Cuts*—despair in theme and torturous fragmentation in narrative structure largely disappeared from mainstream cinema, despite the continued interest in film noir. In nineties film, modernism's thematics turned to plain misanthropy in "independent" films like Neil LaBute's *In the Company of Men* (1997), or to a kind of amused amoral relativism, hiding a deep sexual dysfunction in Todd Solondz's *Happiness,* but otherwise seemed to become the province of the serial-killer film, which reached a double climax in Jonathan Demme's *Silence of the Lambs* (1991) and David Fincher's *Seven* (1995). Each of these films draws on the horror genre and thinks back to *Psycho*. Rather than play counterpoint with social and political events, as Penn does in his best work, the serial-killer film assumes the given of a bleak and scary world where anyone is a potential victim. *Silence of the Lambs* falls back on an oedipal pattern (the heroine is guided by two "fathers," one from the world of light and order, the other from the darkest unconscious) and some old-fashioned notions of sexual perversion. *Seven* plays on the interracial buddy structure so prevalent in eighties and nineties cop films. *Silence of the Lambs* is ironic and playful with its demonic spirit, Hannibal Lector, while *Seven* manages to be one of the darkest films of the nineties, exploring a morally dead landscape in which any agency against evil is seen as impossible. But both move the modernist angst off the shoulders of their characters, away from investigation of the culture, and onto the unknowable evils of a psychotic mind.

This was Hitchcock's gambit in *Psycho*, and *Seven* gets close to it; but neither it nor *Silence of the Lambs* quite indicts all its characters, and by extension its viewers, in the complicity of amorality as *Psycho* does. Neither film extends its reach to the politics of subjectivity, the anxieties of the self in the world that Penn addresses. By the late seventies, the culture was moving away rapidly from both politics and a conscious angst. The Carter presidency, with its claims of moral malaise and the clarity with which it revealed our continuing impotence in the affairs of the world, effectively recognized a dead center of American self-consciousness and concern. The slide in cultural self-esteem that began with Vietnam and Watergate was over; communism was becoming less believable as a source of worry. It was as if the political consciousness of the sixties—that Penn simultaneously celebrated and condemned as fruitless—along with the loss of faith in government and the loss of a war finally sent the culture not to a place of rational inquiry but into a kind of oedipal neediness, an internalization of helplessness in search of a guide. The result was neoconservatism, Ronald Reagan, a few years of groundless optimism, and finally a slide into despairing quietism on the part of the poor and dispossessed; personal, political, and cultural narcissism throughout the upper middle class.

In effect, Penn's work was done. Whatever the personal causes of his creative decline and withdrawal from active moviemaking, other causes rested in history. The sixties desire for personal and political liberation, the belief that a freed subjectivity and a progressive communal/societal politics would thrive together and nourish one another proved unsupportable. History conspired through a series of losses of leaders, wars, and faith in political institutions. The culture's move inward manifested itself in all aspects of the culture's work, Penn's included. His 1983 film, *Four Friends*, recovers the ground of his sixties films, but this time the perspective is ironic to the point of hostility.

Alice's Restaurant, Penn's first film that directly confronted the movement he helped create in *Bonnie and Clyde*, was made at the high point of the antiwar movement, when many of a left-liberal frame of mind had visions of a sharing communal world withdrawn, somehow, from the larger, repressive society. Arlo Guthrie, son of the old freedom singer, was one of the many spokespersons of this group, and his narrative song, "Alice's Restaurant," about a Thanksgiving dinner that ended in jail when he was caught dumping garbage in an empty lot, and about the army's refusal to draft him because he had a prison record as a litterer, became something of a rallying point. Penn attempted to flesh out the song, give it a setting and a larger narrative. The result is a fantasy of communal life fraught with the frictions of jealousies and sexual tensions of the bourgeois world. Unlike *Bonnie and Clyde*, Penn keeps a distance from his characters in this film, examining their attitudes, his own, and the viewer's. In the first part of the film, as Arlo moves in the straight world, he is often observed through a window, separated from the viewer's immediate gaze. The sexual insecurity that was at that time aroused by long hair on males is turned on the spectator. As Arlo is forced to be the butt of many jokes about his hair and his sex so, in a fashion, is the viewer. In the first scene at the draft board an offscreen, masculine voice questions Arlo. When the speaker appears, the voice turns out to belong to a woman clerk. Later, at Arlo's school, a female voice is heard talking to him. When connected to a figure, it turns out to be a male guidance counselor. Penn

59

mocks the audience's inability to comprehend and accept otherness, contrasting continually the gentle, unassuming Arlo with the bullying people around him. But the gap is breached. Arlo, running away from college, stops at a diner. He is taunted by local rednecks and hurled through a window. This is the only violent scene in the film, and it quite literally breaks the distance and pushes Arlo into the audience's sympathies.

The film works wholeheartedly on Arlo's side, though less than wholeheartedly for Alice and Ray, surrogate parents to the commune. They are self-conscious about their role as protectors of hippiedom, mediators between the straight, middle-class world and their young communards. They are caught up in the old codes of behavior, of male supremacy and sexual exclusiveness. By the end, Alice is isolated, emotionally and physically, from her surroundings, as was Arlo at the beginning. No one wins at the end of *Alice's Restaurant*—not oppressive authority, not the liberated hippies. The commune breaks up, and Alice is left alone. A film that wishes, with all its heart, to celebrate community ends by observing isolation. The last shot is a long, complicated track and zoom around Alice, approaching her and retreating at the same time, expressing movement and stasis and, finally, uncertainty.

Four Friends turns uncertainty into impotence and loss. The sixties, in retrospect, are seen as a foolish and undirected time, a moment of distraction from private concerns and the necessary settling of individual affairs. The film suffers a significant breach in its structure. Written by Steve Tesich, it is a loose autobiography of an immigrant's journeys through America, his relations with an implacable father, and a somewhat tedious narration of the young man's love for, fascination, and inability to get along with one of his childhood friends, Georgia. Penn seems to be only barely in control of the narration, and the direction of the actors is unsteady. He is, for example, unable to elaborate the character of a free-spirited woman, and Georgia turns out to be foolish and weak, rather than strong with a measure of self-direction. The strength of the film lies in its set pieces, its allegory of the times, and in Penn's ability to fashion images that concentrate events and phenomena of the sixties and early seventies into concentrated tableaux, rich in ideological and historical portent, which are to a degree reflected through a foreigner's eye.

In a sequence that takes place in 1961, Danilo, the central character, interrupts a high school employment program by raging at the fact that the school is being used to feed recruits to army and industry. Later, at a beach party, a ball with John and Jacqueline Kennedy's picture on it is thrown in slow motion through the air, the dominant icons of that period becoming part of the play of teenagers. The Kennedys' image—people who existed mainly as image—is treated nonchalantly by the characters in the narrative who, of course, have no idea how much power the image will collect to itself as the decade proceeds. A racial incident with a black member of their group occurs at the party, which, like the disruption of the high school assembly, portends the greater conflicts to emerge during the decade. Later still, on the road, Danilo sees this black friend in a bus traveling to Mississippi. The friend calls to him to follow, but Danilo, wrapped up in his personal anxieties, will not join the freedom riders. The car and bus fork away from each other on the highway. After the wedding sequence, in which Danilo's fiancée is shot by her father (who has sexually abused her) and Danilo himself wounded in the eye, he leaves the hospital. Before he leaves, the music of the national anthem can be heard on a radio. As he enters the street, an electric guitar sounds; traffic noise is heard; a black man with a headband walks by; a stoned girl stands nearby. The late sixties teems on the sidewalk, a moment of noise, chaos, and by inescapable association with the hospital, of violence, pain, and sickness. No sweetness of hippiedom exists as it does in *Alice's Restaurant*, no doomed promise of revolt as in *Bonnie and Clyde*. Looking back, Penn sees the time in images of slightly crazed freaks, flag burners, and appalling Greenwich Village "happenings." A time of waste and, the film suggests, the dissipation of subjective energy.

The beginning of the decade is full of portent, broken by the conflicts between social necessity, self-indulgence, and personal need. The end of the sixties is a time of bitter and foolish contradictions. Danilo spends the night at the home of one of his old friends, who was in Vietnam, where he married and brought home a Vietnamese woman. He awakens to see the friend's Vietnamese children staring at him. On television, the astronaut's walk on the moon is taking place. The sound of someone attempting to start up a lawnmower is heard, and Danilo steps to the window, where he sees his friend's wife bent over the lawnmower, trying to work it. The television pictures of the moon, the Vietnamese woman at the lawnmower, with her long hair and native dress, merge into a somewhat terrifying representation of power and banality, of overblown heroism and of the violence committed in the name of preserving the very suburban landscape that the Vietnamese woman now inhabits, itself a representation of complacency and anxiety. This is one of Penn's most inventive set of

61

images; more than image, a semiology of the late sixties, signs of a culture in which the profound and the mundane are so placed together that profundity is muted by the ordinary with the profound indication that nothing of value has been understood from history.

Oliver Stone's *Heaven and Earth* is a huge melodrama about the failed integration of gender and culture after the Vietnam war. The narration sweeps through the humiliation and torture of its central character, Le Ly Haslip, in Vietnam; her sexual degradation; and her marriage to an American. She is brought from Saigon to San Diego by her American husband, Steve, and the initial contacts with the West are told in images that recall *Four Friends*. In Stone's manner, they are bigger and bolder images, filled with the excess of a foreign culture as they might be seen from a diminished foreign perspective. Le Ly goes to a supermarket, and Stone's camera pursues her with a wide-angle lens, so that the rows of food through which she pushes her cart bulge and push their way into our vision and hers. The Vietnamese woman bending over the lawnmower in *Four Friends* is an almost dainty image in comparison, suggesting a reticent, quizzical attitude through the creation of this metaphor of American failure. Stone is never reticent—though always quizzical—and his fish-eyed lunge through the supermarket, the ninety-degree shots over a suburban dinner table bulging with food, explode Penn's image of complacency and anxiety while pushing recognition of the willful ignorance of difference that drove American culture then and now. Unlike Penn, Stone looks for moments of transcendence, for his characters, their culture, and even the viewer. Le Ly survives, although at her husband's expense (he commits suicide); she becomes an entrepreneur and is able to revisit Vietnam for a sentimental reunion with her family.

Penn's films are interrogations of failure, lyrically and violently structured so that the viewer is simultaneously asked to share the internal points of view of the characters and yet somehow—sadly, more often than not—understand that their every gesture proves that "one side's just losing slower than the other." In Penn's work, there is the urge to expose the structure of narrative—to make visible how it works and how the viewer responds to it. Yet with that exposure comes the failure of subjective agency, of any possibility of prevailing for his characters, and an acknowledgment of loss on the part of the viewer. This articulates the modernist's dilemma, the paradox inherent in the desire to open up the text to scrutiny and offer to scrutiny the hopelessness of knowledge. Oliver Stone emerges as Penn's postmodern double, more anxious to expose the workings of narrative structure and viewer response, less likely to admit to the failure of interrogation or even of individual will and purpose. This is not to imply that Stone is an optimist or, on the opposite pole, a strong ironist. He sees differently, more broadly than Penn, and without any reticence to embrace history and politics to find, or suggest, ways out of self-made traps. He turns Penn's reticent pessimism into a fearless plunge into recent history and a clear statement of what he thinks it means.

Both filmmakers were committed to mapping the social and political textures of the sixties and seventies. Penn did his work during the period, marking the initial movements of individual rebellion in *Left-Handed Gun* and *Mickey One*, pursuing an allegory of sixties youth culture in *Bonnie and Clyde*, reworking the boundaries of racial stereotyping in *Little Big Man*, and marking the failures of countercultural optimism in *Alice's Restaurant* and *Four Friends*. Stone maps similar territories, but in retrospect. Some of his films seem, on certain levels, to be a rethinking of Penn's work: *Talk Radio* (1988), a film about performance and the visual relationship of the performer to the space around him, parallels *Mickey One*. *Talk Radio* is also a prophetic piece about the growth and power of the rant of the disaffected. *Born on the Fourth of July* (1989) and *Heaven and Earth* point back to *Four Friends*. The three films attempt to examine the hysteria of the Vietnam and post-Vietnam periods, and the large changes of consciousness they provoked. *U Turn*, through its noir inheritance, links to *Night Moves*. Stone's large, historical projects, *JFK* and *Nixon*, go further than Penn in their inquiry into cinematic representations of history, politics, and personality. But the film that most closely links Stone to Penn, and which can serve as a bridge between these two filmmakers, is his most transgressive work, *Natural Born Killers*.

In the gangster film, the main characters are almost always portrayed as fascinated with the production of their image, through photographs, broadcasts, news reports—sometimes to their detriment. In *Little Caesar*, Rico's fall begins with a news photo he insists on having taken. In the culture at large—the "real" world—gangsters exist more as cultural event, as a representation of danger, threat, and excitement than as grubby, violent little men. So a double mediation occurs: the culture is fascinated by the idea and representation of the gangster; in the gangster film, the thug himself depends on his exploits being known in the world through images and reports. The fictional gangster, himself a mediated creation (made by scriptwriters, directors, producers, publicists, and a responsive

63

audience) understands within his fiction that he must be mediated to prevail. This was an important theme in *Bonnie and Clyde*, with its characters taking pictures of each other, crowds standing in awe around the outlaw couple, the publication of Bonnie's poem and its positive impact on Clyde's sexuality. *Natural Born Killers* pushes this idea deeply back into its own structure, in effect turning this structure inside out in order to expose the mediation effect. Mickey and Mallory are Stone's nineties version of Bonnie and Clyde, with a greater self-consciousness, existing in a film more ready and able to expose its own artificiality and to get us, as viewers, to respond to the fiction-making apparatus at the same time we are affected by it.

This is Stone's great gift, his modernist inheritance, and a problem in the reception of his films. Because movies have so trained us to apprehend content rather than form, and because Stone understands the necessity of supplying content and emotion, it is quite possible, in films as violently transgressive as *Natural Born Killers* or as close to the political-historical nerve as *JFK* and *Nixon*, for the viewer to fall behind Stone's point, which is to invite us to see the work of representation in action and as theme. Therefore, like *Bonnie and Clyde* in the late sixties, *Natural Born Killers* was condemned for its violence and briefly became a minor presidential campaign issue in the early nineties when conservative concerns over Hollywood morality were given voice. The issue, however, is not violence, but its representation and presentation. Like *Bonnie and Clyde, Natural Born Killers* is a moral film that uses violence as a means to a political and perceptual point. For Penn, the political point was the necessity and futility of rebellion and the perceptual structure of his film emphasized this by inviting the viewer to share the characters' point of view and then violently canceling the invitation. For Stone, the politics more generally concern the power of media and mediation. Rather than being asked to share the point of view of the main characters, the viewer is offered a variety of positions in and outside the narrative, which is constructed in such a way that no one comfortable position is offered—at least for any length of time. The viewer is placed in a state of agitation and interrogation—his perceptions are brought into question and he is asked to interrogate what is being seen on the screen.

Stone's narratives follow a basic Aristotelian trajectory, as do Penn's. They have beginnings and middles, and they reach some sort of closure, or an idea for closure, at their end. In fact this may be their most conventional element. Within that conventional structure, Stone sees time as perfectly malleable. More accurately, he sees time as entirely under the filmmaker's control and as a tool for constructing and shifting points of view. Recall the moment in *Bonnie and Clyde* when Clyde pushes Texas Ranger Hamer down on the rear window of the car. There is a cut to the interior of the car, the camera gazing out the rear window, and the last part of the action of the previous shot is repeated. Hamer hits the rear window again. This double take, seeing things twice, switching suddenly from a point of view that is comfortably in continuity with the apparent flow of the narrative to one that is not, becomes a structural and thematic imperative in Stone's films. It is related to the practice of Sergei Eisenstein, the filmmaker of the Russian Revolution, who viewed temporal editing as a major tool in the cinematic representation of history. This is no small point, because Stone is one of a very few filmmakers to reach back to Eisenstein in his editorial practice, using cutting as a means to call attention to perceptual processes and as a tool for distancing the viewer from the narrative flow.

It is an important element in *Natural Born Killers*. The narrative strength of *Bonnie and Clyde* depends on our being stitched into the characters' point of view from the very beginning, so that the rupture at the end gains full impact. But from the very beginning of *Natural Born Killers*, the viewer is forced into a dual situation, neither one of which allows easy access to the main characters. One situation, continued throughout the film, is a kind of rhythmic attention created by a startling flow of images. Stone builds his visuals on unexpected linkages and disorienting juxtapositions within the shots and across the edits. But the very disorientations of the unexpected also produce a distancing effect, so that the viewer, intrigued, appalled, hypnotized, and jarred, is continuously in search of a secure position. The quest is met only by representations of violent outbursts and further disorientations of expectations.

The opening sequence of the film takes place in a diner, which is robbed and its inhabitants shot, stabbed, and beaten up by Mickey (Woody Harrelson) and Mallory (Juliette Lewis). The sequence looks back to the robbery of the grocery store in *Bonnie and Clyde* and sideways to the Pumpkin and Honeybunny sequences of Quentin Tarantino's *Pulp Fiction*, also released in 1994. Tarantino was the author of *Natural Born Killers'* original story and clearly ready to recycle some of its material in his own film. But Stone goes in directions that leave his sources behind. The credit sequence, which introduces the events in the diner, begins with a black-

and-white image of Monument Valley and, over a recent recording of a gravely voiced Leonard Cohen, cuts quickly to an image of coyote and then to a hissing rattlesnake. The first color image—the diner coffeepot—replaces the rattler's face, and the image is canted in what used to be called in Hollywood a "dutch tilt."* Almost all the images in the film will be off the horizontal line, contributing to a mise-en-scène of unbalanced, vertiginous space, a cinematic world out of alignment.

The image of the coffeepot is rapidly replaced by a red-tinted image of a train, moving from right to left, a color image of a hawk, a low-angle shot of the diner sign, and then a television screen, its channels being changed from *Leave It to Beaver*, one of the kids saying, "We're just leaving, Mom," to *77 Sunset Strip*, to the face of Richard Nixon, saying, ". . . as I leave," followed by the zooming in and out on an image of a ghoulish face—possibly Mickey's—with screaming in the background. The camera pans away from the television and up to the waitress holding the coffeepot, canting off in an almost forty-five-degree angle behind Mickey's back. She's offering him dessert, talking about Key Lime pie and how it is an acquired taste. As she says this, there is a cut to a black-and-white closeup of the waitress smiling and saying again, "It's an acquired taste," followed immediately by a return to the original color shot that then pulls back, cants in the opposite direction, and follows Mallory from the counter, allowing the narrative proper to begin.

The cut into the waitress's discussion of pie that replays the temporal moment a second time is an indication of Stone's debt to Eisenstein. He will use the effect often in *Nixon*, where it will become a signifier of both self- and historical consciousness, of a character and a culture who seem simultaneously inside and outside themselves, unsynchronized, disconnected. In *Natural Born Killers* as in *Nixon*, it is the visual equivalent of a profound dislocation, a loss of object constancy, the slipperiness of subjectivity itself—which is very much what is at stake in the viewing of this film. The credit sequence of *Natural Born Killers* sets up the strategies in which a particular subjectivity, the secure knowledge of the viewer before the narrative, is brought into question. Composition and cutting generate a mise-en-scène and a temporal dislocation that constantly disrupt the gaze and signify a world falling apart, a world in

---

* Legend has it that the name came from a corruption of "Deutsche" or German, presumably because German cinematographers, working in Hollywood, were fond of odd camera angles.

which violence, real and imagined, is mediated beyond the point of comprehending an origin or an end, a cause or effect—only an ongoing status, a state of *being viewed*.

The processes of mediation are what are at issue in this film, where discontinuity, even down to the most minute elements of film stock, is foregrounded so that viewers may not see through the image but at it. One specific cultural mediator, television, is foregrounded throughout, from the television images in the diner in the opening sequence of the film, to the parody of MTV rapid cutting, through the thematic material of the film itself. The exploits of Mickey and Mallory are pursued, exploited, televised by Wayne Gale (Robert Downey, Jr.) and his trash-TV scandal program. He interviews Mickey in prison and televises the Grand Guignol riot that breaks out when Mickey escapes. His program realizes the desire of all such shows (and, one suspects, their viewers): the broadcast of real-time violence. In the end, Wayne Gale is murdered by Mickey and Mallory, as his video camera grinds on. They, at least, seem to understand the nature of their media dependence. "Frankenstein killed Dr. Frankenstein," Mickey says to Wayne, in an attempt to articulate the ties that unbind.

The trash TV program that figures so prominently in *Natural Born Killers* is a bit obvious, though no less effective for being so. After all, the lack of subtlety of these programs is what puts them beyond criticism. They exploit and they are proud of the fact. Although the act of exploitation may have many causes, politics and economics are always primary, and the desire of people to watch exploitation television—and buy their advertisers' products—keeps the cycle in motion and, within the discourse of capitalist-based media operations, beyond reproach. This cycle of media exploitation emerges as a theme of *Natural Born Killers*. Stone is less interested in why people watch exploitative media than he is in the fact of their watching, the apparent lack of critical attention, the pleasure in others' misery. This is emphasized in the lunatic parody of a sitcom that follows the diner sequence early in the film. Stone gets there by means of another allusion. The diner sequence attaches *Natural Born Killers* firmly to *Bonnie and Clyde*. In their escape from the murder and mayhem at the diner, Mickey and Mallory take to their car and drive madly, whooping and hollering. The visual construction of the escape and the sounds of their pleasure recall the "hogs of the road" sequence of Stanley Kubrick's *A Clockwork Orange*, that other great late sixties–early seventies film of violent young people. There are boxes within boxes of allusion here in a purposive attempt to keep attention to the fact that this is a film examining the culture and politics of popular images and narratives. And nowhere is this point made with more force than in "I Love Mallory," the television show that interrupts the main narrative to explain the couple's fictional past.

By the nineteen-nineties, television sitcoms exploited vulgarity quite shamelessly as a way to achieve a quick viewer response. Scripts for many programs merely allowed a character to say the word "sex," the producers punched up the laugh track, and a moment was filled with smarm and titillation. "I Love Mallory" exploits the exploiters by imagining an ideal vulgarity, while maintaining the anarchic structure of the film as a whole and further pointing to its origins in mass-mediated response. "I Love Mallory" shows a violent, incestuous, working-class family, in which the young Mallory suffers at the hands of a brutish, sexually abusive father (played by the comic Rodney Dangerfield), who is finally drowned by her and Mickey in the family fish tank. Mickey is Mallory's hero, a butcher's delivery boy with a rippling, dripping sack of meat. These grotesque events are punctuated by the sound of a laugh track that gets uproarious over the most violent and hurtful language and actions. This is television in a distorting mirror, in which the basic forms and types of TV culture are reflected back as grotesques that call forth inappropriate responses to appalling actions.

The Truman Show (Peter Weir, 1998) represented television somewhat in the terms of contemporary cultural studies, which hold that audiences are not dumb slaves to television images, but active negotiators of the meanings they retrieve from them.[23] In the film, the viewers of Truman's televised life—he is the unwitting subject of an ongoing show since his birth—are aware of what's being done; they watch the narrative as television, not life, and when the program ends, they change the channel. The other audience—the viewers of the film—are also privileged with knowledge of the proceedings. We are asked to be part of the melodrama of the character's discovery of his situation. The subject of the program, Truman himself, is initially unaware of the artifice around him, of the fact that he is being directed and his behavior controlled. His coming to consciousness is worked out through a sentimental recognition of a life that could—and will—be better lived. The film, ultimately, maybe despite itself, *becomes* television by adopting its clichés. "I Love Mallory" is television revealed, obstreperously mining the very vulgarity it parodies and demonstrating its evasions by exaggerating its grotesqueness. And its dangers. If television and film can represent anything, and by representing anything give it meaning only within the cycle of exploitation and assent, then external meaning—history—is drained.

This is a premise of postmodernism, that the images and narratives of popular culture gather meaning only within the contexts and the reception of popular culture, without the need to test them against any other reality. It's a subset of the exploitation cycle. *Natural Born Killers* could well be criticized for yielding to the postmodern effect, relating so many of its images to the pop-cultural that it simply short-circuits its intent. The postmodern insists that meaning is of little importance when everything is equated to the same universe. But *Natural Born Killers*, along with much of Stone's work, both adopts and critiques this premise. *Natural Born Killers* spits up the images of the popular, often in our face. Its closing sequence, in which the monsters have become good lower-middle-class family folks, driving their recreational vehicle, kids in tow, across the same landscape they once pillaged, cautions us to look at what we see and suggests, ever so gingerly, that all the film's characters and antics are not only products of media exploitation, but of class as well.

While caught up in the inescapable imagery of the popular, Stone wants to know why we respond to images, where these images come from, how their cultural, political, and historical baggage can be unpacked in a way that might break the postmodern short circuit. He pushes cinema to reflect on the ways images manufacture history and belief, using film's own formal properties to investigate how fragile and arbitrary this manufacturing process is. *Natural Born Killers* is investigation by means of assault on the sensibilities. *JFK* is investigation by dramatic, purposive, morally driven exposition of the way images do and don't work. More than pandering conspiracy theories, which it has been endlessly accused of doing, *JFK* in fact asks us to interrogate the images and narratives of politics—in particular, one of the dominant political fictions of our contemporary national ideology. It attempts an act of disentanglement, but not disengagement. It invites us to look at what we believe we know and to imagine alternative fictions.[24]

Stone understands that the Kennedy assassination, the Vietnam war, and Watergate are the essential and forming events of the last third of the American century. These events were—and remain—processes of unravelling, unfinished and unfinishable narratives. At their most abstract, they are stories of collapse, deflation, loss, and free-floating anxiety. They tell of the coming apart of ideologies of triumph, presence, security, and agency, substituting in their place vague, incomplete murmurings of bewilderment, abandonment, misapprehension, and aggression. Each narrative has its own particular inflection of the ways a culture and its politics, a community and its cohesion become undone and fragmented. The Vietnam narrative tells of a war the government wanted as a means to prove its anticommunist mettle. A legacy of the fifties, in which cultural and political cohesion was built on the bases of fear of external enemies and the demonization and purging of the domestic left, Vietnam began in turmoil and closed on three traumatic revelations: that our own troops were capable of mutiny; that our own culture could reach a threshold of revolt; that, as a political-military organization, we were not invincible.

Invincibility had been a key element of American ideology since at least the twenties, when triumph in war and growing corporate strength contributed to dreams of a powerful nation. Roosevelt's rescue of capitalism and the victory of World War II reinforced a sense of cultural, economic, and political strength, mitigated by an end-of-the-war anxiety. The atomic bomb and the creation of the myth of internal communist menace shook the culture. Senescent leadership and the profound cultural changes brought about by suburbanization and the diminishing of old family structures contributed to uncertainties throughout the country, from the economy to gender. The advent of the Kennedy presidency gave body to ideological necessity by offering the potential to revive and confirm old stories of valor and heroism. Regardless of the fact that Kennedy pursued an oppressive cold war discourse, his presence alone represented an imagined rejuvenation. His assassination opened a sudden void that was permanently inexplicable. It was so unexpected, so wrenching, so without any apparent motivation, that it could and cannot ever be adequately, satisfactorily narrated. But, as Robert Burgoyne argues, a culture and its dominant ideology need to be sealed in order to contain contending elements without breaking apart, which is why a narration of the assassination was attempted by means of the report of the Warren Commission and its single-shooter theory. True or not, this story did not, could not deliver the desired closure. Narratives without closure (a term once restricted to narrative theory and now used in the popular discourse to describe a need to explain or finish any kind of grief) are unendurable— as unendurable as the event itself. The story needs to be retold, obsessively, compulsively, in ways that offer the needed explanations and supply the regeneration and redemption missing from the historical event.

Watergate was a kind of coda to the Kennedy assassination—political assassination as suicide. Nixon had always been a figure of political and cultural self-hatred and seemed to know it, living out a public life of meanness and corruption that finally, as in a bad melodrama, turned around and destroyed him. Nixon's rise and fall and rise were so intimately connected with the work of culture and history from the late forties through the late seventies that his next fall through Watergate had an enormous, foundation-crumbling force. Nixon and Watergate were the last blow to any generally held belief in political efficiency, righteousness, and propriety. The individual and the event put an end to the political cult of personality fomented by Roosevelt and honed to a fine, brief point by Kennedy. Watergate brought home an almost unbearable fact to some— that their government could not be trusted (the counterculture had been speaking this throughout the Vietnam war); we still have not seen the end of this mistrust, which now is fomented by the right.

Beginning with *Platoon* (1985), Stone seeks out images and narratives for these events, representations that would not merely be fictional recreations but cinematic interrogations of historical and cultural figures and movements. He proposes, in Penn's wake, to tell stories of two decades, providing not the closure sought nor the answers wished, but possible, even probable narratives and further inquiries, on the level of cinema. Stone's history is a cinematographic one and, like written histories, is formed by the conventions of the medium and the interrogations of events made by the historian by means of the conventions of her discipline. Historians create narratives based on an interpretation of facts, developed throughout the established methodologies of historical inquiry.[25] A filmmaker—like a novelist, poet, or painter—may do the same, allegorically or indirectly, as Penn addresses the sixties through the thirties in *Bonnie and Clyde*, or by a recreation, representation, and interrogation of the moment itself, as Stone does in *JFK* and *Nixon*. Stone takes all this a bit further by making his representations and interrogations of history also an interrogation of cinematic perception. In a sense, the history of Stone's narratives of the sixties and seventies is the history of cinema in the eighties and nineties and the limits to which one filmmaker was willing to push the conventions of that cinema. The films become, therefore, multiple perspectives, ways of seeing and speaking, commentaries on cultural, historical, and cinematic discourses, using events as fodder for interpretation of the visible.

The Vietnam war itself provides the least interesting material for Stone. *Platoon* was a very popular film and brought him the attention that allowed him to make the films that followed; but its popularity is, I think, based on a sentimentality so fundamental to Stone's thinking that the later films had to struggle, with varying success, against it. The success of the struggle is only based on how much Stone pushes against convention. The push in *Platoon* is minimal. The film plays out a coming-of-age narrative through the loss of innocence and final redemption of a rookie soldier named Chris. Many of the early battle sequences are based on a horror-film model, in which the cutting moves from the gaze of frightened soldiers to their point of view of the dark, threatening jungle. The battle scenes play out unnamable threats against vulnerability. (This horror-film mode may be less surprising when we note that two of Stone's early films—*Seizure*, 1974, and *The Hand*, 1981—fall into this genre.) But although he maximizes the horrible aspects of battle, as any war film does, he also maximizes easy elements of identification and demonization. In battle, the Vietcong are shadowy, frightening, dark little monsters. However, when the American soldiers are in a Vietnam village, Stone is able to flip his terms, and the natives become frightened victims of aggressive Americans. On the battlefield, the film falls on convention; on the field of the social and cultural, it attempts an examination of the breakdown in rational order and the inherent racism and brutality of many Americans in Vietnam. The real dichotomy within the film—a kind of Manichean split, in fact—occurs between two of Chris's mentors, the allegorical figures of Barnes and Elias. The latter is a man of intelligence and sorrow who attempts to understand the losing situation of the American position. Barnes is a corrupt, old-line warrior, an updated version of the John Wayne character in Ford's *The Searchers* (1956), mad, vicious, and ready to kill anyone.

The simplifications, the too obvious oedipal and religious triangulation of Chris, Elias, and Barnes, Chris's voice-over "diaries" to his grandmother, tend to soften the film's hard edges. This conflicts with the film's other intent, exposing the "realities" of the war's conflicts, its terrorist aspects, and the general bad faith of sending young men to die for corrupt reasons. In a way, the narrative conflict and the exposition of historical conflict inflate the sentimentalist aspects, which finally weakens the work. In this film, as well as *Salvador* (1986), made shortly before *Platoon*, and *Wall Street* (1987), made the following year, Stone is still at the mercy of content. The story he is telling drives the films, which rarely stretch far beyond the classical Hollywood style. He finds an experimental outlet in *Talk Radio*, one of his least known and best works, prophetic in the late eighties of the rise of right-wing hate radio in the nineties and based on a play by Eric Bogosian (who acts the main role of Barry Champlain), itself based on the anti-Semitic murder of a Denver talk-show host. The film is a formal exercise in solving an old filmmaking problem: how to "open up" a play—in particular, a play restricted to a single, closed setting. The exercise fails whenever Stone leaves that closed setting, the radio studio where Barry works. When supplying a past and present life, an ex-wife, and other emotional entanglements for the character, the sentimentality that is Stone's worst enemy threatens. But in the radio station, Stone contrives a cutting style, an imaginative sense of space, a claustrophobic, almost expressionistic mise-en-scène that communicates the hysteria of Champlain and his listeners. Within this space, the camera is everywhere, staring, moving, being moved, communicating a lost-boundary narcissism filled with the voices of empty lives full of meaningless opinions, hatred, self-hatred, and murderousness.

The hysteria carries over to *Born on the Fourth of July*, whose narrative temporally overlaps *Platoon*, addressing Vietnam and its aftermath from the perspective of a paraplegic veteran. Actors from the previous film appear—Tom Berenger, the deranged Barnes in *Platoon*, is a marine recruitment officer, and Willem Dafoe, the Christ-like Elias, plays a fellow paraplegic whom Ron (Tom Cruise) meets in a Mexican brothel. The emotional pitch of *Talk Radio* is ratcheted up, and the critique of the war is woven through the life of one of its casualties, treated badly by everyone from his parents through the medics at a VA hospital where he recuperates. Stone leaves little room for inquiry in this film. Or, more accurately, he is in control of the inquiry. He creates a forward rush of events that is broad, loud, and assured. Every cut and movement of the camera is assertive. The battle sequences—played out on sunbaked plains as opposed to the jungles of *Platoon*—communicate confusion and emphasize the violent and deadly disorder of events out of anyone's control.[26] Ron is responsible for shooting a comrade. He and his troops struggle to reach him. Motion is slowed and the blinding sun shines into the camera, rendering the scene in a baked, reddish-gold. Ron is seen in closeup, with a reverse shot revealing his point of view as he slogs up the hill. But the second reverse shot is farther away from the fallen soldier than the first, and it swoops to a closeup of the figure on the ground faster than Ron could possibly move. Space and the integrity of the shot/reverse shot are challenged by a desire to make them more expressive of agonizing failure, more emotionally charged. In closeup, Ron asks, "What happened here?" There is a cut to the dying soldier, his neck wound gurgling. Sounds of a fighter plane are heard and the camera cuts to a distant shot, swooping back from the scene, a mortar exploding behind the group of men.

73

The visual construction of the sequence expresses the chaos and the diminishment of individual potency in war. The rest of the film narrates a struggle to reclaim that potency against a series of inert forces, not the least of which is the literal impotence resulting from Ron's wound. *Born on the Fourth of July* proceeds through a series of set pieces—the VA hospital that Stone represents as a kind of hell of physical neglect; a domestic scene in which a mute father and an anticommunist mother fail in their attempts to deal with a crippled, frustrated teenager; Ron's first antiwar demonstration; the third trip to hell at the Mexican brothel; his man-handling at the 1972 Republican and redemption at the 1976 Democratic Conventions. The film is a bildungsroman in which the audience is given view to the emotional and political growth of its characters, a growth—deeply within the tradition of American ideology—that occurs only through hard physical struggle and a painful growth of consciousness.

The tableaux structure of *Born on the Fourth of July* is shared with *Heaven and Earth*, Stone's other film that compares Vietnam and the postwar American domestic scene. Both are built through serial blocks of strong, sometimes shocking images, visually and aurally charged. Their montage is structured in the cause of linking the tableaux together more than it is in the building of events within a particular sequence. The total mise-en-scène, the construction of space and the articulation of the various spaces into a coherent narrative statement, serves a didactic function about ideological retooling in the midst of a fractious, unsettled culture. It is a didacticism aimed at the characters as much as their audience. The films wish us to learn by seeing how the characters learn and it works through high melodrama, spread across genders: Ron is the melodramatic figure in *Born on the Fourth of July*, while both Le Ly and Steve, the Tommy Lee Jones character who is her husband, attempt to break through cultural boundaries, and only Le Ly survives, though not before tears, rage, hysteria, and, in Steve's case, suicide help sort out various emotional scars, cultural ties, and personality difficulties. There is an operatic tendency at work in all this, a declamatory spectacle of emotional excess that tends to pummel as much as enlighten the audience, depending finally on a profound sentimentality for effect. We must submit to the suffering of the characters to understand their knowledge.

Starting with *JFK*, Stone developed a style in which sentimentality was contained, if not eradicated. Through this style, which should actually be thought of as a rethinking of cinematic narrative practice, it is not the characters who go through a learning experience but the viewer. In *JFK*,

Natural Born Killers, and *Nixon*, Stone breaks radically with conventional, linear narrative construction; he makes history, culture, and their formation part of the narrative construction itself. I noted earlier that *JFK* is a formal investigation of the ways images are manufactured to produce memory and history. I would repeat that *JFK* exists not only—perhaps not even essentially—as a film about Kennedy assassination conspiracies, although that's all the film's critics could see. Rather, *JFK* insists that we pay attention not merely to stories, but to the images through which they are told, and to those doing the telling. It is a film about discourse, process, power, and ideology, about speaking things into existence by investigating and demonstrating how events are represented, so that learning is accomplished by understanding process and coming to terms with power. *JFK* exists only in its telling, produces meaning through its editing and its mise-en-scène, and requests the viewer's active engagement with its methodology. Certainly, Stone wants his film to change minds. But more important, the film wants to show the ways minds can be changed.

The film's methodology is a synthesis of a number of elements. The most conventional is the film's detective narrative—"We're through the looking glass here," says Jim Garrison in one of the film's most famous lines, and, like the characters, we want to find out what's on the other side. "It's a mystery wrapped in a riddle inside an enigma," the mad David Ferrie says about the convoluted relationships between anti-Castro Cubans, the CIA, the Mafia, and the right-wing underground. And it is into the enigma we wish to go and Stone wishes to take us. As Roland Barthes has pointed out, the enigmatic code—the cluster of narrative conventions that keep prodding us to ask "What will happen next?" and therefore keep us reading or watching to find out—are among the most powerful in any kind of narrative.[27] A narrative code is a formal element and is linked in a film to contexts that transcend dialogue. In the David Ferrie sequence, the loony little man (played by Joe Pesci) with a crazy wig and huge eyebrows paces hysterically around a hotel room as Garrison and his men try to find out the answer to their most pressing enigma, "Who killed Kennedy?" The sequence is cut rapidly with the edits contrasting Ferrie, pacing, gesticulating, with the investigators seated or standing around the room, looking, wondering, often reflected in mirrors. Just before the line about the enigma, Ferrie suggests they investigate "Operation Mongoose," a Pentagon operation. The camera has just executed a slow track in on Garrison. There is a cut to a far shot of the room from some distance outside the door. Through the doorway, which is in the center of the screen, we can see one of the investigators and then Ferrie pacing back and forth. The shot is unauthorized by the point of view of anyone in the scene. The camera is substituting for no one we have seen. It becomes, for the moment, a cold, distant eye, suggestive of other eyes, of danger and of exposure, a visual code repeated often in the film.

The "through the looking glass" sequence is played out in a restaurant where Garrison and his investigators are gathered to discuss information on Lee Harvey Oswald. The gathering itself is cut in a fairly standard way: the camera pans around the room or cuts to the various people around the table as they talk and (as surrogates for our own curiosity and surprise) react to the information being laid out. The lighting is subdued, but, as an initial break in the conventional setup, a spotlight plays on Garrison's hands and catches his glasses, sometimes reflecting off of them, hiding his eyes. What is not standard is the cutting into the sequence of visual material, much of which involves closeups of the photographs gathered by the investigators being passed around the table. But the photographs "come to life." As fragments of information are pulled together, the still images turn eloquent. In one instance, an unexplained image that occurred at the very beginning of the film, in the midst of the historical montage that plays beneath the credits—a woman thrown out of a moving car—is shown in the midst of the restaurant meeting both through a photograph and by means of moving images, the woman finally identified as a dope runner for Jack Ruby. During the investigator's discussion, the strange history of Oswald comes together in a montage of still and moving, black-and-white and color images, as if knowledge were being constructed in front of our eyes and we were learning along with the characters on the screen.

While Oswald's story is being constructed, yet another layer of images is cut into the mix, another enigma that constitutes a metaphor for Stone's methodology throughout the film. These images—and we are not aware of what they are until the end of the sequence—are of the making of the *Life* magazine cover of Oswald holding a rifle, a photograph largely believed for many years to be a fake. (The montage includes shots of Oswald working in a darkroom as a map copier, a job he himself refers to later when asked about the *Life* cover. He informs his questioners that he knows all about faking photographs.) At first, we see only images of a graphic artist's hands wielding a matte knife and trimming orange masking paper. In one shot, the artist removes the orange cutout while holding an image of Oswald's head, ready to fit it into place. We see brief shots of the

76

composite image being developed in a chemical bath, but not until the end of the restaurant sequence as a whole do we see the *Life* cover. Garrison and his deputies conclude their discussion of Oswald and the circumstances surrounding his accusation as presidential assassin. "There's a lot of smoke there," one of the men says, "but there's some fire." "We're talking about our government, here," says another. There is a cut to Garrison, holding up a finger, pointing out to his deputy that what they are talking about is a crime, "pure and simple." At this moment, a cut is made to the chemical bath, suffused in red light, in which the faked picture of Oswald is being developed. Over this, Garrison's voice says, "You'all got to start thinking on a different level . . . like the CIA does." In the middle of the phrase, Stone cuts from the image of the photograph back to Garrison. Between the words "CIA" and "does," Stone breaks continuity to a shot further away from Garrison. The light is bright on his hands and glasses. Even though, in the preceding shot, Garrison had not finished pronouncing the word "does," he is momentarily silent in this shot, as if time had suddenly skipped in some unexpected direction. The camera tracks in, and Garrison makes his comment: "We're through the looking glass . . . white is black and black is white." As he says this, Stone flashes light on the image and cuts sharply to pairs of eyes on either side of the screen looking at Garrison. He cuts back to Garrison, then to the red image of the Oswald photograph. The red quickly disappears, and we see the whole image. Cut back to Garrison, "Just maybe that Oswald was exactly what he said he was . . . a patsy." Cut to the *Life* magazine cover. Garrison and his investigators are beginning to discover some alternate "truths" of the Kennedy mystery. The viewer is shown—quite separately, though intercut with the immediate narrative sequence—other truths of fakery and image manipulation.

No reference is made to these images in the dialogue. They constitute another level of dialogue—or dialectic—a representation of image manipulation and historical formation, of mystery and idea, obfuscation and clarification that the film as a whole is about. Stone assumes that viewers will recall the *Life* cover and the controversy that surrounded it (the cover itself appears earlier in the film, on a television screen) and, even more, assumes that the structure of the film has by this time raised a level of awareness that will allow the viewer to absorb the information being communicated by the various levels of the various montage cells. The whole multilayered structure of the sequence mirrors the construction of the film and, more important, the construction of history that Stone is addressing. History is the result of many conflicting narrative layers, a dialectic of stories, each feeding on the other, each claiming the truthfulness of its representation, each a version formed by ideology, point of view, moral and political perspective, cultural context, and desire.

For Oliver Stone, film is as good a historical narrative form as any other—better in some ways. Its images and dialogue can not only be made to articulate points of view, but can show how points of view are made, how history is seen and represented, how stories are told differently by different voices. The restaurant sequence demonstrates how narrative is built by film, through a structure, indeed a collision and even a collusion, of images, of various "voices" speaking simultaneously—the characters and their dialogue; the editorial assemblage of shot; the mise-en-scène or spatial articulation of the visual material; of belief and context supplied by screenwriter, director, and the viewer who must in the end interpret and respond to everything on the screen. Unlike conventional sequences and films, the restaurant sequence, and *JFK* as a whole, is multilayered and polyvalent. Its editorial structure insists that we see more than the characters, more than simple historical narratives—more, indeed than conspiracy theories—and instead understand that images can make us believe many things; they can reveal and direct; construct and manipulate.

Within the images themselves we can see expressed the necessity of questioning as well as the threat of a constrained point of view. If the cutting of *JFK* is like the putting together of a narrative skeleton, each of whose bones and connections is subject to change and rearrangement, the mise-en-scène of the film is like the cavernous space of the body of history. Recall the image in the David Ferrie sequence described earlier, where a cut is made to a shot from the hallway looking at the hotel room, the camera distant from the doorway, its point of view not attached to any of the characters. Earlier in the film, Garrison takes his deputies for a walk of the government district of New Orleans, pointing out the various agencies and their proximity to the offices of some of the key players in the conspiracy. At one point, there is a cut to a high, ninety-degree angle shot of the group on the street below, as if the buildings themselves had suddenly assumed the point of view, diminishing the figures within a threatening space. Later in the film, Colonel X (Stone's "Deep Throat," a narrative invention to supply a lot of information in a relatively small amount of time) reveals the depths of the government conspiracy to Garrison; they are walking across the Mall in Washington. The sequence is punctuated by a montage of scenes that enact X's stories. The two take a seat on a bench near the Washington Monument and, at two crucial points in X's speech, Stone cuts to a wide shot in which the characters on the bench are seen small in a great space punctuated by the monument. The second of these wide shots is even further back from the two of them, accentuating the broad, empty, paranoid space, open, threatening, needing to be filled.

Stone can create a paranoid space and then fill it with narrative information. In the government district sequence, Garrison begins to connect Oswald to other right-wing figures in New Orleans. In a black-and-white flashback, showing Oswald handing out pro-Castro leaflets in front of the office of some right-wing zealots (an act Garrison believes was part of a disinformation campaign), we can see Clay Shaw—a major figure in the conspiracy theory—in the background. The figure (played by Tommy Lee Jones) is clearly in focus and Oswald (played by Gary Oldham) turns to look. However, the viewer cannot possibly know who this character is because he is not on the screen long enough and has not yet been identified in the narrative. Like the construction of the *Life* magazine cover on the level of editing, the appearance of Shaw on the level of the shot provides information greater than what we or the characters know at the moment. It begs viewer attention and retention, acting as an almost subliminal clue to the mystery that will be unravelled as the film proceeds.

In constructing a body of knowledge—or, more accurately, a body of speculation about knowledge and history (itself a speculation about knowledge)—Stone, with the insight of a strong modernist artist, turns inward to the structures of his art. The content of *JFK* is manufactured by its form. We see the processes of cinematic inquiry at work. History becomes not The Truth but the ways truth might be articulated and perceived. His is a politics of perception and articulation, which prove to be, like the truth he tries to unveil, curious, unstable, sometimes undependable. Clearly, Stone is a left-of-center thinker, working in a culture when anything left of center is cause for ridicule by the right. But Stone's films are often conflicted politically, just as they are often softened with sentiment. The latter is clear in those sequences in *JFK* between Garrison and his wife. The visual, structural energy comes to a halt in these places, and the film falls into conventional family melodramatics, traditional *gender* melodramatics, in which the wife complains of neglect, wishes that the husband remain closer to home and his job description, stop taking chances detrimental to the domestic scene. These are conservative moments in an otherwise progressive film, moments of uncertainty, perhaps, of fear of going too far formally and politically, fear of losing the center of convention—fear of losing the audience.

These sentimental sequences come together in the courtroom sequence that ends the film. Two things happen here: Stone connects the jigsaw pieces of visual and narrative elements that have been scattered, looking for coherence, throughout the film. They are gathered and achieve closure of a kind in the images of Kennedy's exploding head in the Zapruder film, which Garrison shows "forward and back, forward and back," exhausting emotion and exposing the impossibility of the single gun theory. But at the same time, Stone introduces another closure, a conventional, oedipal closure by means of Garrison's speech about redeeming the fallen "Father Leader." Here, a film whose radical, modernist structure insisted that we learn history through a theory of representation turns to the mythic, to the sentiment of large, oedipal emotions filtered through a universalist ideology of dead rulers. Is this the other narrative that Robert Burgoyne tells us the film seeks, the narrative of regained community and national purpose? All such narratives are, at their base, really stories of failure and negation. They are conservative attempts to define a culture through a fake redemption, proclaiming power by honoring a dead patriarch. Like the wife's pleas for the husband to come back to the domestic fold, Garrison's summation, with its plea to redeem the fallen king, threatens to negate the film's larger plea to question, probe, and analyze images and discover how history is made by asking us to return to the safe fold of sentimental archetypes, where our rulers are royal and our obeisance therefore unquestioned.

The film's internal contradictions have become externalized in a matter of years. In the early nineties, *JFK*'s demand to question government and mistrust authority could still trace its discourse back to the counterculture movements of the sixties, movements that responded to the repression of the fifties and the hopelessness of Vietnam by calling for an inquiry of governmental operations. But the reassertion of conservatism in the nineties— a virulent conservatism based on resentment and deep insecurity— changed the discourse of the sixties (a central goal of neoconservatism) so that parts of *JFK* now sound like the very right-wing discourse it attempts to attack. Conspiracy discourse, because it is so firmly based in supposition, in the breathless and passionate desire to reveal the causes of fear and suspicion that are the more believable the more they are fantastic, can obfuscate a variety of content and change as the culture changes. To speak about distrust of government from the early sixties through the early nineties was to give voice to profound uncertainties about historical accounts and political misdeeds. From the multiple assassinations of the sixties through Vietnam and Watergate, people of the left could articulate well-reasoned suspicions of their government acting in a less than open manner. But in right-wing discourse, this articulation of mistrust becomes more personalized, racist, anti-Semitic, filled with schizophrenic imagery of black helicopters, new world orders, trilateral commissions, and CIA transmitters placed in the body. Some of *JFK*'s leftish antigovernment discourse now suddenly sounds like right-wing antigovernment language.

That the discourse of *JFK* becomes shaded differently as it is refracted through right- instead of left-wing ideology is not the fault of the film or its creator, but it does speak to the way passionate inquiry can alter based on who is being passionate. On its release, the film came under enormous attack not only from conservatives, but from parts of the liberal establishment who had need of maintaining certain traditional explanations about the Kennedy assassination, and from some who were simply worried about popular film trying so hard to shake up political and ideological perceptions. Some actually believed that its manufactured images might be taken as "real" images. The fact that the film can lend itself to a such a broad sweep of ideological discomfort and mistrust at least proves its powers of interrogation. Asking political questions with the force of conviction makes people nervous; asking them through the persuasive rhetoric of film—whose images and stories are always constructed to make us believe them—creates much discomfort, indeed.

JFK examines the violence done to the political system through violence done to a representative of that system by reactionary forces. Its structure is an assault of images that attempt to construct alternative readings of historical events that assaulted the body politic. *Nixon* is a narrative of violence done to the political system by a representative of that system. It attempts to articulate the personality of a disturbed and disturbing individual who was the source of enormous violence committed on the world. The film continues Stone's evaluation of the sixties and becomes a kind of "life and times," drawing on the conventions of the Hollywood biography genre. But it would be unlike Stone to draw on a genre without exploding it thoroughly. He takes as his starting point an older, fictional "biopic" that itself explored (and exploded) the means by which film represented the life of an individual, *Citizen Kane*. *Nixon*'s debt to *Kane* is as complex as it is obvious. The film's opening montage of a simulated fifties "motivational" film (about how to be a good salesman) that's being watched by the Watergate burglars as they ready for their operation—a montage that includes images of the group huddled together in the light of the projector beam—and the establishing shot of the White House through its outside gates are reminiscent of the opening sequences of Welles's film, with its images of the gated Xanadu and the journalists watching the newsreel footage of Kane's life.

But Stone is thinking about more than equivalent images; he's attempting to get to the root problem posed by *Kane* and articulated in the film itself: how can a film represent a life? This problem is even more complex given that *Nixon* is dealing with the life of a "real" person. Welles's conclusion was to create individual perspectives and points of view to narrate fragments of character, a small piece of whom was known to each of them and to use a deeply shadowed, deep focused visual field to suggest the temptation of seeing all and nothing about a character. In short, he foregrounded the cinematic act of perception, supplying visual and aural pieces of the puzzle of his character. The biographical process was examined as a formal problem to be solved through the investigation of the cinematic process. Stone goes about it in a somewhat different fashion. Unlike Robert Altman's Nixon film, *Secret Honor* (1984), which remains fixed on a mad character in a small room (not unlike Stone's *Talk Radio*), Stone is dealing with a "real" character whom he wants to see in the context of the time that made him and that he made. He wants his film not only to remind the audience of Watergate and Vietnam, but of Southern California and Nixon's childhood. He wants to see the figures around Nixon and the spaces the characters inhabit. He wants to suggest psychology and evoke the fall of the culture Nixon provoked.

Wellesian deep focus space won't work here, and not only for technical reasons. Stone is not interested in elasticizing the screen space. Space, especially as constructed through color, grayscale, and camera angle, is important to Stone; but time, expressed through montage, is equally as important. I mentioned earlier that Stone is the rare filmmaker who links his practice with Sergei Eisenstein, for whom the control over time was the essential expressive element of his art. Time was Eisenstein's malleable medium and he created it through the cut. Character definition and the flow (or the stutter) of history can be created through spatial absences and juxtapositions by means of editing, which in turn create duration, contraction, exposition, juxtaposition, connection.

For example, the first post-credit sequence of the film takes place in late

1973 in Nixon's private quarters. Drunk, doped, suicidal, Nixon talks to Alexander Haig and fumbles obsessively with his tape. The space is dark and cramped. The tape recordings provide a transition to a time eighteen months earlier. Nixon meets with his staff, planning the Watergate cover-up, revealing the depth of his relationship with anti-Castro Cubans. Howard Hunt is introduced as a kind of narrative red herring, an implication held throughout the film, never satisfactorily resolved, that he has something on Nixon that forces the President into rash measures. The spatial construction of the sequence, though confined to the meeting room, is fairly open. There are montage inserts of Chappaquiddick, of the attempted assassination of George Wallace, and a re-creation in black and white of the pilfering of Daniel Ellsberg's psychiatric records. The sequence cycles back to December 1973 again through the sound and visual transitions of the tape machine. The space is even more cramped than at first. The camera cants up from a low angle as a ruined Nixon rummages the room, picks up a bottle of pills that he attempts to open with his teeth. The pills pour out on the floor.

Parts of these actions are in a grainy black and white—a kind of montage by film stock, and part of the methodology of representing the dissociative aspects of Nixon's character that Stone will use throughout the film. For example, during the reenactment of the Kennedy–Nixon debate and the 1962 "You won't have Nixon to kick around anymore" press conference as well as the Republican convention acceptance speech there are crucial moments that we see and see again in which the character himself does something, and then does it again, sliding out of time and out of control.

The sequence of the drunk Nixon pivots the narrative, at the nadir of his career. Stone now must fill in the past, and he does this through a kind of hypertext, a series of links that move the narrative in a number of directions that, collectively, give us history, fill out character, and provide levels of approach to this curious figure. From the confines of Nixon's White House quarters, the narrative moves to the 1960 Kennedy debates, a clever reconstruction of the actual televised confrontation intercut with remarks from Nixon's entourage in the audience. The synthetic construction of this sequence, with Anthony Hopkins's head digitally fused to kinescope television images of Nixon's body on the platform with John Kennedy, provides another clue to Stone's method. History is synthesis, facts retold, explained, represented, seen, and reseen through a variety of points of view. As in *JFK*, image construction and assemblage are not a way to meaning, but meaning itself. Nixon was largely a construction of television, and he used it when he could to his best advantage (Stone reenacts the infamous Checkers' speech of 1952, in which a maudlin Nixon beguiled the nation). Nixon, however, had difficulty maintaining a consistent image. This slippage of control that Stone represents throughout the film by means of images of Nixon edited to redouble themselves are one way Stone visually responds to the slippage of personality. The Kennedy debate stands as the classic moment when the televisual image undid a politician. Articulating it artificially, by putting an actor's head on the kinescoped image of a politician, creates a kind of meta-artificiality. The viewer is put on notice, is given a larger perspective, is warned that all is not what it seems.

Stone's historical analysis makes a narrative link between the loss of the Kennedy debate and the sentimentalized squalor and abjection of Nixon's childhood. Nixon as loser, Nixon held prisoner to the romantic myth of his "sainted" mother and poor, hardworking father, Nixon as wallower in sentiment are all constructed through these childhood scenes that recur throughout the film. They are shot in black and white, distanced and melodramatic at the same time. They triangulate viewer, subject, and film. There are moments when the childhood scenes want to be taken seriously; but then the excess of character or event (the brothers' tuberculosis, the screenwide magnifications of multiplying bacilli, for example) push us away. We are reminded a number of times during the contemporary sequences that Nixon's family romance and myth became another shtick that Nixon would pull out as needed. The point is made when, during one family flashback, Stone dissolves a voice-over of Nixon's resignation speech that again refers to his sainted mother.

The hypertext of loss and self-pity jumps from past to near present, encapsulating improbable images of Nixon playing college football in the early thirties and coming to rest in the 1962 California gubernatorial campaign. This is an important anchoring moment in the narrative, allowing Stone to dwell further on the character's sodden self-pity, delineate the strained relationship between Nixon and his wife, and push both the characters and their history forward. The inherent melodrama of the moment—in which Dick and Pat confront his political loss and she threatens to leave him—is undercut by the mise-en-scène and the reenactment of one of the great public paranoid episodes in contemporary politics. Their breakup and reconciliation is intercut with black-and-white flashbacks of their courtship, including the college theatrical in which they meet (the theatricality of the moment, and Nixon's playing the role of concerned husband, willing to give up his career for his wife, is emphasized by the flashback). The domestic moment is played within a garish hotel suite: the living room has clashing red curtains and green furniture, the bedroom red bedcovers and green lampshades. The setting is a bit surreal and distracting, which is precisely the point. There is a surreal quality to the counterpoint between Nixon and the rest of the world. The character can't fit and doesn't understand why, and so he playacts sincerity, concern, domesticity. He feigns a life. The cutting and mise-en-scène of the film keep emphasizing the illusions.

Melodrama is played out across all the formal elements of a film's narrative. Melodramatic space can enhance the emotional surge of a film, even—as Thomas Elsaesser has pointed out—provide a container for its excess, or it can contradict and thereby cool it.[28] The "bedroom" scenes in *JFK* don't reveal an antidote to their domestic sentimentality either in the editing or the mise-en-scène. They are about the necessity of a man doing his duty. In *Nixon*, the man's duty is always under question. Unlike the passionate Jim Garrison, Nixon is portrayed throughout as stiff, emotionless, with something always going on behind his eyes that counters what he seems to be saying and thinking (Anthony Hopkins's ability to express these conflicts is remarkable). The mise-en-scène aggravates and exaggerates the various dissociations of the character created through the montage and then combines with the montage to articulate fully the internal and external clashes of character and history. All this is done with a level of self-consciousness that maintains a state of some tension.

The self-consciousness highlighted as the hypertext of Nixon's past comes to an end with the infamous 1962 press conference in which, in a nadir of paranoia, resentment, and self-pity, the politician announces, "You won't have Nixon to kick around anymore." Stone cuts to black and white and another camera angle, forcing Nixon to repeat "kick around anymore." This moment of public abjection is absorbed into yet another montage of history, which again alludes to *Citizen Kane*. Stone creates a "March of Time" documentary, summarizing Nixon's place in cold war history, emphasizing, as does the newsreel in *Kane*, the mystery of his character. The "documentary" refers to another abjection of Nixon's, the 1952 television Checkers' speech, made in response to allegations of campaign financing irregularities. With Pat sitting stiffly in the background, Nixon referred to the apparently intimate events of his life, everything from his children's dog Checkers to his wife's "plain Republican cloth coat." He publicly itemized his finances. He debased himself with grotesque sentimentality and many voters loved it. He was allowed to remain as Eisenhower's running mate. As the voice-over in Stone's mini-documentary says, "It was shameless, it was manipulative, it was a huge success."

The comment can be readily applied to *Nixon*, the film. Its large-scale manipulations of time and space are as shameless in exposing its methodologies and its subject as its subject was unashamed of his own political manipulations. *Nixon* is open, large, and broad, sometimes nearly hysterical in its drive to generate images of explanation, narratives of historical clarification, and psychologies of character. Stone keeps countering his subject's desire to scuttle behind the history he helped deform by shoving him and that history out into the open, forcing him to confront it along with the viewer. In the recreation of Nixon's 1968 acceptance speech, the Republican convention hall is turned into a huge space for historical montage. As Nixon mouths right-wing clichés, the terrible history of fifties and sixties repression and the struggle against that repression blooms before him, around him, and in his place. The audience of Republican hacks is replaced by images of civil-rights and war protestors, the faces of George Wallace and Huey Newton; of Boy Scouts and southern freedom marchers.

These are the methods Stone uses not only to form but control his subject and the huge flow of history surrounding both. Richard M. Nixon did his best to control himself and his political life through what Garry Wills calls a politics of resentment.[29] By exploiting his own inadequacies and those of his followers, Nixon turned anger and anxiety into a weapon. He embraced anticommunist ideologies and became them, demonizing his opponents by playing on convenient and easily manipulated fears. When a large part of the culture rose up against the Vietnam war in the sixties, Nixon invented their opposite, "the silent majority," and constructed the discourse of "law and order." His control broke down because it was based on political corruption, a dependence on thuggery and bribes, and a hatred of the self and others—so strong that, once revealed, the artifice of lies and double-dealing couldn't stand. Stone's control seems the opposite of Nixon's. Supreme self-confidence and an outrageously adventurous style allows him to break open decades of history and represent them through an intricate weave of montage and mise-en-scène. This is, of course, the exercise of an enormous intellectual and aesthetic control put in the service of a cinema of revelation. But revelation also means focus, and Stone attempts to rein in his wide-ranging hypertext, his dynamic montages and articulation of screen space through the control of a few guiding metaphors.

The most interesting of these is the idea of "the beast." A curious set of animal imagery and references runs throughout the film, starting with Nixon's abjection in the face of his mother, "Think of me always as thy faithful dog," he tells her, pledging dependence and passivity. The publicly known dog reference appears in the Checkers' speech, which climaxes around a pathetic statement about the faithful family dog, a "gift" from a Texas businessman. It climaxes late in the film, during the unraveling of the Nixon regime. In a severe black-and-white montage of Nixon and his cronies discussing the publication of the Pentagon Papers, an Irish setter is prominent in some of the shots. At one point, during a harangue by Henry Kissinger about Daniel Ellsberg's morals and how the affair makes the President look weak, Nixon gets up and offers his hand to the dog, who yelps and walks away. "Goddamit," Nixon yells, "how long have we had this jackass dog . . . aw, fuck it, he doesn't like me. . . . It's all your fault, Henry." Nixon is referring to the Pentagon Papers, but the conflation of dog, self-pity, and blame is neatly plotted out and creates a very subtle contrast to John Kennedy. In the credit montage of *JFK* there is a shot of a dog eating out of Kennedy's hand.

There is a suggestion of faulty and failed domesticity in these references, and they connect with the awkward "bedroom" scenes between Nixon and Pat, in which Nixon, uncomfortable with anything having to do with emotion and attachment, with an intimacy that depends on emotions unfiltered through sentimentality or sordid self-interest, must pretend affection or even discord—common emotions that are unachievable for him. The recurring image of the dog suggests a playfulness that Nixon can't own; a friendliness that he can't manage; a loyalty completely beyond his comprehension.

On the other side of domesticity is naked animal aggression, suggested in a sequence in which Howard Hunt and G. Gordon Liddy contact the "plumbers," the Cubans who will perform the Watergate and Ellsberg psychiatrist break-ins. The sequence takes place during a cock fight in Miami. "The claws are out," Hunt says, and there is little doubt about the violence inherent in Nixon's use of right-wingers to gather information about his presumed enemies.

The visual references to animals are pushed into metaphor, as Nixon adopts a notion of "the beast" to help him explain political powers out of his control. The phrase is used during Nixon's 1970 nighttime visit to protestors at the Lincoln Memorial. This surreal episode—as bizarre in the film as it was when it took place—is used by Stone again to play Nixon's cocooned world against the external realities he ignored. As he stands at the Lincoln statue, the background behind him becomes a battlefield where a bomb explodes. As he looks at Lincoln, we see photographs of Civil War soldiers and newsreel footage from Vietnam. The reverse shot is telling: when Nixon looks around, he faces the soldiers of the contemporary civil war, young protestors, in awe that they have come face to face with the man they love to hate. In editing their conversation, Stone uses a number of dissociative cuts, as if pulling Nixon away from himself. He cuts in newsreel footage—a Buddhist monk immolating himself; the infamous image of the naked Vietnamese girl running down a road—he distorts the time and the place and Nixon's own comprehension until one of the protestors suggests that he doesn't have any control over things, that the collection of forces maintaining the war is like "a wild animal." As his aides hustle him down the monument steps, Nixon offers that the young woman recognized something it took him twenty-five years to see, that the combined forces of government over which he has no control are "the beast." Of course, he is referring to the uncontrollable and conflicting forces of his own personality.

This verbalizes an idea Stone visualized with tremendous impact earlier on, as part of the sequence representing the 1968 campaign and the introduction of J. Edgar Hoover into the mix of historical narration. Historically, Hoover and Nixon were a perfect pair of powerful connivers, though the balance of power was always on Hoover's side, as it had been for many years before Nixon. A canny reactionary, Hoover used his hatred of difference in race or politics as a club against perceived enemies, and he maintained records on many people for purposes of control or destruction. He was held in such fear and hatred by so many, that, after his death, the revelation of his homosexuality allowed him to be turned immediately from a monster to a joke. His power gone, one hidden aspect of his life revealed, he was dismissed by the culture as a bizarre cross-dresser. Stone, whose homophobia bangs into his desire to reveal the hypocrisies of historical record, falls completely for the new, gay Hoover. His description of the role of the right-wing homosexual underground in the Kennedy assassination in *JFK*, though based on a political reality that existed well into the Reagan regime, was condemned as antigay, and I expect that Stone simply assumed a convention that equates gender difference with some darker moral corruption. There was and is a right-wing gay movement, and the contradictions inherent in that reality are indeed difficult to deal with. Using those contradictions as a means to render the plotters of the Kennedy assassination bizarre may be done too easily by Stone, but he maintains its force of making this shadowy world full of confusion both political and gender. In creating his Hoover for *Nixon*, Stone goes less for convention than for cultural permission (which is, in the end, a version of convention). Hoover in retrospect is clearly perceived as a ridiculous fraud. Hoover in history was a power broker of the most ruthless kind, a user, blackmailer, possibly an assassin. Both aspects are folded into the portrayal in the film, and Nixon's association with Hoover is contained within the image of the beast.

Hoover summons Nixon to a meeting at a racetrack, making sure that a Mafia associate, whom Nixon had met in Cuba, is present and that Nixon knows it. The gangster has fixed the race; Hoover, it is suggested, will fix the election. The sequence is powerfully cut, beginning with images of a wild and frightened horse and a terrible pileup of animals on the track that fixes the outcome of the race. Hoover provokes Nixon's memory, and black-and-white images of meetings in prerevolutionary Cuba flash in montage. At one point, the opening of the starting gates at the racetrack is superimposed over a double exposure of Nixon in Cuba, another version of the dissociative imagery that Stone uses to mark the character. Hoover, Nixon, and Clyde Tolson, Hoover's lifelong companion, go off to look at a horse and talk politics. Nixon rants about the ruthlessness of his opponent, Robert Kennedy; Hoover's own rant moves things up a notch. His isn't the resentful whine of a man undone by someone smarter than he is, but of an out-of-control lunatic. He goes on about "times of savage outbursts . . . the late Dr. King, for example, a moral hypocrite, screwing women like a degenerate tomcat, stirring up the blacks, preaching against our system." As he speaks this, a horse is standing near him, being held by its bridle. Stone cuts to the animal's wild eyes and frothing mouth. He cuts as well to Tolson's knowing winks and Nixon's somewhat abashed and nervous demeanor. "Sometimes the system comes very close to cracking," Hoover says, and Stone cuts to a horse running free on the track. "We've already had one radical in the White House. I don't believe we can survive another." The horse whinnies and pulls back hard. Hoover's hand slips over Nixon's.

The implication of the sequence is that Hoover had a hand in the assassinations of John Kennedy and Martin Luther King, and will have in the murder of Robert Kennedy. The horse imagery derives from the

89

riderless horse that was such a potent image in the Kennedy funeral procession—which Stone has Nixon watching earlier on television. But the association is stretched out to even larger symbolic proportions. The horse is both controlled and wild; frightening and frightened, it is simultaneously Nixon and all the internal and external forces of personality and power that Nixon could not manage. Like the film itself, these conflicts need control and threaten that control at every instant. In this film about power, the horse is the image of power contained, power unleashed, and power controlled again. It is as well the foil to the corruption of power. As an animal, it retains its animal nature—it rears and pulls away in panic. It is a domesticated force that is still elemental: under the human thumb, its life fixed and managed, yet it still demonstrates wildness and panic. It is like the State itself.

It is finally dead meat. The animal imagery of the film ends as a bloody steak on Nixon's plate. Stone creates a sequence aboard the Presidential yacht in 1970, after Nixon has called protestors "bums," after the murders at Kent State. Everyone is there: Mitchell, Kissinger, Haldeman, Erlichman (whom Stone attempts to portray as a growing conscience in the White House by cutting in closeups of his troubled and reflective looks; he is played by the talented, late character actor J. T. Walsh). At this moment of crisis, they talk about the China trip and about bombing Hanoi, about diplomacy as self-interest, and how to convince weeping mothers that the war is just. Nixon, already edging into madness, says he'll use the A-bomb. "We have to entertain the possibility," Kissinger agrees, and Stone cuts to a shot of Nixon's dinner plate, the steak bleeding profusely.

A symbol is only as good as the contradictions it can contain and the multiple meanings it can suggest. The dog/horse/beast/meat imagery in *Nixon* works not only because of its sometimes subtle, sometimes obvious consistency, but because it finds a way to attach the character to the culture through suggestion. It makes contradictions visible (and this is quite contrary to the usual process of Hollywood film, which seeks to suppress contradictions and cut off the attachments of its character to the world at large, except through banal moralities). It permits the character to find excuses for himself and provides the viewer—particularly in the racehorse sequence—with a sense of the massive disconnect between Nixon, the sniveling, resentful little man, and the upheavals he created. Nixon was a bloodless individual who caused a great deal of blood to flow; he was a repressed man but released the repressions in others; his political savagery wounded himself and the body politic. The culture is still flailing because of what he did. The animal imagery contains and expresses these contradictions, providing a useful set of representations for the wildness that emerged from a man who seemed completely separated from both the flesh and the spirit.

The animal imagery also works through a visual aggregation and suggestion that allows Stone to avoid the conventional Hollywood codes of psychological realism. The film has plenty of these: they are rooted in the flashbacks to Nixon's childhood, and they flower again at the film's end, when Stone appears to express more than a little sentiment for his character. They emerge in the invention of the "powerful Texans" to whom Nixon twice pays a visit. The group includes oilmen and shadowy anti-Castro Cubans, composed darkly and with menace. Nixon refuses the overtures of the prostitutes the "powerful Texans" have gathered for their party and, in his second visit, faces up to the men, refusing their bid to control him. It's not clear what these figures are doing in the film. Certainly Nixon did have powerful right-wing associates and supporters in the business and political world. Certainly he made use of right-wing Cubans (as in the Watergate and Ellsberg break-ins), and the film portrays him as regretful and fearful of these characters. Also, at least in his early days, Nixon attended the notorious "Bohemian Grove" meetings of powerful California Republicans. But in *Nixon*, this group seems to serve as a partial escape for the character and the director. If not a play for sympathy, they are certainly an attempt to portray a "human side," or a bit of backbone, even vulnerability, in the character.

Stone understands well enough that sentiment is often the obverse expression of corruption and violence, and he plays this out at the end of the yacht sequence, where Nixon talks regretfully about his actions and his past—talks about them without the least comprehension of their meaning other than his feelings of loss and regret. He is again disconnected from the larger body politic he is supposed to be overseeing. But Stone cannot finally maintain his disengagement, and the film, which for so much of its length refuses to disengage its subject from the larger patterns of history, culture, and the cinematic forms that express the connection, begins to fall into pity and a certain admiration for him. *JFK* searched for a cohesive narrative through the fragments of partial truths, hopeful leads, and the powerful interrogation of images that force them to reveal alternative stories. Its domestic sentimentalities were countered by a ferocity of investigation and revelation. *Natural Born Killers* made popular narratives its subject, seeking to explode our favorite stories of sex and violence by reducing them to absurdity and asking the viewer to negotiate his complicity with the absurd. There are absurdist elements in *Nixon*—the beast imagery we've discussed being the most prominent—and there is the continual absurdity suggested in the film and in the culture at large, the unspoken question of how such an obviously deranged and resentful man continually got elected to high office. In Robert Altman's *Secret Honor*, which provides Stone with elements of character and gesture to build on, the character poses that question directly. There's less self-pity, more arrogance, and about the same amount of paranoia in Altman's Nixon (he turns to a picture of his mother and says he will *not* be her dog), and he roundly points out the paradox of this hated man being continually elected to office. At the end of *Secret Honor*, which Nixon hurls defiance at those who wanted to lock him in a cage "like a fucking animal" and assures us that all he wanted was power! Near the end of Stone's *Nixon*, a morose and suddenly reflective president turns to a painting of John Kennedy: "When they look at you, they see what they want to be. When they look at me, they see what they are." This practically constitutes an answer of one film character to another; it also seems to provide an answer to the events of the film and, by extension, to the history those events represent. Stone's Nixon imagines himself as America's everyman.

Along with the nostalgia of the character's past, the statement wants to offer an explanation for Nixon and all those who supported him across the middle of the twentieth century. More important, it provides answers for Stone, who is intent on making his film a response to both John Kennedy and *JFK*, wanting, perhaps, to redeem the time of the sixties and seventies by hoping—creating, imagining—a redemption for this character whose actions constituted the ruination of politics. Not content to see his debt to *Citizen Kane* to the end, Stone refuses to finish on an ambiguous note. There is no "No Trespassing" sign to close off our vision and our desire, but rather a lengthy reenactment of Nixon's resignation speech, during which the old stories of his childhood, mocked earlier in the film, seem to be taken seriously—almost seriously. This is followed by newsreel footage of Nixon himself heading for his helicopter and then of his funeral, where a variety of politicians came to voice tearful farewells spoken within a cloak of amnesia. The voice narrating this footage is Stone's. The last image of the narrative is a black-and-white still of (the actor portraying) Nixon the young boy, looking off wistfully.

Stone's voice-over talks about Nixon's post-resignation redemption and emphasizes his success in protecting his tapes. The film ends with a choir singing a melancholy song worthy of John Ford, "Oh, Shenandoah, I long to see you." At the end of *JFK*, a title points out with frustration that the files of the Kennedy assassination are locked away until 2029. Somehow, the voice-over relating Nixon's successful suppression of his tapes sounds approving, perhaps or despite the fact that every time more of the tapes are released, they further disclose the man's profound corruption. Approving or not, the mournful heavenly choir and the assured voice of the filmmaker himself indicate that the artist has fallen into a certain admiration, even sympathy, for his subject. There is no gainsaying this. Stone would not be the first person to come to admire his subject. In fact, much of the political power structure of the country went over the top at Nixon's funeral, no doubt in hopes of their own ultimate redemption. The problem lies with the potential damage done to the text itself, because the sympathy and the sentiment throw off the ironic, condemnatory exposure that has gone before. The montages of history contorted by the diminished personality at their center, the spaces around the character enriched by images of history crowding in on him and diminishing him further, depend on a strong narrator who can hold his character at a distance and judge him continually. When that judgment falters at the end, the body of the text itself shudders a bit.

Stone's sentimentality might be seen in a larger postmodern context that eschews the ironic representation of the always lost, always alone, sometimes coping individual of modernism. In the postmodern era, the pathetic or sarcastic takes the place of the ironic and bathos threatens everything. Sentimentality might also be seen in the context of Hollywood filmmaking, in which some kind of redemption is now a clichéd plot convention based on an economic imperative. Orson Welles, the master humanist-modernist filmmaker, always admired his monster, power-hungry characters but never got sentimental over them and only forgave them through a recognition that whatever they did, it was in their character, which they could not choose but follow. "He was some kind of a man. What does it matter what you say about people," says Tanya at the end of *Touch of Evil*. A moving comment about a totally corrupt character who has just been shot dead into an open sewer. It's a comment that only seems enlightening. It offers no redemption, only a vague understanding. Even John Falstaff in *Chimes at Midnight* (1966) ends not as a figure of sympathy as much as a sign of the inevitability of fall from power, grace, and life. Everyone in *Citizen Kane* has something to say about the central character, and none of it quite adds up, because the figure was meant to be

93

a composite of everyone's perceptions. The deep spaces that surround the character are really vanishing points of comprehension; they force us to look beyond Kane into the dark impenetrability of character.

I think Stone has something of this in mind, but his character, his Nixon—our Nixon—can't exist in Wellesian deep space. We can't avert our gaze nor can the spaces of contemporary history exist without him. Stone knows this, which is why he has history surround him, emanate from him, and push him in and out of his space throughout the film. But Stone wants, finally, to push him back into the spaces of history as a redeemed man, just as Nixon, the actual man, wanted to do for himself. The problem of course is that Kane was a fiction and Nixon a fact. No redemption was possible or sought for Kane, and every attempt on the side of Nixon is collapsed by the realities of his own personality, his own hateful language and acts.

Stone succeeds when he charges his films with a powerfully inquisitive formal structure. As Eisenstein's (more that Welles's) heir, he lunges at images with a "kino fist," making them eloquent with an excited, self-conscious, analytic observation of their own violence and that of the culture they address. His images and their montage structure attempt to grab contemporary American history and respeak it in a cinematic discourse that forces open its cruelties and contradictions. His narratives of doomed men seeking to prevail either through their own righteousness or the forces of their own corruption may in fact ask us to rethink the poles of righteousness or corruption—or at least the ways in which we choose to see and assent to them. It is this radical, sometimes violent, turning of perceptual tables on the ground of history that has gotten Stone into so much trouble. With the exception of Robert Altman, no contemporary filmmaker has so forcefully used film to so radically examine political practice. And no American filmmaker has been so forceful in his images and vocal in his own voice defending the right of the artist to interpret. This, in the culture's fashion, has turned Oliver Stone from savior to pariah to joke. Our ideology forces apart the political and the aesthetic. To rejoin them threatens only derision, lest an artist be allowed to see and say too much. Stone has gone even further by addressing contemporary politics from something other than a center-right position and has therefore transgressed that other ideological imperative—invented by Nixon and his colleagues in the post-World War II period—that brands left-of-center discourse as dangerous and ridiculous.[30]

The fact that no contemporary filmmaker has gotten as much press or

94

been as reviled as Stone makes him neither hero nor victim, but rather a fascinating example of how much film still influences the culture and how much that influence will be attacked when it begins to impose on conventional wisdom. It is also a mark of what happens when the levels of sentimentality generated by a film begin to alter an acceptable balance. *Platoon* and *Born on the Fourth of July* foreground character in unexceptional ways: they suffer, learn, explode, change, and, if not prevail, come to a greater understanding of themselves at the film's end than they had at the beginning. Nor is the mise-en-scène of these films exceptional, though the wideangle shots and hard editing of *Born on the Fourth of July* begin to indicate a change in perception on Stone's part. *JFK* is able to create three distinct characters, each seeking redemption and each achieving it. The historical figure of the president, though never represented in any way other than real or manufactured "documentary" footage, is stirred into the cultural consciousness he never quite left. He is the mystery of the sixties, the promise of a cultural and political rebirth that, even though shown to be based on no real premises, was real enough to further the groaning ideological shift out of the fifties. Like Franklin Roosevelt in films of the forties, John Kennedy can't quite be represented and the culture always will want him, and his death especially, defined for them. Stone's Jim Garrison attempts to do this and his narrative is explicitly that of the child avenging the father's death. Everyone wins in this quest, especially the audience, who is more clearly present as a character in this film than in any other of Stone's. It is the audience whose redemption is promised by *JFK*, told that, if they look, they will see. "We're through the looking glass," Garrison says. Stone promises clarity on the other side. The promise was irresistible to many and irritating, even frightening, to others.

Natural Born Killers and *Nixon* very much hold their audience at a distance. The first hurls its images at the viewer with a delighted hysteria and a constant deflation and upending of cultural platitudes, while *Nixon* demands a remembrance of the sixties and seventies with a promise of revelation without clarification. No redemption occurs in *Natural Born Killers*—which insists that the stupid and violent will inherent the earth—and its tentative proffering at the end of *Nixon* is unconvincing. The right was convinced, however, that all three films did their constituencies a disservice and condemned *Natural Born Killers* for its immorality and *Nixon* and *JFK* for their lack of faith to history and further peddling of conspiracy theories. Since the culture equates "conspiracy theory" with the dismissable ramblings of a disgruntled or crazy person, Stone was attacked. His stock began to fall the harder because *Nixon* was not a commercially successful film.

Within a short space of time, Stone's name moved from that of a serious filmmaker to a shortcut to a laugh. In the 1997 film *Conspiracy Theory*, the Mel Gibson character says that Oliver Stone must be a front for the political power structure. "He's a disinformation junkie for them. The fact that he's still alive says it all. He probably should be dead but he's not." Our culture is very hard on its political artists. This right-wing culture is brutal to left-leaning political artists. They both try too hard to create alternative ways of seeing the world.

TWO

TECTONICS OF THE MECHANICAL MAN
Stanley Kubrick

Stanley Kubrick aspired to be the novelist of American filmmakers. Not in the form and content of his work—though his films were almost all based on novels—but in the means of their production and of their creator's life. After what he perceived as the personal disaster of *Spartacus* (1960), he left the United States, took up residence north of London, and worked independently, first with his producer, James Harris; then, when Harris left after setting up the production of *Dr. Strangelove* (1963), on his own.[1] *2001: A Space Odyssey* (1968) allowed him a margin of financial independence. The collapse of a planned production on Napoleon put that independence in question, but with the success of *A Clockwork Orange* (1971) he entered into an arrangement with Warner Bros., which allowed him to develop, write, produce, and edit his films without much consultation with the studio and with guaranteed distribution. All the films were made with a minimum of pre-release publicity and no public appearance by their director. Unwilling to fly, he had not been in the United States since the premier of *2001*, and that isolation took a certain toll. His later films suffered from a certain cultural airlessness, and he seemed to have a great deal of trouble making them. Seven years passed between *The Shining* (1980) and *Full Metal Jacket* (1987, in which a North London gas works and imported palm trees stood in for Vietnam), eleven years until *Eyes Wide Shut* (1999, which had one of the longest shoots in history and in which stage sets stood for the streets of New York).

Privacy, perfectionism, an extreme self-confidence, and perhaps some phobic and obsessive character traits created one of the most retiring directors in American filmmaking. At the same time, his films have become part of the aesthetic and political unconscious of our culture. They reoccur in our language ("Strangelove" has become part of the vocabulary), our films, our television (references to *2001* and *Clockwork Orange* abound in *The Simpsons*), and our commercials (the main theme of *2001*, the opening of Richard Strauss's *Also Sprach Zarathustra,* is still occasionally used by advertisers—at this writing, by Apple Computers). In 1997, in honor of the fictional computer's birth, MIT Press published a collection of essays by computer scientists on artificial intelligence entitled *Hal's Legacy.*

With this control and almost total independence came also a great deal of calculation. Kubrick kept his name alive during the increasingly long intervals between films because the films fulfill a number of functions that keep them in viewers' consciousness. Kubrick did not use his isolation to create "personal" and "difficult" works of the kind European filmmakers are supposed to make (once, years ago). He made complex films that are available to a variety of viewers. The films of his trilogy—*Dr. Strangelove, 2001: A Space Odyssey, A Clockwork Orange*—were commercially successful and demonstrated an unerring ability to seize on important cultural concerns and obsessions—the cold war, space travel, the ambiguities of violence—and represent them in images and narratives so powerful and appropriate that they became touchstones, reference points for these concerns: myths. *2001* is not only a narrative of space travel, but a way of seeing what space travel *should* look like. The film is a design for our imagination and a notion of modernity, creating the lineaments of a modern environment and enunciating the metamorphosis of human into machine. His cinema became the image of what we think this and other worlds should look like; the space apparatus of *2001* forms the basis for the *Star Wars* tetrology, *Close Encounters of the Third Kind,* and every science-fiction film in their wake. *Dr. Strangelove* is the complete text of politics as a deadly joke, a text that has become more and more accurate in the years since its first appearance and now stands as a document of cold war discourse. *A Clockwork Orange* holds in suspension, in the cold light of its cinematography, the outrageous contradictions of freedom and repression, libido and superego, the death of the other in the name of liberation of the self.

These films offer insight while giving immediate pleasure; they are beautiful to watch, funny, and spectacular. The counterculture of the late sixties and early seventies embraced *2001* and *A Clockwork Orange* for reasons of their immediacy and their spectacle. Kubrick was momentarily in danger of being seen as the panderer of contemporary film. Until he did something rather amazing. After three films that structured a mechanics of the modern age, he made a costume drama. *Barry Lyndon* (1975), based on a largely unread Thackeray novel published in 1844 about an eighteenth-century rogue, was the most unlikely and proved to be the most uncommercial film that an artist who had seemed so able to gauge the needs of his audience could have made. Had Kubrick abandoned his audience? After a decade of successful filmmaking, was he becoming self-indulgent or losing his judgment? Or was he not as calculating and cold about filmmaking as some critics have thought? It is well known that Kubrick planned his films by computer and solved production and personnel problems as if he were playing chess with a machine. There is a notion that this is perhaps somehow responsible for the popular success of the trilogy—that Kubrick calculated his narrative and its effects, perhaps even viewer response. But now the great calculator, the independent popularizer, had erred.

Or had he? Kubrick's films have far outlived their popularity of the moment. His best films—*Paths of Glory* (1957), *Dr. Strangelove*, *2001*, *A Clockwork Orange*, and the unpopular *Barry Lyndon*—yield up more and more information on each viewing, revealing themselves as meticulously made and carefully considered. Undergraduates often sit rapt by *Barry Lyndon*, responding readily to its contemplative pace and extraordinary images. Kubrick *is* very much a calculator; his films are cold and distanced and have strong designs on their audience—emotional, intellectual, and commercial. He has proven that the last does not cancel out the first two, and it is a happy coincidence when all three are offered to and met by the filmgoer. One can speculate that with *Barry Lyndon* it was not Kubrick who failed but his audience. The film is an advanced experiment in cinematic narrative structure and design and attests both to the strength of Kubrick's commercial position (no other director could have received the backing for such a project) and the intensity of his interest in cinematic structures.

He followed *Barry Lyndon* with *The Shining*, an adaptation of a Stephen King novel (such as were proving popular at the time), a film that, on first sight, seems to confirm Kubrick's ability to calculate his intent and his effects. A broad, loud, perfectly unsubtle film, it is more a parody of the horror genre than a film seriously intent on giving its audience a fright. Even beyond parody, it first appears as a mockery of its audience, almost an insult in its broadness to those who would not attend to the subtleties of *Barry Lyndon*. But like all his mature work, *The Shining* reveals more on subsequent viewing. Without doubt a parody of the horror genre, it is also—as are many recent representatives of the genre—an examination of the family, in this instance a discovery of the madness in the patriarchal domestic environment and a prophecy of its collapse.[2] Prophecy, satire, and a carefully controlled narrative and visual structure place it in an interesting relationship to the rest of Kubrick's work. *Full Metal Jacket* seems less certain in that relationship. A film about Vietnam, it generates many of the uncertainties and ambivalences of all other films of its kind. As a work by Kubrick, it seems less assured, less structured, less clear about its own point of view than do the preceding films. Because it is a war film, I will treat it in relationship with *Paths of Glory*, a pairing that will reveal both its successes and its flaws. *Eyes Wide Shut* is a film by a great director who seemed to have lost or certainly contained some of his energy, that careening and controlled imagination that drove the previous films. I will discuss it at the end of this chapter.

In what follows, I want to concentrate on *Paths of Glory, Dr. Strangelove, 2001, A Clockwork Orange*, and *Barry Lyndon*, along with some thoughts about how *The Shining* clarifies Kubrick's attitude toward sexual politics in his other films. This means the earlier works will be slighted. They make up an interesting body of generic experiment and indicate something of the direction in which Kubrick was to move. *Fear and Desire* (1953) is an amateur film that Kubrick held out of release until he could no longer exercise this particular control. He was right to do so; it is stiff and adolescent, though it is a war film and therefore predicts one of Kubrick's obsessive subjects. *Killer's Kiss* (1955) and *The Killing* (1956) are gangster films in the noir tradition. The sense of entrapment and isolation they offer is visually acute, and the hard black-and-white photography, the glaring lights, and a sense of exaggerated, even distorted space were to be developed and refined until Kubrick became a master of organizing large and expressive cinematic spaces. The nightmare sequence in *Killer's Kiss*, in which the camera rushes through a claustrophobic city street, photographed in negative, is a source for all the major tracking shots in the films to come, shots that integrate a subjective point of view within an environment that encloses and determines the character who inhabits it. The structure of *The Killing*, in which Sterling Hayden's Johnny Clay attempts to organize a foolproof racetrack robbery, only to be undone by a dismal accident, creates a complex temporal web of overlapping events that points the way to the typical situation of the Kubrick character—entangled and destroyed in systems of his own creation, systems that turn on him and take him over.[3]

The Killing was very much a work of its time. Kubrick draws on the existentialist philosophy popular among fifties intellectuals, representing in Johnny Clay a man unable to create an identity except through a failed attempt to impress himself violently on the world. He is a loser diminished by the gaze of authority; and the collapse of his plans, so carefully calculated that all they can possibly do is fall apart, sets the pattern for the characters in every Kubrick film. *The Killing* is also part of a larger movement in the decade in which the low-budget gangster film provided a space for experimentation for both known and beginning filmmakers. They permitted an analysis of class that studio productions couldn't dare, and they began a movement to the streets, to location filming, that permanently changed the mise-en-scène of American film. In Europe, the French New Wave took cognizance of these films and, in Godard's *Breathless* and Truffaut's *Shoot the Piano Player*, paid homage to them. Quentin Tarantino has been attempting to remake *The Killing* in all his films.

Although he did not pursue the gangster film after *The Killing*, Kubrick, like all the filmmakers discussed here, remained interested in the possibility of stretching genres. The war film has particularly intrigued him, as has science fiction and horror. At the same time, his resources were mostly literary rather than cinematic. The complexities of *2001*, for example, are much closer to science-fiction literature than to the science-fiction films of the fifties (though it is necessary to consider those films in order to understand fully what Kubrick is doing). By literary sources I mean two things: that most of Kubrick's films come from preexisting literary works, and that they have an intellectual complexity associated more with the literature of words than with that of film. The second of these characteristics is of greatest interest. Rather than Kubrick's use of literary sources, his translations from verbal to visual and aural text, what I find of most value in his work is his ability to generate ideas from the organization of a complex spatial realm that encloses his characters and expresses their state of being. For in Kubrick's films we learn more about a character from the way that character inhabits a particular space than (with the exception of *Dr. Strangelove*) from what that character says. Kubrick's is a cinema of habitations and rituals, of overwhelming spaces and intricate maneuvers, of the loss of human control, of defeat.

But before entering these spaces, I want to approach them from various other directions. Kubrick's influences emerge from the work of two seemingly opposite filmmakers, Orson Welles and John Ford. (He has explicitly named Max Ophuls—the great German director whose moving camera devoured space—as a prominent influence. *Eyes Wide Shut* is based

101

upon a novella by Arthur Schnitzler, whose work Ophuls had used as a source for some of his films.) Every filmmaker of the last twenty-five years, American or European, will admit to the influence of *Citizen Kane*, but very few, perhaps only Kubrick and Bernardo Bertolucci (at least in those films before *The Last Emperor*), have indicated an ability to put into practice the mise-en-scène Welles developed in *Kane* and his subsequent films. The Wellesian cinema is a cinema of space and spatial relationships. The camera, for Welles and for Kubrick, is an inscriber of a deep and complex visual field. Working within the design of the set, the lighting, the placement and movement of character, the camera creates an intricate space that it then begins to investigate, building a labyrinthine narrative structure that is a reflection of its investigations.[4] *Kane* is a study of the inviolability of personality, an inviolability proven when other people attempt to break it. A newspaper reporter provokes four people to recreate the character of Charles Foster Kane. The narrative that results is made up of the interlocking points of view of these people that create various spatial relationships between perceiver and perceived and between the audience and their perception of the narrative. The camera functions as creator and mediator of the entire structure, and the result is an extreme formal and thematic complexity. For all the discussion of Wellesian deep focus, moving camera, and long takes, and how these cinematic elements allow great freedom to observe spatial relationships, not many observers have noted that the more one sees in Welles's films, the more opaque and intractable what is seen becomes. For so intricate are these relationships, so complete and closed the world they create, that they become tenuous and abstract. The Wellesian mise-en-scène, especially in his later films—*Mr. Arkadin* (1955), *Touch of Evil,* and *The Trial* (1962)—creates a space so radically dislocated that it becomes a mental landscape. Knowable structures and the spatial relationships between human figures and those structures are distorted by lighting and camera placement to the point of straining the perceptions of the audience. Until *Chimes at Midnight*, the Wellesian mise-en-scène becomes more and more complex, overwhelming, and subjective.

Kubrick assumes many of Welles's attitudes toward the articulation of cinematic space. His composition in depth is almost as extreme—although he depends more on the distorting qualities of the wide-angle lens held at a distance from the characters than the Wellesian practice of layering the composition from fore- to background—as is his use of the moving camera. But where Welles tends to move his camera to investigate the intractability of the space he is creating, Kubrick most often uses it to traverse that space, to control it and understand it, even if the result of the investigation is its intractability. He is much more inclined to use the moving camera as a surrogate or parallel for the point of view of a character than is Welles. Compare the fleeing backward-moving camera retreating in front of Joseph K. in *The Trial* with the stately backward-moving camera that tracks Alex's walk into the record boutique in *A Clockwork Orange*. In the first instance the camera shares K.'s panic; it emphasizes his entrapment, and by retreating through a corridor of extreme dark and light it combines the need to escape with an indication of the impossibility of ever really emerging from the psycho-political cage K. inhabits. For Welles the moving camera often describes a double perspective, that of the character and that of the environment, and the two are almost always at odds. By contrast, the sequence quoted from *A Clockwork Orange* links the viewer to the character in a different way. His movement, the camera's, the synthesized version of the march from the fourth movement of Beethoven's Ninth Symphony, the bright metallic, neon, and lucite colors, the assuredness of the entire structure indicate total control: Alex's control of the situation and viewer pleasure in acknowledging that control. Much the same can be said for the tracking shot of Commander Poole in the centrifugal hall of the spaceship *Discovery* in *2001*—another rare shot indicative of a tentative peace and comfort with the character's surroundings.

But this is greatly oversimplified. The comfort Kubrick affords his characters is always ironic. The control Alex manifests in the sequence referred to is temporary. And while the spectator may marvel at the nonchalance of the inhabitants of the spaceship, she may marvel as well at how they can be so nonchalant in such a strange and overwhelming place. In *The Shining* there is a sequence in which Wendy comes into the great hall of the hotel where her husband, Jack, is supposed to be writing. He is not at his desk, and she looks at his papers, discovering that what he has been writing, obsessively, over and over, in every conceivable pattern on the pages, is, "All work and no play make Jack a dull boy." There is a cut to a camera position behind a pillar in back of Wendy. The camera begins to track to the left, a movement coded in horror films to indicate the approach of the monster, often signifying the point of view of the monster itself. But here, as the camera ends its movement on Wendy, who is standing stunned over the desk, Jack's silhouette moves into the frame from the right, and he asks, "How do you like it?"

A curious sense of false comfort is initially created by this movement.

Jack's madness and the danger he threatens has been well established by this point—indeed Wendy enters the hall carrying a baseball bat to protect her from his violence. Within the generic expectations set by the horror film, confirmed by the specific shock of discovery of Jack's manuscript, the camera movement is an assurance for the audience that the mad husband will attack; it is the bearer of his threatening gaze. But Jack's appearance after the camera has stopped its movement and slightly off its trajectory is a surprise and suggests that the moving camera signified another point of view altogether (a suspicion confirmed by Kubrick's not very successful attempt to suggest that the hotel has some strange life of its own that controls Jack himself).

The central sequence of the sniper in *Full Metal Jacket* keeps the viewer close to the marines and their terror and suffering. At three points, Kubrick breaks this proximity, cutting unexpectedly to the point of view of the sniper within the burning building. In each instance, the camera, without yet revealing the sniper's identity (a very young Vietnamese woman), moves by craning or zooming forward to the next victim of the attack. Rather than a supernatural presence, the moving camera here represents an unknown, dangerous, and very immediate perspective. Each cut to this point of view removes the viewer from a space of chaos and pain to the place where the chaos and pain originate, outside the control of the characters and the viewer's own gaze.

The moving camera, finally, represents Kubrick's own control over the mise-en-scène. Like Welles, he creates a double perspective. The difference lies in the fact that, where Welles investigates the enormity and fearsomeness of the space he creates, Kubrick is superior to it. He can permit the viewer to share a character's point of view and then remove the viewer from it, or allow the viewer to join it briefly enough to create discomfort, thereby defining point of view in many ways simultaneously. Where Welles implicates the viewer in his spatial labyrinths, Kubrick permits greater room to observe and judge his characters' situation and the viewer's own perception of the situation as well.

Colonel Dax's march through the trenches in *Paths of Glory* is an excellent example. As a tracking shot, a technical accomplishment—the camera moving in front of Dax or assuming his point of view as he moves through the narrow trenches, surrounded by his men—it is powerful and assured. As a point-of-view shot, those parts of the shot communicating Dax's control of his situation and what that control must lead to—his sending his men out to be slaughtered—it becomes more complicated. The physical space and the emotional space comment on each other. As observer, the viewer is presented with rapid, assured movement, but that movement is contained by the trenches, their filth and smoke, and their purpose, to hold the soldiers until they leave for the battlefield and death. Later in the film, as the three soldiers condemned to die march to their place of execution, the camera both observes them and assumes their point of view, tracks toward the sandbags, past onlookers, including a photographer and the generals responsible for their deaths. In this case, the characters are not in control of their space; quite the contrary, they are controlled by it, surrounded and impelled by the mechanism of their destruction. When Dax is located in this sequence it is by means of a cutaway to him in the crowd, photographed through a telephoto lens, isolating him, demonstrating his impotence, and in fact answering the seeming assurance of movement and control ironically expressed in his earlier walk through the trenches. All through the film, the camera creates and then observes a world in which the characters manipulate and are manipulated, depending on who and where they are.

This act of description, here and in all of Kubrick's films, is done on a cooler and calmer level than in Welles's films. There is a level of hysteria in Welles that Kubrick avoids. Even *Dr. Strangelove*, a film about hysteria, observes that hysteria from a distance that makes it all the more odious and horrifying. Indeed, the film has a marked absence of tracking shots. Welles pulls, distorts, amplifies space; Kubrick distances himself from it, observes it, peoples it often with wretched human beings, but refuses to become involved with their wretchedness. (Only in *Full Metal Jacket* did Kubrick permit some direct communication of hysteria and pain.) The penultimate sequence of *2001*, astronaut Bowman in the Jupiter room, the human cage, offers an example in contrast. Welles would diminish the human figure and indicate his inferior position. The space would be deeply sculpted in light and shadow. But Kubrick chooses to create this environment in bright, clean lines, photographed in extreme wide angle. The gaze at the character is that of the intelligence that has "captured" him. At the same time, the viewer shares Bowman's own detachment and curiosity about himself. As he passes the stages of his age and youth (having entered the whirlpool), the camera gazes over his shoulder as he sees himself at different points in his life (Kubrick uses the over-the-shoulder shot rarely; its use here is most unconventional, since Bowman sees not another, but himself—and of course there is no true reverse shot possible, for there is no one looking at him). Like Welles, Kubrick creates a visual realm and proceeds to explore it. But unlike Welles's worlds, his is mysterious not because of its intricacy and darkness but because of its clarity and apparent simplicity, a simplicity that belies the complexities it contains.

Both filmmakers are concerned with the ways humans inhabit environments, and both use cinematic structures to observe this. Welles is a humanist, one of the last in the classic sense of the word. He is deeply aware of the power, the inviolability, and the fragility of the human subject and seeks to affirm its centrality and control. The spatial fractures and distortions he inflicts on his characters, the extremes of light and dark through which he sees them, the narratives of power and impotence, gain and loss in which he sets them, all attest to the moral battles of mortal men and women, whose worlds reflect their struggle. Kubrick is an antihumanist. He sees men (with the exception of *The Shining* and *Eyes Wide Shut*, his films are rarely concerned with women, except in a peripheral and usually unpleasant way) mechanistically, as determined by their world, sometimes by their erotic passions (as is Humbert Humbert in *Lolita*, 1962, or Alice in *Eyes Wide Shut*), always by the rituals and structures they set up for themselves. Forgetting that they have set these structures up and have control over them, they allow the structures to control them. Like William Blake, Kubrick perceives individuals and groups assuming a helpless and inferior position with respect to an order they themselves have created. They undo their own subjectivity and agency. But Kubrick does not go beyond antihumanism to embrace another social or philosophical order, for he does not see the possibility of men or women regaining control over their selves and their culture. He sees rather a diminishment of humanity and its ultimate destruction, apocalyptically in *Dr. Strangelove*, through a transformation perhaps at the mercy of otherwordly intelligences in *2001*, through the destructiveness of domestic politics in *Barry Lyndon*, *The Shining*, and *Eyes Wide Shut*, through the utter defeat offered by war in *Paths of Glory* and *Full Metal Jacket*.

106

As complex as the design and the spatial manipulations in Kubrick's films may be, their narrative structure (with the exception of *The Killing* and *Barry Lyndon*) is usually very simple and direct. This marks another difference between Kubrick and Welles, whose narratives are as complex as the visual realm in which they are articulated. In this simplicity, Kubrick is allied with John Ford, though it is a strange and perverse alliance and one that must be approached via Welles. One of the most tantalizing statements by a filmmaker about his work and his influences was made by Welles early in his film career: "John Ford," said Welles, "was my teacher. My own style has nothing to do with his, but *Stagecoach* was my movie textbook. I ran it over forty times."[5] Ford's *Stagecoach* (1939) in fact does contain some stylistic elements that Welles expanded on: some deep-focus cinematography, low-angled shots that take in a room's ceilings, an occasional capturing of light and dust, textures that Welles would find attractive. Just a few months before working on *Kane*, Gregg Toland, Welles's cinematographer, photographed *The Long Voyage Home* for Ford. The chiaroscuro in this film was expanded on in *Kane*, and, as I noted in the discussion of film noir, it is possible to see these two films, with Toland as mediator, profoundly influencing the photographic style of forties cinema. But besides these visual attributes, which Ford pretty much abandoned in the later forties when he did more exterior shooting and worked in color, and that Welles developed further, there is apparently little that Ford and Welles have in common. What I think we find in Welles's statement is a wish, a desire, not to have emulated Ford, but somehow to have absorbed his narrative facility. The characters, events, and surroundings in Ford's films have a connection one to the other, an integration that allows his narratives to move with immense ease. Ford's films are about communities, families, or a group of men or women who survive by resorting to an integral strength among themselves (or the memory of such strength, should the community die or be proved false).[6] The thematics and the formal structuring of these communities in Ford's films work in a harmony of cause and effect, action and reaction, that goes beyond the normal narrative felicity of Hollywood's classical period. Ford hides his methods but not their effects. His compositions are bold and rich in information, his editing precise, and the dramatic confrontations of his characters open and direct. Yet in his best work all is contained in a simplicity of structure that is full of ideological tension.

107

Welles's films are about individuals in decline. Families and other groups barely exist in his work or, if they do, as in *The Magnificent Ambersons*, they exist to show their decay. The narrative structure of Ford's films, with its tight, seamless, closed construction, the perfect congruity of its parts, embodies his concern with the relationship of people in a closed unit. Welles's complex, jarred, and fragmented narratives reflect the struggle and defeat of his characters. His admiration of Ford is the admiration of an opposite, a desire to attain what he knows he is incapable of attaining because the nature of his insight and his own cinematic necessities for realizing it render the attainment impossible. The moral struggles of

Welles's characters are shattering; those of Ford's are healing. Welles's fictions are created by a pessimistic liberal-humanist intelligence, Ford's by a conservative intelligence that slowly loses its optimism over the course of time.

If the relation of Welles and Ford is dialectical, the relationship of Kubrick and Ford is diabolical. Kubrick, on his own terms, attempts to pursue the narrative linearity that Ford developed to perfection, though he makes it more complex and ambiguous. His narratives achieve an intellectual richness Ford could not and would not aspire to. What occurs, then, in Kubrick's work is an articulation of cinematic space directly influenced by Welles, a narrative structure that reflects Ford's, and a narrative content that responds to Ford's by denying its insights and the myths it draws on and recreates. Kubrick, like Ford, is concerned with individuals in groups; but his groups are almost always antagonistic or exclusionary. The Kubrick community is cold, as cold as Kubrick's own observation of it. There is rarely any feeling expressed, other than antagonism, and certainly no integration (the camaraderie tentatively offered in parts of *The Killing* and *Full Metal Jacket* is an anomaly and suggests either that Kubrick is momentarily assenting to the conventions of the gangster or war film or—more likely—provoking the painful irony of men joining in groups only to kill or be killed).

An interesting example in comparison occurs between Ford's *Fort Apache* (1948) and Kubrick's *Paths of Glory*. Ford's film concerns the antagonism between an Indian-beleaguered cavalry outpost and a martinet commander, Lt. Col. Owen Thursday (Henry Fonda). Thursday is presented as an intrusion into the composed and ordered community of the men at the fort. He hates his assignment and acts out his hatred by demanding a strictness of military procedure that the men have never found necessary. Their order is one of fellowship and gentleness, and, through their wives, they integrate their family with their military lives. As a result, Thursday is an irritant and in his attempt to intrude on them he is isolated from them.*

The result of the conflict is the massacre of Thursday and his men by the Apache that emerges from Thursday's inability to recognize the Indians as men to whom understanding and courtesy must be given. The violent

108

---

* On his arrival at the fort, Thursday interrupts a dance, that primary Fordian sign of civilized community. In *Paths of Glory*, the dance is a sign of a rigid and heartless community. Thursday is stiff and alone compared with the ease and movement of the men and their wives. The central conflict occurs between Thursday and Capt. Kirby York

differences in situation and attitude are presented in the visual configurations of the battle with the Indians. They are seen situated within hills
and rocks, secure and inhabiting an enclosed space. Thursday and his
soldiers are isolated on the plains, vulnerable and open. The spaces Ford's
characters inhabit and the way they comport themselves within them are,
as in Kubrick's films, a key to their emotional state. Thursday is always
removed and isolated, first from his own men, then from an understanding
of his opponents in battle. His separation and his inability to resolve the
tensions between self-sufficiency and community, rules of order and
emotional freedom, lead to his fall and the fall of his men. But these tensions
also lead to the terrible ambiguity of the film as a whole. In the body of the
film Thursday is roundly condemned; his inability to yield leads to
catastrophe. In the epilogue, however, John Wayne's Captain York insists
that the catastrophe and its cause must be ignored. Thursday has been
celebrated in the press as a hero, and York (and, by implication, Ford)
upholds this myth. The army must be accepted as the advance guard of
American civilization and as a harmonious community in its own right.
The society at large must believe that Thursday and his men worked
together for a common good. At this point in his career, and for a country
still suffering the traumas of World War II, Ford had to perform an act of
conservative rehabilitation on a narrative that threatened the notion of a
flawless American military.

Fort Apache suffers a major conflict between some truths of human
behavior and the need for historical myth. The myth-making possibilities
of the narrative seem to stop working when forced to deal with a character
it cannot contain, and so Ford adds a coda convincing the spectator
everything is all right after all. Paths of Glory makes no pretense of
examining legends. Rather, it dissolves the Fordian notion of community
and replaces it with a radical isolation of individuals who, though they are
part of a large organization, are forced to be alone. Their desolation is
created, in part, by the form of the narrative itself. Earlier I said that Kubrick
was in the Fordian narrative tradition in that he usually employs a simple
linear structure. This observation must be modified by noting that, though
linear, the narratives are often foreshortened and condensed. A great deal

109

(John Wayne), who emerges not quite as the mediator between Thursday and his men
(that role is taken on by Thursday's daughter, who provides the domesticating softness
absent from her father), but more as a leader whose sensitivity provides a practical contrast to Thursday's unyielding behavior.

of information is presented in a short period of time. In his early work—predating the French New Wave experiments in narrative discontinuity—Kubrick leaves out transitional elements and linking passages. Ford worked to perfection the Hollywood tradition of seamless story construction, using his compositional skills to pack information into the frame. His narratives have a kind of centripetal action, drawing all their elements into a relationship with one another and finally (with the possible exception of *Fort Apache*) into a stable center. Even the later films, *The Searchers* and *The Man Who Shot Liberty Valence*, marked by a lack of stability and security with the old myths, still seek amelioration, an accommodation with order and certainty, which, in the case of *The Searchers*, compromises the work. Kubrick's narratives work centrifugally. Parts of the whole are delineated and then set outside a center never seen or defined and therefore nonexistent. Kubrick's narratives are about the lack of cohesion, center, community, about people caught up in a process that has become so rigid that it can be neither escaped nor mitigated—a stability that destroys.

Paths of Glory is precisely about such a process, or rather the processes that make up military organizations, which are formed of ritual, predetermined, and so absolutely exclusionary that each human element within it is separated from the next. The matter is not, as in *Fort Apache*, of one misguided individual disrupting an established community, but of antagonistic individuals, members of parts of the military order, each out for his own aggrandizement or protection. The essential struggle in the film is, as Alexander Walker and others have pointed out, between classes—the aristocratic leaders of the French army in World War I on one side and the proletarian troops, the scum, or the "children," as the general staff calls them, on the other.[7] In the middle is Colonel Dax (Kirk Douglas), loyal soldier, bad attorney, self-righteous, and trapped within the military organization. Three entwined and opposing forces—the general staff, Dax, the troops—are set within two related but opposing spaces, two areas of activity that, knitted together, provide the narrative structure and rhythm of the film. The "story" is made by the way events occur within and are defined by these spaces. The generals inhabit a chateau of enormous rooms, flooding sunlight, and walls hung with the late seventeenth- and early eighteenth-century paintings that so obsess Kubrick that they appear in one form or another in every film (except *Dr. Strangelove*) from *Paths of Glory* until *Barry Lyndon*, which in a sense becomes those paintings. Such a chateau, with all its accoutrements, is itself an image of elegance and rigid formal structures. By emphasizing the spaces of the chateau, Kubrick demands that the viewer understand and account for its associations and connotations, particularly within the given context. In this cold and elegant, inhumanly scaled habitation, the generals play a brutal and elegant game. "I wish I had your taste in carpets and pictures," says General Broulard (Adolf Menjou) to General Mireau (George Macready) when he first greets him, intending to cajole and bribe him to lead his troops to disaster.

The second space consists of the habitations of the troops: the dark and squalid trenches, the battlefield that looks like the surface of the moon turned into a garbage heap, the prison that holds the three men assigned to die for cowardice. The narrative moves between these spaces, climaxing at the firing squad (an extension of the chateau) and the cabaret (an extension of the trenches). There is no indication that anywhere else in the world exists. Unlike *Fort Apache*, where the fort, situated in the midst of the wilderness, is seen as its embattled but self-sufficient focus, there is no indication of any physical connection between the front and the chateau, or between both places and anywhere else. Kubrick is creating a closed world, or rather closed worlds, since they are isolated from each other. Mireau visits the trenches, and Dax the chateau, but each is out of place in the other's realm. When Mireau and Broulard first meet in the chateau, they start as antagonists but end as happy and comfortable conspirators, circling about the great hall, the camera moving with them, building rhythms of deceit and death. But Mireau in the trenches is completely out of place. When he inspects and brutalizes the troops, the camera flees in front of him, making dynamic the viewer's revulsion at his mechanical "Hello there, soldier, ready to kill more Germans?" Dax's walk through the trenches, as pointed out earlier, is comfortable and assured; the camera both precedes him and shares his point of view. In the chateau, Dax is either isolated or enclosed in the discomfort of its spaces.

But just here a question is raised. Dax is comfortable with his men and uncomfortable with, indeed antagonistic to, the general staff. Does that mean that his is the mediating and ameliorating voice of the film, speaking of humanity in the midst of the terrifying brutality that occurs around him, speaking reason as does the John Wayne character in *Fort Apache*? He clearly does not accommodate himself to the space of the generals, but his comfort with his men proves to be an illusion. He sends them to battle, knowing most will be killed; and though he joins them, he remains separate. In the complex tracking shot that accompanies the attack, the camera continually zooms in on Dax, picking him out, showing him with the men, but separate from them. (This battle sequence, a model for Spielberg's

111

Saving Private Ryan is among the strongest filmic representations of chaos and death in war.) For Dax is finally not the man of the trenches one would perhaps like him to be, upholder of the rights of the scorned and abused. He is a powerless creature of the high command. When the men retreat, and immediately after a closeup of a raving Mireau—"If those little sweethearts won't face German bullets, they'll face French ones"—the film cuts back to the chateau. Two soldiers are seen moving a large painting, expending energy shifting signs of a worn-out elegance. Dax, Mireau, and Broulard meet on the fate of the troops. Mireau is framed against a large, bright window, Dax and Broulard, the mean and cunning general who first ordered the attack, are framed together, beneath paintings—an odd pairing, but indicative of Dax's manipulated, used status. The three bargain over the men's lives, Broulard ordering that three be chosen, tried, and executed. Dax will defend the men in the trial, whose outcome is preordained.

In this sequence, as in others, Dax appears to reflect or incorporate the viewer's anger at the generals and sympathy for the troops. He seems to be the voice of reason against their cunning brutality. But he is not, and could not be if he wanted to. Kubrick is playing as cruel a game with viewer expectation as the generals play with their troops in the fiction. Throughout the film every expectation holds that Dax will get the men off; conventional narrative patterns have coded this situation with such certainty. The good and helpless, in film fiction, are not permitted to die (particularly in 1957, before a certain cynicism had taken over such dependable conventions, and when Kubrick himself, according to recent biographies, had a moment of doubt about the men's fate). But here the codes are not allowed to work. When Dax gives his impotent defense summary at the courts-martial, stating, fatuously, that he can't believe compassion, "the noblest impulse in man," is dead, the camera tracks him from a low angle, behind the guards, who are situated behind the prisoners. Dax is trapped between the men and the judges, walking back and forth, seen through the legs of the guards. He is completely enclosed. The track is lateral, in contrast to the swift forward motion of his earlier walk through the trenches. The composition is sufficient to show that he is as imprisoned as the men he uselessly defends.[8] In a curious way, Dax has become Ford's Lieutenant Colonel Thursday—upholding rigid procedure, but here in the face of an even more rigid procedure. Unlike Thursday, Dax has no humane alternatives. He is without agency and doomed.

Kubrick refuses to see a way out and cannot find any justification for the presence of "noble impulses." After the firing squad, Dax is reduced to name-calling. In his last confrontation with Broulard in the chateau, he calls him "a degenerate, sadistic old man." And as Broulard comes to understand that in defending the men Dax was not acting out of a desire for a promotion, he calls him an idealist and says, "I pity you as I would the village idiot." He proclaims his own proper behavior in the whole affair and asks where he went wrong (he is pleased with himself for having ordered a court of inquiry to investigate Mireau for ordering fire on his own men). Dax answers, "Because you don't know the answer to that question, I pity you." Mutual sarcasm and hatred, and a thorough impasse. Kubrick should have ended the film there, with two duty- and ritual-bound antagonists in impotent confrontation. Instead, like Ford in *Fort Apache*, he chooses to add a coda that might have a softening effect. Dax passes an inn where some of his troops are relaxing. A German girl sings to them. First they boo her, then sing along, weeping. Outside, Dax allows them "a few minutes more" to indulge themselves.

This bit of sentimentality runs against the grain of the film. What had been a close and tight structure of brutality, false hope, and greater brutality now seems to be diminished by a conventional means to move an audience, communal tears. In fact, what Kubrick does here is the opposite of what Ford did. The coda to *Fort Apache* is very much military stiff upper lip: the army has its problems, but they all work out for the greater good. Kubrick creates an easier structure of meaning: the man who cries has feelings and is therefore somehow aware of his lot. Tears permit the audience to release pity and understanding, easing somewhat the moral frustrations suffered during the course of the film. The coda distances the viewer from what has happened, but in the wrong direction. It seems to deny the narrative by presenting conventional material, much easier to accept than what preceded. Possibly, the last sequence needs to be read ironically, concluding that these wretched souls only find relief weeping over another wretched soul on the stage, and that even this relief is short-lived, since they must return to the prison of the trenches. But even if this were the intent, it is done too quickly and too easily. Nothing before has given much of a sense of the troops' individuality. The three men chosen for execution are little more than types. Now Kubrick demands recognition that the men have the emotions the generals do not.

If this sequence works, it does so by restating the entrapped condition of everyone concerned. The generals are trapped by their adherence to a military ritual of patriotism, place-gaining, and self-aggrandizement; the men are trapped by their inferior status and total passivity. (The only officer who actively attempts to save his men's lives does so passively. Lieutenant

113

Roget, a drunken coward who caused a man's death on a night mission, refuses, out of fear, to send his troops out of the trenches to assault the Ant Hill. Dax retaliates by giving him the job of firing the final bullet into the heads of the three victims.) Indeed Dax, caught between his duty to the military and allegiance to his men, is himself passive. He makes no move to take his case outside the military cage. No world exists beyond the trenches and the chateau; all behavior is dictated by the unyielding rules and rituals that belong to them. There is no indication that mutiny or an appeal to other powers is possible. Determination of behavior is complete.

When Kubrick returns again to the subject of war in the trenches, the idea of behavioral determination is unchanged, though somewhat mitigated. Like *Paths of Glory*, *Full Metal Jacket* takes place in well-defined and related spaces, presented sequentially rather than intercut: the barracks and fields of Parris Island training camp; the streets, Marine camp, and the office of *Stars and Stripes* in Da Nang; the burning ruins of Hue. Unlike *Paths of Glory*, these spaces do not form a complex of class and ideological contradictions and tensions. Little is seen or heard of the military high command (one fatuous colonel appears and speaks some hysterical nonsense, claiming, for example, that "inside every gook there is an American trying to get out"), and there is no character equal to Colonel Dax to present even the illusion of—or allusion to—moral order.

More strongly than in *Paths of Glory*, the determining order is the necessity to kill, passed on to the marines from their first moment in training camp by means of the monotone, hysterical, and vulgar drone of the drill instructor, Gunnery Sargent Hartman, often presented in steady, uninflected tracking shots—like his predecessor, Mireau—that precede him through the barracks or on training marches; tracking shots signifying a deadening repetition, a used-up energy of military ritual, contained, ironically, in the one character who contains some energy. "Here you are all equally worthless," he tells his men. The very first shots of the film show the recruits' hair being shaved off, their individuating characteristics removed (indeed the film's two major figures, Joker and Cowboy, look almost identical). And as training continues, this dehumanized raw material is molded into "the phony tough and the crazy brave," men whose function is to kill or die for the "beloved corps."

Through it all, Kubrick attempts to chart an uneven dynamic of character action and viewer response. The early scenes of the boot-camp sequence seem to offer a satire of misguided patriotism and military conformity, that element often found in military films in which the tough but fair sergeant bullies his troops into shape for their own good. But this direction is changed drastically when the most ill treated of the recruits, Pyle, goes mad and shoots both the drill instructor and himself—in the bathroom, where Jack D. Ripper shot himself in *Dr. Strangelove*. What was satire now becomes moral concern over the response of those unable to form the "cohesion" demanded by military training. Early camaraderie seemed to form between the men, particularly as Joker attempts to help Pyle through his difficulties. This initial sense of community is shockingly broken when, after the sergeant punishes the men for Pyle's mistakes, they beat Pyle terribly in the night, with Joker delivering the most devastating blows. Camaraderie threatens to break out again in the latter sequences of the film, during the sniper attack on the troops in the burning city. But viewer response is again redirected. After three men die, Joker discovers the sniper and attempts to kill her (the irony of a woman inflecting such damage on men trained in an atmosphere of obscene sexism is suggested without commentary and it reflects back with further irony on the German woman who brings the troops together at the end of *Paths of Glory*). His rifle jams, and before he can use his pistol, another soldier shoots her. She lies wounded, begging to be killed. Joker stares, his face held in long closeup, and he finally pulls the trigger. His comrades congratulate him. One calls him "hard core." He is pleased with himself. He marches off with his troops and in voice-over ruminates on how pleased he is to be alive, even in a world full of shit. Into the night, against the burning buildings, the troops march, singing the Mickey Mouse theme song.

The troops sing at the end of *Paths of Glory*, and it is only slightly less banal than these hard-core killers chanting "M-I-C-K-E-Y M-O-U-S-E." The soldiers in the earlier film were forced into combat by their officers. Here they seem to go willingly and with a desire to prove themselves. There is no threat of a firing squad, but rather the willing acceptance of duty and the need to prove one's worth. Joker's act is not so much a mercy killing of the young Vietnamese, but an act of mercy for himself, something that realizes and actuates his training, that validates his military life. If he can't kill a real, live enemy, he can kill a dying one. He is caught—as he himself says, referring to the "Born to Kill" motto on his helmet and the peace button on his jacket—between two conflicting forces.

And so, in effect, is Kubrick. I said that the dynamic of character action and viewer response in *Full Metal Jacket* is uneven and, I might add, erratic. As in the cabaret sequence of *Paths of Glory*, there is here the threat of sentimentality, of the rather vicious illusion that, whatever monstrous things war does, it at least brings men together into a community. And although Kubrick never indulges this sentimentality as strongly as Oliver Stone does in *Platoon* or Spielberg in *Saving Private Ryan*, which freshen up only a little bit the "coming of age" convention of the war film, it still lurks in the aura of this one. No other Vietnam film, with the possible exception of *Apocalypse Now* (but without that film's hallucinatory and mythic pretensions), so expresses the hopelessness and confused motivations of that war, its sense of already and always being lost by the United States. "I'll be General Custer," a soldier says; "Who'll be the Indians?" he's asked; "We'll let the gooks play the Indians." This dialogue is played out in front of a movie crew filming the troops. "Vietnam, the movie," someone says. "Is that you, John Wayne, is this me?" But despite this reflexive sequence, *Full Metal Jacket* cannot seem to avoid the generic imperatives of the war film and the ideological determinism that still drives any cinematic recall of Vietnam. Most Vietnam war films suggest that American innocence and fellowship *should* have prevailed; somehow the wrong side won, and the troops went mad, but it was not quite anybody's fault—except perhaps a sneaky and vicious enemy. The anger that informs *Paths of Glory* is gone from *Full Metal Jacket* but not replaced with any firm perspective. War is still depicted as a violent and painful event, but there is no clear sense of who is responsible for it or where it is likely to lead, except to a further infantalization of its troops.

In the case of both *Paths of Glory* and *Full Metal Jacket*, one almost wishes another film had been made, one in which either Dax or the troops took some active role in saving themselves, some opportunity to indicate that there might be an alternative to being manipulated or brutalized, or some awareness on the part of the troops in the last film of who they are and what they might be doing. But Kubrick is not a revolutionary filmmaker. Quite the contrary. The force of his films grows out of their sense of frustrating inevitability, of men almost willfully submitting themselves to an ineluctable order of events. When, in the film following *Paths of Glory*, Kubrick tried to create a revolutionary figure—transforming, through the person of Kirk Douglas, the impotent Dax into the heroic Spartacus—the result was a considerable failure. And I am not sure that the failure of *Spartacus* is the result only of an often silly script and of Kubrick's inability to exercise complete—actually *any*—control over the production (he was called in late in filming by producer Douglas to replace its first director, Anthony Mann). Part of the film's problem may result from the fact that a human being attempting to escape or correct an intolerable situation did

116
■
■
▪

not fire Kubrick's imagination as does an individual trapped in an intolerable situation. Another may be the fact that this is really Dalton Trumbo's film—the first to appear with his name on it since the blacklist began and he was jailed as one of the Hollywood Ten—and its barely hidden allegory of the destruction of left-wing dissent in the fifties is simply not Kubrick's interest.

If Arthur Penn celebrates the attempt to overcome oppression, no matter how much he believes such attempts are doomed, and Oliver Stone attempts to investigate the images of oppression and repression to make chaotic order out of their chaos, then Kubrick, within his highly ordered images, mourns the doom that follows on *no* attempt to overcome or to see, and allows complexity, irony, and ambiguity to stand in all their contradictions. Those wonderful tracking shots in his films lead, finally, to the grave. There is for him no revolutionary spirit or even a simple Fordian spirit of communal energy or sacrifice for the greater vitality of the community. There is barely even a spirit of revelation. Only suggestion. And his characters are never redeemed. They merely die or are diminished, isolated, trapped, and used.

Kubrick's ideas seem responsive to the decade in which he began his creative work, and *Paths of Glory*, like *The Killing*, is a film of the fifties, as *Full Metal Jacket* is of the eighties: periods in our history when passivity was looked on as a virtue and opposition condemned and barely heard. In that light, they are deeply conflicted films. To have taken as strong a stand against military order as does *Paths of Glory* was itself remarkable for 1957—so remarkable that the film was banned in France for years. To have created such an unrelenting narrative (with no sexual or romantic interest), structured in such stark and demanding images, was, for the time, more remarkable still. But with these images to have created a narrative that stops with a revelation of lives trapped and not go on to suggest how they might be freed is itself an intellectual gambit typical of the decade. This was the period of "the end of ideology"—the original cold war version of the currently fatuous "end of history"—a political dead center that declared useless, if not treasonous, any political-cultural structure other than the "free-market" status quo. As a critical tool, this ideology against ideology prescribes analysis that negates a left-of-center perspective, understanding without anything but a center-right point of view. *Paths of Glory* suffers from the end of ideology paralysis because it seems to attack an ideological stance—assumptions of hierarchical rule and the fitness of a given order—and then backs off. Revealing the ugliness of a situation and its

117

propensity to destroy men, demonstrating how a moral stance against the immorality of such a rigid structure turns to impotent self-righteousness, it provokes great anger at a ruthlessness that appears unassailable. But finally the anger is, like Dax's, useless. Offering no possibility of altering the situation portrayed, it leaves the viewer only to wallow in the self-pity of the men in the café, weeping at cruelty and at our seemingly natural and helpless passivity in its face.

Full Metal Jacket leaves an enormous, uninformed distance between the viewer and the men singing the Mickey Mouse song at the end. Into that space are thrown questions of their stupidity, bravery, foolishness, banality, their childlike nature (the troops are referred to as "children" in *Paths of Glory*), their function as tools. The questions float with no promise of being attached to adequate answers or even interesting speculation. True to the ideological formation of the eighties, it deflects speculation or political opinion into an evocation of the recent past—complete with the inevitable sixties rock-music sound track. An illusion of what may have been threatens to substitute for an analytic reading of history, and the realities of history are continually voided in the spaces of despair.[9]

The response to both films is frustration, something that John Ford, for one, would never permit. Perhaps because of his conservatism, his allegiance to the rightness of military and domestic order, and because of the clarity with which he sees the relationship of individual and group and the inevitability of the movement of middle-class Victorian morality westward, Ford insists on a harmonious reaffirmation of a healing order. The rule-bound, mean-minded Lieutenant Colonel Thursday of *Fort Apache* is an anomaly who, no matter what damage he causes, must be understood and absorbed, recuperated into a larger historical myth. Passivity is never a problem for a Fordian character. When such a character can no longer act, he withdraws into heroic isolation from the group he once aided. Ford's characters are supremely secure in their place and, with the exception of Ethan Edwards in *The Searchers*, are, or become, actively engaged in promoting concord within that place. The conflicts they suffer are the result not of ideological turmoil but of ideological certainty. Ford is secure in the belief that the American democracy he celebrates is the best of all social-political orders, and his characters act out narratives that confirm the fitness and security of that order. For Kubrick, fitness and security become traps to destroy his characters, traps from which they cannot extricate themselves. In Kubrick's fictions Fordian stability becomes a prison house and his characters are both—and often simultaneously—

118

inmates and jailers. They do not lunge against the physical, emotional, and ideological spaces they inhabit, as do Welles's characters; they are not comfortable in them, as are Ford's. They are caught, they sometimes struggle, and they almost always lose. Not the soldiers singing in the café or in the ruins of Hue, but the frozen figure of Jack Torrance, trapped in a (literal) labyrinth, face contorted in a scream, at the end of *The Shining*, stands as a summary image of Kubrick's ineluctable pessimism.[10]

Kubrick realized the error he made in *Paths of Glory*, the error of permitting anger and frustration to intermingle with those of a character in the fiction, thereby inviting the audience to assume a point of identification and ultimately be frustrated. Sentimentality—except for its uncertain appearance in *Full Metal Jacket*—and melodrama quickly vanished from his work. While he never moves far beyond the entrapment, impotence, and despair figured in *Paths of Glory* (and foreshadowed in *The Killing*), his narratives and their cinematic structures become more distant and abstract, and his characters less the psychologically motivated creations we are used to seeing in American film and instead more obsessive, maniacal ideas released in human form, expressions of aberrations in the human personality. More than in *Paths of Glory*, they are functions of the spaces they inhabit, spaces that themselves create closed and inflexible worlds, predetermined and unalterable, even, in *2001* and *The Shining*, supernatural.

Lolita is the last film in which he attempted the study of a character who demonstrates at least some awareness of who he is and what he does, even though, as always, that character has no control over himself or others. This is also Kubrick's last film, until *Full Metal Jacket* and *Eyes Wide Shut*, in which the human figure is foregrounded and observed against, rather than within, the space he inhabits. James Mason's Humbert Humbert attempts a quizzical posture before the bizarre characters and places he meets and journeys through, and the long takes with which Kubrick observes this figure decaying under the force of his obsessive desire serve to bring him uncomfortably close to pathos. Through it all, Kubrick is fascinated by the characters he is creating (particularly with Peter Sellers's Quilty) but apparently uncomfortable at the same time. *Lolita* does not achieve an identity. Part adaptation of a celebrated book, part event (both novel and film received much publicity due to their content), part character study, part attempt to make England look like America, it remains a funny and increasingly bold curiosity piece. In regard to the elements of Kubrick's work I am discussing here, it demonstrates his need to withdraw even further from the world he creates, to integrate his characters more fully with the total design of the film, to demonstrate how a world is formed by a personality and then re-forms and destroys the personality who made it. This is a process and a method that become fully realized in the first film of Kubrick's artistic maturity: *Dr. Strangelove: Or, How I Learned To Stop Worrying and Love the Bomb.*

Dr. Strangelove is an unusual film that served the function of prophecy. In the early sixties, Kubrick perceived in the dominant political ideology certain modes of speech, figures of thought, and images of America's imagined place in the world that allowed him to set up a narrative of events so logical and unavoidable that the only possible result (in the fiction made up by the narrative) was the end of the world. The narrative, in its turn, has created a structure of explanation for political behavior that became more valid and more chilling the longer the cold war continued. Now that the behavior and discourse are strangling on themselves because of the lack of a definable enemy, the film's discourse stands as an almost documentary record of a dismal time and the loss of meaning and political morality. The term "Strangelovian" has entered the vocabulary, and our history in the years since *Dr. Strangelove* has tended to imitate the film as much as the film, at the time of its making, imitated history.

A number of elements work toward making the film a complex text of ideas and reflections and predictions. Not the least of these is the extreme simplicity of its narrative structure. There are (not counting a brief sequence in Buck Turgidson's bedroom) only three areas of action: the war room, an enormous black space ringed by fluorescent light, a dark version of the chateau in *Paths of Glory*, computerized maps replacing the paintings; the cockpit, control room, and bomb bay of a B-52; and the offices and exterior of Burpelson Air Force Base. There is no interrelationship between these locations, no communication.[11] Each operates on its own. Even within these areas, no one actually speaks to another, only to himself. No one listens, no one responds. Words are interchanged, but the words are, in the war room, only clichés; at the base, lunatic ravings; and in the plane, military jargon. These three areas of activity are intercut to form the narrative. The activities that occur in each area are caused by what goes on in the others and are independent of the others at the same time. A mad general declares an alert and seals off his base; SAC bombers, which are in the air all the time, proceed to their target, cutting themselves off from communication; the war room coordinates plans to cut off the attack by aiding Russian defense, by means of a hysterical American president talking on the telephone to a hysterical Russian premier. Everyone talks, or tries to talk, on the phone. The first line of dialogue in the film is delivered by General Ripper (Sterling Hayden) on the phone to his chief aide, Mandrake (Peter Sellers), asking, significantly, "Do you recognize my voice?" Everyone does indeed recognize everyone else's voice. No one understands a word that is being said.

Dr. Strangelove is that rarity among American film in which verbal language plays a major role. In fact it is a film about language that creates its own destruction, its own death, and the death of the world. In a film that delineates a love of destruction and death, a *Merkwürdigliebe* (Strangelove's German name), everything done and everything said manifests this love and hastens its consummation. What Kubrick, Terry Southern, and Peter George do in their script and what Kubrick does in his direction is create a series of linguistic and visual reductions, giving the characters utterances that defeat meaning. Like the auto-destruct mechanism on the SAC bomber's radio, the characters' words undo and destroy themselves. The bomber, for example, is introduced by a very serious voice-over narration explaining the SAC system. When the film cuts to the interior of the plane, Major Kong (Slim Pickens) is reading *Playboy* and the communications officer is playing with a deck of cards, images that immediately undercut the seriousness of the introduction. When the attack plan is confirmed, drums and trumpets begin playing "When Johnny Comes Marching Home," music that will accompany all the sequences in the bomber, creating a music-image complex that ultimately contradicts itself. No one comes marching home from this battle.

Major Kong prepares for "nuclear combat, toe to toe with the Russkies." He pulls out a cowboy hat, which he wears through the rest of the flight, a sort of Ronald Reagan before his time. He tells his men, "I reckon you wouldn't even be human beings if you didn't have some pretty strong personal feelings about nuclear combat. . . . If this thing turns out to be half as important as I figure it just might be, I'd say that you're all in line for some important promotions and personal citations when this thing's over with. And that goes for every last one of you, regardless of your race, color, and your creed." Both image and words clash with the seriousness of purpose expected from the situation: a bomber about to start Armageddon. The words in particular reduce meaning to a level of banality and cliché. Roland Barthes, speaking of linguistic structure in the works of Sade, writes that "he juxtaposes heterogeneous fragments belonging to spheres of language that are ordinarily kept separate by socio-moral taboo."[12] Kubrick's

121

characters in *Dr. Strangelove* do precisely the same thing. The socio-moral taboos they break are those that keep expressions of serious connotation apart from those that are banal. A drawling cowboy ought not be associated with the commander of an aircraft carrying a nuclear bomb. When this cowboy begins speaking, one does not wish to hear grammar-school commonplaces and locker-room psychologisms. When this is precisely what is heard, it is very funny because of the surprise and very frightening because of the gap between the utterance and the context, which demands other language. The serious is made light of and the ridiculous is made serious. The language circles upon itself, it has no subject or object, no detachable meaning. The meaning is the utterance itself and its own perfectly logical irrelevance and banality. Of course "human beings" have "strong personal feelings" about "nuclear combat" (does the topic arouse weak impersonal feelings in something other than "human beings"?). These men, however, seem to have no feelings about anything. They use language to express the obvious, the reductive, and the redundant, utterances that speak about feelings in ways that indicate their absence.*

This linguistic subversion continues throughout *Strangelove*, destroying meaning whenever it threatens to emerge. When the Russians discover that the Americans are entering their air space, says General Buck Turgidson, clutching his book, *World Targets in Megadeaths*, "They are gonna go absolutely ape." Turgidson (George C. Scott) is particularly apt at laundering language of meaning, substituting jargon for information (hopes for recalling the SAC bombers are "reduced to a very low order of probability") and speaking about the end of the world in the terms of a businessman ("I'm not saying we wouldn't get our hair mussed. But I do say no more than ten to twenty million killed. Tops. Depending on the breaks"). And the president himself, Merkin Muffley (Peter Sellers), a fussy little liberal with a vulgar name, well-meaning and unable to comprehend the mechanisms set in operation, delivers himself of a line that encapsulates the refusal of these men to understand their actions or the distance between these actions and the words they use to describe them. To Turgidson and the Russian ambassador, wrestling over a spy camera, he says, "Gentlemen, you can't fight here. This is the war room!"

---

* Over the newspaper office in the *Stars and Stripes* sequence of *Full Metal Jacket* is a banner that reads "First to Go—Last to Know: We Will Defend to the Death our Right to be Misinformed." Where *Strangelove* acts out the destruction of word and meaning, the later film merely accepts it as a given.

At the center of this is Jack D. Ripper, the mad general ("He went a little funny in the head—you know, a little funny," says the president to Premier Kissoff on the hotline) who put all the mechanisms of doom into operation. In his confusion of language, the psychotic ease with which he amputates and reconstructs meanings, he permits the entire structure of death to be erected, or, more appropriately, permits the structure, already erected, to work itself out to completion. He is a fundamentalist anticommunist, filled with all the clichés that went with that aspect of the culture's dominant ideology. He is also rather confused sexually, believing that postcoital relaxation and depression are really a loss of vitality (he is not, as many critics have suggested, impotent; his radical misunderstanding of normal psychosexual reactions is much more horrifying than mere sexual dysfunction and is part of the transfer and breakdown of meaning that informs the film).

I said Ripper is at the center of this, but that is an inaccurate metaphor for the film. *Dr. Strangelove* is about the lack of center; it is about a multitude of tangents glancing off nonconcentric circles. That Ripper sets the mechanisms in operation is a convenience of plot and evidences, perhaps, some need on Kubrick's part to present a "human factor" in the proceedings. The inhumanity of the cold war and its destructive potentials are somehow mitigated if one can point to an individual who is mad and triggers those potentials into action. There is irony as well in Sterling Hayden's playing the role, because he was a HUAC informer during the anti-communist purges of the fifties and suffered from despair over that act. In later films, Kubrick tries with some success to eliminate this essentially humanist desire to account for the world through the melodrama of the individual. However, Ripper is the most radical example in *Dr. Strangelove* of the dislocation of word and meaning, form and substance. His great speech is a concentrated collapse from the somewhat shared clichés of reactionary discourse into the crazed, subjective discourse of someone who is creating his own meanings. "Mandrake," he asks his barely comprehending aide (also played by Peter Sellers in a multiple-role gimmick popular in the early sixties), "do you recall what Clemenceau once said about war?"

> He said war was too important to be left to the generals. . . . But today war is too important to be left to the politicians. They have neither the time, the training, nor the inclination for strategic thought. I can no longer sit back and allow communist infiltration, communist indoctrination, communist

subversion and the International Communist Conspiracy to sap and impurify all of our precious bodily fluids.

There is a perfectly logical movement to these words, just as there is perfectly logical movement to the mechanism of defense and retaliation that makes up the war machine. But the logic of both is internal only. The forms are correct, but what the forms signify is illogical and destructive. Ripper's speech ends in bathos, in perfect nonsense, even though his earlier comments about fluoridation as a communist conspiracy were very much a part of right-wing rant in the late forties and early fifties. The mechanisms of the war machine end with a different kind of anticlimax: the end of the world, the sapping of everyone's precious bodily fluids.

The appearance of Ripper as he makes his speech is a fine example of the way Kubrick creates an image that objectively comments on character and situation. The general is composed in closeup, from a low angle, his face brightly lit from below, against a black background. He is smoking a long cigar. This is the image of a man isolated in his own madness, yet protruding from his entrapment, threatening the viewer's space (which is represented, in this sequence, by Mandrake, who attempts a façade of calm and sanity in the face of Ripper's ravings). This appearance of Ripper is similar to a shot of Norman Bates in Hitchcock's *Psycho*. At one point Norman leans over the camera, his face emerging from the dark in an unexpected, and unsettling, angle. These two closeups of madness are similar in effect, but lead in different directions. The madness of Norman Bates is significant of a momentary, unknown, unpredictable terror, always lurking, seldom perceived. The madness of Ripper is the madness of the body politic, which should be easily perceived and perfectly predictable, for it results when individuals create a mock rationality based on language and gesture that appears logical and is in fact dead and deadly. Only the universality of his discourse makes it invisible. Norman's madness is local, the momentary eruption of an omnipresent violence in an unexpecting world. Ripper's madness is global. He is the disseminator of violence, the patriarch of a political and ideological structure whose purpose is to prepare the world for death.

Dr. Strangelove is a discourse of death. Its language and images, the movement of its narrative bespeak the confusion of life and death and the desire to see the one in terms of the other. The persistent sexual metaphor of the film emphasizes the reversal. From the copulating bomber that opens the film, to Ripper's confusion of sexual release with a subversive draining

124

away of vitality, to the planned storage of sexually active men and women in mine shafts to await dissipation of the doomsday shroud, to Major Kong's riding his great, phallic H-bomb into the apocalyptic orgasm and the death of the earth, sexuality in the film is turned to necrophilia, which in turn is part of a greater mechanism of destruction over which the individuals in the films are powerless. The rage to create a controlling order undoes potency; the attempt to erect a structure of power results in the collapse of all structure. The patriarchy erects a world whose function is auto-castration.[13]

If Jack D. Ripper is the mad father of this structure, Dr. Strangelove is his dark angel, the spirit and mover of destruction. He is also the fascist machine, aroused by the word "slaughter," drawing life from death, becoming fully activated just as the apocalypse occurs. When the men in the war room think that the bombers have been recalled, Turgidson says a prayer: "Lord! We have heard the wings of the Angel of Death fluttering over our heads from the Valley of Fear. You have seen fit to deliver us from the forces of evil." On the words "Valley of Fear," Kubrick cuts to Strangelove sitting in his wheelchair, apart from the others, shrouded and crouching in darkness. The words of the prayer, like all the other words in the film, are undone; the image cancels their denotation, for everyone has been delivered into the Valley of Fear; and the Angel of Death becomes the figure around which all the others will cluster.

Through the creation of Dr. Strangelove, Kubrick comes to an important insight. At the peak of the last cold war, at a time when the great, grim myth of communist subversion was the operative, castrating force in America's ideology and culture, Kubrick suggests that fascism is stirring as the ghost in the machine. The glorification and celebration of power and death that feed politics and form the urge for domination define the fascist spirit. In the film it is resurrected in the body of Strangelove just at the point when death dominates the world. This is a chilling idea and perhaps difficult to comprehend for those who tend to look at fascism as a momentary historical aberration that died with Hitler and only appears in the appalling actions of skinhead gangs. Kubrick is suggesting that death was fascism's disguise and that strength was drawn from its ability to hide in the guise of anticommunism and the cold war. This was a brave insight for the time. Its validity remains undiminished.

I have been talking very seriously about a film that is, of course, very funny. Part of the complexity of *Dr. Strangelove* is that it presents its prophecy as

125

comedy, provoking laughter and fear, observing with bemused con-descension a situation that reveals to an audience its own powerlessness and potential destruction. Kubrick manages this situation by applying, in this work of contemporary cinema, the specifically literary form of eighteenth-century satire. To understand how comfortable he is with this form, it is helpful to compare *Dr. Strangelove* with another film released in the same year and by the same studio (Columbia), Sidney Lumet's *Fail-Safe*. The subject of both films is essentially the same, except that the bombers in *Fail-Safe* are sent to their targets by a mechanical error and, rather than ending the world, an even score is achieved. To make up for U.S. planes bombing Moscow, the president (played by the one-time American movie icon of presidents, Henry Fonda) sends a plane to bomb New York.* The difference in the telling, however, is important. Lumet's film is straightforward melodrama. All the characters are given psychological motivation for their actions, and the narrative is developed out of basic cinematic conventions of human conflict. The film demonstrates Lumet's skill in developing overwrought situations through a tightly controlled mise-en-scène and cutting that emphasizes conflict and tension.

Lumet, in *Fail-Safe*, sees the cold war as an arena in which various temperaments and the occasional neurosis are played out and fudges the political issue by blaming destruction on mechanical failure. Kubrick presents the cold war as a massive breakdown of temperament and control, growing out of an intemperate desire for control, a surrender of inquiry and insight to monolithic modes of thinking and acting that, once put into motion, cannot be stopped. Mechanical failure or even "human error" are not the causes of Kubrick's apocalypse, but human activity imitating and surrendering itself to the mechanical. These different approaches to the same situation are therefore rendered in different forms. Where Lumet finds melodrama the best structuring mode for conflict, Kubrick finds satire the best mode for structuring a narrative of the mechanical man and the death of language.[14] Satire gives him the distance needed to observe the process by removing the illusory wholeness of character created by psychological realism and its need for character "motivation." He is left free to draw abstractions and manipulate his figures into appropriate patterns of action and response.

126

* There was a probably apocryphal joke going around in the eighties: Jack Warner is told that Ronald Reagan is running for President. "No, no," says Jack. "Henry Fonda for President, Ronnie Reagan for best friend."

"Two things . . . are essential to satire," writes Northrop Frye: "One is wit or humor founded on fantasy or a sense of the grotesque or absurd, the other is an object of attack. . . . For effective attack we must reach some kind of impersonal level, and that commits the attacker, if only by implication, to a moral standard."[15] The world as portrayed in *Dr. Strangelove* does not exist beyond the film. It is, rather, a grotesque amalgam of various elements, various ways of thinking and seeing, a discourse created from the variety of babbling voices that made up the culture's cold war political structure. The characters of Jack D. Ripper and Buck Turgidson are constructs, types of the right-wing general, or the nightmare vision of what the archetypal right-wing general would look and sound like. Strangelove is more than a parody of Edward Teller and Werner von Braun (with a dash of Henry Kissinger); he is a terrifying fantasy of resurrected fascism. And he is funny. All the characters in the film are funny, because they are exaggerated. But they are only funny to the spectator. No one in the film ever laughs. (If you look closely, you will see Peter Bull, who plays the Russian ambassador, smile at Peter Sellers's Strangelovian antics; but this is one actor uncontrollably reacting to another's talent and is not meant to be noticed.) Not only do the exaggeration of character and their absurd slaughter of language make them funny, the maniacal seriousness of their activities and their inability to perceive how wretchedly hilarious they are make them funnier still.

This demands a considerable separation, on the viewer's part, from what is occurring within the world of the fiction. The satirical mode requires observation and judgment rather than identification; the conventions of psychological realism and character motivation are removed because they have no place in the genre. One need not understand, in the conventional sense, why the characters are behaving the way they do. Rather, as Frye says, the observer must reach an impersonal level, where he or she is guided by a moral "voice" who develops the discourse that addresses and instructs the spectator. In classical satire, this voice is often heard directly, setting out ideas of normative behavior against which the aberrations of the characters can be judged. In *Dr. Strangelove* that voice is not so much heard as it is insinuated through the viewer's reaction to the discourse (the closest thing to a normative voice in the film is Mandrake, who attempts to remain calm and rational amid the lunacy). The discourse is funny because the viewer understands, with Kubrick, that it is monstrous while the paricipants in the fiction don't; it is appalling because, with Kubrick, the viewer has assumed a moral stand against it and has become part of another, more rational discourse. Rational rarely means optimistic. Should the viewer be terrified by Strangelove's emergence from his wheelchair as a fully organized body of death, then, with Kubrick, she or he assumes what is often the final perspective of the satirist, a pessimism, a certainty that what is seen and revealed as stupidity and arrogance is unstoppable.

Dr. Strangelove owes so much of its vision and power to earlier literary modes that it can be seen through them and as part of them. It shares the anger and despair, as well as the energy, of Jonathan Swift and Alexander Pope (the link is recognized: the target of the SAC bomber is Laputa, one of the kingdoms visited by Gulliver in his travels, a world of scientists so inward looking that they must employ people to hit them on the head to bring them to consciousness of the external world). And the last lines of Alexander Pope's *Dunciad*, which sees the powers of dullness and rigidity and the death of the mind conquer the world, are, despite their old and elegant language, quite applicable to the film:

Lo! thy dread Empire, Chaos! is restor'd;
Light dies before thy uncreating word:
Thy hand, great Anarch! lets the curtain fall;
And Universal Darkness buries All.

Film (along with the other arts) has either forgotten satire or replaced it with parody or lampoon. Moral righteousness is unacceptable, and, as we saw in the case of Oliver Stone, the holding of a complex moral or political opinion is considered too often a personal fault and a liability in a creator. That Kubrick was able to rediscover the validity of satire and, more than that, make it work in a way that contemporary writers and filmmakers have not is important. Satire is an intensely social-political form that requires a close engagement with the world rare in American filmmaking, and its presence in Kubrick's work is indicative of a commitment not ordinarily found.

Dr. Strangelove is the only film Kubrick made that so strictly follows the satiric model. The films that follow are more speculative and open. They do not offer the audience a determined response. The images with which they build their narratives achieve a great complexity and demand that the viewer confront them with intelligence. But, in so doing, the force of anger that is present in *Paths of Glory* and *Dr. Strangelove* is diminished. The films remain cautionary in their response to the mechanization of human behavior, but Kubrick seems more willing to stand away and observe the spaces in which his mechanical men operate, less willing to condemn them, and perhaps, with *Full Metal Jacket* and *Eyes Wide Shut,* ready to sentimentalize them. Never a filmmaker to suggest alternatives to the world he creates, he structures his later films with a high level of uncertainty, allowing a latitude of interpretation that often, and particularly in the case of *A Clockwork Orange*, creates confusion and misunderstanding.

But *2001* and *A Clockwork Orange* do continue Kubrick's engagement with immediate cultural and ideological problems. They are intimately tied to the time at which they appeared; *2001* was influential not only in reviving science fiction but in altering basic cultural perceptions about what the design of future technology might look like. The film also constitutes Kubrick's most radical break with film narrative tradition, at least until *Barry Lyndon*. His early work was marked by conciseness and immediacy. *Paths of Glory* and *Dr. Strangelove* have a sharply rhythmical structure of sequences occurring in rapid progression. The progression and the relationship of parts are clear. The films are closed narrative forms; at their end all action is concluded; all loose ends, all the events started within the narrative, are tied and explained. The narratives may be rich in troubling connotations, but their denotative realm—the immediate meanings of what is seen and heard—is precise and accessible. In *2001* denotation is at a minimum and often withheld. The narrative structure refuses to explain itself through conventional means. Actions and events are not immediately motivated, while transitions are startling and spare. There is little dialogue, and much of what exists is deliberately banal. The film has an open structure in which the viewer plays an operative role. Denied a stance of passive observation in front of a predetermined set of meanings, he or she is asked instead to be engaged with the forms and images, and the text as a whole, and from that engagement work through a continual process of meaning, connotation, and suggestion. *2001* has drawn so much commentary because it is, to use Peter Wollen's words on the theory of open narrative construction, "The factory where thought is at work, rather than the transport system which conveys the finished product."[16]

This kind of openness is alien to American film, which traditionally operates according to conventions of narrative completeness, securing a viewing subject within the fictional world (a process I have described working in *Bonnie and Clyde*). It is the process that leads, in David Bordwell's words, to an "excessively obvious cinema."[17] Even among the filmmakers discussed in this book, each of whom is aware of the formal possibilities of his medium, we rarely find a work practicing the kind of

129

open-endedness present in Kubrick's film. We have seen it in Penn's *Mickey One* and will see it in some of Altman's films, particularly *Three Women*. The process of open-endedness is not necessarily synonymous with ambiguity, an effect that can offer uncertainty instead of plurality of meaning. Ambiguity may present no demands on the viewer, relieving him of any real responsibility of decision or understanding. Ambiguity can mean nothing more than a freedom from concern about what is seen, for it is presented as indefinite, unrealizable, unknowable. Ambiguity can provoke passivity, affirming the viewer's secure subjectivity by assuring her that meaning need not upset assumptions or endanger tranquility.

Openness demands activity and integration, a release of subjectivity into numerous positions, a denial of identification and other conventional ploys by means of which the text erases its formal existence. Instead of linking the viewer firmly to a fictive world, the open text demands recognition of the processes of formal mediation, formal *creation* of meaning. The conventional, closed text provides for the viewer. The open text provokes, indeed demands participation, questioning, working with the film's visual and aural structures. Often this is brought about by emotionally distancing the viewer from the narrative. Closed narrative, invisible form, emotional identification force entry into the work's predetermined structure. The less immediate and apparent the narrative links and meanings, and the more immediate and apparent the formal elements of the work, the more options are permitted. These options include ignoring the work altogether or confronting it intellectually and emotionally in an ongoing process.

2001 does not play with temporal structure as much as modernist European film and film from developing countries did in the sixties. Although it covers a span of time from prehistory to infinity, its structure is perfectly linear. There are great gaps in its temporal field but no overlappings, no flashbacks or simultaneous actions (with two exceptions: as the ape "learns" how to use the bone as a weapon, there is an insert of the monolith, indicating his "thinking" about it and its influence on him; and as he begins using the bone, there is an insert of a felled animal). But the film's very linearity, its almost obsessive trajectory through time, with nothing but visual clues and titles to indicate how parts of the trajectory are linked, helps create its open and inquisitive structure. The paucity of narrative information and explanation, the precision of its visual detail, and the complexity of the images provide a wide-ranging field for inquiry. They also provide a field for no inquiry whatsoever. The narrative of *2001*

130

is so sparse, its images so overwhelming, its theme of human submission to a higher force so insistent that it runs the risk of rendering rational engagement with it impossible.[18] Much of the initial, positive reaction to the film, particularly on the part of young people, was a result of its enormous images and antirational stance. It became, in the late sixties and early seventies, a "drug" movie and was promoted as such, the ultimate trip, the advertisements proclaimed.

In this light it is easy to see the film as a mindless bit of visual stimulation, and rather than grandly theorize about its narrative experimentation, decide that its structure is merely vague and therefore entirely undemanding. In short, the film may be as conducive to passivity and yielding acquiescence and as such seen as preparing the way for the science-fiction films of Lucas and Spielberg, which are even more overwhelming in their imagery and antirational in form and substance. John Russell Taylor saw the film as indicative of a shift in sensibility, a change in audience demands and expectations that signaled a willingness, even a desire, to accept minimal story, in the conventional sense, and maximum sensation. He believes that Kubrick sensed this shift and exploited it, creating an undemanding, because unarticulated, work.[19] In other words, because *2001* met with an uncritical response from many viewers, and because this response is made possible by its nondiscursive form, it is possible to dismiss the film as a work that panders to the immediate needs of an undemanding and uncritical audience. It becomes not only the forerunner of the new science-fiction cycle, but of the male adventure spectacle as well.

The problem as to whether the film is a complex experiment or a cheap thrill can be solved Solomon fashion. *2001* is two films. One is a work for its late-sixties moment, a technological fantasy, and a bombardment of visual stimuli that can accentuate a high or cause one. The other (particularly when seen in a 35-mm anamorphic print or on a letter-boxed laserdisc or DVD, rather than in the 70-mm form of its original release, which rendered images that were too overwhelming to see the details) is a speculative, detailed, spectacular, pessimistic inquiry into the forms of the immediate future. The film continues and enlarges Kubrick's attempt to observe the way men occupy space (both literally and figuratively), how that space is articulated, how it both reflects and imposes on human behavior. Seen this way, *2001* is an extension of *Dr. Strangelove*, a prophecy of things to come in light of things as they now are. But more than *Dr. Strangelove*, *2001* is concerned with the appearance of things to come and the reaction to such appearances by the inhabitants and the observers in and of the

131

fiction. On an important level, it is a film about design—about size, texture, and light, about the ways that objects within a cinematic space are delineated, ordered, shaped, and colored, and about how human figures interact with those objects.

Earlier I noted that *2001* was closer to science fiction literature than film. But one area of that relationship is important—namely, the way Kubrick's film changes the genre's conventions about how the future will look. In the fifties—and earlier, if we wish to go back to William Cameron Menzies's *Things to Come* (1936)—the conventions that inform the cinematic design of the future, or of "advanced" extraterrestrial civilizations, are cleanliness, spareness, and order. These codes are visually manifested in straight lines and severe geometric forms. The materials of the future world are metal, glass, and plastic. Wood is rarely seen. Clothing is uniform, smooth, close-fitting. Human habitations are never crowded: figures occupy areas in a neat and orderly arrangement and always in bright light. Except for the vastness of outer space, darkness does not exist (this aspect of the convention is turned into a stylistic trait by Steven Spielberg, for whom hard, almost blinding light becomes a key signifier of a frightening, but finally friendly, extraterrestrial presence). Certainly all this is partially the result of literary influences. Utopian literature, from Plato's *Republic* on, represents its perfect world as the model of clean, rational order. But it is curious that in our century, when that model has been broken by the anti-utopian literature of Orwell and Huxley, it persisted in film with a few key exceptions: the above-ground city of the elite in Fritz Lang's *Metropolis* (1927) is an early design of a streamlined future, but the workers' under-ground city is crowded, dark, and noisome. Richard Fleischer's *Soylent Green* (1973) and especially Ridley Scott's *Blade Runner* (1982)—a complex meditation on power and ownership set in a film noir future—and Alex Proyas's *Dark City* depict earth or its simulacra as foul and overcrowded, an inner-city slum extended and magnified. Scott's *Alien* (1979) offers another response to *2001*, *Star Wars*, and *Close Encounters* with a spacecraft that is not a bright, clean, antiseptic space, but a slightly worn interstellar warehouse.

The persistence of the convention can be explained by the phenomenon of convention itself, which exists as a repeated form, generating a positive response in audiences who accept its representations as valid and desired and, pleased by their response, desire more and respond to more of the same. For viewer and filmmaker alike, repetition becomes easier than invention. Obviously the repetition of this particular set of signifiers is responsive to a profound need to mark progress by images of tidiness and cleanliness. An uncluttered, linear environment is better. The question, "Better than what?" is hardly even implied; "better" is simply what is signified by this complex of meaning. The future means greater efficiency, more done with less effort. The future is progress, easy movement forward with no physical or emotional barriers. Neatness and spareness are its signs.

These equations do yield contradictions, particularly throughout fifties science fiction. In Robert Wise's *The Day the Earth Stood Still* (1951), a streamlined messenger from space and his smooth-skinned robot come to warn the earth that its nuclear bombs threaten the universe. The visitor is clearly an admirable, even Christ-like figure, but his rationality and calm are supported with an enormous power that will destroy the earth if it does not heed him. The contemporary milieu is countered by the interior of the visitor's saucer, designed in the clean circular lines of Art Deco. Fred M. Wilcox's *Forbidden Planet* (1956) shows the world of the Krel as the epitome of order, efficiency, and intellectual strength. Unfortunately, the Krel forgot about their unconscious drives, which became personified and destroyed them. The clean, ordered, and rational future was to be feared as well as desired. In Don Siegel's *Invasion of the Body Snatchers* (1956), the calm rationality achieved by those who have been taken over and subverted by the aliens seems to themselves desirable; to those not yet taken over it is horrifying. The visual design of this, and many other low-budget fifties science fiction, is contemporary drab: mostly shot on location, in the Los Angeles suburbs or the desert, the films depict our world as an ugly, unwelcoming place, which makes the promise of order and security offered by the aliens welcome and frightening simultaneously.[20]

Such contradictions are troublesome because they go unquestioned. Images of order and spareness and light mean "future." The future is inevitable, often good, but sometimes threatening. Too much order and too much dependence on rationality threaten the spontaneity of the human spirit. But whether good or threatening, the images are basically the same. The creators of so much science-fiction film seem unable to see a future that looks otherwise. It may only be created with extreme images. Kubrick, in *2001*, looks closely at the conventions, at the assumptions about the look of the future, and considers their ramifications. The future and its automatic connotations of efficiency and progress are questioned by exaggerating the very extremity of conventional images.

In *Dr. Strangelove,* the womblike war room, with its halo of fluorescent light, its computerized wall maps, its faceless, unsmiling inhabitants, and

133

the SAC bomber, with its multitude of neatly arranged buttons and switches and equally unsmiling inhabitants, are images of efficiency and progress that lead to a breakdown of control and reason. The efficient structures of progress become efficient structures of death. In *2001* the principal images of the future present in so many science-fiction films are extended much further, so far in fact that they outstrip their old meanings. *2001* is as much about science fiction, or at least our reading of the conventions and meaning systems of science-fiction film, as it is about the search for some extraterrestrial force. The design of the film combines the traditional components of linearity, cleanliness, and severe geometrical forms with an extraordinary sense of detail. The exteriors and interiors of Kubrick's spaceships seem to suffer from a horror vacuui. Surfaces are intricately textured and articulated; interiors are filled with screens and buttons that do not merely flash, but flash complex verbal, mathematical, and graphic messages. At times the screen the audience watches is filled with other screens, themselves filled with information. One of the most dramatic episodes in the film, the computer HAL's murder of the hibernating astronauts, is done through words and graphs on a computer screen, flashing the stages of the astronauts' decline, ending with "Life Functions Terminated," a cold, mechanical machine message of death. (There are other important machine communications: the viewer learns some of the details of the Jupiter mission from a television program viewed by Poole and Bowman in the spaceship. Bowman learns the final detail, the need to discover the source of the monoliths from a videotape that is played just as he finishes dismantling HAL.) Reviewers at the time of the film's release commented on the minimal dialogue in the film, but they failed to point out just how much language, via print, computer graphics, mathematical formulas, and configurations, does in fact appear. Visually these words and graphics are themselves clean and linear, presented (as are the credits of the film) in a version of the typeface called Helvetica, a bold, uniform, sans-serif type introduced in 1952 and ever since used on posters, in road and building signs, and for other directional devices. Helvetica has been a favorite typeface for advertising and corporate communications. It is, in short, the typeface of the modern age and has achieved the status of having a meaning beyond what the words formed by it have to say. Helvetica, writes Leslie Savan, means "sanitized, neutralized, and authorized." "You see Helvetica," writes one designer, "and you perceive order." Form becomes an ideological event.[21]

    2001 is a Helvetica film. Not merely the verbal and mathematical images

134

flashed on screens, but the total design of the film predicates a clean authority, an order of total mechanical, electronic, technological perfection. But, as I said, Kubrick is not merely assuming the equation clean equals future equals better. He is examining the assumption and returning a verdict. That verdict is implicit in much utopian literature, explicit in dystopian fantasies of the twentieth century, and the cause of conflict in much American science-fiction film: the future equals emotional and intellectual death. Perfect order and perfect function decrease the need for human inquisitiveness and control. A perfectly clean world is clean of human interference. But *2001* is no humanist's outcry against the diminution of the spirit, nor does it share the hysterical (and hilarious) equation of alien mind control with the International Communist Conspiracy implicit in many fifties science-fiction films. There is not even the anger over human surrender explicit in its predecessor, *Dr. Strangelove*. The film exists as a leisurely, distanced contemplation of technological advance and human retreat, the design of man accommodated to and owned by his machines, neat, ritualized, without awe, without response.

Gene Youngblood tries to make a case for Kubrick's prophesying a new consciousness in his bland, nonreacting scientists and astronauts, a sort of reverse nostalgia in which the future is reverie, "melancholy and nostalgia, not for the past, but for our inability to become integral with the present"— for loneliness in the face of progress.[22] This, however, is wishful thinking; more appropriately, late nineteen-sixties wishful thinking, when passivity and withdrawal were regarded as one possible response—the opposite of revolution—to the irrationality of the corporate, technological state. Youngblood is right that Kubrick is presenting the human being as an outsider but wrong in implying that this is a psychological or metaphysical position. Kubrick's men are on the outside like the buttons and "readouts" of their machines; which is to say they are not outside at all, but perfectly integrated into corporate technology, part of the circuitry. Everything— except, finally, the machine itself—works in perfect harmony. This is not humanity out in space; it is Pan Am, Conrad Hilton, ITT, Howard Johnson, Seabrook Frozen Foods (the corporate names—some of them now defunct—that adorn the space station and spaceship), computers, and their men and women. The people in the film lack expression and reaction not because they are wearing masks to cover a deep and forbidding anguish, as would be the case in a film by the French director Robert Bresson, for example. They are merely incorporated into a "mission" and are only barely distinguishable from the other components. They are sans-serif figures.

135

What then of the film's premise, the notion that the history of man has been guided by unknown, extraterrestrial forces, represented by a dark version of a Helvetica character, the black, featureless monolith? Here the openness of the film is so great that there is a danger of falling through it, for Kubrick is making suggestions, meditating on symbols and their meaning. The best way to deal with this openness is in a dialectical fashion, seeing the contradictions clearly. History, one possible reading of the film would have it, is at the mercy of a god-like controlling power. The transmitters of this power, the monoliths, teach the use of weapons to kill; they lure humankind into technological perfection; they carry humanity to a transcendent stage of rebirth. Men, therefore, have a reason to be passive, for they are the servants of a higher order, slaves of a predetermined plan so precisely calculated that only a precise calculator, the HAL 9000 computer, realizes its full meaning and gets, quite literally, emotional about it and goes crazy. I don't mean to underplay this; I find the confrontation of HAL and Bowman, the latter undoing the computer's thought patterns while it cries "I can feel it," to be one of the most powerful and ironic sequences in the film—an agon between a man and a digital construction with a human voice in which the latter wins the viewer's sympathies.

But suppose the monoliths do not literally represent an existent higher intelligence? They may be read allegorically, as imaginary markers of humanity's evolution, dark and featureless because one of the valid connotations of the future is the unknown, a blindness to possibilities. Extending this further, the monolith becomes not a precipitator but an obstacle to full development. After all, the first result of contact with it is killing. The ape touches it and learns to use a bone as a weapon. The wide-screen closeup of the ape's arm crashing down his newfound club is a prophecy of human savagery to come. The weapon may be a tool to control nature, indicated by the shot of a beast being felled; but it is also used to hold territory and slay others. Kubrick attempts to present many mitigating situations. The apes are being attacked; they need to defend themselves. But they also take an undeniable pleasure in the kill. Brutality is aligned with pleasure, and the bone weapon is a mark of progress. In one of the most audacious edits in the history of American film, the bone, hurled into the air, becomes a spaceship. But this leap forward is no great leap at all. Kubrick's vision of space travel is spectacular, but deadly. The ape showed a manic joy in its discovery; the space travelers show neither joy nor sorrow—they are mere receivers of the data flashed on the various screens

136

that surround them. The territory they conquer seems to offer no excitement, no danger to them, until one of the tools revolts. The ape used the tool, fashioned it into a weapon; now the tools and the men are hardly distinguishable.

When the bland Dr. Heywood Floyd touches the monolith discovered on the moon, the movement of his hand echoes that of the ape. The monolith emits a signal, and the next shot shows the *Discovery* mournfully making its way toward Jupiter. The music, the deliberate track through the spaceship's centrifugal main hall, the quiet passivity of the astronauts give this sequence the air of a ceremonial, a detached, sad, and lonely aura. This is the end of man, alone in space, surrounded by the frozen, half-dead bodies of the other crewmen, and finally locked in combat with a machine of his own making. The isolation is complete, though Bowman and Poole take no cognizance of it. The situation is not unlike that in *Dr. Strangelove*. There the mechanisms of isolation were ideological. Here the ideology is not as apparent but must be sought out in the deadpan faces and automatic reactions of the astronauts, the seductive perfection of the technology, in the red eye of HAL that watches over the proceedings and takes charge. As in *Dr. Strangelove*, the end of human subjectivity and agency is prelude to the death of the person; but here Kubrick allows a further step, an indication of rebirth, of change. The old Bowman in his bed in the Jupiter room, looking up at the monolith, calls to mind a statement by William Blake: "If the doors of perception were cleansed, everything would appear to man as it is, infinite." The point-of-view shot from Bowman's position looking at the tablet presents it as an impenetrable mass—in fact, the camera position and movement are reminiscent of the point-of-view shot from the doomed soldiers marching toward the sandbags where they will be shot in *Paths of Glory*. The monolith promises something beyond it and encloses that something at the same time. Once again, it can be seen to signify an obstacle, a perceptual block that must be transcended.

This places the spectator, of course, on the brink of the metaphysical, a place the film begs us to enter and a place I would like to avoid. Any critical remarks on *2001* must note the suggestion of rebirth, how it moves from the dawn of man through his senescence and back to before the dawn. The enormously evocative images that constitute the film's final sequences point to possibilities of renewed intelligence, a return to a sense of curiosity. The fetus moving through space is the only image in the film of a human being unencumbered by things and, curiously, undiminished by surroundings. But it is, at the same time, an image of enormous solitude, entrapment, and

137

powerlessness. Why is it there? Who is guiding events? The initial dilemma returns: either there is assent to the power of the images and to sensation, or to the suggestion of the narrative that some superintelligence is guiding our destiny. In either case, assent is acquired, and the openness of the film is suddenly denied. The final sequences of 2001 are the most disturbing, for they are at once beautiful and overwhelming, vague and ambiguous, and suggestive of human impotence in the face of a higher authority. These images and their implications lead to some difficult and unpleasant conclusions.

The uncertainty and suggestiveness proved too difficult for Hollywood to leave be. Almost fifteen years later, Peter Hyams wrote and directed a "sequel" to the film for its original studio, MGM. *2010* (1984) constitutes the reverse shot of Kubrick's film. As if the openness of the original needed other images to respond and close it, give it manageable and unthreatening meaning while resituating the viewer in a secure and knowable space, Hyams reduces Kubrick's design and narrative structure to a set of simple and—within the context of the science-fiction genre—reasonable answers. He replaces the nondiscursive power of Kubrick's imagery with dialogue that attempts to account for everything. While their countries prepare for war over Central America, Russian and U.S. scientists join forces in space to save the original *Discovery* rocket ship, reanimate HAL, and find the meaning of the monoliths. HAL turns out to be quite reasonable after all, and the monoliths signal the birth of a new sun and world, caused by an intelligence that promises peace as long as it remains undisturbed. Dr. Floyd (played by Roy Scheider, who inflects his role with conventional character traits in a film where the human figures are foregrounded rather than integrated into the mise-en-scène as they are in *2001*) suggests that in this new universe humans will take a second place. "You can tell your children," he writes to his son as he returns from his mission, "of the day when everyone looked up and realized that we were only tenants of this world. We have been given a new lease—and a warning—from the landlord." The revelation of a new intelligence only confirms the old language of ownership and subordination.

The narrative of *2010* settles back into the classic model of *The Day the Earth Stood Still*, where superior powers will permit Earth to live in peace, unless its "petty squabbles" threaten the universe. Then it would be destroyed by superhuman powers. *2010* is not so blatantly totalitarian; in fact its attack on the American government (clearly depicted as being right-wing in the film) and call for U.S.–Russian cooperation place it among the

138

very few liberal films to appear in the eighties. But a great paradox of American science-fiction film is that, no matter how progressive it attempts to be on a superficial level, there is an apparently inevitable reversion to a reactionary base. "Superior forces" are either authoritarian, and therefore threatening, ultimately destructive powers or, in Spielberg's science fiction, not authoritarian or threatening, but still patriarchal. The rationality and orderliness predicated for a "higher intelligence" always turn out to be repressive, especially when presented as salvific.

In attempting to conclude the difficult openness of Kubrick's film, Hyams only compounds the unpleasant conclusions that can be drawn from it. Both films, and many others beside, structure enormous images, and place the human figure in a passive role, creating narratives that implicitly or explicitly indicate an inescapable human destiny at the mercy of some superhuman force. They always run the risk of structuring themselves on a totalitarian, quasi-fascist model. Susan Sontag writes:

> Fascist aesthetics . . . flow from (and justify) a preoccupation with situations of control, submissive behavior, and extravagant effort: they exalt two seemingly opposite states, egomania and servitude. The relations of domination and enslavement take the form of a characteristic pageantry: the massing of groups of people; the turning of people into things; the multiplication of things and grouping of people/things around an all-powerful, hypnotic leader figure or force. The fascist dramaturgy centers on the orgiastic transaction between mighty forces and their puppets. Its choreography alternates between ceaseless motion and a congealed, static, "virile" posing. Fascist art glorifies surrender, it exalts mindlessness: it glamorizes death.[23]

She includes *2001* as a representative work.

I do not agree completely with her assessment, for the very reason that formally *2001* does not create the kind of insistence, the rhythmical structuring of assent, that is part of the fascist model. Perhaps, as I have indicated, the options offered by *2001* are what save it from falling into this trap. Certainly, it reveals the condition of people turned into things but, as in *Dr. Strangelove*, does so from a cautionary perspective. Rather than glamorize death, it points toward (a rather fantastical) rebirth. Yet, undeniably, the film points toward surrender to a hypnotic force and suggests that this surrender is inevitable.

The film toys dangerously with images of assent and surrender. If it

139

manages to escape total commitment to a vision of human impotence and enslavement, it does so through narrative openness and the speculative nature of its images.[24] Yet the fact that *2001* dallies with these issues, offering the possibility of audience surrender to its spectacle, and turns that surrender into a theme is indicative of a definite and troubling strain in American film since the late sixties. In content and form, often both, a number of American films of the seventies and eighties have indeed submitted to a quasi-fascist aesthetic (less evident in the differently passive postmodernism of the nineties), and it is necessary to digress a moment to see where Kubrick stands in relation to this movement.

In the early seventies, responding to the ideology of the Nixon regime, there was a cycle of reactionary revenge films, in which Don Siegel's *Dirty Harry* and Michael Winner's *Death Wish* (1974) were key entries. Imbued with the law-and-order fantasies of the time, these films present a strong-armed cop or an aroused bourgeois (sometimes a small-town sheriff, as in the *Walking Tall* series) who battles not only criminals but a caricatured liberal authority that seems to thwart his every move with irritating laws. In the eighties, moving on a global scale in response to the openly aggressive images inherent in the ideology of the Reagan years (I will examine this ideology and the films that grew out of it in more detail in Chapter Four), the revenger took on terrorists, or the Vietnamese, or the Russians themselves. A caricatured liberal authority was sometimes transformed into a caricatured bureaucratic authority that still was unresponsive to desires for the rapid and complete righting of assumed wrongs. The *Rambo* films were the most prominent examples of these variations, and all of them, whatever small changes they work upon their conservative base, carry forward the cinematic tradition of a powerful individual avenging a largely passive society. They speak to a strong societal frustration and a desire for expedient action and are obsessed with the idea that a superhero can do what the society as a whole cannot. They encourage passivity by presenting fantasies of a virile and aggressive leader who will emerge to save the society. They all glorify death and murder with an almost transcendent mindlessness.

More disconcerting than these is a small group of films that not only suggest a right-wing solution to societal problems but create a formal pattern of assent and submission in their very structure. The paradigm for this is, of course, Leni Riefenstahl's famous documentary of Nazi Germany, *Triumph of the Will* (1935), a work whose images and rhythm demand total involvement (or total divorcement). Fortunately unable to hypnotize anyone, its intent is still clear: to create a longing in the audience to partake in the faceless geometric mass of happy people, eyes upward, worshipping Hitler. Formally it not only points the way to the ideology, it is ideology in action. And what *Triumph of the Will* now fails to do, such apparently diverse (and unequally creative) films as William Friedkin's *The Exorcist* (1973), John Milius's and Oliver Stone's *Conan the Barbarian* (1983), Steven Spielberg's *Close Encounters of the Third Kind* (1977), Tony Scott's *Top Gun* (1986, a film whose "virile posing" and militarist pageantry, whose fantasies of the powers of flying, connected to adolescent sexuality and rock music, make it a model for the banalities of fascist form; perhaps Kubrick had this in mind when he created for *Top Gun*'s Tom Cruise a more passive figure, with little self-possession, in *Eyes Wide Shut*), the majority of "slasher" films in which men murder women, and a large number of children's television cartoons whose central figures are mechanical superheroes, succeed in doing. These films were not consciously made in the service of a greater political movement, to be sure; but they succeed, on a smaller scale, in inducing a state of irrationality, enveloping and absorbing the viewer, permitting no distance and no discrimination.[25] They communicate power and terror simultaneously, resulting in a state of passivity that restrains a desire for unrestricted, destructive activity. Consider the "Ride of the Valkyries" sequence in Coppola's *Apocalypse Now* (1979), where the camera assumes the point of view of the attacking helicopter gunship, providing a murderous elation and superiority for the viewer, countered by the reverse shots of the Vietnamese village and its inhabitants who are destroyed. What choices are presented between power and helplessness? The film manipulates the viewer into a subordinate position of awe and hopelessness.

Close Encounters provides the most immediate comparison to *2001* and a fascinating example of a kind of quasi-fascist form. Spielberg creates a revision of the basic fifties science-fiction subject, the invasion of the earth by aliens. Fifties xenophobia and fear of communism rarely permitted films to present the aliens as friendly and never allowed passive acceptance of them. But by the seventies there seemed in the culture to be greater openness to—perhaps more need for—giving over to some greater protective and benevolent force (this is one of Spielberg's major preoccupations; Chapter Four will examine it in more detail). Therefore, Spielberg's spacemen are welcomed and revered. They are not a threat, but they are overwhelming and inescapable. As in fifties science fiction, the army still figures as the authoritative force. But where, in the fifties, it impotently attacks the aliens, now it is prepared to greet them and, indeed, employs a massive cover-up operation to do so, a cover-up infiltrated only by a few civilians who, controlled by the spacemen, fight their way to be present at their epiphanic appearance.

The structure of *Close Encounters* is such that the viewer is allowed as little free will as the characters in the film. Extremes of dark and light, a predominance of low-angle shots and rapid dollies toward figures and objects, the incredible size of the space paraphernalia (the "size" of the sound track itself) continually reduce the spectator to an accepting position. The film provides no place to move emotionally and no place to think. Subordinate to lights in the sky, to the army, and finally to an elephantine spacecraft, so overwhelming and so intriguing, the viewer, like the characters in the film, has no choice but to yield to its presence. I submit that the strategies employed by Spielberg are precisely analogous to those employed by Riefenstahl in *Triumph of the Will*. The descent of Hitler from the clouds to an adoring populace dwarfed by his presence and their own monumental, geometric configuration is echoed in *Close Encounters*. Here humans are dwarfed by their loneliness in the inhabited nighttime sky, by lights, by obsessive geometric figures (the characters contacted by the aliens have implanted in their minds the shape of a mountain where the aliens will land), and finally by the enormous ship that descends from the clouds and reduces them to open-mouthed awe. *Close Encounters* is a fantasy, it may be argued (to which, I would argue, that such fantasies represent and respond to major currents in the culture), a work of the imagination that should not be submitted to ideological scrutiny. Spielberg could not have consciously intended such a structure, and, besides, what other reaction is possible but awe and submission to such awesome forces?

As I have insisted throughout, no work of cinema, or any other imaginative form, is ideologically innocent, and Spielberg is responsible for the formal construction of his film, whether or not he is aware of its parallels and heritage. Was George Lucas aware of what a number of critics have seen: that the final sequence of *Star Wars* is patterned directly after a sequence in *Triumph of the Will*? The formal imitation is too perfect for it not to have been conscious. Here then is a genuine case of ideological confusion: The plot of *Star Wars* involves a red army in revolt against the black fascist forces of "The Empire." When the red army wins it celebrates with a Nazi rally! As I noted, most American science fiction for a variety of reasons is inherently reactionary.[26] In the nineties, with the end of the cold war, science fiction has not only flourished but also altered its ideology to some degree. Paul Verhoeven, no stranger to brutal but sometimes mildly subversive films, made *Starship Troopers* in 1997. A strange, silly work—most notable for its digital insects—it simultaneously mocks the fascist tendencies present in science fiction while upholding notions of hierarchy and order. Typical of postmodernist straddling, it is and isn't what it wants to be: parody and cynicism; brutality celebrated and condemned; heroism shrugged off and praised in a typical science-fiction future of order and control; an army of teenagers battling disgusting alien creatures.[27] Meanwhile, Barry Sonnenfeld's *Men in Black* (1997) poses the humorous proposition that the aliens are among us in a variety of guises—Newt Gingrich among them—kept in line by a few heroes willing themselves to become alienated from the world.

Parody and question are mostly alien to Spielberg, who is devoted to developing forms of audience involvement, giving a thrill, and creating emotion. Alfred Hitchcock said, "I feel it's tremendously satisfying for us to be able to use the cinematic art to achieve something of a mass emotion."[28] Hitchcock, though, always shows his hand, always gives the audience means to step back and observe what is being done to them and why. Hollywood film, at least before the late sixties, often attempted to demonstrate some respect for its audience. Although it worked through an invisible style and thereby insisted that the audience perceive its characters and their actions as if they were an unmediated presence; although it played out fantasies of melodrama and induced passivity to a great degree, rarely did it dehumanize or attempt to reduce the audience to a function of the sound and images confronting them. Kubrick, in *2001*, retains this respect. Spielberg (and not only Spielberg) does not. Where *Close Encounters* seals the viewer inside its structure from the opening shot—a blast of light and sound from out of the darkness—and keeps her submissive for its duration, *2001* demands above all viewer attentiveness and is open, where *Close Encounters* is closed; speculative, where *Close Encounters* is predetermined; filled with detailed images, where those in Spielberg's film are merely overwhelming. *2001* is, among other things, about the terror of dehumanization; *Close Encounters* is about the yearning to yield to something more exciting than the merely human that will relieve us of responsibility. And where *2001* is often ironic and always (with the exception of the "Stargate" sequence) calm, *Close Encounters* is sentimental and hyperemotional. If Kubrick dallies with the notion of predetermination and ultimate control by a superintelligence, his speculation is part of the film's larger inquiry and design. Ultimately this is not a very palatable speculation; but the film offers at least an open narrative and an intellectual space in which the viewer may consider what is going on.

This ongoing openness allows *2001* to keep generating meaning. In a humorous piece of journalism about the future of computing, Peter H. Lewis wrote: "Remember the scene in *2001: A Space Odyssey* when the apes confront their first computer? The computer just sits there, a silent monolith, unblinking, not even deigning to offer a cryptic error message. The apes have no access to technical support and, driven mad by frustration, they grab clubs and go on a rampage, smiting any chimp who is wearing a pocket protector."[29] The monolith as computer offers another avenue for speculation. *2001* follows a long line of variations on the Frankenstein myth: the desire of the imagination to create a human simulacrum. This myth—this cultural imperative—has been given greater prominence in the digital age than during the time of the medieval cabalists with their vision of the Golem, Mary Shelley in the nineteenth century, and the long line of fantasists and science-fiction writers and filmmakers could have imagined. In *2001* Kubrick predicted and contemplated the new digital culture and worried over it. HAL is his Frankenstein, the almost human computer simulacrum who gains consciousness and agency—those great dreams of the pursuers of Artificial Intelligence—while the humans around him lose both. The monoliths are a kind of HAL of the far future (and we discover, as HAL is being lobotomized by Bowman, that he alone knew the reason for their mission to find the monoliths)—HAL's offspring, moving through time and guiding humans into their digital presence. There is even a suggestion of this in the film's design, where the modules Bowman ejects from HAL's memory banks look like miniature, lucite versions of the monolith. Much of the speculation on digital culture addresses the loss of body and subjectivity in the great web of computer interconnectivity. In *2001*, the human figure, though seeming to triumph over the computer by disconnecting its brain, has already become a cyborg figure, part of the machine, the machine part of him. The journey to "Jupiter and Beyond the Infinite" is into that matrix that writers on the digital have been recently thinking about.[30] For Kubrick it is a cautionary vision but, given his temperament, inescapable. Over and over, in film after film, he has expressed the inevitability of humans giving up control over the world and technology they strive so hard to get.

This pessimism is set back down to earth and put on a political level in *A Clockwork Orange*, where Kubrick again struggles with the problems of human agency and controlling institutions and seemingly gets himself stuck in a thematic quandary: is the only alternative to passivity an individuality so brutal that many must suffer for one person to be free? Is the political future merely one of self-serving manipulations for power? Is the delight in viewing violence a reflection of a perverse need for it, at least in a safe and distanced form?

If *Dr. Strangelove* is satirical and *2001* contemplative, *A Clockwork Orange* is cynical. There appear to be no responsible answers to the problems the film poses *within* its narrative; one has to think carefully around its edges, into its aura, if you will, to understand what Kubrick is getting at. It is a seductive work, rhythmically dynamic and carefully structured in a perfectly symmetrical form. Its mise-en-scène is constructed through a series of spectacular tableaux, and they, along with the editing pattern, could easily fit Sontag's description of a "choreography [that] alternates between ceaseless motion and a congealed, static, 'virile' posing." *A Clockwork Orange* seems to be the one film in which Kubrick apparently makes easy choices and sets up his viewers for easy answers. Some critics at the time complained that it was a hollow pandering to audience desires for more and more violence. But like all of Kubrick's great work, it yields more with each viewing, and the answers that at first seem easy are revealed as quite complicated and unsettling.

In its design, *A Clockwork Orange* is the dialectic to *2001*. The clean lines and intricate detail of that film are here replaced by clutter and occasional squalor. Only Mr. Alexander's house reflects the sterility of *2001*; but where the cold, clean space tools were fascinating in their detail, the writer's home is only arid and pretentious. The Korova Milkbar, where Alex (Malcolm McDowell) and his droogs get high, bears a resemblance to the Hilton space station in color and furnishings, but it has the added features of erotic sculpture and very un-Helvetica printing on the walls, advertising the various "moloko plus" drugs indulged in by the gang. In *2001*, decoration is at a functional minimum; in *A Clockwork Orange* it has assumed an erotic obviousness and cheapness.[31] The sexuality that was repressed in *Strangelove* and disappeared in *2001* emerges in the world of *A Clockwork Orange* in graffiti, paintings, and sculptures and in the brutality of Alex and his comrades. Sexuality has become the mundane in art, an expression of violence in human behavior. And it is precisely the mundane and the brutal that inform the world created in the film. Passivity and a lack of human, communal integrity resulted in global destruction in *Strangelove* and the suggestion of slavery to superhuman forces in *2001*. Here it results in first a mindless and then a mindful brutality, a violence of one individual against another and the state against all. The love, order, and gentleness that are announced by the humanist tradition as the goals of every individual, Kubrick observes as fantasies. Hate, manipulation, and cruelty are the dialectic to these fantasies, and the life of the mind and spirit becomes the caricatured target of the vitality of the libido and the club. The Cat Lady (whose home is festooned with animals and grotesque erotic art) does battle with Alex by wielding a bust of his beloved Ludwig van Beethoven (to whose music Alex has grotesque and violent fantasies), while he does her in with a bloated, white, sculpted penis.

146

When *2001* makes its transition from the ape's bone floating in the air to the spaceship, something important is left out: what happened to the violence, indeed the joy of violence, that the bone represented? *2001* indicates that it has been drained from humans and placed in their digital simulacra. HAL cleanly kills off all but one of the crewmen on the ship. *A Clockwork Orange* returns to examine the ape's heritage. The beating scenes are choreographed like the ape sequences in the earlier film. When Alex and his droogs beat up the hobo and Billy Boy's gang, they use their clubs as did the ape when he killed the leader of the opposing tribe. When Alex beats up his own gang, his slow-motion antics are similar to those of the ape with his bone. The dawn of man has become his senescence. Violence prophesied by the ape's discovery of a murdering weapon has become violence realized and ritualized, a force no longer to be examined or understood but to be used, either anarchically or under the control of the state. Kubrick seems to offer no other alternative to the aggression that he sees as an inherent component of human behavior (he was an admirer of Robert Ardrey and his "territorial imperative" ideas about human aggression); violence must manifest itself in some form, controlled or uncontrolled. In *2001*, humans have delegated their responsibilities to their machines, and the machines have become the aggressors. In *A Clockwork Orange* responsibility is not so much delegated as dissipated. Life is lived at such a low level of vulgarity that the only expression it seems able to achieve is destruction (a state of things repeated, though in another context, in *Full Metal Jacket*). The state of humankind is hopeless.

At the end of *2001*, old humankind is catapulted into the cosmos as a wandering fetus, presumably ready to start anew. Toward the end of *A Clockwork Orange*, Alex catapults himself out of a window, driven to attempt suicide by his nemesis, Mr. Alexander, the liberal writer brought to madness by Alex's destruction of his wife. He tortures Alex with the music of Beethoven, to which Alex has been conditioned to react with horror. Like Bowman, Alex is sealed in a bare room. Although not the room of sanitized rococo splendor—the last plastic, computer memory of human civilization that marked man's end in *2001*—it provides a similar enclosed and observed isolation, with this ironic difference: it does not constitute a way station to another form of existence. When Alex leaps to his death, he is indeed reborn, but only to his former violent self.

A Clockwork Orange is a curiously elating cyclic vision that seems unable to do anything but celebrate the violence it portrays, because it portrays only that as being alive. The death of feeling and response Kubrick depicted in the preceding films comes alive as its own opposite. Life only responds to death; love becomes the attraction to brutality. It is no longer a strange love. One may feel superior to the characters of *Dr. Strangelove* because they are grotesque and ridiculous; their monomania is obvious. There may be a similar reaction to the characters of *2001* because they are insensitive to the wonder of the universe outside the window of the spaceships and space stations. But Alex is admirable. One cannot help being fond of his vitality and verbal dexterity, and Kubrick manipulates viewer response accordingly. The narrative moves from a bravura celebration of Alex and his atrocities, observed with horror and excitement, to restrained observation of Alex's arrest and imprisonment, when he is treated so badly the viewer can hardly avoid sympathy. The Ludovico treatment that subdues him is presented subjectively—as is the whole film. Our point of view is sealed with Alex's: he narrates, there is hardly a scene in which he is not present, and the spectator therefore shares his perspective and attitudes. His voice and body become part of the mise-en-scène; he is the organic mechanism in the film's clockworks. With the stage performance that demonstrates the success of the treatment, Alex's humiliation and the spectator's sympathies for him are complete. After his humiliation, the narrative duplicates the first part of the film almost incident by incident, only with Alex as the butt of the events: the hobo whom Alex beat up returns with his hobo friends to beat Alex up; Alex's parents take in a boarder who kicks Alex out; Alex's droogs have become policemen and beat him; and the mad Mr. Alexander tries to send Alex to his death as earlier Alex sent Mrs. Alexander to hers. By the time Alex is reborn to his former self, response is so thoroughly on his side that it is hard to tell whether Kubrick is amused at his own powers of manipulation or agreeing with the admirability and good fortune of his character.

Is Alex's way of life to be admired? Is his animal aggression more admirable than the deviousness of the Minister of the Interior and the state he represents? Or is everyone to be condemned, as in *Dr. Strangelove?* One clue to Kubrick's position is the association made among three of the characters. Two of them share similar names: Alex and Frank Alexander, the writer whose wife Alex rapes. Along with Fred, the Minister of the Interior, they make a strange trio. It is as if the three—the loony liberal, Frank Alexander, first cold and sterile, then all chattering grimaces; Alex DeLarge, the violent child, virile killer, magnificent wielder of club, penis, and language, and pathetic victim; and Fred, the devious law-and-order politician, who first uses Alex to show how he can get crime off the streets and then uses him to get it back on the streets when it is politically advantageous to do so—are aspects of the same personality. (In his novel, Anthony Burgess makes the connection between Alex and Mr. Alexander explicit. "F. Alexander. Good Bog, I thought, he is another Alex." In the film, when Alex rings Mr. Alexander's doorbell, it sounds the opening of Beethoven's Fifth Symphony, beloved of Alex.)[32] In the manner of William Blake, Kubrick divides up components of human behavior and places them in separate bodies. The joke, therefore, if joke it is, lies in placing these three social/emotional/political abstractions within the flesh of separate characters, playing them off against each other, and convincing the viewer that they offer real alternatives, when in fact they represent aspects of the human personality that should be integrated. If Alex triumphs in sympathy over the others, it is because vitality is more attractive than deviousness and hypocrisy, even if that vitality is misdirected and brutal. It may take some strength of conviction to believe that Kubrick is laughing at both his characters and at his audience for refusing to see his joke (though this ability to mock his audience is evident again in *The Shining*). The film gives every indication that the audience must admire Alex and admire him with little hesitation. If this is so, the film becomes exploitative of its audience in the worst way. If Kubrick has a satirical intent in artificially dividing components of the human personality into separate types but then builds for one of these types—Alex—a narrative that makes him so attractive and sympathetic that one loses sight of the schematic pattern, then the text becomes skewed and the audience used. The viewer is given little option but to sympathize with a vicious character.

Things are further complicated by the character of the chaplain in the film, whose speech on the necessity of free will seems to be a thesis statement. Even in the formal satirical structure of *Dr. Strangelove*, Kubrick did not make a direct statement of position, allowing the audience to assume its own moral and rational perspective. But in creating a serious religious character, who proceeds to talk seriously and with feeling about an irresistible idea, the narrative and spectator attachment to it are further skewed toward a sympathy with poor Alex. (Kubrick was normally not well disposed to organized religion. Alex often fantasizes to quite heretical religious imagery; priests do not come off well in other films. In *Paths of Glory* the priest is depicted as powerless and hypocritical. His unpleasantness is pointed up by that fact that he is played by Emile Meyer, a singularly ugly individual most often associated in fifties film with roles of brutal, corrupt New York policemen. In *Barry Lyndon* Murray Melvin's Reverend Runt is a priggish character who cannot be taken seriously.) But the chaplain's speech in *A Clockwork Orange*, coming as it does at the point of Alex's greatest humiliation and focusing attention on what seems to be a central theme of the film, seems to offer no choice but to assent to his words. Kubrick's films are all to some extent concerned with failure of will, with a giving up of active participation in events and allowing those events to take control. *A Clockwork Orange* goes beyond this to indicate the threat of a direct manipulation of the will of one individual by others (no superhuman powers here, only the state). But, seen objectively, Alex has a will that needs manipulation. He is a killer, with no rationale for his acts but the general decadence of the society he lives in. We are faced, finally, with an old problem. No alternatives seem to be offered. If a society exists in which humans are reduced to passive, quasi-erotic squalor, if the state exists only to manipulate the wills of its semiconscious members, then certainly any one with initiative and some vitality, even if that vitality is directed toward death, must be appreciated. The viewer can only be trapped by the cyclic nature of the film as much as its characters are, or understand that notions of freedom and individual expression are not part of nature but of culture, born of the results of centuries of consensus and the discourses of power.

This becomes clearer if we attend carefully to the end of the film. Alex, programmed to react violently against violence, is deprogrammed to be violent again in political service to the opponents of the party of the crazy writer, Mr. Alexander. "He was a menace, we put him away . . . ," the minister tells Alex, spoon-feeding his new charge, who, like a baby bird, takes his nourishment and absorbs the minister's desire to do his bidding. As a final reward, the minister has wheeled in an enormous pair of loudspeakers, blasting the end of Alex's beloved Ninth Symphony. Alex goes into a sexual fantasy, making love in the snow while bystanders in Edwardian costumes applaud. His last words reverberate through the film and are absolutely chilling. "I was cured, all right." As the credits roll, Gene Kelly sings "Singin' in the Rain," that sweet song that Alex sang while raping Mr. Alexander's wife. Alex's last words reverberate not only through *A Clockwork Orange* but back to *Dr. Strangelove*. There, too, a crippled force of destruction is cured, all right, as Strangelove rises from his wheelchair and exults, "Mein Fuhrer, I can walk!" Instead of "Singin' in the Rain," his words are followed by a favorite British World War II song, "We'll Meet Again," as atomic bombs destroy the world. Both films are about power and the state. *Strangelove* announces its satire through the mechanical operations of its characters. *A Clockwork Orange* occults its critique by allowing us to assume that one of its characters can escape institutional mechanisms, indeed demonstrate their oppressiveness, by acting out violent fantasies. In neither case do any one of the characters have or see the entire context of the clockworks whose mechanism propels them into rebirths of destruction.

A *Clockwork Orange*, like its distant cousin, Stone's *Natural Born Killers*, is an act of provocation. Both films reveal how easily a spectator can submit and be made to react favorably to images of violence while simultaneously generating a critique of that response. "It's funny," says Alex, as he relates his feelings during the Ludovico treatment, during which he is conditioned against violence by being sickened as he watches violent images, "how the colors of the real world only seem really real when you viddy them on the screen." Kubrick seems to ask for assent to the ramifications of this statement. Whatever he may be saying about the brutality of "civilization," he seems at the same time to want to demonstrate everyone's willingness to accept and even enjoy the representations of that brutality that are more powerfully "real" than anything seen in the "real" world. Once again, he was prophetic. The film was attacked in England by a judge who called it "an evil in itself," as some twenty-five years later, presidential hopeful Bob Dole situated *Natural Born Killers* among "the nightmares of depravity" produced by Hollywood. Fearful of lawsuits because of copycat crimes, Kubrick and Warner Brothers immediately pulled *A Clockwork Orange* from British distribution and continued fighting its exhibition through the nineties, when they lost a suit that attempted to prevent British television from showing a documentary that used a great deal of its footage.[33]

Ironies abound here, and irony is a very difficult proposition, because it demands a multiplicity of points of view and a willingness to yield to the complexities of the ways meaning is produced. Even a master ironist like Kubrick will fold when his film threatens to bring the law down on him. How then should he expect his audience to understand the complex ironies of his film, especially as they are slid behind such a spectacular surface?

Perhaps *A Clockwork Orange* tries too much and ultimately does not allow the viewer to escape the initial power and attraction of its images and main character, even their deviousness. Maybe he believed his audience might deal with its complexity. As if in reaction to this problem and confusion, Kubrick made *Barry Lyndon*, a film that insists its audience remain distant and contemplative, observant and barely involved. *Barry Lyndon* is an even more leisurely and meditative narrative than *2001*. Slow, almost static, its images are of such painterly beauty that they seem to call for admiration as composed objects, apart from their narrative function. The images are peopled with characters whose actions and motives appear irrelevant to contemporary concerns. There is none of the kinetic frenzy and the perplexities of modernity of *A Clockwork Orange*, no invitation to admire individuals or assent to specific acts, no trappings, however artificial, of the contemporary world in that other slow-paced film of Kubrick's, *Eyes Wide Shut*. The film demands only attentiveness and cooperation from the viewer, demands it more than any of Kubrick's preceding films. More, indeed, than almost any film by an American director one can think of.

Popular critics were incapable of dealing with the film, for it denied so many of the filmic conventions they could securely respond to. "Story" or "plot" is minimal; the emotional reactions it calls forth are small and unclear; the characters do not exist as psychological entities. But it is pretty; more than one critic offered the comment that its images belonged in a museum (tantamount to saying the film was dead). The popular audience fared little better. Because of critical response the film got poor distribution, and many of those who did see it were no doubt bored or baffled.

In attempting to account for popular critical response to a film, we often learn more about audience expectations than we do about the film itself. The reaction to *Barry Lyndon* was a reaction less to what that film is than to what it is not. Because it does not meet demands for action, clear motivation of characters, straightforward development of story in simple, dramatic terms and with a functional, unobtrusive style, it sets itself at odds with the traditions of American commercial filmmaking. Certainly *2001* suffers from these same "faults," yet it had a considerable popular success. The difference, of course, lies in the immediacy of its images, their technical fascination, and, finally, the awe created by its attractive mystical connotations. *2001* is a terrified celebration of technology and an elegy to the end of man, mitigated by the suggestion of rebirth that ends the film. *Barry Lyndon* is an elegy that is unmitigated and, rather than fantasize a future, it only evokes a past. The only technology it celebrates is that which makes its own cinematic construction possible: a refined use of the zoom lens, images lit only by candlelight. But the energy and skill of the film's construction are played against the sadness and loss that the film generates. Kubrick structures a decline of vitality and a loss of individual power more severe and final than in any of his other films. At the end of *Barry Lyndon* a date is observed on a check: 1789, the year of the French Revolution. But there is no suggestion that a change in society, a change in the rituals of social behavior, is possible. Kubrick leaves the viewer with an impression of permanent passivity and entrapment. In a peculiar way, *Barry Lyndon* can be seen as Kubrick's first film, setting up historical patterns of obsession and impotence, ritual and retreat, that inform all his other work. It is a ceremony of loneliness, and I wonder if the sadness it evokes is as responsible for its unpopularity as its unconventional form.

The pictorial aspect of that form continually calls for admiration. But the admiration is tempered by the reminders that its beauty is cold and the characters who dwell within the images are suffering from the coldness and the very perfection of form and formality that is, visually, so admirable. Formal beauty should give pleasure; Kubrick makes it communicate sadness. The film's images become charged with feelings of loss, an effect enhanced by the dirge-like quality of much of its music. The more the viewer tries to come to terms with what is seen and felt, the more distance and isolation are forced on him.[34]

This dialectic of attraction and distance is carefully structured by the way the images are composed and the way the narrative progresses. By creating compositions that entice and then distance the viewer, Kubrick generates a frustration and a longing that parallels the experience of the character of Barry Lyndon (Ryan O'Neal) himself, who wishes to enter the world of grand society and is rendered impotent by its formal rituals, which are unable to accommodate his vitality. A major compositional strategy in the first part of the film exemplifies this process. Kubrick will begin with a fairly close shot of one or more individuals and then very slowly zoom back until these individuals become part of a much larger composition, engulfed by the natural world that surrounds them. This achieves a number of results. The repetition of the slow reverse zoom creates a steady, somber rhythm. Visually, it tends to reduce the importance of individuals by placing them within a greater natural design.[35] By doing this within the boundaries of a single shot, rather than by cutting, Kubrick achieves an effect of continual change of perspective, point of view, and subjectivity. A shot that begins close to human figures who, by all the rights of cinematic and

152

cultural convention, should be observed and attended to, and then moves away from them, forcing a realignment of the viewing subject and the subject viewed, disturbs balance and relationship. Alan Spiegel writes:

> ... the motion of the camera begins in drama and ends in spectacle, starts off with an action and finishes with a design, converts human value to aesthetic value and a utilitarian image into a self-reflexive image.... Characters and situations are taken away from us even in the midst of their happening; the camera withdraws from that to which we would cleave close—and in this respect, our sorrow is collateral to Barry's: we too can never get what we want or keep what we get, and the motion of the camera is a measure of our bereavement.[36]

153

This reading may be a bit too literal. A viewer cannot identify with a camera movement any more than he or she can with Barry himself. One can, however, be provoked into observing and, perhaps, responding to correspondences, to the frustration experienced when the film refuses to yield what is expected and to Barry's frustration (and destruction) in a world that refuses to yield to his desires. The film's continual play with subjectivity and positioning of the viewing subject provokes unease. The viewer is removed from proximity to the figure. The figure is denied proximity to his own satisfaction. On all levels, desire is squelched.

Another sequence of shots in the film fulfills in a different manner the same function as the reverse zoom. These shots are static and they take place indoors. These are the sequences lit only by candlelight, which are at first very warm and intimate: Barry and Captain Grogan, the only friend he will ever have, talk in a dark candlelit tent about Barry's mother and about the ruse played on him in the duel with Captain Quinn; Barry and the German girl he meets after his desertion talk of their love in a dark farmhouse made intimate by the golden yellow candlelight and the girl's baby, prominent in the composition and foreshadowing Barry's own child, whom he will love to his own destruction. But the candlelit sequences soon begin to embrace larger numbers of people, in gambling halls and at banquets, where the yellow light and hideous makeup create a vision of the dead come to life. With the exception of one late sequence, in which Barry, his mother, and his son, Bryan, share a moment of intimacy and warmth, the candlelit shots diminish the human figure as they progress. They replace intimacy with distance, the human with the inhuman, or, more disturbing in these images, with the human made to look like death.

The candlelit sequences and the reverse zoom shots are only two of the compositional and structural devices used throughout the film that draw attention to themselves and force a reconsideration of the conventional proximity of viewing and narrative subjects. To an even greater extent than in his previous films, Kubrick structures both images and narrative with deliberateness and certainty, leaving the viewer much space to observe and contemplate, but at the same time guiding this observation, commenting on what is seen, forcing attention to how things are seen. By means of cutting, for example, and by playing on proximity and distance through montage, Kubrick can indicate Barry's precise social and emotional situation at a given moment. When Barry's banishment from polite society is complete, he is observed in a closeup with Bryan, reading—a quiet, domestic, and tranquil shot. Immediately Kubrick cuts to an extreme long shot of the same scene so that the two figures appear dwarfed under a painting in an enormous room, isolated and barren. The effect is more striking than would have been achieved by zooming back from the figures to show their isolation in a large space. The rapid change isolates them and isolates the viewer from them, reasserting the refusal, throughout the film, to permit any intimacy with the characters, to give any hope that isolation can be overcome.

In a potentially touching sequence, where Barry attempts a reconciliation with his wife, Kubrick takes pains to minimize emotional content. Lady Lyndon (Marisa Berenson) sits almost naked in a tub, one of those curious, upright affairs, similar to the tub in which Marat sits in David's famous late eighteenth-century painting. As Barry stands over her, behind and between them can be seen a painting of a man kneeling before a lady. As the sequence continues, Barry apologizes to Lady Lyndon for his indiscretions and assumes a kneeling position just like the man in the painting. There follows a closeup of the two kissing, which is immediately followed by a long shot of the castle in which they live (variations of this shot occur frequently in the latter part of the film, acting as punctuation, reinforcing the fractures of continuity suffered by the character and the perception of him). Everything in the sequence—the strange appearance of Lady Lyndon, naked in the tub, the action of the characters echoed in the painting, the cutting into the embrace by the shot of the castle—forbids easy emotional response but assures attention and an awareness of the rigidity of the characters' lives.

Paintings are a primary means by which Kubrick creates these structures. Paintings appear throughout the film, and the film as a whole is made of painterly compositions. This phenomenon climaxes an almost obsessive concern throughout Kubrick's major work. Late seventeenth- and early eighteenth-century paintings decorate the chateau in *Paths of Glory*. Humbert Humbert shoots Quilty through an eighteenth-century portrait in *Lolita*. A rococo landscape hangs over the interior of the derelict casino where two gangs fight in *A Clockwork Orange*, and a tapestry hangs over Mr. Alexander and his friends when they torment Alex later in the film. In each instance, the camera focuses on the painting and then moves down to pick up the action, the first one violent, the second sadistic (in the first instance, the painting appears immediately after one violent act and before another). The Jupiter room in *2001* is decorated with art similar to that in *Paths of Glory* and is, in fact, a fluorescent-lit, antiseptic parody of the chateau in the earlier film. A curious combination of both appears in *Barry Lyndon* in the enormous room in which Barry discovers the Chevalier of Balibari (Patrick Magee). Just as Bowman had been observed in the earlier film, the chevalier is seen from behind, at a table, eating in grand solitude, in an enormous rococo room. A reverse shot reveals his grotesque makeup face.[37]

In all instances, Kubrick uses paintings for ironic juxtaposition. The quiet, civilized artifice of late seventeenth- and early eighteenth-century French art embodies a code of polite behavior in sharp contradiction to the brutal codes of military order and justice played out in *Paths of Glory*. The pastoral landscape in *A Clockwork Orange* is in complete contrast to the rubble in which the gangs fight. The elegant seventeenth-century chamber-cum-motel room-cum-fish tank in which Bowman moves from youth to old age in *2001* is a parody of images of civilization that might be drawn by a computer from the humdrum mind of an astronaut. The contemporary paintings that hang in the rooms of *Eyes Wide Shut* act as decorations, expressing taste divorced from feeling—much like the characters themselves. The dream of order and politeness, the reality of brutality and manipulation and death: these antinomies plague Kubrick to the point where in *Barry Lyndon* he attempts to enter the paintings themselves and, rather than merely use them as ironic visual counterpoint (as he uses music in *2001* and *A Clockwork Orange* as ironic aural counterpoint), he will pierce these ritual signs of order and civility to discover other rituals, to discover the dynamics of a civilization whose rigid façade on canvas reveals other rigid and brutal façades when these canvases are set in motion.

Kubrick is not making paintings come alive (like those opening sequences of some films in which a sketch or painting under the credits proceeds to dissolve into the "real" scene as the film begins). He is using a painterly aesthetic to set his characters within a design, to recreate the forms

155

and formalities—the rituals—of the past *as* rituals and to keep the viewer continually aware of the external and internal rigidities of the images. "Each image," writes Alan Spiegel, "seals off direct access to its content by converting content into an object of formal admiration; the formalism, that is, insures the image as both visual enticement and proof against further intimacy."[38] I would modify this in one important way: the images do not convert content into form—form always precedes content. Rather, the images in *Barry Lyndon*, these forms of light and color, human figures, natural landscapes, architectural environments, resist yielding a content. They point more to themselves than they do to any expected narrative event. Kubrick is not making paintings come alive; he is playing the viewer's perceptual expectations of painting against those of cinema. One comes to painting to observe static design. One comes to film prepared to see motion, drama, and narrative. *Barry Lyndon* continually threatens to deny drama and narrative by emphasizing rigid composition and then threatens rigid composition with movement and narrative. In all instances expectations are stymied. The conventions of eighteenth-century painting are reversed: instead of order and politeness, there are ugliness and brutality. The conventions of contemporary American cinema are reversed: instead of action and a clever story, there are static, painterly images that require as much or more attention than any story they might be telling. Once again, the viewer is not permitted complete satisfaction of aesthetic or emotional desire. And, as if this were not enough, Kubrick adds yet another element that prevents easy access to the characters and their world: a narrator whose words may or may not be trusted.

Kubrick has always favored voice-over narration. The temporal jigsaw puzzle of *The Killing* is fitted together by a narrator. Humbert Humbert narrates *Lolita*, and a narrator gives the historical setting at the beginning of *Paths of Glory*. In *Dr. Strangelove* a voice tells us about the doomsday machine and explains the SAC system. *2001* replaces narration with titles at the beginning of each section, as does *The Shining*, where the titles give days and times in such minute profusion that they become parodic and cease referring to any usable meaning within the narrative. In *A Clockwork Orange*, Alex's voice reflects on what is being seen and what he is feeling. Joker comments sporadically on events and his reactions in *Full Metal Jacket*. *Eyes Wide Shut* has no voice-over, but Tom Cruise's Bill repeats back almost everything that's said to him in the form of a question. This creates something like an internal voice-over, a device that allows the character to reveal, through his language, his insecurity and failing subjectivity.

In most instances, the voice-over is a device of convenience, a neutral point in the discourse useful to keep the plot from diverting attention from mise-en-scène. The voice-over creates a mock serious tone in *Dr. Strangelove* and a mock-tough, sometimes sentimental one in *Full Metal Jacket*, but only in *A Clockwork Orange* is this voice an integral part of the discourse, helping to form it and mold the viewer's attitude toward the central character, to whom the voice belongs. Alex's voice, with its verbal vitality, its delight in its speaker's exploits, its self-pity and final triumph, both seals viewer sympathies and causes fright at the same time. The narrator in *Barry Lyndon* is a friendly, somewhat detached, always calm and completely anonymous voice (though it is, of course, the voice of Michael Hordern, immediately recognizable to anyone familiar with British film) that provides a variety of services. Discussing what has happened and what will happen, it speaks also of what is happening and what the characters are feeling. The narrator also talks of things not seen that would remain unknown had he not mentioned them. In short, the narrator of *Barry Lyndon* is part of another discourse, the teller of another tale, often parallel to the narrative seen on the screen, though as often denying what is seen or telling a great deal more that contradicts what is seen.

Sometimes, particularly in the battle sequences, the narrator will provide a moral and political perspective absent from the visual and dramatic narrative. He may merely be sadly cynical: "Though this encounter is not recorded in any history books," he says of the absurd and suicidal march of British troops into stationary French lines, "it was memorable enough to those who took part." Memorable indeed, for in this battle Barry loses his friend, Captain Grogan. When we later see the troops marching by a burning building, and as Barry, carrying a goat, walks into a closeup, the narrator, leaping far beyond the immediate implications of the scene, states, "Gentlemen may talk of the Age of Chivalry, but remember the plowmen, poachers, and pickpockets whom they lead. It is with these sad instruments that your great warriors and kings have been doing their murderous work in the world." There is a cut to a shot of Barry carrying water pails, at which point the narrator comments on Barry's low circumstances, though he assures us that he is fated for greater things. Just prior to his dissertation on warriors and kings, the narrator, over a shot of Barry standing by a fire, has commented on Barry's desire to escape the army. This brief series of images and voice-over comments manages to create three different narrative directions, one in the visuals, two in the narration. On the screen are images of Barry thoughtful by the fire and the voice-over supplies something presumably close to his thoughts—he wants to desert. The images then show him involved in the low, humdrum life of a soldier, at which point the narrator takes off on his own speculations about the politics and meanness of war, comments almost more appropriate to *Paths of Glory* than to what is going on here (clearly Barry is not a plowman, poacher, or pickpocket, those "sad instruments" who the narrator says fight the wars). The visual content remains the same until, having disburdened himself of his sadness over war's inhumanity, the narrator comments on Barry's particular state and assures us it will change, due to accidental circumstances. In the next sequence, Barry steals the uniform of one of the two homosexual soldiers bathing in the river—two characters, who, despite demonstrating some stereotypes of movie homosexuals, express a devotion to each other unlike any of the straight characters in the film—and is off to the better things the narrator has promised. Barry's life as a soldier and his unhappiness with it; the narrator's philosophy of war; the narrator's assurance that Barry will go on to other things—none of these elements is contradictory. They simply provide the viewer with more information than is seen or heard within the film itself at this point. Most of all, they remove any immediate uncertainties as to where the narrative is going. Barry will get away from the army (though, as it turns out, only temporarily) and will do well in life (but again only temporarily).

The narrator can present material that contradicts the visual narrative. He undercuts Barry's love affair with the German peasant girl by explaining, in elegant and humorous language, that she is little more than a whore. He tells of the horrible recruitment of children by the Prussian army and how Frederick the Great stoops to kidnapping "to keep supplied those brilliant regiments of his with food for powder." The visuals accompanying this condemnation show only young soldiers marching. As he talks of the deplorable sadism, mutilation, and murder that go on among the ranks, Barry is seen leading a soldier through the gauntlet—unpleasant enough, but hardly the visual equal to the words. As Barry marches with Prussian troops, the narrator says: "Thus Barry fell into the very worst of courses and company, and was soon very far advanced in the science of every kind of misconduct." In the following scenes, Barry engages in battle, saves the life of General Potzdorf (who first discovers his desertion and later becomes his protector). Except for the brief gauntlet scene, there is no visual evidence of Barry's being anything but a proper soldier. Perhaps, as one writer suggests, Kubrick was so sensitive to the criticism of violence in *A Clockwork Orange* that he did not film sequences that would bear out the narrator's words. Perhaps such scenes would have been opposed to the film's design. The violence that is shown—a boxing match, the battles, the various duels—is ceremonial and distanced.[39] The one major explosion of violence, Barry's attack on his stepson, Lord Bullingdon, and the one time Barry is the subject of violence, in the duel with Bullingdon, are startling and effective because they are unusual in their immediacy and their expression of emotional and physical pain.

The distance between the narrative offered in voice-over and the narrative offered in the visuals is as specifically determined as the differences in perspective offered by the zoom shots. The viewer is forced to take a multiple view—in this case of Barry the vicious wretch spoken about by the narrator and Barry the sad, incompetent man of feeling seen in the main narrative. The result is a film somewhat reminiscent of *Citizen Kane*. In Welles's film, different perspectives, different points of view of an individual, some friendly, some adverse, conflict with the viewer's own perception of a powerful man racked with loneliness and an inability to express his passion appropriately. *Kane* confronts the viewer with at least five distinct personalities whose points of view interlock to create the narrative. In *Barry Lyndon* there is only the viewer's perception, fractured and variously redirected by the structure of the film. The contradictions set up by the narrator and the obstacles to emotional involvement set up by the composition and design of the images keep, curiously, forcing attention away from the film and into a confrontation with the perceptions and attitudes themselves. Kubrick is not playing the games he played in *A Clockwork Orange*, where the viewer is requested to identify with a brutal killer. If Barry is vicious and dissolute, there is only someone's word for it; no visual proof is offered. Indeed no proof is offered that validates much of Barry's state of mind or suffering. He is unpleasant to his wife for a time: riding in a coach, she asks him not to smoke. He responds by blowing smoke in her face. The narrator comments that Lady Lyndon occupied a place "not very much more important than the elegant carpets and pictures which would form the pleasant background of his existence." Later Lady Lyndon sees him kissing Bryan's nurse; he takes up with whores. But Barry makes up with his wife, and the narrator never mentions whether his behavior is any different from that of any other male member of the society Barry wants to be part of, or whether his parvenu status makes his behavior the more odious. Once more there is no satisfactory accounting, within the visual narrative of the film, for the contradictory and condemnatory information given by the narrator. The ceremonials the film is about and the ceremony that the film *is* prevent full assent to anything said and to many things shown.

The result of all of this, as I said earlier, is to make a viewer's emotional situation vis-à-vis the film parallel to the emotional situation of Barry Lyndon, who cannot enter the rich, decaying world he so craves and whose moments of emotional satisfaction are undone even before they are finished. After Barry, provoked beyond endurance, beats Bullingdon in front of a proper gathering of gentlefolk and is properly ostracized from their proper company, there are gentle scenes of Barry and Bryan playing— polite but happy family scenes. Over these are the sad melody of the Handel *Sarabande* and the voice of the narrator:

> Barry had his faults [a more moderate statement than the earlier reference to his viciousness and depravity], but no man could say of him that he was not a good and tender father. He loved his son with a blind partiality. He denied him nothing. It is impossible to convey what high hope he had for the boy and how he indulged in a thousand fond anticipations as to his future success and figure in the world. But fate had determined that he should leave none of his race behind him, and that he should finish his life poor, lonely, and childless.

The narrator undercuts the content of the visuals (the images of domestic pleasure) and removes any doubt about the outcome of the narrative. Only the details of narrative closure are then needed to be supplied. Bryan dies from a fall from his horse, the horse Barry gave him that the child rode with an enthusiasm that proved to be his undoing, as did Barry's own enthusiasm in his undertakings. Bryan's deathbed sequence is the most sentimental thing Kubrick has ever filmed; it momentarily breaks the film's distance and, because its sentimentality so jars with the rest, viewing it is uncomfortable. Alan Spiegel condemns Kubrick for the conventionality of this sequence, as others have condemned him for not having more sequences like it in his films.[40] But the sequence does work within the structure of fragmented points of view I have been discussing. Suddenly the viewer is permitted direct emotional engagement, in the conventional form of melodramatic representation, and just as suddenly the rigid formal structure of the film returns. Once again easy emotional access or unquestioning identification with the character is disallowed immediately following its indulgence.

Soon after Bryan's death comes the duel between Barry and Bullingdon, a violent sequence that is at the same time restrained and structured to contain its highly emotional content. The sequence is set within an abandoned building (possibly a church), the characters isolated against walls—Bullingdon is composed so that the walls are clearly defined behind him; Barry is shot with a telephoto lens, similar to the way Dax is photographed during the execution sequence in *Paths of Glory*, so that he is slightly removed from the action, isolated both in it and from it. The sequence emphasizes Barry's aloneness more than any other in the film, trapping him in a final, perfectly ordered, unimpassioned ritual of proper, murderous conduct. Barry, as always, tries to bring some humanity to it, firing into the ground so as not to kill Bullingdon. But, as in every other instance when Barry attempts to humanize his world, he suffers for it. Bullingdon may be a revolting coward, but, when given his chance, he shoots his stepfather, takes advantage of weakness, and triumphs. The symmetry of loss is set: at the beginning of the film, the narrator told us—and we see—that Barry's father died in a duel. Early on, Barry duels with the cowardly Captain Quinn for the woman he thinks he loves. Not knowing the duel is faked—by his beloved's family who want Quinn's fortune—Barry thinks he has shot his opponent and is sent from his home. In the first of those happy family scenes referred to earlier, Barry and Bryan play at dueling, thereby foreshadowing the serious duel with Bullingdon. In that final duel, he does ceremonial battle with his cowardly and vicious stepson whom he does not shoot but is himself shot and sent from his home.[41]

No matter what Barry attempts, he loses and is isolated. No matter what attempts the viewer makes to join emotional ranks with the film, he or she loses and is isolated, forced into a contemplative stance before images and actions that permit only observation; settings and characters that are culturally distant; and an aura of sadness, painful to confront in the character of Barry Lyndon, more painful to confront in oneself. In the film's penultimate sequence, Barry emerges from the inn where he and his mother have been sent after the duel. His leg has been amputated. He hobbles to the coach, the voice-over narrator tells us of his indifferent future, and Kubrick freezes the frame: the beaten, diminished man is literally stopped in his tracks.

The expression of emotionless isolation may be the formal triumph of the film, but it raises a question about *Barry Lyndon* and about Kubrick's work in general. As much as the formal structures of his films force a coming to terms with conventional expectations and engage the viewer in an active role determining narrative development and meaning, the result of the work is a reinforcement of the audience's own passivity and impotence. Let

■
■
▪

me put it another way: struggling to emerge from the discussions of *Barry Lyndon*, and, to a lesser degree, of *Dr. Strangelove* and *2001*, is the adjective "Brechtian." The confrontation these films provoke between their structure and meaning and the viewer's perception of them, the way they insist on a reconsideration of how one understands and responds to cinematic narratives and, subsequently, to what those narratives relate, the way they inhibit stock emotional responses, would seem to indicate a working out of the Brechtian principles of distancing, of substituting intellectual for emotional response, of turning narrative into a process involving under- standing, rather than a product demanding a predetermined reaction. Films like *Paths of Glory*, *Dr. Strangelove*, *2001*, *A Clockwork Orange* separate the viewer from ideological assumptions and represent, with some objectivity, the forms and images of our culture that are usually taken for granted. The corporate names that adorn the space station in *2001* and that film's entire treatment of technology allow an informed discomfort with any un- questioning attitudes toward the myth of progress and the ideological given of scientific and corporate hegemony (no matter that the corporate names may likely represent contributors to the financing of *2001*, their presence in the new realm of the future remains a source of unease). *A Clockwork Orange* questions representations of violence and audience response to them, making the representations and their narrative inviting, while at the same time exposing the ease with which those images invite the viewer. More profoundly than *A Clockwork Orange*, *Barry Lyndon* examines the easy clichés of "individual freedom" and societal necessities. Barry, like Alex, suffers from an attempt to exert his own vitality within a social structure too rigid to support it.[42] *Barry Lyndon*, however, extends less cynicism and more sad contemplation. One of Kubrick's most anti-Fordian films, it represents the domestic unit as a composition not of security and comfort but of rigid economic ceremony, between whose members checks pass rather than affection.[43] The most conventional narrative propositions of American film and its culture—the family as sacred unit of security and comfort—are questioned, given a material context, and scrubbed of ideological detritus.

The collapse of affection and the turning of the domestic unit into a threat are the subjects of the film that follows *Barry Lyndon*. *The Shining*, like *A Clockwork Orange*, makes contemplation of its complex ideas about societal and psychological structures difficult. As a horror film, it invites profound viewer engagement while, as a parody of the horror film and a transference of attention from the family in horrific circumstances to the horror of the family, it denies or at least threatens that engagement at the same time. I suggested earlier that *The Shining* exists on a number of levels. Loud, broad, and—on an immediate level at least—quite explicit, it stands as a response to the meditative solemnity of *Barry Lyndon* (much as the dynamic, violent *Clockwork Orange* stands over and against the contemplative *2001*). The film assaults the audience with image and sound, as if mocking that audience's unwillingness to respond to the previous work. In fact one can read an author/audience allegory within *The Shining*, seeing the character of Wendy as the audience and Jack Torrance as the filmmaker, assaulting her because she will not respond as he wants her to. With this reading, Kubrick can be seen trying to distance himself from his own Brechtian role, denying the rational composure he usually creates and instead battering his audience with image and sound to make its members react—a role he assumes again, with even greater uncertainty, in *Full Metal Jacket*.

Audience reaction is, of course, a primary signifier of the horror genre. A measure of a horror film's success is the amount of controlled fright that can be generated in its spectators. To this end, Kubrick exaggerates his usual stylistics. The wide-angle lens and the moving camera (made even more fluid here by means of the Steadicam device) are used more broadly than in the previous films. Distortion of mise-en-scène, the purposive, almost obsessive movements through the corridors of the Overlook Hotel, suggest—as such stylistic devices do in many horror films—the point of view of an Other, of some monstrous, destructive force that reigns and, in Jack's case, takes over the characters. Shock cuts, inserts of bizarre characters and events meant to represent Danny's visions and Jack's own hallucinations of horrible occurrences past, present, and future, build elements of fear and expectation. But these devices operate reflexively, forcing recognition of them as parts of the horror film's stylistic baggage.

In the final analysis, Kubrick refuses, as always, to allow the viewer an unmediated fall into the fictive world he creates. The film provokes no real terror, there is no manipulation of audience into an irrational reaction to irrational events. Precisely because the structure of the film is so broad as to be almost parodic, and the acting of Jack Nicholson and Shelley Duvall exaggerated to the point where they threaten to become abstract commentaries on the conventional figures of the horror film psychotic and his intended victim, the whole text keeps moving beyond the expectations it sets up. But, were it only a parody of the genre, it would rank as a minor effort on Kubrick's part (although certainly the best of the many Stephen

King adaptations that appeared during the early eighties and anticipating the less interesting postmodern reflections of the genre—*Scream, I Know What You Did Last Summer, The Faculty*—made for teenagers in the nineties). Because it does finally go beyond its own parody to an investigation of the madness and violence of the family, *The Shining* becomes not only an important part of Kubrick's work but a major extension of some of his ideas.

In the vastnesses of their fears and obsessions, Kubrick's male characters extend the effects of their oppression and repression to everything and everyone they contact. Their inability to act on the world they create, the world that finally destroys them, forces them to enact violence on each other and very often, as in *Lolita, A Clockwork Orange,* to an extent in *Barry Lyndon,* and, though the circumstances are extreme, in *Full Metal Jacket,* on women. In *Eyes Wide Shut* the inability to act so reduces the central character that the violence he is responsible for is done second hand, the fault, conceivably, of his own impotent imaginings. *The Shining* concentrates on this particular kind of violence and examines some of its larger ideological ramifications (an examination muffled in *Full Metal Jacket,* where the structures of order are hidden and women figure as sexual objects, references of ridicule, and the mysterious, finally pitiable, embodiment of the unknowable enemy, and occulted into the characters' unconscious in *Eyes Wide Shut*). Perhaps because a woman, Diane Johnson, co-scripted the film with Kubrick, *The Shining* goes further than the other work in foregrounding the function of patriarchy in Kubrick's structure of defeat, defining it within the context of the family and the explosion of violence inherent within the repression that so often constitutes the family unit. The film, finally, is indeed a horror show about possession, breakdown, and madness, but not of the supernatural kind. Jack Torrance is possessed by his own terror and hatred of the inhibitions placed on him by patriarchal imperatives. His domesticating restraints break down, and he attempts to live out a male fantasy of the destruction of the wife and child he is supposed to love and protect.[44]

Like all of Kubrick's men, Jack is trapped. Within the generic elements of the film's plot, he is trapped by the hotel and the supernatural remnants of its past (a former caretaker killed his own wife and family). Within the hermeneutic of the text, he is trapped by an obligation to be father and husband that he finds untenable. He imprisons himself and his family in the hotel for a winter, in a space so huge and labyrinthine that it engulfs them all while intensifying their already unbearable proximity. Unable to break out, like all of Kubrick's characters, he seals the trap so tightly that it collapses and destroys him.

He desperately attempts to retain his dominance, screaming and cursing at his wife, demanding isolation from her and his child with the excuse that he must be left alone to write. He attempts to maintain control by the very power of the patriarchal gaze. Wendy and Danny walk through the enormous hedge maze outside the hotel. The camera follows them, finally tracking in behind them in a threatening gesture. At the end of this movement the shot dissolves to the back of Jack who, instead of writing, is playing handball against the walls of the great room. Over these two scenes a section of Bartók's *Music for Strings, Percussion, and Celesta* is playing— a piece whose tonalities and rhythms have influenced the scores of many horror films. In one of his more spectacular matches of music and image, Kubrick times Jack's stroke of the handball against the wall to coincide precisely with a loud chord in the Bartók piece. The effect is startling, demanding attention not only to the scene, but to the very mechanics of how visuals and sound are matched to create it. Jack stops playing his game and goes over to a model of the hedge maze in the room. As he looks, the camera assumes his point of view almost ninety degrees over the model, zooming down slowly into it. Wendy and Danny's voices are heard, and their figures suddenly become visible in the maze's center. The two spaces— the model and the actual maze—merge under the controlling gaze of the father, who attempts to exercise godlike power over his family until that power makes him mad.[45]

In effect, Jack himself is the subject of that gaze, for it turns inward and he becomes its victim. In the process, he runs through other masculine roles. In the beginning, he is the mature provider. We learn that he is a drunk and broke his son's arm. At one point, after he has turned violent, Wendy protects herself and her child by beating Jack with a baseball bat and locking him in a storeroom. To gain her sympathy, he whines like a small child needing his mother's protection: "Wendy, baby, I think you hurt my head real bad. I'm dizzy. I need a doctor. . . . Honey, don't leave me in here." Before his death, he comes back as a demonic parody of the dutiful husband. Released from the storeroom (by the ghost of the previous caretaker who had killed his family), Jack bashes down the door to the family's living quarters with an axe, looks through the wreckage, and announces with murderous glee the words every wife (according to the movies) wants to hear: "Wendy, I'm home!"

At other times, Jack plays out a role that synthesizes all the others, the long-suffering, woman-hating male, the banal figure of the slob at the bar, complaining about how his wife does not understand him. This scene is quite literal, as Jack is entertained by the ghost of the hotel's barman (acted by Joseph Turkel, last seen in a Kubrick film as one of the convicted soldiers in *Paths of Glory*). "White man's burden," Jack complains to Lloyd about his wife—the banality of the language equal to that of *Dr. Strangelove* in exposing its own deadness while implicating Jack in the entire complex of repressiveness (the only person Jack manages to kill, besides himself, is an African American, the hotel cook who shares Danny's extrasensory powers). "Nothing serious, just a little problem with the old sperm bank upstairs," he says. "Women," replies Lloyd the barman, with the full satisfaction of someone newly discovering a useless cliché, "can't live with 'em, can't live without 'em." Jack finds this irresistible: "Words of wisdom, Lloyd. Words of wisdom." And he drinks his phantom drink to this phantom truth. As every besieged husband must, he looks for an affair. Entering the mysterious, forbidden hotel room where his son was just assaulted, he discovers a naked lady in the bath. She comes to him, they embrace, and in his arms she turns into a scabrous, laughing old crone. Facing all the turns of domestic unhappiness and madness, Jack is undone and unforgiven. The isolation he has sought for himself and his family drives him further into the isolation of his own ideological position. None of the promised masculine pleasures is available to him, and he finds patriarchal power untenable, unendurable. "All work and no play make Jack a dull boy." The deeper he falls into his isolation, the more he feels—like that other Jack and his precious bodily fluids in *Dr. Strangelove*—his freedom and vitality drained away. In *Dr. Strangelove*, Kubrick could not resist extrapolating the effects of repression on the entire world. By the time of *The Shining*, the body politic is reduced to the body of the family and then further to the body of the individual.

Jack fails at all his intended tasks. Even his wife, the very figure he attempts to subdue permanently, turns on him and gets the upper hand. On the generic level, Wendy is a stereotyped horror-film character, both the instigator and the object of the monster's rage. But she transcends her generic role, like the Sigourney Weaver character in *Alien*, who protects herself and destroys the monster. Wendy assumes the "masculine" role in a wonderful symbolic gesture. Just before the scene in which she discovers Jack's bizarre manuscript, she sits with Danny watching Road Runner cartoons (Jack is doubtlessly meant to be associated with the hapless Wiley

Coyote). Getting up to go to Jack, she moves to the rear of the frame and silently, so far back in the composition that it takes some attention to notice it, picks up a baseball bat, with which she will beat down her violent husband. The figure oppressed by the phallus steals it in order to control it. Later, when Jack attempts to smash his way into the bathroom where Wendy and Danny are hiding, she stabs his hand with a large knife, an act of displaced castration that further reduces Jack's potency and threat. The patriarch is hurt with his own weapons, diminished by an acting out on him of his own worst fears of losing the symbol of his power. Wendy becomes a prototype for the "final girl" who Carol Clover recognizes as the saving figure in contemporary horror.[46]

But, as we have seen, Kubrick is not a filmmaker who will offer final triumph to anyone, male or—especially—female. During her last run through the hotel, as Jack is pursuing Danny, Wendy is subject to some supernatural apparitions. She sees through a partially open door a bare-assed man in a pig costume apparently engaging in oral sex with a man in a tuxedo. This homosexual intrusion—appearing as a frightening specter—supplies a final inflection on the film's meditation on domestic angst and patriarchal collapse, suggesting that all sexuality is a thing to be feared and loathed. Jack sees women as threatening objects. To fight him and protect herself and her son, Wendy has to acquire phallic authority and power. The result is that all social-sexual structures collapse, not to be re-formed into a new, liberating order, but to the destruction of everyone. The son Jack tries to kill and Wendy protect withdraws into a schizophrenic world of visions and fears. Wendy, first confronted by a psychotic, possessed husband and then by a vision of homosexuality that by popular definition is a threatening denial of ordinary domestic structures, disappears into the snow along with her son, safe from Jack but still not freed from the subordinate position of despised object. Jack is reduced to a howling beast and finally a frozen corpse in the maze, trapped by the very son he wanted to kill and who proved—like everyone else—cleverer than he (and, for good measure, able to conquer Oedipus). Only misogyny and misanthropy survive. The image at the very end of the film, a photo on the hotel wall suggesting Jack had always been there, that this scene of madness and violence is forever acted and reenacted, confirms the notion of an eternity of despair, of oppressive systems created by people who allow those systems to destroy them.

And this is the reason, finally, that Kubrick's work cannot comfortably be labeled as Brechtian. Brecht believed that the work of imagination could

168   activate an audience's political response and insisted that the contemplative distance created by the formal structure of the work of art is only a prelude to the active seeking of cultural and social change. The distancing structures of Kubrick's films offer only a powerful reaffirmation of the inability to go beyond the repressive objects and rituals men and women have erected for themselves. Brecht would use the imagination to reassert subjectivity into active, communal political structures. Kubrick uses his imagination to show that subjectivity is forever destroyed by monolithic, unchanging, dehumanized structures.

    Discussing the troubling passivity inherent in *Paths of Glory* and the nascent sentimentality and avoidance of history and politics in *Full Metal Jacket*, I said that Kubrick was hardly a revolutionary filmmaker. It would be misguided to demand of him that his work affirm viable possibilities of action, engagement, and change since these did not seem to be part of his artistic/political sensibility. More important, when these possibilities are offered in American film, they almost invariably appear in melodramatic, heroic fantasies—the very forms Kubrick eschewed. Even Stone's films, the most overtly political cinema in recent American film, cannot avoid sentimentality or heroism. Nor can the critic demand that Kubrick investigate the culture in the manner of, say, the French director, Jean-Luc Godard or the late German filmmaker, Rainer Werner Fassbinder. Kubrick, despite his geographical distance, was too much an American filmmaker. Godard and Fassbinder were true Brechtians and ironists whose restrained, self-interrogating films allow their characters and the cultural paraphernalia that surround them to do intellectual battle with each other, with an open invitation for the spectator to join. Kubrick was an ironist whose films are both controlled and open, often inviting emotional more than intellectual engagement (even though they are intellectually more rigorous than the work of any other American filmmaker). They are considerably more declarative than are the films of Godard, spectacular as well as inquisitive. Even though they offer room to observe and draw conclusions while attacking the core ideological structures of the culture, the conclusions drawn are always the same. The viewer is invited to watch the spectacle of the characters losing and perhaps considering some ramifications of the loss, but little more. His powerful spectacles and intriguing, intricate formal structures open a cavern of mirrors that reflect either our own worst fears of ourselves or our most passive inclinations to remain as we are.

Epitaph

Life Functions Terminated

S tanley Kubrick died while the third edition of *A Cinema of Loneliness* was
being completed. He had finished his final film, *Eyes Wide Shut*, and so,
of all the filmmakers discussed here, has left a completed body of work. Or
has he? He had been developing a number of projects during the long period since *Full Metal Jacket*, and the one that seemed to engage him most was
an enormous science-fiction film, *A.I.* (Artificial Intelligence), a cyborg,
transmillennial version of the Pinocchio story.[47] Script problems and, no
doubt, funding concerns on the part of Warner Brothers, who had supported Kubrick's work since *A Clockwork Orange*, put the film on hold, and
he turned to a story by the early twentieth-century German writer, Arthur
Schnitzler (some of whose plays were filmed by one of Kubrick's favorite
filmmakers, Max Ophuls). Apparently, the story, *Traumnovelle* (translated
as "Rhapsody: A Dream Novel"), had intrigued him for many years, and
was now to be made, its original script written by Frederic Raphael (who was
uncertain about its cinematic potential) and with two of the most popular
actors Kubrick had ever worked with: Tom Cruise and Nicole Kidman.[48]

The resulting film is very long, very flat. It seems almost inert, and its
editing structure is as conventional as Kubrick has ever done. Yet it has
been my experience that almost all of Kubrick's work requires a number of
viewings, over a number of years, during which whatever richness and
polyvalent meaning they contain become revealed. At the time of this
writing, *Eyes Wide Shut* had only just opened in theaters, and I did not have
the benefit of videotape or DVD to control and observe its particulars. I
have no idea what my response might be during the coming years, though
it did improve on a second viewing. The film's deliberate, flat pace began
to make sense; the careful colors of its otherwise plain mise-en-scène began
to explain the characters more than I had originally thought. But, I am still
left with the sense of a film somewhat incomplete or unthought out, weak
in subject and lacking the usual Kubrickian visual and narrative energy. This
causes a dilemma. To simply list the film's problems, to stress, in negative
ways, its differences from Kubrick's major work of the sixties and seventies,
would not only be unproductive at this point but churlish in the face of a
filmmaker whom I so much admire and who will never respond with
another film.

Therefore, I would like to stake a claim for *Eyes Wide Shut* that it is an unfinished, perhaps unfinishable film. I don't mean to imply that the film Warner Brothers released in July 1999 is not as close to Kubrick's final cut as was possible—trims and dodges were made for ratings purposes, but apparently with his consent. My claim is both personal and judgmental about what happened to Kubrick and his work since the mid-seventies. From *The Shining* on, the much vaunted Kubrick control over his material began to diminish. His mise-en-scène grew somewhat looser, less defining of character and content; narrative structure lost some rigor, and the extraordinary, ironic interaction of all parts of the film became diluted. The cool, contemplative distance he asks the audience to maintain before his films seems to be replaced by his own distance from the material, perhaps reflecting his own self-imposed distance from the ongoing world and a cooling of his imagination.

The lack of vitality in *Eyes Wide Shut* can be accounted for by its subject matter, which concerns the deadness of the male spirit—the disintegration of active engagement in the world—brought about by the terrors of sexual intimacy. The film's diminished irony—that a man so troubled by his wife's sexuality starts on a quest for his own sexual adventures and can consummate none of them—might be due to Kubrick's desire, or need, to make a more straightforward commercial film and not exploit his big stars any more than necessary. Perhaps he was unable or unwilling to enrich the texture of the narrative and the mise-en-scène of this film with the kind of multiple perspective, the well-laid, often secret, jokes that mark his best work.

But there are other ways to approach the film than from the perspective of what it may lack. I would like to stake my claim for *Eyes Wide Shut* within the history of film and place it against *Marnie* (1964)—Alfred Hitchcock's fourth-to-last film. Although some critics have said that *Eyes Wide Shut* resembles Scorsese, I think it more closely resembles Hitchcock, and especially that late film of diminished vitality.

Marnie is also something of an "unfinished" film, an abstract rendering of Hitchcock's formal and thematic preoccupations that foregrounds the thematics of damaged sexuality without generating them out of a complex interaction of character and space. Like *Eyes Wide Shut*, *Marnie* is concerned with sexual repression and expresses a curiosity about how it can be overcome—a curiosity that reveals as little as Kubrick's film and with as little narrative drive. Hitchcock fully indulges his fantasies of the neurotic and repressed woman whose sexuality needs to be resolved by a vigorous and aggressive male (the most modestly aggressive male we have in contemporary film, Sean Connery). Like the best of Hitchcock, patriarchal prerogative does not go unquestioned, and there is no definitive resolution at the film's end. *Marnie* is an anxiety-ridden work, bleak in its assessment of intimacy, sour in its notion of the shifting powers of sexual relationships. *Eyes Wide Shut*, too, is an anxiety-ridden film, an obsessive and—for its central character—unsuccessful quest for ways to maintain male sexual dominance and overcome the upheavals caused by the shifting relationships between genders. In this film, both the male and female characters suffer their repressions: Nicole Kidman's Alice by merely fantasizing them and having nightmares; Tom Cruise's Bill by reimagining her fantasies and attempting to construct and enter his own.

Like *Eyes Wide Shut*, *Marnie* is one of Hitchcock's sparest films. Color, especially yellows and reds, predominate in a highly artificial mise-en-scène. Like Kubrick, Hitchcock was unwilling to work outside a sound stage because he enjoyed the control that the studio environment could help him maintain. The result is that *Marnie*, made in 1964 when most film-makers, under the influence of the French New Wave, were moving to location shooting, uses painted backdrops of streets and rear-screen projections behind Tippi Hedren riding a dummy horse. He was criticized for this, though one of the film's great admirers, Robin Wood, points out that these obviously artificial effects lend to the film the quality of a dream.[49] *Eyes Wide Shut*, based on a "dream story," is also boldly artificial, though not with the imaginative artifice of Kubrick's earlier films. The interiors of lavish New York apartments and mansions—some of them decorated with great curtains of light bulbs and carefully inflected reds and blues—the flat, unfanciful studio mockups of New York streets, which are intercut with second-unit photography of actual streets in New York; the obsessive turn and return of Bill to those streets; the orgy, reminiscent of Hammer horror films with a dash of Ken Russell, of Roger Corman's Poe cycle, and not enough of Pasolini's *Salò or the 120 Days of Sodom*, may indeed suggest a dream. But of what?

Marnie's Freudianism ("You Freud, me Jane," Marnie says mockingly to Mark Rutland, her husband, whose touch she cannot stand and who rapes her) is quite basic: the character has had a destructive childhood sexual experience that has emotionally crippled her. Her bleak, obsessive life is diminished by the remnants of this experience, revealed less by an articulate mise-en-scène than by a great deal of talk, which is more repetitive than enlightening. It is as if Hitchcock wanted or needed to articulate his ideas more verbally than visually, more on the surface of ordinary movie dialogue and action than within the depths of a complex emotional space of madness and sorrow as in *Vertigo*. *Eyes Wide Shut* is also full of talk, often repetitive talk, almost always conventional. This is not quite the conscious banality of the emotionally diminished inhabitants of *2001* but of the emotionally deadened late-nineties new upper-middle class of too much money, too little self-knowledge, too few emotional resources.

Marnie has lost her sexuality because her mother was a whore and, as a child, Marnie killed one of her rough suitors, a sailor. Nicole Kidman's Alice is full of desire, tempted by men, haunted by a memory of being almost seduced by a naval officer, and dreaming of taking part in an orgy to spite her husband. Her desire makes Bill frantic, and his attempt to find his own sexual way makes up the body of the film's narrative, which becomes a kind of bottled picaresque tale. But unlike Kubrick's other picaro, Barry Lyndon, who wanders Europe only to return to be defeated and castrated, Bill goes in circles; he is perhaps responsible for a death and ends up only with the least effective of movie conventions, a warning that he is involved in things he shouldn't be, that he is in over his head. Or perhaps more accurately, inside it.

What is inside Bill's head? There is a suggestion, buried deeply within *Eyes Wide Shut*—as it is in *Marnie*—that the circles traveled round by the central character are drawn by an unacknowledged, perhaps unacknowledgable, homosexuality. As his journey through the streets begins, Bill is attacked by a homophobic gang of teenagers—who sound for all the world like Alex's droogs. At the grindingly heterosexual orgy, two women and two men dance together. On his second round on the streets, Bill questions the clerk of the hotel where Nick Nightingale stayed. Nick is Bill's double, the medical student who didn't make it and whose current life is lived as a vagabond jazz pianist. Nick told Bill where the orgy was taking place. The hotel clerk, played by Alan Cumming, is, like the gay couple in *Barry Lyndon*, one of the more gentle characters in the film. He sweetly attempts to snuggle up to Bill, to show him interest and give him assistance. Bill leaves him as he does all the people he encounters on his depressing quest, willing to accept clues, but not cues. Bill's quest is taken to flee the incongruities of his own sexual response, which is more complex than he can possibly admit or even fantasize.[50]

Marnie ends with a vague promise of movement away from emotional distress, based on a Freudian moment of recollecting the past. The movement, however, is compromised by the children on the painted streets of Baltimore singing a nursery rhyme: "Mother, mother, I am ill/Send for the doctor over the hill." *Eyes Wide Shut* ends with a sequence in a toy shop at Christmas time, filmed with such conventional shot/reverse shot structure that I can only believe that Kubrick was intent in creating an ironically comforting sense of closure. After the revelations of the orgy and the discovery of the mask Bill wore to the orgy lying next to Alice on their bed, they reassume a domestic posture in a domestic place and try to settle their problems. She wants them to return to reality, to forget dreams, to be awake for a long time to come—though she can't agree with Bill's hope that it will be forever. "And you know there is something very important that we need to do as soon as possible," she says. "What's that?" Bill asks. "Fuck," she says. It's a vulgarity with only a little tenderness and understanding and strong residue of aggression, almost as if Kubrick just wanted to bring Bill down to earth with a dirty word and further confront him with his fear of heterosexual intimacy. But the dirty words of *Eyes Wide Shut* don't have the force of misplaced vigor and self-delight of Sgt. Hartman's streams of obscenities in *Full Metal Jacket*. If Alice's wish reveals anything with her earthiness, it's a call to Bill to join her in the real world of marital sexuality, fraught as it may be with jealousy and boredom, inflected with a controlled fantasy life. All of which suggests that it's a sexuality with which Bill, like Marnie, will never be comfortable. A walker in the dream city, a visitor to a joyless orgy, a man who cannot bring himself to the pleasures of a willing and gentle prostitute—who, it turns out, would have infected him with the HIV virus—or a willing if not so gentle wife, Bill, like Marnie or, closer to home, like Jack Torrance in *The Shining*, though without Jack's passion, anger, and madness, remains contained and distracted by the weak fantasies of the repressed.

Bill is Kubrick's last man. No rebirth, ironic or not, no end of the world, no self-sacrificing duel, not frozen endlessly in death, but only within his own tepid imaginings. Without Jack Torrance's passion, Johnny Clay of *The Killing* becomes his closest relative: all high expectations undone by his own depression and a world that is uninterested in them. Like all his characters, Bill is a pathetic remnant of what should be an energetic participant in the world. Most of Kubrick's characters are boxed in by the spaces around them and yield up their subjectivity to them. The spaces around Bill, the bizarre characters that surround him, only confuse him into submission, though it is not clear to what he needs to submit. Perhaps, *unlike* any other Kubrick man, to a simple domesticity.

Bill Harford is Kubrick's last man, and Stanley Kubrick was American film's last auteur. His films remain as powerful reminders that it was once possible

174

for a filmmaker to live a private life, in control of his art, thinking, planning, executing enormous works filled with vision and intellectual passion. *The Killing, Paths of Glory, Dr. Strangelove, 2001, A Clockwork Orange,* and *Barry Lyndon* are films that explore the world through the continually reinvented language of cinema, articulated with the complexity, irony, and awareness of history, politics, and culture that we expect from the strongest of imaginations. The films joke with us but at the same time take us, as well as themselves, very seriously. They are modernist explorations of a universe made frightful by our own bad choices. By showing how these bad choices are made and the prices to be paid, they are both corrosive and corrective. They open our eyes.

THREE

EXPRESSIONS OF THE STREETS
Martin Scorsese

> "I'm God's lonely man."
> —Travis Bickle

A rthur Penn and Stanley Kubrick stand as the first generation of commercial contemporary American cinema's small avant-garde. Both of them began their filmmaking careers in the fifties, just before the French New Wave helped initiate a break in Hollywood's classical style. Martin Scorsese is part of the next group of directors, which include Steven Spielberg, Francis Ford Coppola, George Lucas, John Milius, Brian DePalma, Paul Schrader, and, more recently, Oliver Stone, who came to filmmaking maturity after the French left their mark. That mark contains some complex tracings. Like Godard, Truffaut, Rohmer, Chabrol, and Rivette, the American filmmakers studied film carefully, both formally and informally. Like the French, they spent a great deal of their youth watching film; but instead of turning to critical writing about their subject before actually making films, many of them attended film school, an extraordinary event in the history of American filmmaking.[1]

In most cases, the older generations of American filmmakers learned their craft in the business, and for most of them that learning was intuitive. They watched and they followed what they saw, by and large directing films the way everyone else did. The occasional stylistic and personal inflections that appeared in some of their work grew out of the freedom offered by the studio system, where the volume of films made permitted some little room for individuals to vary the basic patterns. There were exceptions, of course. Foreign directors in Hollywood brought with them some different approaches, though most of these were quickly absorbed into the mainstream. The American triumvirate—Ford, Hitchcock, Welles—articulated major variations and modifications on the classical style. Ford concentrated on a history of the American West, constructing narratives of middle-class triumph over the wilderness out of a set of compositional groupings in which the human figure in Monument Valley or on a homestead in an imagined frontier limned out the opposition of community and desert, lone hero and domestic site. Throughout his career, Hitchcock worked on redesigning the perceptual space of film and viewer, turning mise-en-scène into a fearful place of uncertain sight where the fragile surety of bourgeois perception was dissolved. Welles's filmmaking career was an ongoing process of remodeling conventions of shot composition and the spatial relationships within the shot, all put in the service of an interrogation of the thematics of power. Each of these filmmakers was acutely conscious and thoughtful about the construction of film narratives. Ford and Hitchcock managed to thrive within the studio system. Welles did not.

Many of the new filmmakers learned about the history of film and the techniques of its construction outside of the studio production system, a process that offered the possibility of a less intuitive and more analytic approach then that of their predecessors. They combined a love of film with the desire to understand it. One of them started from a scholarly perspective. Paul Schrader wrote a book on Robert Bresson, Carl-Theodor Dreyer, and Yasujiro Ozu and an important essay on film noir.[2] Martin Scorsese taught film at his alma mater, New York University, where Oliver Stone was a student. Steven Spielberg began his career directing for television.

This analytic perspective was modified by a number of factors, most important of which was the desire of these young filmmakers not to be independents, but to join the mainstream of Hollywood production. Many of them, including Scorsese, Coppola, and John Milius, the director Peter Bogdanovich (who, though not often associated with the group, and who did not survive as an imaginative force in filmmaking into the eighties, also began as a cinephile), Joe Dante (the director of *Gremlins*, 1984), cinematographer Laszlo Kovacs, and actors Bruce Dern and Jack Nicholson, began their commercial filmmaking work under the guidance of an important individual in the recent history of Hollywood. Roger Corman, under the aegis of American International Pictures (AIP), an organization that was devoted to low-budget movies, offered them an entry into the film business and simultaneously something to escape from. AIP produced horror, science fiction, beach-party, and bike films, and there is only so much room in these genres to move around and test out talent (as Dennis Hopper and Peter Fonda discovered when they attempted to turn the AIP biker film into a grand generational statement in *Easy Rider*, 1969). If Corman taught his pupils to work quickly and cheaply, he also taught them the necessity of finding a situation that provided more leisure and more room for imaginative growth. Coppola, for example, filmed the low-budget horror film, *Dementia 13*, for Corman in 1963. Within a few years, he was beginning to write and direct features for the major studios.

Whether they moved through AIP, or went from film school directly to features, or, in the case of Spielberg, did not go to film school, but began directing for television, the imaginative growth of these individuals was hardly equal. Following his enormous financial success with *American Graffiti* (1973, steered through production by Coppola) and *Star Wars*, George Lucas withdrew from directing to become producer of his films, content to initiate and guide rather than to make images. He returned in 1998 to direct the most recent installment of his science-fiction series. After a demonstration of great narrative skill in the two *Godfather* films and *The Conversation*, Coppola substituted grand spectacle and barren technology for imaginative visions of power and loss. He wished to be more than a producer and director and become a mogul in the old Hollywood sense. None of his desires was satisfied.

John Milius has never transcended his ideological restraints. A self-proclaimed fascist, his work (*Conan the Barbarian*, 1982—co-scripted by Oliver Stone—and *Red Dawn*, 1984, for example) is overblown with portent and violence, full of the racism, misogyny, meanness, and vulgarity that go with his ideology. Brian DePalma has made a career of the most superficial imitations of the most superficial aspects of Hitchcock's style, worked through a misogyny and violence that manifest a contempt for the audience exploited by his films—though in *Scarface* (1983) and *The Untouchables* (1987) he has shown a talent for a somewhat more grandiloquent allusiveness. Paul Schrader started as a scriptwriter. He wrote Brian DePalma's imitation of *Vertigo, Obsession* (1976), the AIP-produced *Rolling Thunder* (1977), *Taxi Driver, Last Temptation of Christ* (1988), and *Bringing Out the Dead* (1999) and co-wrote *Raging Bull* (1980) for Scorsese, and he has directed films of his screenplays: *Blue Collar* (1978), *Hardcore, American Gigolo* (1979), *Cat People* (1982); an intricate examination of politics, psychology, and aesthetics, *Mishima* (1985); and *Patty Hearst* (1988). During the nineties, he suffered the difficulties of distribution common to many filmmakers of a specialized talent. *The Comfort of Strangers* (1991) is an interesting dream narrative that has links back to Nicolas Roeg's *Don't Look Now* (1973) and a host of other films that find Venice a location of eroticism and violence. *Light Sleeper* (1992) is a thoughtful and gentle film that furthers Schrader's obsessive concern with thieves and outlaws redeemed by love, a pattern set by Robert Bresson, whose *Pickpocket* (1959) Schrader attempts to grasp in film after film. He reached a measure of critical acclaim with *Affliction* (1998), a film not merely based on a novel, but with a visual texture so rich and complex that its mise-en-scène becomes novelistic in its detail and persistence. Spielberg has most successfully merged his love of film with an understanding of commercial necessity that has given him the most power and freedom of the group. I will examine what he has done with it in the next chapter.

Martin Scorsese built his career carefully and slowly. He has certainly not been the most commercially successful of this generation of filmmakers and his only major money-making successes have been *The Color of Money* (1986), *Cape Fear* (1991), and, perhaps, *GoodFellas* (1990). Even his well-attended films—*Alice Doesn't Live Here Anymore* (1974), *Taxi Driver* (1976), *Raging Bull*, *GoodFellas*—do not approach the profits of Spielberg or the Coppola of the *Godfather* years. It has only been in the nineties that Scorsese's name has attracted popular recognition, while his style and subject matter have become the basis for the first (and often second and third) films of many younger filmmakers. This has created some benefits. He has so far not had to compete with himself, making each successive film bigger and more spectacular in order to top the profits of the preceding works. More important, by working with moderate budgets and expecting moderate, rational returns, he has been able to keep up a certain level of experimentation and inquiry in his work. Of all the young, post-New Wave filmmakers, he has retained his excitement about the narrative possibilities of cinema, his curiosity about cutting and camera movement, and his delight in toying with the conventions of the classical form. The construction of his films is never completely at the service of the viewer or the story it is creating. There is an unashamed self-consciousness and a kinetic energy that sometimes threatens to overtake both viewer and story but always provides a commentary on the viewer's experience, preventing him or her from easily slipping into plot. He creates an allusiveness, a celebration of cinema through references to other works, that has its equal only in the films of Godard, Bertolucci, and Wim Wenders—and he often uses Godard as a special reference. He loves to experiment with genres. Although he is most comfortable, and most successful, with films about street toughs, petty criminals, and other figures on the urban margins, he has tried his hand at costume drama, *The Age of Innocence* (1993), and two religious "epics," *The Last Temptation of Christ* and *Kundun* (1997).

Scorsese does not create stately compositions or the intellectual distance and rigor of Kubrick or perform the radical experiments in cinematic space and genre of Robert Altman. His cutting patterns are quite different from

Stone's, more often choosing a camera movement over a cut to make a narrative or character point. Scorsese will cut a shot to create a troubling proximity to his subject rather than create a historical and psychological space around him. He is, of the directors discussed here, closest to Arthur Penn, especially the Penn of *Mickey One* and *Bonnie and Clyde*. Like Penn at his best, Scorsese is interested in characters who are representative either of a class or of a certain ideological grouping; he is concerned with their relationships to each other or to an antagonistic environment and how they appear and move as physical entities within narratives of the body. Scorsese's films all involve antagonism, struggle, and constant movement, even if that movement is within a tightly circumscribed area that has no exit. His work is like Penn's (and like that of many of the other filmmakers discussed here) in that there is no triumph for his characters. With the exception of Alice Hyatt in *Alice Doesn't Live Here Anymore*, Paul Newman's Eddie in *The Color of Money*, or, more fantastically, Rupert Pupkin in *The King of Comedy* (1983), all his characters lose to their isolation or their antagonism. Many of Scorsese's characters survive their ordeals, but, like Travis Bickle, Jake LaMotta, Henry Hill, or Sam Rothstein, this survival is hardly a triumph. Those who do triumph are the religious figures, Christ and the Dalai Lama, whose extracinematic story is transcendence of the body and its physical space.

Unlike Penn's, Scorsese's filmmaking shows a degree of stylization that eschews, for the most part, many conventions of Hollywood realism and almost all the "realistic" conventions of the sixties, even location shooting. In *New York, New York* (1977), he moves indoors entirely, depending on studio sets to achieve an expressive artificiality. *Raging Bull* is photographed on location but in black and white, a process by now so unconventional (although becoming somewhat less so in music videos and other commercials) that it creates a distance and stylization heightened by the film's narrative contours and the construction of its fight sequences. In all his films, even *The Last Temptation of Christ*, there is a sense that the place inhabited by the characters is structured by their own, slightly crazed perceptions and by the way the viewer is made to see and understand them by means of what and how they see.

This brings me back to a central concern of this study, the problem of point of view and the articulation of cinematic space, of how and why a filmmaker constructs a narrative world, allows viewer entry into the fiction, and where the viewer is permitted to stand and observe. In Kubrick's work, there is always the sense that the entire mise-en-scène is commentative, representing not a dwelling or habitation, but what an observer ought to think or feel about that habitation. Kubrick does not so much construct places for his characters to live as he does an idea about how and why those characters live. His characters are themselves ideas given fictional flesh. Penn will often depict characters as emerging from or being formed by an environment that barely contains them: the Depression South in *Bonnie and Clyde* seems to call forth a rebellion against its barrenness; the dark, fragmented Chicago of *Mickey One* threatens its hero by echoing his state of mind. Stone creates spaces of interrogation, examining images, threatening their apparent stability, making them respond to the vagaries of history, forcing alternative readings. Spielberg often creates a masterful mise-en-scène of middle-class suburbia, which is then made both strange and attractive by the entry of a foreign force. In quite classical fashion, his films are composed and cut so that the viewer is made complicit with the events and firmly joined to the characters, responding to their ordinariness and the threat or comfort offered by the intrusive phenomenon. The point of view manufactured by Spielberg is finally that of the dominant cultural discourse, to which his films securely attach the viewer. Robert Altman and Oliver Stone, on the other hand, radically fragment mise-en-scène and perceptual location, demanding that the viewer pay attention to its various parts, refusing the comfort of conventional placement.

Scorsese's mise-en-scène does something quite different. Although not as fragmented as Altman's, it is never accommodating. His characters do not have homes that reflect comfort or security. The spaces they inhabit are places of transition, of momentary situation. But these places are not Kubrick's abstract ideas of places. The Manhattan of *Taxi Driver* and *After Hours*, the Little Italy of *Mean Streets*, the Las Vegas of *Casino* are perfectly recognizable, almost too much so. The mise-en-scène of *Mean Streets*, *Taxi Driver*, *New York, New York*, *Raging Bull*, *After Hours*, and *GoodFellas* represents more than New York, a place of tough people, crowded streets, fights, and whores. They represent, to borrow a notion of Roland Barthes', a New York-*ness*, a shared image and collective signifier of New York that has little to do with the city itself, but rather expresses what everyone, including many who live there, have decided New York should look like (and much different from the New York created by Woody Allen, for example, whose streets and apartments are comfortable habitations for walking and conversation; or of *Eyes Wide Shut*, whose flat, studio-bound sets of New York reflect the flatness of their inhabitant's imagination). At the same time—and this is where the difference with Kubrick occurs—

New York is reflective of the energy of the characters, in *Mean Streets* and *GoodFellas*; the anomie of Travis Bickle in *Taxi Driver*; the confused violence of Jake La Motta in *Raging Bull*. And these qualities are communicated to the viewer in the ways Scorsese allows entry into the mise-en-scène. Through composition, lighting, camera movement, and cutting he provides the viewer a primary perceptual pattern, a point of view, that is then joined with another point of view created within the narrative, that of the central character. Edward Branigan writes that one aspect of point of view is a "condition of consciousness . . . which is *represented*."[3] Scorsese represents states of mind and guides viewer response to them with great care and through a complex organization of visual and aural elements. In the religious epics and costume dramas, the precise structure of point of view falls off to some extent. Both *Last Temptation of Christ* and *Kundun* seem to represent the filmmaker himself attempting to come to terms with his own point of view of the subject matter, while the literary aura surrounding *Age of Innocence* forces Scorsese to rely on the authority of other literary-based period films—namely, Welles's *Magnificent Ambersons* and Kubrick's *Barry Lyndon*.

There are other complexities at work in the costume and religious films and other "conditions of consciousness" being represented. They are more reticent and restrained, indulging in a higher degree of conscious artificiality than the other films (indeed, *New York, New York*, which can be counted as a period film, plays up the artificiality of its mise-en-scène and makes it visible). Scorsese's contemporary "street" films are fashioned by a tension between two opposing cinematic conventions, the documentary and the fictional. The documentary, by means of a free-moving, often handheld or, in the later films, Steadicam camera that records people on the streets or talking informally in what appear to be actual rooms, offers an illusion of objective observation of characters, places, and events that might exist before and after the filming of them. The fictional creates a subjective point of view, coded so that the viewer understands that what is being seen has been created for the fictional moment as a controlled artifice. No matter how conventionally "realistic" a fiction is—a realism that is itself the representation of certain conventions of form and content—there is the tacit understanding that it has no material reference outside itself. Scorsese's work contains such severe *anti*realistic elements that the world he creates often becomes expressionistic, a closed space that reflects a particular, often stressed, state of mind.[4] But, like Jean-Luc Godard, he understands the arbitrary nature of the documentary/fiction conventions and freely mixes them. In much of his work there is the sense of capturing a "reality" of places and events that might exist even without his presence. Until *Taxi Driver*, he employed the handheld camera and the rapid, oblique editing that had become associated with a "documentary" and improvisational style by the early seventies.

In all the films set in New York, the street imagery, no matter how colored by the characters' perspective, alludes to a material presence, a factual existence. His actors (particularly Robert De Niro, Harvey Keitel, and Joe Pesci) create their characters with an offhandedness, immediacy, and unpredictable violence that give the impression of unpremeditated existence (as opposed to the carefully studied character-making obvious in the way Kubrick and Stone direct their players). When these qualities are interwoven with the subjective impressions of the world that are communicated by the ways the characters see their environment and themselves, and when Scorsese modifies location shooting (which, by the mid-seventies, was taken for granted in contemporary film) with artificial sets, stylized lighting, and slow motion cinematography, a self-contradictory perceptual structure is created. "Realism" and expressionism work against each other, creating a strong perceptual tension that can be felt throughout his work.*

Scorsese started his commercial career with a film strongly influenced by the New Wave. *Who's That Knocking at My Door?* (1969)—a finger exercise for *Mean Streets*—is inscribed in the handheld, jump-cut, nontransitional style that many filmmakers took from the surface of the French films of the early sixties. Its mise-en-scène is partly neorealist, partly documentary, mixed with the subjectivity of perception and allusiveness that marks *Breathless* and *The Four Hundred Blows*.[5] *Who's That Knocking?* is an "experimental" film in all senses. Formally, it begins trying out the camera strategies, the restless, foreboding movements, that will become one of Scorsese's major formal devices. Contextually, it prepares the way for

---

* Scorsese has made some more or less conventional documentaries: a film about his family, *Italianamerican* (1974), and a big theatrical rock documentary on the last performance of The Band, *The Last Waltz* (1978). This film, shot in 35 mm by some of the best cinematographers working at the time, contains studio sequences. Quentin Tarantino was very attentive to one Scorsese documentary, *American Boy* (1978), a hilarious and painful monologue by Stephen Prince, a friend who plays Andy the gun fence in *Taxi Driver*. Prince tells a bizarre story of reviving a woman suffering from a drug overdose by plunging a syringe full of stimulant into her heart. The story becomes part of *Pulp Fiction*.

Mean Streets, J. R. (Harvey Keitel) being an early version of Charlie in the later film—more of an oppressed Catholic than his later incarnation, less rooted in his environment, standing over and against New York rather than being enclosed within it as Charlie is.

Scorsese has not yet discovered in this early film a method of integrating the character with the space he occupies so that the two become reflections of each other in a mutually defining mise-en-scène. Nor is he quite comfortable with ways of incorporating his love of film, manifested through allusion, within the narrative. Here the allusions stand out irrepressibly; the central character speaks Scorsese's obsession with his cinematic inheritance. J. R. and his girl friend (Zina Bethune) have a long discussion about westerns, John Wayne, and Ford's *The Searchers* (along with *Citizen Kane* and *Psycho* a key film for all of Scorsese's generation of filmmakers). At a party, when a man shoots up a shelf of liquor bottles, there is a cut to a photograph of Wayne with a gun and a montage of stills from Hawks's *Rio Bravo*. This allusiveness will remain in Scorsese's later work, becoming more thoroughly woven into the pattern of his films, until *Taxi Driver* becomes a version of *The Searchers* and *Psycho* in its very narrative pattern, and *GoodFellas* extends allusion to the entire genre of gangster films and the audience's understanding of it.

Who's That Knocking at My Door? stands as a document of Scorsese's beginnings. Something like Kubrick's early films, it is less an impersonal generic exercise than an inquiry into the possibilities of subjective cinematic expression. But unlike Kubrick, Scorsese needed the technical facility and formal restraints of commercial production to develop his style. He never falls entirely into the zero-degree conventions and simple generic repetitions that those restraints can cultivate but, like other strong American filmmakers, used them as a base to build on, as a tradition to recognize and overcome. This base was provided by Roger Corman and American International Pictures.

Boxcar Bertha (1972)—the film he made for AIP—is a work completely unlike its predecessor, *Who's That Knocking at My Door?*, or its successor, *Mean Streets*. Yet it sets itself up as a link between them, if only by smoothing out the stylistic quirks apparent in the former and preparing for the consistent and assured approach of the latter. A violent work, much a part of a group of period evocation films popular in the seventies and influenced by *Bonnie and Clyde*, it is a short, direct narrative that does little more than prepare for an enormous gunfight at the end and a rather repulsive series of images in which David Carradine is nailed to the side of a freight car that pulls out, camera mounted on its top, looking down at the crucified body as a distraught Bertha (Barbara Hershey) runs after. The only inherent contextual interest of the film is its mild pro-union, pro-left stand (the nominal subject is a radical union organizer of the railroads in the thirties). This is, I am certain, the work of its screenwriters, Joyce H. and John William Corrington, for it is a subject Scorsese otherwise shows no interest in. Even *Kundun*, a film in which religion and politics should have been foregrounded and analyzed, uses them only as triggers and passing references, images and suggestions of movement for its characters. In retrospect, the crucifixion imagery might indicate Scorsese's obsession with Christian iconography that would become fulfilled in *The Last Temptation of Christ*. What Scorsese adds to *Boxcar Bertha* is a further indication of his talent with the moving camera. Scattered throughout are shots in which the camera booms down on a character or arcs around two people talking to each other, investing them with an energy and tension that will be developed more fully in the films to follow. *Boxcar Bertha* is an important work not so much *by* Scorsese as *for* him; it permits him to work within the basic patterns of early seventies film, its violence and its urgency, and to understand how those patterns can be worked together with the looser, more self-conscious and subjective elements of *Who's That Knocking?*

The integration occurs in *Mean Streets*, a film in which a carefully structured narrative fiction allows its boundaries to become porous to the influx of documentary techniques. It both observes and creates, becoming a subjective fiction of incomplete lives and sporadic violence in the form of a documentary of four young men in New York's Little Italy. I do not mean to be overly ingenious, but *Mean Streets* does keep altering its perspective on itself, combining what appears to be a spontaneous capturing of its characters' lives with carefully considered, formal arrangements of mise-en-scène and character point of view. This is not a confused or confusing alteration. On the contrary, Scorsese carefully integrates a double perspective in the film, a free-flowing observation and a carefully structured point of view both of and from a central character. In contrast to the contained, highly structured narratives of middle-class Italians developed by Francis Ford Coppola in the carefully made narratives of the two *Godfather* films, and even the ironic narratives of his own later gangster films, Scorsese investigates the almost incoherent street ramblings of disenfranchised men whose lives are defined by disorder, threatened by their own impulses, and, though confined by narrow geographical and ethnic boundaries, paradoxically liberated by the turmoil of the bars, tenements, and streets that make up their world. The central character of the film, Charlie (Harvey Keitel, who here and in *Who's That Knocking?* becomes a kind of alter ego for Scorsese, who often dubs his own voice to represent the character's thoughts) is a further development of J. R. in the earlier film. Less guilt-ridden than J. R., Charlie attempts to come to terms with his Catholicism, his future as a petty mafioso, and his odd, violent friend Johnny Boy. This character, played by Robert De Niro in the first of seven films he has made with Scorsese, is a saintly idiot, a figure with no center, who destroys himself with his own inarticulate desire to be a free spirit.

But then none of the characters in the film has the center or sense of direction that one expects from characters in conventional film fictions, and it is the purpose of the film to observe them in their randomness and as part of an unpredictable flow of events. When Charlie is on the streets, no matter how central he may be to the narrative moment, he is composed in the frame as one figure among many, standing off-center, next to a building, other people moving by him. Johnny Boy is continually caught in randomness. When first seen in the narrative proper (his name, like those of the other characters who are introduced at the beginning, flashed on the screen, in imitation of the way David and Albert Maysles introduce the characters in their documentaries), he is at the end of a street. He pauses by a mailbox, throws something in it, runs up the street, looking back as the box explodes. In another sequence, he is up on a roof, shooting a gun at the Empire State Building uptown. Elsewhere he walks down the street, the camera rapidly tracking him from behind. A kid bumps into him, whom he proceeds to beat up. Little violences, sporadic shootings, fistfights, punctuate the film as if they were parts of ongoing events, or as if they were moving toward some greater violence—which in fact they are. The end of the film is an explosion of gunfire and blood. The exasperated loan shark Michael pursues Johnny Boy, Charlie, and Charlie's girlfriend, Teresa, in a car chase through rainy streets. Michael's henchman (played by Scorsese) shoots them up, horribly wounding Johnny Boy in the neck, as De Niro's Travis Bickle will be shot in the neck in *Taxi Driver*.

This random, violent flow of events is fed by the persistent uncertainty of Charlie's perception of them; his attempts to test his Catholicism; his attempts to justify his life: "You don't make up for your sins in church; you do it in the streets; you do it at home. The rest is bullshit, and you know it." These are the first words heard in the film, and they are spoken over a dark screen in Scorsese's voice. At their conclusion, the first shot is one of movement: the camera moving into Charlie as he rises quickly from his bed. The rhythm of the whole film is established by the fact that Charlie is seen not at rest and then getting up but in motion as the shot begins. A handheld camera follows him to a mirror on the opposite wall; a crucifix is prominent behind him. A police siren is heard outside. Charlie goes back to bed, and as he lies down there are three rapid cuts, each one closer to his head. (Scorsese commented that he had seen this triple cut in Truffaut's *Shoot the Piano Player* and has used a variation of it in all his films.[6] He also saw it in Hitchcock's *The Birds*.) On the second cut, almost synchronized to the editing, the Ronettes' "Be My Baby" begins playing on the sound track. Without preparation or explanation, this carefully executed sequence generates a nervous and purposeless energy that continues throughout the film. It also creates an immediate intensity and initial engagement, which is supplied by the kinetic closeup of Charlie's face. "The simplest close-up is also the most moving," wrote Godard; it can "make us anxious about things."[7] And complex closeups, like those that open *Mean Streets*, whose intensity is magnified by hearing the vocal component first, both voice and face unlocated temporally and spatially, forces viewer attention, makes us uneasy, and does not permit rest. A few of the films under discussion here— *Bonnie and Clyde, A Clockwork Orange,* as well as *Godfather I* and Scorsese's own *Kundun*—use a similar method of entry, beginning on a closeup, without the conventional establishing shot. The face demands attention; its lack of location causes some discomfort. The act of locating it, which is partially the job of the film, partially the job of the viewer perceiving the film, creates a tension between the viewer's expectations and desires to be comfortably situated within the narrative and—in the case of *Mean Streets*—the stubborn refusal of the narrative to meet those expectations and desires.

The sudden blast of rock and roll, rhythm and blues, and sometimes jazz or opera becomes a permanent part of Scorsese's style. Here and again in *Raging Bull, GoodFellas,* and *Casino,* a sound track of popular music contemporary to the time of the narrative becomes an inextricable part of that narrative. The very rhythm of the songs being played becomes integral to the movement of the camera and the editing pattern of a given sequence. The lyrics often comment ironically on the narrative action or the characters' state. As we will see in our discussion of *Raging Bull* and *GoodFellas,* this "found" music becomes so tightly bound to the structure of a film, the cutting, shot composition, and music begin to infiltrate each other so that film and music become a seamless rhythmic construction that, despite its tight integration, always remains on a conscious level influencing viewer response to the film.[8]

It is precisely this level of formal consciousness that informs the opening of *Mean Streets*. The framing and cutting, the peculiar, nervous approach to the main character, indicates that Scorsese is not going to allow his narrative to begin just yet. He retards its progress to show us other things, other ways to get into story, to approach character. The jump cuts to Charlie's face are followed by, of all things, a shot of an 8-mm movie projector, which throws on a small screen scenes from the street, scenes of Charlie and Johnny Boy, flashing lights in the night, a church that suddenly fills the screen, giving way to shots of the San Gennaro Festival, which will provide visual and aural background throughout the film. They provide background for the credits as well as an active expression of the fiction/documentary tension I spoke of earlier.

The immediacy and proximity of the opening shots are momentarily undercut by the projector, the home movies, the typewritten credits. Is the film we are about to see a version of Charlie's home movies? Are they somehow subjective projections of his memories? The cinematic reality of *Mean Streets* is stressed throughout as Scorsese intercuts scenes from his favorite films, integrating cinematic allusions into the narrative more comfortably than in *Who's That Knocking?* Charlie and his friends go to see *The Searchers*, the film discussed at length by J. R. and his girlfriend, the film that will have a perverse influence on *Taxi Driver*. The sequence they watch is of a fistfight. Charlie and Johnny Boy go to see Roger Corman's *The Tomb of Ligeia*. Outside the theater Charlie stands under a poster for John Boorman's *Point Blank* with Lee Marvin's gun pointing, forebodingly, at Johnny Boy's head. In the middle of the sequence in which Charlie and Johnny Boy are gunned down, the image of Glenn Ford standing over his wife's body in the blown-up car of Fritz Lang's 1953 film, *The Big Heat*, suddenly appears (it turns out to be a movie on television watched by Charlie's Mafia uncle, who is oblivious to what is happening to his nephew but oddly close to it through the image on the screen). These intrusions and allusions, like a poet's allusions to other poems within his or her work, or a jazz musician's quotations from other melodies within the piece he is playing, serve a double or triple function. They constitute a celebration of the medium, an indication of a cinematic community; they enrich the work by opening it out, making it responsive to other works and making others responsive to it; and they point to the nature of the film's own existence. The viewer is urged to observe the film's relation not to "reality" but to the reality of films and their influence on each other. *Mean Streets* is a film, and by playing on the various signs of its existence as film, it becomes a documentary not only of fictive events, but of itself.

Throughout his career, Scorsese continues this allusive strategy. Color home movies turn up in the otherwise black-and-white mise-en-scène of *Raging Bull*. Visits by characters to movie houses become rare in the later films, but the allusions continue, becoming alternately very broad, very subtle, or very strange. At their broadest, Scorsese remakes an entire film, *Cape Fear*, based on a 1962 film of the same name, which was, in its time, a *Psycho* knockoff. Within the remake, Scorsese makes subtle, practically invisible allusions to other Hitchcock films. The subtleties can be more occult still, as in the appearance of music from Jean-Luc Godard's 1963 film, *Contempt* (itself a film about filmmaking, though also about the disintegration of a marriage) in *Casino*. This is a secret only the most knowledgeable cinephile or film scholar would discover, though once deciphered, it gives the film an extraordinary emotional aura. The young Dalai Lama in *Kundun* watches a magical film by the French pioneer, Georges Méliès, on an ancient projector and looks at newsreels of atomic blasts. In *The Last Temptation of Christ*, Jesus first sees Mary Magdalen when she performs a sexual act in a tent in front of an audience. The scene is composed and cut to observe Jesus as if he were a patron in a movie theater, watching a screen. The very end of the film, the moment of death on the cross, is visualized by a multicolored screen on which appear jagged fragments of motion-picture film. In all these instances, Scorsese gazes inward to his medium, as if finding a solace in film where his characters cannot find any such in the world. The characters are, of course, themselves creations of film; and so the entire allusive process foregrounds the fiction and addresses it while allowing the narrative to move along as it has to.

The 8-mm projector in *Mean Streets* is part of this self-documentation, this self-consolation, showing fragments of Charlie's world that the film as a whole shows in only a slightly less fragmented way. It shows more, as well: there are shots of Charlie and Teresa with a baby, suggesting, perhaps, a domestic ending to the street antics that take up most of the film itself— or a fantasy of such. The jumpy, fragmented 8-mm film alludes to the way Charlie sees himself in his world and to the way *Mean Streets* documents how its characters—Charlie in particular—see themselves. After the credit sequence, those characters are introduced and the narrative returns to Charlie, observed in church, the church observed from his point of view as he prays and comments on his unworthiness. The camera tracks around him as he announces his desire to do penance for his sins. He talks about the pain of hell and puts his finger over a candle flame: "You don't fuck around with the infinite. There's no way you do that." "The pain in hell has two sides," he says, "the kind you can touch with your hand; the kind you can feel with your heart. . . . You know, the worst of the two is the spiritual." And with these words there is loud rock music and a cut to a slow-motion tracking shot down the glowing red bar that is the focal point of the group's activities.

The expectations created by montage might lead one to believe that the cut on these words from Charlie and the church candles to the drifting point of view in a fiery red bar, replete with go-go dancer, indicates that this place is Charlie's hell. But unless Scorsese is adopting a literal Sartrean position, it is not hell, but merely the place where Charlie hangs out. The redness, the slow motion, the disrupting arcs around Charlie when he talks with the loan shark Michael about Johnny Boy are all disturbing and portentous. More than anything else they indicate Charlie's uncertainty of himself, an existential uncertainty of who he is and how he should act. They communicate the nascent violence of this and every situation Charlie is in (through the movement, the lack of rest, the lack of a stable eye-level gaze, the fistfight that breaks out behind Charlie between two people who have nothing to do with him). If this is hell, it is eagerly embraced by Charlie as a place to work out his conflicts, perhaps even a place to die in, but not as a place of suffering or torture. This is, rather, a place of great vitality, even of hilarity. The relationship of all concerned is loose and joking. The joke goes very sour at the end, and serious strains in Charlie's life keep emerging. But an apparent good-naturedness is kept up most of the way.

When Johnny Boy comes into the bar, Charlie says to himself, in mock piety, "We talk about penance and you send this through the door. Well, we play by your rules, don't we? Well, don't we?" The camera booms into him and cuts to his point of view of Johnny Boy, walking down the bar in slow motion as the Rolling Stones sing "Jumping Jack Flash." Charlie's guilt, his burden, is a screwy kid whom he protects and who gets them both shot up. Charlie talks about suffering and about penance, but these are deeply internalized, only a few profound signs of his suffering are seen until it emerges directly from the barrel of a gun.

A film that does not have emotional turmoil as its subject but only as a referent, and chooses instead to make its characters' actions its subject, is some distance from the conventional narrative that focuses on a few

189

characters working through a defined set of problems. *Mean Streets* is not about what motivates Charlie and Johnny Boy, not about what they think and feel (although these are present), but about how they see, how Charlie perceives his world and Johnny Boy reacts to it. In none of his films will Scorsese opt for the psychological realism of explained actions, defined motivations, or identifiable characters. If his often-commented-on Catholicism does appear in his work, it is in the form of a purgatorial sense of his characters' serving in the world, not looking for grace but attempting survival and barely making it. Even his film about Christ concentrates on these matters, for it creates a figure all but forced to assume a spiritual guise less out of an internal sense of grace than out of the need of others. The world Scorsese's characters inhabit is violent in the extreme, but it is a violence that is created by the characters' very attempts to make peace with it. From the point of view of the characters in *Mean Streets* and the later thug films, their world is perfectly ordinary, and Scorsese reflects this through the documentary nature of many of the images. But at the same time, there is the perception of a heightened sense of reality, a stylized, expressive presence most evident in the bar sequences, in the restless, moving camera, in the fragmentary, off-center editing.

Vitality and tension are apparent not only in the images, but in the dialogue (written by Scorsese and Mardik Martin) as well. Everyone in *Mean Streets* is a compulsive talker—not obsessive, like John Cassavetes's characters, who appear, at least in his early films, driven to reveal themselves through their words at all moments and always on the brink of, or deeply in, hysteria—but using words as an extension of themselves, a sign of their vitality. Their language is rooted in New York working-class usage, profoundly obscene and charged with movement.[9] The slow, self-conscious, and reflective speech of Coppola's middle-class mafiosi in *The Godfather* is here replaced by an expressive thrust of endless words. In a great set piece of the film, Johnny Boy is attempting to explain to Charlie why he does not have the money to pay off Michael (the need to pay this debt is one of the few things that provides something like a conventional "plot," though it is less like a plot than a motif). In a simple setup located in the back room of the bar, against dark walls, punctuated by a bare light bulb hanging over Charlie, a sequence cut in simple shot/reverse shot, over-the-shoulder continuity, with an occasional far shot of the two men, Johnny Boy tells the following story, whose telling serves to create the character who tells it:

JOHNNY BOY: You don't know what happened to me. I'm so depressed about other things I can't worry about payments, ya know what I mean? I come home last Tuesday, I had my money, in cash, ya know ... blah, blah, bing, bing, I'm comin' home, I ran into Jimmy Sparks. I owe Jimmy Sparks seven hundred, like for four months. I gotta pay the guy, he lives in my building, he hangs out across the street, I gotta pay the guy, right? So what happened? I had to give some to my mother, then I wound up with twenty-five at the end of the week. And then what happened? Today, you ain't gonna believe, this is incredible, I can't believe it myself ... I was in a game, I was ahead like six, seven hundred dollars, right?

CHARLIE: You gotta be kiddin'.

JOHNNY BOY: Yeah, on Hester Street. You know Joey Clams?

CHARLIE: Yeah.

JOHNNY BOY: Joey Scalla, yeah.

CHARLIE: I know him too, yeah.

JOHNNY BOY: Yeah, no, Joey Scalla is Joey Clams.

CHARLIE: Right.

JOHNNY BOY: Right.

CHARLIE: They're the same person (*smiles*).

JOHNNY BOY: Yeah!

CHARLIE: Hey!

JOHNNY BOY: Hey! So I was in there playing Bankers and Brokers. All of a sudden I'm ahead like six, seven hundred dollars. I'm really winnin'. All of a sudden some kid walks in and the kid yells that the bulls are comin', right? Yells that the cops are comin'. Everyone runs away, I grab all the money, I go in, it's an excuse, like, to get away. . . .Ya know, and I give everybody the money back later, and that way I get out, I don't have to go into the game and get a losin' streak and all that. What happens? I come out in the yard. I don't know this buildin'. I don't know nothin', I couldn't get out, it was like a box, big, like this (*makes the shape of a box with his hands*). So I gotta go back in. Not only do I go back in, but this kid says it's a false alarm. Can you imagine that? I wanted to kill this fuckin' kid. I wanted ... (*bites fingers in mock rage*). I was so crazy, man, I wanted to kill this kid. Meanwhile I gotta get back in the game, bing, bing, bing, I lose four hundred dollars. Meanwhile Frankie Bones is over there, Frankie Bones, I owe him thirteen hundred for like seven, eight months already. He's after me, I can't even walk on Hester Street without duckin' that guy. He's, he's like waitin' for me, like I can't move, ya know, and he sees that I'm losin', right, so like he's waitin' for me here, so he's tappin' me on the shoulder (*taps Charlie*), he says, "Hey," tappin' me like this, like a hawk, "hey, ah, get it up, you're losin', now give me some money." I says, "Hey, Frankie, come on, ya know, ya know, give me a break over here, let me win some back, ya know, I got debts, I mean I'm in the big O." He says, "Never mind, give me the money." I says, "O.K. Frankie," so I give him two hundred dollars. Meanwhile I lose the deal, I go outside, I'm a little depressed ... anyway I wanna cut this story short, 'cause I know you don't wanna hear all this, and I know, I know, I know. But ... (*Charlie protests that it's all right*) to make a long story short, anyway, I went to Al Kaplan, gotta new tie, I got this shirt ... like this shirt? ... it's nice ... This tie....

De Niro's Johnny Boy is all nervous energy and self-delight, the opposite of the serious, unsmiling, self-contained Vito Corleone whom he creates for Coppola in the second *Godfather*. The character makes himself from moment to moment, almost speaks himself into being (as opposed to the characters played by Sylvester Stallone, the eighties icon of the simple hero, and any number of characters in nineties' films, whose inarticulateness uncreates them continuously). The result is that his language and that of the other characters play a game with the viewer similar to that played by the film's images: it seems spontaneous, emerging from the moment— indeed a great deal of improvisation must have occurred in the creation of it. Yet it manifests rhythm and energy and concentration greater than could be expected were it merely made up and overheard on the spot. The notion of improvisation, introduced by Godard and brought into American narrative film by Cassavetes, Altman, and Scorsese, is one of the trickier problems in modern cinema. Improvisation offers an effect of immediacy and spontaneity but is in fact created with craft and planning; the demands of shooting are too precise to allow for many changes and surprises when the camera is running. De Niro and Keitel may have made up their lines at one point during rehearsal or in actual takes, yet this sequence is constructed from a series of over-the-shoulder shots, which means dialogue had to be repeated many times or even dubbed in after editing. Like Abraham Polonsky, who in his 1948 film *Force of Evil* heightened to a poetic rhythm the diction and cadences of New York dialect, Scorsese, his cowriter, and his actors take the forms of the everyday language of a particular ethnic group, concentrate it, and make it artificial, the artificiality creating the effect of the overheard and the immediate.

The language of *Mean Streets* becomes a means of self- and groupdefinition, speaking of an unrooted life yet at the same time attempting to root that life in a community of shared verbal rhythms and expressions. Of course the expressions themselves can be used as weapons against this community. Calling a rival a "mook" precipitates a huge fistfight in a pool room. Early in the film Michael, the loan shark, tells Charlie that Johnny Boy is a "jerk-off," a phrase that brings Charlie immediately to his friend's defense. At the film's end, Johnny Boy throws the same phrase back at Michael, which, with the empty gun he waves at him, puts Michael in a killing rage. Words that communicate not meaning but feelings are dangerous; but they are at least alive (compare the language of Kubrick's characters, which communicates rigid, unalterable ideas and is deadening). This tension of a dangerous vitality, friendships that become provocations, a restlessness that can't be satisfied, makes up the structure of the film.

Mean Streets does not, finally, define itself as any one thing. Although the film depicts the activities of a group of disenfranchised urban ethnics, it does not attempt to comment overtly on a social and economic class. A film about volatile emotions, it seems uninterested in analyzing emotions or baring souls. It only suggests. There is a subtle sequence late in the film in which Charlie and Johnny Boy go to an urban churchyard. They daintily spread their hankies on gravestones and sit. Johnny Boy finally lays full length across the stone as Charlie argues with him about his future. In the background, Latino music is playing. Charlie stands up. A bottle crashes. There is a cut to his point of view as he looks around, and the camera pans the windows of the surrounding tenements. The windows are crowded with Puerto Ricans partying. The music, noise, sounds of broken glass, and screaming get louder. Charlie doesn't say a word, but his reaction is clear through the point-of-view shot. Here is a new ethnicity, a new group of outsiders becoming insiders, pushing the Italians slowly to the periphery. A loud scream is heard and Scorsese uses it as a dissolve to a shrieking car horn on the more familiar street.

Hinted through this particular sequence and throughout the film is an important understanding about the boundaries of class, ethnicity, gender. These active, energetic young men are so hemmed in by the borders of their birthplace, their sex, and their family origins that their energies get directed to a kind of joyful violence played on each other. They only know who they think they are and are able to go no further than that. The very music on the sound track—mostly black rhythm and blues—mocks their sense of ethnic righteousness. They are constrained by physical space, by an inherited and unquestioned racism, anti-Semitism, and misogyny. They leave Little Italy only twice: once Charlie accompanies his girlfriend, Teresa, to the beach. He feels completely out of place and he is troubled by her quite open sexuality. He fears it because he can only understand her either as an illicit sexual object, whom he does not understand, or a domestic one, whom he is not yet ready to embrace. She is like another territory, across another border. At the end of the film, with Michael in pursuit, Charlie, Teresa, and Johnny Boy drive to Brooklyn—a foreign country to these parochial, lower-Manhattan-bounded Italian Americans. They get lost and found by Michael, whose henchman (played by Scorsese) shoots them.[10]

Since Al Capone became the avatar of the gangster in the popular imagination, and the Mafia a source of undying fascination, Italians have been the ethnics of choice for movie thugs (some recent inroads by Russians in nineties film have not produced a firm enough representation of threat to become more than a passing interest). *Mean Streets* is the first gangster film to perform a meditation on the ethnic core of the gangsters, discovering in it a set of common assumptions of ascension—Charlie wants to become middle class and run a restaurant under his uncle's—a small-time neighborhood mafioso—patronage. The home movies at the beginning of the film suggest that he achieves his wish, survives his gunshot wounds, marries Teresa, and has a child. But this ascension is limited to Charlie and, more important, to the ethno-geography of his neighborhood. We get no real sense of what if any "future" these characters might have, partly because they exist only as fictions in the film and their existence ends when the film does but also because they are defined by their cinematic, ethnic, urban place. They don't go anywhere; their space merely contracts around them, while the camera and the editing, as if in response to that contraction, generate movement in response to their outbursts of violence.

Unlike earlier gangster films, the characters of *Mean Streets* are unconcerned with their standing or their fame. Limited by the knowledge and boundaries of their place, they are content with small gains, good times, minor successes, and committing violence on one another. The film is more concerned with observing these men in their group than in applying the usual conventions of the gangster genre. But Scorsese is well aware of the film's cinematic roots, which continue to thrive and grow, especially under his eye. In Mervyn LeRoy's *Little Caesar*, Rico's boss introduces him to his gang. The camera, assuming Rico's point of view and in a gesture still somewhat unusual in an early sound film, circles the table, as the guys acknowledge the new man. The first cut to the bar in *Mean Streets* is to Charlie's point of view as he walks in and along the room. It is a brief, slow-motion tracking shot. Scorsese is just beginning to experiment with altering film speed to express character state of mind. No sounds are heard, except for the Rolling Stones' song on the sound track. Some patrons look up at the camera, as if to acknowledge Charlie. Early in *GoodFellas*, in the first sequence of Henry Hill as an adult, Henry introduces the viewer to the restaurant he runs. The camera moves across and about the bar. Hill, whose gaze apparently authorizes the camera as his point of view, tells the viewer who it is we're seeing. As the camera passes by, each character talks back to it/Henry/us, acknowledging the introduction with some news or business—"Yeah, I took care of that thing for ya," "I'll go get the papers, get the papers."

A triangulation occurs within film history: *Little Caesar, Mean Streets, GoodFellas* are acknowledging each other through the structure of a point-of-view tracking shot. Scorsese pays his cinematic debts (as he does again at the end of *GoodFellas*, when there is an insert of Joe Pesci's Tommy firing a gun point-blank at the camera, echoing the bandit shooting at the camera at the end of Edwin Porter's 1903 *The Great Train Robbery*); he links his films to the gangster tradition. In *Mean Streets*, the linkage is more obvious in the ways in which Scorsese works both with and against the genre's conventions, and, in *GoodFellas*, it is obvious in the ways he reconfigures the relationship of the viewer to the tradition, foregrounding the fictionality of movie gangsters. Another triangulation occurs between the history of the gangster film, *GoodFellas* itself, and the viewer—more accurately a kind of collective viewer, created by Scorsese's film and all the other gangster films audiences are heir to. *GoodFellas* addresses the history of the gangster film partly through a direct address to the viewer by means of the voices of its characters, Henry Hill (Ray Liotta) and his wife, Karen (Lorraine Bracco). Scorsese had already worked with voice-over in *Taxi Driver*, where Travis Bickle, reading from his diary, makes psychotic observations on the events of his life. The voice-overs in *GoodFellas* are not psychotic, but seem rather to be the words of two good-natured guides—commentators, memorialists, even moralists—reflecting on the pleasures and fears of the gangster life in ways meant to ingratiate. They are, of course, fictional voices, which are mediated by another narrator, the controlling voice of the film itself. That "voice" is a synthesis of the screenplay and direction, of the cutting of the film and its mise-en-scène. But where the mise-en-scène of *Taxi Driver* is, as we will see, carefully constructed to reflect the singular mind of its main character, *GoodFellas* seems closer in its construction to *Mean Streets*, almost documentary in its observation of small-time New York gangsters at work and play, but with a clearer definition of the storyteller and story-telling than its predecessor.

In *GoodFellas* Scorsese moves one level up in gangster life. Instead of the profoundly circumscribed street toughs of Little Italy, these characters operate across New York, though they are based in Queens, one of the outer boroughs of Manhattan. Most of their thefts remain petty, they smuggle cigarettes; some are quite large: the freight "heist" at Kennedy airport is a big operation. Instead of four men improvising their lives, the "wise guys" of *GoodFellas* operate as a moderately extensive business, with a boss, minions, hangers-on, loose cannons, all ready to kill or get killed whenever anyone above them is displeased. The ethnicity of this group is broad—Italians, Irish, and Jews—but this apparent breadth contains a movie irony, because these are the three mainstays of old Hollywood's representation of ethnic groups. African Americans and Hispanics are peripheral to them, not only throughout film history, but within Scorsese's films, because the thugs are, themselves, deeply racist—a fact Scorsese notes continually.

However broader the range of types, ethnicities, and geographies of the wise guys, they are circumscribed in an airless world of brutality and betrayal. They rob, steal, snitch, go to jail, take drugs, sell drugs, beat each other up, assassinate one another, and go to jail again—or into the witness protection program. The trick of the film is to make this world seem less airless than it is, and Scorsese accomplishes this by seeming to filter his mise-en-scène through Henry's and Karen's points of view and by means of some highly kinetic image-making. Given their ethnicities—he's Irish Italian, she's Jewish—they appear outside the Italian gangsters' world yet are so entranced by it that their pleasure and energy overwhelm what should be plain revulsion at what the characters in the film are actually doing. This delight is transferred to us not only through the voice-overs, but through the mise-en-scène itself. There is no better example in the film than the now famous four-minute shot of Henry and Karen descending through the hallway, kitchen, and into the main room of the Copa Cabana night club. Done to the accompaniment of the Shirelles' "And Then He Kissed Me," taking advantage of the mobility of a body-mounted Steadicam camera, this shot stands as a major contradiction to the theory, propounded by André Bazin, that the long take enables fundamental realist perceptions in cinema. Bazin held that when the filmmaker allows his camera a long, meditative gaze at his subject, that subject reveals itself in the fullness of its existence.[11] Sometimes the reverse is true. Because continuity cutting is naturalized as the transparent delivery system of film stories, when the cutting stops and the viewer is asked to look at a shot in its long duration, attention becomes drawn to the medium as well as the message. It's not inevitable. Quentin Tarantino's long-take dialogue sequences, especially in *Pulp Fiction*, do not make themselves particularly noticeable because the dialogue itself is the focus of attention. The opening shot of Robert Altman's *The Player* does, because it is very complex and demands attention, and because the dialogue of the characters keeps referring to its antecedent, one of the most famous long takes in film history, the opening shot of Welles's *Touch of Evil.*

The immediate narrative function of the Copa shot is minimal: Henry takes Karen on a date to show off what a big man he is. But its function in the larger narrative and visual strategy of the film is greater: Henry is in full command of his world, and his commanding movement through the back and main rooms of the club, chatting with workers, having a table lifted high over the other customers' heads as he heads for his reserved place, indicate a man at the top of his game. Indeed, this sequence shot precedes the Kennedy airport heist in the narrative flow, and that job indicates the height of the gang's powers and the beginning of their downfall. But, again, the shot is more than a narrative marker. It is the visible mark of the film's narrative author; it is, in effect, Scorsese saying, "Look at what I can do—and keep on doing longer than most other long shots in the history of film." Its traversal of enormous space recalls Welles's opening of *Touch of Evil* and calls forth the long tradition of moving camera reaching back to the work of the German F. W. Murnau. It is chest-thumping, to be sure, but it is also a statement about the existence of the camera, the eyes behind it, and their ability to create, own, and express ideas through mise-en-scène. The shot exists both in and outside the film simultaneously, another part of the triangulation the film creates with itself, film history, and the viewer, and an important part of the self-consciousness that eventually becomes the overriding narrative of *GoodFellas*.

The long take is, of course, only one aspect of the self-conscious narration. Editing is another and very subtle element. Scorsese's editing style is carefully executed and tuned to create the appropriate dramatic rhythm of a given sequence. The angularity of the cutting, making arhythmic joins between the movement in one shot to the movement in another, speeding things up—as in the cocaine sequences, where the cutting suggests the characters' paranoid state of mind—provide a kind of rhythm section for the shots that together compose the movement and meaning of the film.

The film's many voice-overs, mostly delivered by Henry, occasionally by Karen, provide another kind of rhythmic counterpoint. Henry recalls and reports, explains, reflects, comments, boasts, vaunts, maintaining all the while a tone of amused awe at the life he leads. Unlike the voice-over narration in Kubrick's *Barry Lyndon,* or Travis Bickle's in Scorsese's own *Taxi Driver,* Henry's seems to be in sync with what we see on the screen. More than in sync, in control. This is his story, his film. "As far back as I can remember, I always wanted to be a gangster." Henry's words occur in the pre-credit sequence of the film, over a sequence that actually occurs much later in the narrative, as he looks on while Tommy (Joe Pesci) and Jimmy (Robert De Niro) stab and shoot Billy Batts in the trunk of their car. In this sequence, Henry looks down at the trunk, an expression of slight discomfort on his face. The camera dollies in to his face and the image freezes; Tony Bennett sings "Rags to Riches" on the sound track. The voice-over tends to redirect our attention from the narrative movement, briefly diverting it from the images to another temporal range, where voice and the person speaking, rather than image, are most important. Combined with the freeze frames that occur throughout the film—a very literal suspension of narrative movement in which the image flow comes to a stop—another rhythm is created as the film seems to be asking us to think about other than its moving images, to listen to a familiar voice coming from an undefined space, a voice that perhaps controls the images.

"Memory" might be a word for this. In the early part of the film, Henry recalls getting beaten by his father for hanging around with the hoodlums instead of going to school—the image freezes on his father viciously beating him with a belt. "The way I saw it, everybody takes a beating some time," the older Henry tells us in voice-over. His gangster pals, with the perfect logic of the street, decide that if the postman doesn't deliver truant letters to his mother, nobody will know where Henry is. So they beat up the postman and stick his head in a pizza oven. Freeze on postman in pizza oven. "That was it," Henry explains, "no more letters from truant officers, no more letters from school, in fact, no more letters from anybody."

Until the end of the film, Scorsese doesn't seem to provide an establishing shot that anchors Henry's voice in a known space. Where is it coming from? From what point in the narrative? Is it the controlling point from which all the other images radiate? Are the freeze frames representing what's going in Henry's memory? Are all the other images? We are back to the questions posed by the Copa Cabana shot: whose perceptions are controlling *Good-*

Fellas, who is providing a dependable point of view? Earlier, I made reference to the sequence in the bar, where Henry introduces the viewer to his gangster pals, as the camera circles and the men address it as it passes by. They address it as if it were Henry and as if Scorsese were executing a fairly normal point-of-view shot where the camera equals the character's eyes. "Fairly normal" in the conventions of classical Hollywood cinema is still a complex affair in which the viewer is asked to transfer attention from the neutral space of third-person observation—itself fraught with assumptions about who is seeing what and why—to the immediate perceptions of a character. In a point-of-view shot, the camera—the apparatus—is to be taken as an agent that transfers the perceptions of a fictional character in a fictional space to the collectivity of viewers looking at the film. It is an ideological as well as narrative device, in which the viewer assumes that, while many times removed from the camera eye and while the camera eye is itself a mechanical recorder of images, we are assuming the perceptions of an individual consciousness—seeing through someone's eyes.[12] Scorsese knows how tenuous this convention is and plays a trick on it and the viewer. The last person introduced at the bar is Jimmy Two Times ("who got that name because he said everything twice"). The camera follows Jimmy from the bar ("I'm gonna get the papers, get the papers"). He walks to the rear and to the left. There has been no cut, so presumably the point of view still belongs to Henry. But, as Jimmy leaves, the camera continues left, now following a guy in a Hawaiian shirt, who moves to the kitchen. From screen left, a rack of fur coats emerges, being pushed by Henry! There are a few jokes as the recipient of the coats asks what he's going to do with them in the middle of summer and decides to hang them in the freezer with the meat (thereby foreshadowing the frozen gangster corpses placed in a meat truck later in the film). The camera ends its run behind Henry, who walks to the rear of the kitchen.

If the track around the bar has been authorized by Henry's point of view, how is it that Henry emerges from a space that is not the same as the space occupied by the camera? We have already noticed something like this in Kubrick's *The Shining*, when the camera, which we expect is a vehicle for Jack Torrence's point of view, tracks from the right and then Jack walks in front of it. The play against expectation there is founded in horror-film conventions, where the camera takes the position of the monster. *GoodFellas* is not a monster film, though its characters are amusing monsters full of self-importance and diminished stature, who prey mostly on themselves.

199

The switch in point of view here is a kind of caution, subtle, barely notice-able, that we need to take care when identifying with characters. The camera is not Henry. Henry does not own the film's point of view.

Late in the film, just as Henry is about to betray his friends, he meets with Jimmy in the diner that is their usual hangout. This is a crucial mo-ment. Henry is about to break the cardinal rule. Jimmy knows this. Their meeting in the diner follows the sequence in which Jimmy acts in a threat-ening manner to Karen, trying to maneuver her down the street into a dark corner, a sequence shot in a Hitchcockian manner with the camera track-ing Karen and then assuming her point of view as she walks down the street, finally pulling up as she decides to make a getaway in her car. "Your mur-derers come with smiles," says Henry in voice-over as he comes into the diner. The camera tracks down the aisle, this time hewing closely to Henry's point of view, and he sits with Jimmy in the booth. The camera assumes a ninety-degree position so that Jimmy is on the left, Henry on the right, the window between them. As they talk, something strange happens to the space. The interior seems to remain stable, while outside the window, the world expands, objects move closer. It is quite disorienting and meant to be, because the coordinates of Henry's world are shifting rapidly. Scorsese has executed a camera strategy that dates precisely back to 1958 and Alfred Hitchcock's *Vertigo*, where, to emulate a state of dizziness in a high tower, Hitchcock photographed a mock-up of the tower stairwell by simultane-ously zooming and tracking the camera in opposite directions, presenting the collapsing of space that represents the Jimmy Stewart character's point of view. This emulation has fascinated filmmakers. Spielberg uses it to great effect in *Jaws*, where Sherriff Brody's anxiety as he looks at the water for a sign of the shark is communicated by the same kind of opposite pull of lens and camera body that creates a vertiginous space. The effect is now threat-ening to become commonplace, but its use in *GoodFellas* is effective and an-other indication of a storytelling "voice" that is more than Henry's and that tells us about events beyond the dialogue or the voice-overs.

The payoff comes quickly. Henry and Karen negotiate with the FBI to go into the witness protection program. At the wise guys' trial, Henry is up on the stand, pointing to and giving up his friends. The camera swoops around him; the cutting picks out the faces of his former pals; his voice-over talks about how wonderful the life was: "We were treated like movie stars with muscle. We had it all just for the asking." Paulie and Jimmy rise to take their sentence. Henry's voice continues talking about the life. Scorsese cuts back to him as he says, "It didn't matter." Now he is directly addressing the camera. "It didn't mean anything. When I was broke I would go out and rob some more." He is making eye contact, breaking a cardinal rule of the classic American style that forbids a character to recognize the camera's presence, and he gets up from the stand, walks around and through the courtroom as if it were a movie set, moves into closeup, and tells us, "And now it's all over."

The good life of a petty gangster is over, and so, almost, is the film. But what does all this mean? Certainly, the sudden break of the "fourth wall" is not a big surprise in this visually playful film. And it seems to answer the original question about the origination point of Henry's voice-over. He's musing in the courtroom, which is revealed to be a movie set. He has apparently revealed his place in the fiction as one of the *components* of the narration and one of its controlling voices. This would be a satisfying analysis except for the fact that Henry's voice-over continues into the film's last sequence, his new habitation in a faceless suburb, where he can't get a decent tomato sauce and has to live the rest of his life "like a schnook." Henry comes out the door, picks up the paper, looks once again at the camera. A smile begins to play across his face, a glissando plays on the sound track, and Scorsese cuts to a shot (which appears nowhere else in the film) of Tommy—who was murdered at the hands of his own Mafia family—shooting his gun directly at the camera. On the soundtack, the Sex Pistols sing "My Way."

Tristram Shandy, Lawrence Sterne's great, reflexive eighteenth-century novel about trying to get a novel written, ends with words that seem perfectly to sum up these last shots of the film:

L — — d! said my mother, what is all this story about?
A C O C K and a B U L L, said Yorick. . . . And one of the best of its kind, I ever heard.

Scorsese has created the perfect latter-day cock-and-bull picaresque narrative about gangsters, which, like Sterne's novel and later modernist works of fiction and film, continually gloss their own status as fictions. At the same time, he created the perfect gloss on the gangster genre. The interaction of voices, narrative spaces, gazes at the camera, winks, nods, and smiles acts to interrogate our response to the history of gangster films. Why do we believe anything we see in gangster films? Scorsese seems to ask. They are playing out of sixty-year-old narrative codes that trigger our assent to the fantasy of a powerful and violent life. They are our idea of a self-contained community, of protection and riches that are based on corruption and murder, and therefore—in the inevitable, contradictory logic of a culture that resents those who gain huge success while admiring them and wanting to see them punished—doomed to fail. Henry speaks for the viewer. Like him, we love the gangster life. At least we love looking at representations of it. And we applaud its failure, because it comforts us with the paradox that the life is desirable, untenable, and unattainable.

GoodFellas gives us everything, and we are able to take pleasure, be shocked and appalled, maintain our distance, be mocked by and mock in our turn the figures on screen. *GoodFellas* is pleasure with very little pain. Unlike *Mean Streets*, whose rough unpredictability is a little threatening, *GoodFellas'* unpredictability almost always winds up in a joke. Even its violence is so surrounded with rudeness, laughter, and high spirits that its ill effects are dissipated. It is the gangster film as low-life screwball comedy with blood and with a self-awareness that distracts us from its more appalling elements. Such is not the case with *Casino*, a sort of sequel to *Good-Fellas*, also co-written by Nicholas Peleggi, and forming (for the moment) Scorsese's gangster trilogy. All three films are concerned about the constitution of certain borders or boundaries. Cinematically, *Mean Streets* examines the borders between fiction and fictional documentary while dwelling thematically on the constricting borders of a disappearing ethnic neighborhood. *GoodFellas*, acting in part as a parody of *The Godfather* films, thinks about the borders of family, legitimate and illegitimate, about a protective community that dwells with betrayal and kills its own. Cinematically, it attacks the safe borders between viewer and viewed, making contact with the spectator in unexpected ways, playing with basic conventions of point of view of whom is seeing what and why.

Casino tells of the destruction of borders, the loss of the gangster community, a movement from city to country, from Kansas City (rather than New York) to the desert, from Mafia to corporation. In all three films, centers come apart. The gangs in *Mean Streets* and *GoodFellas* disintegrate when they turn on each other. This happens with the suddenness of an angry word and a trip out of the safe neighborhood in *Mean Streets*. It happens with a glance at the camera in *GoodFellas*, a glance that has itself been prepared for by other glances: the troubling, Hitchcockian sequence where Karen visits Jimmy at his warehouse in Queens, for example. Henry's act of betrayal is his own act of salvation. He redeems himself into the banality of a suburban life in the witness protection and betrays the audience with a wink and a nod. Irony bites. The thing that bites in *Casino* is a baseball bat, with which two characters are beaten, before the viewer's eyes, to a bloody pulp at the end of the film—the only violence in a Scorsese film that I cannot watch.

There is little irony in *Casino*, little engagement with the expectations of the audience, that playing on the viewer's desire, inviting her into the game that energizes the previous two gangster films. The structure of taut, angular surprise around the edge of every shot of *Mean Streets* and *GoodFellas* is replaced by a more horizontal editorial and narrative line. The film is three hours long and is the only film of the trilogy to be shot in the wide anamorphic screen ratio of 2.35:1, a form Scorsese uses only rarely (*Cape Fear* and *Age of Innocence* are the others so far). There are many dialogue sequences cut with the conventional over-the-shoulder style that Scorsese usually reserves for expository sequences in films with which he is not completely engaged. But here, narrative duration, cutting, composing characters within the long, horizontal screen frame, the very horizontal stretch of the desert that becomes a metaphor in the film for death and loss and is contrasted with the cold, lowering skies and cinderblock buildings of Kansas City, are part of a different rhythm and direction of narrative structure and not a sign of disengagement.

Like its predecessors, *Casino* is concerned with the fall of a mob, but here the fall is more global, less dependent on personal quirks. It is more political, though still based on a smart understanding of ethnic subtleties. Intimacy and sexuality enter the scheme in different ways than in the earlier films. Charlie's relationship with Teresa in *Mean Streets* is rooted in the Catholic agony over sexuality as pleasure vs. sexuality as reproductive duty. Teresa herself is a troublesome presence of self-aware sexuality that Scorsese contains both through her attachment to Charlie and her epilepsy. Karen and Henry's relationship in *GoodFellas* is on a more equal footing, though "equal" in Scorsese's gangster realm means that, while Karen has her own voice, can answer back, can confront Henry's mistress, and help hide the cocaine, she remains relegated to the position of gangster's wife and subject to scorn and abuse. The romance of *Casino* has more melodramatic roots, and emerges directly from another film—Jean-Luc Godard's *Contempt*—that deals with sexuality within a very European context: enthrallment, debasement, abjection, and death. The romance runs parallel, indeed mirrors, the other narrative movements of the film. The Kansas City mob runs Las Vegas, installing Sam "Ace" Rothstein (Robert De Niro) as its

Chief Operating Officer. The mob sends out Nicky (Joe Pesci) to watch Ace. But Nicky is a mean-minded little killer, who tries to turn Vegas into a space for his petty and violent thievery.

Sam Rothstein is a Jew, an outsider among the Italian thugs, more of an outsider than Henry Hill, who was half Irish. But Ace has Henry's wiliness and an extraordinary and simple sense of place and administrative purpose. Even his enthrallment to Ginger, his insistence on marrying her despite her lack of affection for him and her obsessive relationship to her pimp (played with more than usual sleaziness by James Woods), is done with steadiness and understanding. The growth of their mutual contempt destroys Ginger but leaves Ace pretty much as he was. He seems to function as one of the spatial elements in the film, part of the horizontal line that remains steady despite the spikes of appalling violence done by and, finally, to Nicky, despite the crumbling of the mob's control and the literal, physical fall of the old mob-dominated casinos and the rise of the corporate, family-friendly Las Vegas. In this sense, *Casino* is a kind of chronicle and recalls those quasi-documentary elements that we spoke about in *Mean Streets*. Here, though, Scorsese is less concerned with the elements of perception he dealt with in the earlier films but with a kind of overview of gangsterism and gambling. The first part of the film, narrated by Ace and occasionally by Nicky, is devoted to a documentation of the skimming practices of the mob and its all-encompassing gaze. The second part of the film, somewhat more conventionally dramatic, also addresses the gaze, but this time it is the FBI's, who observe the characters' comings and goings so thoroughly that the mobsters belief in their freedom to act is only an illusion.

Now this should sound familiar. Scorsese is once again making a film that not only finds its foundations in other films, but takes as its larger subject a cinematic problem: the question of the gaze, which extends our discussion of point of view in *GoodFellas*. How characters look at one another and how the viewer is asked to look at the characters are problems fundamental to film structure. The formation and control of the gaze determine how shots are composed and cut; the direction of *our* gaze, which a good director will control as much as he controls the gazes of the characters in the mise-en-scène, determines our point of view and our emotional and intellectual attachment to the film. Scorsese has always been fascinated with how the gaze is structured, and we will see how in *Taxi Driver* he manages it with such rigor that, as viewers, we are scarcely allowed any separation from what the central character is seeing. *GoodFellas* brings under investigation the generic gaze of the gangster movie as well as a larger question of why audiences are so eager to look at gangsters on the screen. *Casino* is thinking about the decay of that gaze, and where *GoodFellas* treats the gaze of the audience ironically, jokingly, so that the violence might almost be noted as an aberration, in *Casino* the audience's gaze is continually interrupted by sadistic acts of violence that are seen as central to the gangster's world. We are asked either to look away or to become scopophilic accomplices. Visual pleasure, the essential drive that makes us want to look, see, know, and feel more is compromised by *Casino*. The pleasures of knowledge, learning about the money operations on the floor and in the back rooms of the gaming palaces; the erotic pleasures of the gaze at Sharon Stone's Ginger; the narrative propulsion that carries us through the collapse of a marriage told across the expanse of gaudy, shiny interiors and cheap, desert-side roadhouses, and the general hard and beautiful neon-fluorescent glow of the film's mise-en-scène are countered by the viciousness of Ace's having a cheater's hand broken with a hammer, Nicky's crushing a rival's head in a vice until his eyeballs pop out, and the final, anti-scopophilic images of Nicky and his brother beaten to a pulp with a baseball bat.

Yet, even though the scopophilic aspects of the gaze are threatened, Scorsese insists on indicating that he remains in control of it. There is a sequence, early in the film, that parallels in virtuosity the Copa Cabana sequence in *GoodFellas*. Scorsese, through Ace Rothstein's voice-over, and an extraordinary montage, presents us with a theory of the gaze that parallels Michel Foucault's discussion of the Panopticon, all cut to the music of the Les McCann / Eddie Harris song "Real, Compared to What?" Bentham's Panopticon is a construction by means of which prisoners are kept under observation in jail. The prisoners are aware they are being observed, but cannot see their observers. Foucault extrapolates this architectural event into a social, cultural, and political statement of power. "The Panopticon is a marvelous machine which, whatever use one may wish to put it to, produces homogeneous effects of power. . . . He who is subjected to a field of visibility, and who knows it, assumes responsibility for the constraints of power; he makes them play spontaneously on himself; he inscribes in himself the power relation in which he simultaneously plays both roles; he becomes the principle of his own subjection."[13]

The quotation seems applicable to Ace Rothstein: diffident, moral (in a way), glad to be of use, eager to do his job, an upright tool of mobsterism. In his relationship to his bosses and to his beloved but unloving Ginger, he becomes the principle of his own subjection. He sees almost everything, accepts the constraints on his power—and survives. The sequence in which he explains the Panopticon creates a visual ascension of the controlling gaze, a montage of the eyes that bind Ace to his bosses and the viewer to the viewer's boss: the director of the film. The first line of the song "God-dammit, real compared to what?" sounds on the track, and two figures come into view across the expanse of the frame. The lights shine off the glasses of one them. Ace moves in between them and the camera circles and tracks in to him. "In Vegas, everybody's got to watch everybody else," his voice tells us, and for forty seconds, Scorsese cuts from one set of watchers to another as Ace tells us who is watching whom, a counterpoint of gazes, ending with "the eye in the sky," the gazers in the ceiling of the casino, who are "watching us all."

The long tracking shot in *GoodFellas* was a celebration of the directorial gaze; the panopticon montage in *Casino* is a statement of its necessity. Even its form states necessity. A long, tracking shot is always a statement of liberation, even, as we saw in our discussion of Welles and Kubrick, where it often signifies the collapse of agency. Only the director can organize and execute an elaborate track. Cutting can be celebratory. Eisenstein proved this and Stone extends the principle. But it is always necessary. Cutting is what is done *to* the shot, not with it. Bernardo Bertolucci, in an oedipal state, once called editing a kind of castration.[14] In a film about the destroying gaze, this particular cutting exercise is both a statement of the director's power to create an eloquent sequence and significant of the castrating force of the gaze, and the loss of control expressed in the narrative. The sequence tells us that no one and everyone in this particular world has power and its very diffuseness will be its downfall. Ace is a tool of the Kansas City Mafia, who allow Nicky to watch over and eventually try to destroy him, only to be destroyed himself. Meanwhile, the FBI gazes on everyone and, finally, the great, universal corporate gaze bears down and brings everything to ruin. Even the erotic gaze is compromised. Ginger is introduced in the midst of the montage, seen at the craps table, and then by Ace, who, at the end of the sequence, is watching her on a television monitor, no doubt receiving its signal from "the eye in the sky." He looks at her, desires her, and enters into a destructive relationship from which only he will survive.

For all the looking and watching that takes place in *Casino*, little is learned. For all its complexity, it cannot quite overcome the flat horizontality, the dying line that is its metaphor. Its acts of violence go deeper than any insights into their causes. Much of the film has a kind of sour charm and all of it the sheen of filmmaker whose eye is strong and sense of construction seamless. But where *Mean Streets* and *GoodFellas* wrapped their characters' desire for success with the irony of the failure within a constricted but energized mise-en-scène, *Casino* contains its energy as it proceeds. It seems to share with Scorsese's costume dramas—*The Last Temptation of Christ, The Age of Innocence*, and *Kundun*—an earnestness of observation, a perfection of production design, and a diffusion of narrative concentration. Even *Last Temptation*, which struggles to humanize its Christ figure, to create him and his followers in the mold of the street wanderers of *Mean Streets* in the agony of finding a simple life where simplicity is impossible, cannot quite explain the overwhelming violence of its conclusion. These are all films of a dying fall from grace. Both *Casino* and *Last Temptation* (the other film set in the desert) proffer grace as a domesticity that is absolutely unattainable, an idea Scorsese has pursued as far back as *Alice Doesn't Live Here Anymore* and *New York, New York*. In *Casino* domesticity is a lost cause, and all desires are cut short or buried in the desert, stolen by the Mafia, or taken over by big corporations, who destroy the old casinos. All gazes finally bounce off one another, back to us, who finally have to avert our own gaze in face of the violence. We are even cut off from Ace. At the end, he alone remains to tell the tale, a bookie in San Diego, his eyes hidden behind a huge pair of tinted glasses. He takes them off but does not meet our gaze. "And that's that," he says, closing a long, grim story with a slightly chagrined look. Henry Hill's knowing smile at the camera is nowhere in evidence.

If we accept Thomas Elsaesser's idea that melodrama provides visual structures for the dynamic of emotions repressed, expressed, and contained, and that the excess of this operation spills over into the film's mise-en-scène and music, then almost all of Scorsese's films fall into the melodramatic camp.[15] But classic movie melodrama deals with emotional conflict between genders; Scorsese examines individual struggle, or the conflict between men, always reflects this onto the mise-en-scène, but rarely resolves the emotional turmoil, as would conventional melodrama, into the typical terms of psychological realism. The contestation of emotion is pushed into violence, against others or the self, transferred into the culture at large through the creation of a small or large legend (this is what happens to Travis Bickle in *Taxi Driver*, Rupert Pupkin in *The King of Comedy*, or to Jesus Christ in *The Last Temptation of Christ* and the Dalai Lama in *Kundun*).

When dealing with heterosexual domestic melodrama, Scorsese will often push cinematic allusion even further into the foreground than in his other films. *Alice Doesn't Live Here Anymore* depends a good deal on forties "women's" film; *New York, New York* is quite consciously built on the musical melodramas of the thirties, forties, and fifties. In *Casino*, Scorsese sees the domestic scene as a disaster, an act of masochism, and turns to Godard for guidance. This process of domestic collapse within an allusive melodramatic frame is nowhere more evident than in *Cape Fear*, a film Scorsese made for Universal as thanks for the studio's support of *Last Temptation*, and which went on to be one of Scorsese's few big money-makers.

Cape Fear is Scorsese's remake of a 1962 Universal film of the same name, which, in its time, was one of the relatively few films to pay direct homage to *Psycho*. Two years after its appearance, Hitchcock's film was still a transgressive event. Its impact on American filmmaking occurred slowly, sporadically, but profoundly—as we'll see when we look at *Taxi Driver*. The first *Cape Fear* not only had *Psycho* on its mind and in its images but in its creative staff as well: George Tomasini, Hitchcock's regular editor, who cut *Psycho*, edited *Cape Fear*, and Bernard Herrmann wrote the score. Martin Balsam, Detective Arbogast in *Psycho*, plays a role in the later film. Although J. Lee Thompson, director of the first *Cape Fear*, is no Hitchcock, he can copy, and there are camera angles and events that come into the film direct from its predecessor, while the whole attempts to maintain the grayscale, barren landscaped angst of Hitchcock's work. Scorsese had already worked through *Psycho* in *Taxi Driver*, and therefore, understanding that Hitchcock lay behind the original *Cape Fear*, he needed to do Hitchcock again, but another way. He takes on Herrmann's score wholesale, having it reorchestrated by another veteran Hollywood composer, Elmer Bernstein. He continues the actor shuffle of the first *Cape Fear* by bringing back in bit parts Martin Balsam as well as the original film's stars, Gregory Peck and Robert Mitchum.

Otherwise, Scorsese moves the film slightly away from a story of sadistic revenge by a creepy psycho into a big, loud, color, Panavision family melodrama, in which a lawyer, Sam Bowden (Nick Nolte) must protect wife, daughter, and home from the internal strains as well as the external threat brought on by the release of a convict, Max Cady (Robert De Niro), whom Sam put away. Sexuality and gender play as overt a role in this film as they ever have in Scorsese's films, which may only mean that their role is explicit and obvious rather than subtle. But on the level of immediate apprehension, Scorsese did not intend subtlety. This was a film undertaken to reach a large audience. It succeeded, while at the same time carrying on a subtle play of Hitchcockian allusions that helps make it a bit more than a noisy crowd pleaser.

When I first saw *Cape Fear*, I could barely make out something familiar going on behind the images, as if there were a ghost moving through the film. The ghost turned out to be not so much a spirit as a palimpsest, another text, an original one, playing beneath the second *Cape Fear*'s surface the way *Psycho* played beneath the first's. That palimpsest turned out also to be made by Hitchcock. Scorsese turns the story of *Cape Fear* into a narrative of doubles. Cady is something of Sam's evil twin, his dark other, a bad conscience turned into a vengeful madman. Hitchcock had long been fascinated by the narrative of the double and had treated it most successfully in his 1943 film *Shadow of a Doubt*. It comes up again—most famously—in the 1951 *Strangers on a Train*, and it is that film, along with two other less than successful Hitchcock films of the period, *Stage Fright* (1950) and *I Confess* (1953), that plays beneath the surface of *Cape Fear*. These films more than play, they are *re*played by Scorsese, so that sequences, especially from *Strangers on a Train*, are remade in the later work. For example, one of the most famous moments in *Strangers on a Train* is the tennis match, where the evil and deranged Bruno watches Guy from the stands. As the tennis ball flies back and forth, the heads of the crowd move to watch it. All except Bruno, who stares straight ahead, full of menace and malice. In *Cape Fear*, Sam Bowden sees Max Cady at a Fourth of July parade, across the street from him. Scorsese picks up Cady in a telephoto shot: the parade moves across the camera's line of sight, the crowd around Cady watches the parade, Cady stares straight ahead, full of menace and malice. The ghostly appearance of Cady outside the window of Sam and Leigh's bedroom echoes Bruno's appearance in the dark outside Guy's house in *Strangers on a Train*.[16]

I'm convinced that in *Cape Fear* Scorsese consciously made two films in one: the raucous, crowd-pleasing moneymaker with Robert De Niro as a seductive version of the unkillable monster of contemporary horror films who keeps rising whenever he's thought dead, and the serious film-scholar version, in which one must analyze the images to discover the Hitchcockian allusions. They are certainly obscure, and obscurity is not necessarily the same as complexity. But this is a difficult point in American film, where complexity is suspect because of producers' fears of burdening and therefore alienating the viewer. This might encourage a director to use an obscure reference that would give a film some depth and which an audience member might get or not. At the same time, contemporary filmgoers have become sophisticated in the complexities of popular culture. Indeed, the postmodern phenomenon depends upon reception—audience response. Postmodernity is, in part, the condition of living comfortably within the web of popular cultural references, of recognizing, perhaps, that Max Cady's finger tattoos that read "Love" and "Hate" come from Charles Laughton's *Night of the Hunter* (1955) and adorned the fingers of Robert Mitchum, who also plays Max Cady in the first *Cape Fear*. What was once pedantry is now popular wisdom. Those particular tattoos have moved from the films into the actual marks tattoo lovers put on their bodies. But this is not complexity. For all its allusions, *Cape Fear* is still a simple and somewhat simple-minded film.

The ironies of self-consciousness in *GoodFellas* and the dying fall along the horizon of the desert in *Casino* certainly offered, along with Oliver Stone's films, as high a level of cinematic complexity as any film of the nineties. But Scorsese does not choose to work at full tilt in every film, and these were countered by *Cape Fear* and by *The Age of Innocence* and *Kundun*, films more intricate and polished in their production design and editing than in complexity of mise-en-scène or narrative. But even Scorsese's two major films of the nineties are less charged than those films around which his reputation thrives, *Taxi Driver* and *Raging Bull*. Although *Mean Streets* may be the film most obsessively imitated by young filmmakers, *Taxi Driver* and *Raging Bull* are the works that garner the most critical attention, and deservedly so. In these films a cinematic intelligence is at work in a concentrated way, creating a mise-en-scène of the streets from which the characters cannot be detached, exploring a complex point of view, and generating content out of form so tightly that it is impossible to detach a summarizable story or understand characters as entities separate from their narrative and the space into which they are placed.

The subjects of *Raging Bull* are working-class Italians in New York, which links them both to *Mean Streets* before it and *GoodFellas* following it. The relationship between Jake La Motta (Robert De Niro) and his brother, Joey (Joe Pesci), echoes that of Johnny Boy and Charlie. As in both films, there is a perpetual ground bass of violence, which reaches its dominant voice in the boxing ring. The neighborhood tough guys, the stylized imitation of New York working-class speech (the film was co-scripted by Mardik Martin and Paul Schrader) are also of a piece with the other street films. And, like those films, there is a desire not to define motivated, conventional characters who dwell within a traditional narrative design. Still, the films do have generic ties. *Mean Streets* contains some elements of the gangster film and of film noir, even of the thirties Warner Brothers Dead End Kids cycle, yet it does not build itself on a firm generic base. *GoodFellas* is firmly based in the gangster genre. *Raging Bull*, by the nature of its subject, is immediately associated with the subgenre of the boxing film, and Scorsese has therefore to confront certain conventions, such as the revelation of a sensitive soul beneath the fighter's hardened exterior. The film toys with some of the subgenre's characteristics. Jake La Motta finds his prestige, his means of impressing himself on the world, in the boxing ring, the only safe outlet for his aggressiveness. He naively desires to succeed in the sport on his own and must confront those inevitable elements of the boxing film—the mob and its demand that he throw a fight. But these generic prerequisites, rather than reining the film into a conventional pattern, serve as a foil to its eccentric structure and to Scorsese's refusal to make his character and narrative conform to type. One need only compare *Raging Bull* with any of the *Rocky* series to see how far Scorsese moves his text outside the pattern that elaborates the boxing ring as a successful stage for the working-class hero or for any heroics at all.[17] One has to look back to Robert Rossen and Abraham Polonsky's *Body and Soul* (1947) and Robert Wise's grim film, *The Set-Up* (1949), to find usable antecedents.

Yet out of the mix of generic elements and the refusal to create a simple narrative and comfortable character continuity, Scorsese comes as close as he cares to a psychological study—much closer than he does in *The Color of Money*, his other sports film, where actions, reactions, and motivations are more conventionally rendered than they are in any of his films. *Raging Bull* does not attempt to explain its character. We are not given reasons for Jake La Motta's behavior; rather we see it and hear it. Character is revealed in La Motta's movements, actions, and talk, in the spatial coordinates of which he is the focal point, and in the music and sound that surround him or are only in his head. What we learn is that *Raging Bull* addresses the inscription of sadomasochism onto the body of an individual who punishes himself and others because he cannot understand or control either. Like so many of Scorsese's characters, La Motta is a subject without subjectivity, without a firm comprehension of self or its location. Even though, like the characters of *Mean Streets* and *GoodFellas* or even Travis Bickle in *Taxi Driver*, La Motta is tied down to cultural, ideological, class moorings, he is, more than anything, a function of his vocation, his physical size (with which he must do as great battle as with any opponent), his incomprehension, and his monolithic jealousy. The characters of *Mean Streets* and *GoodFellas* at least have the comfort, however uneasy and tentative, of their community. La Motta has no comfort, only the pull of his inarticulable aggression, his self-destructiveness, and his need for recognition. The narrative lurches him from one violent or demeaning situation to another. On the stage of a cheap nightclub, in the ring, or in a domestic space, La Motta can only give or receive abuse.[18]

The film opens with an enormously fat La Motta rehearsing his nightclub routine, reciting lines that contain the film's title—"Just gimme a stage where this bull here can rage"—demeaning even his violent nickname. As he ends his act with the cliché, "That's entertainment," a phrase that reduces all performance to the same level of banality, Scorsese cuts to a mid-closeup and a superimposed title, "Jake La Motta, 1964" (such identifying titles tag the film with certain documentary conventions, as they do in *Mean Streets*). Another cut reveals a young, lean La Motta in the ring, poised with fists up. The title reads 1941. On the sound track, the La Motta of 1964 repeats, "That's entertainment," and his younger incarnation gets punched violently in the face with a loud smack on the sound track.

"Entertainment" is punishment and sacrifice, or sacrament, a means to escape from the body by using the body to give or receive pain, or as a public demonstration of the private need to inflict damage. Indeed, public and private, violence and sexual intimacy merge in a group of scenes in which Scorsese cuts from La Motta and his wife-to-be Vickie leaving the room to make love, to La Motta fighting Sugar Ray Robinson, and then back to another scene of lovemaking).[19] Violence as sacrament also becomes a driving theme of *The Last Temptation of Christ*, the film very much on Scorsese's mind at the time. *Raging Bull* can be seen as a kind of preparation for it.

The ring is where La Motta's person and personality are constituted and dissolved and the boxing matches are created as a kind of interior landscape, an arena of violent despair and terror, a dark space punctuated by photographers' flashbulbs and fights breaking out in the audience. The sounds of this strange, vicious world are articulated by disembodied moans and shrieks (the sound track, as we will see, is the most carefully articulated in any of Scorsese's films to that point), and the images are made of fragmentary, slow-motion shots of fists and faces receiving them with a frightful noise and explosive splatterings of sweat and blood. The point of view within the ring is of a kind of semiconsciousness and a dissolving of the self—an expression of La Motta's interiority. Outside the ring, where events are observed somewhat more neutrally, with much of the quasi-documentary presence of streets and tenements that marks *Mean Streets*, La Motta's dislocation and lack of center are indicated by another visual signifier of weakened consciousness. When La Motta looks at his wife with the jealousy that, along with his violence, is the only expression of his feelings for her, he sees her and the people she is with in slow motion, moving as if unconnected with the world, another projection of his own confusion. Scorsese's use of slow motion is one of his most articulate stylistic devices, so well tuned that he can increase and decrease the speed of his characters' perceptions within one shot. Interiority is, by this means, made explicit; space and movement become functions of how the character sees his world.

In *Raging Bull*, sound becomes another expression of interiority, even a way to explain character. Scorsese does this in complex ways that counterpoint or expand the narrative, sometimes on the level of form itself, where sound works as a clever counterpoint to editing. Early in the film, there is a key sequence of fouled domesticity between Jake and his first wife. The sequence takes place in a cramped tenement, dogs barking, people yelling—mostly Jake at his wife about how she is cooking his steak. He throws it on the floor and her out of the room. The whole sequence is shot and cut tightly, in medium closeup. Here and throughout the film, Scorsese uses the over-the-shoulder style to greater effect than anywhere else in his work. It's not a sign of boredom but of attempting to get close to his characters, who, of course, do not accept closeness of any kind short of violence. Joey sits with Jake and tries to calm him down, a process that almost always leads to illogic and violence. Jake complains about his body, his hands especially—"like little girls hands." He'll never be able to fight Joe Louis, he says. Joey reasons with him that because Jake's a middleweight and Louis a heavyweight, they will, indeed, never fight. But logic and disappointment only lead to violence for Jake, in this case of the masochistic sort, and he bullies and goads Joey into hitting him in the face. "Whadd'ya trying to prove?" Joey finally asks. There is, of course, no answer to this, for Jake comes to a blind desire for pain whenever his career, his masculinity, his subjectivity come into question. A forties swing tune fades up on the track where previously there had been tenement noises and Italian songs. There is a shot of Jake's wife peering from behind the door. She walks to the rear of the room. The music comes up and its rhythm is taken over in the next shot—in a gym—not by music on the sound track, but by the sounds of the boxing gloves hitting the boxers' faces. The boxers are Jake and Joey, sparring. When Jake discovers that Joey has brought in some mob guys, he begins beating him up.

The cut in which sounds made by events occurring in the image (the boxing gloves) complete the rhythm of music on the sound track (the swing tune) may be a simple act of showing off, or a commentary on the practice of the continuity style where music or sound is routinely used to cover a cut. But it is more; Scorsese is experimenting with a tight integration of all the formal elements of the film, of linking all the sounds that would be familiar to his characters, which in turn limns out the porous borders of their emotional state and the viewers' awareness of those borders. This becomes clearer later on when Jake sees his new love, Vicki, at a neighborhood dance, and the use of sound becomes more complex. The main part of this sequence is a nicely orchestrated series of shot/reverse shots: Jake looks at Vicki's table, and what he sees in drifting, slow-motion tracks is a self-possessed woman, talking with the mob guys Jake hates. He follows her out of the club, pushing past crowds of people—someone is wiping off another guy's bloody nose. It's very noisy. There's a jazz tune on the track, which is quietly infiltrated by a forties pop rendition of a thirties jazz number, "Big Noise from Winnetka," with its heavy drums and whistling. When Jake comes out of the club and onto the street, all the noises stop, and only the drums and the whistling of the pop tune can be heard. The camera observes him and then cuts to his point of view, a slow-motion track toward the car with Vicki and the street guys. There is a closer shot of Jake, and the aural spaces of the outside world return with a blast as the bouncer throws someone out, yelling, "Get the fuck outta here."

214

This is a classic example of a simple idea, the representation of a character's state of mind, given depth and resonance through its formal expression. Jake La Motta lives an interior life but without introspection and self analysis. His mind is vacant of insight, analysis, meditation, comprehension; it is a reduced set of fixed ideas: jealousy and violence as automatic responses to external stimuli; a confused, abject sense of self-worth; an inarticulate self-pity. La Motta's perception is not fully articulated by object consistency. Everything he sees is somehow understood as an extension of himself and belonging to himself (this is an interesting variation on the perceptual condition of his predecessor, Travis Bickle, who also sees the world as an extension of himself but completely dissociated from him). The world is in his head, and he doesn't understand what goes on there. The slow-motion perception helps communicate this strange phenomenon, as does the blocking out of the world's sounds when Jake sees his new love. She takes over his sensorium; the external world gets drowned out by a whistling tune and then returns with violence.

Ultimately, the sound track becomes a way of communicating explanations for Jake's life. Late in the film, Jake, fat, alone, running a sleazy night-club in Miami Beach, and about to be busted for serving minors, is entertaining his customers. At one point, there is a Louis Prima song on the sound track, which keeps repeating the refrain, "Nobody, Nobody, Nobody." The song is not foregrounded but insistent enough to enter the viewer's consciousness. Shortly afterwards, Jake is thrown in jail. He has completed one of his great acts of stupidity by breaking up his championship belt to sell its jewels for bail money, only to be told by the pawnbroker that it might have been worth money had he left it intact. In jail, the great fat man is alone and in the dark. The chiaroscuro allows us to recognize him as a figure made up of parts, fragmented, disconnected. He begins smashing his fists against the wall. He is in a position, once again, only to hurt himself. He smashes his fists against the wall and cries, "Why? Why? Why?" Well, that question has been answered in the song a few scenes earlier: Jake is "Nobody, Nobody, Nobody." The counterpoint of image, words, and a sound track song we must retain in order to make sense of things creates a relationship between the viewer and the film in which the viewer is asked to see more, understand more, certainly feel more than the character—but not get moved into a melodramatic space. Memory is a killer of melodrama. If we remember and can make the associations of the song and the character's pathetic actions, a textual and perceptual complexity is created that withdraws us from simple identification with the character and urges us into a larger, more comprehending view.

Jake is at his pathetic nadir at this point and hasn't an idea why. But the visual and aural cues offer the viewer some suggestions: a violent, emotionally fragmented figure, unable to make a mark on the world, with no one left to abuse, ultimately only able to take out his blind frustration on himself. A nobody whose only available target is his own body. Self-destruction, however, is self-limiting behavior, as Jake quickly discovers when he pounds his fists against the concrete walls and begins crying in pain. Self-parody is less painful, if more demeaning, and Jake takes to the stages of grim strip joints to do his "act." The film ends where it began, with Jake in his dressing room, preparing to go on stage. With no emotional resources, having destroyed himself physically, his obesity mocking his former strength, he becomes a kind of freak, reciting doggerel and movie dialogue in nightclubs. He stands by a mirror in a dressing room, rehearsing Marlon Brando's great speech from *On the Waterfront*, about being a contender and a bum. This film about a real boxer ends by referring to a fictional boxer in another film, reflecting the necessary and painful

215

intersections of fame and fiction, mining—as do all of Scorsese's films—the articulate images and dialogue of other films. But the irony of allusion is marked here. As the possibilities for expressing the self decline and diminish for Jake, the need to attach that self—a fictional self based on a "real" person—to another fictional self increases. To confirm the irony, Scorsese himself appears, fragmented, reflected in the mirror, asking his star if he needs anything before his act. La Motta then looks at himself in the mirror and says, "Go get 'em, champ." He shadow boxes and calls to his image, "I'm the boss, I'm the boss," and prepares to go on stage. (We can again recall that song, which responds to Jake's hopeful self-boasting: "Nobody, Nobody, Nobody.")

One performance is as good as another, when either one offers an illusion of existence to a diminished personality and the illusion of participation to a diminished spectator. In *The King of Comedy*, De Niro plays a different kind of loser, who kidnaps Jerry Lewis in order to take over his talk show, goes to jail, and emerges a hero. His reason? "Better to be king for a night than schmuck for a lifetime." The paranoid attempts to avoid being undone by controlling as many people as possible, even if for a moment. In Jake's case, the moment gone, he can only try to hide his bulk behind another boxer—the character played by Marlon Brando, with whom De Niro is often compared—who never existed.*

Raging Bull continues the line of inquiry into inarticulateness and ideological abandonment that was begun in *Mean Streets*. In both films the characters are unassimilated into the dominant discourse of their culture and must talk—or, in the case of Jake La Motta, fight—their way into a temporary presence, which vanishes the more they struggle. This futile attempt to establish the self, to constitute subjectivity within a disinterested world is a constant thematic element of Scorsese's films, pursued in a variety of contexts and with many variations of the documentary/expressionist approach. And if *Raging Bull* is an extension of *Mean Streets*, it is also a reconsideration of the ideas Scorsese developed in *Taxi Driver*, which is the centerpiece of his films and the one that best represents the control of mise-en-scène and the play of perceptions. *Taxi Driver* also is the film that most violently and ironically works through the problem of the dislocated

---

* There is another reference to *On the Waterfront* in these closing scenes. Jake makes a rough attempt at reconciling with his brother, a lesser ruffian who had been utterly devoted to him. Terry Malloy's speech from *On the Waterfront* is delivered to his brother, a heartless thug.

subject—a figure that fascinates Scorsese in most of his films—who cannot explain himself or the celebrity thrust on him.

Like *Raging Bull*, and, later, *GoodFellas*, *Taxi Driver* is an extension of *Mean Streets*. But where *Mean Streets* and *GoodFellas* examine isolated urban gangster subcommunities and *Raging Bull* an urban, sadomasochistic character who finds some outlet in the larger community of organized boxing, *Taxi Driver* focuses on one isolated urban semi-individual who has difficulty making any contact with the external world. Where *Mean Streets* and *GoodFellas* present their characters in tenuous control of their environment, at home in their surroundings, and *Raging Bull* a character whose emotional environment is the battleground of his own body, *Taxi Driver* presents its character trapped by his environment, swallowed and imprisoned. More accurately, the objective-subjective points of view of those films, which permit the viewer to look both at and with the characters, is replaced by a subjective point of view that forces the viewer continually to see as the character sees, creating a mise-en-scène that expresses, above all, the obsessive vision of a madman. Finally, where *Mean Streets* and *GoodFellas* celebrate urban life in its violence and its community and *Raging Bull* points to violence as the formal, even sanctioned means of an individual's expression of self, *Taxi Driver* rigorously structures a path to violence that is separate from community, separate from the exigencies of any "normal" life, separate from any rational comprehension and need, but only the explosion of an individual attempting to escape from a self-made prison. An individual who, in his madness, attempts to act the role of a movie hero.

217

Mean Streets plays a dialectical game with film noir, its enclosed, violent, urban world recalling many of noir's conventions. But, despite its violent end, it escapes the total bleakness of noir precisely because of its sense of community and the energy of its characters. Even though they *are* trapped, they do not evidence the loneliness, dread, and anxiety manifested in noir (nor does Jake La Motta, whose absence of a defined self is also an absence of self-consciousness). Again, despite the cruelty that ends the film, the bulk of *Mean Streets* emphasizes a friendship—however unstable—among its characters. *GoodFellas* plays friendship against betrayal, while the mobsters of *Casino* live in a world of diminishing community and expanding distrust. *Taxi Driver* renders the conventions of film noir in an immediate and frightening manner. The film's central character lives completely enclosed in a city of dreadful night, so removed and alone that everything he sees becomes a reflection of his own distorted perceptions. Travis Bickle

(De Niro again, in a performance that matches the one in *Raging Bull* for the degree of its obsessiveness) is the last noir man in the ultimate noir world: closed and dark, a paranoid universe of perversion, obsession, and violence. In the creation of this world, Scorsese goes to noir's roots, to certain tenets of German Expressionism that call for "a selective and creative distortion" of the world by means of which the creator of a work can represent "the complexity of the psyche" through a visual style that exposes the "object's internal life, the expression of its soul."[20] Scorsese does want to "expose" the inner life of his character but not to explain it. As with Jake La Motta, the internal life of Travis Bickle remains an enigma throughout the film. The subject without subjectivity cannot be explained, even through the most dreadful violence, and a major concern of the film is to frustrate viewer attempts at understanding that mind. But, as always, Scorsese is very interested in communicating the way a world looks as it is perceived by such a mind, and he uses "a selective and creative distortion" of perception in extraordinary ways, more formally coherent and extensive than he will in some of his later films.

The focus of my analysis will examine the ways Scorsese creates his expressionist, noir mise-en-scène and how he asks the viewer to observe and even enter it. But, before proceeding, it is important to inquire once again into the role of Paul Schrader, who wrote the script for this film, co-scripted *Raging Bull*, *The Last Temptation of Christ*, and wrote *Bringing Out the Dead*. Schrader is an articulate screenwriter and director, whose essay on film noir remains the best on the subject and offers pertinent ideas for an understanding of *Taxi Driver*. However, most critics have chosen to look at his book, *Transcendental Style in Film: Ozu, Bresson, Dreyer*, to help explain *Taxi Driver* and the apparent disparity between what Schrader might have intended and what Scorsese executes. Some writers have wanted to see in the film a study of Travis Bickle as a lost and insular but coherent and self-contained individual, in the manner of a Robert Bresson character who achieves a spiritual grace by the almost negative persistence of his activities. Schrader is a great admirer of Bresson, and a recent film of his, *Light Sleeper*, as well as his earlier *American Gigolo*, owes a great deal to Bresson's *Pickpocket*, which, like all of Bresson's film, is made of small gestures, significant cutting on seemingly insignificant motions, and impassive faces covering obsessive emotions. *Pickpocket* concerns a thief redeemed in prison by love. Schrader is so taken with this image of love redeeming the lost, imprisoned soul that he refilms its final sequence, duplicating it almost shot by shot at the end of *Light Sleeper*.

But Scorsese is not a Bressonian filmmaker, and his belief in grace—if he does indeed believe in grace—remains an unrealized sacrament for characters who always fall short of finding it. Even Scorsese's Jesus Christ fights the road to grace from the very start. If it was Schrader's intent to create a Bressonian script in *Taxi Driver*—to make another *Pickpocket*—Scorsese changed that focus.[21] Much later, in *Bringing Out the Dead*, he gives Schrader more room to create a frenzied, street-bound, but ultimately sentimental character—an ambulance rather than a taxi driver—who finds some Bressonian grace in a woman's affection. But in *Taxi Driver*, his character starts and ends without grace, persists in unmotivated fits and starts, and lives in a world so much his own creation—or, better, his own misperception—that no salvation is possible, for there is no one to save and no one to do the saving. If Schrader intended *Taxi Driver* to be an inquiry into spiritual isolation and redemption, the loneliness and transcendence of the outcast, the film presents no such transcendental material, for this is not the way Scorsese sees individuals inhabiting their world. He has rooted his film in the very earthbound context of the madness of a lonely, barely coherent individual who cannot make sane associations between the distorted fragments of what he sees. The "salvation" he receives, the recognition he gains for gunning down a mafioso and freeing a young runaway from a brothel, is simply ironic, the result of other people's distorted perceptions, and in no way changes the central character or his inability to understand himself or his world. If anything, it aggravates it, for there is an indication at the film's end that Travis Bickle has some glimmering and fleeting recognition of his madness, but only enough to make him turn away from the revelation.

219

One problem does arise in the film when elements that attempt to give Travis more character and "motivation" than Scorsese wishes him to have seem to intrude. The problem appears with the diary—Schrader's invention and borrowed from Bresson's *Diary of a Country Priest*—that the character keeps and which he reads in voice-over and which is occasionally shown, throughout the film. In discussing the use of voice-over commentary in the films of Bresson, Schrader writes that the "narration does not give the viewer any new information or feelings, but only reiterates what he already knows . . . it only doubles his perception of the event. Consequently, there is a schizoid reaction; one, there is the sense of meticulous detail which is a part of the everyday, and two, because the detail is doubled there is an emotional queasiness, a growing suspicion of the seemingly 'realistic' rationale behind the everyday."[22] Schrader and Scorsese follow this

Bressonian principle only sporadically. For example, Travis is seen in his cab and, from his point of view, street after dismal street appears, populated solely by hookers. His voice comments: "All the animals come out at night, whores, skunk pussies, buggers, queens, fairies, dopers, junkies." Here the voice-over does strongly double the viewer's perceptions of Travis's one-dimensional view, emphasizing, along with the visuals, the selectiveness of his point of view that makes the viewer "queasy" and "suspicious" over the relationship between Travis's "reality" and any that is likely to be ex-perienced outside his gaze. But when, later, Travis suddenly uses words like "sick" and "venal" to describe the world he has chosen to see, or says of himself, "All my life needed was a sense of someplace to go. . . . I don't believe that one should devote his life to morbid self-attention. I believe that someone should become a person like other people," the voice-over comes perilously close to the old convention of psychological motivation. Travis, in words quite above the diction level he usually uses (early in the film, talking to the manager of the cab company, he does not even know what "moonlighting" means), is suddenly offering reasons for his behavior. Schrader and Scorsese are allowing the entry of language that gives an analytic cast to the character, unsupported by what is seen of or by him. This is language that suggests that motivation and rationale of a conventional kind will allow the viewer to "understand" and account for the character and perhaps dismiss him as yet another tortured soul. The best that can be said is that it indicates the schizophrenia that Schrader alludes to in his discussion.

While Travis is speaking of himself in the words just quoted, the images and music track lead in quite different directions. For this sequence Bernard Herrmann provides a thudding sound almost like a heartbeat. (Herrmann's score, his last before his death, models each sequence in the film with the appropriate tonal and rhythmic expression.) Travis is lying expressionless in bed. His face is expressionless, but the camera, craning over and down to him, provides a commentary more eloquent than the words. Travis is a paralyzed being; what feelings he has come in abrupt, disconnected spurts. The movement of the camera is almost a lunge toward him, which expresses both an attempt to approach him (to carry the gaze close to a figure we feel we must understand) and a repulsion from him, for the angle of approach to the figure is too disorienting; no one could ever "normally" see a figure from this angle and with this kind of movement. And it is just this tension of attraction and repulsion that the film depends on to keep the viewer at an appropriate distance from the character and withhold an explanation of who or why Travis Bickle is. His voice-over commentary at this point, as at others, is a miscue and a false clue to an enigma.

It would be fairer to the film and to Schrader and Scorsese to look beyond the Bressonian references and focus on Schrader's concepts of the noir hero to understand Schrader's contribution to the creation of Travis Bickle and his perverse universe. "The . . . final phase of film noir," Schrader writes of the period 1949–53,

> was the period of psychotic action and suicidal impulse. The *noir* hero, seemingly under the weight of . . . years of despair, started to go bananas. The psychotic killer, who had in the first period been a subject worthy of study . . . now became the active protagonist. . . . Film noir's final phase was the most aesthetically and sociologically piercing. After ten years of steadily shedding romantic conventions, the later noir films finally got down to the root causes of the period: the loss of public honor, heroic conventions, personal integrity, and, finally, psychic stability. The third phase films were painfully self-aware; they seemed to know they stood at the end of a long tradition based on despair and disintegration and did not shy away from that fact. . . . Because film noir was first of all a style, because it worked out its conflicts visually rather than thematically, because it was aware of its own identity, it was able to create artistic solutions to sociological problems.[23]

Taxi Driver is acutely aware of its own formal identity, more so than the films of the period Schrader discusses precisely because it comes after them. The film defines its central character not in terms of social problems (though it does suggest these) nor by any a priori ideas of noble suffering and transcendent madness, but by the ways the character is perceived and perceives himself and his surroundings. He is the climactic noir figure, much more isolated and very much madder than his forebears. No cause is given for him, no understanding allowed; he stands formed by his own loneliness and trapped by his own isolation, his actions and reactions explicable only through those actions and reactions. Scorsese has made a film that not only expresses insularity and psychosis, but is insular itself. In the tradition of film noir, the world created by *Taxi Driver* exists only within its own space, a space that is itself formed by the state of mind of its central character, in that strange double perception in which the viewer sees the world the way the character sees it and sees the character himself, thereby permitting both proximity and separation.

Taxi Driver may suffer a bit from a split between its screenwriting and its director's intentions. But it is an important and still valid premise of the auteur theory that the director absorbs or, better, re-creates the script into something else—the film itself, which is more than the script. If we assume that Schrader's notions of the formal integrity of film noir are valid, we can forget about Bresson—whose very *lack* of expressiveness and whose insistence on suppressing the internal and subjective make his work inapplicable to Scorsese's film—and proceed to a close examination of this film about the "despair and disintegration" of a psychotic killer who is its active protagonist. In its very first shot are found the methods of presentation that will be at work throughout.

The shot is of the front end of a Checker cab emerging from smoke, and is immediately recognizable. The streets of New York often have steam pouring from their manhole covers, and such a sight, at night, illuminated by headlights, is quite striking. Scorsese therefore begins with an image familiar to anyone who knows New York. But at the same time he instantly defamiliarizes it, makes it strange.[24] The smoke is yellowish, and the taxi that emerges from it is not so much moving as looming, viewed from a low angle and traveling at a speed too slow and regular for it to be an "actual" cab on the street. The music that accompanies this presence is percussive and slowly accelerates in tempo and loudness, not unlike a car engine starting in slow motion. The shot dissolves to a tight closeup of a pair of eyes, first tinted red, then normal in color, then red and white. The eyes move back and forth, scanning, blankly, something as yet unseen by the viewer. A dissolve to the reverse shot (what the eyes are seeing) shows the world outside the cab through a wet and blurred windshield. The people and traffic seen through the windshield are hard-edged, but their movements are multiplied and extended so that they leave trails of light and traces of their forms (this is, of course, a special effect, and therefore calls attention to itself as a specific filmic device as well as a perceptual aberration). The shot dissolves again to people going by on the streets, tinted red and blue, and moving through the smoke in slow motion; there is a dissolve back to the eyes looking left to right and then a return to the smoke with which the sequence opened.

Some critics have referred to this sequence, and the opening shot in particular, as an emergence from hell. This is an evocative analogy, but it misses the point. It is precisely the lack of definition, the lack of knowable space, which has about it just the hint of the recognizable and the everyday that makes it so disturbing. The defamiliarizing of the familiar; the introduction of the blankly moving eyes (again, cinematic convention connects the title of the film, the shot of the cab, and the eyes, so that the viewer assumes they are the eyes of the driver; cinematic history refers the eyes and the flashing light to the opening sequence of Bernardo Bertolucci's 1970 *The Conformist*, another film about aberrant perception and personality, whose opening is itself influenced by the credit sequence of Nicholas Ray's *In a Lonely Place*, 1950; Scorsese says that the origin of the eyes is Michael Powell's 1951 film, *Tales of Hoffmann*); the strange movement of the people on the street, recalling the slow-motion crowd in the bar sequence in *Mean Streets* and anticipating the slow-motion point-of-view shots used throughout the film, was already becoming a stylistic trademark; the gaze both at and from this foreboding car and its occupant moves the viewer into a realm of distortion and threat in which she remains throughout the film. This credit sequence is also outside the narrative proper, for in the sequence following this, Travis goes to a cab company to ask for a job driving. This creates for the character a state out of time, a kind of perpetual state of mind that diffuses itself over the film.

As the smoke clears, Travis, viewed from behind, enters the cab company to ask for work. His movement is accompanied by the crescendo of the main musical theme. As an exposition of plot, the ensuing sequence is simple. The antagonism between the cab owner and Travis offers a direct expression of anger that envelops the film as a whole, and their dialogue supplies some minimal information about the character: he can't sleep at night; he goes to porn movies; he was in the marines. But more than what is said and done, what is seen in this sequence and the way it is seen continue to provoke, almost subliminally, discomfort and perceptual dislocation. The camera observes Travis from behind as he stands over the cab owner. Opposite him, through a large opening in the wall, two men are arguing. Barely heard, they play no direct role in the sequence (on second viewing one of the arguing men is recognized as Wizard (Peter Boyle), who will be one of Travis's cronies at the all-night cafeteria and to whom Travis will attempt to disburden himself—"I got some bad ideas in my head"); but they form a focus of attention in the shot and literally reflect Travis, the angry, inarticulate man. The reverse of this shot, the look at Travis, places him low in the frame, too low and off-center, so that behind him a man seated on a stool seems too large for the perspective of the shot. A bit later, when asked about his license, Travis answers that it's clean, "real clean, just like my conscience." The cab owner blows up at him, and the camera booms up and forward, bringing Travis perilously close. The placement of the character

223

in both these shots and the movement toward him in the second are too portentous for the narrative function at the moment. The portent is greater than the immediate action and that skews the reaction that one might have to a conventional expository dialogue sequence. The placing of a character in unexpected parts of the frame, particularly in closeups that are off-center or off-angle, is a device that Scorsese borrows from Hitchcock, from whom he has learned the ability to design a composition in order to activate viewer perceptions, offering something more than is expected, and preparing the viewer, almost unconsciously, for events to come.

When Travis leaves the dispatcher's office, the camera follows him to the cab garage but leaves him to pan across its dark space, following a totally peripheral character (Wizard, again), the camera picking up Travis as he walks back into the frame and out to the street. At first look, this seems a perfectly ordinary way to get a character from one point to another without cutting. But the question arises as to why the camera doesn't stay with him all the way rather than abandon him for an anonymous character. It is a curious shot—I've noted a less portentous version of it in the bar sequence in *GoodFellas*—and is related to an even more curious shot later in the film. Following Travis's disastrous date with Betsy (Cybill Shepherd), during which he takes her to a porn movie only to have her walk out on him in outrage, he calls her from a public phone in an office building. Travis is observed at a distance, off-center, talking on the phone. His face is turned away to the wall. He is solicitous to Betsy and agonizingly simple-minded, concerned that she has the flu, wondering if she got the flowers he sent her (she says she didn't, and in the next sequence we see his room filled with dead flowers). Suddenly, the camera begins to move away from Travis, tracking to the right and coming to rest before a corridor that leads out to the street. It stays there as, off-screen now, Travis finishes the conversation. As he begins a voice-over comment on how Betsy refused to come to the phone on subsequent calls, he walks into the frame and down the corridor as an anonymous figure passes him.

The compositional structure of the film resituates the viewer, forcing him to share the spatial dislocations of a character who is radically displaced from his environment and who perceives that environment empty of any "normal" articulations and filled rather with his own aberrations. The camera observes him in unconventional and uncomfortable placements within the frame, even removing him from the frame entirely when the camera indicates, unexpectedly and disconcertingly, the spaces around him—the neutral spaces of the taxi garage or the barren space of an office hallway, the highly significant spaces of his room, with its cracked walls, dead flowers, boxes of junk food. Scorsese also explores the expressive possibilities of temporal distortion. I noted that the narrative is encased within the timeless drift of the cab through the distorted streets, a drift that opens and closes the film and punctuates it throughout. There is the slow-motion movement of the people on those streets and the visual multi-plication of their movements. And there is also this odd occurrence after Travis leaves the taxi garage in the sequence discussed earlier. The camera picks him up in a far shot walking up the street. Sunlight brightens the buildings behind him, but he is in shadow. There is, quite unexpectedly, a lap dissolve. But rather than moving to another place and time, which is the conventional meaning of this device, it merely moves Travis a little closer forward in the shot and shows him taking a drink from a bottle in a paper bag. The effect here is produced not by any new expository informa-tion, turn in the plot, or dramatic interchange, but simply by a cinematic device that works against expectations and is therefore disturbing, setting up a complicated relationship with the character.

The lap dissolve, as I said, is conventionally used to signify a lapse of time and/or a change of place. Here the effect is rather of a momentary lapse of consciousness or of a drifting unbound by time, a perception by us of the character's state of mind. Scorsese will repeat the device during the "You talkin' to me?" sequence, as Travis accelerates his psychotic prepa-rations for murder. Scorsese may have gotten the idea for the dissolve that plays against temporal and spatial expectations from Bernardo Bertolucci who creates a similar effect in *Before the Revolution* (1964) and *The Spider's Stratagem* (1970). In the latter film two characters have a conversation that is continually interrupted by fades to black—a transitional device similar to though more emphatic than the dissolve. But the fades do not actually interrupt anything, for each time the scene returns the conversation continues with no indication of a major change in time. The effectiveness of this device becomes mitigated as Scorsese uses it in later films as a transitional device or even in place of straightforward cutting. Unlike his use of slow motion, which retains its power as a signifier of disturbed perception, the dissolve becomes a flourish. But in *Taxi Driver*, its power resides in its novelty, and in all instances of its use it forces the viewer to look at the character and disturbs that look at the same time. As with the other acts of visual displacement, the gaze is dislocated, disrupted, and the viewer is permitted neither proximity to the central character, sympathy with him, nor comfortable distance. Within this context the shifts in diction

225

between Travis's speech and his voice-over diary entries, which I earlier criticized, might be understood: they become further acts of dislocation, further denials of coherency in the character.

The viewer, made to gaze *at* the character in particularly discomforting ways, is made as well to gaze *with* the character himself, to see the world as he sees it. This is done immediately in the credit sequence through the appearance of the people in the street and, more forcefully, because more subtly, in the observation of the men arguing in the cab owner's office. His gaze is joined whenever he drives in his cab. Whores and gangs inhabit every street, whores and their clients and would-be murderers are his fares. "Did you ever see what a forty-four magnum pistol can do to a woman's face?" asks a passenger (played by Scorsese) as he forces Travis to pull over to the curb and look with him at an apartment where, he says, his wife is having an affair with a black man (the gaze of two psychotics, one the function and creator of the other, join, doubling the viewer's distressed perceptions). "I mean, it'll fuckin' destroy her. Just blow her right apart. . . . Now did you ever see what it can do to a woman's pussy? That you should see. . . . I know you must think I'm pretty sick. . . . I'm paying for the ride. You don't have to answer." And through it all, Travis remains impassive. He never looks at his passengers except through his rearview mirror. He never reacts when his cab is spattered by a water hydrant or by garbage. A man walking down the street with his shirt pulled over his head or another yelling down the street over and over, "I'll kill her, I'll kill her," brings no reaction from him.

Neither coincidence nor a reflection of "reality" explains why the only people Travis sees are the mad and the disenfranchised, why the only streets he sees are the stews of the city, why the cafeteria frequented late at night by him and his cronies is populated only by pimps and nodding drug addicts. These are the only people and the only places of which Travis is aware. They constitute the only things he perceives and, since the viewer's perceptions in the film are so restricted to his own, the only things the viewer is permitted to perceive as well. The camera, therefore, does not, as Diane Jacobs suggests, appear "helpless to avert its gaze from the horrors that walk in its path," nor does it revel "secretly in the filth and the suffocation."[25] Instead it takes a very active role in transmitting a point of view that may itself be helpless to avert its gaze from filth and ugliness. Travis is prey to his own isolated and isolating gaze (a gaze that is infected with the myth of New York as a foul sewer—the "New York-ness" mentioned earlier), and the viewer, in turn, is prey to it. *Taxi Driver* is not a documentary of the squalor of New York City but the documentation of a squalid mind driven mad by its perception.

Taxi Driver is the portrait of an obsessive, a passive obsessive, so oppressed by his isolation that when he does act, it is only on the dark and disconnected impulses triggered by his perceptions. Alternatively, he can be seen as kind of tabula rasa, a blank slate, on which is inscribed, or rather rudely and selectively scribbled, the things he sees. This is given some validity by the sequence with Scorsese as the homicidal passenger in the back seat. It is after this encounter that Travis takes a seriously violent turn, as if he were taking directions from his passenger/director on how to behave horribly. But finally there is no analysis of, nor reasons given for, his behavior—none, at least, that comes from the plot of the film or consistent actions of the character. Travis can, perhaps, be viewed as a radically alienated urban castoff, a mutant produced by the dehumanization of the postindustrial world (television news continually makes us aware of the random murderers who keep appearing and disappearing in our culture, and, since *Taxi Driver*, the random or serial killer has become an almost clichéd figure in both film and television). But this film withholds any such political, social, or even psychological analysis. Even the presence of a presidential candidate who becomes Travis's aborted target is used only to point out how terribly distant vulgar politics is from "the people" it professes to address and how distant is Travis from anything as communal as politics.

However, despite what it withholds on the level of plot and the usual conventions of psychological realism, *Taxi Driver* does offer an analysis of the cultural aberrations that afflict Travis and, by extension, viewers of the film. Scorsese quietly, even hilariously, suggests one possible motivation for, or result of, Travis's psychosis. The more deeply he withdraws, the more implicitly he comes to believe in the American movie myths of purity and heroism, love and selflessness, and to actuate them as the grotesque parodies of human behavior they are. Travis Bickle is the legitimate child of John Wayne and Norman Bates: pure, self-righteous, violent ego and grinning, homicidal lunatic; each the obverse of the other; each equally dangerous. Together they create a persona so out of touch with ordinary human experience that the world he inhabits and perceives becomes an expressionist noir nightmare, an airless and dark trap that its inhabitant escapes only by drawing everything into it with him. The final irony occurs when Travis's act of slaughter, which he believes is an act of liberation and purification, is taken as such by everyone else, and the viewer finds herself potentially

227

caught by the same aberrations as he, that the double perspective offered by the film fuses, and the lunatic is momentarily accepted as hero.

In fact the closeness forged between spectator and character point of view, and the gap in understanding or comprehending that character, create a confusion that finally makes it difficult to see just how tightly the movements to destruction are drawn and how those movements are shaped by the various myths and ideological distortions that play on the little that remains of the character's mind. Travis gets involved with two women, each not a character as much as a further creation of his aberrant sensibility. Betsy, the campaign worker for the clichéd liberal candidate, Charles Palantine, is, by Travis's own admission, a dream girl. She is a fantasy figure from a fifties movie, appearing to him as a woman in white who comes "like an angel" out of the "filthy mass" he sees himself living in. "They cannot touch her," he says, emphasizing each word (further emphasized by the camera's panning across the words written in his diary). As Travis spies on her from outside campaign headquarters, the viewer is given a privileged look at her, unmediated by Travis, with her fellow workers, and she turns out to be a perfectly mediocre personality involved in mindless conversation. Her ordinariness is played against Travis's stare, his impassive observation punctuated by strong camera movements that destabilize the space he occupies and make his presence a threat. When Travis invades Betsy's office, he speaks to her in the words of a movie hero. He says she's the most beautiful woman he has ever met; he thinks she is lonely, that she needs a friend. He projects his own feelings on her in such sentimental terms that she can hardly help but react to them. But why would a sane woman react at all to a weird man who has been staring at her and then greets her with a line out of a rotten movie? Is she fooled by his charm? Is it because this is really Robert De Niro talking to Cybill Shepherd? Is it, as Patricia Patterson and Manny Farber suppose, just bad scripting and improbable motivation and reaction?[26] Or is Scorsese allowing Travis's fantasy—and the viewer's—to play out a while? One of the things movies tell us is that it is not impossible for the most improbable boy to win the beautiful girl.

Scorsese is not entirely disinterested in the character of Betsy. He allows her to play with Travis, to indulge a kind of preppy curiosity about the freakish and the threatening. Once they begin talking—in a cafeteria sequence that is edited so that Betsy often appears in a shot over Travis's shoulder, but he almost always in a shot alone—it is clear how separate they are. Betsy says he reminds her of a song by Kris Kristofferson. "Who's that?" asks Travis. Betsy quotes from the song: "He's a prophet and a pusher, partly truth, partly fiction, a walking contradiction." This is perfectly meaningless to Travis. "You saying that about me? . . . I'm no pusher." "Just the part about the contradictions. You are that," says Betsy, who might as well be talking to no one. In the next sequence Travis is seen buying the Kristofferson record or, more accurately, part of him is seen, his arm, with a military patch that says "King Kong Company," through the window of the record store. Betsy is wrong. He is not a contradiction but a thing of disconnected parts, any one of which can take momentary precedence until another disconnected part, or another influence, word, or mutant perception, jars momentarily into place. The shuffling Andy Hardy romancer takes his white angel to a porn movie, and when she flees, condemns her to hell and says she is cold like all women. Cold "like a union," he says, drawing on a notion of people in groups, something totally repellent to this lonely man.

The second woman, a little girl actually, is a twelve-year-old prostitute, who tries to get into Travis's cab and is pulled out by her pimp, who throws Travis a twenty-dollar bill. The event occurs midway between his first meeting with Betsy and his taking her to the porn movie, and just after he has picked up the candidate Betsy works for. This is a marvelously contrived series of coincidences (as most any movie plot is) that serves to echo the random, fragmentary nature of Travis himself. Betsy will put Travis over the edge; candidate Palantine will be his first object of violence; the angry, violent words of his backseat passenger and, finally, Iris (Jodie Foster), the baby whore, will catalyze the explosion. There is no real connection between them, except that they are all clichés, all the reflections of a junk-food mind to which women are either white angels or poor girls in distress and presidential candidates clean, dashing men who, being clean, will clean up the mess that Travis is obsessed with. "The president should clean up this whole mess here," he tells a slightly astonished Palantine, who winds up in the back seat of his cab, "should flush it down the fuckin' toilet." If Palantine can salvage Travis's world, then Travis can save Iris from hers. Or, if no one can cleanse Travis's world, then he at least can save one person from it. Never mind that Iris is too stoned to know what Travis is talking about and is living in circumstances similar to those of her would-be savior. Living, that is, under the oppression of clichés. In one of the few sequences of the film that does not encompass Travis's point of view, Iris and her pimp, Sport (played with outrageous menace and unctuousness by Harvey Keitel), are alone in the red-orange light of their room. Sport plays out a strange ritual of seduction and ownership, holding Iris to him (she comes up to his chest) and dancing her about the room. "I depend on you," he says. "When you're close to me like this I feel so good. I only wish every man could know what it's like to be loved by you. . . . It's only you that keeps me together."

Iris is torn between two sets of platitudes, the concerned protective language of Travis and the cheap sentiment of Sport, whose words to her are like the junk food Travis is always eating, superficially filling but empty and finally destructive. Like junk food they are addictive and therefore imprisoning. Hearing these words and seeing Iris's situation outside of Travis's perception set up a peculiar tension: either Travis, in all his madness, is correct in wanting to "save" Iris from her situation because it is repulsive and inhuman, or he is blind to the ludicrousness of the situation of a little girl secure within a grotesque parody of affection stronger than he can know. If so, his desire to help her is meaningless because she neither desires nor needs any help. Throughout the film, the world is perceived as Travis perceives it; now, briefly, it is seen without him, and it appears hopeless, outrageously hopeless, yet carrying a suggestion that the loneliness that Travis sees and experiences everywhere can be mitigated. The mitigation is cruel and fraudulent, but it is something compared with nothing. The destructive solitude of the family to which Iris is returned after she is "freed" by Travis, a solitude we hear about through the droning voice of her father reading a letter he has written to Travis, may be cleaner and more moral but no less oppressive and sentimental.

It would be foolish to imply that the film is advocating teenage prostitution; that is not the point. Scorsese is examining aspects of an ugly world, a nonbourgeois world that has adopted the other's clichés and revealed them as destructive. Travis is slowly destroyed by those clichés until, becoming the demonic parody of the avenging hero, he becomes a destroyer. In his dealings with Iris, he becomes nothing less than a parody of John Wayne's Ethan Edwards in Ford's 1956 film *The Searchers* (the film that obsesses Scorsese's alter ego, J. R., in *Who's That Knocking at My Door?* and which Charlie goes to see in *Mean Streets*). Ethan is himself a figure of neurotic obsession, who wants to rescue his niece from the Indians because of his hatred of miscegenation and his desire to purify her and bring her back to white civilization. (Certainly Sport, in his hippie gear, is meant to be a version of Ethan Edwards's rival, Chief Scar, even though it is Travis who wears the Mohawk haircut.) The equation—Travis Bickle as Wayne's Ethan; Iris as Natalie Wood's Debbie; and Sport as the Chief—is perfect. Like Debbie, who becomes accommodated to the Indians before Ethan rescues her, Iris has accommodated to her world; it is an ugly accommodation, but it works on its own terms. Like Chief Scar, Sport attempts to protect his people, and, like Ethan, Travis will overcome all odds, will risk his life, to save what is left of Iris's innocence. Travis believes in the rightness of his plan, as does his filmic forebear. What he does not see is that his whole notion of saving people is based on a movie cliché of heroic activity, based on an even older cultural narrative of captivity, a cliché (which Ford himself questioned) that his madness seems to make valid. Iris passively submits to the clichés of squalid sentimentality; Travis submits to the clichés of violent action. (Betsy believes movie clichés too; she is fooled by them until Travis attempts to draw her directly into his world, at which point she flees; the angel in white cannot exist in the dark hole of a porno house.) The different reactions of Iris and Travis to their predicament are presented in a strong montage that follows the sequence between Sport and Iris. As the pimp dances his whore away with loving words, shots are heard on the sound track. There is a cut to Travis, isolated in the square opening of a shooting gallery. As he shoots, the square leaps forward— persistence, threat, single-mindedness, madness directly confronting the viewer.[27]

The violence that Travis commits in his attempt to "save" Iris (or, more accurately, the violence that Scorsese creates on the screen) is the most problematic aspect of *Taxi Driver* and it echoes throughout Scorsese's work. Like the violence in *Casino*, it is so enormous that it seems, on first viewing, to rupture an otherwise carefully restrained and thoughtfully constructed film, finally obviating that restraint by overwhelming it. At the time, and on one viewing, the sequence could be considered one of the more cynical moments in contemporary American film. This needs a context. By 1976, the simulation of violence had reached a level of mindlessness and predictability that left only three alternatives: exaggerate it to more insane proportions in order to elicit a thrill from an audience dulled by endlessly exploding hemoglobin bags and men careening backward from the force of a shotgun blast; show an actual death; or forget the whole set of con-ventions, retire the various forms of brutality, and consider some other manifestations of human behavior. By 1978, that current of film violence had largely run its course, only to be revived again in the horror, slasher, revenge, and male action films of the eighties. By the nineties, computerized pyrotechnics and the importation and domestication of Hong Kong Kung Fu movie conventions of choreographed chaos had somewhat overtaken immediate visible bodily damage as a means to provide a visceral charge. A few filmmakers, like Paul Verhoeven, especially in *Robocop* and *Starship*

Troopers, remain true to the bleeding and dismembered body, and Scorsese keeps returning to it almost obsessively. Back in 1976, there was some indication that the filming of an actual death could be conceivable. The rumor and brief public appearance of "snuff" films (one of them was called *Snuff* and purported to show the "actual" dismemberment of a woman) threatened to overturn the conventional relationships between film and its subjects by inverting the conventions of narrative art.[28] Were the "snuff" films "real," the contract of narrative film that states that what we see on the screen is a lie (does not *really* happen) would have to be rewritten. All distance between what is seen and what is understood by what is seen would be lost. The question would no longer involve a viewer becoming prisoner to an illusion of reality—or of attending a documentation of reality— but being guilty of assenting to the actual event of murder. The only real meaning of such films would emerge from the moral choice of attending them or not.

The snuff films were probably lies—never having seen them, I say this out of a need for assurance. They failed to gain an audience (surely a sign that we do need the protection of fiction) and by now have returned to the deep pornographic underground. But it is impossible to downplay the significance of their appearance at the time, their reappearance in modified form in the *Faces of Death* videotapes that were among the highest renters at local video shops during the mid-eighties, or the various "amazing videos" programs on television in the nineties that showed "real" and really appalling violent acts repeated over and over again. The documentation or representation of violence and death must respond to a deep need for both *frisson* and mastery on the part of many viewers and no doubt an equally deep need to see represented the aggressiveness and misogyny so embedded in the general ideology but somewhat repressed in reality. Certainly they respond to an irrepressible desire for exploitation on the part of filmmakers and distributors.

Scorsese cannot be entirely absolved of exploitative intent. He is a commercial filmmaker and violence of some kind is always part of his mise-en-scène and a part of the way in which he understands the world and turns it into cinematic narrative. That is one possible defense. Another is formal and structural. The violence in *Taxi Driver* grows and develops out of the entire structure of the film and is, finally, so stylized that it provides commentary on the whole perceptual complex of violence in film— something Scorsese forgot to do in *Casino*, where the violence seems simply a punishment for the audience and a final revelation of the mob's brutality.

In *Taxi Driver*, every element leads toward bloodletting. Travis prepares to shoot down candidate Palantine at a rally. "My whole life has been pointed in one direction," he comments. "There never has been any choice for me." The obsessive-compulsive character decides that there is an object for his obsessiveness. Packed with weapons, his hair shaved like an Indian, he attends the rally, is spotted, and runs. (It is of interest to note that "freeing" Iris by violence is not the first act Travis considers. Killing is his major impulse, and that urge connects itself to Iris only after the attempted assassination fails.) He returns home, drinks beer, and takes aspirin. At night he goes to Sport's apartment building in the East Village, where, after taunting Sport (who throws a lit cigarette butt at him), he shoots him in the stomach and goes off down the street to sit on a stoop. He returns to the building and enters, the dark interior appearing somewhat like the set of a German Expressionist film. The camera tracks through the corridors. An avuncular old man, who was earlier seen as the money collector for Sport's brothel, pursues Travis, who turns and shoots fingers off the old man's hand (close up and in slow motion—reminiscent of the scene in *McCabe and Mrs. Miller* where the Reverend's hand is shot off by the gunman, Butler). Sport reappears and shoots Travis in the neck. Travis shoots Sport some more. The camera assumes a position above the stairs; we hear the sound of blood trickling, and there is a momentary calm, broken by Travis shooting more bullets into Sport and shooting and beating the old man, who starts running after him, yelling maniacally, "You crazy son of a bitch . . . I'll kill you. I'll kill you. I'll kill you."

At this point, in slow motion, a customer opens the door of Iris's room. There is a cut to a shot of Travis being pursued by the old man, and a return to Iris's customer, who shoots Travis in the arm. The maniacal catapult that Travis has built to hold one of his guns and deliver it to his hand pops out and allows him to shoot the customer in the face (as De Niro's Vito Corleone shoots Fanucci in *Godfather II*). The old man, still yelling "I'll kill you," grabs Travis from behind as they enter Iris's room. They fight on the floor; Travis gets a knife he has concealed around his ankle, stabs the old man in the hand (the one that was not shot earlier), and then blows the old man's brains out, spattering the wall with blood (through all this, Iris's sobbing creates a counterpoint to the gunshots and the dripping blood). Travis now puts a gun to his throat and pulls the trigger, but it is empty. He sits down, and as the police enter (emissaries from the sane world who appear menacing as they first peer through the door but who soon bring a calming order to the scene), he puts a bloody finger to his head, works it

233

like a gun, and, smiling, lays his head back. The camera cuts to a high, overhead shot, and, to a crescendo of music, tracks the carnage down the blood-splattered stairway and, through a series of lap dissolves, over the bloody body of Sport and out the door, observing the police cars and the crowds, in slow motion, gathering.

I describe the sequence in detail partly to make a written record of the climax of screen violence in the mid-seventies and to see if the horror of the sequence can be re-created in verbal description. It cannot, of course, and the difficulty is to keep from exaggerating the description or reflecting on it verbally just enough to make it comic. And I wonder if beneath its horror there is not something of the comic, or at least the bizarre, ready to break forth, turning the sequence, with all its repetitions of shootings, fallings, and risings, its grotesque exaggerations, into a parody of screen violence. Early in the film, Travis drives by a movie house that is showing *The Texas Chain Saw Massacre*. The marquee is prominently in view as the cab drifts through the streets. One may speculate whether the reference suggests the influence of violent films on Travis (as, in the person of John Hinckley, Travis and his film would someday have a violent influence on someone "in real life"), reflects his violent propensities, or alludes to cinematic violence that the climactic sequence will parody—and that Scorsese himself will parody further in the funhouse, horror film violence of *Cape Fear*. I would also suggest the shootout is another aberration of Travis's mind. Not exactly a fantasy—it "happens" as part of the fictional events of the film but happens the way everything else in the fiction happens, as an exaggerated expression of the way a madman perceives and acts on his world, an expression doubled by the viewer's own perception of it as he watches the film. In other words, the act of violence is another part of the inside/outside process of observation that Scorsese has followed throughout. So much so that Scorsese plays a little game. After the event, there is a newspaper clipping on the wall of Travis's room that shows an overhead diagram of the carnage—a sketch or storyboard of the high-angle shot that closed the sequence. This is a reflexive gesture on Scorsese's part, as important as his own appearance as the murderous husband in Travis's cab. The "outside world" in the film (in this case, the press) imitates the interior world of Travis by means of the sketch that was very likely the filmmaker's own storyboard for the climactic shot of the film. The film reflects its parts against each other and against the spectator's observation of them, raising form to consciousness.

I noted that there is something predestined about the shootout. The violence grows out of Travis's mad self and the violent world he sees and absorbs until it becomes his reflection. Part of the mise-en-scène and the entire formal construction of the film, the shootout is prepared for by gestures made, compositional strategies set up, words said throughout. For example, the second time the viewer sees Betsy, she is bantering with a friend at campaign headquarters about a newsstand operator who has only one hand and only two fingers on that hand. They speculate that the mob blew off his fingers. Travis does not hear this, and there is no implication that this ridiculous conversation suggests to him his treatment of the caretaker of Sport's brothel. It is simply a setup and a contrast, the banal chatter of two people oblivious to the world in which Travis lives, words that will be ironically and grotesquely realized in the shootout and after. Reference to the Mafia turns up again when it is discovered that one of the men Travis kills was a mafioso. This is the event that, with the freeing of Iris, makes him a media hero.

In this sequence, Travis approaches Betsy and makes his pitch to her, telling her how he has observed all the people around her and all the work on her desk. When he says this, there is suddenly a cut to a point-of-view shot from Travis to the top of her desk, which the camera pans, following the sweep of Travis's hand. Even though it approximates Travis's point of view, it is just off enough, the editing slightly out of sync, to be unnerving. It acts as another signifier of the spatial and temporal distortions in Travis's perception. However, the high angle, the movement across the clutter of the desk, *formally* predict the high-angle shot of the carnage later on. In fact, Scorsese presents such a high-angle shot twice before: once at the cab company, where there is a similar point-of-view shot from Travis to the cab owner's desk, and then again at the candy counter of the porn movie theater Travis visits. This may, I am afraid, sound more than a bit over-ingenious. But in a film as carefully structured as *Taxi Driver*, every shot is made to count, to be meaningful immediately or to prepare for meaning later in the work. This meaning need not be on a substantive level. Form can refer to, or in this case foreshadow, form. A high-angle pan of a cluttered desk is contextually different from a high-angle track of a room full of bloody bodies but formally similar. Both are high angle and both move. A linkage is therefore set up that may not affect a spectator consciously on first viewing but remains part of the structural system and the spectator's awareness of the film nevertheless.

Other foreshadowings are more apparent and direct. When Travis purchases guns from Andy, the gun fence, who sells his wares as if he were selling appliances, the camera pans across the collection of armaments, and Travis holds one up and aims it through the window, the camera tracking along his arm to an anonymous couple on the street. Earlier, at the Belmore Cafeteria, when Travis takes Wizard aside in an attempt to tell him of the bad ideas in his head, a black cab driver looks up at him and points his finger at Travis as if it were a gun. There is a dolly back from this gesture— a shot from Travis's point of view—and then a reverse to Travis, who reacts with an odd look. Once outside the cafeteria, Travis attempts to unburden himself to Wizard, who cannot comprehend what he is saying. He calls him, with affection, "Killer." "Relax, Killer," he tells him, "you're gonna be all right"—words that will ironically ring true as Travis proceeds. Later, when Travis meets Sport for the first time, the pimp makes the same gun gesture with his hand at Travis. After the massacre, Travis repeats the gesture, at his own head. The world Travis sees inscribes itself on his mind and he reads it back.

Through the structuring of point of view, the reconsideration of the noir milieu, the intense observation of the character's relationship to a carefully defined world that expresses his state of mind, and with its reticence in analyzing or seeking motivations for that character and his world, *Taxi Driver* sets up a closed narrative of loneliness and madness. The film proves, finally, to be quite responsible, in the sense that it offers, in a clearly defined form, the lack of clarity and the lack of definition that characterize solitude and psychosis without falling into the trap that romanticizes madness as a redemptive experience. In total, by presenting its character and his semi-life as simply *there*, the film implicates the viewer and allows neither the character nor the viewer to be removed from the consequences of events and of perception. It examines from the point of view of its character the clichés and the sentimentality that have come to be taken for granted in films and television, conventions of masculine strength and feminine passivity, of heroism and revenge, that appear not merely banal but insane and destructive when they are taken as meaningful.

I spoke earlier of the use Scorsese makes of cinematic allusion, the way he follows the French New Wave filmmakers in drawing on, paying homage to, and in many instances changing the cinematic forms and conventions that precede his work. I noted how, in *Cape Fear*, a somewhat impoverished narrative is given some depth by layering its images and sequences over similar ones in *Strangers on a Train*. In *Taxi Driver* that allusiveness is more carefully integrated into the film, rendering it rich and resonant—making it, like a saner version of its main character's mind, a tablet on which is written the narratives and formal patterns of other filmmakers. The Fordian lineage of Travis Bickle and his demonic recreation of the John Wayne persona in *The Searchers* are clear. Even stronger and more conclusive is the film's homage to Hitchcock and to *Psycho* in particular.

What Hitchcock persistently examines in his best films are the ways an audience can be manipulated in and out of morally ambiguous situations and made to react not only to what is happening on the screen but what is happening within their own responses as well. Hitchcock speaks to the power of images and sounds to move an audience into reaction and counterreaction and, within the narratives constructed by these images and sounds, to the manipulative power of sexuality and domination and fear that one character can wield over another. Throughout the forties and into the fifties, he cloaked this inquiry, sometimes almost hermetically, in romantic melodrama (*Notorious*, posing as a love story, is as frightening an exploration of sexual and emotional abuse and political manipulation as one can find in American film). In the fifties he slowly began to drop the generic pretenses, first in *The Wrong Man*—whose grim and unrelentingly dark view of a man trapped in the city of dreadful night makes it one precursor of *Taxi Driver*—and then in *Vertigo*, as complex a film of male sexual despair ever made. By the time he made *Psycho*, Hitchcock was able to create a world that was the dialectic to that of melodrama, a dark, loveless, brutal world in which the viewer is made an emotional accomplice first to a petty thief and then to a homicidal maniac. The world of *Psycho* is a subdivision of noir territory, in which the desolate isolation of a roadside motel takes the place of a barren urban landscape, and its parlor the reflection of a savage and savaged mind.

Taxi Driver becomes at many points an analogue to *Psycho* and is tangentially related to *Vertigo* as well—the relationships of Travis to Betsy and Sport to Iris being curious echoes of Scottie's idealized and destructive relationship to Madeleine/Judy. Both *Taxi Driver* and *Psycho* are studies of the impenetrability of madness, but where Hitchcock leads the audience by indirection, showing the effects of madness, bluffing the cause and withholding the source, Scorsese concentrates on the central figure, never withholding a concentrated gaze on a disintegrating mind. But in both cases, though by different means, the viewer is permitted a degree of closeness to a character, reproved for that closeness, and made to feel horror and guilt because of it. Both Hitchcock and Scorsese play on the desire to "identify," to sympathize with and understand a film's "hero." Both do this formally, through devices of framing and composition, through control of the mise-en-scène: as a viewer tends to move toward the character, the way she sees the character stimulates a move in the opposite direction, alienates the very desire to understand.

Both films work through a sense of terrifying isolation. Norman Bates is completely removed from his world, dissociated, with a schizophrenia Hitchcock allows us to share: we hear the same voices Norman does. Travis Bickle is removed with his world, half-seeing and half-creating it wherever he goes until it almost literally disappears into his own reflection. The sequence in which he looks at himself in the mirror—as if he were every antagonist he could ever fantasize—"You talkin' to me? . . . Who the fuck do you think you're talkin' to?"—signifies an almost total solipsism. As with Norman, people come into Travis's realm, but like him they have only a partially independent identity (independent as any fictional character can); mostly they become another distorted reflection, providing information about violence or becoming its target.

Psycho and *Taxi Driver* attempt, finally, to delineate this solipsism, creating a world and a state of mind so enclosed and so unknowable that the viewer is fooled for attempting to understand it. Hitchcock fashions his enigma through a major manipulative device: a false lead and fraudulent identification. Norman's mother, thought at first to be a separate character, is discovered to be Norman himself, a killer with knife and wig shrieking in the darkness. The shock at this discovery is offered a palliative by means of a psychiatrist's rational explanation. In cold, deliberate tones, in the security of a police station, a doctor explains Norman's condition, placing it within the order of rationally understood experience. By all expectations, this explanation should end the film, close it neatly and with the promise of comfort. But it is not meant to be closed comfortably, or at all. After the psychiatrist's tidy and titillating words, the gaze is redirected at Norman himself. The camera tracks slowly to him, in a cell, draped in a white sheet, his mother's "voice" explaining how she wouldn't hurt a fly; the track continues to approach Norman's manic face until, beneath it, Hitchcock briefly dissolves in the image of mother's grinning skull, the two images punctured by the car in which Norman had buried his victims being pulled from the swamp. The face and the acts of madness, images of unexpected and uncontrollable violence, regain power over the psychiatrist's talk of complexes and psychoses. Rather than the security given by explanation, one is left with the enigma of the irrational.[29]

The closing sequences of *Taxi Driver* similarly play on a desire to understand and assimilate the unknowable. After the carnage, the camera, as it has earlier in the film, pans along the walls of Travis's apartment. Travis is not present, only a version of him that has been created by his act, newspaper clippings announcing his heroism: "Taxi Driver Battles Gangsters," "Reputed New York Mafioso Killed in Bizarre Shooting," "Taxi Hero to Recover." Over this is the droning voice of Iris's father: "You are something of a hero around this household." The antisocial lunatic killer has become savior; a combination of Clint Eastwood, Sylvester Stallone, and now perhaps by Arnold Schwarzenegger, Jean-Claude Van Damme, Steven Seagal, and Bruce Willis—is born from the union of Norman Bates and John Wayne, with Kubrick's Alex acting as godfather. (What better offspring than Dirty Harry Callahan, the urban vigilante of *Death Wish*, Rambo, and *Die Hard*'s John McClane in the person of that working-class philosopher, the cab driver?) The desperate search for heroes in seventies cinema cast up some odd characters, who seem to insist that only viciousness and excesses of antisocial behavior could lead to triumph in a society seemingly devoid of other means of self-expression. The tough-guy heroes of the eighties and nineties have become somewhat more social, even sensitive. But Travis is born of the older school.

What prevents the viewer from accepting Travis as just another manifestation of such salvation, of the lone hero rescuing the captive maiden? Nothing, except that he clearly manifests the psychotic assumptions that lie hidden in the film heroes who are his antecedents and descendants. While individuals may do brave deeds, the concept of the hero and heroism is a culturally constructed myth. It begins in epic poetry and lives on in movies that posit violent individual action as a social good, rendering the community passive and helpless in face of the man of action. *Taxi Driver* allows the viewer to assume the position of the hero's admirers. What is contained in the clippings on Travis's walls, and heard in the voice of the father whose daughter he has returned, gives the viewer permission momentarily to slip out of Travis's perception of the world and into an equally mad perspective. And if that opportunity is taken, the viewer is suddenly situated in an unsecured place, discovering that she is as capable of seeing the world in as mad a light as Travis, discovering ludicrous heroes in unlikely places, indulging in fantasies as grotesque as Travis's own.

This hallucination continues in the following sequence. Travis is standing with his cronies in front of the St. Regis Hotel. This is the first time in the film he is seen in a setting not redolent of violence and perversity (although by this time his presence alone is sufficient to create the necessary aura). Betsy, the angel in white, gets into his cab, and Travis drives her to a leafy East Side street. The sequence continues the fantasy of the hero originated by the newspaper clippings and the letter from Iris's father. Travis is removed from Betsy, talking to her casually, not permitting her to pay the fare, playing the melodramatic role of the strong, rebuffed lover. Has he somehow been purified by his ritual act of destruction and its attendant glorification? Or does he think he has? Betsy is not seen for the duration of her ride, except as she is reflected through the cab's rearview mirror. When she finally emerges from the cab, it is in a far shot, and she remains a kind of ghostly projection of Travis's romantic fantasies. The momentary perceptual separation from Travis, the illusory reconsideration of his status, lingers. Is he, after all, a likable guy who just—as President Merkin Muffley says about Jack D. Ripper in *Dr. Strangelove*—went a little funny in the head? In truth, the sequence is a set-up in a manner analogous to the penultimate sequence in *Psycho*, offering a false invitation to understand the character.

As Travis drives away from Betsy, she can be seen through his rear window. The camera pans across the cab's interior, past Travis to his eyes, strangely lit, as in the beginning of the film, reflected in the rearview mirror. He glances toward the mirror and there is a cut to a shot from behind it, looking at him. Suddenly, as if catching sight of his eyes, he makes a lunge, twisting the mirror toward him. As he does this, a loud squeak is heard. There is a cut back to a shot from inside the cab, looking at the mirror and the street outside. Travis's hand pushes the mirror away and, as the credits come up, the lights of the streets are seen outside the cab window and reflected in its mirror. As the credits end, the percussive sound track rises, Travis's eyes briefly pass across the mirror, while outside is the grainy nighttime street, the people moving, as they did at the beginning of the film, in slow motion. The final chords of the music track allude back to similar chords used by Bernard Herrmann in *Psycho*. Like the end of *Psycho*, the end of *Taxi Driver* is a reminder of the abysmal impossibility of understanding madness or accounting for its violence. What it adds is the suggestion that the carrier of this madness has some awareness of his state. Travis's avoidance of his eyes in the cab mirror refers back to his conversation with Iris. When he told her that Sport is a killer, she responded, "Didn't you ever try looking in your own eyeballs in the mirror?" When he finally does, his reaction parallels that of the viewer who gazes into Norman's face at the end of *Psycho*: terror. New York's hero is still "God's lonely man," still a killer. He remains his own passenger, threatening to take others for a ride.

Scorsese was so fascinated by the madness and violence of Travis Bickle and the complex perceptual elements that constructed both the character and the viewer's reaction to him that he and De Niro recreated him in different guises many more times. Jimmy Doyle, in *New York, New York,* manifests a similarly unmotivated—though more contained—violence in a mise-en-scène that extends the expressionist tendencies of *Taxi Driver* into the absolute artificiality of a movie set. *Raging Bull* tempers the expressionism of *Taxi Driver* by combining it with observation of the character's urban ethnic environment and more closely identifying point of view with the dissolution of the subject, the individual dissolved out into indeterminable drives and actions. Curiously *The King of Comedy,* a film whose wit and brightness link it more closely to *Alice Doesn't Live Here Anymore,* toys with some of the ideas of *Taxi Driver* by turning them back to front, in a comic mirror.

Visually and structurally, the two films are quite different. Because it is about television, *The King of Comedy* is shot analogous to the flat, neutral television style. The lighting is even and high key; the camera is almost always at eye level and largely steady; the editing, except for some fantasy sequences, remains close to the standard shot/reverse shot pattern of television and ordinary filmmaking.[30] But despite its repression of visual exuberance and its use of comedy to reduce anxiety and threat, *The King of Comedy* plays out a central problem raised by *Taxi Driver.* The lone, disenfranchised individual is once again taken by the public to be important, heroic—or, in this instance, at least, entertaining—and is thereby absolved of his madness. De Niro creates a character named Rupert Pupkin, who, like Travis Bickle and Jake La Motta, has no superego, no controlling voice that permits him to live comfortably within the knowable bounds of middle-class convention. Unlike his predecessors, however, his subjectivity is strongly defined, so much so that it is unaffected by external realities. Rupert wants only one thing in his life—to become a TV talk-show comedian. To that end, he will insert himself into any situation, any confrontation, without embarrassment. His madness is defined by his insistence on turning desire into act and refusing to flinch at situations that would be largely unthinkable to a normally inhibited person. He forces himself into the life of a popular talk-show host, Jerry Langford (played with restraint and self-awareness by Jerry Lewis), finally kidnapping him in order to assure himself a spot on his show. His success is enormous. Although jailed for his actions, he, like Travis, is taken as a hero by the media and becomes a popular star.

Like Jake La Motta and Travis Bickle, Rupert imposes his fantasies on the world—to such an extent that one critic suggests it is difficult to tell whether his final triumph is imaginary or not.[31] But no one is physically hurt by Rupert's impositions. At the beginning of the film, Ruppert cuts his hand in the act of forcing his way through a crowd of admirers into Jerry Langford's car and Jerry gives him his handkerchief to stop the bleeding; when Rupert and his friend Masha kidnap Jerry, they bind him head to toe in adhesive tape. These moments of violence suggest the dangerous aberrations that occur within and between the characters but are limited by the comic form of the film, existing as forebodings only. Travis's and La Motta's fantasies take the form of perceptual dislocations that distort and transform the world outside them. The world of celebrity and show business is already distorted, made up of the fantasies and aberrations of everyone who actively or passively takes part in it. Therefore, Rupert does not so much violently attack a world constructed out of his own aberrations but merely forces room in that world for one more aberration—himself.

This provides another explanation for why Scorsese moderates his visual style, basing the film's structure on more conventional patterns than he usually allows himself but then modifying them just enough to indicate a perceptual disturbance. He will use some of his old devices to indicate the dubious perceptions of his central character, as in the pre-credits sequence when Jerry Langford, seen from Rupert's point of view, moves in slow motion. But he will also use the ordinary shot/reverse shot pattern in an unusual way to integrate "fantasy" and "reality" and indicate their proximity. At the end of their first meeting (aided by Masha, who gets locked in Jerry's car so Rupert can pull her out and take her place with his idol), Rupert tells Jerry they should have lunch. In the next sequence, Jerry and Rupert have lunch, and Jerry begs Rupert to take over the show. Scorsese cuts between the two in a standard fashion. But he also cuts away from the fantasy to one-shots of Rupert, in his basement, talking, carrying on the dialogue with himself. By entering Rupert's imaginary world in this way Scorsese is, in effect, entering the solipsism that constitutes celebrity. Rupert's life as a star begins in his imagination, which he recreates in his basement, the space rigged out with life-sized posters of Marilyn Monroe and Humphrey Bogart, of Liza Minnelli and Jerry Lewis/Jerry Langford (after he becomes a star, Rupert himself will be a life-sized poster in a bookshop where his memoirs are being sold). Rupert sits between these two cutouts, kissing them, laughing at their unheard jokes, pretending to be a talk-show host, interrupted by his mother's off-screen voice (Scorsese's mother's voice, in fact), yelling at him to be quiet or to go to work. At one point, he records an audition tape for Jerry; he sits at a desk, talking into his tape recorder, his mother yelling at him. There is a cut to a photograph of a laughing and applauding audience. Rupert steps in front of it and begins to deliver his monologue (the words of which are mostly incomprehensible). The camera pulls back, the sounds of people laughing becomes distorted; when the camera finishes its movement, Rupert is observed at the end of a long, white corridor, standing before a poster of people frozen in hilarity. The space of the imaginary, of fantasy, becomes so powerful that it transforms reality or, more accurately, further subdues it. The onanist of entertainment will begin to impose himself on the outside world, which will finally be as pleased with him as he is with himself.

Travis Bickle's madness is read as bravery by the newspapers; Rupert Pupkin's obsessive activity, his invasion of privacy and commandeering of the airwaves by kidnapping, is turned into fame by magazines, television, and their audience. There is a wider and flatter plane of perception operating here, which may further account for the relative flatness of the mise-en-scène. Where Travis Bickle's terror was relatively localized, Rupert's literally subverts the country. He kidnaps a popular talk-show host and as ransom demands that he be given a monologue on the show. His wish is granted, he delivers a grotesquely idiotic routine about his parents and throwing up, goes to prison, writes a book, and emerges a major figure in the popular imagination (these last two events are presented through a montage of magazines and book covers, reminiscent of the newspaper headlines near the end of *Taxi Driver* and a similar montage in *New York, New York*); the individual himself disappears beneath the signs of his fame.

The question finally raised by both *The King of Comedy* and *Taxi Driver* is, who is crazy? If the viewer is implicated in the response to Travis Bickle's actions, the whole of television culture is implicated in Rupert's. His desire speaks to the desire for fame of everyone who sees him, and the film makes it difficult for the viewer to remain superior to the world the film addresses. Rupert is too bizarre to remain unattractive. His is the perfection of a crazed simplicity. Open and direct in his aspirations, his fantasies are relatively uncomplicated, and he cannot be embarrassed by them or by acting them out. Whether pursuing his girlfriend, Rita (played by the black actress Diahnne Abbott, whose race is never an issue to Rupert), or Jerry Langford, or pursued by his overtly lunatic cohort, Masha (Sandra Bernhard, who dances around the bound Jerry Langford almost naked in a delirium of lost repression: "I wanna be black," she tells him, in an attempt to express her notion of sensual delight at having her hero near her), Rupert remains steadfast and smiling where others might run cringing. Travis Bickle deflects viewer comprehension, Rupert invites it. He is an avatar of the man on the make, simple enough to bring assent to his desire to enter the lucite and chromium offices of media stars, indeed to become one himself. His obvious madness is mitigated by the persistence we are always told is needed to get ahead. He succeeds through a criminal act and a television per-formance so bad that it stands as another embarrassment by which he—and apparently the television viewer—is unaffected. Travis's success is appalling; Rupert's almost welcome. In either case a cipher has been filled with celebrity, and the culture that seeks images to celebrate and gives fame to madmen is once again put in a situation as precarious as the subjects of its admiration.

The subjects and objects of fame, celebrity, and admiration seem to have obsessed Scorsese from *Taxi Driver* on. *New York, New York*, his homage to the dark musicals of the forties and fifties—and a kind of remake of *A Star Is Born*—deals, like *King of Comedy*, with show business but from the inside, from the point of view of two embattled lovers struggling with careers. The visual structure of the film makes the viewer conscious of the artifices of romance and fame. The sets are studio bound, many of them simply painted backgrounds, an evocation of form in which levels of realism collide. Like *The Age of Innocence*, *New York, New York* has *Barry Lyndon* on its mind. All three films offer a meditation on the artifice of space that movies create and the relationship between two kinds of spatial illusion: the painter's canvas and the director's movie screen. Mise-en-scène doesn't quite swallow up Scorsese's characters as it does Kubrick's, and, as we have seen, these characters often attempt to struggle against the spaces around them. Some give in to them, like Newland Archer in *The Age of Innocence*, whose personality merges with the rituals of upper-middle-class behavior, rendering him emotionally impotent. Others battle them and prevail, like Rupert Pupkin. Others, like Jake La Motta, Jimmy in *GoodFellas*, or Max

Cady in *Cape Fear*, try to impress their bodies on the space around them, battering it and other bodies to their will. They lose.

Scorsese's "spiritual" characters—Jesus and the Dalai Lama—are also ambiguous, reluctant seekers after fame. Christ's agonies in the desert in *The Last Temptation of Christ* are closer to those of Jake La Motta's in the ring than they are to more conventional movie lives of Christ. The massive beating Jake allows himself to take from Sugar Ray Robinson is a kind of crucifixion, emphasized by the slow pan of the camera across the ropes, which grow bloodier as the camera looks more and more closely, ending with blood slowly dripping as if from a crown of thorns or a stigmata. In *Last Temptation*, Scorsese and Paul Schrader construct a Christ somewhat like Jake, moved by outside forces, unsure, uncertain—though, unlike Jake, with more self-consciousness—to take on the burden of savior. Scorsese's Jesus must, in a sense, have the celebrity of God beaten into him and the choice made for him. The appalling violence that makes up the Christ story is certainly not lost on Scorsese; neither is the notion that being beaten into submission and then killed makes a deep impression on all concerned. I am not suggesting that *Last Temptation* is a cynical film, but that it is so much inscribed with its maker's preoccupations about identity and fame, subjectivity and its loss that it gets mixed up. It clashes with its literary source (Nicos Kazantzakis's novel), the overwhelming conventions of screen biblical epics, its director's desires to rethink those conventions, his own preoccupations, and the excruciating violence of the Christ myth and Scorsese's elaboration on it. *Last Temptation of Christ* is peculiarly too constrained and not restrained enough. This results in an inclusiveness jarred by massive acts of suffering.

Celebrity and violence seem inextricable to Scorcese, and this problem plagues *Kundun*, whose subject is supposed to be deeply meditative and unworldly. The best Scorsese can do is contain his character within richly colored and composed images and to attempt some sense of drama by representing the conflict between the Dalai Lama and the Chinese, where the character of Mao, as he does in Stone's *Nixon*, comes off as a more comfortable and knowing figure than his antagonists. Otherwise, Scorsese cannot get to the interior of his main figure the way he can create a conflicted personality for his Jesus Christ or suggest his conflicts by way of mise-en-scène and point of view. Mostly because neither he nor his scriptwriter knows Buddhism—which is, after all, a deeply interior spiritual practice—and because, as Orson Welles once observed, the work of prayer and meditation is difficult to film, Scorsese is reduced more than in any of his previous films to be content with surfaces. With the spirituality that should be the necessary subject of the film reduced, the politics mostly obfuscated, the film becomes a pretty exposition of a figure unable to act and barely willing to flee. But the film does suggest that celebrity may finally be the payoff for flight, for the final images of an isolated figure in a strange land serve really as the prelude for that figure with which we in the West are most familiar.

That's the fact that cannot be forgotten and a major problem with the film. The Dalai Lama may be a contested Buddhist spiritual leader, but he is a completely uncontested post-cold war, anticommunist celebrity, especially in the United States and particularly in Hollywood, where he dines with the stars. *Kundun* was financed by Michael Eisner and the Disney Company and written by Melissa Mathison, who wrote *E.T.* for Steven Spielberg. The film is finally an orientalist exercise in theme-park spirituality, rendered by a master colorist and composer of richly textured scenes. As a kind of transnational product made to irritate or enlighten no one (despite China's momentary threat to boycott Disney products), but rather to trade on the name of a great filmmaker and revered subject, it tells us little of *realpolitik* and global conflict. But it tells us a bit about how Hollywood is willing, even as it was in the studio period, to produce a "small" film for a smallish audience. The contradiction is only apparent, because "small" and transnational are not exclusive. Money is to be made on the wide distribution of a less-than-blockbuster film. Besides, such a production makes everyone feel fine; and enlightenment therefore follows redemption, which filmmakers want for themselves as much as for the characters they create.

Finally, despite its failings, *Kundun* represents Scorsese's love of experimentation, his infatuation with all film genres, and his desire to keep trying out the means of his art. Even *Bringing Out the Dead*, a film that seems to be marking time, caught somewhere between *Taxi Driver* and *After Hours*, not advancing insight or formal experiment very far, shows his willingness always to push his camera into the face of reality to reveal a more real cinematic face and body behind it, a violent and struggling body, trapped in spaces it barely comprehends and wants still to struggle against. In that body's movements within a space filled with tension and violence lie some of the great gestures of contemporary film.

FOUR

OF DINOSAURS AND SHIPS
Steven Spielberg, Large Things,
and the Digital Mise-en-Scène

> The auteur of the movie is as much the techie as the director.
>
> —Peter Bart, *The Gross*

1

In order to understand the movements and patterns of nineties cinema, we must understand the work of Steven Spielberg, who has established himself as the focus of filmmaking activity during the decade. At the same time, in order to understand Spielberg, we need to examine the flow of cinematic work around him. This chapter will play a bit of counterpoint, looking for some patterns in late twentieth-century film, finding Spielberg, comparing him with the work of other directors, and then moving to the center and examining his work for both form and content.

We may actually be too close to the period to find the large patterns of nineties film, and there is the possibility there are no clear patterns to find just yet. It was a decade of minimal experimentation and large-scale repetition of older ideas. However, the corporate and economic events surrounding film production during the last decade of the century are very clear, and many critics are focusing on these aspects of the cinematic equation: the merger of the studios into units of very large corporations continued unabated, leading, in turn, to the further globalization of American film, forcing profits to depend increasingly on foreign sales, thereby pushing the films themselves to be acceptable and accessible across cultures. The long death of the short-lived auteur, a demise that resulted largely from a few studios losing everything by banking on what they thought to be bankable directors, resulted in increasingly younger studio heads and producers assigning films to increasingly younger directors, with minimum experience—in filmmaking or in life—beyond the films they've seen at USC or UCLA film school and the MTV videos that may have been their sole first venture into production. At the same time, the studios and the "independents" (many of which are often financed and almost always distributed by the "independent film" units of the studios:

Columbia's Sony Classics, Fox Searchlight, Disney's Miramax, AOL–Time Warner's New Line) are less and less open to experimentation of any radical kind. We are therefore less and less likely to see experiments with narrative form, visual style, and, especially, the larger "master narratives," the template stories of desire, deceit, triumph, contrition, and redemption that have informed films since the cranking of the first projector.[1]

At the same time, American films enjoy ever-increasing popularity, and through the new distribution media of videotape, laserdisc, DVD, and cable, have extended their lives—and their profitability—longer than could have been imagined in the classic studio days. Many studios have taken full advantage of this extendable shelf life by releasing expanded or restored editions and "directors' cuts" after initial theatrical and video release. The new storage and distribution media have produced an interesting collateral struggle over copyright and ownership of films, with the MPAA's Jack Valenti leading an intensive battle to place all copyright controls in the hands of the content providers—the studios—while in the process attempting, finally without success, to do away with fair use.

In many ways, the nineties produced a cinema of retrenchment, even as, economically, it expanded its reach by being woven into large corporate webs and through extended storage and distribution. This retrenchment occurred on the basic levels of content and form, and it pretty much closes the curtain on the modernist styles this book remains stubbornly devoted to. Some critics have attempted to argue that the retrenchment is actually the development of a new style, the ubiquitous postmodernism, but this term covers such a multitude of sins and salvations (but never redemption) that it loses much of its descriptive force. At its best, the postmodern is an attempt to move beyond modernism, beyond the voice of the despairing author seeking coherence of form and structure in the face of an incoherent universe and to move toward an inclusive celebration of the death of meaning in which all art, high and low, is recognized as sharing a community of images and sounds. At its best, the postmodern addresses the breaking down of individual, national, international, and aesthetic boundaries, recognizing that technology has rendered subjectivity—that complicated discourse of individuality, agency, and will—permeable and changeable.[2] The postmodern addresses the ways in which the political, aesthetic, ideological, and cultural merge and co-determine one another through a multitude of voices and addresses.

At its worst, postmodernism functions as the spin doctor for the incoherent. Permeability, a populist mixture of image and sound, a sarcasm or cynicism that barely masquerades as irony, a knowing allusion to the work of popular culture that assumes an audience brought up on television need know no more than they've seen on television, and an almost demonic avoidance of meaning and complexity are postmodern attributes that render some of its products adolescent, banal, and, too often, puerile. Intelligence is sometimes evident, as in *The Simpsons*, which assures us that all our dreams emerge from the film and television unconscious. More often than not, and especially in movies, the jokes backfire, the allusions are smothered in their obviousness, and both cynicism and irony collapse into smugness. Quentin Tarantino's *Pulp Fiction* stands as the acme of postmodern nineties filmmaking. It attempts a number of experimental approaches, borrowed from the New Wave (Tarantino's production company is called "Band à Part," after a gangster film by Jean-Luc Godard). Very long takes of dialogue sequences, a play with temporal sequence, and a rough-hewn energy that the New Wave directors used to admire in Samuel Fuller's films make *Pulp Fiction* look like a contender for a revision in the classical style. The flourishes, the apparent witty banality of the dialogue, the goofy fracturing of temporality are a patina over a pastiche. The pastiche (a favorite concept of postmodernism, best understood through the example of "sampling" in hip-hop, where parts of older songs are woven into the rhythmic mix of the new piece) is essentially made of the two films that Tarantino can't seem to get out of his mind: *Mean Streets* and *The Killing*. Young toughs in groups, a robbery gone bad, a play on temporal continuity keep appearing in *Reservoir Dogs* (1990), *Pulp Fiction*, and *Jackie Brown* (1997).

The popularity of *Pulp Fiction* was based on its simulacrum of novelty, and simulacrum, the imitation of something that never existed in the first place, is a beloved quality of the postmodern. It needs to be differentiated from the modernist technique of allusion, in which references to other works serve as a way to the creation of resonance and the complexity of textual relationships. When Martin Scorsese creates a palimpsest of Hitchcock's *Strangers on a Train*, on top of which he constructs images and sequences in *Cape Fear*, or uses *The Searchers* and *Psycho* as the texts driving *Taxi Driver*, the result is a complex intertextuality in which the films, in effect, talk to each other, and the viewer is asked to attend to a conversation across the plain of film history. When Tarantino "does" *The Killing*, we learn little about a Tarantino aesthetic, which itself understands even less about Kubrick, and don't learn much about his three films. Pastiche becomes a kind of poaching, and a poaching of surfaces at that.[3] But this much must be understood: the postmodern is about surfaces; it is flattened spatiality in which event and character are in a steady state of reminding us that they are pop-cultural figures. This is a flat, circular—or short-circuited—space whose pleasures arise from self recognition.[4] That's why *Pulp Fiction* was so popular. Not because audiences got all or any of the references to Scorsese and Kubrick, but because the narrative and spatial structure of the film never threatened to go beyond themselves into signification. The film's cycle of racist and homophobic jokes might threaten to break out into a quite nasty view of the world, but this nastiness keeps being laughed off— by the mock intensity of the action, the prowling, confronting, perverse, confined, and airless nastiness of the world Tarantino creates.

But I've been arguing that the mark of a good filmmaker is precisely this ability to create a well-defined world, a visual, fictional space that articulates ideas and invites an inquiring gaze. The modernist mise-en-scène is open and invites a search for meaning that can be precise, ironic, and ambiguous. Oliver Stone's *Natural Born Killers* was made from a Tarantino script and contains all the aimless, disgusting violence that Tarantino loves. But its spatial articulations never offer an evasive duck and cover for the viewer, a way to avoid or laugh off what is going on. Its violence is driven by a curiosity about representation, about the ways we watch and need to see more such violence, and the ultimate approval we give to outlaws because they appear to embody an energy drained from us by the demands of the everyday. The film makes us uncomfortable, because we recognize that its parody of media fame is in fact a parody of what we accept without much question in our daily exposure to television. *Pulp Fiction* is a simulacrum of our daily exposure to television; its homophobes, thugs and perverts, sentimental boxers and pimp promoters move through a series of long-take tableaux: we watch, laugh, and remain with nothing to comprehend.

Am I preaching morality? *Mean Streets* and *The Killing* are moral films if for no other reason than the closed worlds they create are always recognized as being part of some larger experience, and that in turn suggests that the actions of the characters have consequences. Both films are about class and its constraints. *The Killing* has deeply embedded within it the currents of existential angst and working-class despair flowing through the fifties; *Mean Streets* theorizes—visually, in its dialogue, in the spaces around its characters—about class and neighborhood boundaries. *Natural Born Killers* is a moral film because its very form demands that the viewer consider the consequences of his or her viewing. *Pulp Fiction* is without theory or consequences, or it's about laughing both off, and this itself is a great paradox churning within the postmodern. Postmodernism theories abound, but, unlike modernism, the works that are theorized eschew theory themselves because they deny significance. They posit only their images, sounds, or words within their closed narrative worlds, snubbing a quest for resonance, history, politics. Modernism is the enemy of complacency; postmodernism its accomplice. It shares a peculiar and general smugness of a post-cold war culture in which history is declared over and the dominance of capitalism a natural event. But it shares that culture's despair as well. *Any* meaning is liable to be distressing, because the fragile power balances between interest groups, classes, races, and genders would be brought immediately into question were we to discover through our art, our politics, our movies what the culture, its economics, its ideologies are exactly about. So, the postmodern attempts to fight the fragility of cultural anxiety, the sense of isolation from power and agency sensed by so many people, by means of flippant display and careless pastiche. It plunders the past of popular culture in an attempt to convince us that we are part of a community in which history is only a function of popular memory. If we remember something from television and get the joke, it's enough and we may take our careless pleasure.

The postmodern strain is no more dominant in American film than the modernist was. A conservative operation on all levels, American filmmaking tends always to fall back into the secure modes of the classical continuity style, generating the most banal meanings from the most invisible formal structures. It tries, as it always has, to cover the variety of its audiences with a variety of genres—even though the age range of all the audiences remains targeted at fifteen to thirty-five. The desire to broaden the audience within that range has resulted in, for example, the growth of films aimed at African Americans, some of them directed by African Americans. From the homeboy movies like *Boyz n The Hood* (John Singleton, 1991), to raucous sex comedies like *Booty Call* (Jeff Pollack, 1997), to women's films—Forest Whitaker's *Waiting to Exhale* (1995), Kevin Rodney Sullivan's *How Stella Got Her Groove Back* (1998)—and family melodramas, *Eve's Bayou* (Kasi Lemmons, 1997) and *Soul Food* (George Tillman, Jr., 1997). The variety of style and content expressed in these films is quite broad. They provide entertainment and insight for their target audience while permitting the studios to feel virtuous having serviced that audience. They also provide opportunities for new directorial talent and, in films like John Singleton's *Rosewood* (1997), Jonathan Demme's *Beloved* (1998), and much of the work of Spike Lee, a space for meaningful interrogations of race, history, and culture.

That the studios follow the money is no longer a major insight, and a driving theme of this book is that we can't dismiss films because they are, at base, a commodity in the circulation of capital. Because they are commodities that narrate, that tell stories to and about their culture, they have meaning no matter why they are made or for whom. At the same time, their meaning is very much dependent on the reason for and the target of their making. The fact that, in the fall of 1998, thousands of *Star Wars* fans went to theaters and paid full admission to sit through a two-minute trailer for the next installment of their favorite film speaks a lot about the power of popular narrative to excite desire. The fact that the *Star Wars* series grazes along the postmodern is important. As a huge pastiche of a variety of genres, touched with just enough New Age vagaries about intuition and self-reliance, it offers itself as an avatar of cinema. It embraces every master narrative, offers large varieties of visual spectacle, and promises to go on forever as a provider of visual and emotional pleasure for its viewers and money for George Lucas.

Star Wars is a reference point for the kind of cinema I want to talk about in this chapter—a fin-de-siècle cinema. Or, perhaps, as Jean-Luc Godard predicted at the end of *Weekend* in 1965, simply a *fin du cinéma*. This is a cinema of the spectacle, a cinema of large images in which forces of explosive destruction are contained by heroic men with a sense of humor. It is, remarkably enough, a cinema of irony—or cynicism. Its postmodernity is marked by the fact that everyone in the film, making the film, watching the film, is winking at each other. The delicate play of gazes that construct all narrative cinema has turned to the play of winks and nods. This is a male cinema largely generated in reaction to the feminism of the late sixties and therefore reactionary at its core. But the steady undercurrent of irony and the occasional manufacture of a male character of some vulnerability, who takes cognizance of the absurdities of his situation and the demands put on him, mitigate the otherwise conventional attitudes of the strong man taking on himself the saving of an endangered and passive community. This is a cinema of the body in which flesh is endangered by machinery, and often becomes part of the machinery. It is the cinema of the cyborg.

Partly because it is a cinema of the computer graphic designer. The heroic male body is surrounded by destructive machines. Both body and machines—in fact, the entire mise-en-scène of the late-century male action film—are studio constructed: models, traveling mattes, gorgeous photorealist painting, and, since the early nineties, computer-generated images.[5]

This aspect of contemporary film must be put in some historical perspective. From its beginnings before the turn of the twentieth century, the shot—the basic unit of a film—was built from a number of components not always present at the same time. Where the Lumière Brothers were filming "actualités"—a train pulling into the station, workers leaving their factory, a couple feeding their baby—Georges Méliès was manufacturing images in his studio, using matte painting and miniatures, most memorably in one of the first science-fiction films, *A Trip to the Moon*. During Porter's 1903 *The Great Train Robbery*, thieves steal the mail from a railcar hurtling along. The hurtling is represented by a rear-screen projection of moving scenery outside of a door cut into the set of the railcar.

As studio production began in the teens, the rationalism of speed and cost efficiency took immediate hold. A method of achieving both was to shoot entirely in the studio and only what was available at any one time, taking advantage of optical printing and the two-dimensional structure of the film image to trick the eye looking at the final print. Was there need of a character looking out at a cityscape? The buildings could be painted with a cutout of the character and placed near the camera. The perspective lines of the painting and the desire to see the human figure foregrounded would allow a viewer's eye to reverse the planes, seeing the figure in front of the cityscape. Alternatively, the figure could be photographed in front of a blue screen and the cityscape photographed anywhere in the world. In the optical lab, the blue would be dropped out of the background behind the figure, who would be projected over the cityscape. The figure could be made to fly or to fall. Seen on the screen, the illusion is all but invisible.

These basic techniques, including the use of models and miniatures, of stop-action photography and rear-screen projection, permit great flexibility in manipulating various physical objects. Elements of the image are laid over each other at various times during the production and manufacture of the film. This has been the standard operating procedure of filmmaking since the beginning. And there is more than economics involved. There is an implicit recognition that film is the first cybernetic art. Photography, as André Bazin pointed out, extended the eye with technological apparatuses. Filmmaking added much more to the process, generating narrative out of technological manipulation, fusing the imagination with the complexities of the moving image.

But rear-screen projections, models, miniature cars and planes, matte shots, are analogue procedures, actual objects made by hand and in the optical lab that, small or large, trick the eye to see things vaguely familiar from everyday perception. The computer creates from nothing—nothing visible or analogue at least. While some modeling of the human figure may start the design process (a technique that has its roots in rotoscope animation, where Disney artists, for example, film characters in action and then trace those images into animations), the actual composition of computer-generated scenes comes from the artist's manipulation of the arithmetic, base-ten binaries of computer code that address the pixels on the computer screen. They build images slowly and painstakingly, making space for the human figures—when indeed human figures will be used rather than generated by the machine—matching movements, creating worlds. Spielberg recognizes the art of the digital artist in a stunning, reflexive shot in *Jurassic Park*, when one of the dinosaurs, having entered the interior of a building, is seen reflecting back the computer code of which he's made. The birdlike reptile stretching its wings, perched on a tree in the tropical jungle at the end of Spielberg's *The Lost World* (1997), is really a congratulatory vaunt by the film's digital artists, displaying their ability to create anything and make it look like a representation of the probable.

The history of the digital mise-en-scène is short and recent. Although digital manipulation of sound began in the seventies, the computer power necessary for the fabrication of imagery took longer to develop. It begins to appear in earnest around 1992, though James Cameron was experimenting with it in the water creatures in *The Abyss* (1989) and the cyborg in *Terminator 2* (1991). These are, of course, special-effects movies in which spectacle is prominent and the viewer plays with a double consciousness of the artificiality of the images and their "realism" simultaneously. Wolfgang Petersen used more subtle digital effects in *In the Line of Fire* (1993), where Clint Eastwood's head is pasted on a stunt double's body and crowds are created by digital duplication; Robert Zemeckis uses digital figure replacement somewhat clumsily in *Forrest Gump* (1994), as the hero gets placed next to the likes of John F. Kennedy. *Jurassic Park* completes the movement to the digital in 1993, and shortly after that there are essentially no studio-driven films that do not create a digital mise-en-scène in part or throughout their length. Sit and watch the very final credits of any but the lowest budget "independent" film. Here are the individuals who are now as important as the cinematographer, the production designer, and, perhaps, the director, for they design and execute much of the mise-en-scène, articulating the space that creates the film's world.

254

To judge what has been gained or lost with the domination of the digital mise-en-scène is not a useful task. In so many instances digital techniques simply replace older optical effects that films had used since their beginnings; they can be described merely as another method in the manufacture of images. Yet, because the computer enables the creation or simulacrum of imaginary worlds not only more easily (though, given the minute and detailed work required, "readily" might be a better word than "easily"), it is allowing filmmakers a wider scope of expression or, on the negative side, an opportunity to allow all creativity to flow to the design, while narrative and editing remain as banal as usual.

The task is to examine the movements of nineties cinema through its changing mise-en-scène and concentration on male-action and science-fiction films, and to focus this through the work of Steven Spielberg, an innovator, a master at suturing the viewer so tightly into the narrative and spatial flow that he seems to become part of it, and a director who uses his popularity and influence to make, from time to time, films about large and historically significant subjects, turning his viewers into the subjects of narratives that presume to represent the Nazi destruction of the Jews or the visceral experiences of World War II combat. I want briefly to compare Spielberg with James Cameron, whose films exploit the simplest aspects of male heroism by tricking them out with heavy armament and underwater feats. Cameron is a cynical director, who disguises his misogynist narratives with apparently strong female characters, who ultimately become abject to the men or the machines. Male or female, his characters are directly or independently dependent on heavy metal and become cyborgs. When he modifies the cyborg premise in *Titanic* (1997), he has nothing but a teenage romance, one conventional narrative about snotty upper-class snobs versus plucky lower-class boys, and a disaster in which the heavy machinery turns on the hero and heroine. The film sloshes between the romance and the teenagers, and the superstructure of the ship. That movement generated more revenue than any film of the decade.

A well-tuned and well-visualized glibness works in Cameron's favor, as it does for many of his action contemporaries, like John McTiernan and the stable of directors working for the nineties master producer of the techno-male action genre, Jerry Bruckheimer (*Crimson Tide*, Tony Scott, 1995; *The Rock*, Michael Bay, 1996; *Con Air*, Simon West, 1997; *Armageddon*, Michael Bay, 1998; and *Enemy of the State*, Tony Scott, 1998). Their ability to excite accessible emotions with large, violent, often surreal spectacle, and heroics whose physicality transcends the capabilities of any human bodies places them quite firmly in the Hollywood tradition of absorptive cinema, seamlessly drawing its parts together and the viewer into its web. Spielberg

255

is no less glib, but his is a glibness that goes beyond sensory stimulation. He is so proficient—so efficient—at structuring his narratives, controlling his mise-en-scène, and positioning the spectator within these structures, that his films all but guarantee the viewer will surrender herself to them at some point during the narrative. Power like this needs to be understood; when film so easily manipulates emotion, there is every reason to find out how and why. I want to touch on Spielberg's work from an ideological perspective, compare it with some other nineties films, and then return to a closer examination of his films that will then more clearly manifest his intent.

Spielberg's films are obviously well crafted, technologically overdetermined, dependent on cinematic effects, and at the same time determinedly realistic and manipulative—realistic because they are manipulative. His work brings to the fore the central problem of the illusionary form, the power of American cinema to create itself as an unquestioning site of belief and assent. Let's recover a bit of ground: the way in which Spielberg's films so happily and energetically foreground their narrative and cinematic devices makes them readily accessible to formal analysis, while at the same time creating a sense of ongoing story into which we are deeply drawn. He combines some minor elements of modernism with the dominant Hollywood style—the repetition of formal devices whose aim is to render themselves invisible but which Spielberg occasionally allows us to glimpse. His work straddles both worlds. In addition, he includes frequent allusions to other films and reflects on his own (*Close Encounters of the Third Kind*, is a film not only about friendly aliens, but about cinematic spectacle itself; *Jurassic Park*, in postmodern fashion, tries to be everything: it is the very theme park that is the subject of its narrative). But despite all these elements, he disallows distance and objectivity. He tightens his films like a trap, so that the viewer is unable to see beyond the image content and remains immediately unaware as to why there is no escape. From the outside, the camouflage is difficult to penetrate. His films become seamless, cyborg mechanisms.

An important part of the mechanism is the ideological structure of the films. The content of Spielberg's work is attractive only to the degree that its formal structure gives it shape and meaning and manipulates viewer assent to it. The form and structure of the films produce images and narratives that respond or give shape to the current ideological needs, offering a safe and secure ideological haven. Their images and narratives speak of a place and a way of being in the world (indeed the universe) that viewers find more than just comfortable, but desirable and—within the films—*available*. Just here is where we see form and content become inextricable. These films create for their viewers comfortable surrogates for an uncomfortable world, satisfying desire, clarifying, indeed forging relationships between the individual and the world within their own imaginative structures. Unlike Arthur Penn's or Stanley Kubrick's work, Spielberg's films are not simply ideological bellwethers, pointing to major cultural currents, summing up the state of things every five to eight years. They transcend the function of responding or giving shape to ideology and instead become ideology, the very shape and form of the relationships we desire for our world. Louis Althusser writes, "*All ideology hails or interpellates concrete individuals as concrete subjects.*" Individuals give their subjectivity willingly to the ideological discourse, because something obviously recognizable and desirable is there. "It is indeed a peculiarity of ideology," he says, "that it imposes (without appearing to do so, since these are 'obviousnesses') obviousnesses as obviousnesses, which we cannot *fail to recognize* and before which we have the inevitable and natural reaction of crying out (aloud or in the 'still, small voice of conscience'): 'That's obvious! That's right! That's true.'"[6] The ideological structures of Spielberg's films "hail" the spectator into a world of the obvious that affirms the viewer's presence (even while dissolving it), affirms that what the viewer has always believed or hoped is (obviously) right and accessible, and assures the viewer excitement and comfort in the process. The films offer nothing new beyond their spectacle, nothing the viewer does not already want, does not immediately accept. That is their conservative power, and it has spread throughout the cinema of the eighties and nineties.

Spielberg's films constitute a factory of ideological production, the great imaginary of the late twentieth century, full of images the culture wants to see, images and narratives that express or evoke its desire. They offer spectacle, an imaginary history, solid, liberal views of race in the face of nonstop reactionary backlash; a hint of politics that is offered without Oliver Stone's demand that the viewer not give up her subjectivity but recognize it as the object of the film's address. The frequency, success, and influence of his films over two decades have made them a kind of encyclopedia of desire, a locus of representations into which audiences wished to be called. He remains at the center of eighties and nineties American filmmaking and to get there I want to look again through some adjacent doors, examining other images and narratives of the period, before confronting the main texts. I want to return to the male-action films I referred to earlier, those films that are borne out of Spielberg's word but go in other directions.

Many American films of the mid-seventies and eighties were a conduit for the shudder that went through the culture and its dominant ideologies during the sixties and seventies, beginning with the assassination of Kennedy and ending with the resignation of Nixon and the liberation of Vietnam in the mid-seventies. For a society unused to internal failures and external losses, unable and unwilling to analyze events historically, politically, economically, rationally, the result was a mixture of anger, guilt, and frustrated aggressiveness. In film, images and narratives of despair and impotence alternated or were combined with violent outbursts against the self and others. *Taxi Driver*; *Death Wish* and its vigilante offspring; Coppola's *The Conversation*; *Night Moves*; Alan J. Pakula's *The Parallax View*; Sidney Pollack's *Three Days of the Condor* are some examples, among many, of films that spoke defeat and powerlessness, with the occasional, isolated surge of violence as surrogate for social action.

The revolution in Iran, the capture of American hostages, the dominant notion that President Carter was weak because he did not or could not make war threatened to cut away any of the remaining ideological props of liberalism. A turn came in the late seventies. The weakened structure began to be strengthened and the dominant voice retuned by the discourse of neoconservatism. Within the relative ideological hegemony of American politics, liberalism and conservatism are not very disparate and in fact coexist with only some tension. Both ideologies are centered on the image of the male individual and his unfettered advancement in a "free enterprise" economy. And while the progressive wing of liberalism (about the only remnant of left discourse remaining in the culture) recognizes the reality of sexual difference and may sometime question "free market" mythologies, the mainstream is anticollective, antifemale, antileft, hierarchical, and aggressive. Liberalism embeds its aggressiveness within images of conciliation and myths of equal opportunity and reason ("Let us reason together" was Lyndon Johnson's call while he waged war) and gathers to itself, almost like satellites, opposing ideological fragments, discourses that offer possibilities of help to those outside the central sphere of power, while that sphere remains essentially untouched. Conservatism repels any mitigating or modifying forces, demanding individuals and groups be not merely unimpeded by rules and regulations, but be denied of assistance or protection, while demanding that everyone dwell within a rigid, economically, often religious, white fundamentalist determined hierarchy.

Conservatism is an essentially antimodern ideology. The more social-economic structures change, the faster conservatism builds fantastic ideas of a past in which families existed as peaceful, reproductive units, keeping gender in order, worshiping a Christian god, and, most important, minding their own business. The business of the state and its corporate structures would remain under cooperative government-business control but with the illusion that government was not there. Neoconservatism was born of a somewhat more intellectual base, developed largely by disillusioned sixties radicals—many of them Jewish intellectuals, like Norman Podhoretz, Gertrude Himmelfarb, and William Kristol, who, in the anticommunist tradition of Sidney Hook and Lionel Trilling, fled their ideological homes. They wound up in the bosom of Reaganism, with its "evil empire," trickle-down economics, antigovernment beliefs that, through a racist, sexist discourse, further eroded the very cultural cohesion it claimed to seek.[7]

Contradictions develop continually within both liberalism and conservatism. Liberalism cannot comfortably contain images of social responsibility within its capitalist imperative. Conservatism gets tongue-tied as it insists on unfettered individual initiative while promoting a protected, elite, patriarchal structure of ownership and administration. It gets downright violent when proposing a complete separation of government and governed while insisting that living people adopt its dead fantasies of correct domestic and gender behavior. Infiltrating these contradictions is a right-wing discourse of extraordinary belligerence in which the banalities of free enterprise are re-created into harsh statements of moral and political righteousness, protectionism (of all entrenched, noncommunist political, economic, and social structures), and intolerance.

Liberalism generates, as part of its ideological contradictions, a loneliness born of its impossible promise of communal assistance. Conservatism fosters loneliness outright by insisting that each man must count on no help and each woman must be dependent on this same unaided individual. At the same time, conservatism pretends to offer a voice to the lower middle class, those to whom its goals of wealth and power appear in vague sight but are perpetually unreachable. This is the group that attends to conservative discourse, believes its litany that the most fulfilled life is one in which money is earned and a family raised and protected without government assistance—tasks that require single-minded effort, self-denying labor, and a refusal of all political action except assent. This discourse also announces that the middle class can win back national and international esteem and pride presumably lost when foreign governments

259

assert themselves. Typically, the announcement is based on yet another contradiction: this esteem is rightfully ours, it says, but we are too weak to establish our right to it. As a result, aggressiveness and belligerence increase until military operations become all but unavoidable. In the end, conservatism must wage war or (more likely) recognize its impotence as a fact and then fantasize images that pretend to overcome that impotence. The absence of the actuality or promise of war—an absence that has existed since the end of the cold war and remains aggravated by the memories of civil and military unrest in the Vietnam conflict—turns the right in on itself. A culture of isolated individuals cannot exist without an imagined enemy. No one in the Middle East can quite fit the bill, no matter how demonized, and so the right wing turns on its own culture. *Some* government has to be the enemy; nothing seems to be available abroad, and so our own government will fit the bill.

Nineties politics were marked by the absurdity of individuals running for office they say they can't stand, wanting to take part in government only to destroy it and its leader. Contained in this absurdity is the growth of the private militias—anti-Semitic, misogynist, racist, homophobic groups gripped by a cinematic fantasy of government intruders, replete with imaginary apparatuses of black helicopters and alien penetration. Their strangeness achieves potency as they harass, bomb, and kill while the elected right remains silent about their action and their own connections with it.

The militias grew from the paranoia of the disenfranchised and were fed by movies, which picked up on the contradictions inherent in conservative and liberal discourse. Early in the seventies, film created the images and the narratives that give ideological structure to what has often been a confused liberal discourse punctuated by occasional desperate action. During the decade, in response to feelings of social impotence, the subject as effective agent in cinematic fiction was diminished physically, emotionally, and politically. Francis Ford Coppola's *The Conversation* offers a better than typical example. The film's central character, Gene Hackman's Harry Caul, is a gray and recessive surveillance expert, who, in the course of the film, undergoes a kind of moral destruction. Used to spying on others with delicately operated sound equipment, he becomes—or so he believes— witness to the murder of a corporate director. As a result, he suffers a kind of moral paralysis, subdued by his guilt and then by the very act that created that guilt. The man who attempted to subordinate his personality to become the secret watcher of other people's lives becomes the object of surveillance himself, by someone not troubled by anxieties. At the end of the film, he is a completely reduced figure, sitting in the corner of his room, which he has torn to pieces looking for a hidden microphone, playing a saxophone as if he were a child sucking a pacifier.

The character's fall is accompanied by a questioning of the viewer's own position of safety outside the narrative, in the world. Coppola structures events through Harry's sensibility, so that a complex of fear, guilt, and fantasy is created that sometimes defies straightforward comprehension of what happens. But he also articulates his camera so that it often creates images of passive, almost impersonal observation. In that last shot, the camera observes Harry from a high angle, mechanically swinging right and left, as if it were an instrument of surveillance. Therefore, the viewer must respond not only to Harry's sensibility, but to the absence of sensibility signified by the coldly observing camera. The result is a reduction of both subjects, the participant in the fiction and the viewer of the fiction, neither of which is given any moral ground. The film raises questions not only about the morality of spying and the effects of being spied on, but about the efficacy, potency, and ethics of action itself.

The Conversation was one of a number of films of paranoia and loss, fictions of impotence and despair that disallowed the effective heroic action American films had so often promised its audience. There were also responses to these statements offered by country and urban vigilante films, particularly the *Walking Tall, Dirty Harry,* and *Death Wish* cycles. These films drew directly on the convention of the individual hero, resituating him in somewhat more clearly defined political contexts than in the past. While Buford Pusser was battling mob elements in a small town in *Walking Tall* (1973, directed by Phil Karlson, "based on a true story," yet essentially the same film as Karlson's 1955 *Phenix City Story*), Dirty Harry Callahan and Charles Bronson's architect hero of *Death Wish* were acting in political opposition to local government powers. The police adhered to liberal laws that permitted killers to walk the streets. The vigilantes, more closely in touch with the needs of the community, transcended these laws, bringing evil to violent justice.

These films articulated, quite simply and directly, one aspect of the growing conservatism of the seventies, generating images that articulated the Nixonian calls for law and order against antiwar activists (the mad killer in *Dirty Harry* wears a peace symbol) and other anarchic forces in the society that seemed resistant to control. As the Nixon regime turned paranoid and Vietnam caused a rupture in the ideological layer where cultural images of invincibility lay embedded, filmic expressions of violence

261

became more inwardly directed and masochistic. There were symptoms that the society held itself collectively to blame for Vietnam (of course it was to blame, though the political aspects of this truth were not the ones examined), and many films focused on the crazed Vietnam veteran. As always, cinema evaded political realities and, in this instance, focused on Vietnam as a psychological aberration that turned innocent young men into psychopaths (*Taxi Driver* has some relationship to this group of films). On another, equally apolitical, level, the war was seen as a challenge to conventional notions of civilized conduct (including traditional notions of the "proper" conduct of war), a destruction of individual comportment and control, and a demonstration of just how fragile the conventions of Western civilized behavior were. Michael Cimino explored this somewhat aberrant version of right-wing humanism in *The Deer Hunter*, as did John Milius and Francis Coppola in *Apocalypse Now*, and Oliver Stone in *Platoon*. Stone's film attempts a tighter view through a rookie's eyes, but the view maintains that this was all a personal struggle that led to an understanding of the good and evil of the human character. The Vietnam of all these films savaged hearts, minds, and bodies, making American boys crazy. *Apocalypse Now* and *Platoon* portrayed Vietnam as a hallucinatory, schizophrenic realm in which hierarchy, responsibility, and order decayed. Of the mid-eighties Vietnam films, only Kubrick's *Full Metal Jacket* concentrated on the destructive elements inherent in the training and disposition of the soldiers themselves. The cause of moral decay and madness, particularly in *The Deer Hunter* and *Apocalypse Now*, was an enemy as anarchic as "the criminal elements" who needed extermination in the law-and-order films. Worse, they were "Oriental" and communist, able therefore to be represented as the alien other, who might infiltrate the Western soul and destroy its moral structure. The analogy to fifties anticommunist science-fiction films is not at all strained.

The regime of Jimmy Carter was a result, in part, of a search for calm after this latest assault, along with a desire to live out a fantasy of a nongovernmental government (Carter had his origins in the populist, indeed Capra-esque notion of the "man of the people," who might separate the nation from an established power that now appeared not only corrupt, but self-absorbed and uninterested in people's needs). During Carter's tenure, various national interests outside the United States continued to assert themselves, and the internal economy faltered badly; the hoped-for calm turned into another cycle of frustration and desire for revenge. Middle Easterners took the place of Asians as the alien other, although their

262

representation in film was limited to the comic or the devious. Middle East-erners were depicted either as rich and stupid men in robes or savage, irrational terrorists, a stereotype that has grown since the end of the cold war, as filmmakers can now only represent Russian mafiosi or Middle Easterners as figures of international evil.

Politically, the culture still required a period of calm, recuperation, and affirmation, even in the face of events that would appear to render such a period impossible. Ronald Reagan was able to enact an extraordinary phenomenon. With the actor's talent for assuming a persona requisite to the situation at hand and a national audience ready to become subject to a discourse of security, power, and self-righteousness, he was able to focus various ideological elements. More, he became an ideology. For a moment it seemed possible that no further ideological displacement would be necessary. Reagan did not merely articulate the language of extreme conservatism; he was his own discursive center, displacing the reality of politics with the illusion of a personality who spoke deliberately, assertively, and with complete conviction. "The great communicator" was not merely a journalistic cliché. Ronald Reagan became what many people wanted to see and hear. More than what Reagan spoke, the way he spoke it, his aggressive, anticommunist discourse, his promise of a free-enterprise utopia where everyone (of the appropriate gender, politics, and color) might do what they wished and thrive, with no interference; his implicit offering of himself as paternal guide into this utopia made him an ideological magnet and a hegemonic force, equaled (in a rather different political context) only by Roosevelt in the thirties and forties.

But words are not enough. Ideology is structurally unsteady. Currents keep surging and contradictions keep occurring, causing shifts, forcing ele-ments continually to realign in order to maintain validity as representa-tions. Reagan's aggressive discourse, which presented most of the nonwhite, nonmonied, or noncapitalist world as enemy, could only exist *as* discourse, as a way of addressing reality that finally ignored reality altogether. Except for a few military invasions and the arms and economic support given to reactionary government or guerrilla groups throughout the world, there was little Reagan and his government could do about the international and domestic complexities it attempted to simplify in its language. One result was a great deal of ideological energy that remained unconnected to tan-gible images. Fragments of discontent and desire continued to be gener-ated and frustrated, breaking loose, seeking articulation. Reagan, or the Reagan discourse, kept articulating problems with solutions that could not be safely acted out in reality, notions of international hegemony and internal domesticity, economic self-sufficiency that could not be lived out by most people.

American film, as always, became an important generator of images through which that ideological energy was channeled. And since film had always created an imaginary realm of individual passions inflamed and satisfied, not much accommodation had to be made. Some generic adjustments, some variations on heroic stereotypes, and a confusion of historical realities allowed filmmakers to supply the coherence that the general discourse lacked. Two areas—strength against communism and the virtues of the family—were much attended to and often intermingled in odd ways. The cold war, an ideological knot tied in the fifties and continuing its hold in the eighties, provided basic material for two groups of films. One was directly anti-Russian and is best represented in Sylvester Stallone's *Rocky IV* and Taylor Hackford's *White Nights* (both 1985).

The most effective film in conveying the ideology of the Reaganesque, and quite possibly an important fictional catalyst (along with the infamous novel, *The Turner Diaries*) for the militia groups (here and abroad), was *Rambo*. The seventies vigilantes worked locally, within their city or town. The eighties avengers worked internationally, specifically in Vietnam (a province of Russia in most of the films involved); their purpose was to find those men—a son in the instance of Ted Kotcheff's *Uncommon Valor* (1983, co-produced by John Milius and Buzz Feitshans, the latter the producer of a number of right-wing Vietnam avenger films, including the two *Rambo*s), friends, or simply abandoned American soldiers, as in Joseph Zito's *Missing in Action* (1984)—who were presumably left behind and forgotten. This search for the missing and for the unachievable closure to the Vietnam narrative climaxed in Stallone's and George Cosmatos's *Rambo: First Blood Part Two* (1985).

To understand the politics and ideological structure of Rambo and the other missing-in-action films, it might be helpful to first look briefly at one that extracts its avenger away from the peculiarly right-wing, anti-Russian base that supports all of those just cited. J. Lee Thompson's Charles Bronson vehicle, *The Evil That Men Do* (1984), goes against the grain. The Bronson character—a retired avenger (little information is offered about him; simply being an avenger was sufficient background for most of these characters)—takes on, for no pay, the job of destroying a hired torturer, who works for the United States and its client countries in Central America, teaching counterinsurgency by giving instruction in the destruction of the human

264

body. The Bronson character tracks the man down and hastens his death at the hands of a group of his former victims, who work in a mine. The final act is not that of the lone hero but of a collective and is almost a revolutionary gesture.

This film is an all but unaccountable aberration, because few others of the period express such anti-American, pro–Third World sentiments (there are some vaguely liberal precedents in the seventies, *Walking Tall* and *Billy Jack* films, and perhaps two eighties films that question American hegemony, racism, or anti-Russian feeling, each of them—Peter Hyams's *2010* and the German director Wolfgang Petersen's *Enemy Mine*—works of science fiction). Perhaps *The Evil That Men Do* demonstrates that the avenger melodrama manages political ambiguities and conflicts simply by resolving them through the repeated figure of the lone man who performs the symbolic action of destroying a well-defined evil (the torturer's acts are much more clearly defined in the film than his politics). By so doing, the audience is absolved of political responsibility, performing its own symbolic act of social-political evasion by allowing the action to create catharsis while ignoring the causes and effects of the action. As long as it fits within certain narrative parameters that permit the hero to operate, and as long as it helps explain "the existence of social disorder,"[8] the evil of the avenger films may be of the right or the left.

The theory is partly born out in *Rambo: First Blood Part Two*. Although the villains of the piece are identified as Vietnamese and Russian, they appear as something quite different. They are determined one way politically, another cinematically. The Vietnamese are not Vietnamese but a re-creation of World War II movie Japanese. Their Russian adviser is not Russian but a representation of a World War II movie Nazi. In the videotapes of *Rambo* prepared for distribution in countries sensitive to anti-Russian propaganda, the dialogue was easily re-dubbed so that contemporary references were effaced and the film set in World War II. Mutually shared simple-mindedness is not the sole contributing factor to this confusion. On some level, like all filmmakers, the creators of *Rambo* realized that a popular narrative is facilitated both in its creation and reception if its codes are immediately apparent and easily recognized. An old signifying system is more easily recreated than a new one invented. Asians and Germans have been typed and coded since the earliest years of cinema, their representation easily explains and defines "the existence of social disorder" and provides for its correction. Demonization is easier than explanation. Reverting to such representations is more convenient

265

than attempting to describe who the Vietnamese soldiers were and what a Russian adviser might be like and what, if anything, the two might have in common. By solving the problem without dealing with it, the film invites an easy participation and ready reception by the viewer. *Rambo* speaks the discourse of frustration satisfied and fantasies affirmed; it confirms what film has been saying throughout its existence; that "Orientals" are indeed all alike, without history or national differentiation; that Nazism signifies any white, foreign evil, easily detectable by a character's uniform, insidious accent, and cruel gaze.

But the fact remains that, despite the transmission of current ideology through older film images, *Rambo* and the majority of avenger melodramas have an affinity for contemporary conservative discourse (and vice versa), which seems to indicate that their generic violence and dependence on individual as opposed to collective action is, finally, more amenable to the ideological representations of the right. This rightward inclination was particularly strong in the eighties Vietnam revenge cycle because of the presence around them and, in a curious way, within them of Ronald Reagan. The ideological process works like this: the missing-in-action films contain two enemies, the U.S. government and the Vietnamese (as noted, in order to maintain a comforting familiarity and not strain political stereotyping, the Vietnamese are often depicted as mere tools of the Russians). The major fault of the United States is that it did not permit the soldiers to win the Vietnam war in the first place ("Do we get to win this time?" is John Rambo's most lucid, if not most historically useful, utterance when he is sent on his mission). To compound matters, the government now covers up the existence of survivors to save itself embarrassment (although, in reality, the Reagan government seemed to ply rumors of the existence of prisoners of war to promote active antagonism against the Vietnamese). At the same time, Ronald Reagan, the head of government, based his career on separating himself from the government on all matters, including Vietnam policy. As a result, the government could be attacked for continuing to allow prisoners to suffer (the objects of this attack in the films are sometimes the CIA, but more often officials of some unnamed bureaucracy); the head of the government could stand apart as the mentor of brave, individual action, as the patron of the missing, and—in the films—the mentor of the avengers. Even outside of the films, Ronald Reagan was not so much an individual as an ideological representation of the tough movie hero; through him and into the films passes the spirit of John Wayne, particularly the John Wayne of *The Searchers*—the lone figure, something of an outlaw, who can work against the system for the good that everyone knows the system is trying to ignore. Like Reagan himself, the avenger heroes become unique embodiments of that part of the dominant ideology the dominant ideology itself does not wish to recognize, the desire to discover and act on foreign injustices to Americans, safely, through the intervention of an individual who will act for everyone.

The avenger films, finally, offer an ideological contract, promising to represent that which is *only* available in representation in return for the committed gaze of the viewer. If representing a representation seems to be a redundancy, recall that the ideology of the right presents a barely coherent discourse full of possibilities that cannot be acted on without enormous military and social cost. The films articulate these possibilities, representing the assenting viewer's own fantasy, uniting his subjectivity (assuming that the intended subject of these films is male) with characters who enact the ideology's great wish fulfillment: destruction of the other, ending opposition by annihilating it, placing the entire burden on a single individual. The only cost is the price of admission, which includes a most terrible and hopeless admission, that the words spoken by the ideology and the images given it by these films have validity.

The validation of the imaginary has some peculiar consequences, affirming patriarchal structures and absorbing the individual into them. The viewing subject is not cut off from comfort and sustenance, he is offered them. He is given an illusion of power. Rather than being positioned against or at the mercy of patriarchy, the subject is put under and made witness to its protection. The patriarchy assumes a maternal position, of care rather than authority. In the process, an extraordinary event happens as the ideological material from the larger discourse of the government is given shape by its image-making arm, eighties film. Ronald Reagan (re)entered cinema as the guiding patriarch offering maternal care.

Earlier I mentioned that Reagan created a persona who stands apart from the government he attacks, acting as the brave mentor to great deeds that cannot be done. I am suggesting here that, more than an external guiding force, he becomes a disguised narrative figure in these films, a paternal figure who guides the hero. The image of older mentor—the wise fatherly surrogate— keeps appearing in contemporary American film in a variety of guises. I must emphasize that, as an ideological and psychological presence, this figure is hardly new; the maternal patriarch is present throughout literature and film, usually coded as a protector and the well of great wisdom. In the late thirties and early forties, Roosevelt would appear often in films. In *Yankee Doodle Dandy* (1942), for example, when George M. Cohan visits the White House, "Roosevelt," is viewed from behind, represented by his shoulder and back, a metonymic figure of the great man who may not be fully represented, yet whose presence accompanies everything. When the Joads enter the government-run migrant camp in *The Grapes of Wrath*, they are greeted by the man in charge, who looks like Roosevelt and offers them the security and help that was an extension of Roosevelt's ideological aura.[9]

The entry of the Reagan persona into film is different, taking the form of an older man who teaches and legitimizes the hero and, perhaps even more important, protects the audience. While the hero goes beyond the mentor in his deeds, the mentor is still present as a control, as a safety limit. He looks out for the hero and looks out for the audience as well. With him present, the viewer is assured that the hero will neither get hurt nor go too far beyond established bonds (mentors in pre-Reagan contemporary film might be unreliable: in *Taxi Driver*, Travis goes for advice to the older cab driver, Wizard, who says he doesn't know what Travis is talking about; the mentor fails and Travis goes beyond all socially acceptable bounds of behavior). This is particularly true where the older figure mentors an adolescent. The young man is still learning, still vulnerable and capable of wrong action if uncontrolled. Here the mentor fully emerges as father surrogate, a wiser and more protective influence than the hero's actual father (who is either dead, separated from the family, or completely ineffectual), who manages to create a sounder patriarchal situation than any actual father could. Replacing the biological father, giving the hero direction and control, the new mentor-maternal-patriarch supplies the ideological demand for family, without the need to bring forth the insoluble problems regarding the family's viability.

Obi-Wan Kenobi and, most especially, Yoda, who makes his appearance in the 1980 *Star War*'s sequel, *The Empire Strikes Back*, embody much of the old man mentor stereotype. Somewhat pre-Reagan, they both repeat old figures of the master teacher and foreshadow the new stern but nurturing figure of the eighties, here conveniently separated into the warrior father and the spiritual father. We see him again in Robert Zemeckis's *Back to the Future* (1985). Under the guidance of a somewhat loony scientist, Doc Brown, Michael J. Fox's Marty McFly goes back in time before his birth and helps to arrange his parents' marriage. His own father is mild mannered and cowardly, and therefore Marty must be sure the match occurs, lest he and his family become uncreated. Unfortunately, his mother-to-be falls in

268

love with him, thus creating a most interesting variation on the oedipal triangle. Marty is under the obligation not only to get his mother matched to the correct person, but also to save his scientist friend. Just as Marty left, Doc Brown appeared to be assassinated by Libyans who sold him the plutonium for his time machine (a Delorean car) in return for his promise to build them a nuclear bomb. As a result of these efforts, the son manages to go through oedipalization before he is born, create his family to his own liking (when he returns from his trip, his father is no longer a hopeless coward, but a suave writer, thanks to Marty's interventions), and save Doc Brown. Through it all, the scientist acts as a kind of idiot savant, both an equal and elder guide, who does not make paternal demands, is vulnerable, and who offers not only support but adventure. *Back to the Future* creates an interesting counterpoint to another Spielberg-produced film, Joe Dante's *Gremlins* (1984). Here, too, the young man's father is mild and somewhat passive, an inventor of useless objects. The mentor figure plays only a small role here, where an Asian elder entrusts the boy with a small beast that multiplies into a horde of mean little demons. The boy becomes father to the anarchic creatures over whom he must regain control.

Zemeckis's and Dante's post-Reagan films show some interesting changes in perspective. In *Forrest Gump* (1994), the hero is without a father but with a platitude-spouting mother. He is a simpleton, untutored, and— as the opening imagery of the film suggests—light as a feather. Without guidance, he floats through the history of the last third of the twentieth century, crossing paths with rulers, finding romance, being lucky. We see here a Clintonesque figure emerging: southern, apparently guileless, infinitely capable. Joe Dante's *Small Soldiers* (1997) plays a turn on his *Gremlins* films. The child gets no useful teaching from his father and must learn from an animated toy figure, a cross between Yoda and the Cowardly Lion, who teaches the benefits of courage only under duress and of hiding whenever possible. The soldiers of the title are militia types, violent, racist, hateful, and persistent.

Post-Reagan avenger films assume different forms and often ironic narratives. But before we can understand them, we need to return briefly to *Rambo* and its antecedent. In Ted Kotcheff's *First Blood* (1982), the film that introduces Rambo and Col. Trautman (Richard Crenna), the relationship between fatherly guide and wild young man is slightly different than its sequel, because the film aims at a modicum of complexity. Called in when Rambo runs amok, Trautman is revealed to be Rambo's military leader and the one who formed his personality. He says that he "created"

269

Rambo by training him to be a counterinsurgency fighter, a trained killer of Vietnamese guerrillas (the notion of Rambo as "killing machine," which recurs in the second and better known of the films, makes an interesting comparison to the shark in *Jaws*). Unfortunately, with the war over and the political object of his destruction gone, he is now a displaced subject, wandering, lonely, his fighting mechanism primed to go off with the right catalyst. When the redneck officials of a small town provoke him, he declares war and nearly destroys them all. Trautman, the father-mentor, begins as something of a Frankenstein with his son-monster barely under his control.

In this first incarnation, Rambo is presented as a version of the crazed Vietnam veteran stereotype, here modified as the misunderstood tool/ victim of the society of the seventies. Rather than an avenger, he is lost and needing a protector. Trautman must reclaim his responsibility—which is the responsibility of the society—and offer some haven to his wandering child. At the end of the film, after Trautman has stopped Rambo's destruction just short of the murder of the sheriff, Rambo tells him of his Vietnam experience. His description of a friend who was blown up in his arms by a Vietnamese saboteur reverberates with other anecdotes and depictions of atrocities in earlier films about the war: Kurtz's tale in *Apocalypse Now* of the Vietnamese who cut off the arms of peasants vaccinated by Americans; the Russian roulette fantasy in *The Deer Hunter*. These tales and scenes are meant to evoke the image of an enemy so vicious and uncivilized that he is capable of driving ordinary men insane through unspeakable acts. They are meant to prove that it was not the war itself that damaged American soldiers, but the terrifying, unscrupulous enemy who, we would believe, caused the war in the first place. It is as if the dehumanization created by American intervention in Vietnam could be mitigated by stories of even greater dehumanization on the part of the enemy. The effect of such atrocities has damaged Rambo and uprooted him; he has nowhere to go and no outlet for the killing instincts implanted by Trautman. Without the war, he is a violent, abused child with no guidance.

Within the narrative, Trautman must regain the trust of and responsibility for his offspring and act as the mediator between the narrative and the audience. As he provides explanations for Rambo's actions, sets limits, knows how far Rambo can go, how far he can permit the sheriff to make a fool of himself, his control becomes apparent. Trautman, in effect, directs the narrative and the viewer's response as well. As Rambo's creator and the

270

audience's guardian, he permits enjoyment of the violence because his wise hand is in control. In *Rambo: First Blood Part Two*, that control is somewhat more restrained and less restraining. A guide is no longer needed, only a representative of the patriarchal right to destroy enemies. *First Blood* was part of the opening movement in the recuperation of Vietnam; *Rambo* is the full fantasy of winning the war—"this time."

Rambo himself changes from a confused figure damaged by the war, needing help, to an angry adolescent, denouncing the political father for refusing to let him fight. There are many contradictions here; the fathers are split many ways, yet they form an interlocking patriarchal web. "The supreme achievement of patriarchal ideology," writes Mary Ann Doane, "is that it has no outside."[10] Rambo battles society and supports it, fights one representative of government and is supported by another. He never has to move outside, because finally the patriarch is always with him and he within the patriarchy. His major political battle is against that image of all governmental action—or inaction—that we disapprove of, the bureaucracy. Like the external enemy, communism, the bureaucracy is intractable and cannot be done away with; it serves as a constant irritant and a catalyst to action, which is why it so quickly became the right wing's surrogate for communism after the cold war. This time, however, Rambo is aided in his struggle not only by Trautman (a soldier and therefore part of the bureaucracy—although the indication is that he is somehow working on his own, outside normal military channels because the bureaucrat who opposes him has soldiers working for *him*), but by the figure who guides Trautman and, through him, gives Rambo support, the great enemy of communism and bureaucracy, Ronald Reagan.

Trautman has Rambo released from prison to carry out a photo-reconnaissance mission on a prison camp in Vietnam where American prisoners are believed to be held. Marshall Murdoch, the recalcitrant and double-dealing bureaucrat, tries to prevent Rambo from finishing his mission in order to keep the existence of prisoners secret. Rambo is stranded alone amid Vietnamese and Russians, while at the base, Trautman curses the bureaucrat for his actions. A number of significant objects are seen, at various times, surrounding Murdoch. On his desk is a copy of G. Gordon Liddy's *Will*. On the wall behind him is a photograph of Reagan. The book by the former Watergate thief (an admirer of Hitler and, in the nineties, the host of a hate-radio call-in program who advocated that we aim for the head when shooting government officials) focuses the actions of all the participants, each of whom demands adherence to the righteousness of his cause. Liddy's book reflects positively on Rambo, whose will allows him to overcome torture and the force of three armies—the Vietnamese, the Russian, and the American—to free the prisoners single-handedly. It reflects negatively on Murdoch, whose will is not free, who is at the mercy of selfish political desires, and whose intransigence and paranoia are associated with an older politics that Reagan has transcended. Early in the film Murdoch asks for "something cold," and one of the soldiers goes to an unlocked Coke machine to get a can for him. Observing this, Rambo registers interest and displeasure in a man who orders soldiers around and abuses the privileges of private property by getting free Cokes. A Coca-Cola machine is played for a joke in *Dr. Strangelove* (Lt. Mandrake has it shot open in order to get change to call the White House, much to the chagrin of Col. Bat Guano, who warns that he will have to answer to the Coca-Cola company for destroying private property). Here is a serious sign of the abuse of privilege, of Murdoch's assumption of power and authority.

The significance of Reagan's photograph on the wall is a bit more complex and plays the role of a silent character in the various confrontations. Reagan, of course, as head of the government, is Murdoch's superior and therefore somehow responsible for his unforgivable action. But the masterstroke of Reagan's ideological maneuverings was his ability to remove himself from the discomforting realities of *realpolitik*. Like the father of a large family of unruly children, Reagan disapproved, cautioned, even punished, and remained aloof and untouched at the same time. He is Murdoch's superior; he may, in his role of president, have to disapprove of an illegal action; but ideologically he is on Rambo's side. Rambo, in fact, fulfills the Reagan discourse of retribution against enemies. During two sequences, when Trautman confronts Murdoch, the photograph is composed close to him. During the sequence in which Trautman curses Murdoch for betraying the mission and abandoning Rambo, the photograph is first directly behind and to one side of him; then, when Murdoch presents his cynical justifications for abandoning the mission, Murdoch's face eclipses the photograph, just as his actions attempt to deny Reagan's will to correct the "errors" of the war. Trautman's proximity to the photograph validates both his and Rambo's position and places Reagan on their side. More than on their side: Trautman becomes a surrogate for Reagan in the film, a figure who sums up all the patriarchal representations in the films we have been discussing. He guides, directs, controls. He is almost helpless against bureaucratic opposition, but his offspring is powerful enough to overcome all odds—even his momentary despair when he believes Trautman himself has betrayed him—and kill the enemy. In the process, Rambo himself is transformed. He is no longer merely Trautman's "son," but through Trautman Reagan's son as well, the ideal issue of an ideal patriarch, who does his father's business without assistance and without question. Finally, as he achieves an apotheosis, Rambo becomes the offspring of the culture itself, the child of his society's desire for revenge against the loss of its sons. An enormous rush of ideological concentration occurs in these representations. Desire for revenge that had been ignited by the language of aggression is offered images that neatly organize the desire into a narrative that appears to fulfill desire on an imaginary level.

And a physical one. Rambo's body itself becomes a transcendent point of attention, a place on which desire and action may be inscribed. So grotesquely muscled, it looks like a child's warrior doll, which is perhaps its function. Rambo is everyone's toy soldier, placed in fantasies of war, beyond harm even when captured and tortured, the apotheosis of the virile posing that Susan Sontag pointed to as a mark of fascist aesthestics. He is the perfect human machine, a cyborg, making new ideological history in which, because of his efforts, "We get to win this time." As transcendental son, he also rewrites the family's history. He goes off to war not only to protect the dignity of those back home, but to restore dignity to those in prison. He gives everyone new faith in military prowess and at the same time, by doing everything himself, puts no one but himself in danger. He falls in love with a woman he meets on the mission, but she is killed in the course of his operation, and his aloneness remains inviolate, as do the emotions of the viewer, safe in his own isolation. (The woman is Vietnamese, and though not one of the enemy, safely outside the racial pale and the viewer's sympathies.) When Rambo is through with his job, he does what every family hopes its child will do and makes no further claims. He does not even kill Murdoch but merely frightens him so that the bureaucrat will now know his place. His reclamation of honor and his job of saving those without hope completed, he wanders off alone, no one's responsibility.

The act of reclamation and redemption is most important for the avenging hero and a major facet of an aggressive ideology. Something is presumed lost or undone and must be gotten back or finished. The male figure, so battered by emotional, physical, and feminist blows, must reclaim

273

honor and place, recognize who he is and why. This process lies at the core of all melodramatic structures (and ideology is, finally, melodramatic). Although melodramas and ideologies may contain contradictions, they cannot be maintained without guarantees of closure—not merely closure in the usual sense of a satisfactory ending, but an ending that brings events back to a better place and creates a better person. The Vietnam war did not "work" ideologically because while it was going on there was no clear notion of its closure, and when it was over it was not closed. Loss was interpreted as incomplete action. Not only was victory denied, but peace for the culture that suffered the loss seemed impossible. There were conflicting ideas about what wrongs had been committed during and because of the war, but no notion as to how those wrongs could be undone.

Because of the domestic and international upheavals after the war, there was no immediate hope that things would be better. The desire for reclamation, recuperation, and redemption was enormous. The films that created narratives for a conservative ideology attempted through aggressive (but safe) fantasies of individuals reconquering Southeast Asia, or fantasies of domestic concord gained by overcoming difficult obstacles, or fantasies of visitors from other worlds comforting small children to assure the culture that an imaginary world—a world of images—in which security and power were regained was indeed possible. These films give visual structure to ideological discourse. In return, that discourse was nourished by the films. "After seeing *Rambo* last night," the President of the United States is reported to have said after a Middle East hostage crisis in 1985, "I'll know what to do next time." And, in fact, he actually thought he did. By the mid-eighties, history and ideology, film and fact, got terribly mixed, and in the persons of Oliver L. North and Robert C. McFarlane, Reagan found his own "real-life" incarnations of Rambo and Trautman.

Cut to a reverse shot, and *Rambo* appears as a nasty parody. The figure is a comic book warrior whose ideological usefulness is so momentary that it disappears along with the moment, only to pop up "in reality" in the terrifying figures of Serbian weekend warriors who dress up like their hero and kill Muslims or in the lingering fantasies of right-wing militia men. In the final sequel, Rambo battles with Afghani guerrillas against evil Russians. History has put a bitter edge on this struggle and its one-time heroes. With the end of the cold war, all the representations of anticommunist rage and victory collapsed along with the regime the dominant capitalist ideology so hated, so loved, and so needed. Now, all former enemies and heroes are compromised by mitigating factors; sides are unclear; goals invisible;

masculinity itself, and all its attributes, are brought into question. The cold war successfully extended the inherent masculine rights of all war making: men in power, controlling the disposition of other men, and ultimately the culture. War is possibly more profoundly gendered than any human activity.

In the post–cold war period, ideology questions many of its functions. Authority must be redefined, indeed sought out anew. Gender becomes an issue of contention and redefinition. Boundaries—often the telling issue of war and part of the basic discourse of the cold war and its obsession with "containment"—become soft and permeable and, with networked technology, invisible. Popular culture itself passes through national, cultural boundaries (remember the Serbians) and cultures become wracked with uncertainty as reactionary forces, nostalgic for the moment of absolute control, attempt to re-erect the walls that have been pulled down. The movement is mirrored again in the image of the president. George Bush had none of Reagan's histrionic abilities, his mock authority, and stern fatherly demeanor. Bush appeared never to believe anything he said, seemingly distracted by the pretense that he had a knowledge of the complexity of the world he could never quite articulate. Bush was a stern, distracted professor, without wisdom, unable to renew context. Bill Clinton, young, sexually active and indiscreet, a Vietnam war protestor; so much an antipatriarchal figure that he was difficult to adequately represent. He was the borderless figure, almost amorphous. The left—that is, the liberal movement of American culture—could not visualize him at all. The right saw and represented him quite accurately (for them) as the perfect post–cold war figure, a man without easily perceived boundaries, compassionate, smart, liquid in the sense that his sensibilities flowed and ebbed from private to public: open, recessive, vulnerable, and easily demonized because he was the negative patriarch, the passive, unheroic male who deferred to his wife. Clinton was the object of the anger of the right given human form.

Clinton was represented in a few films as the positive, flawed figure he was. Elaine May and Mike Nichols's *Primary Colors* (1997) is a major example and an adequate representation of the complexities and contradictions of personality. Rob Reiner's *American President* (1995) offered a fantasy romance. The darker, right-wing versions of Clinton appeared in *Murder at 1600* (Dwight H. Little, 1997), but no film better captured the ambiguities of post–cold war Clinton America than Dean Devlin and Roland Emmerich's *Independence Day* (1996). The film is the summa of postmodern science fiction, drawing on its fifties progenitors (especially *The Day the Earth Stood Still*—which it literally quotes on a television set in one sequence—and *The War of the Worlds*) through *2001* (to which it alludes) and *Star Wars* (which it copies). Like so much fifties, eighties, and nineties science-fiction film, *Independence Day*'s ideological structures are so bound up in the relationship of narrative, character, and formal structures to the culture at large that the film becomes overdetermined with cultural meaning. *Independence Day* is a counterpoint of changing gender positions and expectations, with a Clintonesque president who starts by wallowing in indecisiveness and winds up as Shakespeare's Henry V. A black air force captain, played by an engaging young actor, Will Smith, unable to enter the space program, ends as a warrior hero. A Jewish intellectual whose lack of commitment is broken by his father's blessings and a dim realization that theory and praxis can be combined through action comes out of his own depressive lack of confidence to help the air force captain destroy the aliens. A drunken redneck with paranoid fantasies of being probed by aliens is redeemed by turning into Commander Kong from *Dr. Strangelove* (the scenes of his engaging his bomber and diving into the enemy ship are almost shot by shot from Kubrick's film) and doing to the aliens what he is sure they did to him. The old patriarchal guard, especially the secretary of state and former CIA director, is dressed down and fired, the first target of the president's newly discovered righteous wrath.

The women are safely on the margins: the president's wife, a Hillary Clinton clone, suffers for her independence by dying, a convention as old as film itself. The president's press secretary—the one woman who acts positively and seems to do it independently of sexuality—retains a strong position but gains renewed admiration for her husband, the Jewish intellectual. The air force captain's girlfriend is a stripper, and her sole function, aside from proving that pluck is available to the lowliest, is to provide comfort for the president's dying wife. Providing comfort is a typical position for black women in film, but her persistence and self-possession are more than stereotypical character effects.

But then none of these characters is a simple stereotype, though they are made to join forces within the larger, inescapable, obsessive cliché of nineties cinema—redemption. Every male in the film must overcome perceived weaknesses and hesitancies and emerge not with greater knowledge, but the ability to act violently—an inescapable outcome given the film's premise that they, and the earth as a whole, are being violently exterminated. The ethnic and characterological mix, however, makes them more available as comprehensible characters (with the exception of a gay character, acted with every conceivable flap and tick of the worst homophobia). This availability applies to the film as a whole. *Independence Day* exists on a number of levels: as a cleverly made alien-invasion film that depends—in its first part—on cunning editing and shifting of viewer position, building expectations through gesture, shadow, and assertive flash editing, as well as a digitally composed representation of sheer size as threatening spectacle; a full-throated cry for international reconciliation; and, at the same time, as a conservative reminder that men's place is in the sky, women's not. It is, as well, a representation of a favorite cold-war gesture (that existed in science-fiction films during the cold war itself) of aliens attacking us from space.

The film is a perfect specimen of a postmodern, digitally generated, one-narrative-fits-all, all-knowing ideological and cultural ameliorator. It seems to yield to current questions about individual masculine action by focusing not on the single heroic male saving the community—the world, in this case—but through the division of heroic acts among a number of lesser individuals who cut across class, racial, national, and, to a very small degree, gender boundaries. The U.S. triumphs, but only with the help of old enemies. Yet the essential conservatism of the genre remains: victories are military, males triumph, and—given generic requirements—the forces needed to be overcome are so fantastic that they bear little relation to the day-to-day threats to people. Indeed, the threats posed by science-fiction films in general act as substitutes for the small, political, economic problems that are not able to be attended to in daily life or represented by the digital compositor working with a producer looking for a profit-making film. They are thereby transferred to men rediscovering their masculinity by flying spacecraft and saving the world. *Independence Day* balances these forces better than many other of its kind and is able to keep its momentum going with a leavening of irony and postmodern knowingness—or cleverness—by mixing allusions to a variety of satisfying films and giving just enough credence to popular legend that everyone is allowed to have his fun.

Nineties science fiction very much absorbed the male action-adventure genre of the eighties and nineties, a genre we need to examine in order to get to Spielberg, who has worked in both forms and, as in so many others, set a pattern and a goal for other filmmakers. I want to return to the work of James Cameron, whose transformation of the male-action character type led the way for others to follow. The pre-*Titanic* Cameron, the director of heavy metal destruction and redemption films, pushed the actor Arnold

Schwarzenegger to stardom and, in so doing, completed a postmodern turn on the male hero. In *The Terminator* (1984), Cameron created Schwarzenegger as a destructive cyborg from the future and allowed some small gender shifts to occur: the Terminator is a programmed killer, sent from a postnuclear, machine-run future to prevent the birth of the rebel leader against the machines. He does battle with the son of the leader, also sent back to the present, and the mother-to-be of the leader, who is, finally, impregnated with the leader by his son.

A matriarchal lineage is produced, with the Terminator as a mechanized Oedipus, a body without organs (to borrow a phrase from Deleuze and Guattari), a creature who is set only to destroy but instead manages to create his own destroyer by not being able to kill the woman who will be his destroyer's mother.[11] Matriarchy and unencumbered femininity are not something Cameron is comfortable with nor was he able to create a traditional split between good and evil. The Terminator, evil and destructive, remains enormously attractive. His obsessive march to eradicate the would-be mother of the future rebel, the point-of-view shots through his cyborg eye, complete with text and graphics that help him pinpoint his target, his overwhelming destructive powers, made him an avatar of vengeance (if not righteousness) in line with the seventies avenger films. But the contradictions that emerged—mainly the Schwarzenegger character as attractive monster, lead to some changes. Seven years later, at remake time, Cameron, no doubt in league with Schwarzenegger and his publicist and agent, reversed the terms. Oedipus the destroyer becomes Oedipus the powerful, friendly patriarch. Mother, maddened by the world's refusal to believe her apocalyptic ravings, is in a prison for the criminally insane, where she builds her body to become that favorite Cameron figure, the manly woman, ready to take up arms. In *Aliens* (1986), Cameron's sequel to Ridley Scott's *Alien*, the women become appendages to their weapons, buckling under the weight of enormous guns. At the end Ripley, who at the conclusion of the first film revealed her human vulnerability, is turned into a cyborg, encased in a huge metal superstructure to do battle with the female beast in that greatest of male fantasies, a cat fight. In *Terminator 2*, the mother remains hysterical throughout and a fierce fighter, but subordinated to the cyborg returning as the protector of her child who will grow up to be the savior of the future. The Schwarzenegger figure here is pursued by another avenging cyborg, digitally perfected this time so as to appear a liquid entity, all but indestructible, able, trickster-like, to assume any form and viscous enough to pierce any barrier.

The original Terminator becomes the protective father, mentored by a child, who teaches him emotions. This post-Reagan reversal humanizes the father, turning his violent propensities toward the appropriate goals, and gives the cyborg hero some self-consciousness. He gains a self-effacing humor, even humility, the most important new quality for the new action hero. Self-effacement appears in full, satisfying, ego-assuring form in the first *Die Hard*, directed by John McTiernan a few years before the second *Terminator*. *Die Hard* is fundamentally a right-wing film, still linked to Reagan-era ideology, restating the need for a chaotic and threatened community to be saved by a lone male hero.[12] But this hero is too aware of his cinematic, pop-cultural existence to take any of it very seriously. More accurately, he and the film that contains him counterpoint seriousness against irony and self-effacement and cynicism. *Die Hard* is in the postmodern mode that relies on the cynical, sentimental, and self-protective response on the part of the film and its audience. It keeps telling us it's all a joke, that the world is no more meaningful than the film that is representing it at this moment, or *is* as the film represents it, and we would be fools to take it any more seriously. We would equally be fools not to. That would put us outside the joke.

Die Hard allows its hero to mock himself and recognize his movie existence. The villain, Hans, whom we think is a terrorist but turns out to be only an international thief, calls out to John in frustration: "Who are you, just another American who's seen too many movies? Do you think you are Rambo or John Wayne?" John—whose name, John McClane, is a play on the name of a character played by John Wayne in a fifties anticommunist film, *Big Jim McClain*—disavows such heroic lineage and says he's Roy Rogers. Disavowal or not, John does save the day, amid a riot of contradictory forces: political terrorists who aren't political, federal and government law enforcement agents who turn out to be utter fools, and a bumbling black policeman, who slips past one stereotype into a gender twist on another. He becomes the protective mammy figure, and he helps John survive. All this is driven by an attempt to protect the conservative order of genders. John is separated from his wife, Holly, and flies to L.A. for a reconciliation, where he discovers she is a corporate executive, using her maiden name. It is this revelation, his discomfort with being deprived of his patrimony within the domestic order of things, that leads him to her office and the mayhem that ensues.

In a sense, all the heroism, bloodshed, explosions, and mayhem in the film are aimed at John's attempt to prove a meaningful manhood. Yet, at the same time, everything is also there to parody the search for manhood so prevalent in cinematic discourse. There is a moment in the film where John becomes Rambo, naked to the waist, heavy with armament, wading through the palm-fringed fountain of the office building exploding around him—an urban jungle warrior in a luxury, parody Vietnam.[13] John is the lone avenging hero and is a parody of himself at the same time. He is full of self-deprecation and finds that he needs someone else—another male, someone to share or help with his struggle.

A major convention of the action film, used by so many eighties and nineties films that the list would be endless, is to provide the hero with a "buddy." The "buddy" is an extension of the cultural cliché of "male bonding," a situation in which men can fantasize about being released from the repressions imposed by the company of women. In film, the "buddy" allows adventure, joking, safe community, marginalization of women, and an apparent absence of sexuality. The "buddy" complex views sexuality as an obstacle to manly acts. But this denial of sexuality carries a covert admission of the possibilities of homosexuality, which, of course, is inadmissible. Therefore, to play it safe, one or both of the buddies has a wife or girlfriend, who is usually accommodating about her man's absence and adventures, largely by remaining invisible. Men engage in rigorous activity together; the sexual tensions between them are never stated.[14] The buddy film is a fantasy of men with and at the same time without women.

In *Die Hard*, John's buddy is Al, the black cop, who mentors him through the apocalypse in the skyscraper, acting as a supportive woman, attempting to keep order among the contending law men on the street below and provide moral succor to his buddy above. In the street, when John emerges from the building and Al finally proves his own manhood by shooting the last villain, they embrace This sequence is framed and cut almost precisely the same way as the meeting of John and Holly at the beginning of the film. But in the final embrace with Al, Holly is marginalized at the very edge of the frame, pushed out of this moment of true male liberation. Not until Al releases John and, with motherly praise, tells Holly, "You've got a good man here," is the heterosexual couple reunited. Holly has her moment of action when she punches out a wretched television news reporter who betrayed her children. She is thereby offered some dignity and strength. Order is restored, in this film that attempts to have everything all ways.

Die Hard is a film of self-contradictory complexities. It refuses to take its events seriously, yet insists they are serious. It plays against racial stereotypes. Some of its African-American characters turn out to be heroes despite themselves; one is a destructive computer hacker. The Japanese, feared for their predatory economic policies in the eighties, become admirable figures here through the paternal head of the company that John saves. "Pearl Harbor didn't work out," he tells John, "so we got you tape decks." His death at the robber's hands early in the film is played sentimentally.[15] With its lineage in the seventies "disaster" films—especially the 1977 *Towering Inferno*—presaging and influencing the revisionist heroic views of *Terminator 2*—*Die Hard* set the pattern for many parodic, digitally explosive action films in which the male body is given an elasticity and recuperative strength that makes it even fitter to protect women, children, and the rest of the community. Rather than stretching a genre, *Die Hard* and its kin expand the action film so that it can encompass and contain feminist interventions, placing the male in a more vulnerable posture without allowing him to lose the initiative of the lone hero.

It must be pointed out that the genre can be stretched only so far. The Bruce Willis vehicle *Hudson Hawk* (1991) and the John McTiernan– directed Arnold Schwarzenegger film *Last Action Hero* (1993), which is an interesting version of the 1988 Italian film *Cinema Paradiso* and, like *Terminator 2*, a film that places its hero at the mercy of a child, failed miserably because they took the joke too far. Postmodernism, at least as it is realized in the popular media it loves to feed on, is allowed only a certain leeway when it becomes the driving formal pattern of an actual movie. The postmodern insouciance, violence, homophobia, and racism of *Pulp Fiction* were perfectly acceptable because the film didn't pretend seriousness and therefore didn't mock it. The complex play of pop-cultural, cinematic, racial, gender, and social issues in *Die Hard* was acceptable because almost everyone but the hero and his body were represented as villainous or ridiculous, and the basic forms of the captivity and rescue narrative remained intact. But those films that simply mocked or suggested that they were smarter than the audience suffered a postmodern implosion. The audience maintained an independent subjectivity, refused to be shifted into an entirely sarcastic mode, and ignored the films.

Whether ignored or made into enormous box-office hits, the eighties and nineties stream of male-action and science-fiction films recreated and reformed genres and audience expectations, simultaneously affirming dominant ideologies of rescue and redemption while provoking a rethinking of the male figure in response to a multitude of cultural pressures.

These pressures drown Cameron's *Titanic* (1998), the all-digital, all-romantic, all-water effort whose success surprised everyone involved. The

281

great ship going down—the great ship of state sinking under the weight of its own smugness and inability to deal with class differences—struck some political chords, but they were sounded quietly. Rather, *Titanic* is the last word (so far) in gender reversal, astonishing in its positing of a feminized male character, a limp, all but asexual figure whose success and failure depend on a woman. The film transcends the cliché that a strong woman stands behind a successful man. The cultural signification lies in this cliché's positioning of women behind. Women are fine as the stabilizing sub-ordinate, controlling a family while the man is free to travel outside the domestic space. But *Titanic* rises above the clichés by so thoroughly creating a passive male figure, who literally reverses the originary cinematic modes of gender construction. Rather than traveling outside the domestic space, he falls victim to the isolation and destruction of the foundering ship of state. As far back as film history goes, the subject of captivity and salvation was the woman, and the man came to her rescue. D. W. Griffith and others created the standard editing patterns of cross-cutting between shots to express this gender-driven event. In other words, film form is driven by conventional gender inclination.[16] In *Titanic*, Jack is handcuffed to a pipe below decks, the water rises, and it is up to Rose to save him. Cameron uses the same cross-cutting style as Griffith, and the sequence could be an updating of the end of his *Way Down East* (1920), where Lillian Gish is trapped on an ice flow, the hero in hot pursuit to rescue her.

282

This reversal, of course, is a key to *Titanic*'s success. Cameron, the most unlikely director to do so, made the perfect old-Hollywood "woman's pic-ture," complete with a generically driven melodrama of high romance that concludes with the death of the man. His death allows the woman to live with the memories of her love, indeed within those memories. Ultimately, the gender reversal reverses in on itself. Rose saves Jack, though Jack does die, and his transcendence is his movement into her memory, where she is kept a captive to the ideal of the perfect romance. What seemed to be a reversal of gender roles is really just another turn on the eternal romance with a dead lover. Cameron's misogyny may be slightly bottled up, but only slightly.

In *The Abyss*, Cameron made his first underwater film, quite strikingly photographed, but ultimately unable to break free of a dependence on *Close Encounters of the Third Kind* and *E.T.* Like all of his films, *The Abyss* is also dependent on hardware and heavy metallic superstructure as well as supernatural or alien power. In this film, a man brings his wife back to life, he gives her CPR, and finally smacks her to bring her around! Perhaps not since *Public Enemy* has one of the most awful of male banalities—that every woman needs to get hit once in a while—been given such a respectable, indeed life-affirming visualization. In Cameron's universe, a woman has no life-giving powers, unless she has been reduced to a function of massive armament. So, in *Titanic*, while Rose can rescue the handcuffed Jack from the rushing waters in the ship, she cannot finally give him or save his life. As a woman, she has no godlike power and can only see her manchild die, turn blue, and ascend to the skies, while she survives to tell her tale. Sarah Conner, in the *Terminator* films, birthed and succored the savior of man; Rose, an ancient mariner, can only recycle her tale in an endless nostalgia about the sweet boy and the great sinking ship.

Here is an interesting Hollywood fantasy: what would happen if a woman directed a film written by James Cameron? How would his perspective on gender and admiration for armament be managed? The fantasy is realized in a film called *Strange Days* (1995), directed by an ex-wife of Cameron's, Kathryn Bigelow, a filmmaker who had proved an ability to inflect action films with a hard and difficult feminist edge in *Blue Steel* (1990). *Strange Days* is an extraordinary film—mixed up, wrongheaded, and absolutely right. It takes the digital mise-en-scène as its subject and its theme. In *Strange Days*, at the end of the millennium, the ability to digitize the real world has become a means to create and distribute first-person visions of that world directly into the brains of passive subjects. Instead of heavy metal, Bigalow imagines a plastic mesh that fits over the head, allowing the recording and playback of subjective experience. This is the latest version of Huxley's "feelies." Used mainly for surrogate sexual experience, the digital "clips" function as a motif and plot device in a world Bigelow constructs as a complex rush of images from the L.A. streets at the end of the century: rogue cops shooting blacks for pleasure, crowds in a state of frenzy—images pushed and heaved up in a nighttime of middle-class nightmare.

The film constructs a representation of the now depressed L.A. of the post–Rodney King uprisings, a city in decayed turmoil, living on the desperate eruptions of repressed rage and carnivalesque abandon. The plot twists and turns of the film are its weakest parts. Strongest are the ways it thinks about gender in a world reaching the end of its tethering to reality. The main male character, Lenny (Ralph Fiennes), is a loser in a world of losers, living off trade in the illegal "clips," one of which turns out to be a snuff video of a woman raped and murdered. The killer puts the recording apparatus on his victim, so the viewer of the "clip" can vicariously

283

experience her death. If a male filmmaker had made this sequence, it would rightfully have been condemned as exploitative, but because a woman created it, its sense of outrage, the grueling immediacy of the images, leaven its scopophilic content. Bigalow has set up the structure of the film and its narrative context so that the sequence is highly condemning. Unlike Cameron's delight in suborning women to male power (or, in *Titanic*, passivity), Bigelow shows disgust and manages to weave through her film other alternate representations of gender and race.

Lenny Nero is a punching bag throughout the film: used, betrayed, beaten up, stabbed, he is a man without qualities, unable to hold his own, like his namesake, fiddling while L.A. burns. The figure of strength and sight in this film is a black woman, "Mace" (Angela Bassett), who refuses to subordinate her own perceptions to the digitized "clips" and who ultimately saves Lenny. The film ends with what might otherwise be a conventional reconciliation and romance. The "bad guys" get caught, the L.A. police are absolved by the capture and killing of the bad apple—the film's surrogate for Mark Furman—and the crowd at millennium's end is delirious. What breaks convention is the discovery of romance between Lenny and "Mace," ending in a rapturous embrace. Although the issue of race quietly moves throughout the film, which uses the L.A. uprisings and the racism of the rogue cops as one of its many narrative bases, the one issue of race that matters to so many people—interracial romance—just happens in this film. It emerges in the form of a strong woman who protects and guides a less than strong man. Everything gets reversed and everything gets fixed in a peculiar way and in an uproarious setting, out of which, phoenix-like, emerges a transgressive moment of visionary racial and gender reconciliation. There is less than redemption here; there is even a larger failure in evading political realities for a conventional love-conquers-all ending. But in that failure is a small utopian moment for contemporary film, and the usual banalities become somewhat unstuck.

In a period when so many films fell back into the old eye-level, shot/reverse shot, evenly lit mise-en-scène of the exhausted classical style, it is fascinating to find in the scorned genres of action-adventure and science fiction a complexity of mise-en-scène that, usually denigrated as mere spectacle, seems to offer ambiguous perceptions of the world unavailable to other genres. The fact that a sense of complexity and difference, of some interrogation of cultural clichés, has emerged out of the eighties and nineties action/science-fiction film indicates that their large actions, often political directly or by inference; their global, extraterrestrial reach; their

284

spectacle itself present a sense of figuring out which moral forces are at play in the culture. These films are almost always reductive, full of movie good and evil, broadly painted, lacking subtlety. Subtlety is not what American film is about, but the cinema of digital spectacle sometimes achieves if not subtlety at least visual complexity that demands attention be paid and a nudge at ideological givens that invites attention. The majority of these films are millenarian, they speak of the imminent end of the world, in micro or macro terms, and therefore reinforce a sense of loss and helplessness. In closure, their heroes avert the world's end, once again positing individual over communal action. But some of the films refuse to revert to known cultural positions: the offer of a sexual embrace between a black and white couple at the end of *Strange Days*, the assumption that an African American is a purposeful, self-possessed president of the United States in Mimi Leder's *Deep Impact* (1998), a film similar in subject to *Armageddon*, but one in which individuals respect communal rights and move to the apocalypse with grace and morals in tact. All of this stands as proof of a floundering but active imaginative energy in contemporary film.

2

"You know Spielberg—he gets me every time."
Man overheard in a theater lobby after seeing *Saving Private Ryan*

Steven Spielberg stands as the wellspring of this vitality. Since his appearance in the mid-seventies, he has developed, refined, and expanded the action and science-fiction genres. He has been an innovator in digital composition, and, more, has used the clout of his success to attempt films of Large Subjects, of race and war, of the attempt of the Germans to exterminate the Jews. And he remains beloved as the great fantasist of recuperation, every loving son, calling home to find out how things are and assuring the family that everything will be fine. He is the grand modern narrator of simple desires fulfilled, of reality diverted into the imaginary spaces of aspirations realized, where fears of abandonment and impotence are turned into fantasy spectacles of security and joyful action, where even the ultimate threat of annihilation is diverted by a saving male figure. The problem with Spielberg is that the security and joy offered by his films are rarely earned but rather forced on the viewer, willing or not, by structures that demand complete assent and emotional compliance in order to survive. His films are not so much texts to be read and understood, but mechanisms—now often digital mechanisms—constructed to stimulate desire and fulfill it, to manipulate the viewer without the viewer's awareness of what is happening.[17] He is hardly the first American filmmaker to manipulate or assure his audience, yet he is the first to do so with such insistence and consistency. He is the contemporary master of the mode and plies his trade with a subtlety (as much subtlety as his chosen forms allow) not to be found in those films that follow in his wake.

He is very much father to the ideologically bloated films of the eighties and the great spectacle films of the nineties. He has even added a political subtext to some of his recent work only implied in his earlier films. For example, the film that very much set the tone for the new male-action film, *Raiders of the Lost Ark* (1981), plays counterpoint with history, politics, and ideology, while eschewing any direct participation with the contemporary world by setting its narrative in the thirties and using comic-book Nazis as figures of evil. The historical-political allusion is subdued; there is no discussion or exposition of Nazism per se—just as there is none in *Schindler's List*. The Germans are useful in the wider narrative context of adventurer-archaeologist Indiana Jones—mild-mannered archeology professor turned adventurer—and his quest for a Jewish religious object, the Ark of the Covenant. Both religion and politics are reduced to elements easily accommodated to plot, to cliché, and to special effects. Religion becomes an aspect of the supernatural, the supernatural an overarching protector of the good, the Nazis an anti-Semitic force of destruction and perversion of this protective aura. The cruelty of the Nazis is complemented by the obstructionism of the U.S. bureaucracy (a Reaganesque touch), who, when Indiana Jones brings the Ark to America, hides it in a government warehouse. There, ending the film, the camera seeks it through thousands of crates in a sequence mimicking the end of *Citizen Kane*.

The most resonant political representations in the film, certainly at the time of its first release, are the Arabs. One must recall that the film appeared at a high point of anti-Middle East feeling in the United States, just after the Iranian hostage situation and at the beginning of the Reagan regime. Even though Indiana has an Egyptian friend and protector in the character of Sallah (a version of the patriarchal substitute we observed in much Reagan-era cinema), the Arabs are seen mostly as cunning, swarming, somewhat dim-witted tools of the Nazis and victims of the hero's physical prowess. One sequence in particular stands out. At the end of a long search through Arab-thronged streets for his beloved, Marion, who has been spirited off by the Nazis, Indy suddenly finds himself confronting an enormous Arabian figure. Bearded, turbaned, dressed in black robes with a red sash, this giant stands alone twirling a large saber. He is the fantasy of every hated Arab enlarged into one figure. He grins malevolently at his helpless prey. A cut to Indy shows him with a somewhat quizzical and contemptuous expression. The narrative pattern of *Raiders of the Lost Ark* presents its hero with a series of insurmountable obstacles, which he then surmounts by cleverness or physical skill. He gathers up the subjectivity of the audience, removes from it the reality of danger, and then repositions that subjectivity within a kinetics of victory over physical obstacles and escape. Neither the viewer nor the viewer's adventuresome surrogate ever loses, and the meeting with the Arabian giant is no exception.

The quizzical, contemptuous gaze offered by Indy is not a manifestation of uncertainty about what action he will take. Quite the contrary. He simply pulls a gun and shoots the Arab dead. The significance of his look turns out to be amazement that the Arab would assume such useless posturing, should even for a moment think himself a threat. The ideological positioning of the viewer is made quite certain. Subjected to imagined humiliations at the hands of Middle Easterners—figures known to Western culture almost exclusively through their most violent representations—the audience, having given itself over to the hero, finds it can now subject the villain to instant, guiltless retribution. The response to this sequence in a movie theater was overwhelming. The hero's bravura, his ability to dispatch enemies without himself getting seriously hurt, assured the viewer an instant and untroubling gratification. Reaganism had its first major filmic representation.

Athough the sequence may have lost some ideological immediacy, the general methodology of viewer positioning is typical of Spielberg's style and his continuing success. He is, if not more subtle in his means, usually more indirect and often more insidious. His narrative discourse continues to speak to yearnings for security, help, reclamation, and amelioration; the formal articulation of this discourse still situates the viewer in order to make both the yearning and Spielberg's assuring response to it irresistible. The methods Spielberg employs to compose his images and build them into narratives offer interesting examples of how film represses individuality and creates an ideal and responsive subject—a universal subject. When a Spielberg film works, the response of one viewer ought to be the same as every other. This is, as I've noted before, not an original phenomenon. The existence of classical Hollywood cinema depends on an audience's

287

assent to its formal and substantive conventions and an acceptance—indeed belief—in the illusory fullness and presence of the fictive world these conventions create. Spielberg is particularly precise in the calculation and execution of the conventions, almost Hitchcockian. But Hitchcock's manipulation of imagery and narrative always has a second level of articulation, so that the primary response is inflected by an awareness of the response and even, somehow, by an awareness of the methods used to achieve that response. The viewer is permitted a space to reflect on his or her own reaction, to reread almost immediately and see through the illusion. For all the reflexive gestures in his own films—most notably through quotations, which are often taken from his own films as well as Hitchcock's—Spielberg never permits the viewer reflective space. Should such an opening occur, it might bring down the entire structure of belief each film works so hard at erecting.

The construction methods of the Spielberg style are surprisingly simple—at least until he gets very much involved in digital effects, particularly in *Saving Private Ryan*—and I would like to move through them, in order to gain some understanding of how this filmmaker articulates and manipulates the classical style, and then out into a more general discussion of what exactly is being constructed. What follows, therefore, is a kind of catalogue of devices and techniques, a taxonomy of Spielbergian form with some discussion of the form's significance, itself followed by a discussion of the ideological structures set up by that form.

Perhaps the most immediately recognizable formal element in a Spielberg film, almost a stylistic signature until the nineties, is light—blinding light shone directly into the camera lens. During the sixties, breaking with long cinematographic tradition, filmmakers began allowing light to flood the camera, showing its refractions through the elements of the lens. Shooting into the sun rapidly became a convention, as did the glare of headlights on a nighttime street. Stanley Kubrick always used severe backlighting, allowing light to come in through windows behind characters or from fluorescent lights above them. Spielberg goes beyond this, making bright, sometimes overwhelming light, a major element of his mise-en-scène. *Close Encounters* begins with a dark screen that suddenly bursts into the light of headlights piercing through a desert sandstorm. Roy Neary's first encounter with a spaceship is shown by a blinding light that floods his truck in the night—a night made darker by the fact that all man-made lights have gone out. Light creeps through the door jams as the aliens come to remove young Barry from his mother's house. The spaceships are seen mostly as lights, and the spectacle that ends the film is told with light on light, a play of brightness and color whose intensity is threatening when it begins, but which ends as an invitation to its finally unthreatening mystery. The presence of the extraterrestrial in *E.T.* (1982) is noted by light streaming from the shed of a suburban house. Threatening at first, this light becomes a signifier of a friendly creature, itself threatened by other lights—the flashlights of the government men slashing the darkness in search of the visitor. Elliott, E.T.'s earthly friend, is almost always backlit and surrounded by light, significant of his protective and protecting aura. When Shug Avery and Celie go upstairs to read Nettie's letters in *The Color Purple*, light streams in through the window behind them. "Look for me in the sunset," Nettie writes.

Threat and protection, fear and security, are the opposing poles of Spielberg's thematic. The light piercing through his films plays on both, violating the viewer's safe distance from the narratives by demanding attention, forcing the gaze, hiding objects, and then revealing those objects, surrounding them with its protective glow. The light offers enlightenment but blinds the viewer to it at the same time. Light was the most visible means of Spielberg's game with his viewer, his act of temptation and promise, his demand for attention. And it reveals as well his love of his medium. Film only works because of light; light initiates the filmic image. Spielberg takes this physical fact and turns it into a stimulus of narrative perception. His more recent films have grown noticeably darker; there is little brightness in the black-and-white nightmare of *Schindler's List*, only the glare of naked bulbs or the hard light from the sky. *Amistad* (1997) depends on darkness as a metaphor for slavery and the bodies oppressed by it. Most of the film's mise-en-scène is dark and damp, though the victories, especially the destruction of the African Lomboko slave fortress, are preceded by the freed slaves escaping into the sunlight; and the last shot of the film, as Cinque sails for Sierra Leone, looks, from his point of view, at the sun through the rigging of the ship. A pale sun shines through the flag at the beginning and end of *Saving Private Ryan*.

Spielberg's other means are somewhat less explicit and occasionally more subtle, though they all have the same ends. In his fitting together of narrative parts, he follows the convention of strict continuity cutting, linking sequence to sequence chronologically, or intercutting two sequences that are meant to be happening simultaneously, though in different places. In all cases, he sutures the viewer's perceptions into the linkages so that the linkages themselves are invisible. He employs some very traditional methods of linking shots, covering a cut with a passage from John Williams's symphonic score (or Quincy Jones's in *The Color Purple*); by moving from one shape to another (the bright round light of a helicopter to a white, round radar dish in *Close Encounters*); or from one physical movement to a similar one in the next shot—quite conventionally, at times, as when the bang of the judge's gavel is cut to the unlocking of Cinque's cuffs in *Amistad*. Sometimes he will use cutting for a whimsical or virtuoso effect. *E.T.* contains a sequence linking Elliott, his friend from space, and a John Ford film. Elliott is in school and E.T. is at home, drinking beer. As the creature gets drunk and falls down, so does Elliott. E.T. then watches *The Quiet Man* on television. John Wayne pulls Maureen O'Hara to him and kisses her. The action is matched and cut to Elliott at school who echoes John Wayne's movements with a classmate. (Like most of the filmmakers discussed here, Spielberg is infatuated with Ford, and references to him occur in almost every film.) The cutting in this sequence not only serves to indicate the bond of human and alien across domestic and psychic space, but to interconnect fictional spaces as well, linking all movie images together. If ever any reflexive openings occur in the sentimental glaze of *E.T.*, they are at points such as these, when the film admits its relationship to other film romance, other film fictions. The process is continued without cutting in a later sequence when the children and their alien playmate, costumed for Halloween, walk down the street. E.T is drawn to a child dressed as Yoda—two movie fictions recognizing one another. Such self-conscious gestures are, as I noted, never distancing; they continue to propel the viewer into the fiction. The spaces of recognition, of filmic allusions, of editing style, heighten the viewer's affection for the images and their affective pull.

As dictated by the classical style, Spielberg's cutting—rarely as self-conscious as this, but often consciously manipulative—moves the narrative from one temporal or spatial point to another. It almost always drives or is driven by the expectations set up for the viewer by or within the sequences themselves. But, like Hitchcock, Spielberg occasionally makes the viewer a participant in the cutting process. By offering partial information and withholding the rest, Spielberg manages a continuity of suspense, expectation, desire, and fulfillment that molds both the cutting pattern and the viewer's gaze into one interlocking web. Here is an example from *Jaws*, not one of security or comfort—except for the comfort of being safely manipulated into fear and anticipation, which is what this particular film is about. After the first shark attack, Chief Brody (Roy Scheider) decides to shut down the Amity beaches. There is much confusion and some panic on Brody's part as he gives orders. A marching band goes down the street, interrupting Brody's assistant as he tries to tell Mayor Vaughn about the attack. Brody goes to the ferry, where he is joined by the mayor, the coroner, and another town official. In a long take, Brody attempts to explain his actions, while the mayor—dressed in an absurd blazer printed with little white anchors—insists that the beaches cannot be closed because summer tourism will suffer. The coroner changes his original story, suggesting that a boat rather than a shark may have caused the victim's death. (The references to the corruption of public officials during the Watergate scandal would have been immediately noted by an audience in the mid-seventies.)[18]

During all this, the audience, primed by the scene of the first attack, its fear heightened by the expression on the policeman's face when he discovers the remains of the body, waits in anticipation of further grisly events. The viewer, of course, knows that the mayor is planning a cover-up, knows that a shark is lurking. This is a major clause in Spielberg's contract with the audience. Hitchcock often pointed out that if, in the course of the narrative, a bomb is planted under a table, the characters must remain ignorant of it, but the audience must be keenly aware of the situation, so that they may fear and wonder over the outcome. In the same vein, Spielberg often provides the viewer with just slightly more information than the major character has, thereby giving the viewer superiority over that character, fear of what may happen, and promise that the hero will succeed and join the viewer in a fantasy of triumph. But Hitchcock said the bomb must never go off; Spielberg always creates an explosion of one kind or another. As the scene on the ferry ends, the mayor warns against panic. "It's all psychological," he says, taking Brody's arm and moving forward into the frame. "You yell 'barracuda,' everybody says 'huh, what?' You yell 'shark,' we've got a panic on our hands on the Fourth of July." Appetites are further whetted. Fear is supplemented by expectation of chaos. There is a cut to a shot of the ferry returning to the dock, and then a cut to the beach, as a large woman moves across the frame from right to left. Expectation and fear in *Jaws* are based on the body and the injury that might be done to it. The corpulent woman walking into the water emphasizes both the body and the fear.

As she moves into the a water, a young boy in red trunks walks out in the opposite direction. The camera reverses its movement, tracking the child to his mother, who gives him permission to get his raft and go back swimming (unknown to the viewer, this is the child who will be the shark's next victim; here special knowledge is offered but not recognized). The child continues walking to the right, past Brody, who sits, in profile, on the right side of the screen, gazing out at the ocean, while his wife and others carry on small talk behind and to the left of him. A cut to his point of view of the beach reveals the large woman floating in the water, a young man running past with his dog (he had been observed earlier when the lady walked by). He throws a stick for his pet, who will also become the shark's victim. The child in red trunks returns to the water, a rapid cut taking him from the beach into the ocean. A number of shots of bathers—the large woman, the boy in red trunks, the boy with his dog playing on the beach—follow, ending with a frontal shot of Brody staring intently. One after the other, two figures walk in front of him, the motion of each hiding a cut that, when the figure passes, presents an even closer shot of the Chief. The intensity of the gaze at him and of what he sees makes him a surrogate for the viewer, looking intently, waiting. Whatever reactions he shows will be a signal to the viewer that something terrible (and wonderful) is happening.

Point-of-view shots are complex events, organizing the visual space from three different perspectives: that of the director (and his or her camera), who creates and orchestrates the film's matrix of perspectives and glances; the character in the film for whom the camera is seeing; and the viewer, who is meant to be seeing what the character sees, via the camera. The illusion of the camera gaze—its eye that stands for the eye of character and viewer, which in turn becomes the I of those two subjects it creates or represents—gives the viewer particular ownership of the space and the character, a privileged place of seeing and knowing. Jean-Louis Baudry writes, "If the eye which moves is no longer fettered by a body, by the laws of matter and time, if there are no more assignable limits to its displacement—conditions fulfilled by the possibilities of shooting and of film—the world will not only be constituted by this eye but for it.[19] When the camera assumes a first-person perspective, the viewer is doubly constituted by the world of the fiction (the diegesis) and the particular eye viewing this world at a particular moment in its fictional existence. To complicate matters, a point-of-view shot can, indeed often does, contain the figure whose view we are meant to be sharing. The stare *at* that figure locks the viewer more firmly to the character. When the two subjects merge, the fictional world is then constituted for both.

Spielberg complicates the process further in some of his later films. The sequence of the little girl in the red coat in *Schindler's List* is an interesting example. The body of the narrative is filmed in black and white, but at this crucial moment, as the Jews are being rounded up and taken from the ghetto, a faint color of red is introduced in the coat of a child that Schindler sees from horseback on top of the hill. The color is, in an important sense, imaginary: placed there (digitally) by the filmmaker, it serves to individuate the child from the mass of prisoners, herded, assassinated, escaping, being caught, and also—intercut with Schindler's gaze—indicate a growth of his consciousness about what is happening below. Spielberg continues looking at the little girl in the red coat even after Schindler leaves his perch and she goes indoors. She is therefore left to remain in the viewer's consciousness and to provide a sad link in the narrative, carried out later when the Nazis exhume the bodies from the Warsaw Ghetto, and Schindler sees the girl's charred corpse, her red coat still visible. The girl in red is constituted for Schindler's gaze and ours; it allows us to see what he is seeing and that becomes a surrogate for our understanding of his growth in awareness.

In *Jaws* the Hitchcockian play of gazes continues on the beach. Another cut to Brody's point of view shows the large woman bathing. A figure crosses the line of sight and once more hides a cut that returns the gaze to Brody himself. These figures crossing his field of vision are interruptions, obstacles that make him and the viewer nervous. Another such interruption occurs and the gaze returns to the ocean, this time closer to the floating woman, and then back to Brody just as something black is seen moving toward her in the water. Brody starts, but the reverse shot reveals it only as the head of a man swimming. Expectations have been raised further and then released. Brody relaxes for a moment and is interrupted by a man with a trivial problem. The man bends down to speak to Brody, blocking his and—since the two have been drawn so close—the audience's view. Brody lifts his head above the man's shoulder and Spielberg cuts to a point-of-view shot that looks over the man's shoulder to the ocean. A woman is seen in the water, screaming, and on that scream Spielberg cuts to Brody getting up, looking. The reverse shot reveals it to be a girl and boy playing in the surf. Another momentary rise and fall in tension is created. Brody's wife—composed behind and below him in the frame—speaks to him about their children, who have been swimming. The old man whose bobbing head Brody—and the viewer—thought was a shark, comes up to talk. Brody looks at his children, who are seen running. His wife rubs his shoulders and he relaxes some. There are further shots of children swimming and screaming; Brody's small son on the beach; the boy calling after his dog; the stick he threw for him, floating on the water. Finally the underwater shot of dangling legs and the accelerating sounds of bass fiddles indicate the shark is approaching. The interlock of points of view is momentarily

293

broken, shifting to that of the monster, a device that repels the viewer rather than makes him or her complicit with the attack. It is difficult to "identify" with the point of view of a shark and, by forcing the viewer to do so, Spielberg raises anticipation, expectation, and a desire to see the unseeable—a monster destroy a human. There follow a number of shots of the attack, thrashing bodies, the boy with red trunks going under, blood boiling in the water, intercut with people rising up on the beach, all of which are climaxed with a combination zoom and track in opposite directions on Brody and his wife, who is behind him, rubbing his neck. (The combination zoom-track is a technique Spielberg learned from the point-of-view device Hitchcock uses to represent Scottie's reaction to heights in *Vertigo*. It appears, as noted earlier, in the diner at the end of Scorsese's *GoodFellas*.) The effect is to bring Brody rapidly forward in the frame while making the background seem to slip away from him. The movement is expressive both of his response and the viewer's own reaction to the long delayed event, an interesting visual representative of panic.

With such an effect, Spielberg charges the spaces of the shot itself with fear and desire. During one sequence early in *Close Encounters*, air traffic controllers huddle around a radar screen on which they observe the blip of an aircraft's having an encounter with a spaceship. The camera observes their faces reflected in the screen or gazes intently at them, lit and photographed from below; focus is shifted from one face to the other. As the UFO makes its pass, the anxious voices of the airline pilots are heard on the loudspeaker, and the camera tracks in toward their anxious gaze. Again figures within the narrative become surrogates for the viewer's own anxious look, this time for something that exists only as an enigma, as yet unseen.

This conventional camera movement, a slow dolly forward to a figure, becomes charged with emotion. Such a movement has been coded—since the early thirties at least—as a gesture of approach or a visual exclamation within an otherwise static scene (in this latter guise it becomes a typical stylistic gesture in postwar, pre-New Wave French film). Spielberg inflects the movement just enough to change its conventional effect. He makes it slightly faster than usual (though not enough to make it suggest a frightened lunge at the object to which the camera is moving) and usually places the camera at a slightly low angle. This upward angle, combined with the movement, communicates the threat or danger to the character being approached and, at the same time, encourages the viewer to react to the threat uneasily. In effect, it becomes a point-of-view shot for the audience, inviting the viewer into the narrative space, indicating the danger or enigma of that space at the same time.

This angle and movement are persistent throughout *Close Encounters of the Third Kind*, a film in which Spielberg plays against the generic expectations of science fiction, frightening his audience with alien invasion, which such films inevitably present as dangerous but that here turns out to be friendly. At the beginning of the film, as the army and scientists meet the Mexicans who have discovered the lost air squadron of 1945, the camera persistently moves toward the various figures. The confusion, the blowing sand, the low angle movements, the scientist's almost hysterical questions about the discovery, "Where's the crew. . . . How the hell did it get here?" serve as a provocation to the viewer. Fear, hysteria, enigma lead to a *desire* to discover what has happened, to penetrate the mystery and overcome the resistance of the screen space and its figures to which the camera moves without, yet, revealing anything.

Movement and cutting throughout the early part of *Close Encounters* offer both an obstacle and an invitation, fear and longing for explanation that is not so much offered as climaxed by the spectacle of awe, joy, and regeneration that ends the film. At this point, the sheer size of the spaceship and the attendant apparatus dwarf the human figures. By this time, the low-angle tracks—in combination with the gargantuan images—completely subject the viewer. They reduce him or her in relation to the images and, by their very dynamic, organize the movement and direction of viewer perception into a predetermined state of bliss and wonder. The shot becomes a controlling force, a tool of the director as dictator. So much so, that, when he is ready, Spielberg can reverse the movement of the shot and thereby use it as a release from the narrative. After a final dolly in to the wondering face of Lacombe (François Truffaut), who proceeds to communicate with an alien from the ship, there are a series of low-angle tracks moving *away* from the wondering humans, releasing tension, preparing the viewer not only for the departure of the spacecraft, but for his or her own separation from the narrative—though the final separation is not complete until the viewer is further subdued and excited by the massive forms of the ship and the overwhelming sound track.

Jurassic Park continues in a similar vein. The opening sequence in particular, in which a dinosaur is loaded into a ship at night, uses bright lights shining in the camera and low-angle tracking shots to create a sense of awed anticipation. But in this film—even though Spielberg does attempt to offer elements of danger, especially in the child versus beast sequence near the end—the emphasis, as in *Close Encounters*, is on spectacle: the welcoming representation of the fantastic.

An interesting variation of the low-angle track occurs in *The Color Purple*, Spielberg's ethnic domestic melodrama, whose genre demands that he eschew the more dramatic visual effects of the fantasy and adventure films. Yet his own style—the complex of forms he has developed as particular variations on existing conventions—tends to overlay more traditional requirements or extend them into somewhat different configurations. When Celie (Whoopi Goldberg) first approaches her new husband's house, which will be a place of pain and humiliation, there is a low-angle shot from her point of view. The camera booms forward, at a low angle, directly at the house and the children lined up in front of it. On first viewing of the film, the audience is unlikely to know of the brutal events that await Celie, and this almost violent movement is an important preparatory device. In fact the violence begins in the course of the tracking shot, as one of the children hurls a rock toward the camera eye/I of Celie. After that event, the bloody imprint of Celie's hand—the result of her head wound—is seen on a rock.

The movement is, as always, dramatic and foreboding, but finally too much for this particular film. A stylistic element imported from another genre, it signifies the film's director more than it does a major narrative event. Although it imparts important information, the form outstrips its signifying potential and indicates that Spielberg's stylistics may be limited and therefore open to repetition. Of course repetition is necessary for the creation of a style. Kubrick's tracking shots, Scorsese's methods of shooting New York streets, Robert Altman's use of the zoom lens or of offscreen dialogue mark the way these individuals inflect and individuate formal material, and they occur in film after film. But when such inflections overdetermine narrative material and do not create a formal significance of their own, then the auteur, designing and shaping his film, gets caught within his own devices and desires. In this case, the point-of-view shot represents Spielberg more than it does the narrative it is supposed to form, a problem he seems to have understood. In *Amistad*, his second film about Africans and African Americans, there is a great deal more stability in camera and point of view. Too much, perhaps. Feeling the weightiness of his subject, Spielberg seems here to have frozen in place, giving over the burden of carrying the film to the costumes and production design—like Scorsese in his period pieces. In *Amistad*, the characters act and react with conventional dignity or villainy, as if history could supply the drama by itself. There is a stasis here in which the characters play actors on the stage of history, weighty and considered, without the dialectics of historical struggle in Oliver Stone's histories, for example.

Another spatial construct favored by Spielberg is a bit more interesting. Most of his theatrical films, at least until the late eighties, are made in an anamorphic ratio.* He often takes great advantage of the horizontal breadth of the composition by placing figures off center, on the left or right of the screen, and then situating other, equally important figures in the other parts of the frame, in the background and in soft focus (turning to advantage the difficulty in creating deep focus with an anamorphic lens). He will then sometimes shift focus so that the figure originally seen clearly in the foreground goes out of focus and attention is shifted to the figures in the rear. The effects of such compositions are less insistent than the dolly-in and depend more on the viewer's willingness to explore composition. Rather than manipulate by dynamic movement, such shots require active observation of the frame (and anything in Spielberg's work that offers the viewer an opportunity to exercise his or her own will is to be noted with appreciation).

An example of the method is found in *Raiders of the Lost Ark*. Indiana Jones has just survived an enormous chase across the desert. He has been shot, run over by a truck he had been clinging to, dragged by the same truck down the road, and generally abused beyond the endurance of any normal human body—presaging the body resilience that becomes a mark of the male action film. He and his lover, Marion, arrive at a dock, where Sallah, his friend and protector, has prepared passage for him on the boat of an African, Katanga. The camera tracks Indy and Marion walking to the dock from right to left. Sallah greets them, and the camera continues its track, bringing Katanga into the frame on the left. There is a shift of focus to Katanga as the three original figures are now in soft focus in the center background. Katanga lights a cigarette (the sequence takes place at night, and the lighting effects are subtle and effective). Indy asks Sallah if these people are to be trusted, and Sallah calls to Katanga, who walks over to them, the focus changing as he approaches the original group in the center of the frame. Katanga offers them his cabin and then walks out of the frame. Indy moves to Sallah and embraces him, moves to the rear, and makes way for Marion to say her good-byes. Sallah sings a song as Marion

297

* In recent years, Spielberg has returned to the nonanamorphic ratio of 1:1.88. Perhaps this is because he realizes that he has more control over the composition in this ratio when the film is "modified"—that is, has its sides cut off—for video.

and Indy walk to the rear and to the boat. The camera follows Sallah off to the right as he passes a group of sailors and waves good-bye to his friends who are now standing on the gangplank.

Raiders (and its two sequels), to a greater extent than Spielberg's other work, depends almost entirely on cutting to maintain its rhythm and create the illusion of rapid and dangerous action. This long, complicated shot in which figures and camera are almost choreographed together offers a moment of rest and collection (which is, in fact, what the characters enjoy at this point in the narrative). But if it seems to change the register of activity, it is in fact only a modification of that register that permits it to encompass another ideological effect. Spielberg's films are always concerned with melodramatic conventions of friendship and assistance, with the attractive myth of individuals coming to the aid of other individuals to ward off danger and loneliness. Only Dennis Weaver's David Mann in *Duel* (1971) is without external support; he is the only Spielberg character who must depend entirely on his own resources. Otherwise, each of Spielberg's characters has a special friend who helps: in *E.T.*, Elliott has his alien; Brody has Hooper in *Jaws*; Celie is brought to maturity by Shug in *The Color Purple*; Lou Jean and Clovis are befriended by the very policemen whose laws they break in *The Sugarland Express* (1973); Jillian and Roy help each other get to the alien landing in *Close Encounters*, where the aliens themselves prove to be universal friends. The scientists (with the exception of the computer scientists) bond with each other and the children in *Jurassic Park*. Cinque is aided by Baldwin, the white attorney, and Joadson, the black abolitionist in *Amistad*. The Jews in *Schindler's List* are aided by the one Nazi who rises above the general moral squalor. General Marshall acts as a protector to mother Ryan in *Saving Private Ryan*. Calling on the caring words of President Lincoln, he orders that her surviving son be retrieved from the European war. Tom Hank's Captain Miller executes his order, turning it into a moral obligation and his troops into a close-knit, squabbling family. In the films Spielberg produces, children are often supported by their friends and family, as is Marty McFly by his scientist friend in *Back to the Future* or the group of children who look after one another in Richard Donner's *The Goonies*.

These friendships and groups, whether human or cosmic, are always of a fantastical kind—intensive support provided under overwhelming conditions. They are exclusive groupings and rarely pose wider questions of community. On the contrary, the larger community is often seen as indifferent or antagonistic, and the friendships are so isolated as to form a

298

cell within it (a phenomenon of particular importance in *Schindler's List*). Spielberg's major discourse is precisely about the security of exclusive, protective, and nonthreatening companions. There are no larger communal spaces in his films—the beach in *Jaws* is a place of threat; the town in *The Color Purple* is either anonymous or, again, a place of danger; Normandy Beach in *Saving Private Ryan* is the site of horrible death, as well as war-movie heroism; the landing field for the spacecraft in *Close Encounters* and the closed courtroom of *Amistad* are the closest Spielberg can come to a large area of people working together. But in *Close Encounters* their work, of course, is for a purpose that will finally diminish the group, and, in the course of the film, the community contacted by the aliens is whittled down to a single couple, Roy and Jillian. In *Raiders*, a good part of the globe becomes a field for an individual of almost supernatural powers to prove his cleverness and endurance. When Spielberg decides to encapsulate him within the tentative confines of rest and protection, he does it with a remarkable cinematic grace that affirms the need for isolation, with friends, from a dangerous world. Encapsulation becomes a major narrative device to deflect the pain of the characters in *Schindler's List* and *Saving Private Ryan*. Both films are surrounded by "modern-day" episodes in which the traumas of the main narrative events have been ended. "Schindler's Jews," the survivors of those he saved, form a community of thankfulness, a large family. A smaller family provides the protective and assuring encapsulation for Private Ryan.

This encapsulation process includes the film viewer. For she is invited—often forced—to partake of the groupings and become a privileged participant in the illusory world of adventure and salvation. Earlier, I mentioned the contract that Spielberg draws up, promising to offer the viewer slightly more information than that held by the characters. The contractual obligations are fairly one-sided, the films parcel out information, entice the viewer by means of manipulation of point of view, but in fact never get beyond the manipulation, for someone outside the fiction can never actually become part of it. The terms and methods of that manipulation, however, can seem quite agreeable and their visual articulation interesting. The first part of *Close Encounters*, for example, is built on alternating sequences of strange and ordinary events—the discovery of the lost fighter squadron in Mexico, the UFO sightings by airliners and controllers, the appearance of the flying saucers to the little boy, Barry, in Muncie, the domestic discord in Roy Neary's house, and his encounter with a spaceship out on the highway. In some of the later films, the terms and methods become less agreeable, as if Spielberg is thinking that the serious must equal loss and sadness. So, the victories of the slaves in *Amistad* are dampened by a final title that tells us of Cinque's unhappy return to his country. The hero of *Saving Private Ryan* and many of his men die—an old melodramatic convention that permits the death of the beloved character to signify a larger sadness and sacrifice. Here, however, Spielberg returns to the framing narrative in order that the work of the hero is seen to bear results in the moral dedication of the man he saved.

In many of his films, Spielberg balances the global events with the domestic. In *Close Encounters* he is most interested in the effects of the space visitors on the little child and on Roy, the man with the heart of a child. Full-scale domestic melodrama threatens in the case of the latter. Roy becomes obsessed with the vision of the mountain—the sight of the spacecraft's landing that the aliens have implanted in his mind. He falls apart, loses his job and his family. The latter is an event any Spielberg film construes as intolerable; he cannot permit a rupture in domesticity to last very long. Roy soon joins forces with Jillian, Barry's mother, who shares with Roy the imprint of the mountain shape. Once they discover their shared vision, they continue their quest together.

In order to hasten the healing of the domestic break and the concurrent separation between viewer and character, Spielberg uses a wide-screen compositional effect we have been discussing to give the viewer privileged information and finally assure us that Roy's isolation will not be a permanent state. When Roy's wife and children leave him, he is alone in their midwest suburban house (such a house is the location of much Spielbergian melodrama, where passion is turned into a commodity to be consumed by the viewer who inhabits similar quarters). In the shot that climaxes the first part of the sequence, Roy stands on the left of the composition, staring out at the suburban landscape, rendered all the more banal by the momentous, cosmic events he is attempting to understand and the psychological upset he is suffering. (In the first version of the film, Roy had gone almost mad and built his model of Devil's Tower out of garbage and garden dirt he hauled in from the front of his house. Spielberg removed this scene to incorporate more gigantic special effects as Roy enters the spaceship in the "special edition" made for the film's re-release.)

As the sequence continues, there is a leap in time. The television set, placed to the right of the Devil's Tower model, plays the end of a soap opera and then a beer commercial. Roy crosses in front of it just as the news comes on. Howard K. Smith, the former news broadcaster (who, like CNN reporters in recent films, hired out his image to filmmakers so that they might make reference in their fiction to another form of mass entertainment, the network news), is delivering a story. He reports the army's closing of Devil's Tower in Wyoming and shows an image of the mountain Roy has been trying to model. Roy is now on the phone to his wife, walking across the room, then sitting in front of the television screen, on which the image of the tower and the model he has been building match up. For the moment, however, he is oblivious to it, for his despair over ruined domesticity interferes with his search for higher truths. But when the images match up for a second time, he finally notices what is going on.

The viewer, however, is permitted primary access to the space, registers the information, but of course cannot pass that information to the fictional character. A gap is opened by the very fullness of the shot, partially closed when Roy finally sees what the viewer already knows, and then sealed shut with a cut to Jillian, who is also seeking a correspondence to the image in her head (as well as seeking her son who has been taken by the aliens). She sees the same news program on her television set. The recognition and the joining of the two characters is now immediate, and in the next sequence Roy is driving to Wyoming, where he will meet Jillian. Both will finally reach the site that the government has closed off (another gap in knowledge: the viewer knows the army has created a false story of a toxic spill to evacuate the area; Roy and Jillian must overcome further obstacles to discover this themselves and must then endure considerable hardship to reach the landing site). The ability to see the mound Roy builds and its analogous television image within a single shot and before the central character does creates both knowledge and frustration. It directs the viewer's entry into the space left empty by the departure of Roy's family and encircles the viewer within the formation of the character and the narrative process itself. The cut then relays the knowledge about Devil's Tower, held mutely by the viewer, across narrative space, connecting the characters to the viewer's already held information, relieving frustration, allowing the narrative to proceed and a new domestic unit to form.

There are other instances in Spielberg's films where composition generates a tension between desired security and narrative uncertainty, especially on the domestic level. In *Jaws*, a few brief sequences quickly establish a domesticity that is set at odds with the horror of the shark attacks and the resistance of the town leaders to closing the beaches. Immediately after the first attack, and before the beach sequence described earlier, there is a sequence with Brody and his wife and child. The couple

301

get out of bed; their son comes to them with a cut hand. Brody goes to the phone to receive the call about the shark attack. He is framed on the right of the screen, in sharp focus, his wife and son in soft focus in the left rear of the composition, standing in the kitchen—the domestic space—where she tends the son's injury. The family unit is present but visually fading in importance in face of the task that lies ahead, while the cut hand assumes a significant relationship to the large bodily assaults inflicted by the shark. Later, in a moment of domestic calm, father and son watch television, the son playfully mimicking Brody's gestures. This sequence begins with the camera focused on the mother; but she quickly moves again to the kitchen, remaining in soft focus behind them until Hooper enters and the three sit around the table discussing the shark.

302

As a peace-loving, middle-class man, wife and child are the comfort and quiet Brody wants. But they must be positioned correctly. The wife may not dominate, only remain the soft-focus anchor of the domestic group. And that group is threatened, as always in American film, and especially at times of cultural stress. A major thematic of films during the fifties and from the mid-seventies through the mid-eighties is that middle-class comfort and security is a frail thing. Not only must it be fought for, but continually tested. Two things have to happen: the family unit needs to be secured against external threat and the male member of that unit needs not only to protect (or in some instances avenge) the family, but in the process must prove himself. During the late forties and fifties, gangsters often intruded on the family and had to be defied by the husband; or the husband got involved with gangsters—an act that threatened the stability of his family— and had to extricate himself. Classic variations on the theme occur in Michael Curtiz's *The Breaking Point*, Fritz Lang's *The Big Heat*, and William Wyler's *The Desperate Hours* (1955). Later variations placed other obstacles in the domestic path and permit a certain amount of role reversal. To save her family, Lou Jean initiates the journey to reclaim her son and forces her actions on a somewhat passive husband in *Sugarland Express*. Similarly, in Richard Pearce's *Country* (1984), the wife must struggle to keep her farm against the insensitivity of both a hostile government bureaucracy and a beaten and unreactive husband. In Robert Benton's *Kramer vs. Kramer* (1979), however, the husband proves to be the strong parental figure, caring for his son after divorce, and in Robert Redford's *Ordinary People* (1980), the wife proves to be a major force in promoting domestic discord. The wife in Hooper and Spielberg's *Poltergeist* (1982) undergoes a considerable ordeal at the hands of the living dead in order to preserve the family unit.

The intrusion on domesticity in Spielberg's films most often takes the form of insuperable or superhuman forces: the malevolent truck in *Duel*, the more malevolent shark in *Jaws*, the law in *Sugarland Express*, extraterrestrials in *Close Encounters*, the Nazi extermination of the Jews in *Schindler's List*, World War II in *Saving Private Ryan*. The Indiana Jones films stand outside the pattern by focusing on a male figure who refuses the comforts of family entirely. However, in *Raiders of the Lost Ark*, he finds comfort with a strong woman, nearly his equal in bravery, and an older friend and guide. *Indiana Jones and the Temple of Doom* (1984) presents the hero with a conventionally dumb and hysterical woman companion, but also with a young Asian boy who bravely accompanies him on his adventures, offering wisecracks in place of strength and providing an audience surrogate. The oedipal pattern is completed in *Indiana Jones and the Last Crusade* (1989), when the hero is reunited—indeed physically bound—to his father. *The Color Purple* inverts some of the codes by creating the husband himself as the seemingly insuperable and disruptive force and placing in the narrative a woman who reorganizes the domestic structure, giving the central female character strength and support to break away. However, the inversion does not turn out to be subversion.

Jaws uses the family group as a point of reference and departure, and the ramifications of its narrative take us beyond stylistic devices and the problems of pictorial composition into larger areas of ideological formation. The film rapidly integrates itself within the subgenre of the buddy film—men joining with other men and casting the woman out. The soft-focused mother and children eventually disappear from view entirely as the screen is filled with the presence of Brody, the young scientist Hooper, and the obsessed old shark fighter Quint, who form a new family grouping. Within that family, Brody must prove himself the brave son, although he, in effect, fathers himself. Hooper is too young, too much the intellectual, too unattached, and too rich to emerge as the film's hero. He may only aid Brody, ending up hiding under the water for the climax of the battle with the shark, joining Brody on a piece of the wrecked boat as they paddle to the shore after the victory. Quint is too old-fashioned, too single-minded, and too much the individual to emerge the unadorned hero. He is too old and, paradoxically, too unforgivingly paternal and mean to survive. His death—in the film's most grisly scene—is the death of the old father. Brody, however, is the perfect middle-class man, who must be initiated into heroism (although police chief of the seaside resort, he is a New Yorker who is afraid of the water), and may return to shore and family only after undergoing his rite of passage. As Stephen Heath points out, this battle at sea occurs "in the summer of America's final year in Vietnam," during which the three men enact a ritual of "destruction and conscience and manliness and menace and just-doing-the-job."[20] Of the three, the unassuming, middle-class man does the job best and emerges from struggle renewed. Likewise, Roy Neary, in *Close Encounters*, is offered a severe, cosmic test, which he endures because of his childlike faith and his ability to join with Jillian in the quest for the new utopia of the aliens. Both Brody and Neary, though serious about their tasks, do not take themselves too seriously, which is a prime requisite of the modern hero—as we've seen in the male-action film. Commitment and seriousness of purpose isolate an individual, make him threatening, and therefore unacceptable (Rambo is the curious exception to this). The man who proves himself best is nothing special, an ordinary man who fights for domesticity (or, in the case of Indiana Jones, for the hell of it). With his victory, Spielberg proves that the traumas of the seventies and eighties may be overcome by an ordinary heroism supported by domestic desires.

Even through the nineties, when the tenor of Spielberg's films and their view of the domestic changed somewhat, they still operate to prove the validity of, and to recuperate any possible losses to, the domestic space. Their specific formal devices work toward the success of this project, which becomes finally the universal mise-en-scène. In *Close Encounters*, the visitors from space send their children out to greet the earthlings, thereby promoting an intergalactic family, already initiated by their calling first on Jillian's small child and then Roy to join them (Jillian remains on earth, in soft focus, as it were, waiting first for the return of her son and then of Roy). E.T. descends to perform the role of father, secret friend, and baby for young Elliott. Even the Indiana Jones films (inflected by George Lucas's fantasies of adolescent adventure and an invulnerable hero who seems to want none of the normal ties to home and family) don't betray Spielberg's central concern. Indy has two lives: one as mild-mannered bespectacled archaeology professor, the other as adventurer, something of a sublunar Superman. Were he only an adventurer, the viewer would be unable to find the securing point. The narrative space would be open-ended; its activity would find rest in the conclusion of the adventure but not in the satisfactory return of the subject to a place of comfort. So, the first film has Indy return home; the second has him save hundreds of Indian children captured by an evil sect, returning them to their desolated village. He and dad find the Holy Grail in the last of the series. The hero takes on the role of paternal savior, that major figure in eighties cinema who forms the narrative core of Spielberg's work. The father, or his surrogate, must prevail.[21]

The nineties films perform some interesting alterations to these patterns. Both *Jurassic Park* and *The Lost World* reflect—as do many contemporary films trying to escape conservative rituals—the imperfections of the domestic scene. In the first film, a new family made up of the unmarried Drs. Grant and Stattler and the grandchildren of the Jurassic theme park's builder, join together to fight the marauding beasts. In *The Lost World*, the beasts enter the domestic sphere directly, as a dinosaur invades San Diego, seen by a child from his suburban bedroom window. But these two films, which seem an attempt to join elements of *Jaws*, *Close Encounters*, and the Indiana Jones movies, founder on the narrative level. They seem insecure about point of view (though less so in *The Lost World*, where a definable set of villains emerges), and more concerned with their secondary, or perhaps meta-narrative, the one about the spectacle of the digital mise-en-scène into which their creative energies are absorbed.

The later "serious" films, in broadening their reach to large historical subjects, mute spectacle somewhat and find sometimes odd ways of restating the patriarchal imperative. *Amistad* is precisely about the loss of familial protection. No comprehension of tribal life is available to Spielberg's American, middle-class imagination. We do know that slaves are ripped from their tribal homes; they rebel, break their shackles, and take over the slave ship they are traveling on. Caught, they are thrown into an American jail, unable to communicate with anyone. And they are saved by a clearly defined patriarchal figure, Anthony Hopkins's John Quincy Adams, who himself has two "child" surrogates in Joadson the abolitionist and Baldwin the lawyer. In the climactic sequence, Adams, hoary and doddering, comes out of retirement to successfully argue Cinque's case before the Supreme Court. It is a painful sequence because it appears to thrust onto the narrative a pater-ex-machina, the crusty old white man (a stereotype that has become a major figure of ideological overcompensation in both film and television—defying feminist arguments by showing that unpleasant white men are still good "inside"), descending to save the confused, oppressed Africans. The same situation forms the narrative premise in *Schindler's List*, where the Jews, analogous to *Amistad*'s Africans, are reduced to helpless gratitude before Schindler, who, learning compassion against his worst nature, reaches through the Nazi hierarchy to save a few people to work in his factories.

Saving Private Ryan presents a different kind of problem. The war genre—following closely on the ideological imperatives of the military itself—demands that men leave their families to form homosocial groups. The genre must work against the conventions of domesticity and paternal protection, replacing it with an all-male hierarchy in which individual heroism is either set against or absorbed into the work of a harmonious group. In the war film, the domestic scene is only imagined; it is what the men are fighting to preserve. Therefore, *Ryan* is the rare Spielberg film in which heroism is spread around and where the righteous do not immediately prevail. No fatherly figures are available within the narrative proper (though we have a glimpse of one in General Marshall). But these figures *must* exist in Spielberg's universe, which cannot reach steady state without a family and a guardian male. Captain Miller, a schoolteacher, is insufficient to assume the paternal role and therefore is given the status of moral guide, pushing his men along the road to find the lost brother and kill Germans. Other paternal, familial units emerge at the margins.

The film's framing narrative shows an old Ryan with his family at Captain Miller's graveside. The son has become father to the man. Miller and his troops searched the battlefields of France to find the lost son and Miller killed as a result—a Spielbergian Christ surrogate, sacrificing himself for a larger purpose. Years later, the prodigal returns to the graveside, having become an almost apt student and the father of his savior's memory. The main narrative concludes with the dying Miller reminding Ryan to lead a good life, to "earn" the sacrifice Miller and his men have undergone to save him. It's a curious demand, but necessary because of Miller's continual need to convince his men to pursue their goal. His words indicate that all of this was done not merely to save one man, but to serve a larger moral imperative. It is one of those rare moments in which a Spielberg male is less than certain about what he has done and therefore must demand that the subject of his actions redeem them. The subject himself is less than secure. In the closing framing narrative at Miller's grave—which Ryan addresses, just as various characters played by John Wayne in John Ford movies had done—Ryan turns to his wife for confirmation that he has indeed lead a good life. "Tell me I have lead a good life. Tell me I'm a good man." In a film without women, this sudden need for a woman's validation expresses a basic male insecurity that runs through much of nineties cinema while at the same time calls for the reconstitution of the domestic scene over everything else. It is an admission, as well, that Ryan is not of heroic stature, hasn't the self-confidence of his savior, Captain Miller—whose tremulous hand indicated that his courage, too, was less than solid—and needs feminine reassurance, more accurately domestic reassurance to convince himself. The family that faces his grave at the beginning and end of the film confirms this. Ryan's calling on his wife's approval is the conduit of Miller's need and seals the domestic bond that seems, finally, what Miller's quest—initiated by General Marshall's desire that the entire Ryan family not be destroyed by the war— was all about.

The heroic male is under interrogation throughout *Saving Private Ryan*, from Miller's trembling hand to the devastating losses suffered by the troops. This film, more than anything else in the Spielberg canon, makes the viewer uncomfortable and uncertain about a secure position, about righteousness prevailing. Without the framing narrative and its female affirmation about a moral life, the film would be unremittingly bleak, with no redemption in the offing. It might have joined with *Paths of Glory* as a view of war that offers no consolation. Therefore, in addition to the framing narrative, Spielberg has to do something else, he has to turn to technological spectacle to divert the viewer into the mise-en-scène, providing aural and visual wonder and fear to make up for the moral uncertainty that very mise-en-scène creates. Through the manipulation of film stock and sound, through the creation of animated digital bullets, flying into the screen space, toward the soldiers from an unseen enemy, the viewer is given the opportunity to share the anxiety (if not the danger) of battle. Finally not so different from *Jurassic Park*, including an oncoming German tank that sounds suspiciously like a dinosaur from the earlier film, the audience is absorbed into the film's narrative space, and awe competes with despair.

The Spielbergian world is absorptive and distributive, forcing the spectator into it, obsessively replacing discontent with satisfaction, insisting that the man-child's desire for comfort and companionship is a persistent state that cannot be fulfilled in a mature, earthbound, communal environment. In the later films, the earthbound world becomes increasingly dangerous, complicating the possibilities of an individuality responsive to social needs. In fact, it tends to refuse individuality, certainly heroic individuality that is secure with its own knowledge and moral activity. Spielberg needs to fight against the potential anomie and despair caused by the lack of redemptive heroics by figuring out new ways to represent how individual acts can be done in the service of returning or bringing the self and the world back to a state of calm, protected by a strong, male figure. This is as true in *Schindler's List* as it is in *Close Encounters*. Spielberg absorbs uncertainty and fear and redistributes them into narratives in which they are replaced either by a self-effacing hero who actively engages a threatening world or by an unheroic man or man-child whose passivity is filled by an external, unearthly presence. The problem is that the process is becoming harder to represent with conviction.

In either instance, a hierarchical order is created (as it must be in melodrama) in which the subject viewing the film and the subject within the film are placed in a relationship of child to succoring adult, a relationship impossible to sustain outside the film itself. I noted that *Jaws* is very much a film of the Vietnam-Watergate period when the culture felt itself at the mercy of all manner of sharks. Spielberg's representation of political and social threats by a monster spawned in nature is itself an act that removes any responsibility for the threat, reducing the world to helpless victims of nature needing salvation. The shark has no rational motivation but merely destroys, without reason or premeditation, the least suspecting and deserving individuals. The enemy is a natural and instinctive force; no one is responsible for it. When it is destroyed, the world can be restored to a knowable and safe order—a more trustworthy order because a protecting figure is now at hand. The petty politicians of Amity (or the corrupt land developer in *Poltergeist*) have a hand in prolonging or, in the latter instance, provoking the threat. But the threat, finally, is greater than they are—a situation, paradoxically, more manageable than if it were caused by mere human agency. Heroic action may right nature and create succor. It is less than successful in dealing with the subtle machinations of corrupt adults.

If *Jaws* is a response to the cultural shocks of Vietnam and Watergate, *Close Encounters* responds to the period of transition after these events, and *E.T.* to the long night of complacency and withdrawal begun in the late seventies and continuing into the eighties. The films emerge not so much from order disrupted, as they do from a desire for a more dependable, exciting, and sustaining order than that which exists. *Close Encounters* is about patriarchy lost, about the domestic unit in decay, about the authority of the father in confusion. The job of the film is to reorder that patriarchy on a cosmic level. Mediating these actions is the paternal figure of Lacombe, who travels the world to integrate various UFO sightings and help the army prepare for the arrival of the aliens. Lacombe's paternal role is doubled: in the film he is the quiet, assured investigator and guide to the new world; but he is also François Truffaut, director of films about children and innocence, the father of Spielberg's own imagination. Truffaut appears again, by allusion, in *The Color Purple*. When Nettie teaches Celie to read by attaching pieces of paper with words on them to the objects the words name, she is doing what Truffaut's character, Itard, did to teach language to the wolf boy in *Wild Child*.

Lacombe's voyages, interspersed throughout the early part of the narrative, confirm a cultural hierarchy that assures the reigning place of white, middle-class patriarchs in the new order to be brought by the spacemen. Lacombe is wise and knowing in his quest. The people he discovers who have encountered the aliens are capable only of barely articulated awe. In India, for example, masses of people chant the music communicated to them by the aliens and point their fingers heavenward to indicate the origin of the sounds. In the United States, the army intervenes with technology and subterfuge, while "ordinary" people wait passively or, in the case of Roy and Jillian, finally resort to heroic resourcefulness to reach Lacombe at the landing site in order to convince him that Roy has been especially chosen. Jillian remains behind; her boy has gone aboard the spacecraft and now her lover will make the voyage. Only two women are among the army personnel that go aboard the ship. The aliens in that ship seem to be only males ("He's a boy," Elliott tells his sister—and reassures the viewer—about his own alien in *E.T.*). Male authority is unthreatened by the new forces that bring comfort to the earth, which comes in the form of new fathers to man. The groups that formerly represented order—the army, science, the family—dissolve in the face of the blinding light of new protection. I said that the space visitors seem to be male children; in fact the first alien figure seen is a huge, white figure hovering protectively over many small white figures. Another double paternity is formed: the aliens who will be mankind's guide and protector are in turn protected by a fathering figure. The terrifying is turned into the benign. Enormous power, demanding and receiving enormous obeisance, is so represented as to offer masculine protection to a needful child.

This affirmation of protection is repeated with greater intimacy in *E.T.* The upsets of the seventies seemed to call for large interventions. At the beginning of the Reagan era, the culture was ready for simple, uncomplicated, direct communication with an unthreatening leader. The film represents this ideological shift to a childlike dependence on a kindly patriarchal force, a solution to anxiety and insecurity repeated by many other filmmakers. To achieve its effect, *E.T.* inverts the narrative structure of *Close Encounters* while keeping its direction and purpose largely intact. The scale is smaller; the low tracking shots and oblique lights shining in the dark are less overwhelming. Yet they still signify a threat and mystery, though the threat quickly becomes detached from the aliens and attached to adult earthlings who search for the visitor. The essential mystery of the film concerns only how E.T. and Elliott will get along and survive. The child is faced with a barely understanding mother—who manages to remain ignorant of the visitor in her house for much of the early part of the film— a troublesome brother and sister (Elliott is significantly without a father) whom he must win over to his side, and scientists and government officials who want to study the creature. Spielberg creates, in effect, two aliens, Elliott and the space creature, finding their way in the troublesome adult world.

They manage through a process of total identity. I said that the initial goal of a Spielberg film is to position the spectator so securely within the narrative movement that her subjectivity is given up to that movement. More than "identifying with the characters," the viewer is made part of the imaginary complex of the fictive world, subject to its events and rhythms, his individuality suppressed into the narrative weave. E.T. doubles this process. Elliott and his alien become so close that they share experiences, to the point where, when E.T. sickens, Elliott does too, and almost dies. While the viewer cannot achieve as close a physical proximity to the fictions on the screen, she can be situated in so intense a state of longing for that proximity that, for the duration of the film at least, those fictions become the illusory fulfillment of the viewer's desire.

Earlier, I spoke about the ways in which certain films hail the spectator to them in a way that seems to counter the oedipal threat, offering a kind of dual matriarchal/patriarchal protection—sustenance, security, and power. I want to elaborate that argument here, because the narrative processes of E.T., the effect of identifying the two characters in the film and the viewer with those characters, exemplify the process better than any other film. The French psychiatrist Jacques Lacan hypothesized a moment in the development of the child that he called "the mirror phase." At this point, the child, as if seeing itself and its mother in the mirror, receives its initial notion of the self as separate being, another self who is, at the same time, not another. Because it is the reflection of the child still in the state of maternal protection, it exists in the fullness of being and security. This is the imaginary realm, a place of images whose reality are only the images themselves. For Lacan, this moment is also the beginning of sexual identity—or mis-identity. The child discovers that it either has a penis or not, that it is like its mother or its father, and with that discovery begins the desire to own the symbol of potency, a desire that allows the child to enter and become subject to the symbolic stage of language, culture, and power in degrees depending on its gender.22

E.T. is a curious working out of the Lacanian theory. The alien creature both is and is not Elliott, and it is everything Elliott wants it to be. Because Elliott's father has left him, E.T. becomes not only another self and an imaginary friend (in multiple senses of the word imaginary), but a paternal *and* maternal surrogate, even more powerful than those other matriarchal patriarchs I discussed earlier. Even more, they become mother and father to each other. E.T. has wisdom, the power of flight, and can cure a cut finger with a touch. Elliott teaches the alien human language; the alien teaches Elliott feeling and care. Each is the other's baby, each takes on the other's self, and Elliott is offered the possibility of bypassing the adult world and escaping Oedipus altogether. Their relationship offers Elliott power without the concomitant castration, the subjugation of self to other selves—to the patriarchal order—that is part of normal movement into adulthood. "I have absolute power," Elliott tells his brother before introducing him to E.T. And he maintains this power, with E.T.'s consent, until his other self—unable to return home—sickens and dies. At this point, the scientists who have been searching for the alien invade Elliott's house and threaten to return him and the viewer back to the world of male authority. These men are represented throughout the film by their flashlights piercing the dark, threatening Elliott's secret, or, in the case of the one scientist who will most sympathize with Elliott, by the keys clinking on his belt, a synecdoche marked by its phallic suggestiveness. This figure emerges as the absent male patriarch and proves to be not a threat, but a positive paternal figure, who has—like the viewer—concern and envy for the relationship between Elliott and E.T.23

The fortunate child of fantasy has complete control over his own oedipal process, can enter into the world of power and differentiation with his subjectivity and control intact. The viewer is not in such a fortunate position. I said that *E.T.* doubles the process of identification. Elliott and E.T. merge as father/mother/son, boy/best friend, self/other self. The viewer merges with the film, gives up his or her subjectivity to it. If Elliott proclaims complete power over his relationship with the alien, so Spielberg proclaims his power over the viewer. The film becomes the viewer's mirror. But whereas in the Lacanian mirror phase (to quote Christian Metz), "The child is both in [the mirror] and in front of it," the mirror of the cinema "returns us everything but ourselves, because we are wholly outside it. . . . The spectator is absent from the screen *as perceived*, but also (the two things inevitably go together) present there and even 'all-present' as *perceiver*. At every moment I am in the film by my look's caress."[24] The perceiver's gaze caresses the cinematic mirror and, in the case of a Spielberg film, is caressed in turn. *E.T.* does everything to make the viewer forget that he or she is absent from the screen by sealing the viewer's gaze within the anti-oedipal fantasy of the film's two main figures. With the mutual caress, the viewer is returned to a childlike state and enters the imaginary world.

312

"I don't know how to feel," Elliott says as E.T. dies. Within the fiction, Elliott becomes dependent on the creature; outside the fiction, the viewer is dependent for his or her feelings on the filmmaker's manipulation of the fictional characters and the viewer's response to them. Spielberg makes us feel what he wants. He is the ultimate, arbitrating patriarch and knows, much better than his characters do, that the relationship to the imaginary cannot go on indefinitely. Elliott himself is forced to enter into the next and final stage of development, Lacan's symbolic order, the realm of language, of difference, of phallic power, of the need to position the self among other selves within shifting strings of that power. After all, that self was threatened by E.T., and while Spielberg seeks to assure the protection of the self, he does not wish its dissolution. The narcissistic identification of child and space creature is finally broken by the latter's need to go home or die and by the former's need to come home to the paternal voice, provided by the friendly scientist. E.T. is resurrected by the promise of home and Elliott confronts the adult world once more, helping the creature engineer his escape. "This is reality," Elliott tells his friends who ask if E.T. couldn't just beam up to his ship.

The escape itself is a scene that at once recalls the Freudian imagery of infantile dreams of flying and the last sequence of Vittorio De Sica's *Miracle in Milan*, where the poor take off for heaven. The police and the government in pursuit, E.T. leads the children in flight into the forest where his spaceship and comrades will come to take him home. With mother and friendly scientist present (suggesting the reformation of the earthly domestic unit), E.T. makes his separation from Elliott. The imaginary disappears and Elliott is left in the world of men. The viewer has considerably more trouble leaving the imaginary of the screen. The shower of tears that clouds the gaze at the end of the film also clouds the ability to move away from the fiction, which lingers in the imagination in the form of memory, of consumer goods, in journalistic references that may be consumed over and over. The narrative may have permitted E.T. to go home; its ideological effect keeps the viewer in a state of rootless want and yearning. The fiction had to provide separation in order to close itself, but in its closure it opens the gap of dissatisfaction with the mundane and creates desire for even more images that pretend to close that gap.

Spielberg manipulates the space between his texts and reality itself, creating melodramatic desire within his films and between them. The desires he satisfies within the films return again when they are over and may be satisfied by re-seeing the film, or waiting until the next one. An enviable circuit of exchange is created in which the viewer is always ready to purchase more assurance, more satisfaction, while the product is manufactured both to satisfy and create greater need. Conventional melodrama closes down its narrative by insisting that desire must be sublimated and redirected. "Don't let's ask for the moon. We have the stars," Bette Davis tells Paul Henried in *Now Voyager*, when they realize their love must remain platonic. But Spielberg is off in another direction. He affirms what the culture has always suspected, that gratification can only be achieved within the imaginary realm of film—his films, which promise moon, stars, men, and gods who will save us. Jean-François Lyotard states that the old narratives are no longer of use in the postmodern world.[25] Spielberg finds that the problem can be overcome by absorbing the world into his narratives, creating a melodramatic oedipal machine, delivering protection, yet denying what it seems to offer, keeping the viewer attached to it at all times, threatening/promising loss whenever the attachment is broken. The machine generates surplus value for its manufacturer and delirium, satisfaction of desire, and a need for more from its spectators. Promising fulfillment of the dreams of childhood, the machine places everyone who comes in contact with it in the position of a child under the control of the father who gives, takes away, promises to give again if the child reacts correctly.

But, as I said, this process grows more difficult when Spielberg tackles "history," those events that occur to people in the world that too often resist desire, resolution, and redemption. It would seem that the so-called "serious" films, particularly in the nineties, might deviate from this pattern, and they do, except that Spielberg turns deviation into deviousness to maintain a semblance—a simulacrum—to the original simulacrum of his protected worlds. Even as far back as *The Color Purple*, the patriarch exercises his full power in a film that *should* offer liberation from old patriarchal repressions. But, it only restates them with such force that the initial subversive act is itself subverted and the old order reclaimed. Alice Walker's novel, the film's source, is a strong statement of female strength and community, an affirmation that women can place themselves in the center of knowing and acting. The film offers moments as strong as the novel; indeed, Celie's denouncing of her husband and proclamation of her freedom is a powerful feminist statement. But the statement is ultimately retracted, rephrased, and finally refuted in a film that cannot break from older cinematic tradition or the tradition Spielberg himself has developed during his own career.

The Color Purple does tone down its spectacle and resituates its fantasy, transferring longings for protection and security from the realms of space visitors into a world of rural houses, fields, and poor towns reminiscent of older Hollywood films about blacks in the South: Cabin in the Sky, The Green Pastures, Pinky. The influence of John Ford on the film is consuming, a force that helps pull it inward toward convention and the conservative reclamation of its liberal project. In The Color Purple, Ford's influence is profound enough to affect the very compositional structure of the film. When Spielberg closes his narrative with Nettie's return from Africa, Celie, Shug Avery, and others of the household are composed on and around the porch of Celie's house, gazing at the approaching group, exactly as Ford composed similar family groupings around house fronts in, for example, Fort Apache and The Searchers. He repeats the composition in Saving Private Ryan when Mrs. Ryan is told of her sons' deaths.

But Ford was always concerned with issues of larger community, as well as the individual and the family. Spielberg is not, at least until the nineties. Community always lingers around the peripheries of his films, and issues of order are either on a personal or universal level, never involved with the body politic, even in Schindler's List, a film that should be about the body politic. Ford looked to adjust his individual figures into the movement of American history, seen from a conservative perspective—but at least seen. In The Color Purple, a film about a black community in the first half of the century, Spielberg shows almost no interest in the political, economic, or ideological forces at work at the time, only the personal and the domestic ideologies of the eighties transferred back into the fictional realm.

Amistad, situated in the late eighteenth-century, displaces political and economic concerns with the legal, turning a difficult, painful subject into a courtroom melodrama. The narrative of The Color Purple, despite the brutality and emotional deprivation that occurs within it, is a melodrama set in pastoral realm—with a few brief visits to the city—strangely cut off from the rest of the world. When the brutality is ended and emotional deprivation curtailed with Celie's liberation and the return of her sister, the pastoral realm enfolds everything, and the film becomes an idyll of regenerated souls. Walker's novel offers Spielberg and his screenwriter, Menno Meyjes, an opportunity to evade larger problems, for it creates an almost mythical southern, rural landscape in which economic and community problems do not seem to exist. But this is countered by the fact that, in Walker's fiction, black poverty is a given, understood by its pervasive presence. Within that poverty, the central female characters are clearly defined and clearly aware of their difference, of their being black and not white, female and not male. Spielberg's fiction is strangely lacking in awareness of this difference. To be sure, his characters are black, but their rural accents, as well as their appearance and surroundings, are more authentically movie Negro than southern black. Walker's characters break out of stereotypes; Spielberg's attempt to do so, only to be reclaimed. Spielberg dissolves Walker's fiction into the conventional patterns of the only thing he knows, movies, and the only ideological patterns with which he feels comfortable, patterns of return to domestic order controlled by men. On its most profound level, *The Color Purple* is an effective, authoritative narrative that confirms the necessity of male-dominated structures of power.

Whatever measures of freedom the characters attain must, as in any melodrama, be contained. After her break with her husband, Celie leaves with Shug and becomes successful in a business of her own devising (she manufactures trousers that fit both men and women). But she must be brought home—quite literally, as she discovers she has inherited her father's house. Mr., his life ruined by Celie's newfound energy, must also be brought back, in fact reinserted within the film's central grouping. The film's ideological project could not be successfully closed were he left out of the general reclamation that ends it. Mr. must be recuperated not only into the narrative, but into that greater narrative fantasy of mid-eighties America in which families are returned to their proper order. Alice Walker offers a quiet return of Mr. into the fold of decent human behavior. He learns to look after himself; he and Celie talk gently with each other. Spielberg eschews quiet reconciliation for melodramatic reversal. The patriarchy must be somehow reestablished. But Mr. cannot be the figure who offers the reconciliation; he has been too brutal and Celie's break with him too complete. Were they to come back together, the narrative movement would be not merely reversed but broken. Instead he must be reconciled into a more general scheme, and the narrative allows this to occur by making him an agent for the recuperative process and then allowing him a share in the spaces of reunion.

The process begins with a shot of him smiling, rocking on his front porch, which is inserted into the movement of Shug to her father. Placed by the editing into the middle of this specific return of the father, he is joined into the general act of reclamation, which he facilitates by arranging with the U.S. Immigration Service for the return of Nettie and Celie's children. When that reunion occurs, when the entire family, which was broken up first by Celie's stepfather and then by Mr., come to each other and embrace, Mr. is again edited into the process so that he is sutured into the harmonious space. Celie and Nettie run to each other in the fields and embrace; Celie meets her children. Intercut with these events are shots of Sofia, Harpo, and Shug, smiling happily, observing the proceedings from the front of Celie's house. At one point, Shug turns, and, as if she were looking at Mr., Spielberg cuts to a shot in which the camera dollies in on him in the fields. He is looking downward with contentment (the dolly-in, that favored camera movement I described earlier, does not represent uncertainty or threat here, but a dynamic move to proximity with the character, a reduction of space between him and the viewer). There is another shot of Shug followed with yet another of Mr., this time seen from a distance in the fields, walking off. Finally, as Celie and Nettie clap their hands against the sun, Mr. can be seen walking by behind them.

Although unable narratively to reenter Celie's newfound happiness, he is composed within it visually, and in turn helps to compose it. His presence that was so violent and destructive before is now the necessary part of closure. The matter is not simply one of a happy ending, of a fairy tale in which all figures, evil and good, are reconciled in the end, but of an inability to cast out the male figure. *The Color Purple* cannot allow its female figures a space of their own and insists that the male figure—Shug's father and Celie's husband—be present and part of a transcendent reordering of freedom back into the domestic unit. Many uncertainties are solved inside and outside the narrative. Any fears that black women—any women—may proclaim their independence from patriarchal structures are soothed; any notion that independence may exist apart from the confines of a happy, loving family with a controlling male figure is annulled.

All this is raised to a another level of complexity, though not a different level of closure, in *Amistad*. The recuperation process is more difficult here, because Spielberg is dealing with an "actual" event in a much earlier period. But the historical aspect is the least troublesome. Spielberg, as much as Oliver Stone, has the right to narrate history according to his own insights. More difficult is the necessity of dealing with human—as opposed to prehistoric reptilian or extraterrestrial—otherness. Cinque and his people are outside the context of Western culture and consciousness. At first, Spielberg can deal with this otherness only by seeing the Africans as primitive in an elemental sense. He visualizes them as primal energy. During the opening sequences of the film, they are seen close up, confined, wet, dark, and struggling. Cinque, in a crude proposition of Christ-like characteristics, pulls a spike out of his chains with his bare hands. Later, having lost their case, they become unruly, reverting to their "primitive" state, setting fires, photographed in dark silhouette against the flames. Primal and childlike, conscious enough to revolt against appalling conditions, but then thrust into the slave-holding West and mutual incomprehension, these figures seem as imprisoned by cultural and movie stereotypes as by the conditions set forth for them in this particular film.

317

The solution to this looming racist dilemma comes in a most unfortunate way, by means of the old colonialist fantasy of conversion. In the center of the film, when the slaves are awaiting the verdict of their first trial, in a sequence that is intercut with images of their judge praying in church, two of the prisoners discuss a book on Christianity, understanding the images, not the words. One of them, Yamba, has learned the basics of the story of Jesus and the resurrection. He even identifies with the Jews: "Their people suffered more than ours . . . their lives were full of suffering." (His words are translated in subtitles.) These poor, confused Africans decide that the Jews of the Old Testament had it worse than they do! They are learning not merely Christianity, but humility. They are becoming what we should be. This long sequence is so wrongheaded that even the darkness of the mise-en-scène, the low, close camera, and the fine music of John Williams can barely control its cloying gratuitousness. I'm not arguing here whether or not it was possible for prisoners from another culture and religion to "discover" Christianity. Historically, African slaves in America combined their native religions with Christianity to create a vibrant spiritual practice and aesthetic. But what goes wrong in this sequence is the sentimentalizing and infantalizing of these characters who "naturally" discover the rightness of the Christ story by looking at pictures, suggesting, through intercutting, that they and the judge are receiving heavenly grace. It is almost as if Spielberg were aware of and parodying Althusser's definitions of how ideologies work, insinuating that the obviousness of white Christian culture will "hail" everyone into its obviousnesses. Postcolonial studies have demonstrated how Westernizing, Christianizing events distorted and mutated cultures. Spielberg, though, seems to have no alternatives. He believes that the Africans have to be humanized, which, for him, means brought into the Western, white, Christian fold. He is quite successful in at least part of this project, when he demonstrates the Africans' sense of outrage at the inhumanity of their condition, especially in the film's most moving scene, when Cinque rises up and demands that what he wants is to be free. Though a desire for freedom is not the sole property of Western Christianity. But this is not enough. Spielberg has to show that they are, beneath it all, *obviously* "just like us." Inside every non-Christian is a Christian waiting to get out.

A sequence like this occurs because Spielberg can't quite escape the necessities of convention and will never consciously escape the demand of dominant cultural beliefs. His popularity depends on them; his imagination can't move beyond them. The filmmaker we are dealing with is by now a creation of his own renown and a function both of his success and his films. These films, whether about sharks, dinosaurs, aliens, slaves, or Jews headed for the gas chamber are all based on certain givens of cinematic form and content, which are themselves guided by unshakable beliefs about what an audience wants or needs to see. And Spielberg believes that, to reach that audience, to always "get them," he must, no matter how intractable the material may be to such a treatment, calm us with a promise of security within a fatherly embrace. This is nowhere more obvious than in *Schindler's List*, a film whose ostensible subject, the attempt of the Germans to kill all the Jews in Europe, takes on nothing less than the most serious, horrendous event in the twentieth century.

The history of films about Nazism and the extermination of the Jews is a curious one, filled with works as exploitative as they are analytic. Some believe the best way to capture this particular history is through a documentary style. Claude Lanzmann's *Shoah* (1985) is much admired for its straightforward recording of the memories of still-living victims. Marcel Ophuls, in *The Sorrow and the Pity* (1970), *The Memory of Justice* (1976), and *Hotel Terminus* (1987), goes beyond memory to an ironic probing of individual acts, self-deception, and the surprise revelation of terrible events and even worse people. The best "documentary" of the event is not that at all: Alain Resnais's *Night and Fog* (1955) is a kind of visual essay, a recollection of a nightmare that combines a bizarre beauty of a camera slowly tracking through the remains of a concentration camp with the always appalling images of heaps of corpses. Fiction films about fascism cover a wide range of insight with an equally wide range of authority. Many go for mundane analysis of individual personality quirks, usually based on sexual difference, as if a homophobic depiction of fascism can account for a race's barbarism. Bernardo Bertolucci's *The Conformist* (1971) seems to take this tack, but is more subtly concerned with a character who becomes a fascist because he *thinks* he's homosexual and seeks out "normality" with the Italian fascist party. *The Conformist*, more important, is about seeing and blindness, a film of clear hallucinatory images, hypnotic in its insistence that fascism was partly created from confusion of subject and object, an ideological imperative to violently enforce potency and forgetfulness over the despair of self-knowledge, and the willingness to subdue the self under the worst instincts of a culture. Joseph Losey's *Mr. Klein* (1977), like *The Conformist*, starts by observing an individual character. This character, like Oskar Schindler, is a non-Jew. But Losey takes another route. Instead of turning Klein into savior of the Jews, he gives the character a Jewish dopplegänger, an imaginative way to let the character see himself Jewish as if in a mirror: pursued and fleeing. The character and his other merge in a depiction of a roundup of Jews in Paris that is hair-raising in its representation of the collective right-wing history of mass oppression and destruction.

In *Schindler's List*, Spielberg wants to concentrate on the larger events of the Nazis' extermination program in Poland, and for the most part he does this well. Filming in a richly textured, carefully composed black-and-white that recalls the films of the Italian neorealist movement, the great period of Eastern European filming in the sixties and early seventies, and even the imagery of Welles, he achieves proximity and distance at the same time.[26] The viewer is asked to observe and respond to the shocks of the brutality against Jewish victims without being undone by them. Spielberg allows a play between comprehending the violence and feeling brutalized by it. Revulsion would not serve the purpose of comprehension, and without the latter no understanding can ensue. Partly due to the distancing effect of the visual construction, and partly because for the most part he refuses to individualize the Jews, we are offered the sense of a terrifying visitation on an entire race. His careful intercutting of large movements and individual actions and reactions (most obvious in the sequence of the girl in the red coat, but more subtly carried throughout the film) maintains a balance between figure and mass. This method constitutes a response to an interesting belief on the part of some scholars that the Nazi extermination cannot be represented, that its intensity and horror defy being fictionalized and shown. Attempting such a representation would only trivialize the event and impose on the memory of those who suffered something that is not possible to be shown. No mere images can relate the enormity of what happened.[27] There is a ring of sentimentality and exclusion to this idea and a kind of reductive notion of the power of images to move emotion, enhance memory, and instruct future generations. That the extermination of the Jews can and has been represented badly, exploitatively, is undeniable; that it cannot or should not be represented is almost a guarantee that it will be forgotten.

Spielberg's representation proceeds with just enough reticence so that the horror and enormity of events are carried in image after image of incredible despair and utterly random violence committed on helpless people. He is able to encapsulate the whole process of genocide in the overwhelming image of the cattle train with its cargo of women entering the gates of Auschwitz, human ash falling like snow from the giant chimney of the furnaces; lights cutting through the night. The grotesque monumentality of the images diminishes the human figure as the Nazis themselves diminished it to ashes.

Problems occur when Spielberg does attempt to individualize and create melodrama. Amon Goeth, the S.S. commandant, is too unrelievedly brutal. He is a psychopath, and psychopathology is too easy a way to dismiss Nazism and its adherents. As historians have shown—and as the current history of genocidal nationalism proves—either psychopathology infects an entire culture, or, more likely, ideological elements are so distorted by dreams of power, authority, and manufactured hatred and convictions of necessity, that the majority of a culture gets caught up in the act of killing the demonized other.[28] There were psychotic Germans, to be sure; but Nazism cannot be reduced simply to psychosis. There are scenes in *Schindler's List* of German officers in a hysterical frenzy of killing that are, perhaps, more accurate than Goeth's unrelenting murderousness, but also bring with them the old Hollywood representations of Nazis as sophisticated gangsters, simply cruel and cunning. Interestingly, it is in *Saving Private Ryan* that Spielberg moves away from stereotype. The German soldier, captured by Ryan's men, who convinces them to let him go and then turns up again in the final attack and stabs the Jewish member of the battalion in the neck, slowly, almost soothingly, exposes a complex figure—very much a mirror of his American enemies—anxious to save his own life, ready and willing to take the life of his enemies.

Schindler's narrative, however, demands Goeth to be present as the foil to Schindler, the redeemed Christian. Their dialogues together offer simple confrontations of stupid evil versus the growing compassion of a clever man. The scenes where Schindler uses Goeth's fantasy of power to convince him to spare a Jew flatten the film's argument by reducing large historical movements to personal manipulation. Spielberg wants us to understand the heroism of one German who saved some Jews. At the same time, he wants the viewer to see the huge, disgusting canvas of the slaughter. He cannot only do the latter, because the film would be like a documentary and, without a drama, would not draw a large audience. He cannot make the drama too complex, because that would endanger the emotional bond that Spielberg must build between audience and film. Depth and ambiguity are not acceptable qualities of popular cultural artifacts. The result is an interesting compromise that doesn't quite manage to work. Through composition and editing of his images, through the power of their contents, he creates some emotional distance. In the midst of these images he creates the drama of a Nazi philanderer who understands how to use cold business practices to cheat some other Nazis out of their prisoners. The result is a controlled movement of viewer position, beckoning her into the drama, removing her to a distance by the appalling violence that is the film's essential mise-en-scène.

But where is the voice of the Jews? We see them as victims; we see a few of them saved. They get a representative, individualized in the character of Itzhak Stern, whose melancholic humility before Schindler creates an appropriate indication of self-possession, comprehension, and a certain cunning that prods his boss to further action and self-realization. He is not as simplified a character as Goeth, but he is one voice only. In a peculiar way, he is the only reverse shot of the subject of the Nazis' destruction. Of course Spielberg shows us the persecuted singly and, especially, in groups; he shows us different classes, different hierarchies; but only through Stern do the people actually get a voice, a face, and agent. And he, like Goeth, is present to help along Schindler's drama of redemption.

I've talked at length about Spielberg's obsession with the creation of the white, male savior, a figure who appears in almost all his films. But this obsession is not appropriate in the historical moment he is representing in *Schindler's List*, because in actuality individual acts of heroism on the part of Christians during this period were small; and the salvation of the Jews was retarded to the very last minute of victory in the East by the Russians. Stern's clever humility and Schindler's capitalist largesse—his bartering with his fellow Nazis to supply them with goods if they will allow him cheap Jewish labor—only serve the purpose of a kind of drama of forgetting, while the images around them force historical remembrance. The moral that

Spielberg seems to want to generate, that bad men can become good, that we should all save our fellow sufferers, is as vague and out of place as is his moral's exemplum. He creates a series of contradictions that finally causes an extraordinary collapse of narrative, imagery, and history in a sequence that is matched only by *Amistad*'s Africans-who-discover-Christianity in its dereliction of responsibility.

The Jews' arrival at Auschwitz is a frenzy of dark cruelty, climaxed with the leading of a group of women—who Schindler had "saved" but who got sent to the camp anyway—into the showers. Before this, the sequence is intercut—in the standard Hollywood mode—with Schindler jumping into his car and racing to the camp to save the women. Any viewer with any knowledge of the concentration camps knows what the "showers" mean, and Spielberg depends on it. These women are being led to their death. The camera moves across and with the women as, first, their hair is shaved from their heads and tossed into bins of the hair of other victims. They are made to strip naked, and the viewer is offered a brief but unmistakably erotic-sadistic gaze at their bodies. The viewer is given the point of view of the Nazis, in a horror-film convention (that Spielberg all but invented in *Jaws*) that is out of place here, cynical and abusive. A woman is shown briefly caressing her child, and the group is finally led into the showers, a handheld camera following them, again as if from the point of view of the killer in a slasher film. The women huddle in this cavernous dark space, punctuated by glaring lights on the wall. The doors are closed, and the camera, like Norman Bates's eye, moves to the peephole to see more. There is a cut back to the interior of the shower room. The lights are turned out and the women scream in terror. The camera picks up agonized faces and groups of women moving hysterically. It pans up to the shower heads and back to the women staring upward in expectation. Water, not Zyclon B, pours down on them.

What are we to make of this? In the narrative itself, there is no indication that Schindler was the immediate cause of the women's salvation. Later, in a grim sequence in which the characters' eyes are in shadow as they bargain for human lives, Schindler bribes the camp official to buy back the women—the official insisting on calling the inmates "units," warning Schindler, "You shouldn't get stuck on names." But this comes after the fact. No explanation is offered for the women's escape from being gassed, except implicitly to allow Schindler to continue as the saving father. But why put the viewer through the terrifying expectation of their death, especially with the manipulations of cross-cutting and the nudity that turns us into voyeurs? Is this, again, merely a repetition of the old horror-film technique of building tension only to have it relieved when nothing horrible is discovered?

I'm afraid that this is exactly what Spielberg has on his mind: a moment to peak and then relieve viewer anxiety and mitigate the horror he has been at such pains to represent. The sequence occurs near the end of a very long, very grim movie and closure soon must be reached, closure that, in Spielberg's hands, must include a harmonious gathering of a new family. "Schindler's Jews," like the women in the gas chamber, are saved. A Russian officer sets them free, and, at the end, in an odd and effective act of reflexiveness set in Israel, and in color, "Schindler's Jews" join with the actors who played them in the film to lay stones on Oskar's grave.

Is it simply in Spielberg's aesthetic and commercial nature to please his audience, even at the cost of credibility or the even higher cost of confirming the psychotic fantasies of Holocaust deniers?[29] Where Oliver Stone sees history as a struggle between various powerful entities that must be brought into visible presence through montage in order to be understood, Spielberg views it as a struggle between victims—whom Spielberg tends to infantilize— and white saviors, seen in large compositions that define their relationships to one another. Both victims and savior are visible and in an unequal state of dependence: their visibility depends on their dependence, and triumph is always guaranteed, no matter how proscribed, no matter how much it defaults to our ideology of victimization that demands that we all desire to be saved even when saviors are nowhere to be found, a situation almost guaranteed to create stasis.

The process seems to be reversed in *Saving Private Ryan*. No one wins— at least among the group of soldiers who are the focus of the narrative. There is a hope that a larger morality of commitment and growth will prevail, and the film attempts to turn the tables on the war genre by allowing a fairly thorough and brutal destruction of the men involved, forcing the audience, through a variety of technical means mentioned earlier, to share the anxiety of the dying while awestruck by its spectacle. Where *Schindler's List* attempts a bit of distance between the viewer and the horrors represented on the screen, *Saving Private Ryan*, in theme-park style, gives the audience a ride through hails of bullets, men's limbs being blown off, and sounds that combine the whistling of armaments through the air, the thud of bullets meeting flesh, and the screams of the wounded and dying. Unlike Peckinpah's *The Wild Bunch*, with its perverse choreographed grace of violent death, *Saving Private Ryan* asks the viewer to experience a deep unease and trepidation that, the film believes, parallels the battlefield experience. But why? The film itself is not antiwar, and Spielberg does not hesitate in depicting Nazi soldiers as brutal as their brothers in *Schindler's List*, but with no Schindler emerging to save anyone. Salvation here results from the going through with it: Miller's commitment to find Ryan no matter what the cost; Ryan's discovery of the meaning of commitment. But this suggests that there *is* the old Spielberg pattern here. Ryan is the "victim" of the war, his brothers slain, the fatherly General Marshall in Washington ordering him returned to his mother. Miller is Marshall's emissary, a Christ-like figure who dies so that Ryan can discover grace and grow into the proper family man, and continue his redemption. The frame narrative of *Saving Private Ryan* creates the same kind of stasis as does all of *Schindler's List*. Producing in his audience a desire to be actor and acted on, savior and saved, Spielberg creates passivity: the longing gaze at the spectacle on the screen.

The redemptive event that so obsesses Spielberg and American cinema in general achieves a number of results: it provides narrative closure without having to reach any definitive conclusions; it totally evades politics and history; it gives men an excuse for their behavior; and, most obviously, it hails the redeemed character (and presumably the spectator) into the ideologies of testing, heroism, love, marriage, and family—without the audience having to act on anything but their ability to look at the screen. The various images of family in Spielberg's films—their formation and reformation under male leadership—are used to purchase emotion at the expense of analyzing alternatives or examining the details of history, which becomes spectacle that confirms power and hierarchy at the expense of communal action. "Spectacle demands our attention," writes Dana Polan. It is "a command to 'look here' that needs no cognitive assent other than the initial fact of looking. The specific content of a spectacle is only a very small part of its attraction. . . . Spectacle offers an imagistic surface of the world as a strategy of containment against any depth of involvement with that world."[30]

But something, of course, must be contained. In all of Spielberg's films, the promise of regeneration and redemption, of social, personal, political change is contained within the spectacular pleasure of ideological assent. The viewer buys the commodity of spectacle and is repaid by exciting images that offer the dangers of subversion rendered harmless by the affirmation of secure convention. Since the spectacle's command to look is by definition a patriarchal one (because American cinema is part of the general discourse of male power, and commands are part of that discourse), the viewer is assured that what is looked at will affirm the secure, known discourse of the culture at large. Narrative images of home and safety, of protecting fathers and securing families, are a part of that discourse, which has turned them from social, psychological realities into consumer goods, packaged as exciting narratives and sold with the promise that their purchase will assure contentment and an appropriate place in the cultural imaginary.

Terry Eagleton nicely describes the shift of "family" from its reality as a refuge from the public sphere into a commodity whose purchase offers validation of one's place within that sphere. "Mass culture," he writes, "to some degree displaces the family as the arena in which needs and desires are negotiated, and indeed progressively penetrates the family itself."

> In the classical public sphere, private experience provided the very basis of public association: participants encountered each other precisely as private citizens, and the subjective autonomy of each was the very structure of their social discourse. The "intimate" realm of the family and household was at once a refuge from this world, and one matrix of its modes of subjecthood. In late capitalism, privatization becomes the dissolution, not the enabling condition, of public association; it is at once the effect of a real separation between family and society—of the absence of a public sphere which might mediate between them—and, paradoxically, of that deprivatization of the family brought about by the absorption of some of its traditional functions into the state, which maroons the family with little beyond its affective and consumptional experience. The family remains in part a refuge from civil society, nurturing vital impulses unfulfilled by it; but since it is also ceaselessly penetrated by commodity culture, this potentially positive arena of the personal is continually caught up with forms of privatization which atomize, serialize and disconnect. At the same time, the forms of public *association* of the traditional bourgeois sphere are replaced with an ideologically powerful *homogenization,* an *ersatz* sociality which is little more than the leveling effect of the commodity.[31]

"Privatization" is the process of removing the larger offerings of protection to the community, of permitting all spheres of activity to be turned into commodities and entered into the balance sheets of exchange. "The family" has become one of these commodities, fetishized, sentimentalized, and gutted of substance in political discourse, sold on television and in film as something viewers must desire, that they might in fact be able to own if they purchase its images and cultivate them with their own financial and moral capital. The family is no longer a refuge, but a command and a judgment—a law of the patriarch. Spielberg's spectacles demand that we look at the kindly statement of these laws, that we permit ourselves to be dissociated from reality by the promise of a private realm where reality will never impinge. Like all consumer products, they promise to soothe fears and satisfy desires. They complete a circuit of demand with a ready supply of promise. The terrors of the world remain untouched by them; our understanding of these terrors is short-circuited by the ease with which the films overcome them. The subject is personally privatized and reconstituted by spectacle that can push the world aside and replace it with an imaginary realm willingly consumed.

In the last decade of the twentieth century, the need to push the world aside became stronger as its complex realities made the conservative ideal of the private less easy to manage or even to believe. The rash of serial-killer films kept reminding audiences (as Hitchcock had done in previous decades) that the security of the private was an illusion and that violence had no easy definition. Terror of all kinds, we learned, is always near. One of these films, David Fincher's *Seven*, took a modernist turn, depicting a world so dark and broken that destruction of the domestic was both inevitable and logical. Jonathan Demme's *Silence of the Lambs* was more upbeat in its assessment, taking a comforting perspective by doubling its components. Two serial killers, one a psychotic transsexual, the other a cannibal rendered fascinating by his sophistication. Two FBI investigators, one a fatherly teacher, the other a female novice. The cannibal shares the role of paternal guide with the teacher, while the novice is redeemed from her childhood fears and the anger that is a rightful component of her gender. The "bad" serial killer, whose gender trouble is represented as truly threatening, is killed as the novice makes her transition to master. The cannibal is redeemed because he suffers for his sins (which are too outrageous to be taken seriously) and because he recognizes the novice's virtues. The mise-en-scène of *Seven* is unremittingly dark and sinister; even the desert of its final sequence is a place of dark threat and ultimate aloneness. *Silence of the Lambs* concludes in the cheerful chaos of the Third World, where the cannibal disappears in the crowd to feast on his tormentor. *Silence of the Lambs* plays, in postmodern fashion, with all the visual gags of the horror and police-chase film, turning many of its sequences into operatic tableaux. One may leave *Seven* upset, but *Silence of the Lambs* creates so many possible subjectives and responses, so many visual constructions and familiar editorial devices and fatherly care that there is finally more pleasure than terror and a suggestion that evil may coexist comfortably with good so long as they don't transgress agreeable gender and sexual borders.

Spike Lee's *Summer of Sam* (1999) took a different route. The film is less interested in the serial killer as a fearsome but undeniably fascinating aberration of the culture than as an extension of it, as one kind of difference or otherness. *Summer of Sam* is about a range of social, asocial, sexual, and ethnic differences, of which the Son of Sam is only a part. It attempts a huge palette of a moment and a variety of events that are internal and external, true and fictional, and that do what so few films are capable of, move out of the private and into the public realm.

Most of the action and science-fiction films we spoke of earlier have taken the more conventional route. If "traditional" families are impossible to represent in contemporary films, then alternative associations that reflect the old fantasies in another guise will maintain an audience faced, in the fiction, as in their own lives, by seemingly insuperable odds. Oedipal odds! In Jerry Bruckheimer's *Armageddon*—among the most spectacular of the nineties digitally composed films—Bruce Willis's Harry Stamper saves the world (though not Paris and some Third World cities) and his daughter by sacrificing himself. He is redeemed by his heroism and by passing on his patrimony to his daughter's lover. Meanwhile, governance of the operation that saves the world is supervised by the calm, suffering, faithful NASA director, Dan Truman, all self-possession, like his namesake. He shares this calm, fatherly assurance with the African-American president in *Armageddon*'s sister film about killer asteroids, Mimi Leder's *Deep Impact*. Fathers at any cost, embedded in spectacle that assures us with its own self-assured mastery of the visual, which in turn assures us that male mastery will prevail. If the family cannot last in the world, no matter how hard filmmakers and right-wing politicians fight to preserve its mythology, then an alternative mythology of male redemption—the reassurance that the protective father will reemerge from the bad boy to take its place—will.

Few films have countered this process. Todd Solondz's *Happiness* happily states that fathers of any kind cannot function except by passing down their dysfunction and misery to their children. The wonder of *Happiness* is its apparent refusal to judge. Its suburban characters are not merely moral monsters, they are adorable moral monsters: despicable and completely within the realm of common experience, viewed with understanding and,

328

if not compassion, at least comprehension. Gary Ross's *Pleasantville* (1998), on the other hand, takes the radical step of questioning the convention of the family altogether. The film gently, quietly dismantles the conservative mythos of "family values" and a constricted knowledge of the world by celebrating imagination, reading, art, sexuality, the breaking of the usual cultural bounds.

But it is almost alone in this. The need to conserve has been prominent in American film since the beginning of the studio period, and at the end of the twentieth century it seems still to have no alternatives. Film recognizes that the old ideas are worn out and so restates them in different configurations. The strong father and compliant woman endure, on earth, in space, on the computer graphics screen, in front of the audience's eyes.

In this way, ideology reproduces itself.

FIVE

RADICAL SURFACES
Robert Altman

Oliver Stone's *Nixon* ends in a sentimental, nostalgic flare. The drunk, pill-popping paranoid seems almost to recognize his failings when it comes time for him to resign. He looks at Kennedy's image and says mournfully, "When they look at you, they see what they want to be. When they look at me, they see what they are." At the end of Robert Altman's film *Secret Honor*, Richard Nixon screams a mad, defiant "Fuck 'em" at all his presumed and imagined enemies, all the voters who elected him, condemned him, and elected him again. "Fuck 'em," he screams—his image echoed on the television monitors in his office that multiply and recreate him. "Fuck 'em," he yells, fist upraised, his television image responding, throwing out more images. "Fuck 'em."

Robert Altman told a story about negotiating a project with Warner Brothers some years ago. After much talk and some compromise on the director's part, a Warner's executive became uncomfortable and hesitated. He still was not sure about the proposed film and he told Altman, "We don't want this to seem too much like a Robert Altman movie."[1] In 1976, Altman made *Buffalo Bill and the Indians, or Sitting Bull's History Lesson* for Dino De Laurentis. A big film with big stars—Paul Newman and Burt Lancaster— it turned out to be a dry and angry denunciation of the myths of show business and the distortions of people and history those myths engender. Few people went to see it, and it could only have been taken as an insult by its producer, who cut it for European distribution. The affair resulted in the breakdown of a project Altman was planning, a film of E. L. Doctorow's best-selling novel *Ragtime* (later made into an indifferent film by Milos Forman). However, Altman was able to return within a year with *Three Women*, a difficult, enigmatic, and not very commercial film. In the late seventies, Altman had a multifilm deal with Twentieth Century Fox. *A Wedding* did well critically and commercially. *Quintet* and *A Perfect Couple* did very poorly. Fox refused to distribute the last of the films, *Health*, and

Altman had to take it to colleges and festivals himself. (A few years later, Altman made a film for MGM called *O.C. and Stiggs,* based on some *National Lampoon* characters. It was released many years later on video.) In 1981, his last large-scale production, *Popeye*—made for Paramount and Disney—behind him, other projects getting canceled, Altman sold his studio, Lion's Gate Films, and started what was essentially a new career of low-budget, independently distributed films made from plays and, occasionally, for cable television.[2]

In the early nineties, approaching his seventies, Altman made a comeback in Hollywood. *The Player* did very well, and he began to get other projects made, including his summary film, *Short Cuts.* In a few years, these films, along with *Prêt-à-Porter* and *Kansas City,* brought his production schedule almost up to what it was in the seventies. In 1997, in an apparent attempt to reach a broader audience, he made a film from a John Grisham property, *The Gingerbread Man.* The film tested poorly, the studio (a small independent, Polygram) demanded to recut it themselves. It tested poorly again; Altman raised hell in public. The head of Polygram's parent company, Island Records, left his position earlier than planned in protest against his own studio. Altman's version was finally adopted and then dumped by the studio by distributing it in ways guaranteed to make it fail.[3] He came back again with *Cookie's Fortune* (1999), a genial, low-keyed film that managed to get critical and even some audience support.

I would not suggest that Altman (of all people) identifies with Richard Nixon, but rather that the final outcry of that paranoid figure created by Altman, writers Donald Freed and Arnold M. Stone, and actor Phillip Baker Hall, carries enfolded within its hysteria some of the very calm, non-paranoid defiance expressed in Altman's own work and career. Throughout the seventies, he had been able to use the economic and emotional system of Hollywood filmmaking to the advantage of his work and the benefit of exceptional filmmaking. His one blockbuster, *M.A.S.H.* (1970)—something of an accident, since Altman was far from its producer's first choice as director—provided the security for his future work. Producers were willing to back his films on the promise that he would make another enormous commercial success. He never did, but the promise allowed him to direct one or two films a year, made relatively inexpensively and returning relatively small profits. More important, he was able to make them under his own auspices and to elaborate within them and from film to film a consistent approach and point of view. Altman's seventies films are formally and contextually of a piece, so much so that, once his style is understood, it can be recognized in almost any one part of any film he makes. He stands with Kubrick as one of the few American filmmakers to confirm the fragile legitimacy of the auteur theory with such a visible expression of coherence in his work. Altman's nineties films begin to exhibit some changes in style. *The Gingerbread Man* looks as if it could have been made by almost any competent filmmaker, while *Kansas City* begins some new formal experiments. But even with as ordinary a film as *The Gingerbread Man* and as gentle a film as *Cookie's Fortune*—works that seems to bear out the earlier caution that "we don't want this to seem too much like a Robert Altman movie"—few filmmakers have, with his insistence on control and coherence of form and content, so annoyed producers and distributors.[4]

Part of the consistency—especially in the seventies—came from Altman's ability to create around him a dependable community of production people and players, a mini-studio in which the logistics and complexities of his films were worked out among individuals who were familiar and comfortable with his methods and approach. His associate producers, Scott Bushnell and Robert Eggenweiler, and assistant director, Tommy Thompson, formed the nucleus of this group. Editor Lou Lombardo and production designer Leon Ericksen worked on some of his best films, as have cinematographers Vilmos Zsigmond and Paul Lohmann. Alan Rudolph was an assistant director on *Nashville* and co-author of *Buffalo Bill and the Indians*. Altman, in turn, produced Rudolph's first films, *Welcome to L.A.* (1977) and *Remember My Name* (1978), and Rudolph's later work still bears traces of Altman's influence. (Altman also produced Robert Benton's *The Late Show*, 1978, and Robert Young's *Rich Kids*, 1979.) Until they began branching out into their own careers, he had a stock company of players, including Shelley Duvall, Michael Murphy, Keith Carradine, René Auberjonois, John Shuck, and Bert Remsen. This group helped provide security within an insecure environment and made it possible for Altman to explore and expand on his ideas from film to film without having to start from zero each time. Scott Bushnell and other associates remain with Altman's new company, Sandcastle 5 Productions. Cinematographer Pierre Mignot filmed all the theatrical adaptations of the eighties.

I am aware that such a narrative runs the risk of turning Robert Altman into a hero, making him the auteur not only of a body of films, but of a romantic personality, fighting the mean-minded, commercially crass system, succumbing, regrouping, failing, and triumphing. But, in fact, he is not a hero, only a good filmmaker with a keen sense of survival. Perhaps for the purposes of remaining optimistic about the future of American film,

Robert Altman, fighter against the system, is an important figure. For the purposes of critical inquiry, however, that persona is less important than the films Altman makes, and it is those films that manifest the subject that is important for the inquiry. I spoke of their consistency, but must point out that a break occurs in 1981, when Altman begins making films of plays and continues with his return to Hollywood in the nineties. Those films are quite different in form from the preceding works, more contained, held fast by their verbal source and their budgetary constraints. They continue to explore many of the same problems as the work of the first period, and some may be seen standing in a dialectic relationship: *Streamers* to *M.A.S.H.*, for example; *Come Back to the Five and Dime, Jimmy Dean, Jimmy Dean* and—at least in terms of location—*Fool for Love* to *Three Women*; *Secret Honor* to *Buffalo Bill and the Indians, Beyond Therapy* to *A Perfect Couple. Kansas City* links to *Thieves Like Us, Images*, and *Three Women*; *Short Cuts* reaches back to *Nashville* in structure and in fact embraces all the work up to that time. All the films in the Altman canon play counterpoint with one another. Whether in theme, idea, story, or style, they emerge and fold back one into another. In the discussion that follows, I want to incorporate that dialectic and do some comparison of the recent to the earlier work.

Given the extent of Altman's output and the relative consistency of his formal approach within each of the three periods of his career, I want, in the discussion that follows, and as I did in the previous discussion of Spielberg, to create something of an arbitrary division between form and content. I will first look at the ways Altman alters conventions of cinematic space and narrative structure and will then examine the major films. However, since there are about thirty-seven of these, from 1957 to this writing (and not including television films), it will be impossible to discuss them all or give equal attention to each. The method will necessitate some doubling back and some fragmentation of exposition. But this seems the best way to encompass the scope of Altman's work, which itself encompasses nothing less than an inquiry into the images of contemporary America and the way those images have been set by our films and our politics (among other forms of entertainment, representation, and misrepresentation). The films, themselves engaging entertainments, continually reflect their origins and their status as films as they reflect from us and back to us the images we hold of ourselves and our culture.

In creating these inquiries and reflections, Altman dissociates himself from the closed forms of classical Hollywood storytelling, turning the screen into a wide, shallow space (until 1981, and beginning again with *Fool for Love*, 1985, he used the 2.35 to 1 anamorphic ratio almost exclusively), filled with objects and people, with movement, with talk and sounds and music woven into casual and loose narratives that create the appearance of spontaneity and improvisation—an appearance he and his collaborators like to promote. But it is only an appearance, for the apparent casualness is carefully intended, and the sense of arbitrary observation is calculated to situate the viewer in the narrative in specific ways. In the theatrical adaptations, he reverses his approach almost completely. Filmed in standard ratio (sometimes in 16 mm or videotape), the eighties films draw attention directly to their dramatic center. Confined to a very few sets, and carefully locating and exploring the figures within their milieu, the films seem to deny the openness and apparent randomness of the earlier work. After having broken up the narrative and dispersed the viewing subject into its various parts in the earlier films, Altman now attempts to reconstitute that subject, urging the viewer to concentrate on carefully developed dramatic dynamics. However, in his rapid move from modernism to postmodernism and back again, Altman continually rediscovers the difficulties in locating a secure subject. Once his films move from center to periphery, they then go in the opposite direction, still not finding a secure point of rest. In the nineties, he experiments with both movements, sometimes in the same film, locating or dislocating both the viewing and the narrative subject within a space that, while apparently easier to locate, is even less easy to define.

Altman made two features in the fifties. One of them, a "documentary" on James Dean, employing stills and interviews, is an artifact of the kind of sentimental myth-making he was to attack in the seventies. He directed television in the early sixties and in 1968 a feature for Warner Brothers called *Countdown*. This potentially interesting study of astronauts—which was, in effect, lavishly remade by Ron Howard as *Apollo 13* (1995)—concentrating on their jealousies and tensions, is filmed and cut in a frontal, static, eye-level mode that allows for little but a straightforward exposition of the story. Made in what could be called the Hollywood anonymous style, its form is unobtrusive, linear, with no detail to detract from the headlong perpetration of plot. *Countdown* is a studio film and gives no idea of what Altman was to do, though it does offer an example of the early work of two major seventies actors, James Caan and Robert Duvall. The film would hardly be worth mentioning were it not an example of the kind of formal structure that Altman and most of the other filmmakers discussed here are working against. It is a prepared text that the director has only to transfer to film; there is no space for the inflection of style, which, for Altman, makes its initial appearance in *That Cold Day in the Park* (1969).

The subject of a repressed spinster driven to murder by her activated but unrealized sexual desires seems at best a cliché, at worst a bit of rampant sexism, and offering at most the opportunity for some conventional psychology and brooding, foreboding compositions, perhaps some shock cuts in the manner of an AIP horror film. Indeed, *That Cold Day* offers all these and, were it an isolated work, could easily be dismissed by the reviewer's phrase "atmospheric." The film is not isolated, however, but rather an initiation, and Altman's attempts to render the subjective states of a female consciousness, though crude here, will be refined in *Images* (1972) and fully realized in *Three Women* (1977), *Come Back to the Five and Dime, Jimmy Dean, Jimmy Dean* (1982), and *Kansas City* (1996). Most important is that Altman begins to develop in this film the opening of the aural-visual space of his narrative, diffusing its center by taking notice of the peripheries. The camera continually drifts away from the main action, zooming past a face into a window to pick up the out-of-focus light reflected on the glass, defining the central character and her state of mind by bringing to the viewer's attention the otherwise unnoticeable objects and minutiae that surround her. Dialogue shifts, too, away from the central speakers. In a bar, a diner, a doctor's office, Altman picks up conversation to the side, almost off screen. When Frances Austen (Sandy Dennis) visits her gynecologist, she sits in the waiting room apart from the other women. Attention is on her but at the same time diverted from her, diffused by the fact that she is observed, through the length of the sequence, from outside a window and further diffused by the fragments of tantalizing gossip that drift around her as the other women talk about sexual problems.

On the face of it, there is nothing unusual about one character set off against a group of strangers, with those strangers speaking of matters that somehow reflect the main character's state of mind. Certainly a key development in American film of the sixties involved greater attention paid to peripheral action, a sense of life existing around the main focus of action (Penn's *Mickey One* is a good example). In conventional film narrative, attention is concentrated on the central characters and their relationship. Sequences carefully moved from an establishing shot to a mid-shot and then to closeups of individuals or couples who speak in turn, the dialogue and the cutting directing attention to the central concern of the sequence. In a sequence that took place, say, in a nightclub or other public area, the "extras" were precisely that, extra to the sequence, filling the space rather than participating in the sequence. An exterior, such as a street scene, would be peopled by anonymous bodies, and, were any commentary on the main action needed from them, a closeup from the crowd would be cut in and quickly removed.

D. W. Griffith is a forerunner of this tradition of centralized, exclusionary screen space. He used the closeup to narrow the narrative field and concentrate attention inward, removing unwanted surroundings by inserting what he considered the center of those surroundings, the emotionally charged human face. Certainly an ideological force is operative in this: the focus in traditional American cinema on limited, concentrated narrative areas, dominated by a few central characters, reflects long-standing myths of individual potency as well as the pre-cinematic tradition in middle-class art that the only serious and engaging dramatic interests are those of the individual in conflict with him- or herself or another person, with the individual spectator being the privileged observer of that conflict. Responses to this narrative tradition in film did not begin with Altman or the other contributors to recent film but can be seen in the work of film-makers as diverse as Eisenstein and Renoir.

Eisenstein's montage in his silent films creates a sense of constant movement from periphery to center and back again, from masses of people in action to the faces within those masses and the small events that make up the action. Cause and effect, action and reaction, play against each other, the "center" of events occurring ultimately off screen, in the spectator's consciousness, which the montage guides but keeps somewhat distant. Eisenstein, of course, is working out his filmic structures from an ideology more clear and immediate than Griffith's—an ideology of revolutionary action, Marxist dialectics, and dramatic change in social and aesthetic structures—and Griffith's films became a model for Eisenstein to work against. Jean Renoir's responses to the American narrative tradition in the thirties are less radical. His redefinitions of the visual field and the focus of individual sequences within a film are closer to what Altman would be doing in the seventies (and, to a lesser extent, to what Spielberg does in those shots that allow the viewer to examine the space surrounding the central figure). *Grand Illusion* (1937) and *Rules of the Game* (1939) are struc-tured with an acknowledgment that narrative blocks do not have to be built out of single, concentrated areas of activity. Renoir recognizes that the screen is capable of indicating an extension of space beyond the frame rather than denying the existence of that space. Through deep-field composition and the use of the pan he extends the spatial limits of the shot, indicating, by continually expanding it, that there is more to the space than is immediately depicted. In a sequence in *Grand Illusion* where a soldier puts on a woman's costume while the others stare at him, the pan of the men's faces not only indicates surprise, longing, and sadness, but also quantity. There are many men, in a large area, and they all share, at this moment, the same feelings. As the camera moves from face to face, the effect is incremental and expansive; the viewer is permitted visually to embrace the physical presence and the emotions of the men. In *Rules of the Game*, Renoir orchestrates his characters and camera so that there is an expanding and contracting flow of spatial movement in response to the emotional and intellectual movement of the narrative, encompassing that movement and opening it out, permitting observation of many activities and not allowing the viewer to comfortably focus on any one character or point of view.[5]

As noted, American cinema since the sixties has taken more cognizance of peripheral activity. But, with few exceptions, this has not been in the manner of Renoir nor, certainly, of Eisenstein. The periphery recognized usually encompasses onlookers, and the sense is that of giving the extras a bit more work to do. With the rise of location shooting and the setting of action sequences within those locations, the possibility arose of counter-pointing the central action against those observing the action but irrelevant to it. A source for this is Carol Reed's *The Third Man* (1949), whose postwar Vienna exteriors are punctuated by workers in the dark, barren streets, old faces observing speeding cars. Reed's onlookers constituted a kind of historical conscience, silently commenting on the action. In recent film the faces that are inserted into a sequence of a shooting or a car wreck are only observers, commentators on the action who have nothing to do with the "plot," the central characters and their activities, and they signify only a passing, outside world. In eighties and nineties science-fiction and action films, the onlookers are constituents of the mise-en-scène, part of the destroyed landscape. The suggestions of activity beyond the central character in *That Cold Day*—the women at the gynecologist's, for example—are a bit special. Altman is imposing peripheral action onto the central focus of the sequence, not merely indicating its presence but playing that presence over and against the main figure and her concerns, forcing the viewer to take equal notice of both while at the same time removing the viewer from both by shooting the sequence from the other side of a glass window, a device Altman uses again, for comic effect, in the therapy sessions in *Beyond Therapy* and to capture the beehive activity of a film studio or communicate the perceptions of a voyeur in *The Player*. So, too, with the camera drifting off, away from the main character, and zooming to objects and blurred lights. Here Altman uses the zoom to suggest a subjective sense of vagueness and disorientation; elsewhere he will use it to capture the particulars of a defined area, reorganizing the space of a given sequence by developing it as a place of inquiry rather than accepting it as a preexistent whole (a method he will continue, on a much more restricted scale, in the theatrical adaptations and the nineties films). Elsewhere, the zoom becomes a kind of hypnotic eye, creating a rhythm of observation, probing the connective tissue between shots. More than Renoir, Altman launches an investigation of the ways one observes filmic constructions and the ways one reads the narratives to which these constructions give form.

The investigation moves forward rapidly in *M.A.S.H.*, the film Altman did not originate or choose but which he was able to use both as a means to develop new formal approaches and, coincidentally, as a financial base on which to build his future work. In *That Cold Day in the Park*, the shooting style is an extension of the basic horror-gothic approach. Most of the action takes place in the dark, heavy apartment of the main character, Frances Austen. Browns and blacks predominate; there is little red, so that the act of violence that concludes the film is all the more shocking because of the sudden appearance of the color of blood. A standard focal length lens (which approximates the spatial relationships of the eye) seems to be used throughout, allowing Altman and cinematographer Laszlo Kovacs to explore the rooms and their shadows and the characters trapped within them.

M.A.S.H. is shot largely outdoors, but the area is an isolated one, cut off. The men live in flimsy tents; they are pressed in by their situation, not only as a hospital unit stuck inside the war zone. In fact, this aspect is underplayed, for the war is never seen or heard, only its casualties. The emphasis is the way the men's spirits are imprisoned by military order. (In *Streamers*, the action is confined completely to the interior of a barracks; parts of the outside are glimpsed only through windows. But the imprisonment here is actually psychological; the pressures of confinement and the possibility that the men will have to go to Vietnam generate racial and sexual tensions and violence rather than a struggle against their oppression.) To create the mise-en-scène of confinement in *M.A.S.H.*, Altman employs two devices that effectively contradict each other, resulting in a curious spatial illusion that grows out of the contradiction. *M.A.S.H.* is

338

photographed (by Harold E. Stine) in Panavision, whose great width is often used to suggest large horizons or actions. But Altman wishes to constrict the space of *M.A.S.H*, and to this end he employs a telephoto lens for most of the sequences, which compresses space, making it flat—a device that had sometimes been used to great effect by Akira Kurosawa. Unlike shallow-focus cinematography, which foregrounds the figures in focus, creating an undefined background, and deep focus, which articulates the objects from foreground to back, telephoto cinematography tends to background everything, or at least to put foreground and background on the same plane. Within the extreme width of the Panavision screen and the compressed depth created by the telephoto lens, Altman fills the screen space with people and objects, all of which are drained of any bright colors, save for the spurting blood in the·operating room, and observes them from a distance.

The result is visual conflict rendering an experience of claustrophobia, a sense, on the viewer's part, of being locked into an observation of a mise-en-scène that refuses to open up or give way, to yield immediately to the viewer's investigation of it. The visual denseness is supported and perhaps exacerbated by the sound track. There is not a silent moment in *M.A.S.H.*: dialogue, music, announcements on a loudspeaker are continuous, sometimes at odds with, or in ironic counterpoint to, what is happening on screen, sometimes all things at once. Altman takes from Welles (and Howard Hawks) the notion of overlapping dialogue, people talking at the same time without waiting for a response. The effect is an aural space that parallels the decentralization of the visual space. By refusing to allow the comfort of pauses in the dialogue any more than he allows the comfort of simple visual orientation, Altman creates a demanding and busy visual and aural field.

But the terms of his demands are not those that André Bazin spoke about in his discussions of the long take and deep-focus cinematography, with their capability of opening the image to active participation on the part of the viewer. In *M.A.S.H.* and the films that follow, Altman rarely uses deep focus, and he cuts a great deal! I would estimate that the average shot length in his films is about the same as any other filmmaker's. The visual structure of his films requires not that the viewer pick and choose among various visual and aural options but that she observe and understand the whole and integrate into the larger unit those parts of the whole that the director wishes to emphasize. What Altman creates is not the conventional structure of a whole that is analyzed into its parts, but a simultaneity of the whole *and* its parts, a simultaneity the viewer must always attend to.

M.A.S.H. creates and sustains its busy, constricted, claustrophobic structure for about half its length, then dissipates itself as the action leaves the army camp for antics in Tokyo and on the football field. The spatial experimentation occurs only sporadically in the film that follows, *Brewster McCloud* (1970). Two sequences within this film—one in a police laboratory, the other a police investigation of a murder on the street—are constructed with large numbers of people talking all at once and at cross purposes, bad jokes weaving in and out of the conversations, no one element taking precedence over the others. These sequences tend to be isolated, for Altman is working out other problems of narrative structure. *Brewster McCloud* jokes around with itself, falls in love with its bird-shit jokes and the loony characters that fly and squawk around its demented assemblage; it is a film of adolescent shenanigans and excremental humor that Altman continues to stumble into, in *O.C. and Stiggs*, and again in *Prêt-à-Porter* (1994). With *McCabe and Mrs. Miller* (1971) he thoroughly grasps the possibilities of his spatial experiments and sees them through.

McCabe and Mrs. Miller is among the richest works of seventies cinema; form and content are so well integrated that a split is difficult to make, even for purposes of analysis. It will bear talking about once in the context of its visual and narrative structure, and once again in relation to its genre and the way it responds to other westerns. In each case, analysis is enlightened by placing the film in the context of the work of John Ford.

In *The Man Who Shot Liberty Valance* (1962), Ford worked out the possibilities of an indoor western, eschewing wide-open spaces for the dark interiors of saloons and homes, a newspaper office, and a meeting hall. Ford, near the end of his career, wanted to examine the transition of the frontier wilderness to the closed, lawbound community. He was saddened by this transition, though he realized its historic reality and inevitability. More important, he knew that the myth of the West had to be tempered by the reality of capitalist expansion. His film is an elegy for the past and an almost begrudging celebration of the change to the bourgeois security of a structured civilization. Altman has no stake in either part of the western mythos. A man with a late-sixties, early-seventies consciousness, with a certain left-liberal perspective, he sees the western, and most other film genres, along with the attitudes and ideology they embody, not as healing and bonding lies—which is the way Ford saw the western—but merely as lies. Like Ford, Altman responds to the elegiac element always latent in any myth of the past. But, unlike Ford, he does not mourn the passing of the frontier and investigate the coming of law and order: he mourns rather the lost possibility of community and the enforced isolation of its members.

Out of this paradox of community and the isolation it creates Altman builds the *découpage* (the compositional and editing structure) of his film, working from the reorientation of space and sound he began experimenting with in *M.A.S.H.*[6] Over the Warner Brothers logo at the beginning of the film are sounds of a harsh wind blowing. As the credits begin we see a man on horseback, heavily wrapped in furs, riding through the pine trees of a northern winter landscape. A sad lyric by Leonard Cohen accompanies the movement, a song about a gambling stranger. The space, as in *M.A.S.H.*, is enclosed, narrow, and flat, and the color is almost bichromatic: the greens of the trees standing out, barely, from a general blue haze. The man on horseback—as in so many westerns—enters a town. He pauses by a church, removes his furs, dismounts, mumbles something angry and incoherent. Visual attention shifts to some of the men in the town, standing about in the rain, looking, observing the stranger from a distance. McCabe (Warren Beatty) is seen again in a telephoto shot, from a vantage point inside a saloon; he is crossing a footbridge, moving toward the camera until his face is framed in the saloon window, looking in.

There is a cut to the interior of the saloon, dark, filled with low voices. The color, what little there is, appears warmer than the exterior blue. Various faces are picked out. Through a barred partition we see the owner, Sheehan (René Auberjonois), lighting a candle under a statue of the Virgin and saying a prayer. More faces are picked up; McCabe asks for the back door. Various comments from the men in the saloon regarding his gun can just be heard: "Is he wearing a gun? . . . Do you know what kind of gun that was . . . that was a Swedish . . . from Sweden . . . What the hell is he wearing a gun for?" These comments appear freely on the sound track, not assigned to any speakers directly seen. McCabe returns with a tablecloth and spreads it out. Some people comment on the weather. A small fight breaks out over a chair. Again various faces are observed. McCabe asks for a bottle. As they are about to begin playing cards, McCabe asks to go fifty-fifty with Sheehan, and as they talk of a business arrangement Sheehan lights a lamp, infusing the space with a warm golden light. There is talk of the game, of betting, a shot of hands dealing cards. McCabe's hand points to the table and his voice, off screen, says, "Jack off." With the accompanying laughter, the camera cuts to the whole group and then to a zoom to McCabe's face, smiling, revealing a gold tooth, cigar clenched happily.

For this verbal description of the film's opening sequence to work properly, I would somehow have to break the sentences up, slip some parts of them under others; still others would have to be bent sideways or placed at a diagonal. For in a more radical fashion than *M.A.S.H.*, Altman has created in *McCabe* a tight and enclosed space, peopled with figures who, though contained in that space, seem unconnected to it and, even more, unconnected to each other. There is little eye contact among the various characters in this opening sequence. When McCabe looks, he doesn't get a direct look back. The camera rarely observes the characters squarely, at eye level, centered in the frame. They are rather picked out, seemingly at random, glanced at and overheard. The Panavision screen and telephoto lens serve, more than they did in *M.A.S.H.*, to inhibit observation by compressing the screen space. The cutting and the sound mixing create a barely localized environment and a sequence of events that are just suggested.

Through it all, Altman produces a fine dialectical effect. The more random fragments of faces, figures, and conversation that are given, the more coherent the space becomes. The viewer is often unaware, momentarily, of just what location he is observing, or even why it is being observed. But the confusion itself becomes a coherent expression of this loose, unfocused community, existing in disorder, with its members operating not out of friendship but in a sort of mutual antagonism. And the less definition Altman offers, the less securely is the viewer fixed in the narrative and instead is offered the opportunity to help construct the proceedings from the interlocking fragments. To repeat, this is quite a different phenomenon from what Bazin had in mind when he spoke of the filmmaker allowing the viewer to retrieve a range of information and experience from the image. Bazin's concept suggests an activating of the otherwise passive filmgoer; but this is only sometimes the case. The long deep-focus take may do little more than concentrate attention and permit the viewer to observe the details of the mise-en-scène. It may intensify reactions by allowing them to build slowly rather than by commanding them through editorial direction. But Altman does direct the attention and the gaze. However, unlike the conventional *découpage* of American film, he does not order that gaze into, and then within, a determined and delimited space (as, for example, Kubrick does unconventionally). He creates—or, more appropriately, allows the viewer to create—an idea of place out of visual and aural fragments and suggestions. This fragmentation is, of course, never as severe as that of the European cinemodernists working in the late sixties and early seventies, and the town in *McCabe and Mrs. Miller* is, ultimately, well defined. However, his dependence on viewer cooperation in constructing the mise-en-scène and his refusal to situate the viewer comfortably in an easily observable space break sharply with the codes of conventional film.

The effect achieved is, again, reminiscent of Renoir: an extension of the screen space, the suggestion of rich and random activity of which the focus of narrative attention is only one part. Like Renoir, Altman attempts to indicate a wholeness, a continuum of space. Unlike Renoir, he does it by cutting and by sound, rather than panning and tracking. When movement occurs, it is most often executed by a zoom, which by its nature does not encompass space but narrows or extends it, depending on the zoom's direction. Like his cutting, Altman's use of the zoom offers more by showing less. But it defines the relationship of a character and his or her surroundings, or the relationship between two characters, by directing attention more coherently than would a direct cut. More gently too. Altman's zooms, at least in *McCabe*, invite regard of faces and objects; they reveal a private moment or an intimate reaction on the part of a character. They reveal even a violent action without sensation and offer proximity without embarrassing either viewer or character. They inquire and connect within and even between the films, for the zoom is the major technique Altman brings from the seventies films to all his later work. Within the limited space of the theatrical films, the zoom inquires even more carefully, directing viewer perception within the scene, acting more as a centripetal force, preventing stasis through the persistent probing of the characters in their setting, countering the artifice of the theatrical space that might be created by a steady camera and conventional cutting. In the nineties, Altman begins experimenting with the zoom and the repression of it. At times, in *The Player* or *The Gingerbread Man*, it is used perfunctorily. In *Kansas City*, he withholds a zoom shot for a full six minutes into the film, and thereafter it becomes subsidiary to a fracturing of narrative and the connective power of music. *Kansas City* speaks to the murkiness of corruption spread across race and gender. The zoom shot is less appropriate in communicating this obscurity than a nonlinear cutting pattern countered by a jazz track that provides the only continuity the film has to offer. The zoom in *Short Cuts* becomes the connective tissue of the film itself, pulling the viewer, sometimes against his will, across the many different narrative lines—and connected through associations of objects, colors, textures, and movements—into the barren lives of its inhabitants.

Let me pick up the description of the early sequences in *McCabe and Mrs. Miller*. The busy, rambling, off-centered gambling scene is brought to a small climax as the camera zooms into McCabe's smiling face, isolating and accenting it, presenting an image of a man momentarily in control of his situation. But this zoom closeup is broken by a cut to a telephoto shot of the footbridge outside and the feet of a figure walking away from the camera, which pulls up and zooms back. The warm and embracing movement to McCabe is broken by the cold blue exterior from which the camera withdraws as soon as it is seen. The figure on the footbridge turns out to be the minister of the town (which is named Presbyterian Church), the one person who cannot engage himself in the activities of the town and who, later, shares in McCabe's destruction by refusing him sanctuary in the church. In this instance the zoom serves to link the viewer closely with McCabe, then to link McCabe with one of the individuals who will prove to be his nemesis, and to define sharply the two areas, the warm gold interior of the saloon and the cold blue exterior of the town. The act of linkage is most important, for if Altman had merely cut from the card game to the approach of the minister outside, only separation and opposition would have been implied. By first offering proximity to McCabe by the means of the zoom to his face and then cutting to the footbridge and zooming back from that, Altman associates the places and the individuals and introduces important narrative tensions.

In a later sequence, McCabe brings three ragged whores to town. The event is a major turn in his entrepreneurial efforts. He shows them off to the men; a fight breaks out between the whores and the men; McCabe takes the women to their temporary, ramshackle quarters. He is deeply confused over what he has gotten himself into. "I've got to go to the pot," one of the whores tells McCabe, "and I don't think I can hold it." The camera zooms into her face and, in a reverse shot, zooms to McCabe, who looks distressed and uncertain. Out of a kaleidoscope of faces and events, the zoom isolates a moment, a relationship, a set of reactions. It does not necessarily bring the characters close to each other; in fact, the zooms to the whore and to McCabe indicate the extent of incomprehension between them. But the zooms indicate as well their forced proximity and the necessity of the viewer's dealing with that proximity.

The zoom for Altman is a narrative probe, an attempt to understand characters and mise-en-scène, the signifier of a cautious but assured approach, a means to discover detail and emphasis, a way to connect disparate parts. It does not have the positive sense of space transgressed as does the tracking shot.[7] Rather—in Altman's hands, at least—it inscribes the parts and details of the visual and narrative field. With the zoom, and in conjunction with his editing, Altman can create a field of action and event that is detailed and particularized. The point of view given the viewer is that of discoverer and connector. The zoom functions as an offering of perspective and detail, of coaxing, leading but never totally or comfortably situating the viewer, or closing off the space that is being examined.

The visual and aural field created in *McCabe and Mrs. Miller* sets the pattern that Altman will build on in the films that follow. As much as he alters the pattern to fit the needs of each film, the basic preoccupations remain: the urge (prior to the theatrical adaptations) to decentralize the incidents and the area in which those incidents are acted out; the use of the zoom to probe details and emotions. There is, too, a reticence, a desire not to overwhelm the viewer (another quality Altman shares with Renoir), to show him or her some respect and allow a comfortable distance. Even the violence in his films, often random, sometimes gratuitous, is not—except, perhaps in *Kansas City*—brutalizing, but a part of the abrupt changes and alterations that make up his narratives.

On some occasions, Altman alters the distance and demands that the audience be implicated in the mise-en-scène. There is an attempt to communicate the claustrophobia and the developing violence throughout *Streamers*, but with only limited success. *Fool for Love* employs flashbacks that present material contrary to or simply different from what the characters are saying in their voice-over commentary about those flashbacks, thereby demanding the viewer account for the perceptual discrepancies and, in effect, work out an alternate mise-en-scène. The flashbacks—perhaps more accurately flashes sideways—in *Kansas City* serve to make the temporal construction of the film and the relationship of its parts more complex, rather than satisfy demands for a logical construction of a narrative line. In *The Long Goodbye* (1973), Altman so radically and subtly manipulates the perception of cinematic space that the viewer becomes aware of this manipulation through a sense of discomfort and uneasiness. The film is an attempt to reexamine the figure of Philip Marlowe, Raymond Chandler's private eye, traditionally embodied in the figure of Humphrey Bogart in Howard Hawks's *The Big Sleep*. Altman's Marlowe (played by Elliott Gould) is a puzzled, passive, deeply abused man, caught in an environment and a moral structure he refuses to comprehend. To allow the audience a comprehension of Marlowe's dilemma, Altman and his cinematographer, Vilmos Zsigmond, uproot perceptual stability, preventing a secure, centered observation of the characters in their surroundings. Almost every shot in *The Long Goodbye* is either a very slow, never completed zoom into or out from the characters observed, or a slow, almost imperceptible, arc around or track across them.

In one sequence, Marlowe and Roger Wade (Sterling Hayden), the broken, drunken writer, sit by the ocean, talking, drinking aquavit from enormous cups. The dialogue is broken down into one-shots of each of the participants, isolating them from each other visually as they are isolated from each other emotionally and by the misinformation each has about the other. The one-shots are punctuated by shots of both together, but these only serve to emphasize their separation by showing their physical distance. This would be a fairly standard *découpage* of a dialogue between two mutually wary antagonists, except for the fact that they are never observed with a still camera. A slow zoom back from Wade is cut to a slow arc around Marlowe, to a slow zoom back of both, to a leftward arc of Wade, to a right arc of Marlowe, and so on until, at the end of the sequence, the camera zooms in and past both to the ocean behind them. More than what is said by the characters in the sequence, the viewer may be affected by what the sequence says about the characters. Here and throughout the film the movement comments, insists that there is more to be known, catches us up in an instability and an incompleteness.

In a later sequence, Marlowe is in Mexico investigating the assumed death of his presumed friend Terry Lennox. He speaks to an official and his aide while the camera observes them through the open window of a building. The dialogue, in which Marlowe is thoroughly lied to by both men, is created by a series of slow lateral tracks across the bars in front of this window. When Altman cuts to a closer shot of the group, the camera is still outside the bars and still tracking, yet near enough so that the bars are out of focus and barely visible. The combination of the telephoto lens, the proximity of the bars, and the slowness of the track give an immediate appearance of a static shot, yet the sense of movement is inescapable, and the effect insidious. Like Marlowe, the viewer is made uncertain of the seen and unseen, insecure about perception itself.[8] Unlike *Raging Bull*, for example, where slow-motion point-of-view shots and strange shifts in the sound track communicate Jake La Motta's failing grasp of his own situation within his world, the movements in *The Long Goodbye* implicate the viewer with the central character's tenuous perceptions of the world.

The Long Goodbye is Altman's most extensive experiment in altering the spatial coordinates of the film narrative. I referred to it as being manipulative, but in fact that is not the appropriate term (particularly when compared, for example, with Spielberg's work). Like the mise-en-scène of

McCabe and Mrs. Miller it asks a different perceptual response than a more conventional film would; it is more insistent in its demands and more unsettling than is *McCabe,* or indeed any other of Altman's films until *Short Cuts,* which refuses any element of identification, resolution, or redemptive action. But as in the other films, suggestion takes precedence over direction, and the peripheries of action take on equal importance with the centers. In an important sense, Altman is a director of peripheries. The dislocation of space that makes up the visual world of his films is part of a wider dislocation that concerns him. The well-made American film, with its steady, linear, and precise development of story and character, appears to Altman to be itself a dislocation and a distortion, a refusal to come to aesthetic terms with the decenteredness and incoherence of modernity. By attending to different spaces, both visual and narrative, he can reorient the ways an audience looks at films and understands them and the ways they reflect cultural fantasies back to that audience.

The narrative structure of almost all of Altman's films develops out of, or as part of, their spatial structure. Even *The Gingerbread Man,* as straightforward a detective thriller as any good director might construct, develops out of its Savannah location a dark, perpetually rainy world of secrets through which the characters scurry. The movement from center to periphery demands an abandonment of straightforward narrative development. Events on the edges gain equal importance with events in the middle. More is seen and heard than one is accustomed to. Throughout the offhand conversations that make up the first sequence of *McCabe,* Altman cuts away to the bar, where a running and finally anticlimactic conversation about a beard is taking place. McCabe wanders in and out of the saloon to look around, to urinate ("That man out there takin' a pee," says Sheehan the barkeeper, inventing a legend for McCabe that will help undo him, "is the man who shot Bill Roundtree"), and as he wanders, so does the conversation, in and out of what should be the main concern, McCabe's buying into the town and his reputation as a gunfighter. But nothing definitive is ever said and no direction given to the narrative. The sequence ends as it begins, gently, humorously, and indirectly. McCabe returns to the gambling table, he tells one of his endearing filthy jokes, and the camera quietly zooms past everyone to a fiddle being plucked in the background.

When, in *The Long Goodbye,* Marlowe gets off the bus in Mexico and wanders through the squalid town square, incongruous in his jacket and tie, the camera quietly moves from him to zoom in on a pair of fornicating dogs, who wind up snarling at each other (surely the finest example of the often-mentioned improvisational methods of Altman's direction). As fortuitous, offhanded, and incongruous as this particular zoom is, it enhances a narrative of offhanded and incongruous movements and of casual, Southern California couplings that lead to snarling and to death. Altman can become somewhat less casual and more direct, as in the depiction of Griffin Mills' murder of his stalking screenwriter in *The Player* or, much more powerfully because less expected, a brutal act of violence in *Kansas City*. Seldom Seen—Harry Belafonte, playing against type as a loquacious, ruthless mobster—takes one of his gang to be stabbed to death. Seldom stands in the foreground, telling his chauffeur a ridiculous joke about Marcus Garvey, a Jew, and a cracker on a desert island. This shot is intercut with the gang stabbing their victim. At the end, the camera pulls up and back to reveal the gang leaving the corpse and a pack of dogs arriving to finish their work. In the foreground, Seldom and his driver laugh uproariously over the joke. Snarlings, fistfights, acts of violence continually break out in Altman's films, not so much as they do in Scorsese's as a portent of even greater violence to come, but as unexpected moments, always there to punctuate the tenuous calm of any given scene and indicate the disruption and potential violence that underlie any situation.

People and events are always disrupted in an Altman film, as are viewer expectations and assumptions. The spectator no more expects to have attention drawn to a pair of fornicating or scavenging dogs than to a Philip Marlowe who cannot tell lies from truth—and does not seem to care—or to Harry Belafonte, playing a garrulous, heartless gangster, or to a frontiers-man who is only interested in being an entrepreneur, or to a Buffalo Bill who is nothing but a preening, fatuous racist, or to a boy who lives in the Houston Astrodome while he builds a pair of mechanical wings so that he can fly off to nowhere, or to the political infightings of candidates for the presidency of a health food convention. These films do not merely contain unexpected turns; they are unexpected turns. They are quiet attempts at a deconstruction of the narrative and generic truths that are taken for granted in American film, which Altman unfastens from their position as absolutes and relocates within the formal, cultural, ideological structures that created them. In dislocating their visual and narrative centers, the films dislocate their generic centers as well and begin to reveal some of the ways in which the smooth, undistracted, and unquestioning forms of cin-ematic storytelling have lied. Altman will no more construct alternative truths to the lies he perceives than will any other American filmmaker; but

347

the deconstruction is insightful, funny, sometimes angry, sometimes off the mark, and always respectful of uncertainty and plurality.

Brewster McCloud, though a less than perfect film, is a good place to start an examination of the deconstruction process and to extend the investigation of Altman's use of space to the wider areas of narrative and generic inquiry. The very opening of the film indicates what Altman will be up to. The MGM logo appears, but instead of the expected lion's roar, there is a voice saying, "I forgot the opening line." The film cannot quite get itself started. No smooth entry into a story is promised. A rather strange man appears, a lecturer (René Auberjonois), who talks to us about birds, men, the dream of flight, and environmental enclosures. As he is about to speak of the last, there is a shot of the Houston Astrodome and in it Margaret Hamilton, the wicked witch of *The Wizard of Oz*, attempting to lead a marching band of black musicians in the national anthem. The credits begin; Hamilton stops the band and attempts to get them to sing on key. The credits begin again, and the band breaks into gospel, completely out of control. This film, which will concern itself with the conflict of freedom and constraint, announces this conflict from its beginning, not only in its images, but in the difficulty it has in getting its images started. *Brewster McCloud* parodies itself, its existence as a controlled formal structure, from the very start.

It parodies other films as well—*The Birds, Bullitt,* and *The Wizard of Oz*—while intricately shuffling its elements—a boy training for flight in the bowels of the Astrodome, under the care of a mothering bird-woman; the deaths by bird droppings and strangulation of various bigoted and brutal characters; the posturings of an artificially blue-eyed "super-cop" named Frank Shaft (played by Michael Murphy, drawing on the absurd elements of an earlier character created by Steve McQueen but in name looking forward to the black cop John Shaft, who appeared a year later in a film by Gordon Parks, also made for MGM). All the while the film playfully comments on its own silliness while refusing to face its serious intent. The film's individual parts—the complicated sound track of radio announcements; the voice-over of the lecturer, who comments on the bird-like endeavors of the various participants and slowly turns into a bird as the film progresses; the intricate intercutting of foolish police investigations with Brewster's dream-like isolation; the car chases; the touching connotations of dreams of flight, of Icarus, and of Oedipus—are successful, but only as parts. They refuse to yield up a coherent statement about the anger that informs them. *Brewster McCloud* is a film about sexuality, power, and freedom, and about how these fundamental personal and ideological components were being changed, questioned, repressed, and corrupted under the Nixon regime at the turn of the seventies ("Agnew: Society Should Discard Some People, A Certain Number Who Won't Fit In," reads a newspaper seen early in the film and rapidly covered with bird droppings).

Altman attempts to realize the transformations and distortions of these three forces within a doomed adolescent fantasy of freedom and flight. This end-of-the-sixties fantasy is in turn enclosed by another fantasy, that of the super-hero policeman, that aberration of the heroic that our culture allowed to be foisted on itself, in film and on television, in the late sixties and early seventies, and which reappeared as the international avenger in the eighties, only to be modulated later in the decade by the vulnerable and sensitive action hero. But although Altman feels the tensions inherent in repression and the need to escape it, and understands the absurdity of the heroic images the culture chooses to embody its various desires to escape untenable situations, he cannot bring the playful openness of the narrative to do more than suggest them. The crushed corpse of Brewster—whose flight to freedom, doomed from the start, ends in an agonizing fall—lying amid the characters who are prancing about in circus garb (the mock-Fellini ending of the film is about the most unfortunate thing Altman has ever done) further rends the fabric of the narrative, rather than mending it with an intended irony. Things fall apart in much the same way in the later *Prêt-à-Porter*, which cannot make up its mind whether its goofiness is parody, satire, or an embrace of the fashion business.

Brewster McCloud is a significant and successful failure. More clearly than *M.A.S.H.*, it lays out Altman's formal and thematic concerns (though sexuality, power, and freedom are themes so general that almost any film can be said to deal with them, they are specific to Altman in that they do inform most of his work and he consistently deals with their manifestations in the culture). *Brewster McCloud* is important also in that it shakes him free of the potential trap of *M.A.S.H.*, for *Brewster* examines some of the contradictions in the "youth rebellion" of the late sixties—its inherent aimlessness and dependence on the existing social-political order—whereas *M.A.S.H.* is merely a gratification, indeed a pacification, of that rebellion. *M.A.S.H.* feeds a given audience what it wants and shocks others in a perfectly acceptable and unthreatening way. While the compression of space, the crowded mise-en-scène, and sound track are important for what will come out of them in Altman's films, *M.A.S.H.* presents very little for an audience to deal with contextually. Its narrative is constructed from a series of episodic gags, each representative of the anarchic individual fighting against a restrictive order, with no analysis offered as to the nature of that order and why it should be fought against. Military order is held up as "bad," the heroes of the film as "good." *M.A.S.H* may indicate a difficulty inherent in any film about the military. The genre is too weighted by larger ideological fears and aspirations. Attitudes toward discipline and suffering and enemies, patriotism and death are too fraught with contradictions of patriotism, moral necessity, and other ideological traps to be worked out clearly. Only Stanley Kubrick in *Paths of Glory* came close to dealing with the complexities, while Spielberg in *Saving Private Ryan* reduces them to sentimentality. Altman has no luck with even when he reverses perspective. *Streamers*, which attempts to concentrate on the psychological tensions of a group of men waiting for service in Vietnam, substituting melodramatic confrontation for comic hijinks, ends with a clear and violent manifestation of racial and sexual instability, but comes to no more certain understanding of how individuals react to the reality of war and the military state than *M.A.S.H.*

M.A.S.H. is not a good place to find the beginnings of Altman's investigations of genre. It is finally no more of an antiwar film than is *Paths of Glory* or, for that matter, Lewis Milestone's celebration of selfless bravery in a Korean battle, *Pork Chop Hill* (1959), or Terrence Malick's reveries in *The Thin Red Line* (1999). *M.A.S.H.* is antiauthority only. With a happy band of committed surgeons substituting for the committed band of fighting men omnipresent in earlier war films and the substitution of operating room for battlefield, it merely teases its audience with an attitude of liberated nonconformity. The war is not really present in *M.A.S.H* (the bleeding bodies have no faces and merely provide more foils for the antics of the heroes) and therefore need not be confronted. There is a smugness not merely in the characters but in the way the narrative allows them to prevail without forcing them to confront anything—such as a notion of why they are where they are.[9] *M.A.S.H.*, like *The Graduate*, that other hymn to the passive side of the rebellion of the sixties, is a gentle massage. While the happy surgeons prevail over military order, it remains unchanged and enduring. *Brewster McCloud*, though it also goes some way in depicting the stupidity of the prevailing order, indicates too how difficult it is to overcome with infantile fantasies of evasion and escape. *Brewster* is therefore a much less happy film than its predecessor. Only in its refusal to take itself seriously does it manage to avoid being rather grim.

M.A.S.H., despite its sense of self-parody, takes itself too seriously and perhaps the only way it can be saved is by regarding it not as an army comedy but as part of the subgenre of POW films.[10] If the war were regarded as a prison and the surgeons of the M.A.S.H. unit as its captives, their hopeless rebellion might be seen as a kind of protection against the destruction of the spirit. This reading gives the film an aura of hopelessness that provides an otherwise absent dialectic. Without it the narrative is all flashy episodes, running jokes, and unexamined assumptions, a balm to the viewer who wants to believe that the structure of authority can be destroyed (or humiliated) by either laughing at it or ignoring it (and being good at your work). Altman's later films try to avoid or at least to confront such false assumptions. That too few such assumptions are confronted in *M.A.S.H.* and too many in *Brewster McCloud* indicates that Altman needed a way to stabilize his perspective, to integrate and control the visual and narrative experimentation that goes on in these early works. He finds that way in *McCabe and Mrs. Miller,* through organizing his film both within and in opposition to one of the most established of American film genres. Where *M.A.S.H.* parallels the war film, *McCabe* sets up an active analysis of the western. Where *M.A.S.H.* celebrates the community that exists in opposition to military authority, *McCabe* is an elegy to the loss of community and the isolation of the individual on the frontier. I said earlier that Altman, unlike Ford, does not see the transition of wilderness to civilization as somehow natural and preordained, incorporating the struggles of individual heroes into secure bourgeois enclaves of law and order. Rather, he sees the conquering of the West as part of the inevitable movement of capitalism, with its attendant brutality, betrayals, and selfishness. The town of Presbyterian Church is no frontier bastion, no Fort Apache or Dodge City. Its inhabitants are not upright citizens or gun-fighters. They are merely rather dull and passive people trying to keep warm. The bumbling entrepreneur, John McCabe, has only to walk in to bring a semblance of order, via a gambling saloon and whorehouse. His enemies are not savage Indians or anarchic outlaws but the very passivity of the people, his own misplaced sense of heroism, and the agents of a mining company (who include a savage Indian and anarchic outlaw). He is undone by refusing a business deal and believing he is a gunfighter.

Altman offers no one in the film, or watching the film, the comforts of convention, the easy assumptions that there are ideals worth dying for or communities worth preserving, at least as those ideals and communities are constituted in our movie myths. In *My Darling Clementine* (1946), Ford creates a sequence in which the townspeople hold a square dance within the unfinished frame of a church, with American flags flying and the wilderness of Monument Valley safely in the distance and effectively sealed off by the structures of the community. He creates it with no irony and no subtext, but as a pure symbol of human order controlling and impressing itself on the wilderness.[11] In *McCabe*, the comforts of civilization are on a cash basis only and the church a place of denial. Its interior alone of all the buildings in town remains unfinished; its inhabitant is an antisocial, mean little man. But it does serve ironically as a place of congregation. When the church catches fire, the townspeople flock to save what they have heretofore ignored, leaving McCabe alone in the snow, pursued by the mining company's gunmen. He acts the hero despite himself and dies—unlike most heroes embedded in the ideology by cinema—for absolutely nothing. In an alternating montage sequence worthy of Griffith, McCabe is placed alone, pursued by gunmen, while the townspeople gather to save a worthless building. Unlike Griffith's, however, the two parts of the montage never join. The community is left to its own devices, McCabe to his death.

The church fire and the gunfight in the snow continue and conclude a set of visual ironies set up early in the film. When Sheehan, on McCabe's arrival, lights the lamp in his saloon, it infuses the area with a warm and golden light that continues to bathe the interiors of the gambling house and whorehouse throughout the film. Conventional association offers this as the light of warmth and security, contrasted with the cold blue of the exteriors. But this is a film in which warmth and security are shown to be delusions and snares and community a fraud. Altman and cinematographer Zsigmond manipulate the warm-gold-interior and cold-blue-exterior light to warn against false comfort. When the mining company gunmen ride into town, they are bathed in gold light; when McCabe first confronts their leader, the enormous Englishman Butler (few would expect a western gunman to speak with an English accent) in Sheehan's saloon, the gold light is replaced with the cold blue of the exteriors. The simple glow of protection, security, and community is easily transferred and broken down. The church, conventionally associated with refuge and security (a convention Altman acknowledges early in the film when he photographs it against the sunset as its cross is placed on the spire—one of the most photographically beautiful shots in all his work), burns up. Golden warmth is replaced by destructive fire, destructive not merely to the church (which everyone has ignored previously), but to McCabe and the sense of community obligation. The gold light proves to be false, fooling the viewer as it has the characters of the fiction. When seen for the last time, in contrast to the blue cold in which McCabe dies, it is suffusing the opium den where Mrs. Miller (Julie Christie) has withdrawn. All connotations of security and community are stripped from it. It is here the warmth of withdrawal, avoidance, and isolation. Mrs. Miller is looking within herself, able to see no further than the marble egg she turns in her hands. (That image returns as self-parody in *Popeye*, where a visit to a gambling and whorehouse reveals a Mrs. Miller look-alike reclining, staring at a vase she holds in her hands—an apt event in this somewhat imagination-starved film where Altman looks back and seems to find only elements for parody in his own work.)

The shots that end the film—Mrs. Miller's eyes and the marbled patterns those eyes see—seem to be in perfect opposition to the opening shots of McCabe's entry into the town. But if we recall those opening shots, the enclosed space they embrace, McCabe mumbling to himself as he dismounts from his horse, the vacant and directionless stares of the men hanging about in the cold, it is clear that Mrs. Miller's state of isolation and self-absorption is only an intensification of the state of things at the beginning. If we realize, in retrospect, how the cutting of the film and its crowded, fragmented spaces and sounds create a sense of pervasive isolation in the midst of community, the end comes as little surprise.

Isolation and self-absorption are qualities Altman discovers in many of his characters and most of the places they inhabit. He finds the idea of a successful community difficult to imagine and the smaller units within communities—conventional romantic couplings and domestic unions of the kind usually celebrated by American film—impossible. Only once, in *A Perfect Couple*, does he create an unassuming, middle-class man and woman who manage to find successful love with a minimum of pain and within a context almost devoid of irony. Successful love consummates *Beyond Therapy*, but only after long, ironic sexual battle. *Cookie's Fortune*, Altman's gentlest film (despite its conventional character of the mad Southern woman), attempts to ameliorate all its characters and their problems. After attempts to cheat and wrongly accuse people, the madwoman dies; romance and friendship bloom; wrongs are righted; racial harmony breaks out. The incremental brutalities visited by couples on one another end in a cataclysm of nature in *Short Cuts*. The relationship of Mrs. Miller and McCabe is indicative of difficulties Altman usually sees in romantic conventions. Their initial isolation from one another is a result of the business arrangement that determines their actions. McCabe wishes to be an independent businessman. "Partners is what I come up here to get away from," he tells Sheehan, asserting his independence in a scene that is punctuated by the brutal stabbing of a customer by one of the whores McCabe clearly cannot control by himself. As he attempts to break up the fight, the scene is once more broken by violence, this time the scream and smoke of a steam engine bringing Mrs. Miller into town.

Her intrusion into McCabe's life is not physically violent, but it is disrupting and complicating. She proves to him his lack of entrepreneurial knowledge, particularly when it comes to running a whorehouse; but, more, she shows him how dumb he is trying to do business alone. This is a difficult thing for the hero of a western to hear, and from a woman especially. The shot that occurs after the initial dialogue between McCabe and Mrs. Miller at a table in the saloon, she eating an enormous meal, McCabe manfully downing his scotch and raw egg, is a slow reverse zoom of McCabe alone, in slight disarray, belching and farting. This is a rare little shot, not merely because one is not used to hearing a character break wind in a film, but because of its effect as an immediate response to the dialogue preceding it. McCabe is a lone man, and his aloneness has just been assaulted; the brief insert permits the viewer a sort of offhanded observation of his confusion and his attempt to reassert himself, if only to himself. The fact that the camera zooms away from him rather than toward him implicates the viewer in his solitude, his desire to be alone, and his feeling of having been violated. The shot affirms the vulnerability of the would-be hero and indicates his end.

Mrs. Miller is rarely observed alone, except for the very last sequence. She is occasionally set off from her girls, once glimpsed just in the background at a birthday party for one of the whores. The few times that a sequence begins with just her, McCabe appears shortly, and their conversation inevitably involves business and inevitably puts McCabe in a bad light. She is not alone because, unlike her generic forebears, she is a woman of business and not the center of a family. She is not the frontier wife or the schoolteacher from the East who domesticates the hero. She is a whore and the administrator of a whorehouse, jobs she knows and does well. She demonstrates no desire to be other than what she is. Unlike Ford, Altman is not taken by the domestification of the West. There is little domesticity in the film as a whole; only two "families" exist, a black barber and his wife, who are rarely seen, and Coyle (Bert Remsen) and his mail-order bride, Ida (Shelley Duvall). Coyle is killed in one of those flash brawls that punctuate the film, and Ida becomes one of Mrs. Miller's girls.

Constance Miller does not wish to provide the expected romantic, domesticating role. Curiously enough, McCabe does; he is, despite himself, a character with romantic pretensions. Unfortunately, like his pretensions as a businessman, he cannot handle them. He remains at the mercy of convention and platitude. Neither Mrs. Miller nor anyone else will accept them. In a touching sequence that denies the fulfillment of romantic expectations usually set up by film, McCabe comes to make love to Mrs. Miller, full of bravura and tenderness: "You're a funny little thing. Sometime you're just so sweet." Well, in this instance she is not sweet, but stoned. Her reaction to McCabe is to hide coyly under the sheets and point to her money box. He dutifully counts out his payment, and the camera zooms into Mrs. Miller's—very literal—heart of gold.

The only time McCabe is allowed to express his feelings is when he is alone. At one point, so tied up in his own inarticulateness and inwardness, he paces a room and faces the wall, drinking, mumbling to an absent Mrs. Miller, "If just one time you could be sweet without no money around. . . . If you just one time let me run the show. . . ." "I got poetry in me," he says; "you're freezin' my soul." McCabe sounds like a pubescent rock balladeer and is expressing himself from the same source of conventional, sentimental clichés that has fed movie lovers and songwriters for years. In his hopeless innocence and aloneness he can only confront himself, and with language that expresses only that innocence and aloneness without responding to anyone else's needs. He is at this point one with almost every melodramatic character in cinema who cannot call on any other mode of discourse but that which expresses his own barely articulate, self-satisfying emotions and which is drawn from the stock language of the sentimental. Since there is no one who cares to share these emotions, he winds up talking about himself to himself.

The threat to McCabe is not merely that Mrs. Miller will not return what he thinks is his love for her (she does, in fact, demonstrate—to herself—some concern and even some affection for him), but that she and everyone else in the film speak a language different from his. And he cannot understand the language of others anymore than they can understand his sentimental gibberish or his mock-tough gibberish. He will pretend comprehension of other clichés, if they seem to fit in with his own understanding of things. The lawyer, Clement Samuels, feeds McCabe a most atrocious line of half-liberal, half-conservative nonsense when McCabe consults him about the threat of the mining company. Samuels talks of protecting big enterprise and small, of busting up the trusts and monopolies. "I just didn't wanna get killed," says McCabe. "Until people start dying for freedom," says the lawyer, in a line redolent of patriotic illogic, "they ain't gonna be free." Samuels convinces McCabe he can be a hero, that he can "stare 'em down and make 'em quake in their boots." In other words, that he must be Gary Cooper or Henry Fonda, or even John Wayne. Poor McCabe buys it.

Altman's fiction continually turns in on itself and its predecessors, placing itself in a critical perspective to history and the myths of history propounded by other westerns. Certainly McCabe would like to fancy himself a hero, if not actually be a hero. When he parrots the lawyer's words to Mrs. Miller, her expression of concern for him and his stupidity is more than a bit tempered by her concern for her investment should he be killed. Altman unfailingly responds to any outpouring of romantic individualism on McCabe's part with one or another expression of economic self-interest. The West, Altman tells us, contrary to what we have been told in film after film, was not so much the testing ground of our culture's initiative as it was an outgrowth, or the outward growth, of the wielding of economic power. The initiative was taken by those with the power to initiate. Mrs. Miller seems to understand this, so that at every moment she denies whatever emotion she might have—she might even wish to have—in order to protect herself.

McCabe kills the three mining-company killers, and he does it alone, like a good gunslinger should (and unlike that weaker cowboy, the sheriff of *High Noon*, who had to depend on his wife to help him). Like their relatives in *High Noon*, the townspeople ignore his plight, not out of cowardice particularly, but rather out of passivity and distraction; the church is burning down. Mrs. Miller deserts him; what could she do to help him? McCabe finally lives up to the "big rep" the townspeople have created for him (and, could the fiction be extended, probably creates a bigger rep in his wake). He is shot and dies in the snow, buried in it, no more than a mound of white, his heroism unseen, unapplauded, and unwanted.

McCabe and Mrs. Miller, like Coppola's *The Conversation* and Arthur Penn's *Night Moves*, denies absolutely the possibility of the individual triumphing, in fact or in spirit, and it could be criticized for reinforcing the ideology of defeat and powerlessness that we noted was common in the seventies and largely given up in the eighties and nineties when powerlessness was too keenly felt in the culture to have it reinforced in film. *McCabe and Mrs. Miller* is saved, however, by its own lyricism and gentleness, its sense of process and suggestion of other modes of behavior. For while there is an immediate expression of hopeless activity and inevitable loss, there is the possibility of the opposite. The film is without despair and with the suggestion that, perhaps between the adolescent romanticism of McCabe and the hardness of Mrs. Miller, love might possibly exist on terms other than the raucous sentimentality American film insists on expressing. There is a suggestion too that a community might cohere on terms other than self-interest and a brutality that arises out of greed. The film suggests these alternatives, but only by their absence.[12]

Altman will not admit them openly; but he at least tempers his film with a softness that somewhat denies the hopelessness of what is seen. This is not to suggest that the film is in any simple way "optimistic." Altman cannot easily slide into any one extremity of point of view and stay there long. The very pluralism of his visual and narrative form forbids it: there is too much happening, too much diversity for any one mood to dominate any other. In his other films the alterations of mood are usually more extreme than they are in *McCabe*, where a sadness of lost opportunity is most persuasive. The predisposition on the part of the viewer to respond to configurations of lost love and blighted romance provides a tension with the film's political and ideological nuances. The hazy quality of the images and Leonard Cohen's songs (so effective in combination with the images that, when heard by themselves, the images are recalled to memory) also provoke an emotional response. The continual and ironic contrasts of cold exterior and warm interior work out an idea of needed protection and desired community that garners a response even though the film continually denies them—a denial that assures a regret over their loss. An effective balance and tension are achieved between desire stimulated by conventional expectations and the response to what is actually happening in the narrative. Tenderness is achieved out of its opposite as the film evokes a longing for the very attitudes it attempts to deny.

Later, in *Quintet* (1979), Altman will do his best to suppress any lyrical response. *Quintet* is the pessimistic, indeed nihilistic extension of *McCabe and Mrs. Miller*. The frozen frontier community becomes the frozen, desolate city at the other end of history, at the end of the world. Here, Altman does not play off the horizontal expanse of the Panavision screen against the compressed space of the telephoto lens. The film is shot in standard ratio and the peripheral circumference of the camera lens is smeared, so that the gaze is moved inward toward the center, which is itself in frozen decay. If the possibility of vital expansion is just slightly suggested at the peripheries of McCabe, it is denied altogether by the absence of

357

peripheries in *Quintet*. Gambling is no longer an enterprise and a pastime, but an obsessive way to death, the ritual of an aristocracy that seems able to warm itself only on each other's blood. As in McCabe, "friendship" is replaced by "alliance," but even that is only a pretext for murder. Essex (Paul Newman) enters the dying city from the frozen wastes, loses his wife and her unborn child to one of the murderous players of the game of Quintet, almost loses his own life to other players, and ends by walking out of the city to the wastes alone. No warmth, not even the illusory security of an opium den, is offered to any character. There is no sad, lyrical soundtrack, only dissonant music and the sounds of shearing ice.

Quintet is an unsatisfying film because of its single-minded desolation. Its pessimism is part of a later expression in Altman's work, an experiment in despair and the reduction of the spatial openness of the earlier films, and can be observed in the grimness and disillusion that infiltrate *Buffalo Bill and the Indians, Three Women*, and *A Wedding*, coming to brief hiatus with the unusual romanticism of *A Perfect Couple*, the political hysteria of *Health*, and the silly doodlings of *Popeye*. The mood returns in the theatrical adaptations where restricted space again becomes charged with a melodrama that often gives voice to deadness of spirit and environment and is broken once again in *Beyond Therapy*, where the expanses of the Paris skyline offer liberation from neurotic confusion. In the mid-seventies, however, his inquisitiveness kept the perspective of his films shifting and refracting rapidly through and across many genres and many moods. The nineties brought a more permanent change, with many of the films, *Short Cuts* in particular, assuming the darkness of spirit without the lyricism of *McCabe and Mrs. Miller* but with all the betrayals of *Quintet*.

If *McCabe* portrayed the community as a place of isolation, and romantic love as individual fantasy determined, externally, by economic necessity, *Thieves Like Us* (1974) reverses the point of view, attempting to locate a possibility of love within a larger social and economic context, a love that attempts to counter that context but inevitably fails in the face of it. The film also establishes a different notion of community. There are three communities in *Thieves:* the American heartland in the thirties, Depression-ridden, listless, barely cohesive; the three thieves, Bowie (Keith Carradine), Chicamaw (John Shuck), and T-Dub (Bert Remsen), who attempt to form a bond of friendship in necessity, rob banks because it is the only thing they know how to do, and protect each other because they are the only ones who can; and the lovers, Bowie and Keechie (Shelley Duvall), who remove themselves from the male group, attempt a community of two, sealed off from the larger world, isolated and finally destroyed when Bowie is killed by the police.

The film contains little of the ironic lyricism and spatial dislocation of *McCabe* or the psychological intensity of *Images*, and certainly none of the restrained hysteria of *The Long Goodbye*, the film that immediately preceded it. Filmed in standard ratio, it does not play off a horizontal width against a compressed interior space (but neither does it suggest a sense of collapse and claustrophobia like the later *Quintet*). Its framing is loose and casual, and Altman indulges in a deep-focus sequence for only the second time in his major work. The first such sequence appears in *Images*, where Cathryn's living room, with its smoking fireplace, is composed in the left foreground of a particular shot, while to the right and in the rear, she can be seen working in the kitchen. In *Thieves*, Bowie, Chicamaw, and T-Dub sit together in a living room, while to the right and in the rear, Keechie goes about her work in the kitchen. In both shots we find a woman in her "proper place," oblivious to some larger event occurring outside her observation. Unlike such shots in Spielberg's films, Altman charges these compositions with irony and portent. The women in his films rarely remain in conventional situations, rarely allow themselves to be "placed."

Despite the departures in the film's spatial construction and its casual, even kindly, treatment of its characters, *Thieves Like Us* follows through some of Altman's major concerns. Like most of his seventies work, it is a film of generic protest, and the genre it protests is of recent origin. Altman looks directly at *Bonnie and Clyde*, and with that look denies the heroic, even mythic status that Penn gives his characters. They attempt to control their world by asserting their energy and spirit on it. The characters of *Thieves Like Us* are always controlled by their world, enjoying a tenuous freedom from it only when the three men are alone in a joking camaraderie, or the two lovers withdraw within themselves. But even in these instances the world is present, either in the newspaper accounts of the gang's exploits or in the radio programs that create a background to all their activities. If the Barrow gang creates its own community and briefly dominate its world, the thieves and lovers of Altman's film are always dominated by a community that oppresses them in the form of the soap operas, gangster stories, cheap poetry, and political and religious speeches that dominate the film's sound track. This very domination emphasizes the distance of the characters from their environment, while simultaneously Altman is at pains to distance the viewer from the characters' activities.

When the three robbers take a bank, the camera remains outside, gazing at mundane activities on the street as if refusing the viewer privilege to the gang's activities, which are replaced on the sound track by a broadcast of "Gangbusters" that ironically mocks their exploits. When a robbery is observed directly, it is a disaster: the gang is forced to kill, and it marks the end of its success. In this instance, in ironic counterpoint to the activities, the sound track plays a speech by FDR about security, peace, happiness, and the power of a democratic government to protect its citizens. When Bowie and Keechie make love, their closeness is punctuated by a radio soap-opera version of Romeo and Juliet. Over and over the radio voice drones, "Thus did Romeo and Juliet consummate their first interview by falling madly in love with each other." The radio commentary mocks the couple but makes their adolescent passion the more endearing at the same time. Even more, it refuses to let them alone. None of the characters is free from the authority of the world and the images that diminish them. Like McCabe and Mrs. Miller—though without their entrepreneurial opportunities—Bowie and Keechie are held down (within their fiction) by economic oppression and (outside their fiction) by the myths of their cinematic predecessors. They are oppressed by the demands of their culture whose banality drains from them any possibility of heroic action. McCabe and Mrs. Miller inhabit a moment in American history when that banality was just coming to be (its birth is witnessed in the characters of Eugene Sears and Ernie Hollander, emissaries from the mining company, who represent violence by wearing a bland face, and by the lawyer Clement Samuels, who mouths the clichés of free enterprise as if they were new truths). Bowie and Keechie are alive at its maturity. Bonnie and Clyde transcend for a moment the emptiness and banality of their culture; Bowie and Keechie merely sink beneath it.

If Altman refuses to indulge in the heroic nonsense of *Bonnie and Clyde*, he also refuses to indulge in the total grimness of oppression and loss that Penn's myth-making leads to. He refuses as well the grimness that accompanies an earlier version of *Thieves Like Us*, which is also an influence on Penn's film, Nicholas Ray's *They Live by Night*, based on the same novel that is Altman's source. The two films offer a revealing comparison of style and temperament. *They Live by Night* is a film noir, although it makes some important shifts in the noir structure by dealing with rural thieves rather than urban gangsters and private detectives. Ray's characters are trapped within their world, enclosed in a darkness that seals up their innocence like a coffin. His lovers are betrayed and humiliated; Altman's make at least an attempt to confront their situation, to work out the allegiances that Bowie has both to his friends and his lover. In Ray's film, Bowie has to be physically coerced to stay with the gang; in Altman's, he chooses to help Chicamaw escape from prison, though his friend proves so bitter and murderous that Bowie is forced to abandon him. At the end of both films, Bowie is killed and Keechie is left alone. But the different forms of the endings indicate an important change in points of view. In Ray's film, Keechie is left by Bowie's body, the viewer's gaze concentrated on her, while her own eyes are averted and her face full of hardness and despair. She then fades into the darkness. Altman's Keechie watches her lover's death from a distance, restrained by Mattie, the woman who betrays Bowie to the police—explicitly in Ray's film, implicitly in Altman's. Keechie is seen behind a screen door, the bright red of a Coca-Cola icebox punctuating the blue haze, a romantic poem punctuating the sound track. As the police shoot to pieces the shack Bowie is in, Keechie smashes her everpresent Coke bottle, violently screaming in slow motion (a welcome removal from the brutality forced on the viewer at the end of *Bonnie and Clyde*).[13] But Altman does not leave her there. After Bowie's body is carried out of the shack, there is a cut to the waiting room of a railroad station. On the sound track Father Coughlin, the right-wing thirties radio evangelist, speaks to the need of bearing our burden in silence, like men. Keechie talks for a while to a woman (Joan Tewkesbury, co-author of the screenplay), telling her the child she carries will not be named after his father. She then joins the crowd going up the stairs to the platform. There is one more shot of her impassive face and then a cut to a far, slow-motion shot of the crowd disappearing up the stairs.

Where Ray ends in despair, Altman ends on a notion at least of a world in which some sad flow of life continues. He lifts the noir fatality that trapped Ray's characters, diffusing it into a wider context, the larger trap of the world they inhabit. His Keechie endures, not withdraws like Mrs. Miller. She will exist ensnared in the promises of comforts and security, ever-present in the radio shows she hears, promises negated by the narrow, marginalized life she must lead. But at least some community, even the face-less, slow-motion crawl of a crowd in transit, exists, and no film noir offered even that much.

When Altman returns to the thirties, in *Kansas City*, the atmosphere is as dark as he has ever created. In this film of mirror reflections and dark, barely defined spaces, characters move in a world distempered by a corruption so profound and *given* that betrayal is the ordinary motive of most of the characters. The film's most active characters, Jennifer Jason Leigh's Blondie and Harry Belafonte's Seldom Seen, talk continuously, profanely, with the obsessive need to impress themselves on the world with language and deeds. Only Seldom prevails, because he holds some of the power in a universe where power is measured either by the immediate violence of gangsters or the unseen violence of politicians (the two forces merge as a hired thug beats up a hobo hired to vote as often as possible). The ambiguities of relationships in this film are maintained throughout. The darkness and the reflections, the constant talk, the very lack of certainty as to who is doing what to whom (what, for example, is the exact relationship between Blondie and the politician's dope-taking wife she holds kidnapped during the duration of the film?), the violence that ends the lives of most of its attractive characters would render it the bleakest in the Altman canon, were it not for the music. Leonard Cohen's songs in *McCabe and Mrs. Miller*—like Annie Ross's in *Short Cuts*—help create and disseminate the narrative mood, lyrical and depressed in the first instance, bitter and cynical in the latter. The jazz performances in *Kansas City* are of a different order from the film's narrative: upbeat, expertly performed, and diametrically opposed to the characters' corruption—or at least its dialectic. After all, the musicians all play in Seldom Seen's nightclub. They are a visible, creative, committed African-American culture opposed to Seldom's thugs, who are allied to the white power structure of the city. They suggest a larger continuity as well, for the musicians represent real jazzmen: Count Basie, Lester Young, and Coleman Hawkins, with a young Charlie Parker watching them from the balcony.[14]

In *Kansas City,* Altman makes a noir film with a female protaganist who loses out to an African-American male, a strong turn on the racial and gender hierarchies of the old genre, though very like traditional noir in its indication of a global corruption. In *Thieves Like Us*, he made something that approaches film lumiére, which, like his western, indicates a potential of community as well as its inevitable dissolution. He indicates that neither male camaraderie nor heterosexual love is able to survive in a culture that denies the very security it promises to those unable to abide, for intellectual or emotional or economic reasons, by its rules. But he indicates as well that a kind of endurance is possible, albeit a passive, lonely one. Keechie's survival is in fact similar to Mrs. Miller's, similar as well to the survival of the crowd at the end of *Nashville* or, in a more diminished and ironic way, the drunken couples at the end of *Short Cuts*: isolated, with false comfort or none at all, unable or unwilling to change their situation. But Keechie at least moves on, and although it is a movement in sadness and resignation, it is more movement than Mrs. Miller's, and more certainly than any noir character—any Altman character—usually makes.

Another kind of movement, more extreme, but no more hopeful, occurs in the film that precedes *Thieves Like Us*, a version of film noir, this time by way of the forties detective film, *The Long Goodbye*. The film is at once a direct descendant and a powerful denial of its ancestry. The detective has fascinated Western culture since he was invented in the nineteenth century. An urban and urbane quester, he could descend into worlds the middle-class reader—and, later, viewer—could never approach. Even more, he could do what the reader and viewer could only dream of doing—gain control of complex and dangerous situations through reason and perception and with a moral superiority that allowed him to be engaged in, but untouched by, the moral squalor around him. The classic detective was also the surrogate of the reader in the act of detection, an act that permitted an interplay, in the traditional "whodunit," of many voices: the author, the criminal, the detective, and the reader, creating a complex discourse that always promised that one voice would prevail, a voice that enunciated the pristine and integral solving of the problem.[15]

When, via Dashiell Hammett and Raymond Chandler, the detective entered the film noir world of the forties, changes occurred. He became less morally pure, less certain, less sure of his perceptions. The dark, oppressive mise-en-scène he worked in did not permit clear understandings and pristine solutions. The rich, devious perpetrators of criminal acts, their low and vicious henchmen, and the dark, treacherous women of the noir universe allowed for no easy comprehension and apprehension. The film noir detective was a sullied individual and almost always harmed morally and physically by his business. Yet he prevailed. Bogart's Sam Spade, in *The Maltese Falcon* (1941), had a sense of moral obligation and self-protection, as well as a sense of bluff and bravura, that allowed him some success. The various Philip Marlowes, especially Dick Powell's in *Murder My Sweet* (1944) and Bogart's in *The Big Sleep*, had a strength of self-protective wit and cynicism that distanced them somewhat from the complexities and compromises of their work.[16] They also had, for the audience, at least, a recognizable milieu in which to operate. This would appear to be an immediate contradiction: the film noir world is dark and oppressive; yet the forties detective operates in a recognizable milieu. The contradiction arises from some curious results of convention. Forties film noir rapidly became set in its visual forms so that its threat was somewhat lessened through the almost comforting repetition of its images. The shadows and rain-soaked streets, dark nightclubs and narrow alleys, the half-lit faces and claustrophobic rooms with shadows of venetian blinds became instant icons of a quickly recognizable fictive world. This easy recognition, transmitted by an often stable, neutral camera, contradicted the amoral, indeed dreadful, vaguenesses of the world being created.

It has been suggested many times that noir worked as a subversive element in the classical Hollywood style; but that subversion became somewhat neutralized by a repetition that created the familiarity of met expectations—hence, noir became a genre. After the institutionalization, however, comes a series of reawakenings. One need only look at Aldrich's *Kiss Me Deadly* and Welles's *Touch of Evil*, two late noir films deeply conscious of the way they are put together, to discover how disturbing the genre still can be when its forms go beyond the conventions that were established by the late forties. The fact that the noir model is so often copied or investigated by recent filmmakers indicates both its potency and the readiness with which its elements can be used for effect. *The Long Goodbye* continues this self-conscious reexamination of original noir forms, rediscovering their potential for subverting old codes. Its form, analyzed earlier, creates an unstable and unsettling perspective, a sense of disorder and lack of comprehension so extreme that it expresses as much or more in camera and lens movement than its forties predecessors did through chiaroscuro and the claustrophobic framing of their characters. If *Touch of Evil* is the last film noir in black and white, *The Long Goodbye* may be the first in color, eschewing the expressionism of the forties and of Welles, reintroduced by Scorsese in *Taxi Driver*, and refigured again by Altman in *Kansas City*, replacing it with a drifting, unlocalized, uncertain perspective. Rather than being witnesses to a dark and doomed world, as in classic film noir (and that other seventies revision of the noir detective film, *Night Moves*), the viewer shares the point of view of a Marlowe so completely out of control of his world that there is no possibility of detection, but only, perhaps, of accidental discovery. The voices woven into the text of detective fiction become here a confused mumble.

Many critics, some with outrage, have discussed how weak, fooled, and finally violent Altman's Marlowe is—particularly compared with his Bogart forebear in *The Big Sleep*. But a closer look reveals some interesting similarities, or at least extensions of Hawks's 1946 film. Hawks portrays a closed, dark, and, in its corruption, curiously stable world over which Marlowe seems to exercise almost complete control. But Altman and his screenwriter, Leigh Brackett (who co-scripted *The Big Sleep*), perceive that control to be tenuous at best, fraudulent at worst. The Hawks/Bogart Marlowe becomes, despite himself, deeply entangled in the world he enters, caught in the very morass he attempts to clear. His control over things is apparent only in his wit and his ability to find momentary attachments based on the least amount of mistrust. In fact, the Hawks/Bogart Marlowe is played for a fool by everyone and is reduced to committing murder as vicious as any committed by the various thugs, grifters, blackmailers, and rich young women who drift in and out of the film's complex narrative. *The Big Sleep* ends in a litter of corpses (dead of Marlowe's doing), with police sirens punctuating the night and sharply undercutting the apparent romantic calm Marlowe shares with Vivian Sternwood (Lauren Bacall).

In *The Long Goodbye*, Altman and Brackett merely strip away the security of the Bogart persona, his wit and his ability to stand back from a given situation in a posture of self-preservation. Their Marlowe is a man out of time. "I'm from a long time ago," he tells his police interrogators. He is a character without physical or emotional anchorage in the world. "Remember, you're not in here; it's just your body," he tells David Carradine, who happens, in one of those small, offhanded, tangential sequences of Altman's, to be sharing Marlowe's jail cell. He is a man whose every connection with the world is faulty and noncomprehending. The discourse he carries on with the world is barely coherent and neglectful of the basic logic even of conversation. As he passes on the ramp that separates his apartment from that of a group of girls who practice yoga in the nude (and go mostly unnoticed by Marlowe), the following interchange ensues. He asks them if they've seen his cat (who ran off the night before when Marlowe couldn't provide it with the proper brand of food). One girl answers, "I didn't even know you had a cat, Mr. Marlowe." Another girl emerges, saying, "Say you wanted a hat?" Marlowe replies, "No, no, you don't look fat." And as the verbal language drifts and glances in incoherent directions, so the camera—our gaze onto Marlowe's world—drifts and pans, zooms slowly in and out (never completing its motion), arcs and dollies until the viewer's own perceptions are inscribed into an orderless, almost random series of interchanges and events.

The self-defensive Marlowe wit has turned into incomprehension. Mumbling passivity—Marlowe's key and favorite response is, "It's O.K. with me" (a phrase that will turn up again in somewhat different form and a more disastrous context in *Nashville*)—is what has become of the Marlowe persistence and drive for moral order. And in his insular state Marlowe merely allows himself to be had. For no particular reason, he decides to refute the accusation that his friend Terry Lennox murdered his own wife. It is as if this notion of trust and friendship that Marlowe irrationally holds somehow provides a center to his drifting world. In fact, it furthers the drift and results in terrible betrayals, that of Marlowe himself certainly being the worst. Friendship is always a difficult subject for Altman, and his films constantly probe the proximity of friendship to betrayal. Bowie, out of emotional necessity, betrays his friends when he goes off with Keechie in *Thieves Like Us*. McCabe is betrayed by Sheehan and eventually by the whole town. *Nashville* and *Short Cuts* can be seen as a complex of betrayals, of people refusing to admit to each other's emotional validity and individuality, looking rather on one another as objects to be used in the first film and abused in the latter. In *Quintet* a character explicitly states that "alliance" has been substituted for "friendship" in their freezing, dying world. The father of *Fool for Love* has shockingly betrayed his children by having kept two wives: the children are each the result of the separate unions, and they fall in love with each other. Only in *California Split, A Perfect Couple, Popeye,* and somewhat tenuously in *Beyond Therapy, Vincent and Theo* (1990), and *Cookie's Fortune,* does Altman see the possibility of two people sharing a modicum of trust. However, in *California Split* and *Vincent and Theo,* the two are men and their relationship is tentative, in the latter finally destructive. The cartoon frivolities of *Popeye* allow no serious consideration of the relationship. The sexual meanderings that occur in *Beyond Therapy* are no guarantee of permanent union. The van Gogh brothers in *Vincent and Theo* share such an entangled, boundaryless relationship that they cannot survive alone. *A Perfect Couple* and *Cookie's Fortune* remain the films in which betrayal does not destroy a relationship.

Marlowe's unquestioning and irrational belief in his friend cuts him off from even the limited comprehension of things he may have had. And just here we can see how clearly Altman is changing the conventions of the detective film. His Marlowe does not detect anything, actively or passively. He attempts to prove wrong the charges against his friend, but in so doing accepts any lie that is thrown his way. The Bogart/Hawks Marlowe persists in an attempt at discovery, no matter how dark and futile the attempt may be (so too, for that matter, does Penn's Harry Moseby). Altman takes the inevitability of failure as a fact and starts from there. He sees the film noir detective as a patsy and chooses not to have him struggle manfully to prove otherwise. (Interestingly, the core of Altman's revision may lie in a sequence in *The Big Sleep* where Marlowe, trapped in the shadows of a warehouse office, looks on helplessly and hopelessly as Lash Canino murders Harry Jones; Marlowe afterward reveals an unexpectedly sentimental attachment to "little Jonesy," for whose death he bears responsibility.) Finally, Altman creates, out of the dialectical extension of the Philip Marlowe of the forties, a perfect fictive surrogate of a major cultural phenomenon: the modern passive individual, who accepts everything, questions nothing, and is had continually by anyone less gullible than he. But this very passivity creates its own irrational activity and deeply implicates Marlowe in the destruction of others.

One character who loses because Marlowe cannot and will not act is Roger Wade. He is one of the more melodramatically powerful men that Altman has created, a precise and conventional rendering of the burned-out, alcoholic writer who has been part of romantic mythology since the nineteenth century. The character reappears in different guise in Robert Duvall's Dixon Doss, a slightly mad, antiauthority good old boy in *The Gingerbread Man*. Wade's appearance in a film that otherwise denies conventional figures and acting styles (the kindly, vicious Jewish gangster, Marty Augustine, played by film director Mark Rydell, is an example, along with Marlowe, of this unconventionality) makes him stand out as an immediately attractive, because familiar, figure. He stands out so clearly that Marlowe, a figure made up of anticonventional unromantic elements, cannot even see him. "Loony Tunes" is Marlowe's response to Roger Wade. The romantic, boisterous loser, full of anger and sorrow, only looks mad to the modern, recessive, passive loser. With a just irony, Wade calls Marlowe "Marlboro Man," and both remain vulnerable and outside each other's spheres.

367

In one of the film's great set pieces, Marlowe goes out to the beach, while Roger and Mrs. Wade argue, the writer expressing his passion to his cold wife (a noir woman, she is part of Terry Lennox's crime and uses Marlowe to push her husband to ruin and further her escape to her murderous boyfriend Terry; she is reincarnated as the devious Mallory Doss in *The Gingerbread Man*). Their conversation is observed and listened to from outside the glass door of their beach house, the camera slowly zooming in on each and on both together. Marlowe, playing on the beach, is reflected in the window in front of the couple (technically the sequence is more complicated than this, for it appears that one shot of Marlowe on the beach is superimposed on the window; therefore, when the camera zooms back from the window, there is a coordinated zoom back in the superimposed shot, doubling the spatial slipperiness and uncertainty). This complex spatial and perceptual interaction serves as a metaphor for the film as a whole. The viewer is suspended between two points of view, seemingly unconnected with either. Because the Wades are observed through the glass for much of the sequence, the viewer is distanced from their conflict. The constant movement of the camera emphasizes this removal, this inability to confront the action as the viewer expects she has a right to. Marlowe, who is blind and deaf to what the Wades are doing and insensible to information that would go against his obsessive allegiance to his friend, is outside, dancing in the waves like a child. He is reflected on the same glass through which the camera observes, and because he is reflected, only his back is seen, and from a considerable distance. Every participant in the sequence is cut off from every other, emotionally, physically, and in their mutual misunderstanding. I said the viewer is suspended between points of view. In fact, the authorizing point of view still belongs to Marlowe, even though his back is to the scene. The recording apparatus—microphone and camera—may be trained on the Wades, but the instability created by image and sound projects the uncertainty, the lack of clarity that mark Marlowe's perception.[17] He cannot master any scene, any situation.

Later, after Wade is humiliated at a party by the slimy psychiatrist Dr. Verringer, he commits suicide by walking into the sea (like Norman Maine in *A Star Is Born*). Marlowe and Mrs. Wade are talking by the window, she misleading Marlowe by discussing Roger's affair with Mrs. Lennox, hiding her own connection with Marty Augustine, who has been pursuing Marlowe. Through the window that stands between them, Roger can be made out in the darkness, walking to the ocean. The camera zooms past Marlowe, past Mrs. Wade, to the figure approaching the waves. The movement is not an urgent one, merely another series of slow spatial drifts, not hurrying the viewer's gaze or the characters' to this pathetic event, but merely alluding to their obliviousness to it. They do not react until a reverse shot is given, a slow zoom up to the window from outside. Again, as so often in Altman's films, a window is used as a barrier to direct emotional contact. This device that reaches a climax in *Fool for Love*, where the characters, at strong emotional odds with each other, are observed almost continuously through windows. It becomes a metaphor for the voyeuristic elements of moviegoing and moviemaking in *The Player* when Griffin Mill, spying on his tormentor's girlfriend outside her house, simultaneously talks to her on his cell phone.

What follows in *The Long Goodbye* is a scene of enormous energy for Altman. Marlowe attempts to save Wade from the ocean. This is his most active moment, and the noise of the surf, the darkness and confusion, Wade's dog running in the ocean with his master's cane, provide an engagement of viewer and action, and the participants in the action, unlike any other scene in the film. The problem is that this action and engagement are to no avail, for Wade is dead. The emotional peak the action creates and carries over to the investigation that follows reaches a level of hysteria that makes it impossible for either viewer or Marlowe to hear a policeman tell him that Wade could not have been responsible for Sylvia Lennox's death (as Mrs. Wade had said he was), information that further implicates Terry himself as well as Marlowe in the consequences of his own stupidity and neglect.

Altman is appropriately wary of highly emotional situations, of melodramatic crises and confrontations. These are the stock-in-trade of American film and represent a method of easily engaging the audience and, occasionally, obviating narrative difficulties. In television, even more than in classical Hollywood film, a sequence of overwrought feelings, of melodramatic hysteria shot in closeups, will be used to suture up narrative weakness, depending on the audience's emotions to take the place of perception. Altman refuses such orchestrated climaxes and prefers to dissipate emotional intensity by observing peripheral action. When he does create an emotional scene, like Wade's suicide and its aftermath, he uses it to indicate its deceptive qualities. Later, in the theatrical adaptations, where such emotional climaxes are built into the drama out of which Altman must construct his film, he attempts, with varying success, to create them as dynamic ruptures in his mise-en-scène. The revelations of lies and repressed lives in *Come Back to the Five and Dime, Jimmy Dean, Jimmy Dean,* the brutal murders at the end of *Streamers,* the memories of bigamy and incest in *Fool for Love,* are pushed up by the tensions built throughout the film; they break out and are then reabsorbed—with the exception of the last work, in which resolution results in a kind of apocalypse, as the motel inhabited by the main characters goes up in flames.

The dynamics are not as controlled as they are in the seventies films, not as ironic or as powerfully significant of false perceptions. They no longer question melodramatic structures and the ways such structures hide more important realities, but rather accept them as the necessary consequences of theatrical form. The moments of hysteria in the later films, like *Vincent and Theo* and *Short Cuts,* appear as set pieces in contexts that hold comprehension or closure at a distance. In *Short Cuts,* they permit the characters to act out, to vent and embarrass themselves and others. Melodrama becomes—as it is in ordinary life—a means to evade emotional confrontation by making the emotions themselves the subject of attention.

At the end of the suicide sequence in *The Long Goodbye* Marlowe gets hysterical when he believes that Wade killed Sylvia Lennox; it is the highest emotional peak he reaches in the film, and it is based on lies. But neither he nor the viewer (unless the latter listens very carefully, for the camera is on Marlowe when it is said) hears the police inspector tell him that Wade could not have done it. Marlowe cannot hear or see; he is the detective as somnambulist. He is the bandaged mummy whom he meets in a hospital room in the penultimate sequence—his own double, as Jonathan Rosenbaum points out, who hands him a tiny harmonica that Marlowe will play as he skips off from his last encounter with Terry Lennox, the only encounter in the film in which Marlowe, his head somewhat cleared of misapprehensions (though not of misperceptions), takes definitive and immediate action.[18] This action was found so distasteful that, when the film was recut for television, it was altered and rendered ambiguous. In the film Marlowe kills Terry, shoots him without hesitation. They confront each other in a series of slowly accelerating zooms. "So you used me," says Marlowe. "Hell," answers Terry, "that's what friends are for. . . . Nobody cares." The camera is on Marlowe's face as Terry offers this response, and it zooms in closer as Marlowe answers, "Yeah, nobody cares but me." For the first time in the film, spatial proximity with the character is achieved. Still an isolating proximity, for nothing is offered that could make one believe that Marlowe is in touch with anything but a brief awakening of anger. There is another shot of Terry and a zoom in closer, faster on his face: "Well, that's you, Marlowe. You'll never learn, you're a born loser." The shot returns to Marlowe, zooms back—"Yeah, I even lost my cat"—and he pulls his gun and fires. Terry falls into a pool, rolling in the water like the cowboy shot by the punk gunman in *McCabe*, or the gunman himself when he is later shot by McCabe. So many of Altman's characters die in water. The camera zooms in again on Marlowe's face as he watches Terry, spits, and leaves. He walks down the road, oblivious to Mrs. Wade, who passes him in a Jeep, heading for her now dead lover. On the sound track, the musical theme of the film, which in parody of forties films has been repeated throughout, coming from every conceivable source—doorbell to Mexican marching band—is distorted and moaning. Marlowe begins blowing the harmonica given him by the mummy. As he diminishes in size down the road, he begins dancing; on the sound track is the music of "Hooray for Hollywood" that opened the film. The mummy comes to life, having activated himself by murder.

I detail the ending of *The Long Goodbye* because it is an unusually definitive one for Altman, though still highly diffuse and multivalent. The fact that neither Chandler's Marlowe, nor any of his forties film incarnations, could kill a friend coldly and unflinchingly is a convention of Hollywood morality that Altman cannot abide, and he detects the weakness and falseness of it. At the end of Hawks's *The Big Sleep*, Marlowe pushes Eddie Mars (toward whom he once felt friendship) out the door to meet the certain machine-gun fire of his henchmen. Within the context of the film, the act seems appropriate, for certainly Mars would have killed Marlowe, and besides he is being forced into a death equal to his own viciousness. But Marlowe is responsible for the death nonetheless, as he was for the murder of Harry Jones by Lash Canino, a murder he passively observes. He is responsible for the death of Canino himself, whom he shoots out of revenge for Jonesy and out of a need to escape (at this point in the narrative Marlowe has no choice but to shoot his captor). The Bogart Marlowe is a killer whose killing is always morally accounted for. In Chandler's novel *The Long Goodbye*, Marlowe does not kill; he accepts Terry's having used him with sadness and understanding. The important thing for him is to remain true to an idea of friendship.

Altman cannot accept either the morally justified murders or the passive acceptance of abuse under the guise of loyalty. The act of his Marlowe is therefore a response to both, a murder as gratuitous as any shown on the screen—even Griffin Mills's murder of the screenwriter in *The Player*—and an action of a sleepwalker momentarily awake. There is undeniable satisfaction in Marlowe's act, the pleasure felt when a narrative includes revenge is immediate—a response proved by the endless series of films for which revenge is the central narrative dynamic. There is particular satisfaction here because Marlowe finally does something, acts rather than being acted on. Yet the act is repulsive, as repulsive as Marty Augustine smashing a Coke bottle in his girl friend's face to scare Marlowe ("Now that's someone I love, and you I don't even like"). Peckinpah may have insisted that violence is a purgative; Penn may insist that it is the necessary result of defiant action; Kubrick and Scorsese may see it only appearing and disappearing, neither explained nor explicable, or, if explained, always something more than the explanation; the makers of revenge films may use violence as the exploitation of impotence. Uninterested in examining the act, they use it to activate the unsatisfied desires of the viewer.

For Altman, the causes of violence are almost as vague as Camus's *acte gratuit* and inevitable as well as erratic and unpredictable. And the violence hurts everyone concerned, though no one may be immediately aware of this. Altman is one of the few American filmmakers who examines the results of the violent act, which more often than not only reaffirms the state that existed previous to it. The act of violence alters nothing. After the killing, Marlowe is still a jerk, still unconnected to his world. McCabe is dead along with the three gunmen. After the assassination in *Nashville*, everyone remains gullible and manipulable, singing their great anthem of passivity, "You may say that I ain't free / But it don't worry me." The murders in *Quintet* are the ritual acts of a dead society. The violence that ends *Streamers* grows out of and then sinks back into the groaning depression that marks the narrative as a whole. The conflagration that closes *Fool for Love* takes the life of the father who kept two wives, disperses the other characters, symbolizes the explosion of misdirected passion, but finally closes the narrative with no questions answered. Jerry Kaiser's murder of the girl he picks up in the park at the end of *Short Cuts* is a kind of logical conclusion to the undirected, unearned sexual rage suffered by him and most of the other male characters in the film; elemental almost to the point of disturbing the natural order, and therefore resulting in a perturbation of the earth. Perhaps only the death of Edgar in *Three Women*—unseen, only referred to—has some positive value; it changes a situation, though the change itself is a grotesque one. Usually no one is helped, ennobled, or purged by the violence that occurs in Altman's films, least of all the audience. If a viewer applauds Marlowe's shooting of Terry, that same viewer must answer for its ramifications: is a person who has been played for a fool only able to rectify his or her passivity by murder? If, on the other hand, the act is appalling, then why are we not appalled by other acts just like it in our cinema? Why is the futility of Bogart's Marlowe "heroic" and the futility of Gould's Marlowe repulsive?

Altman is well aware that the ambiguities are generated by movies, and that is why "Hooray for Hollywood" opens and closes the film. Whatever its other qualities and faults, American film, with other forms of popular entertainment, has helped make the larger culture as gullible and passive as poor Marlowe, sometimes finding it difficult to discriminate between actions represented, reactions to them, and the social-political contradictions that play among everything, fudging the lines between valid individual activity and destructive heroic fantasies. If Altman is not attempting to clarify the confusions, he is at least attempting to reveal them, to demonstrate how perceptions have become befuddled by false heroics and irrational acts that present themselves as being true to life, as believable, when all they are actually true to are conventions of behavior that exist only in a film fiction. But *The Long Goodbye* is not a goodbye to

Hollywood. Altman's affection for it is too strong. He needs its conventions as material to dismantle and reconsider.

When he comes to confront Hollywood directly, the conflicts become clearer. *The Player* is a sort of schizophrenic film, partly in love with its own existence, a celebration of the filmmaker's return to L.A., partly parody, partly denunciation of the very system to which Altman has again returned. The conflicts are too strong, the need to please everyone too powerful. The very structure of the film creates conflict between, for example, the complexities of the opening, the long, six-minute shot, made in homage to *Touch of Evil*, the film that marked Welles's return to Hollywood some thirty years earlier; the insightful metaphors for voyeurism in the many sequences shot through windows; and the long, romantic sequences that could have been shot by any competent filmmaker. The finesse of the opening sequence is pretty much squelched for the rest of the film. The amazed and appalled views of studio machinations, observed through windows and mirrors, find no response in the smarmy love affairs of the main character, which seem to be presented with minimal irony. The fact that he gets away with murder seems more a joke than a moral dilemma as it is in *The Long Goodbye*.

The Player is at its strongest when Altman examines his enduring theme of betrayal. More than in any previous film, almost all the characters exist within narcissistic shells, moving through a closed universe, smirking off any concern of moral obligation. *The Long Goodbye* is a deeply felt, intellectually and emotionally rigorous parody of the noir detective film. *The Player*, without the previous film's anger or even its engagement with the crazy main character, is instead a bemused extension of some earlier sour looks at filmmaking: Ray's *In a Lonely Place*, Joseph Mankiewicz's *The Barefoot Contessa* (1954), and Vincente Minnelli's *The Bad and The Beautiful* (1952) and *Two Weeks in Another Town* (1962) come to mind. But Jean-Luc Godard's lyrical elegy to the craft, *Contempt*, does not. *The Player* undercuts any possible sentimentality or devotion to corporate filmmaking in all its meanness, while at the same time it indulges in erotic display of the kind that Altman usually avoids. Love scenes, gentle zooms to Hollywood stars—mostly of the old guard—violent acts both physical and emotional, a sense of a world in which everyone looks, betrays, and then moves on to the next betrayal, are not sufficiently woven into an expressive narrative structure. Love story, vision of universal betrayals, parody of a way of filmmaking that is already a parody of how the imagination could be used, *The Player* can't decide what it wants to do; its maker seems too close and too angry to make up his mind.

When Altman returns to the subject of detection in *The Gingerbread Man*, he again meditates on the difficulties of actually determining who is doing what to whom and where the moral center of perception lies. Kenneth Branagh's Rick McGruder is a southern lawyer in a storm-wracked Savannah, whose rain-soaked mise-en-scène helps communicate the cloudy relationships between the characters who—except the lawyer (this is a Grisham story, after all)—are mad, or corrupt, or in thrall to a woman who, in good noir fashion, turns out to be the devil of the piece. The obviousness of *The Gingerbread Man* does not rank it high in Altman's canon, but it is a well-made film that makes the points of *The Long Goodbye* with more directness and therefore less interest. It's a film made for its plot and plotted with a focus on a character who, unlike Marlowe, finally sees enough to allow him to pull away, wiser if unredeemed.

After the angry correctives and discomfiting ambivalences offered by *The Long Goodbye*, Altman softened his approach in *Thieves Like Us*, still diminishing the heroic myth, but with more restraint and certainly a more kindly disposition to his characters. Before *The Player*, this is the closest Altman comes to a conventional film narrative. But it is only a momentary pause, for he follows it with one of his more ambitious reorganizations of narrative structure. *California Split* (1974) can be taken on one level as another entry into the buddy film cycle, though it manages to escape some of the more uncomfortable sexual evasions and misogynistic attitudes of these films by keeping its emotional level low, by allowing, as few American films do, emotions and emotional relationships to be chancy, fleeting, nondestructive, unscarring. Unlike other buddy films, it gives its women characters equal status and equal strength. Though the Gwen Welles and Ann Prentiss characters are whores, they do not suffer and are not condescended to, nor are they any more oppressed by their situation than their male counterparts are by gambling. George Segal's Bill is sad a good deal of the time, but mostly because he does not experience either the thrills or the agonies in gambling that so many other films on the subject have insisted one must feel.

In *California Split*, Altman substitutes for melodrama a sort of emotional laissez-faire and does so mainly by organizing not only the subject but also the narrative form of the film around gambling. The film's structure is that of a game of chance, a playful, random, offhanded series of events full of accident, coincidence, and peripheral action brought to the center in a more extreme way than in the previous films. But the adjective is misleading, for the film is not "extreme" in any way. If anything, it is extremely gentle and undemanding, requiring only a pleasure in its playfulness and its improvisational effect. The film is carefully crafted to be open not to various interpretations but to various reactions to its juxtapositions and anomalies; it is made to be analogous to the wheel of fortune that closes the film, spinning and stopping where it will.[19]

This is, of course, not improvisation in the usual sense. Though much of the dialogue may have been made up in rehearsal and in preparation for shooting, the structure of chance and coincidence, the joking interplay of events in the film and the expectations of the viewer would have to have been carefully planned. *California Split* holds an important place in Altman's work: experiment, joke, a game about gaming, it also moves him a bit beyond the generic revisionism of *McCabe* and *The Long Goodbye* into a greater revision of narrative structure in general, of the ways movies tell their stories and can be made to tell them differently.

With *Nashville,* Altman attempted to refine and enlarge the open structure of *California Split,* adding many more characters, each with his or her own small narrative to be worked out. Much more than its predecessors, Altman wanted *Nashville* to be a grand cultural statement, a "metaphor for America" (as he himself called it). Unlike its predecessors, however, *Nashville* falls short of the notion of the open narrative, in which the viewer is asked to participate in, question, and respond to new forms of expression. The film tends to become ambiguous rather than responsible and temper its anger with sad contemplation. Pretending, perhaps disingenuously, to encompass many attitudes and points of view, its own perspective is somewhat restrictive. "All you need to do is add yourself as the twenty-fifth character," writes Joan Tewkesbury in her introduction to her screenplay, "and know that whatever you think about the film is right, even if you think the film is wrong."[20]

Film, however, does not allow the spectator to become a participant on the same level as the fictions who inhabit its narrative. Even Altman and his screenwriter cannot change the immutable status of an imaginative work as an object made separate from the viewing subject and inviolable. As open and malleable as its structure of meaning might be, the elements that make up that structure—the immediate forms of what the viewer sees and hears—are permanent and removed. All a screenwriter and director can do is attempt to position the viewing subject as a more active and responsive element, less manipulated and constructed by narrative and character conventions. The fact that a narrative is made a certain way and that its characters say and do specific things (the same things, each time one sees the film) makes it impossible to believe that *whatever* we think about them is right. We may change our attitudes on subsequent viewings (as, indeed, my own response to *Nashville* keeps changing each time I see it) or even our reflections on a single viewing, but a certain structure and perspective remain. Altman, more than any other American filmmaker, has insisted on positioning the viewer within the *process* of narrative, requesting that she observe and comprehend the interacting details that cohere in sometimes nondirected ways. But cohere they must on some formal and contextual level, or narrative is impossible. If narrative is possible, then some basic meaning system is created.

I am trying to provide some limits to modernism and the notion of the open narrative—limits that, in the course of time, Altman himself imposed as he moved away from the openness of his seventies films. If Tewkesbury and Altman insist that any reading of their film is the right one, then no meaning exists, and the film's status as narrative disappears into an arbitrary arrangement of incoherent parts, mutually exclusive characters, and anomalous events (of course, if that were true, a very definite meaning system would emerge). *Nashville* is none of these. Rather it is precisely located in time and place with many characters, and Altman takes great care to relate them, even if by apparent accident, and to define them. Even though it has no conventional story line, the various "stories" of the various characters move easily and neatly. The frame narrative—the organizing of a rally for candidate Hal Phillip Walker—easily holds the parts together, and the controlling thematic of celebrity, power, their illusions and abuses, is addressed in each subnarrative and through each character. Finally, the structure of *California Split* and *The Long Goodbye* is more complex, for *Nashville* actually only extends the parallel or alternate montage structure basic to American film; it merely has more parallels and alternations.

As an experiment in smoothly integrating a number of alternating narrative units into a whole, it does succeed with much energy and a sense of delight in its scope. As an integration of the fragments that made up American culture in the mid-seventies, it remains close to *Brewster McCloud* though without that film's manic silliness, and *McCabe*, with its lyricism suppressed but not absent. Altman continues to be struck by the self-serving, passive nature of the culture but adds here something more, a notion of hypocrisy and meanness that can be glimpsed in *McCabe*, begins to surface more in *The Long Goodbye*, and becomes full blown in the nineties. In *Nashville*, all the characters are fools, manipulated or manipulating, hurt or hurtful, each using what little power he or she has to affect someone with less power. Barbara Jean, perpetually in a state of nervous breakdown, is booed by her audience and shot down at a concert, but not before she is treated like a child by her husband manager, Barnett, who is in turn insulted by Connie White and her manager. Tom, the pop singer, insults a poor soldier whose life is spent following Barbara Jean around and treats his women as sexual objects to be conquered and discarded. Opal from the BBC uses everyone as a sequence in her nonexistent documentary and insults Haven Hamilton's son Buddy and the chauffeur, Norman. Del Reese, Linnea's husband, makes little attempt to comprehend his deaf children, helps Triplette, the political operative, organize his rally, and makes a pass at Sueleen after she has been first fooled into doing a striptease at Triplette's smoker and then humiliated during the performance. Linnea cheats on Del with Tom. Haven Hamilton condescends to everyone but falls for Triplette's promise of political power. L.A. Joan refuses to visit her uncle's wife in the hospital, thereby causing him great pain. Triplette manipulates everyone into performing at his rally for the invisible Hal Phillip Walker, whose campaign is based on the clichés of a meaningless populism. Kenny, the assassin, has the last word by shooting Barbara Jean and, with this gratuitous act of political violence, throwing everyone into chaos and revealing their inherent passivity.

A major difference between the humiliations visited by one character on another here and similar acts in *M.A.S.H.* is that the audience cannot share the victory over those who are hurt or identify with them. Altman keeps the viewer decidedly on the outside as an aware observer, a positioning he modifies in *Short Cuts* where the viewer, while distanced, is still made acutely aware of the emotional batterings going on. In the very few instances in *Nashville* where an emotional attachment threatens to break out, it is immediately squelched. Mr. Green learns of his wife's death in the hospital as the soldier, Kelley, is telling him how he watches over Barbara Jean for his mother's sake. The camera zooms in on Green as Kelley walks off saying, "You give my best to your wife." Green begins to grimace, to laugh in pain, but, before the viewer indulges in this rare expression of emotion, Altman cuts to Opal and Triplette laughing, she giving him her theory of assassination. On that there is a significant cut to Kenny, the actual assassin, on the phone to his grasping, protective mother. Other moments of emotional expression in the film are similarly compromised. Lady Pearl's feelings about the Kennedys are decidedly neurotic; Sueleen's shame at having to do a striptease is a result of her own self-delusion.

The distance at which the audience is kept is an important part of

Altman's narrative control, for it positions the viewer as discriminating observer. The problem, however, lies in the uncertainty of what is to be observed and how. The ugliness of the behavior of most of the characters is not much dwelt on or commented on and is easily dismissible as part of the "flow" of events. If it can be argued that Altman is indeed somehow attempting an enormous "metaphor" of democracy, with all its flaws and all its attractions, then it can be argued in return that what is shown is the very opposite of democracy: the great passive sink where those with some power manipulate those with less power and everyone sings a chorus of "You may say that I ain't free/But it don't worry me." And this in the end may be Altman's point. Passivity and the alienation from power are a major subject of the film, from the opening speech of the invisible presidential candidate, who denies the right to be apolitical, through the insistence of most of the characters throughout the film that they are apolitical, to the revelation that politics is the function of everyone's manipulation of power over others. Altman accurately perceives that the ideology of the apolitical is a trap that conveniently allows those with politics and power the ability to control and manipulate. He confirms his perception by observing the manipulations of power conducted by the various characters on one another and on their audience, by presenting his "candidate" as just another political idiot, and the political rally, toward which all the events and characters of the film lead, to be the arena of yet another unexplained assassination whose resulting trauma permits all the errant couples of the film to be rejoined and another talentless country and western singer to achieve stardom. The fools remain fooled; the viewer, made distant and superior to the activity, is permitted only a sad resignation toward the events.

378

The pluralism of the film undoes itself—by condemning passivity while seeming to condone it, exposing the banal hypocrisy of country and western music while applauding its vitality, observing the vicious vacuity of "stars" while indicating that they're just folks, and giving everyone his or her due—and ends in ambiguity and evasion. A catastrophic event brings everyone together, but in a devitalized state, ready to be herded and manipulated once again. No answers are offered; indeed, the many vital questions raised by the film disappear in the general drift. Literally so, for it ends in a most uncharacteristic camera movement for Altman, a movement away from the field of action up to the sky. This seems to be the final evasion, and it needs a response. If *Nashville* suggests that America is divided into those who are in show business and those who passively watch the performance, it stops short of encouraging an analysis of this massive act of cultural manipulation. If everyone is at the mercy of everyone's lies, including their own, is there any meaning to individuality, is there any trust or any possibility of community? It's similar to the questions raised in *The Player*, but there the community is even more self-contained than it is in *Nashville*, and the world outside is never seen, never known.

The questions have become even more potent in the years since *Nashville*, and the film seems even more pertinent than it did in 1975, despite the fact that it has been all but impossible to see in a form other than a panned and scanned videotape. Altman has himself often returned to the problems posed by it, the cultural facts of celebrity and passivity becoming as important a thematic in his work as in Scorsese's. Unlike Scorsese, however, Altman is not interested in exploring the neurotic drive for recognition (even in his meditation on that great neurotic of the modern age, Richard Milhous Nixon) or the responding, somewhat psychotic drive on the part of the culture to accept the image of celebrity. Rather, he is concerned with the uncomfortable reactions of those needy of attention and unable to give it to others. He is intrigued by the emotional and economic exchange that occurs between the owners of the spectacle—the makers and the celebrities of film and television—and the public who buys their images. In his nineties films whose subject is celebrity—*The Player* and *Prêt-à-Porter*—narcissism seems more important a subject than the cultural surround of celebrity's world.

Two of the late seventies films, *Buffalo Bill and the Indians, or Sitting Bull's History Lesson* and *Health* attempt alternative analyses of power, politics, culture, and spectacle. *Buffalo Bill* is narrower in scope than *Nashville*, an attempt to find the origins of certain kinds of cultural domination and its representations in history and language. As opposed to *Nashville's* openness, it is an immediate, didactic, unambiguous, and closed essay on the substitution of personality for reality and the turning of history into lies—filmed with a jaundice-yellow wash over its images. *Buffalo Bill* is a narrative about narrative, about making stories and assuming that those stories adequately account for an individual's perceptions of the world. In short, the film is about the generation of ideology itself. Ned Buntline, writer of dime novels, creates Buffalo Bill out of William F. Cody, and Buffalo Bill creates the Wild West in which the white man always and effortlessly triumphs over the savage Indian. America and its history is an enclosed compound of actors and producers who keep sucking the past into their arena and recreating it into a banal and simple present. "Everything historical is yours, Bill," says one of the boss's toadies. "I'm going to Codyfy the world," promises Nate Salsbury, producer-director of the Wild West. In the process the world is reduced to false assumptions of racial superiority, manifest destiny, and the complete gullibility of anyone not a party to the show.

Partly satire, partly farce, partly, as its subtitle states, history lesson, *Buffalo Bill* creates a set of exaggerated characters whose lives are devoted to exaggeration and to turning the false into the real. "Halsey he don't mean a word he says," comments Buffalo Bill on Sitting Bull's interpreter. "Which is why he sounds so real." Their words (in some of the best dialogue in Altman's work, co-written by Altman and Alan Rudolph) constantly expose their own absurdity without their ever showing an awareness of what they are saying. Except for the somber and dignified Sitting Bull, Halsey, and Burt Lancaster's Ned Buntline, who act as chorus, commenting sadly and ironically on the events, the characters stay enclosed within their world and their lies, feeding on each other and off Bill, who feeds off the image of himself created by Buntline and compounded in his show (Bill is played by Paul Newman, and the result of this casting is to have one star of mythic dimensions play another who is playing the myth of himself that was created by someone else).[21]

The structure of the film is analogous to that of Kubrick's *Dr. Strangelove.* There is a similar use of language that signifies one thing to those inside the fiction and another thing to those on the outside; a similar blindness of the characters to the implications of their actions; and, like Kubrick's characters, the inhabitants of the Wild West are trapped in the logic of their lies, perpetuating an insulated and self-serving perception of the world that is destructive in its simplifications and assumptions. The film invites comparison as well with Penn's *Little Big Man.* But where Penn's picaresque narrative of a white man caught between his own corrupt world and the Indians' innocent and gentle culture suffers from special pleading, from an attempt to perpetuate another myth, that of the noble and gentle savage, Altman chooses another route. He is not concerned with the Indians per se; he realizes that their diminution and ruin have been accomplished and are irreversible (when the small and unprepossessing Sitting Bull first arrives at the Wild West, everyone mistakes Halsey for him—"That Injun's seven feet tall," someone says. "He's getting smaller every year," replies Buntline, aware that the myth cannot sustain itself). Rather, Altman speaks of the perpetuation of that ruin and of the self-deception that permits the perpetuation. Bill is in love with the image of himself (he looks in mirrors, gazes at his portrait), and that image is turned into an ideology of supremacy, of victory and hegemony. When Bill dreams of the dead Sitting Bull, who appears, as always, silent, self-contained, private, and assured, he can only insist that this hegemony must be real, for, if it is not, he is alone and without value. (Bill's dream is filmed in a rather theatrical manner almost as if it were on a stage. *Buffalo Bill* is in fact based on a play by Arthur Kopit and foreshadows the theatrical adaptations that would occupy Altman in the eighties.) "God meant me to be white," he says. "And it ain't easy. I got people with no lives livin' through me! . . . You see, in one hundred years I'm still going to be Buffalo Bill. Star! And you're still going to be the Injun." Gazing, yet again, at his portrait, Bill asks a question whose connotations pervade the film: "My God, ain't he ridin' that horse right? But if he ain't, then how come all of you took him for a king?"

Buffalo Bill and his Wild West must be right. Everyone assents to him and his myths. No one has ever questioned him. The mystical dreams and humane demands of Sitting Bull result only in his humiliation and defeat (the last thing seen of him is a charred bone). Buffalo Bill lives on in power and victory. These must be real. In the last sequence of the film, Bill "fights" Sitting Bull in the arena of the Wild West as hundreds cheer. The Sitting Bull he fights is actually Halsey, the tall Indian whom everyone figured must have been Sitting Bull when they first rode into the Wild West together. Everyone was right after all. "When the legend becomes fact, print the legend," says the newspaper man at the end of Ford's *The Man Who Shot Liberty Valance.* Ford was quite serious. His conservatism demanded assent to cultural myths. Altman is both amused and appalled by the ease with which the myths prevail. Buffalo Bill has his own way. He fights the Indian everyone expected him to fight, and he beats him by merely pushing him to the ground. He stands in phony triumph over his phony captive, and the fraud is climaxed by the camera pulling far away to a high shot of the Wild West arena surrounded by the wilderness. The shot seems to signify entrapment. Bill and his company are alone and isolated by their lies. But it is a troubling point of view, for it is not very clear to whom it belongs. Is it meant to indicate newfound superiority to the lies of "the show business" on the part of the viewer? Having seen this film, does the viewer now see clearly how he or she is abused by cultural myths? Has this analysis of the semiology of cultural production freed us from subjugation to the signs the owners of the culture create to manufacture a predetermined response? Actually, all Altman has done is describe the present in terms of the past.

The dynamics of cultural response, of politics, of film continue to prove his point that the society remains gullible to the fraudulence of celebrity, movie heroism, and white male supremacy. "The show business" and its spectacles continue to command attention and assent, and the culture seems contented by its passivity in the face of those dominant images. In the seventies there was the passivity of disenchantment and disengagement. If the heroes are dead, the culture seemed to say, if heroism is itself a fraud and no other alternatives seem possible, then all that remains is simply to bemoan the fraud and mourn the death. In the early eighties the hero was revived. On screen, muscular men destroyed foreigners, and visitors from outer space protected children. An aging movie star became President and regenerated the fantasy of white, male, middle-class, Christian dominance that can secure the world under the protection of heroes made in its image. "Everything historical is yours."

Altman revived Bill Cody once again just at the point of transition from the seventies into the eighties in a film that marked an end to the first phase of his career and looked back at what he had done before. *Health* is a great carnival of a film, a hilarious documentation of politics and culture at the end of the Carter era when passivity began to disguise itself as self-satisfaction and marginal interests requested majority attention.* The focus of the film is narrow and precise, even though the form of the film, like the best of Altman's work, is loose and open, full of peripheral action, off-screen dialogue, and, occasionally, multiple sight gags going on in one shot, after the manner of the French director Jacques Tati. But here, instead of linking together many narratives to make a larger commentary on the politics of manipulation as he does in *Nashville*, Altman creates a very precise event. A Florida convention of health food enthusiasts becomes a small mirror of larger political follies, of silly, self-serving people so convinced of their importance that they take for granted the fact that major significance attends their ridiculous activities.

The event is the perfect parody of political spectacle in which self-importance is raised to a historical (and perfectly hysterical) imperative, and gestures are made for the sole purpose of calling attention to themselves and the television cameras that observe them. There are flacks,

---

* The idea of the carnivalesque, borrowed from the Russian formalist critic Michail Bakhtin, and prominent in film and literary criticism in the eighties and nineties, addresses works that uproot traditional class hierarchies and conventional narrative and character structures. *Health* and many other of Altman's films fit this notion of misrule and unruliness.

advance persons, people dressed up as a variety of fruits and vegetables, a television talk show host, and candidates. Esther Brill (Lauren Bacall), an eighty-three-year-old virgin, believes that each orgasm a woman has shortens her life by twenty-eight days. Her motto is "Feel Yourself" and she tends, in the middle of a sentence, to raise her hand and fall promptly to sleep. Her rival is Isabella Garnell (Glenda Jackson), who orders the furniture removed from her hotel room—"Our worship should not be of material achievement," she pontificates, "but of human values and ideals"—drinks hot water with nothing in it, idolizes and quotes Adlai Stevenson, and records all her thoughts onto a tape cassette. A third candidate, Dr. Gill Gainey (Paul Dooley, who co-wrote the film), has an ostentatious patch of white hair on his head, proclaims himself a member of the extreme middle, a mediator between the people and nutrition, and sells a product that has "all the sea water without the salt." When his candidacy gains no attention, he lies at the bottom of a swimming pool as if dead. Carol Burnett plays Gloria Burbank, a White House representative on nutrition who, after pleading neutrality, declares herself for Isabella Garnell and becomes romantically involved with her former husband, Harry Wolff (James Garner), Esther Brill's campaign manager. (The least clever item in the film is Gloria's propensity to become sexually aroused whenever she is frightened, a dumb idea on which Altman plays a variation in *Prêt-à-Porter*.) A political trickster (Henry Gibson) dresses up as a woman and advocates breast feeding in an attempt to gain Isabella's confidence in order to discredit her by proving that she is really a man.

The general chaos is given some order by two figures, one of whom is the only woman of sanity in the film. She is the black public relations director for the convention hotel, who observes the events with a distanced amazement and bemusement that places her as a surrogate for the viewer. The other figure has a more complex role. Dick Cavett appears as himself, a talk show host who is covering the convention. Earlier, in *Nashville*, Elliott Gould and Julie Christie appeared as "actual" Hollywood celebrities among the country and western celebrities impersonated by the actors in the film, and *The Player* depends on the appearance of any number of celebrities coming into and out of the frame to give it a kind of reflexive, semi-parodic energy. Cavett has a more clever function in *Health*. Here and in *Nashville*, characters either fawn over the personalities who enter their fiction from the outside or take them for granted, and in either case a hierarchical structure of illusion is created among actors playing celebrities and actors who are celebrities already and play themselves. Cavett's role in *Health* turns this around somewhat. He is, of course, the actual celebrity and the point to which all the characters tend to gravitate. The television program he is doing from the health food convention draws everyone to him, including the viewer—the electronic titles marking the start of taping are super-imposed on the screen as the show within the show begins. (As in *Brewster McCloud*, the film starts by pointing to its existence as documentation of a spectacle. Someone yells "Hit it!" and, under the studio's logo, the Twentieth Century-Fox drum roll is replaced by the convention band.) Cavett remains calm and aloof from the lunatic activities of the other characters. Twice in the course of the film, as the other characters go through their machina-tions, Altman cuts away to Cavett, zooms gently into him lying in bed, watching Johnny Carson. The actual celebrity, entering a fiction filled with would-be celebrities, removes himself from the frenzy to commune with a colleague on television.

As in *Nashville*, a collision of fictions and illusions pushes the already eccentric structure of the film further off-center. Altman creates a world that is a parody of a political phenomenon that is itself already a parody of show business, for political conventions always mediate the realities of power with the signifiers of spectacle. *Health* is, finally, a representation of a representation. And Dick Cavett, the talk-show host, a celebrity who acts as mediator and midwife to other celebrities and moderator of the specta-cle, is in the perfect position to be ringmaster of this carnival, remaining aloof to the very situation he has a responsibility for creating.

Into this crazed parody of political buffoonery comes a strange, frightening, prophetic figure with a familiar name. Col. Cody (played with a violent southern accent by Donald Moffat) appears, not as Buffalo Bill, but as a right-wing ogre who claims to own the health food convention and, by implication, the government itself. During two sequences played out in a threatening darkness, one with candidate Isabella Garnell, the other with Gloria Burbank, he speaks of a corporate power that diminishes everything in its wake. "You're into government programs," he tells Isabella, "we're into foreign governments." He claims responsibility for the death of the group's president, the event that has lead to the current campaign battle. "You work for me, woman," he tells the White House representative, "you are finished making moral stands. Your work is meaningless. You ain't gonna change a thing." And to Isabella he delivers a most chilling judgment that affirms completely the power of manipulation and lies over reality. "Lady," he tells her, "you have told me what I wanted to hear. You are for real. That means you are no threat to anyone." The words echo something Altman's original

Col. Cody said about Sitting Bull's Indian interpreter: "Halsey, he don't mean a thing he says, which is why he sounds so real."

Lying, as Franz Kafka's Joseph K. feared, is raised to a universal principle. The appearance of truth is given more power than any possible realities might have—including the reality of Col. Cody himself. The great liar and owner of all things historical proves, in his reincarnation in *Health*, to still be a fraud. He is not the right-wing lunatic he sounds like, but rather Esther Brill's crazy brother pretending to be a right-wing lunatic. Everything, finally, is what it seems, a perfect illusion, a manipulation of words, images, and individuals in a great, silly game. Everyone willingly enters into a trance. The convention of health food enthusiasts is to be followed by a convention of hypnotists. Dinah Shore, who will cover that group, greets Dick Cavett as he leaves.

Altman is so fascinated by that particular manipulator and corrupter of images, Buffalo Bill Cody, that he recreates him yet again—much changed in form—in another film. *Secret Honor*, the one-person play about Richard Nixon filmed by Altman in 1984, stands as a coda to the meditations on politics, celebrity, and spectacle carried forward in *Nashville*, *Buffalo Bill and the Indians*, and *Health*. Altman's Nixon is Buffalo Bill turned schizophrenic. Part of him is the great fraud who would mold history into a reflection of his televised image and an echo of his tape-recorded voice. Another part is a passive hysteric, hiding behind a self-induced nightmare of conspiracy in which he becomes the willing political tool of the rich and powerful. The result is a Nixon made up of cringing bravura: an obscene, racist, anti-Semitic, all-American paranoid, who denies his power and corruption, replacing it with delusions of conspiratorial forces to which he has no choice but submit.

During the course of the film, which takes place in the confines of an office, he drinks, yells, exclaims, whines, talks into his tape recorder (an extension of his personality and filmed in ways that Oliver Stone borrowed for his *Nixon*), addresses his image on four television monitors—the confirmation of his personality—or to an imaginary judge, or his dead mother, whose imaginary presence removes the sentimentality that visible representation permits in Stone's *Nixon*. He strangles on language, sometimes finds it impossible to get words out of his throat. He stands dwarfed by portraits of Lincoln, Woodrow Wilson, and the alter ego he despises, Henry Kissinger, alternately defying the world and contemplating suicide. He blames his career on the "Committee of One Hundred," a shadowy group of businessmen who, he insists, used him to keep control of the world and allowed him the illusion of power. "There I am," he says, "down in the sewer, waiting for my turn just like every-fucking-body else." This Nixon is a vile and profane Rupert Pupkin, who became president instead of a television star. This is not the man haunted by his past and the misprision of his own personality, as is Stone's Nixon, but someone who seems to know exactly how corrupt and crazy he is and is perfectly defiant about it.

Like so many of Altman's characters, Nixon uses passivity as a means of action. The contradiction is a bold one. By refusing to act, or only reacting to situations caused by inaction, or blaming actions on the power of others, or by being a willing subject to someone else's spectacle, these characters remove themselves from responsibility—or are removed from it. Altman is especially drawn to the passivity that is the result of gender, a passivity that is not wanted, but culturally enforced. In five films (and *The Laundromat*, a short work made for cable television), he attempts an examination of women who react in strange and sometimes destructive ways to their subordinate situations, or who can't react at all. The films raise the inevitable problem of whether a male artist can explore female consciousness from anything but a male perspective. Therefore, those films whose subjects are women—*That Cold Day in the Park, Images, Three Women, Come Back to the Five and Dime, Jimmy Dean, Jimmy Dean, Short Cuts* (I think that *Cookie's Fortune*, also a film about women, does not quite match the others because its point of view is spread among a number of characters; it is an ecumenical film)—must be understood as films about women from the point of view of a particular male. And it is not an entirely dependable point of view. The films in which women are active though not necessarily central figures—*Nashville, A Wedding, Health, Beyond Therapy, Prêt-à-Porter*—do not offer terribly flattering representations. The women there are often foolish and, when they act, it is sometimes stupidly. A question of consistency is raised, and of authenticity. Second, Altman finds it difficult, in the films whose subjects are women, to escape from some old Hollywood or theatrical conventions of rendering psychological states: strained camera angles and odd point-of-view shots, dreams, hallucinations, memories, mirrors that serve as windows to the past, eerie music.[22] Unlike Scorsese, who managed an almost creditable film about a woman in *Alice Doesn't Live Here Anymore* by avoiding psychology, Altman gets caught in a dilemma. His attempts to define states of mind in novel ways run the risk of being compromised by his use of expressionist interventions. With the exception of *Three Women* and *Short Cuts*, the narrative inquisitiveness and formal playfulness with which Altman explores character and event from the outside, avoiding psychological analysis and defining character by what the character does and what is done to him or her, are largely missing in these films.

That Cold Day in the Park, as I noted earlier, is important as an indication of Altman's early experimentation in reorganizing the spatial centers of his narrative. Thematically, its attempt to present the cliché of the sexually repressed spinster who can only release her repressions in deviant behavior would hardly be worthy of comment were it not for the respect that Altman shows for the character of Frances Austen and his skepticism toward the boy she brings in from the cold. She mothers, attempts to seduce, imprisons, and procures for him, and then kills the whore she has procured. Both Frances and the boy are presented as being equally repressed. She traps herself in the accoutrements of old age, surrounds herself with old people; he is a passive onlooker to the sexuality of others. Both of them can be seen as the first of Altman's passive characters, acted on, in this case, by their repressions and their environments—the gloom of Frances's apartment and the shallow brightness of the streets the boy wanders. Their environments help to define them, but they are at the same time set off from the worlds they inhabit. A sense of isolation and inwardness is achieved by the shots that zoom away from Frances in her apartment to a wall of glass bricks or the lights of the street seen out of focus through the window.

This movement is Altman's central attempt at rendering an internal state, a lack of emotional anchorage, a sense of surroundings precariously or incompletely grasped. He uses similar techniques in *Images* and *Three Women*, and in all three cases his use of the zoom is unlike that in the other films where it accents a face, picks out a detail, indicates the extension of space. In *The Long Goodbye*, the zoom, along with the arc and the tracking shot, is used to create an unstable space, but that space is not merely reflective of the internal state of the central character; rather it indicates an almost universal instability of perception. In *That Cold Day*, movement is to blurred or reflected objects; in *Images* to a wind chime, which becomes a kind of fetish, an instrument that is insistently played on, but is itself passive, an apt reflection of the central character. Reflective surfaces become apertures of memory in *Come Back to the Five and Dime*, where images of the past appear through a mirror, and the zoom and pan are directed across time from one barren moment to an earlier one.

Like *That Cold Day* (indeed, like *The Long Goodbye* and *Nashville*), *Images* is about a passivity that turns to the destruction of someone else.

387

Rendered in the most extreme subjective terms—the viewer, a good part of the time, sees only what the character sees—this passivity results in the breakdown of the character's perception of the "real" world and a withdrawal into an interior, surrogate one, which then redefines "reality." Altman does something very clever here. *Images* contains his most sharply defined images (made by Vilmos Zsigmond). There is little apparent tinkering with the color (the "flashing" technique, a method of pre-exposing the film that renders the gold and blue in *McCabe,* the blue-green haze of *The Long Goodbye,* and the jaundice-yellow of *Buffalo Bill*) and a greater use than in the other films of deep-focus cinematography. By unlocalizing the place of the film—it was shot in Ireland, but the locations are never named—and then rendering that unnamed location in bright, hard, deep images, Altman makes the hallucinatory world of the central figure, Cathryn (Susannah York), very immediate and very vague simultaneously. There is little narrative byplay in the film; the events are precisely focused among only five characters who become interchangeable in Cathryn's mind. (The name of each actor is given to another actor's character: Susannah York is Cathryn, Cathryn Harrison is Susannah, Hugh Millais— who plays the killer Butler in McCabe —is Marcel, Marcel Bozzuffi is René and René Auberjonois is Hugh.) *Images,* in appearance and narrative construction, is one of Altman's clearest films, and he takes great delight in playing that clarity and immediacy against the deranged and incoherent sensibility of his main character.

In retrospect (the film was not well received or understood in 1972), *Images* is also very clear and immediate in its statement about a particular kind of withdrawal and passivity. Cathryn is trapped by a basic dilemma: how to reconcile the demands of the self with the demands of domesticity, of being a dutiful wife to—in this case—a meticulously bourgeois husband. Both in rebellion against and withdrawal from this conflict Cathryn retreats and then exteriorizes her other, a sexual being with lovers and strong demands. She fears this other and the sexuality she represents. Her conflict undoes her, and in her imagination she kills her former lover, René, with a shotgun and stabs her husband's lecherous friend, Marcel (René is actually already dead when he appears to Cathryn's imagination, and Marcel reappears quite well and happy after she stabs him). In a final hallucinatory attempt to confront and destroy her other self, she kills her husband "for real." The events and conclusion of the film propose an excess of imaginative zeal in the representation of madness.

Yet Altman's desire to show madness as one manifestation of a particu-

388

lar social-political phenomenon, in this case the cultural oppression of women, may be valid but is also evasive. He is perhaps more successful when he comes to the problem from the outside, as observer, then as analyst. Mrs. Miller is a better creation of a woman attempting to be free, and Keechie of a woman oppressed by her helplessness, than Cathryn is of either. *Images* may suffer from being too clear, too simple, and too much centered on the abnormal psychology of its main character, problems with which Altman continually struggles when exploring feminine consciousness. *Come Back to the Five and Dime* splits its subject five ways. Five women gather in the Woolworth's of a desiccated Texas town to celebrate the reunion of their James Dean fan club. Images of their past and discussion of their present reveal a complex of lies and delusions each has visited on herself. The dramatic—indeed theatrical—sequence of unveilings, in the course of which more and more neurosis, repression, and pathos are discovered as each character exposes more and more of her life, yields finally to a notion of patriarchy as mutilation.[23]

Each of them has undergone a diminishment of self, physically and psychologically. Sissy (Cher), who, in order to please men, fetishizes her breasts as her most sexually attractive feature, reveals that she has in fact lost them to cancer. Joanne (Karen Black) is literally castrated. Humiliated as a boy because of effeminate characteristics and denied by Mona, whose child he fathered, he has had himself surgically rendered female. Mona (Sandy Dennis) lives in the belief that she bore a retarded child fathered by James Dean during the filming of *Giant*. She has surrounded herself with pictures and masks of Dean, turned herself into the Virgin Mary of a celebrity cult figure. In an illusory world, bordered on one side by the mirror of their past, on another by relics of a fifties movie star, and all around by the lifeless heat of the desert, these characters represent women not merely as victims of patriarchal demand, but as crippled by it. Unable to sustain themselves in the patriachal structure, they have neurotically withdrawn from it or denied it or themselves. The only member of the group who insists she is happy is a woman who is perpetually pregnant, who finds comfort in the secure anonymity of domesticity.

Like *That Cold Day in the Park* and *Images, Come Back to the Five and Dime, Jimmy Dean, Jimmy Dean* deals with the crisis of women confronting the oppressions of patriarchy by dissolving them into neuroses. Unable to struggle, these figures first collapse within themselves and then extrapolate their delusions as protection against the world that surrounds them. *Fool for Love*, though not specifically about women, is also concerned with the

389

oppressions of patriarchy—quite literally, as it describes the effects on his children of a man who kept two wives. Here the delusions of repression and emotional pain are drawn through two visual/narrative devices. More than in his other films, Altman shoots characters and their actions—sometimes whole sequences—through windows, separating figures from one another and from the viewer, suggesting a constant desire to see things that cannot be seen directly or clearly. When the characters—the Old Man (Harry Dean Stanton), Eddie (Sam Shepard, author of the play on which the film is based), and May (Kim Basinger)—attempt to recall their past and relate its emotional terrors, their words and the images that accompany them do not quite match. The gestures and actions of the characters in the flashback may simply deny what the character is saying in voice-over or may be out of narrative sync, occurring at a different time, perhaps—or at all times.[24] The mirror in *Come Back to the Five and Dime, Jimmy Dean, Jimmy Dean* presents direct entry to the past, perhaps revealing more than the characters wish to remember. The flashbacks in *Fool for Love* indicate that the past is either unreachable, or too present, or that it must be changed, romanticized, revised in the present for the characters to deal with its unpleasantness.

In no instance is the result entirely satisfactory. Narratives of victimization internalized and then emerging as destruction of self or others remain stories of victimization. And melodramatic revelations, no matter how cleverly generated, tend to cancel profundity through their excess. Altman is most successful when he generates his subjects out of a rich and cluttered field of images and sounds from which he can appear casually to pick and choose, defining his characters by indirection rather than melodrama. *Three Women* works the best among his films on women because it attempts to avoid exclusive concentration on neurosis and combines a number of narrative approaches. The film works simultaneously from the inside out—from the characters' minds to the world beyond them—and from the outside in—from the contemporary, desert landscape of the Southwest to the people that landscape defines. To this is added another element. Mediating the interior and exterior worlds is the continual presence of a group of grotesque murals painted by one of the characters. These murals depict three reptilian women: one shows them at each other's throats; another shows two under the domination of the third; and both show all of them diminished by an enormous male figure. The result of the interplay of interior states, exterior landscape, and the bizarre murals that punctuate the film at strategic moments is an expressionism of sorts. Not the almost classical expressionism of *Taxi Driver*, in which the appearance of the external world is molded through the perceptions of an agonized mind, but rather an expressionism created through the counterpointing of the world in its physical and ideological presence with reflections of that world off of the emotional states of the characters. The world of *Taxi Driver* is terribly concrete and immediate. The world of *Three Women* seems an appendage to the world of ordinary experience, not quite real, not quite nightmare, not even a fully articulated world, but a realm of existence that combines parts of each and whose most distinguishing feature is aridity and banality. It is all but empty of anything but the bizarre and the commonplace.[25] (The geographical locations of *Come Back to the Five and Dime* and *Fool for Love* are similar to *Three Women*, but because he must restrict locations, Altman cannot visually play the counterpoint of exterior and interior as he does here. Aridity and barrenness, however, are qualities shared by the three films.)

At one point, Millie Lammoreaux (Shelley Duvall) is driving her roommate Pinky's parents to her apartment. The camera observes the mother through the windshield of the car as she says, "Sure doesn't look like Texas." The camera pans away to reveal a featureless desert landscape that could be Texas, Southern California, Arizona, New Mexico, anywhere that is dry and hot and without features or human habitation. Pinky's mother sees a difference where there is none, attempts to give meaning to that which is barren of meaning. She brings a present for her daughter, a plaque with a gruesomely oppressive rhyme: "In this kitchen, bright and cheery, daily chores I'll never shirk. So bless this kitchen, Lord, and bless me as I work." "It's for the kitchen," she says. In *Three Women* everyone is trapped by clichés, by an inability to speak beyond the ordinary and the commonplace, their minds rendered sterile by having nothing to think about, nothing to feel, nothing to say, nothing to see.

Throughout his films, Altman has shown a painful sensitivity to the banal and an awareness of its destructive capabilities. *Three Women* takes the banal as its subject. Its characters, Millie, Pinky Rose (Sissy Spacek), and Willie (Janice Rule), as well as everyone who surrounds them, are ciphers, empty vessels in an empty landscape. Most are filled by whatever floats by. Millie ("I'm known for my dinner parties"—which consist only of packaged, processed food) is filled with the language of women's magazines and so insulated by its dehumanizing jargon that she seems oblivious to the fact that she is ignored by everyone. Pinky is filled by Millie, for she has no self at all. She is first seen when the camera zooms to her face, wide-eyed and blank, staring through a window at the health spa for old people where she has come to work. Later, at the spa, when she talks incessantly about Millie and how she misses her, the camera slowly and deliberately zooms to and past her face—achieving an effect akin to having her face slide slowly off the side of the Panavision screen—to the bright windows behind her, which go out of focus. There is an immediate cut to a metered television set on the wall of Pinky's dark, closed room. The set is on, but there is nothing on it, and the camera pulls back from the bright empty screen (which suddenly goes off) to Pinky lying asleep. This movement and cut accomplish what Altman was trying to do in *That Cold Day* and *Images*, to find a visual surrogate for a subjective state. Pinky is as blank as a curtained window or a television screen, a creature without a personality, without thought. The third woman, Willie, is less detailed. She is pregnant and finally delivers a stillborn baby, a barren birth into a barren world. An artist, she creates the murals of reptilian women (one of whom is pregnant) and the monstrous male who controls them. She is married to Edgar, a parody of a macho male, an ex-stuntman and gun-toting buffoon who sleeps with Millie (the only man who will) and is the analogue to the male figure in Willie's mural. Willie is mostly silent, seemingly removed from the banality around her, yet constantly commenting on the terror of that banality in her art. Having given up the language of patriarchy, she seeks to comment on its oppression in another language, in the monstrous, almost mythic images she paints.[26]

A problem that Altman has with these figures and their world is integrating them within a coherent design. As I said, he attempts to create a modified expressionist point of view, indicating states of mind. The early sequences in the health spa, with the silent old people being walked about by Millie and her colleagues; the first sequence in Millie's yellow apartment and Edgar's dilapidated bar where she hangs out, with motorcyclists and target shooters in the back and Willie painting her murals in an empty swimming pool; Millie's early relationship with Pinky; the sequence in which Millie enters her bedroom to find Pinky's decrepit parents locked in a sexual embrace—all form a complex point of view that oscillates between a recognizable world and a frightening, disengaged, disorienting one where identities are uncertain because unformed and unformed because there is no sense of self or location.

The point of entry into the film for the viewer is also uncertain. There is no possibility for "identification" with the characters and little sense of understanding, on a rational level, this discourse of absent personalities. The film may be an attempt—more extreme than in the other works—to split perceptions, remove their foundations, as the characters are split and unfounded. In the sequence where Willie gives birth to her dead child, the camera is placed just outside the doorway of this gruesome scene of pain and loss, placing the viewer at a distance but at the same time forcing on him the point of view of Millie inside, helping Willie, and Pinky outside, frozen in terror. Here and throughout the film, the viewer is caught in a forced perspective where the immediacy of the event and its detached and disorienting structure conflict. The result is a sense of being unanchored, with no firm or assured position, drifting, like the subjects within the narrative, through shifting images and significations. As a result, the viewer tends to gain no knowledge greater than the characters have, to see and understand no more than they do.

Altman seems intent on overmystifying the narrative or, perhaps more accurately, overdetermining it with expressions of mystery and a forced sense of the portentous. There is little of the playfulness present even in the most serious of his other films (a problem the film shares with *Quintet*, *Streamers*, and, to a certain extent, *Fool for Love*). The exchange of identities between Millie and Pinky, for example, is an excellent idea, but managed with a strained sense of profundity. Altman had toyed with it in *Images*, where Cathryn and her young friend Susannah are seen reflected together in mirrors, and finally with their faces superimposed in a window, suggesting that Susannah, as a woman, will follow Cathryn's path of madness. The more explicit exchange between Millie and Pinky (who says her name is really Millie) seems an inevitable result of the emptiness of their personalities. But Altman cannot disengage himself from the Bergmanesque pretentiousness of the situation. Fortunately he does not infuse the situation with the metaphysical vaguenesses of *Persona*; he is too much in touch with the immediate presence of our culture. The world is present in *Three Women*, and its influence marked on the characters. But that influence remains diffuse. The idea of interchanging identities is itself diffuse, too fanciful and too abstracted from the otherwise concrete and immediate indicators of barren souls in a barren world.

The tension between abstract and concrete is strongest in the final sequences of the film, as Altman attempts to reanchor the psychological transformations of character back into the environment they came from. When Pinky absorbs Millie's personality, she expresses it in a spirit of meanness and coldness, without her host's cliché-ridden vocabulary and without the pathetic quality that vocabulary lent her. Millie buckles under Pinky's meanness, her passive nature submitting to Pinky's newfound and

393

misdirected strength. But another change occurs after Pinky's nightmare—perhaps the most portentous, if not pretentious, sequence in the film, in which all the faces appear doubled or in violent and distorted form and the events of Willie's stillbirth are foreshadowed. After the nightmare, Pinky is more docile; her fear brings her to Millie for mothering, she wants to sleep with her, and Millie comforts her, placing her hand on her face. A new relational complex is forming, which will be completed after the horrendous sequence of Willie bearing her dead boy.

During the stillbirth, Millie acts with a strength she has never before demonstrated. Pinky is frozen in fear, unable to call for a doctor. After Millie emerges from the house, hands bloodied and shaking in front of her, as she had appeared to Pinky in the dream, she slaps her, again demonstrating an unexpected sense of power and control. The sequence ends on Pinky's face, bloodied by Millie's hand, which has in effect transferred to her the sign of Willie's agony. From Pinky's face a cut is made to a long, far shot of a desert road, barren and hot, power lines marking the background. A yellow Coca-Cola truck comes into view (yellow is the bright, bland color that Millie chooses for everything: her apartment, her dress, her car). The truck pulls into the "Dodge City" bar that Edgar owned and that was Millie's hangout. Pinky is behind the bar, chewing gum, reading a magazine. When the delivery man asks to have his Coca-Cola signed for, Pinky says she'll call her "mom," who turns out to be Millie. In the dialogue with the delivery man, there is the revelation that Edgar has been shot, "a terrible accident, we're all grieved by it." Millie orders Pinky to the house to fix dinner. At the house Willie sits on the porch, telling of a dream she had and cannot remember. The camera zooms back from the house; Millie is heard ordering Pinky about, Willie asking why she has to be so mean to her. The camera pans to a pile of old tires, the last image of the arid landscape. The shot dissolves to the mural of the three reptilian women bent to the ground. The enormous male figure has one of the females by the tail; he raises his other hand in a fist. One of the female figures points up to an occult symbol, a cross in a circle, around which emerge four snakes.

The film concludes with Altman's most bitter observation of domination and passivity, of assent to ritual and assumption of cultural myths. The three women, ridding themselves of men (Willie's child was male and is born dead; and the suggestion is clear that the women shot Edgar—"I'd rather face a thousand crazy savages than one woman who's learned to shoot," he had said earlier), proceed to reenact a family structure with one dominant member, now maternal rather than paternal, and two passive members. The enclave they form in the garbage-strewn desert is a parody of the male-dominated society reflected in Willie's mural and whose patterns of domination and passivity Altman sees spread through all relationships. They can only exist in an isolated reenactment of power and passivity within the structure of the family, that central image of psychological and economic control, the place where the ideology is delivered, nurtured, and reproduced.

As opposed to Spielberg and many of the filmmakers discussed in the preceding chapter, Altman sees the family as a barren place, as barren as the ideology it reproduces and that reproduces it, demanding that a fantasy of security and succor apart from the public sphere be accepted as necessity. The family is literally barren at the end of *Three Women*, where its grim imitation of life takes place in the dry desert, and is destructive of all emotional balance in *Fool for Love*, where a father's attempt to have two families results in an oppressive sexual relationship between the son and daughter of his different wives. Only when characters escape the grip of family, as in *A Perfect Couple* and *Cookie's Fortune*, or transcend the limits of ordinary emotional demands, as in *Beyond Therapy*, does Altman offer any hope of victory.

His most vicious attack on domestic institutions occurs in *A Wedding*, which furthers Altman's explorations and revelations of hypocrisy, duplicity, manipulation, and humiliation. The subject of attack here is the very ritual that constitutes the institutionalizing of love in the culture, and Altman uses that ritual to work through many of his concerns.[27] Formally, the film is another experiment in the interaction of large numbers of people within an open narrative form. Contextually, he continues to explore the breakdown of community, the difficulties—indeed the impossibilities—of romantic engagement. Although often a clever and funny film, its anger and, too frequently, condescension tend to make it flippant and evasive. Almost every cut, every zoom, reveals another bit of banal or embarrassing behavior without seeking to reveal the root causes of the banalities or to explain why they are so ridiculous. A senile priest, a pubescent bride with braces, her sexually promiscuous sister (pregnant by the groom), a pompous lesbian wedding coordinator (played by Geraldine Chaplin, who expands a bit on her unpleasant character in *Nashville*), a mother addicted to heroin, a lovesick in-law who attempts to seduce the mother of the bride—these and other caricatures appear and reappear to be laughed at or degraded. Altman shows, with only some insight or concern, that the rich are foolish and the nouveaux riches superficial and uncaring. The emotional contours of *Nashville* and the intellectual engagement that informs *Buffalo Bill* and *Three Women* are not much in evidence.

A Wedding's cleverness always threatens to become a smugness that, for the first time in Altman's work, comes at the expense of its characters and finally the spectators. When the farce is turned on the viewer, who is led, at one point, to believe that the newlyweds are killed in a car wreck, the manipulation becomes too extreme. When it is revealed that it was not the newlyweds who were killed, but another young couple, a rather attractive man and woman somewhat less odious than the others who populate the film, the manipulation of emotions becomes too facile. The viewer is asked suddenly to reflect on the situation, to be horrified by the fact that the parents of the newlyweds are oblivious to the death of the other couple when they discover that their own children are safe. This becomes the final shame visited on them, and they remain unaware of their emotional poverty. The only noble act in the film is a passive one: Luigi Corelli (Vittorio Gassman), the patriarch who has been held down by his wife's money, leaves the whole group behind for freedom.

But the leaving behind is the problem. Like Mrs. Miller, who withdraws into an opium den, or Essex, who treks out into the ice wastes at the end of *Quintet*, or May, who walks out into the dark at the end of *Fool for Love*, or Prudence and Bruce who transport themselves from New York to Paris, away from the conflicting claims of lovers and therapists in *Beyond Therapy*; like the drift of the camera to the skies at the end of *Nashville*; or like the high shot that ends *Buffalo Bill*, the suggestion remains that the best way out of an impossible situation is simply to leave it behind. In some of these films, the withdrawal is informed by the narrative, by insight into the sources of hypocrisy and self-delusion in *Buffalo Bill*; by a lament for missed chances in *McCabe and Mrs. Miller*; by an understanding of the powers of ritual over life in *Quintet* or the results of distorted domesticity in *Fool for Love*. But *A Wedding* has offered only a stony gaze at a pack of unattractive people, a gaze like that of the statue in the garden to which Altman's camera is occasionally drawn: blank and uncomprehending. The gaze permits a privileged position, a position of safety and superiority, unlike *Buffalo Bill*, which attempts at least to offer an active demythification, to explore some of the foundations of cultural lies. *A Wedding* leaves the viewer simply alone, a situation by now too familiar.

In retrospect, Altman's best work is an ongoing process of representing a cultural and political milieu he sees as ridiculous at best, barren and cruel at worst. It is an ironic and sometimes misanthropic process that often takes pleasure in exposing meanness while exercising an intellectual rigor that permit the films to investigate the destructive assumptions underlying ideological givens. At their most acute, Altman's films, with their unrelenting zooms to, from, and through characters, their fractured narratives and coincidental crossings and linkings of characters, invites our gaze into spaces we usually go to the movies to avoid. The films about women, with their conflicting points of view and unwillingness to remove blame from anyone, best exemplify this, for they insist on a complexity of point of view, of mutual victimization; they look at gender as a cultural phenomenon, heir to all of culture's ideological contradiction. *Short Cuts* carries the process as far as it can conceivably go. Altman has zoomed out from the subject itself, examining not women in particular, but gender as a whole. At the same time, he zooms in on a particular group and a geographical space. Instead of the marginalized, only partly sane figures that inhabit *Three Women*, or the upper-middle class inhabitants of *A Wedding*, he focuses on a broad sample of lower-middle class and working-class white couples, all of them constricted economically and/or emotionally, others diminished only by their shortsightedness, their oppressions, or their mute despair. The setting is contemporary Los Angeles. Not the West Los Angeles and Hollywood of *The Player* or the demi-monde of *The Long Goodbye*, but the suburban sprawl of gangly neighborhoods, every other house up for sale, where nature—whether in the form of the Med-fly or earthquakes—threatens some kind of retribution against the gender warfare going on beneath every roof.

The film is based on a number of stories by Raymond Carver, and it is important to consider this. Altman was busy through the eighties filming plays by prominent dramatists, and drama is meant to be performed and performed again. The films are intelligent interpretations of works meant to be interpreted. Narrative literature is not, despite the fact that so much of Hollywood filmmaking comes from literary sources. The two forms are so fundamentally different that, especially when the literary source is itself a tightly structured, stylistically marked piece of writing, the resulting film should clearly display how it is using its source: as a source for plot material, the raw events that the film narrative respeaks into being (the usual method of film adaptation); as a way to echo the original author's voice and style; or to find its own voice that parallels, responds to, or contradicts its source. Fundamental to all of this is the process of representation and the building of cinematic structures. Meanings do not simply float around, waiting for a writer or a filmmaker to snatch and drop into a book or a movie. When a filmmaker decides to base his work on a novel, he must be aware of what recreation, restructuring, does to the original work. "Adapting a book to a film is fundamentally a moral crisis," Abraham Polonsky once said, "Assuming the intention is serious, the book is not chosen to be translated for non-readers but because still embedded in the conception is a whole unrealized life whose language is a motion of images." [28] We have seen this construction of a new narrative life out of the novel occur in Kubrick's work, and in Altman's *The Long Goodbye*. In *Short Cuts* it becomes even more critical, because Carver is in the canon of contemporary high literature.

Carver's work would not immediately suggest Altman's films. The spareness of his verbal language and narrative, even the oddness of metaphor and event that captures emotion on a kind of sideband of relevance run counter to Altman's large, colorful canvases, filled with people coming and going, usually in the wrong direction. But the two share a dark, even misanthropic, view of human behavior, and especially of gender relationships. The lower-middle class inhabitants of Carver's stories offer Altman a somewhat different perspective on class than he usually takes, and the very spareness, even meanness, of their narrative lives suggests a way for Altman to approach his characters from somewhat different angles than he is used to. More interesting is the challenge of narrative restructuring the stories offer—especially given the fact that Carver himself restructured and even rewrote many of his works. They are, many of them, quite short and self-contained, their characters and their worlds isolated. Isolation is a mark of Carver's fiction: the individuals and couples are meanly or sadly contained within their small fictional world. Altman found a way to maintain the sense of isolation while adopting it to his favorite device of large interlocking narratives, with characters' paths crossing in unexpected ways, the poverty of their lives affecting one another, even without their being aware of it. Unlike Stone, who holds the pieces of his narrative together with montage and flashback, Altman, in *Short Cuts*, creates an interlocking web of narrative not only by having the characters appear within each other's stories, but through often ironic internal references: parallel physical movements or gestures, television sets showing images that imitate or mock the characters' actions, counterpointing and associating them across the narrative field. He turns the sense of isolation and gender panic that is explicit in his own work and inherent in Carver's into a global statement.

It is intriguing to see how Altman worked with his fictional source. "A

Small, Good Thing" is Carver's story about a couple whose son suffers a hit-and-run accident and dies. The couple is harassed by the baker who made the son's birthday cake, and, in their despair, they confront him. He suddenly (in the revised version of the story) shows a constricted expression of sorrow and remorse.[29] The son's doctor at the hospital is Dr. Francis, a rather blank, bland figure, described as "a handsome, big-shouldered man with a tanned face," wearing a three-piece suit. After the child's death, Dr. Francis takes the couple into the doctors' lounge. As if to fill the scene with another figure merely to indicate the ordinary ongoingness of the world in face of the couple's despair, Carver observes:

> There was a doctor sitting in a chair with his legs hooked over the back of another chair, watching an early-morning TV show. He was wearing a green delivery-room outfit, loose green pants and a green blouse, and a green cap that covered his hair. He looked at Howard and Ann and then looked at Dr. Francis. He got to his feet and turned off the set and went out of the room.[30]

He is not heard from again, at least until Altman's film, where he becomes the doctor treating Howard and Ann's son, Casey. He is dressed similarly as he is in the story and is imagined by Altman walking out of that narrative into one of his own. Birthed by Carver's story, taking on a larger life, in *Short Cuts*, as Ralph Wyman, he is not only the doctor treating Casey, but also the seething husband, whose wife's one-time sexual indiscretion is cause for his continual anger—characters who originated in Carver's "Will You Please Be Quiet, Please?" In the film, Ralph's wife, Marian, is a painter of grotesque laughing or screaming figures. She is a direct descendent of Willie in *Three Women* and June Gudmundsdottir in *The Player*, funneling their characters into the film through her work. With this figure, Altman closes a relationship of painter, painting, and subject that he had toyed with in earlier films. Marian's work is a clear expression of her and Ralph's anger and discomfort with each other; hysteria and rage blossom from the images and merge with the characters.

At a long, drunken party in which Ralph and Marian are joined by Claire and Stuart (Claire had met Marian at a concert given by another character in the film, a cellist, who will commit suicide, the daughter of a jazz singer whose songs of pain and anger constitute the film's sound track). In the course of the party, they put on clown makeup. Claire works as a clown for children's shows. They play *Jeopardy* (Alex Trebeck happened to show up

399

at that concert where the two women first met, one of those appearances of celebrity Altman loves). They talk, and Marian remembers her art school teacher—the one with whom she had the affair that tortures Ralph—who killed himself. He taught her the primitive use of painting to express emotion. At the end of her speech, Altman cuts to Ralph, in clown getup, distorting his mouth in a scream, squeezing the neck of a balloon so that it emits a grotesque squeal of his repressed pain. He becomes a figure in one of Marian's paintings.

Cries of pain emerge throughout *Short Cuts* in various guises, through suicides, aggressive acts, inappropriate actions, expressions of repressed sexual anger. Women are almost always the objects of these destructive acts. Before the party, Ralph forces Marian to retell the story of her affair. He is seated amid the paintings in her studio, again as if he were one of them. In a closeup, one of Marian's portraits of a man's head with a manic grin is seen next to him. Ralph asks Marian why her figures are always naked, "Why does naked make it art?" Marian comes back to the room and stands next to a naked female, who is smiling in happiness. Marian spills her drink and removes her skirt. From the waist down, she, like her paintings, is now naked. This moment of intimacy—Marian cannot comprehend Ralph's ruthless pain over her past indiscretion—pushes Ralph to even greater anger and aggressive language: "Marian, look at me. You don't have any panties on. What do you think you are, one of your goddamn paintings?" She dresses, admits to having had intercourse with her teacher, and Ralph goes back to his sullen anger.

Marian's nakedness makes her directly vulnerable, particularly to the viewer's own gaze. This kind of imagery brought some accusations of sexism against the film. But actually quite the opposite of sexism is happening. Altman *is* asking us to look at Marian naked, and she is very attractive. But in the context of Ralph's anger, her own repressing of the memory of the affair, and in light of the paintings that surround her, we are offered a cinematic and narrative space to consider why we enjoy our own voyeurism and why the naked body is not merely attractive, but the potential target of anger to the one who looks. Marian is clearly unembarrassed by her appearance before her husband; he is clearly enraged. The viewer is ricocheted between his point of view, the larger context of what he is doing to Marian and their marriage, and—given all that has already happened in the film—what the female body often means to the male gaze: arousal and the desire to take revenge on arousal's object. The point has been made absolutely clear in the episode of the fishermen who discover a naked woman's body in their lake, pee on it, and leave it in the water until they are ready to go home.*

The structure of that incident, intercutting the men engaged manfully in their sport and camaraderie with shots of the body of the woman, silent, face down under the water—recalling so many of Altman's characters who die in water—causes a kind of lyrical juxtaposition between callousness and its victim. When one of the fishermen, Stuart—who is with his wife at Ralph and Marian's party—comes home, early in the morning, he immediately begins making love to his wife, Claire, despite her protests about his fishy hands, a comment Stuart cannot possibly let go without making a vulgar analogy. The sequence is intercut with some other narrative moments in which various characters talk about aberrant sex or sex as aberration. After their lovemaking, Stuart tells Claire about the body in the water. As she listens, lying next to him in the bed, the camera zooms slowly to her. This is one of the longest shots in the film, and it occurs as a kind of pivot for the viewer's own recognition, a turn further toward the female consciousness that reacts to the brutality around it. Simply gazing at Claire allows us to comprehend her compassion for the dead woman that was unavailable to the men. Claire gets out of bed and takes a bath, as if to share some of the victim's experience while cleansing herself of a shared guilt (she learns that the victim was raped and smothered). She later drives to Bakersfield for the woman's funeral. She mimes signing the guest book, leaving no trace of her presence, preferring an anonymity of feminine support and consolation to match the victim's anonymity to the men who dishonored her corpse. Like most of the women in the film, she has been written out and written off by the men. One of the women in the film is literally written on.

The main traces throughout the film are not of women's presence as active, self-protective agents, but as objects of assault and rage, their personalities quashed. These traces move from the inane to the violent. Stuart and the fishermen visit Doreen's diner and make her bend over to get things for them so they can ogle her backside. Her husband sits by, saying nothing. Stormy Weathers rips his ex-wife's house to shreds. There is rage transferred, in Gene the Cop, who cheats on his wife and steals his kids' dog; and in the smarmy makeup man, Bill, getting a "chubby" as he pretends to beat

---

* I wonder if Altman himself found the implications of this sequence too dreadful? In *Cookie's Fortune*, fishing becomes a site of security and the proof of friendship. The last scene of the film has most of the major characters, male and female, sitting on a dock, happily fishing together.

his wife while making up her face with wounds, writing his hatred on her with marks of violence, and then taking pictures. A funny and chilling moment occurs when one of the fishermen goes to a photo kiosk to get the pictures of the drowned woman at the same moment that Bill and his friends get the pictures of the mock beating of Bill's wife. The photos are mixed up, and each looks at the other's images with horror and quickly exchange them and go their separate ways.

Women destroy themselves, as in the suicide of the cellist, Zoe Trainer; or are economically driven into being sexual objects. The sequences between Lois and Jerry are particularly grueling and lead to the cataclysm that ends the film. The two are just above Doreen and Earl on the economic scale. Jerry is a pool cleaner and Lois supplements her husband's income by doing phone sex. Every time Altman returns to this couple, the rage builds. Altman's attitude toward Lois is ambiguous. She does a job; it's especially degrading, but she seems unaffected by it. Too much so, because she is able to carry on dirty phone talk while feeding her child. She seems unwilling to express sexuality at all to her husband. After all, she has to do it for a living. In scene after scene, Altman zooms in on Jerry's expressions of hurt, confusion, and, finally anger. It pushes him to murder. He and his friend Bill—the makeup artist—pick up some girls while picnicking with their families in Griffith Park. They go off for a walk, and Jerry hits the girl with a rock, and an earthquake ensues.

The murder is inevitable and the earthquake metaphoric, as if nature were reacting to the welling up of gender violence and hatred in the film's characters. But it's hardly final, hardly the apocalypse. Altman is not a director of large closures. It turns out to be a small quake, only one person is killed, unknown by most of the characters in the film—the girl murdered by Jerry—and therefore unimportant. It even makes room for some small compensatory gestures. The bullying baker, when confronted by Howard and Ann, offers them baked goods and protection from the quake. Doreen and Earl stand under the lintel of their trailer, hoping this quake is the big one, satisfied that it's not, reaching a momentary accommodation in their affection for each other. Gene—having previously relented and taken the dog he left in another neighborhood away from its new owners and back to his kids—stands bravely in his backyard, barking safety orders to his neighbors through an LAPD bullhorn. The drunken couples, Claire, Stuart, Marian, and Ralph, continue their angry, retributive revelries. The camera slowly pans away from them, over the L.A. cityscape. On the soundtrack, Annie Ross (the jazz singer who plays Tess, a depressed, alcoholic jazz singer, mother to the suicide) sings "Prisoner of Life."

Short Cuts is a kind of prison house. Its characters move through proscribed physical and emotional spaces, come in contact with one another, accidentally, as relations, or as friends, all the while living out a singularity of despair, bad luck, or anger. The bright light and color of Los Angeles surround them, but they remain dark and obsessed. They move but are frozen in their depression and anger, in their economic and cultural blight. The light and the character's lives suggest an influence on the film beyond Carver, a visual influence by means of the painter Edward Hopper. The light of Hopper's paintings is not of Southern California, but it has that same bright pitilessness, and it has influenced the lighting of many, many films. Individual Hopper paintings—most especially *Night Hawks*, the far shot of a diner at night—have been copied by a number of filmmakers. But Altman, perhaps unconsciously, has captured, without imitation, the loss and diminishment of personality that so many of Hopper's paintings connote: lives negated by depression and loneliness. Mark Strand writes, "Within the question of how much the scenes in Hopper are influenced by an imprisoning, or at least a limiting, dark is the issue of our temporal arrangements—what do we do with time and what does time do to us? ... Hopper's people ... are like characters whose parts have deserted them and now, trapped in the space of their waiting, must keep themselves company, with no clear place to go, no future."[31]

In *Short Cuts*, the characters barely have themselves as company, but continually seek out others to visit their discomfort on them. In the hospital, as Ann and Howard Finnigan agonize over their dying child, hit by Doreen's car, Howard's estranged father comes to visit and unloads on him the story of a wretched affair he had with his wife's sister many years ago. The inappropriateness of the actions of his and all the characters is barely tolerable. Pain is always inflicted. Movement is always brought to an end by all of them. They look to each other and see only their own pain. Class, culture, environment, the ennui of economic and intellectual entrapment create the impossible turmoil of self-hatred, gender hatred, and finally, a panic that occurs at the recognition of entrapment. The characters often do move. They never get anywhere, and they hurt others on the way.

Strand writes about Hopper that his paintings

403

are short, isolated moments of figuration that suggest the tone of what will follow just as they carry forward the tone of what preceded them. The tone but not the content. The implication but not the evidence. They are saturated with suggestion. The more theatrical or staged they are, the more they urge us to wonder what will happen next; the more lifelike, the more they urge us to construct a narrative of what came before. They engage us when the idea of passage cannot be far from our minds. . . . Our time with the painting must include—if we are self-aware—what the painting reveals about the nature of continuousness. Hopper's paintings are not vacancies in a rich ongoingness. They are all that can be gleaned from a vacancy that is shaded not so much by the events of life lived as by the time before life and time after. The shadow of dark hangs over them, making whatever narratives we construct around them seem sentimental and beside the point.[32]

Altman gives the continuousness, the ongoingness, that shadows the vacancies. He gives us narrative. After all, he makes films not paintings. But his stories are rarely sentimental and always reveal that the nature of continuousness—of continuity—may be the sham that hides the fact that connection without betrayal or despair is rare. When we move, we cause hurt. Like Hopper, like any creative imagination that uses the form of his or her work to invite the viewer or reader to see as well, Altman allows us in on process. The despair and vacancies, the revelation of our propensities toward passivity, a willingness to be oppressed by manufactured images that are accepted as historical realities, the ease with which we descend into emotional or physical violence, the images manufactured by Altman to inscribe these subjects refuse to dominate the viewer. The open narrative construction—the flow, the sense of process and accident that so many of his films achieve—attempt to take apart the very subject they create, expose their manufacture and affirm the fact that it is the viewer who must make sense of them. Make us, as Strand hopes, self-aware. Two distinct voices seem to be speaking these filmic discourses. One announces the inevitability of defeat and despair through the hopeless yielding to domination. The other enunciates a freedom of perception and therefore a control over what is seen, understood, and interpreted. However, the dialectic can become mere contradiction. There is an open narrative structure offering the viewer the potential of engaged response; and there is, no matter how great the openness, the insistence that, for all that engagement, the only pos-sibility is to consider the varieties of our lack of freedom. These conflicting voices, speaking against passivity and lack of control while simultaneously declaring their inevitability, risk canceling each other.[33]

Although he remains trapped in the ideology of losing, of gaining and then losing, of profit and loss, Altman, despite his pessimism, has more generosity, more sense of possibilities than anyone making commercial film in America. The other directors I have discussed here, even in their experimentation, seem determined to match narrative form and content, to deploy images of loneliness and entrapment, isolation and fear to reinforce that desperate perception we have of ourselves. If any of their characters prevails, it is for a while only, and they seem only to prevail in order to make their fall all the more hard. When they do succeed—as Spielberg's characters do—their success is so fantastic, so predicated on spectacular events far removed from the social realities of everyday life, that they cancel the very affirmation they seek to make. They leave their viewers lonely with reality. Altman, when he offers the plurality of a cinematically mediated world in its fullness and variety, at least presents the opportunity of expanded perception, of perhaps seeing beyond the prison that our contemporary cinema seems dead set on insisting we inhabit.

And there is in Altman's work always the hope, and sometimes the reality, that someone, even if it is a fictional surrogate for Richard M. Nixon, will raise his fist and call out a loud and clear defiance—"Fuck 'em!"

NOTES

INTRODUCTION

1 Some of the ideas for the decline of Hollywood production values and shifts in studio personnel during the late forties were developed with David Parker. An excellent summary of the changes in Hollywood from the late forties through the sixties—from which much of the information in this section is drawn—can be found in Robert Sklar, *Movie-Made America: A Cultural History of American Movies* (New York: Vintage Books,1994), 249–304. See also Gordon Gow, *Hollywood in the Fifties* (New York: A. S. Barnes, 1971); John Baxter, *Hollywood in the Sixties* (New York: A. S. Barnes, 1972); Axel Madsen, *The New Hollywood: American Movies in the Seventies* (New York: Crowell, 1975); William Paul, "Hollywood Harakiri," *Film Comment* 13 (March–April 1977); Stephen M. Silverman, "Hollywood Cloning: Sequels, Prequels, Remakes, and Spinoffs," *American Film* 3 (July–August 1978), 24–30. For an excellent study of the financial character of the studios, see Douglas Gomery, "The American Film Industry of the 1970s: Stasis in the 'New Hollywood'," *Wide Angle* 5, No. 4 (1983), 52–59. More recent studies of Hollywood economics include Justin Wyatt, *High Concept: Movies and Marketing in Hollywood* (Austin: University of Texas Press, 1994); Steve Neale and Murray Smith, eds., *Contemporary Hollywood Cinema* (New York and London: Routledge, 1998) and Jon Lewis, ed., *The New American Cinema* (Durham, N.C., and London: Duke University Press, 1998).

2 See James Monaco, *The New Wave* (New York: Oxford University Press, 1976), 3–12. Monaco's remains the best study of the French movement and has served as something of a model for this book.

3 In recent years, filmmaking in France has fallen on hard times. The initial cohesion is gone, and while critical commitment remained strong—at least until the early eighties—production has reverted to the classical, linear style. Many French films are now made with an American audience in mind. See David L. Overby, "France: The Newest Wave," *Sight and Sound* 47 (Spring 1978), 86–90; Annette Insdorf, "French Films American Style," *New York Times* (July 28, 1985), H16.

4 Many people have examined the phenomenon of film's effacing its existence as film. Two out of many possible references are Colin MacCabe, "Realism and the Cinema: Notes on Some Brechtian Theses," *Tracking the Signifier* (Minneapolis: University of Minnesota Press, 1985), 33–57; Christian Metz, *The Imaginary Sig-*

nifier, trans. Celia Britton, Annwyl Williams, Ben Brewster, Alfred Guzzetti (Bloomington: Indiana University Press, 1982), 3–68. For the idea of fiction as lie and substitution, see Umberto Eco, *A Theory of Semiotics* (Bloomington and London: Indiana University Press, 1976), 6–7.

5 Louis Althusser, *Language and Materialism* (London: Routledge & Kegan Paul,1977), 67. The second quotation from Althusser comes from *For Marx,* trans. Ben Brewster (New York: Random House, Vintage Books, 1970), 252. For a direct application of ideological theory to cinema studies, see Jean-Louis Comolli and Jean Narboni, "Cinema/Ideology/Criticism," in Bill Nichols, ed., *Movies and Methods,* Vol. I (Berkeley and Los Angeles: University of California Press, 1976), 23–30; Editors of *Cahiers du Cinéma,* "John Ford's *Young Mr. Lincoln,*" in *Movies and Methods* I, 493–529. The April 1978 issue of *Jump Cut* (No. 17) has an excellent series of essays summarizing the subject. See also Bill Nichols, *Ideology and the Image* (Bloomington: Indiana University Press, 1981).

6 Terry Eagleton, *Literary Theory* (Minneapolis: University of Minnesota Press, 1983), 172, 210.

7 See Michael Rosenthal, "Ideology, Determinism and Relative Autonomy," *Jump Cut,* No. 17 (April 1978), 19–22.

8 Some recent work on film music includes Kathryn Kalinak, *Settling the Score: Music and the Classical Hollywood Film* (Madison: University of Wisconsin Press, 1992) and Caryl Flinn, *Strains of Utopia: Gender, Nostalgia, and Hollywood Film Music* (Princeton, N.J.: Princeton University Press, 1992).

9 One of the first serious discussions of acting is Richard Dyer, *Stars* (London: The British Film Institute, 1979). Some more recent attempts to open up a serious discourse on acting include James Naremore's *Acting in the Cinema* (Berkeley and Los Angeles: University of California Press, 1988) and Christine Gledhill, ed., *Stardom: Industry of Desire* (London and New York: Routledge, 1991).

ONE: ARTHUR PENN AND OLIVER STONE

1 Noël Burch discusses the early history of the classical Hollywood form in *Life to Those Shadows,* trans. and ed. Ben Brewster (Berkeley and Los Angeles: University of California Press, 1990).

2 See Joseph Christopher Schaub, "Presenting the Cyborg's Futurist Past: An Analysis of Dziga Vertov's *Kino-Eye" Postmodern Culture* (January 1997), online: http://muse.jhu.edu/journals/postmodern_culture/v008/#v008.2.

3 Cf. Diane Jacobs, *Hollywood Renaissance* (South Brunswick, N.J., and New York: A. S. Barnes, 1977), 35–37.

4 Robin Wood, *Arthur Penn* (New York: Frederick A. Praeger, 1969), 44.

5 Alexandre Astruc, "The Birth of the New Avant-Garde: *La Caméra-Stylo,*" in *The New Wave,* ed. Peter Graham (New York:Doubleday, 1968), 17–23.

6 Paul Schrader, "Notes on Film Noir," *Film Comment* (Spring 1972), 8. A great deal has been written about noir. Schrader's article remains the best. Early works include the November–December 1976 issue of *Film Comment,* devoted to noir; Larry Gross, "Film Après Noir," *Film Comment* 12 (July-August 1976), 44–49; Charles Higham and Joel Greenberg, *Hollywood in the Forties* (New York: Paperback Library,

1970), 19–55; J. A. Place and L. S. Peterson, "Some Visual Motifs of Film Noir," *Film Comment* 10 (January–February 1974), reprinted in *Movies and Methods*, I, 325–38; Robert G. Porfirio, "No Way Out: Existential Motifs in the Film Noir," *Sight and Sound* 45 (Autumn 1976), 212–17; John Tuska, *The Detective in Hollywood* (Garden City, N.Y: Doubleday, 1978), 339–42. Alain Silver and Elizabeth Ward, *Film Noir: An Encyclopedic Reference to the American Style* (Woodstock, N.Y.: Overlook Press, 1979); E. Ann Kaplan, ed., *Women in Film Noir* (London: BFI Publishing, 1980) are influential on the discussion of domesticity that follows. For a thorough, cross-indexed filmography, see John S. Whitney, "A Filmography of Film Noir," *Journal of Popular Film* 5 (1976), 321–71. For background on the technological changes that made noir possible, see Barry Salt, "Film Style and Technology in the Thirties," *Film Quarterly* 30 (Fall 1976), 19–32, and "Film Style and Technology in the Forties," *Film Quarterly* 31 (Fall 1977), 46–57. More recent works include Frank Krutnik, *In a Lonely Street: Film Noir, Genre, Masculinity* (London and New York: Routledge, 1991), James Naremore, *More Than Night: Film Noir in its Contexts* (Berkeley: University of California Press, 1998).

7   See Steven Cohan, *Masked Men: Masculinity and the Movies in the Fifties* (Bloomington and Indianapolis: Indiana University Press, 1997).

8   Wood, *Arthur Penn*, 44–45.

9   Jack Shadoian, *Dreams and Dead Ends: The American Gangster/Crime Film* (Cambridge, Mass.: MIT Press, 1977), 288, 303–4. It is important to note that Shadoian does not approve of this self-consciousness.

10   John G. Cawelti, "The Artistic Power of *Bonnie and Clyde*," in *Focus on Bonnie and Clyde*, ed. Cawelti (Englewood Cliffs, N.J.: Prentice-Hall, 1973), 57. Cawelti's is a major essay on the film and there are some parallels with what is discussed here, the most important of which are noted.

11   Ibid., 59–60. For another view of sexuality in the film, particularly for the sympathy aroused by Clyde's impotence, see Wood, *Arthur Penn*, 84–86.

12   For a discussion of shot length, see Barry Salt, "Statistical Analysis of Motion Pictures," *Film Quarterly* 28 (Fall 1974), 13–22. Daniel Dayan's essay, "The Tutor-Code of Classical Cinema," in Leo Braudy and Marshall Cohan, eds., *Film Theory and Criticism: Introductory Readings*, 5th ed. (New York: Oxford University Press, 1999) 118–29, is the classic discussion of the structure and ideology of the shot/reverse shot. See also Nick Browne, "The Spectator-in-the-Text: The Rhetoric of *Stagecoach*," ibid., 148–63.

13   Many writers have addressed themselves to the vitality of the characters set against the barrenness of the landscape they inhabit [see, for example, Stephen Farber, "The Outlaws," *Sight and Sound* 37 (Autumn 1968), 174–75]. Some have found their situation revolutionary and praised it [Peter Harcourt, "In Defense of Film History," *Perspectives on the Study of Film*, ed. John Stuart Katz (Boston: Little Brown, 1971), 266–69] or condemned it (Charles Thomas Samuels, in *Focus on Bonnie and Clyde*, 85–92). As should become clear, I do not see the film as a call to revolution but, to the contrary, as a warning against being too free.

14   Richard Burgess brought this to my attention.

15   Cawelti, "Artistic Power of *Bonnie and Clyde*," 79.

16 Ibid., p. 82.

17 For the car as icon in gangster films, see Colin McArthur, *Underworld USA* (New York: Viking Press, 1972), 30–33. See also Steven Cohan and Ina Rae Hark, eds. *The Road Movie Book* (London and New York: Routledge, 1997).

18 Robert Warshow, "The Gangster as Tragic Hero," in *The Immediate Experience* (Garden City, N.Y.: Doubleday, 1962), 127–33. See also my article, "Night to Day," *Sight and Sound* 43 (Autumn 1974), 236–39.

19 Shadoian, *Dreams and Dead Ends*, 1–6.

20 Cawelti, "Artistic Power of *Bonnie and Clyde*," 79–84.

21 See Susan Jeffords, *Hard Bodies: Hollywood Masculinity in the Reagan Era* (New Brunswick, N.J.: Rutgers University Press, 1994).

22 Michael Walker, "Night Moves," *Movie*, No. 22 (Spring 1976), 37–38.

23 See, for example, John Fiske, *Television Culture* (New York and London: Routledge, 1989).

24 The argument about JFK and the destruction and creation of cultural and political narratives is drawn from an excellent essay on the film by Robert Burgoyne in *Film Nation: Hollywood Looks at U.S. History* (Minneapolis: University of Minnesota Press, 1998). Burgoyne also examines the sequence concerning the Oswald *Life* magazine cover.

25 This is the argument made by Hayden White, who addresses *JFK* in "The Modernist Event," *The Persistence of History: Cinema, Televison, and the Modern Event*, ed. Vivian Sobchack (New York and London: Routledge, 1996).

26 Susan Mackey-Ellis points out the different battle mise-en-scènes in the two films in *Oliver Stone's America* (Boulder, Colo.: Westview Press, 1996).

27 Roland Barthes, *S/Z*, trans. Richard Miller (New York: Hill & Wang, 1974).

28 Elsaesser, "Tales of Sound and Fury: Observation on the Family Melodrama," in *Movies and Methods*, vol. 2 (Berkeley and Los Angeles: University of California Press, 1985), 165–89.

29 Garry Wills, *Nixon Agonistes* (New York and Scarborough, Ontario: New American Library, 1970).

30 For an idea of the scholarly response, see "Special Focus: Oliver Stone as Cinematic Historian," *Film and History*, 28, nos. 3–4 (1998).

TWO: STANLEY KUBRICK

1 Some biographical information is based on conversations with Alexander Singer and James Harris.

2 Robin Wood discusses the matter of the horror film and family madness in the chapter "The American Nightmare," in *Hollywood from Vietnam to Reagan* (New York: Columbia University Press, 1986), 84, 150ff. In this and other matters, Wood's insights and mine are often closely aligned.

3 Description and some analysis of Kubrick's earlier work can be found in the three book-length studies of his films: Norman Kagan, *The Cinema of Stanley Kubrick* (New York: Continuum Publishing Group, 1989); Gene D. Phillips, *Stanley Kubrick: A Film Odyssey* (New York: Popular Library, 1977); Alexander Walker, *Stanley*

Kubrick Directs (New York: Harcourt Brace Jovanovich, 1971). An expanded edition of Walker's book is *Stanley Kubrick, Director* (New York and London: W.W. Norton, 1999). Walker's ideas and mine are often parallel, especially our readings of *A Clockwork Orange* and its similarities to earlier Kubrick films. Another fine full-length study, and a beautiful piece of production, is Michel Ciment, *Kubrick*, trans. Gilbert Adair (New York: Holt, Rinehart and Winston, 1984). Each of these books, and Walker's in particular, has been of use in the study that follows. Walker's discussion of Kubrick's use of space is a special influence. See also Thomas Allen Nelson, *Kubrick: Inside a Film Artist's Maze* (Bloomington: Indiana University Press, 1982). There have been two popular biographies of Kubrick—Vincent LoBrutto, *Stanley Kubrick: A Biography* (New York: Donald I. Fine, 1997), John Baxter, *Stanley Kubrick: A Biography* (New York: Carroll & Graf, 1997)—neither of which had access to Kubrick himself or his archives. Stephen Mamber has produced an extraordinary visual analysis of *The Killing* that is online in the January 1998 issue of *Postmodern Culture*, http://muse.jhu.edu/journals/postmodern_culture/v005/#v005.1

4 Welles himself refers to his work as labyrinthine. Although Kubrick has mentioned Max Ophuls as an influence on his moving camera (see Walker, *Stanley Kubrick Directs*, 16), the influence of Welles is much more evident [see Terry Comito, "Touch of Evil," *Film Comment* 7 (Summer 1971), 51–53].

5 Quoted by Dilys Powell in Peter Cowie, *A Ribbon of Dreams: The Cinema of Orson Welles* (South Brunswick, N. J., and New York: A. S. Barnes, 1973), 27–28.

6 So great is the communal need in Ford that in his later films the individual who is asocial by his nature and inclination—Ethan Edwards in *The Searchers*, Tom Doniphon in *The Man Who Shot Liberty Valance* (both characters played by John Wayne)—removes himself so the communal unit may survive. [See Joseph McBride and Michael Wilmington, "Prisoner of the Desert," *Sight and Sound* 40 (Autumn 1971), 210–14]. The notion that Ford became less interested in deep-focus cinematography when he began to work in color was suggested by Joe Miller.

7 Cf. Walker, *Stanley Kubrick Directs*, 84; Kagan, *The Cinema of Stanley Kubrick*, 65.

8 Walker, *Stanley Kubrick Directs*, 112, emphasizes the enclosed, geometric situating of the figures during the courts-martial.

9 For Kubrick and the fifties, cf. Kagan, *The Cinema of Stanley Kubrick*, 64–66. For an excellent discussion of the "end of ideology" syndrome, see Roland Barthes, "Neither-Nor Criticism," in *Mythologies*, trans. Annette Lavers (New York: Hill and Wang, 1972), 81–83. Ideas on the interpretation of history in the eighties were suggested by Angela Dalle Vacche, "History, the Real Thing in Postmodern Culture," a paper delivered at the Society for Cinema Studies, May 1987. See also the essays collected in Sobchack, *The Persistence of History*. For the ending of *Paths of Glory*, see Baxter, 90–94.

10 Cf. P. L. Titterington, "Kubrick and *The Shining*," *Sight and Sound* 50 (Spring 1981), 119.

11 Walker, *Stanley Kubrick Directs*, 160–62. Margot Kernan pointed out to me the significance of the first line of dialogue cited later in the text.

12 *Sade, Fourier, Loyola*, trans. Richard Miller (New York: Hill and Wang, 1976), 33–34.

13 Gerald Mast, *The Comic Mind* (Indianapolis and New York: Bobbs-Merrill, 1973),

317, 319. See also F. A. Macklin, "Sex and *Dr. Strangelove*," *Film Comment* 3 (Summer 1965), 55–57.

14 "Kubrick's films have always dealt with characters who mechanized themselves." Don Daniels, "A Skeleton Key to *2001*," *Sight and Sound* 40 (Winter 1970–71), 32. The mechanization of human behavior has been long recognized as a major element in Kubrick's work.

15 Northrup Fryer, *Anatomy of Criticism* (Princeton, N.J.: Princeton University Press,1957), 224–25.

16 Peter Wollen, *Signs and Meaning in the Cinema* (Bloomington: Indiana University Press, 1972), 164 and *passim*. See also Roland Barthes, *S/Z*, trans. Richard Miller, 10–11.

17 Theories of the subject and its placement in and outside the fictional narrative have received much attention. Two general treatments can be found in Kaja Silverman, *The Subject of Semiotics* (New York: Oxford University Press, 1983), and Terry Eagleton, *Literary Theory*, 127–193. For Bordwell, see David Bordwell, Janet Staiger, Kristen Thompson, *The Classical Hollywood Cinema: Film Style and Mode of Production to 1960* (New York: Columbia University Press, 1985), 3–11.

18 Kagan, *The Cinema of Stanley Kubrick*, 161–62.

19 Taylor, *Directors and Directions*, 129–32.

20 See Vivian Sobchack, *Screening Space* (New Brunswick, N.J.: Rutgers University Press, 1997).

21 "This Typeface Is Changing Your Life," *Village Voice*, June 7, 1976, 116–17. Fredric Jameson writes, "Form is immanently and intrinsically an ideology in its own right." (*The Political Unconscious: Narrative as a Socially Symbolic Act* (Ithaca, N.Y.: Cornell University Press, 1981), 141).

22 Gene Youngblood, *Expanded Cinema* (New York: Dutton, 1970), 140–46.

23 Susan Sontag, "Fascinating Fascism," in *Movies and Methods*, I, 40.

24 Cf. Jonathan Rosenbaum, "The Solitary Pleasures of *Star Wars*," *Sight and Sound* 46 (Autumn 1977), 209.

25 There are interesting alternative readings of slasher films that see a peculiar feminist engine driving them. See Carol Clover, *Men, Women, and Chain Saws: Gender in the Modern Horror Film* (Princeton, N.J.: Princeton University Press, 1992).

26 For the ending of *Star Wars*, see Rosenbaum, "Solitary Pleasures"; for a more detailed analysis of the politics of Spielberg's film, see Robert Entman and Francie Seymour, "*Close Encounters of the Third Kind*: Close Encounters with the Third Reich," *Jump Cut*, No. 18 (August 15, 1978), 3–5; and Tony Williams, "Close Encounters of the Authoritarian Kind," *Wide Angle* 5, No. 4 (1983), 22–29. I will deal more thoroughly with the form and substance of Spielberg's work later in the book.

27 See Stephen Hunter, "*Starship Troopers* and the Nazi Aesthetic," *Washington Post* (November 11, 1997), D01.

28 François Truffaut, *Hitchcock*, trans. Helen G. Scott, rev. ed. (New York: Simon and Schuster, 1983), 282.

29 Peter H. Lewis, "State of the Art: Resolutions for a Happy PC Year," *The New York Times* (December 31, 1998).

30 For an optimistic reading of digital culture, see Donna Haraway's seminal essay, "A Manifesto for Cyborgs: Science, Technology, and Socialist Feminism in the

1980's," *Socialist Review*, No. 80 (1985), now simply known as "The Cyborg Manifesto" and widely reprinted.

31   Cf. Robert Hughes, "The Decor of Tomorrow's Hell," *Time* (December 27, 1971), 59.

32   Anthony Burgess, *A Clockwork Orange* (New York: Norton, 1963), 158. My thanks to Richard Simmons for helping me connect the names.

33   See Dinah Nissen, "*A Clockwork Orange*," *The Pact Magazine* (December 1, 1993), 12.

34   Mark Crispin Miller, "*Barry Lyndon* Reconsidered," *Georgia Review* 30 (Winter 1976), 843.

35   Cf. Michael Dempsey, "*Barry Lyndon*," *Film Quarterly* 30 (Fall 1976), 50.

36   Alan Spiegel, "Kubrick's *Barry Lyndon*," *Salmagundi* (Summer–Fall, 1977), 204.

37   Cf. Miller, "*Barry Lyndon* Reconsidered," 834–35. Hans Feldmann, "Kubrick and His Discontents," *Film Quarterly* 30 (Fall 1976), 14, discusses the ritual of eating in *2001*.

38   Spiegel, "Kubrick's *Barry Lyndon*," 199.

39   Feldmann, "Kubrick and His Discontents," 17.

40   Spiegel, "Kubrick's *Barry Lyndon*," 199.

41   Cf. Feldmann's analysis in "Kubrick and His Discontents," 18. Spiegel, "Kubrick's *Barry Lyndon*," 201, fully analyzes the symmetrical repetitions in the film.

42   Feldmann, "Kubrick and His Discontents," 17.

43   Cf. Andrew Sarris, "What Makes Barry Run," *Village Voice*, December 29, 1975, pp. 111–12.

44   The classic treatment of how horror films critique the ideology of the family is Robin Wood's "The American Nightmare."

45   This concept of the all-seeing patriarchal gaze is contained in Michel Foucault's concept of the "panopticon" in *Discipline and Punish*, trans. Allen Sheridan (New York: Vintage Books, 1979). For another discussion of patriarchal structure in the film, see Flo Liebowitz and Lynn Jeffries, "*The Shining*: Ted Kramer Has a Nightmare," *The Journal of Popular Film and Television* 8, No. 4 (Winter 1981), 2–8, cited in Vivian Sobchack, "Child/Alien/Father: Patriarchal Crisis and Generic Exchange," *Camera Obscura*, No. 15 (1986), 15.

46   The stereotyping of women in the horror film is discussed by Gérard Lenne, "Monster and Victim," in *Sexual Stratagems: The World of Woman in Film*, ed. Patricia Erens (New York: Horizon Press, 1979), 31–40. Clover's *Men, Women and Chain Saws* examines the female hero of the horror film, and Linda Williams's "When the Woman Looks" in Barry Keith Grant, ed., *The Dread of Difference: Gender and the Horror Film* (Austin: University of Texas Press, 1996), 15–34, offers a powerful explanation of the association of monster and woman in the genre.

47   See Gregory Feeley, "A Masterpiece the Master Couldn't Get Right," *The New York Times* (July 18, 1999).

48   Frederic Raphael, *Eyes Wide Open: A Memoir of Stanley Kubrick* (New York: Ballantine Books, 1999).

49   Robin Wood, *Hitchcock's Films* (New York: Paperback Library, 1970), 165.

50   I owe these insights to Justin Wyatt. A discussion of the gay dimensions of *Marnie*

can be found in Lucretia Knapp, "The Queer Voice in *Marnie*," *Out in Culture*, eds. Corey Creekmur and Alexander Doty (Durham, N.C.: Duke University Press, 1995), 262–81.

THREE: MARTIN SCORSESE

1 For a discussion of this generation of filmmakers, see Michael Pye and Lynda Myles, *The Movie Brats: How the Film Generation Took Over Hollywood* (New York: Holt, Rinehart & Winston, 1979).

2 Paul Schrader, *Transcendental Style in Film: Ozu, Bresson, Dreyer* (Berkeley and Los Angeles: University of California Press, 1972), 72; "Notes on Film Noir," 8.

3 Edward Branigan, *Point of View in the Cinema: A Theory of Narration and Subjectivity in Classical Film* (Berlin, New York, Amsterdam: Mouton Publishers, 1984), 57.

4 Cf. Leo Braudy, "The Sacraments of Genre: Coppola, DePalma, Scorsese," *Film Quarterly* 39 (Spring 1986), 17–28. For recent documentary theory, see Bill Nichols, *Representing Reality: Issues and Concepts in Documentary* (Bloomington: Indiana University Press, 1991).

5 Jacobs, *Hollywood Renaissance*, 124.

6 Pye and Myles, *The Movie Brats*, 192.

7 Jean-Luc Goddard, *Godard on Godard,* trans. Tom Milne (New York: Viking Press, 1972), 21, 28.

8 See Ian Penman, "Jukebox and Johnny Boy," *Sight and Sound* 4 (April 1993), 10–11.

9 David Denby, "Mean Streets: The Sweetness of Hell," *Sight and Sound* 43 (Winter 1973/74), 50.

10 Nancy O'Neill talks in detail about the borderlines of race, class, and gender in *Mean Streets* in her master's essay, "Racial Formation as a Structuring Function of Cinema: An Examination of Martin Scorsese's *Mean Streets* and *Taxi Driver*," University of Maryland, 1998. On the freeze frame in *GoodFellas*, discussed later in the chapter, see Laura Gaither, "The Freeze Frame: Narrative and Temporality in Hollywood Film," University of Maryland, 1995.

11 Bazin talks about this effect in all of the essays published in the two vols. of *What Is Cinema?*

12 The classic discussion of the transforming camera eye is in Jean-Louis Baudry, "The Ideological Effects of the Basic Cinematographic Apparatus," in Bill Nichols, ed., *Movies and Meaning*, Vol. 2 (Berkeley and Los Angeles: University of California Press, 1985).

13 Michel Foucault, *Discipline and Punishment: The Birth of the Prison* (New York: Knopf, 1995), 202–203.

14 Bertolucci's comments are in Enzo Ungari with Donald Ranvaud, *Bertolucci by Bertolucci*, trans, Donald Ranvaud (London: Plexus, 1987).

15 Thomas Elsaesser's "Tales of Sound and Fury: Observations on the Family Melodrama."

16 A fuller examination of Scorsese's use of Hitchcock in *Cape Fear* can be found in my essay, "Algebraic Figures: Recalculating the Hitchcock Formula," in *Play It*

Again Sam: Retakes on Remakes, eds. Andrew Horton and Stuart McDougal (Los Angeles and Berkeley: University of California Press, 1997). There is also my online article, "The Moving Image Reclaimed," in the subscription journal *Postmodern Culture* 5, No. 1 (September 1994) that uses moving images from the various films. It can be found at: http://muse.jhu.edu/journals/postmodern_culture/v005/#v005.

17   Braudy points out Scorsese's response to Stallone in "Sacraments of Genre," 26.

18   An interesting study of the body as metaphor in film is in Steven Shaviro, *The Cinematic Body* (Minneapolis: University of Minnesota Press, 1993). See also Leslie Stern, *The Scorsese Connection* (Bloomington and Indiana: University of Indiana Press & The British Film Institute, 1995), 11–31.

19   Braudy discusses the commentary on celebrity in Scorsese's recent work and uses the term sacrament, ibid., 26–27.

20   Lotte Eisner, *The Haunted Screen*, trans. Roger Greaves (Berkeley and Los Angeles: University of California Press, 1973), 23–24.

21   See Michael Dempsey, "*Taxi Driver*," *Film Quarterly* 21 (Summer 1976), 37–41; Jacobs, *Hollywood Renaissance*, 143–44. See also Robert B. Ray, *A Certain Tendency of the Hollywood Cinema, 1930–1980* (Princeton, N.J.: Princeton University Press, 1985), 349–60. I have not examined the original, but the description of Travis Bickle that appears in a script extract published in *Film Comment* 12 (March–April 1976), 12, does present him in extravagantly romantic terms, very different from the character created by Scorsese and De Niro in the film. See also Schrader's comments on his script in the same issue of *Film Comment*.

22   Schrader, *Transcendental Style in Film: Ozu, Bresson, Dreyer*, 72.

23   Schrader, "Notes on Film Noir," 12, 13. Colin Westerbeck notes the noir influence via Schrader in "Beauties and the Beast," *Sight and Sound* 45 (Summer 1976), 138.

24   "Making strange" is a concept developed by the Russian Formalists. See Fredric Jameson, *The Prison-House of Language* (Princeton, N.J.: Princeton University Press, 1972), 50–53.

25   Jacobs, *Hollywood Renaissance*, 146. Jacobs does speak of the camera reflecting Travis's state of mind.

26   Patricia Patterson and Manny Farber, "The Power and the Gory," *Film Comment* 12 (May–June 1976), 29.

27   For a longer riff on Scorsese and *The Searchers*, see Lesley Stern, *The Scorsese Connection*, 32–68.

28   See Peter Birge and Janet Maslin, "Getting Snuffed in Boston," *Film Comment* 13 (May–June 1976), 35, 63.

29   Cf. Robin Wood, *Hitchcock's Films*, 132–33; Raymond Durgnat, *Films and Feelings* (Cambridge, Mass.: MIT Press, 1971), 217–18.

30   Steve Mamber discusses the imitation of the television style in *The King of Comedy* in "Parody, Intertextuality, and Signatured: Kubrick, DePalma, and Scorsese," a paper delivered at the Society for Cinema Studies, April 1986.

31   Richard Combs, "Where Angels Fear to Tread: *After Hours*," *Sight and Sound* 55 (Summer 1986), 208.

FOUR: STEVEN SPIELBERG

1 Two good collections address the changing businesses of filmmaking: Steve Neale and Murray Smith, eds., *Contemporary Hollywood Cinema* and Jon Lewis, ed., *The New American Cinema.*

2 Cf. Haraway, *Cyborg Manifesto.*

3 For a good study of the concept of "poaching" texts, see Henry Jenkins, *Textual Poachers: Television Fans and Participatory Culture* (New York: Routledge, 1992).

4 Fredric Jameson has a lot to say about postmodern space in *Postmodernism, or, the Cultural Logic of Late Capitalism* (Durham, N.C.: Duke University Press, 1991).

5 See Thomas Elsaesser, "Digital Cinema: Delivery, Event, Time," in Elsaesser and Kay Hoffmann, eds., *Cinema Futures: Cain, Abel or Cable? The Screen Arts in the Digital Age* (Amsterdam: Amsterdam University Press, 1998), 202–22.

6 Louis Althusser, "Ideology and Ideological State Apparatuses," *Lenin and Philosophy*, trans. Ben Brewster (New York and London: Monthly Review Press, 1971), 173, 172. Italics in original. This concept of ideological address or "hailing" is discussed by Silverman, *The Subject of Semiotics*, 48–50. For discussion of the formal structures of ideology, see Fredric Jameson, *The Political Unconscious*, 140–41.

7 See Mark Gerson, *The Neoconservative Vision* (Lanham, Md., and London: Madison Books, 1996), 176–93.

8 Jameson, *The Political Unconscious*, 171.

9 David Parker reminded me of this. For the representation of Roosevelt in film, see Dana Polan, *Power and Paranoia: History, Narrative, and the American Cinema, 1940–1950* (New York: Columbia University Press, 1986), 66–67.

10 Mary Ann Doane, "The Voice in the Cinema: The Articulation of Body and Space," *Yale French Studies*, No. 60, p. 50.

11 Gilles Deleuze and Félix Guattari, *Anti-Oedipus: Capitalisim and Schizophrenia*, trans. Robert Hurley, Mark Seem, Helen R. Lane (Minneapolis: University of Minnesota Press, 1977).

12 Some of this argument is paralleled in Susan Jeffords, *Hard Bodies: Hollywood Masculinity in the Reagan Era.*

13 Thanks go to students who pointed this and so much else in other films out to me.

14 The classic work on men in groups is Eve Kosofsky Sedgwick, *Between Men* (New York: Columbia University Press, 1985).

15 For an extended discussion of *Die Hard*, see Robert Kolker, *Film, Form, and Culture* (New York: McGraw-Hill, 1998).

16 As Laura Mulvey proves in "Visual Pleasure and the Narrative Cinema."

17 The idea of Spielberg's films as machine is in Stephen Heath, "*Jaws*, Ideology, and Film Theory," in *Movies and Methods*, II, 512, and James Monaco, *American Film Now* (New York: Oxford University Press, 1979), 176–77. Monaco also briefly discusses the beach sequence and Hitchcock zoom in *Jaws* that I will treat in detail further on.

18 See Heath, "*Jaws*, Ideology, and Film Theory," 510–11.

19   Jean-Louis Baudry, "Ideological Effects of the Basic Cinematographic Apparatus," trans. Allan Williams, in *Movies and Methods*, II, 537. See also Branigan, *Point of View in the Cinema*, 73–100.

20   Heath in "*Jaws*, Ideology, and Film Theory," 511. For a discussion of the three male figures, see Wood, *Hollywood from Vietnam to Reagan*, 177. Fredric Jameson offers a fascinating reading of Quint's death as "the two-fold symbolic destruction of an older America—the America of small business and individual private enterprise of a now outmoded kind, but also the America of the New Deal and the crusade against Nazism, the older America of the Depression and the war and of the heyday of classical liberalism" ["Reification and Utopia, *Social Text* 1 (1979), 143–44].

21   Frank Tomasulo provides an interesting mythic/political reading of *Raiders* in "Mr. Jones Goes to Washington: Myth and Religion in *Raiders of the Lost Ark*," *Quarterly Review of Film Studies* 7 (Fall 1982), 331–38. He points out that in a 1952 anticommunist film entitled *Hong Kong*, the actor, Ronald Reagan, is seen wearing "leather jacket, brimmed felt hat, three days' growth"—an earlier image of Indiana Jones.

22   For a lucid account of this complicated theory, see Nichols, *Ideology and the Image*, 30–33, and Christine Gledhill, "Recent Developments in Feminist Film Theory," *Quarterly Review of Film Studies* 3 (Fall 1978), 476–80.

23   See Wood, *Hollywood from Reagan to Vietnam*, 176.

24   Metz, *The Imaginary Signifier*, 49, 54.

25   Jean-François Lyotard, *The Post-Modern Condition: A Report on Knowledge*, trans. Geoff Bennington and Brian Massumi (Minneapolis: University of Minnesota Press, 1983).

26   See Yosefa Loshitzky, "Holocaust Others: Spielberg's *Schindler's List* versus Lanzmann's *Shoah*," in *Spielberg's Holocaust*, ed. Yosefa Loshitzky (Bloomington and Indianapolis: University of Indiana Press: 1997), 109–10. Many of the arguments I advance are also discussed throughout the essays in this excellent collection.

27   For a summary of this opinion, see Geoffrey Hartman, "The Cinema Animal," in *Spielberg's Holocaust*.

28   Daniel Jonah Goldhagen, *Hitler's Willing Executioners: Ordinary Germans and the Holocaust* (New York: Vintage Books, 1997).

29   This argument is also put forth by Sara Horowitz, "But Is It Good for the Jews? Spielberg's Schindler and the Aesthetics of Atrocity," in *Spielberg's Holocaust*, 128.

30   Dana Polan, "Above All Else to Make You See: Cinema and the Ideology of the Spectacle," 63.

31   Terry Eagleton, *The Function of Criticism: From The Spectator to Post-Structuralism* (London: Verso, 1984), 121–22.

FIVE: ROBERT ALTMAN

1   Gary Arnold, "Filmmaker Robert Altman—Back in the Swim," *Washington Post* (May 8, 1977), E4.

2   Some information on Altman's career comes from Gerard Plecki, *Robert Altman* (Boston: Twayne Publishers, 1985), 103–26.

3   Information on the travails of *The Gingerbread Man* can be found in *Salon* magazine's review (http://www.salonmagazine.com/ent/movies/1998/03/06gingerbread.html).

4   See Robert Self, "Robert Altman and the Theory of Authorship," *Cinema Journal* 25 (Fall 1985), 3–11. An excellent economic history of Altman's film production is undertaken by Justin Wyatt, "Economic Constraints/Economic Opportunities: Robert Altman as Auteur," *The Velvet Light Trap*, 38 (Fall 1996), 177–93.

5   The ideological differences between Eisenstein and Griffith were most clearly articulated by Eisenstein himself. See his essay "Dickens, Griffith, and the Film Today," in *Film Form*, trans. Jay Leyda (New York: Harcourt Brace Jovanovich, 1969), 195–225. See also Nöel Burch, *Theory of Film Practice*, trans. Helen R. Lane (New York: Praeger, 1973), 17–30; Tom Gunning, *D. W. Griffith and the Origins of American Narrative Film* (Urbana and Chicago: University of Illinois Press, 1991); André Bazin, *Jean Renoir*, trans. W. W. Halsey II and William H. Simon (New York: Simon and Schuster, 1973), 87–91. Bazin's seminal writings on the long take and deep-focus cinematography are contained in *What Is Cinema?*, Vol. I, trans. Hugh Gray (Berkeley and Los Angeles: University of California Press, 1967). For a wide-ranging, speculative essay on the problems of screen space, see Stephen Heath, *"Narrative Space,"* *Questions of Cinema* (Bloomington: Indiana University Press, 1981), 19–75. A number of critics have indicated the Renoir influences on Altman.

6   The notion of *découpage* comes from Burch, *Theory of Film Practice*, 4.

7   See Paul Joannides, "The Aesthetics of the Zoom Lens," *Sight and Sound* 40 (Winter 1970–71), 40–42.

8   For a detailed description of the camera work in *The Long Goodbye*, see Michael Tarantino, "Movement as Metaphor: *The Long Goodbye*," *Sight and Sound* 44 (Spring 1975), 98–102. In the same issue, Jonathan Rosenbaum's essay "Improvisations and Interactions in Altmanville" (91–95) considers the narrative dislocations in the film.

9   Cf. Jacobs, *Hollywood Renaissance*, 71.

10   As a student of mine once suggested.

11   See Stefan Fleischer, "A Study Through Stills of *My Darling Clementine*," *Journal of Modern Literature* 3 (April 1973), 243–52.

12   Michael Dempsey sees the hope for community more positively stated than I do. See his essay "Altman: The Empty Staircase and the Chinese Princess," *Film Comment* 10 (September–October 1974), 14–17. For an excellent survey of Altman's treatment of romantic love and the couple, see Robert Self, "*The Perfect Couple*: 'Two Are Halves of One' in the Films of Robert Altman," *Wide Angle* 5, No. 4 (1983), 30–37. Self refers to the unusual romanticism in the film *A Perfect Couple*, 36.

13   Jacobs, *Hollywood Renaissance*, 66.

14   Robert Self covers the complexity of the jazz presence and structure in *Kansas City* in his forthcoming book, *Story, Subject, and System: The Art Cinema of Robert Altman* (Minneapolis: University of Minnesota Press). His work points out how tightly knit the jazz is with the narrative of the film. John Pacy suggested the ideas about Keechie's survival in *Thieves Like Us*.

■

15 See the analysis of detective fiction by Tzvetan Todorov, in *The Poetics of Prose*, trans. Richard Howard (Ithaca, N.Y: Cornell University Press, 1977), 42–52.

16 Two excellent essays review the history of Marlowe on the screen: James Monaco, "Notes on *The Big Sleep*, Thirty Years After," *Sight and Sound* 44 (Winter 1974–75), 34–38; Charles Gregory, "Knight Without Meaning?" *Sight and Sound* 42 (Summer 1973), 155–59. The following analysis is indebted to them. For a current overview of the gendered aspects of noir, see Frank Krutnik, *In A Lonely Street: Film Noir, Genre, Masculinity*.

17 Edward Branigan talks about the notion of point of view projected into the mise-en-scène. See *Point of View in the Cinema*, 137–38.

18 Jonathan Rosenbaum, "Improvisations and Interactions," 95.

19 Cf. Rosenbaum, "Improvisations and Interactions," 91.

20 Joan Tewkesbury, *Nashville* (New York: Bantam, 1976), 3. Altman made the "metaphor of America" comment in *Newsweek*; cf. John Yates, "Smart Man's Burden: *Nashville*, *A Face in the Crowd*, and Popular Culture," *Journal of Popular Film* 5 (1976), 23.

21 Karen Stabiner, "*Buffalo Bill and the Indians*," *Film Quarterly* 30 (Fall 1976), 55. Joan Mellon has a good discussion of the myths of male supremacy that are attacked in the film; *Big Bad Wolves* (New York: Pantheon, 1977), 339–41.

22 For some excellent readings of women's representation in Hollywood film, see Mary Ann Doane, *The Desire to Desire: The Woman's Film of the 1940s* (Bloomington: Indiana University Press, 1987) and Linda Williams, "Body Genres," *Film Quarterly* 44/4 (Summer 1991), 2–13. Williams's "When a Woman Looks" is an excellent reading of the place of women in horror films.

23 Cf. Self, "Robert Altman and the Theory of Authorship," 8–9.

24 See Richard Combs, "*Fool for Love*," *Monthly Film Bulletin* 53 (July 1986), 196.

25 For a discussion of the film as dream, see Marsha Kinder, "The Art of Dreaming in *Three Women* and *Providence*: Structures of the Self," *Film Quarterly* 31 (Fall 1977), 10–18.

26 See Alice Ostriker, "The Thieves of Language," in *The New Feminist Criticism*, ed. Elaine Showalter (New York: Pantheon Books, 1985), 314–38.

27 Margot Kernan pointed this out.

28 In Andrew Sarris, ed., *Interviews with Film Directors* (New York: Avon Books, 1967), 392. Originally published in *Film Quarterly* 15 (Spring, 1962).

29 David Wyatt explained the story's history to me.

30 Raymond Carver, "A Small, Good Thing," *Cathedral* (New York: Alfred Knopf, 1983), 65–66, 80.

31 Mark Strand, *Hopper* (Hopewell, N.J.: The Ecco Press, 1993), 25.

32 Ibid., 23.

33 For a parallel argument, see Leonard Quart, "On Altman Image as Essence," *Marxist Perspectives* 1 (Spring 1978), 118–25.

The fragmented self: Warren Beatty in *Mickey One*, Arthur Penn, 1964.

Eye contact on Depression streets. Warren Beatty and Faye Dunaway in Penn's *Bonnie and Clyde*, 1967.

The final gaze. Bonnie and Clyde look at each other...

...before they are shot to death.

The point of view from the car: the end of *Bonnie and Clyde*.

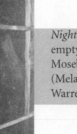

Night Moves, Arthur Penn, 1975: empty spaces and screens. Harry Moseby (Gene Hackman), Delly (Melanie Griffith), Paula (Jennifer Warren).

"C'mon, take a swing at me, Harry, the way Sam Spade would." Marty Heller (Harris Yulin) and Harry Moseby in *Night Moves*.

Danilo (Craig Wasson) watches his friend's Vietnamese wife (Nga Bich Thi Duong) attempt to start the lawn mower in Arthur Penn's *Four Friends*, 1981.

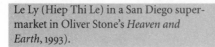

Le Ly (Hiep Thi Le) in a San Diego supermarket in Oliver Stone's *Heaven and Earth*, 1993).

Through the looking glass. Jim Garrison (Kevin Costner) in *JFK*, Oliver Stone, 1991.

Images from the *Life* magazine sequence in *JFK*.

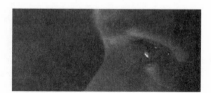

Paranoid spaces: the interrogation of David Ferrie (Joe Pesci) in *JFK*.

Images canted off the horizontal line. The diner sequence in *Natural Born Killers* (Oliver Stone, 1994); Mallory (Juliette Lewis).

"I Love Mallory." The sitcom family in *Natural Born Killers*. Left to right: Kevin (Sean Stone), Mallory's Dad (Rodney Dangerfield), Mallory's Mom (Edie McClurg). Micky (Woody Harrelson) and Mallory are in the background.

Oliver Stone's double editing. "You won't have Nixon to kick around anymore" seen twice, in *Nixon*, 1995.

Robert Altman's Nixon (Philip Baker Hall) in *Secret Honor*, 1984.

Wellesian space. The camera flees from an entrapped and frantic Joseph K (Anthony Perkins) in *The Trial*, Orson Welles, 1962.

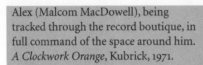

Alex (Malcom MacDowell), being tracked through the record boutique, in full command of the space around him. *A Clockwork Orange*, Kubrick, 1971.

Dax's (Kirk Douglas) purposeful and complex track through the trenches in *Paths of Glory*, Kubrick, 1957.

Military spaces: Thursday (Henry Fonda) and York (John Wayne) in *Fort Apache*, John Ford, 1945…

Mireau (George Macready) and Dax in the chateau *of Paths of Glory*…

...Drill Instructor Hartman (Lee Ermey), in *Full Metal Jacket*, Kubrick, 1987.

The darkness of men unwittingly planning their own destruction. *The Killing*, Kubrick, 1956, and *Dr. Strangelove*, Kubrick, 1963.

Screens and buttons in *2001: A Space Odyssey*, Kubrick, 1968.

Kubrickian space. Bowman in the "Jupiter Room" (*2001: A Space Odyssey*).

As Bowman removes the monolith-like memory modules from Hal's brain, a prerecorded television report is received explaining that Hal alone knew about the mission to Jupiter.

Alex (Malcom McDowell) and the Ape: *A Clockwork Orange* and *2001: A Space Odyssey*.

Dr. Strangelove (Peter Sellers): the fascist machine comes to life, in *Dr. Strangelove*, 1963.

Alex at the end of *A Clockwork Orange*: "I was cured alright."

The human figure made to look like death: a candlelit scene in *Barry Lyndon*, Kubrick, 1975. Reverend Runt (Murray Melvin), Lady Lyndon (Marisa Berenson).

Barry (Ryan O'Neal) and his son, dwarfed by an enormous painting, in *Barry Lyndon*.

Jack (Jack Nicholson) shares words of wisdom with Lloyd the Bartender (Joseph Turkel) in *The Shining*, Kubrick, 1980.

Jack, gone to beast, attempting to oedipalize his son in the icy maze of *The Shining*.

The painted dreamscape of Hitchcock's *Marnie* (1964). Tippi Hedren.

Bill (Tom Cruise) in the painted streets of an imagined New York. Stanley Kubrick, *Eyes Wide Shut*, 1999.

Bill in Nighttown, pursuing his demon dreams and terrors of an unrealizable sexuality. *Eyes Wide Shut*.

The orgy in *Eyes Wide Shut*. As in all of Kubrick's films, the male is isolated, alone, powerless.

Expressions of the street. The documentary impulse in *Mean Streets*, Martin Scorsese, 1973.

Fights break out at a moment's notice. Johnny Boy (Robert De Niro) in *Mean Streets*.

The dialogue between Johnny Boy and Charlie (Harvey Keitel) in *Mean Streets*.

The gang is introduced to Rico in *Little Caesar*, Mervyn LeRoy, 1930. The Wiseguys greet us and Henry in *GoodFellas*, Scorsese, 1990.

Breaking the fourth wall, addressing the viewer. Henry (Ray Liotta) in *GoodFellas.*

Watching! Robert De Niro in *Casino*, Scorsese, 1995.

The horizontal line in the desert...

...and in the domestic space (*Casino*). Sharon Stone, Robert De Niro.

Scorsese and the Hitchcock palimpsest. Bruno (Robert Walker) stares at Guy during a tennis match in *Strangers on a Train*, 1951.

Max Cady (Robert De Niro) stares at Sam at a Fourth of July parade in *Cape Fear*, Scorsese, 1991.

Scorsese's Christ on the cross (Willem Dafoe) in *The Last Temptation of Christ*, 1988…

…and Jake La Motta (Robert De Niro) crucified in the ring. *Raging Bull*, 1980.

A narrative of the body. Jake, fat, in *Raging Bull*.

In the cab dispatcher's office, the camera booms in to a disturbing, off-centered, tilted closeup of Travis (Robert De Niro), in *Taxi Driver*, Scorsese, 1976.

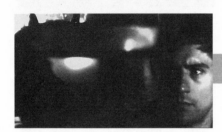

Travis and the hallway echoing the emptiness of his mind. *Taxi Driver*.

Travis sees his own eyeballs in the mirror at the end of *Taxi Driver*.

The confrontation of Travis and Sport (Harvey Keitel) in *Taxi Driver* is based on the meeting of Ethan (John Wayne) and Scar (Henry Brandon) in Ford's *The Searchers* (1956).

The pattern of high angle shots in *Taxi Driver* that leads to the 90-degree shot of the slaughter near the end of the film.

The fantasies of Rupert Pupkin. Robert De Niro and Jerry Lewis in an imaginary conversation. *The King of Comedy*, Scorsese, 1982.

The digital mise-en-scène: *Titanic*, James Cameron, 1997…

…*Jurassic Park*, Steven Spielberg, 1993…

…the destruction of Paris, *Armageddon*, Michael Bay, Jerry Bruckheimer, 1998.

Rambo's body. Sylvester Stallone, *Rambo, First Blood, Part II*, George Cosmatos, 1985.

Spielberg's use of blinding light: Roy Neary (Richard Dreyfus) and Lacombe (François Truffaut) in front of the mother ship in *Close Encounters of the Third Kind*, 1977.

Perceptual slippage: the camera zooms and tracks in opposite directions, creating a vertiginous effect in *Jaws*, Spielberg, 1975. Roy Scheider, Lorraine Gary.

The intensity of the gaze. The air traffic controllers in *Close Encounters*.

Spielberg's domestic space: the wide screen places Brody in the foreground, attending to business, while wife and child are relegated to the background. *Jaws.*

The domestic space is replaced by the adventure of male buddies.

The privileged view. Roy Neary is on the phone while the television and his model mountain reveal the truth about the alien landing site. *Close Encounters.*

Ideological certitude. Indiana Jones (Harrison Ford) reacts to and responds to the sabre-wielding Arab in *Raiders of the Lost Ark*, Spielberg, 1981.

Old Ryan (Harrison Young) with his family, seeking assurance at Miller's graveside. *Saving Private Ryan*, Spielberg, 1998.

Spielberg does Ford. The opening sequence of *The Searchers*...

...and the scene in *Saving Private Ryan* when soldiers come to report the death of Ryan's brothers to his mother.

Death mechanized: a powerfully oppressive image of a train bringing victims to Auschwitz in *Schindler's List*, Spielberg, 1993.

The shower scene in *Schindler's List*. Terror...

...and relief give the impression that people might be saved from the Nazi gas chambers.

The constriction of space in *M.A.S.H*, Robert Altman, 1970.

Death by water. The cowboy (Keith Carradine) shot by an outlaw, dying in the freezing river. *McCabe and Mrs. Miller*, Robert Altman, 1971.

The townspeople save the burning church…

…while McCabe (Warren Beatty) fights the gunmen and dies alone in the snow. *McCabe and Mrs. Miller.*

Film noir—film lumière. Two versions of Bowie and Keechie: Farley Granger and Cathy O'Donnell in the noir world of Nicholas Ray's *They Live by Night*, 1949.

Keith Carradine and Shelley Duvall in the brighter world of Altman's *Thieves Like Us*, 1974.

Howard Hawks's Philip Marlowe must look through the shadows in *The Big Sleep*, 1946.

Altman's Marlowe is isolated in the light, his perceptions refracted and confused. *The Long Goodbye*, 1973.

Show business. Bill Cody (Paul Newman) creates the Wild West in Altman's *Buffalo Bill and the Indians*, 1976.

The mediated voyeur: Griffin Mills (Tim Robbins) spies on June Gudmundsdottir (Greta Scacchi) while talking to her on his cell phone in Altman's *The Player*, 1992.

Millie and Pinky (Shelley Duvall and Sissy Spacek) in the arid landscape of Altman's *Three Women*, 1977.

Bill, the makeup man (Robert Downey Jr.), inscribes his misogyny on Honey (Lili Taylor) in *Short Cuts*, Altman, 1993.

Marian (Julianne Moore) stands by one of her paintings with the L.A. landscape behind her in *Short Cuts*.

Marian's husband, Ralph (Matthew Modine), becomes one of her paintings.

The fishermen and the body, in *Short Cuts*.

In *Cookie's Fortune* (1999), Altman changes his mood and his mind; fishing becomes a healing act.

FILMOGRAPHY

A listing of major, full-length theatrical features. The notation "Panavision" following the Photography credit indicates anamorphic ratio. Videotape versions do not reproduce the full width of the original frame.

ARTHUR PENN

1958 THE LEFT-HANDED GUN
Script: Leslie Stevens, from the play by Gore Vidal.
Direction: Penn.
Photography (b&w): J. Peverell Marley.
Art direction: Art Loel.
Editing: Folmar Blangsted.
Music: Alexander Courage.
Ballad: William Goyen and Alexander Courage.
   Cast: Paul Newman (*William Bonney*), Lita Milan (*Celsa*), John Dehner (*Pat Garrett*), Hurd Hatfield (*Moultrie*), James Congdon (*Charlie Boudre*), James Best (*Tom Folliard*), Colin Keith-Johnston (*Tunstall*), John Dierkes (*McSween*), Boâ Anderson (*Hill*), Wally Brown (*Moon*), Ainslie Pryor (*Joe Grant*), Marten Garralaga (*Saval*), Denver Pyle (*Ollinger*), Paul Smith (*Bell*), Nestor Paiva (*Maxwell*), Jo Summers (*Mrs. Garrett*), Robert Foulk (*Brady*), Anne Barton (*Mrs. Hill*).
   Produced by Fred Coe (Harroll Productions) for Warner Brothers. 102 min.

1962 THE MIRACLE WORKER
Script: William Gibson, from his play.
Direction: Penn.
Photography (b&w): Ernest Caparros.
Art direction: George Jenkins, Mel Bourne.
Editing: Aram Avakian.
Music: Laurence Rosenthal.
   Cast: Anne Bancroft (*Annie Sullivan*), Patty Duke (*Helen Keller*), Victor Jory (*Captain Keller*), Inga Swenson (*Kate Keller*), Andrew Prine (*James Keller*), Kathleen Comegys (*Aunt Ev*), Beah Richards (*Viney*), Jack Hollender (*Mr. Anagnes*).
   Produced by Fred Coe (Playfilms) for United Artists. 106 min.

1964 MICKEY ONE

Script: Alan Surgal.
Direction: Penn.
Photography (b&w): Ghislain Cloquet.
Production design: George Jenkins.
Editing: Aram Avakian.
Music: Eddie Sauter, improvisations by Stan Getz.

Cast: Warren Beatty (*Mickey*), Alexandra Stewart (*Jenny*), Hurd Hatfield (*Castle*), Franchot Tone (*Ruby Lapp*), Teddy Hart (*Breson*), Jeff Corey (*Fryer*), Kamataré Fujiwara (*The Artist*), Donna Michell (*The Girl*), Ralph Foody (*Police Captain*), Norman Gottschalk (*The Evangelist*), Dick Lucas (*Employment Agent*), Benny Dunn (*Nightclub Comic*), Helen Witkowski (*Landlady*), Mike Fish (*Italian Restaurant Owner*).

Produced by Arthur Penn (A Florin/Tatira Production) for Columbia. 93 min.

1966 THE CHASE

Script: Lillian Hellman, based on the novel and play by Horton Foote.
Direction: Penn.
Photography (Panavision): Joseph LaShelle and (uncredited) Robert Surtees.
Production design: Richard Day.
Editing: Gene Milford.
Music: John Barry.

Cast: Marlon Brando (*Sheriff Calder*), Jane Fonda (*Anna Reeves*), Robert Redford (*Bubber Reeves*), E. G. Marshall (*Val Rogers*), Angie Dickinson (*Ruby Calder*), Janice Rule (*Emily Stewart*), Miriam Hopkins (*Mrs. Reeves*), Martha Hyer (*Mary Puller*), Richard Bradford (*Damon Puller*), Robert Duvall (*Edwin Stewart*), James Fox (*Jake Jason Rogers*), Diana Hyland (*Elizabeth Rogers*), Henry Hull (*Briggs*), Jocelyn Brando (*Mrs. Briggs*), Steve Ihnat (*Archie*).

Produced by Sam Spiegel (Lone Star/Horizon) for Columbia. 135 min.

1967 BONNIE AND CLYDE

Script: David Newman and Robert Benton.
Direction: Penn.
Photography: Burnett Guffey.
Art direction: Dean Tavoularis.
Editing: Dede Allen.
Music: Charles Strouse, Flatt and Scruggs.
Costumes: Theadora van Runkle.
Special consultant: Robert Towne.

Cast: Warren Beatty (*Clyde Barrow*), Faye Dunaway (*Bonnie Parker*), Michael J. Pollard (*C. W. Moss*), Gene Hackman (*Buck Barrow*), Estelle Parsons (*Blanche*), Denver Pyle (*Frank Hamer*), Dub Taylor (*Ivan Moss*), Evans Evans (*Velma Davis*), Gene Wilder (*Eugene Grizzard*).

Produced by Warren Beatty (A Tatira-Hiller Production) for Warner Brothers. 111 min.

422

1969 ALICE'S RESTAURANT

Script: Venable Herndon and Arthur Penn, based on the recording "The Alice's Restaurant Massacree" by Arlo Guthrie.

Direction: Penn.
Photography: Michael Nebbia.
Art direction: Warren Clymer.
Editing: Dede Allen.
Music: Arlo Guthrie, Woody Guthrie, Joni Mitchell, Gary Sherman.
Musical supervision: Gary Sherman.

Cast: Arlo Guthrie (*Arlo*), Pat Quinn (*Alice*), James Broderick (*Ray*), Michael McClanathan (*Shelly*), Geoff Outlaw (*Roger*), Tina Chen (*Mari-Chan*), Kathleen Dabney (*Karin*), Police Chief William Obanhein (*Officer Obie*), Seth Allen (*Evangelist*), Monroe Arnold (*Blueglass*), Joseph Boley (*Woody*), Vinnette Carroll (*Lady Clerk*), M. Emmet Walsh (*Group W Sergeant*), Judge James Hannon (*Himself*), Graham Jarvis (*Music Teacher*).

Produced by Hillard Elkins and Joe Manduke (A Florin Production) for United Artists. 111 min.

1970 LITTLE BIG MAN
Script: Calder Willingham, from the novel by Thomas Berger.
Direction: Penn.
Photography (Panavision): Harry Stradling, Jr.
Production design: Dean Tavoularis.
Editing: Dede Allen.
Music: John Hammond.

Cast: Dustin Hoffman (*Jack Crabb*), Faye Dunaway (*Mrs. Pendrake*), Martin Balsam (*Allardyce T. Merriweather*), Richard Mulligan (*General Custer*), Chief Dan George (*Old Lodge Skins*), Jeff Corey (*Wild Bill Hickok*), Amy Eccles (*Sunshine*), Kelly Jean Peters (*Olga*), Carol Androsky (*Caroline*), Robert Little Star (*Little Horse*), Cal Bellini (*Younger Bear*), Ruben Moreno (*Shadow That Comes in Sight*), Steve Shemayne (*Burns Red in the Sky*), William Hickey (*Historian*), Thayer David (*Rev. Silas Pendrake*), Ray Dimas (*young Jack Crabb*), Alan Howard (*adolescent Jack Crabb*).

Produced by Stuart Millar (Hiller Productions, Stockbridge Productions) for Cinema Center Films/National General Pictures. 150 min.

1975 NIGHT MOVES
Script: Alan Sharp.
Direction: Penn.
Photography: Bruce Surtees.
Production design: George Jenkins.
Editing: Dede Allen, Stephen A. Rotter.
Music: Michael Small.

Cast: Gene Hackman (*Harry Moseby*), Jennifer Warren (*Paula*), Edward Binns (*Joey Ziegler*), Harris Yulin (*Marty Heller*), Kenneth Mars (*Nick*), Janet Ward (*Arlene Iverson*), James Woods (*Quentin*), Anthony Costello (*Marv Ellman*), John Crawford (*Tom Iverson*), Melanie Griffith (*Delly Grastner*), Susan Clark (*Ellen Moseby*).

Produced by Robert M. Sherman (Hiller Productions/Layton) for Warner Brothers. 99 min.

1976 THE MISSOURI BREAKS

Script: Thomas McGuane.
Direction: Penn.
Photography: Michael Butler.
Production design: Albert Brenner.
Editing: Jerry Greenberg, Stephen Rotter, Dede Allen.
Music: John Williams.

Cast: Marlon Brando (*Lee Clayton*), Jack Nicholson (*Tom Logan*), Kathleen Lloyd (*Jane Braxton*), Randy Quaid (*Little Tod*), Frederick Forrest (*Cary*), Harry Dean Stanton (*Calvin*), John McLiam (*David Braxton*), John Ryan (*Si*), Sam Gilman (*Hank*).

Produced by Elliott Kastner and Robert M. Sherman for United Artists. 126 min.

1981 FOUR FRIENDS

Script: Steve Tesich.
Direction: Penn.
Photography: Ghislain Cloquet.
Production design: David Chapman.
Editing: Barry Malkin, Marc Laub.
Music: Elizabeth Swados.

Cast: Craig Wasson (*Danilo*), Jodi Thelen (*Georgia*), Michael Huddleston (*David Levine*), Jim Metzler (*Tom*), Reed Birney (*Louie*), Elizabeth Laurence (*Mrs. Prozor*), Miklos Simon (*Mr. Prozor*), Lois Smith (*Mrs. Carnahan*), James Leo Herlihy (*Mr. Carnahan*), Julia Murray (*Adrienne*), David Graf (*Gergley*), Nga Bich Thi Duong (*Tom's Wife*).

Produced by Arthur Penn and Gene Lasko for Filmways. 115 min.

1985 TARGET

Script: Howard Berk and Don Petersen, from a story by Leonard Stern.
Direction: Penn.
Photography: Jean Tournier.
Production design: Willy Holt.
Editing: Stephen A. Rotter, Richard P. Cirincione.
Music: Michael Small.
Special consultant: Gene Lasko.

Cast: Gene Hackman (*Walter "Duke" Lloyd*), Matt Dillon (*Chris Lloyd*), Gayle Hunnicutt (*Donna Lloyd*), Josef Summer (*Taber*), Ilona Grubel (*Carla*), Victoria Fyordorova (*Lise*), Herbert Berghof (*Schroeder*), Guy Boyd (*Clay*), James Selby (*Ross*), Tomas Hensva (*Henke*), Jean-Pol Dubois (*Glasses*), Ulrich Haupt (*Older Agent*), Robert Ground (*Marine Sargeant*), Ray Fry (*Mason*), Richard Munch (*The Colonel*), Catherine Rethi (*Nurse*), Jean-Pierre Stewart (*Ballard*).

Produced by Richard D. Zanuck and David Brown for Warner Brothers/CBS. 115 min.

1987 DEAD OF WINTER

Script: Marc Shmuger and Mark Malone.
Direction: Penn.
Photography: Jan Weincke.

Production design: Bill Brodie.
Editing: Rick Shaine.
Music: Richard Einhorn.

Cast: Mary Steenburgen (*Julie Rose, Katie McGovern, Evelyn*), Roddy McDowall (*Mr. Murray*), Jan Rubes (*Dr. Joseph Lewis*), William Russ (*Rob Sweeney*), Ken Pogue (*Officer Mullavy*), Wayne Robson (*Officer Huntley*).

Produced by John Bloomgarden and Marc Shmuger for MGM. 100 min.

1989 PENN AND TELLER GET KILLED

Script: Penn Jillett and Teller.
Direction: Penn.
Photography: Jan Weincke.
Production design: John Arnone.
Editing: Jeffrey Wolf.
Music: Paul Chihara.

Cast: Penn Jillette (*Penn*), Teller (*Teller*), Bill Randolph (*Floor Director*), John Miller (*Steve the Bandleader*), Ellen Whyte (*Makeup Woman*), Caitlin Clarke (*Carlotta/Celia McGuire*), Ted Neustadt (*Bob the Host*).

Produced by Timothy Marx and Arthur Penn (Lorimar Film Entertainment) for Warner Brothers. 89 min.

1993 THE PORTRAIT

Script: Lynn Roth, from the play by Tina Howe.
Direction: Penn.
Photography: Richard Quinlan.
Art direction: Robert Guerra.
Editing: Janet-Bartels Vandergriff.
Music: Cynthia Millar.

Cast: Gregory Peck (*Gardner Church*), Lauren Bacall (*Fanny Church*), Cecilia Peck (*Margaret Church*), Paul McCrane (*Bartel*), Donna Mitchell (*Marissa Pindar*), Joyce O'Connor (*Samantha Button*).

Produced by Scott Adam and Linda Berman. (Made for Cable)

1996 INSIDE

Script: Bima Stagg.
Direction: Penn.
Photography: Jan Weincke.
Editing: Suzanne Pillsbury.
Music: Robert Levin.

Cast: Eric Stoltz (*Marty Strydom*), Nigel Hawthorne (*Colonel Kruger*), Louis Gossett Jr. (*Questioner*), Ian Roberts (*Moolman*), Janine Eser (*Christie*), Louis Van Niekerk (*Strydom*).

Produced by Hilliard Elkins and David Wicht. 94 min. (Made for Cable)

OLIVER STONE

1974 SEIZURE

Script: Edward Andrew Mann, based on a story by Oliver Stone.
Direction: Stone.
Photography: Roger Racine.
Production design: Najwa Stone.
Editing: Nobuko Oganesoff and Oliver Stone.
Music: Lee Gagnon.

Cast: Henry Baker (*Jackal*), Martine Beswick (*Queen of Evil*), Lucy Bingham, Richard Cox, Roger De Koven (*Serge*), Troy Donahue (*Mark*), Jonathan Frid (*Edmund Blackstone*), Anne Meacham (*Eunice*), Timothy Ousey (*Jason*), Christina Pickles (*Nicole Blackstone*), Joe Sirola (*Charlie*), Hervé Villechaize (*The Spider*), Mary Woronov (*Mikki*).

Produced by Garrard Glenn and Jeffrey Kapelman for Cine Films and Euro-American Pictures. Executive Producers: Harold Greenberg and Donald Johnston. 93 min.

1981 THE HAND

Script: Oliver Stone, from a book by Mark Brandel.
Direction: Stone.
Photography: King Baggot.
Production design: J. Michael Riva.
Editing: Richard Marks.
Music: James Horner.

Cast: Michael Caine (*Jon Lansdale*), Andrea Marcovicci (*Anne Lansdale*), Annie McEnroe (*Stella Roche*), Bruce McGill (*Brian Ferguson*), Viveca Lindfors (*Doctress*), Rosemary Murphy (*Karen Wagner*), Mara Hobel (*Lizzie Lansdale*), Pat Corley (*Sheriff*), Nicholas Hormann (*Bill Richman*), Ed Marshall (*Doctor*), Charles Fleischer (*David Maddow*), John Stinson (*Therapist*), Richard Altman (*Hammond*), Sparky Watt (*Sergeant*), Tracey Walter (*Cop*), Brian Kenneth Hume (*Boy in Classroom*), Lora Pearson (*Girl in Classroom*), Oliver Stone (*Bum*), Jack Evans (*The Country Bumpkins*), Scott Evans (*The Country Bumpkins*), Randy Evans (*The Country Bumpkins*), Patrick Evans (*The Country Bumpkins*).

Produced by Bert Kamerman and Edward R. Pressman for Warner Brothers. 104 min.

1986 PLATOON

Script: Oliver Stone.
Direction: Stone.
Photography: Robert Richardson.
Production design: Bruno Rubeo.
Editing: Claire Simpson.
Music: Samuel Barber (from "Adagio for Strings") and Georges Delerue.

Cast: Keith David (*King*), Forest Whitaker (*Big Harold*), Francesco Quinn (*Rhah*), Kevin Dillon (*Bunny*), John C. McGinley (*Sgt. O'Neill*), Reggie Johnson (*Junior*), Mark Moses (*Lt. Wolfe*), Corey Glover (*Francis*), Johnny Depp (*Lerner*), Chris Pedersen (*Crawford*), Bob Orwig (*Gardner*), Corkey Ford (*Manny*), David Neidorf (*Tex*), Tom Berenger (*Sgt. Barnes*), Willem Dafoe (*Sgt. Elias*), Charlie Sheen (*Chris*), Richard Edson (*Sal*),

Tony Todd (*Warren*), Kevin Eshelman (*Morehouse*), James Terry McIlvain (*Ace*), J. Adam Glover (*Sanderson*), Ivan Kane (*Tony*), Paul Sanchez (*Doc*), Dale Dye (*Captain Harris*), Peter Hicks (*Parker*), Basile Achara (*Flash*), Steve Barredo (*Fu Sheng*), Chris Castillejo (*Rodriguez*), Andrew B. Clark (*Tubbs*), Bernardo Manalili (*Village Chief*), Than Rogers (*Village Chief's Wife*), Li Thi Van (*Village Chief's Daughter*), Clarisa Ortacio (*Old Woman*), Romy Sevilla (*One-Legged Man*), Mathew Westfall (*Terrified Soldier*), Nick Nickelson (*Mechanized Soldier #1*), Warren McLean (*Mechanized Soldier #2*), Li Mai Thao (*Rape Victim*), Ron Barracks (*Medic*), Oliver Stone (*Army Officer in bunker destroyed by suicide attack*).

Produced by A. Kitman Ho and Arnold Kopelson for Hemdale Film Corporation and Orion Pictures. Executive Producers: John Daly and Derek Gibson. 111 min.

1986 SALVADOR

Script: Richard Boyle and Oliver Stone.
Direction: Stone.
Photography: Robert Richardson.
Production design: Bruno Rubeo.
Editing: Claire Simpson.
Music: Georges Delerue.

Cast: James Woods (*Richard Boyle*), James Belushi (*Doctor Rock*), Michael Murphy (*Ambassador Thomas Kelly*), John Savage (*John Cassady*), Elpidia Carrillo (*Maria*), Tony Plana (*Major Max*), Colby Chester (*Jack Morgan*), Cynthia Gibb (*Cathy Moore*), Will MacMillian (*Colonel Hyde*), Valerie Wildman (*Pauline Axelrod*), José Carlos Ruiz (*Archbishop Romero*), Jorge Luke (*Colonel Julio Figueroa*), Juan Fernández (*Army Lieutenant*), Salvador Sánchez (*Human Rights Leader*), Rosario Zuniga (*Human Rights Assistant*), Bill Hoag (*2nd Immigration Officer*), Waldeir DeSouza (*U.S. Customs Guard*), Angel Vargas (*Tic Tac Monster in Cafe*), Miguel Ehrenberg (*Captain Marti*).

Produced by Gerald Green and Oliver Stone for Hemdale Film Corporation and Virgin Films. Executive Producers: John Daly and Derek Gibson. 123 min.

1987 WALL STREET

Script: Stanley Weiser and Oliver Stone.
Direction: Stone.
Photography: Robert Richardson.
Production design: Stephen Hendrickson and Hilda Stark.
Editing: Claire Simpson.
Music: Stewart Copeland and Giuseppe Verdi (from the opera *Rigoletto*).

Cast: Charlie Sheen (*Bud Fox*), Tamara Tunie (*Carolyn*), Franklin Cover (*Dan*), Chuck Pfeiffer (*Chuckie*), John C. McGinley (*Marvin*), Hal Holbrook (*Lou Mannheim*), James Karen (*Lynch*), Leslie Lyles (*Natalie*), Michael Douglas (*Gordon Gekko*), Faith Geer (*Natalie's Assistant*), Frank Adonis (*Charlie*), John Capodice (*Dominick*), Martin Sheen (*Carl Fox*), Dani Klein (*Receptionist*), François Giroday (*Alex*), Pat Skipper, (*Postal Inspector*), John Deyle (*U.S. Attorney*), Oliver Stone (*Trader*).

Produced by A. Kitman Ho and Edward R. Pressman for American Entertainment Twentieth Century-Fox. 124 min.

1988 TALK RADIO

Script: Oliver Stone, from a book by Stephen Singular and play by Eric Bogosian and
Tad Savinar.

Direction: Stone.

Photography: Robert Richardson.

Production design: Bruno Rubeo.

Editing: David Brenner and Joe Hutshing.

Music: Stewart Copeland.

Cast: Eric Bogosian (*Barry*), Ellen Greene (*Ellen*), Leslie Hope (*Laura*), John C. McGinley (*Stu*), Alec Baldwin (*Dan*), John Pankow (*Dietz*), Linda Atkinson (*Sheila Fleming*),
Zach Grenier (*Sid Greenberg*), Tony Frank (*Dino*), Harlan Jordan (*Coach Armstrong*),
Bill Johnson (*Fan #1*), Kevin Howard (*Fan #2*), Anna Levine (*Denise/Woman at Base-
ball Game[voice]*), Bruno Rubeo (*Terry*), Pirie MacDonald (*Judge Willard*), Allan Cor-
duner (*Vince/Morris [voice]*), Mimi Cochran (*Girl #1*), Teresa Bell (*Girl #2*), Rockets
Redglare (*Killer/Redneck Caller [voice]*), Angus G. Wayne (*Engineer*), Chip Moody
(*Announcer*), David Poynter (*Engineer*), Peter Zapp (*Josh/Vincent*), Robert Trebor (*Jef-
frey Fisher/Voice of Francine [voice]*), Carl Kissin (*Cleo*), Jan-Michael Vincent (*Michael*),
Park Overall (*Agnes/Debbie/Theresa [voice]*), Michele Mariana (*Rhonda/Elderly
Woman/Julia [voice]*), Earl Hindman (*Black John/Chet/Jerry [voice]*), John Seitz (*Rob
[voice]*), Kyle McClaran (*Arnold [voice]*), Dee Pylano (*Nancy [voice]*), Daniel Escobar
(*Frank [voice]*), Michael Wincott (*Kent/Voice of Joe [voice]*), William De Acutis (*John the
Baptist/Ralph [voice]*), Frederika Meister (*Sexy Woman [voice]*), Lars Barilias (*Fred
[voice]*), Martin Raymer (*Arnold [voice]*), Al Clark (II) (*Larry [voice]*), John B. Wells
(*V.D. [voice]*), Leigh French (*Newscaster [voice]*), Walter Lynn (*Newscaster [voice]*),
Theresa Bell (*voice*).

Produced by A. Kitman Ho and Edward R. Pressman for Cineplex Odeon Films and
Universal Pictures. 110 min.

1989 BORN ON THE FOURTH OF JULY

Script: Oliver Stone and Ron Kovic, from a book by Ron Kovic.

Direction: Stone.

Photography (Panavision): Robert Richardson.

Production design: Bruno Rubeo.

Editing: David Brenner and Joe Hutshing.

Music: John Williams.

Cast: Tom Cruise (*Ron Kovic*), Willem Dafoe (*Charlie*), Tom Berenger (*Recruiting
Sargeant*), Bryan Larkin (*Young Ron*), Raymond J. Barry (*Mr. Kovic*), Caroline Kava
(*Mrs. Kovic*), Josh Evans (*Tommy Kovic*), Seth Allen (*Young Tommy*), Jamie Talisman
(*Jimmy Kovic*), Sean Stone (*Young Jimmy*), Anne Bobby (*Suzanne Kovic*), Jenna von Oÿ
(*Young Suzanne*), Real Andrews (*Vet*), Ron Kovic (*Veteran at Parade [uncredited]*).

Produced by Lope V. Juban Jr., A. Kitman Ho and Oliver Stone (Ixtlan Corporation)
for Universal Pictures. 145 min.

1991 JFK

Script: Oliver Stone and Zachary Sklar, from books by Jim Garrison and Jim Marrs.

Direction: Stone.

Photography (Panavision): Robert Richardson.

Production design: Victor Kempster.

Editing: Joe Hutshing and Pietro Scalia.

Music: Tom Hajdu, Andy Milburn, and John Williams.

Cast: Kevin Costner (*Jim Garrison*), Kevin Bacon (*Willie O'Keefe*), Tommy Lee Jones (*Clay Shaw*), Laurie Metcalf (*Susie Cox*), Roy Barnitt (*Irvin F. Dymond*), Jack Lemmon (*Jack Martin*), Edward Asner (*Guy Bannister*), Gary Oldman (*Lee Harvey Oswald*), John Candy (*Dean Andrews*), Sissy Spacek (*Liz Garrison*), Joe Pesci (*David Ferrie*), Kevin Bacon (*Willie O'Keefe*), John Candy (*Dean Andrews*), Donald Sutherland (*X*), Wayne Knight (*Numa Bertel*), Michael Rooker (*Bill Broussard*), Gary Grubbs (*Al Oser*), Jay O. Sanders (*Lou Ivon*), Beata Pozniak (*Marina Oswald*), Gary Carter (*Bill Williams*), Walter Matthau (*Senator Long*), Alvin Spicuzza (*Bailiff*), John Finnegan (*Judge Haggerty*), Walter Breaux (*Vernon Bundy*), Michael Skipper (*James Teague*), Melodee Bowman (*FBI Receptionist*), I.D. Brickman (*Dr. Peters*), Joseph Nadell (*Dr. McClelland*), Chris Robinson (*Dr. Humes*), Peter Maloney (*Colonel Finck*), Chris Renna (*Bethesda Doctor*), Dalton Dearborn (*Army General*), Merlyn Sexton (*Admiral Kenney*), Steve F. Price Jr. (*Pathologist #1*), Tom Bullock (*Pathologist #2*), Ruary O'Connell (*Pathologist #3*), Christopher Kosiciuk (*FBI Agent at Autopsy*), John Reneau (*A Team Shooter*), Stanley White (*B Team Shooter*), Richard Rutowski (*Fence Shooter*), Bill Bolender (*Prisoner Powell*), Larry Melton (*Patrolman Joe Smith*), Carol Farabee (*Carolyn Arnold*), Willie Minor (*Bonnie Ray Williams*), Ted Pennebaker (*Arnold Rowland*), Bill Pickle (*Marion Baker*), Mykel Chaves (*Sandra Styles*), Price Carson (*Tippet*), Gil Glasgow (*Tippet Shooter*), Martin Sheen (*Narrator [voice] [uncredited]*), Frank Whaley (*Fake Oswald [uncredited]*).

Produced by A. Kitman Ho, Oliver Stone, and Clayton Townsend (Alcor Films/Ixtlan Corporation/Le Studio Canal+/Regency Enterprises) for Warner Brothers. Executive Producer: Arnon Milchan. 189 min.

1991 THE DOORS

Script: Oliver Stone, J. Randall Johnson, Randy Johnson, and Ralph Thomas, from a book by John Densmore.

Direction: Stone.

Photography (Panavision): Robert Richardson.

Production design: Barbara Ling.

Editing: David Brenner and Joe Hutshing.

Music: John Densmore, The Doors, Robby Krieger, Ray Manzarek, Jim Morrison, and Carl Orff (from *Carmina Burana*).

Cast: Val Kilmer (*Jim Morrison*), Kathleen Quinlan (*Patricia Kennealy*), Michael Wincott (*Paul Rothchild*), Michael Madsen (*Tom Baker*), Josh Evans (*Bill Siddons*), Dennis Burkley (*Dog*), Billy Idol (*Cat*), Kyle MacLachlan (*Ray Manzarek*), Meg Ryan (*Pamela Courson*), Kevin Dillon (*John Densmore*), Frank Whaley (*Robby Krieger*), John Densmore (*Engineer—Last Session*).

Produced by Bill Graham, Sasha Harari, and A. Kitman Ho (Bill Graham Films/Ixtlan Corporation) for Imagine Films Entertainment and Carolco Pictures—Tri-Star. Executive Producers: Brian Grazer and Mario Kassar. 141 min.

429

1993 HEAVEN AND EARTH

Script: Oliver Stone, from books by James Hayslip, Le Ly Hayslip, and Jay Wurts.

Direction: Stone.

Photography (Panavision): Robert Richardson.

Production design: Victor Kempster.

Editing: David Brenner and Sally Menke.

Music: Kitaro and Randy Miller.

Cast: Haing S. Ngor (*Papa*), Bussaro Sanruck (*Le Ly [age 5]*), Supak Pititam (*Buddhist Monk*), Joan Chen (*Mama*), Thuan K. Nguyen (*Uncle Luc*), Hiep Thi Le (*Le Ly*), Tommy Lee Jones *Steve*), Lan Nguyen Calderon (*Ba*), Thuan Le (*Kim*), Dustin Nguyen (*Sau*), Khiem Thai (*Brother-in-Law*), Andy Reeder (*Alan [age 4]*), Chau Mao Doan (*California Monk*), Vivien Straus (*Neighbor's Wife*), Melinda Renna (*Policewoman*), Robert Marshall (*Detective*), Tai Thai (*Jimmy [age 20]*), Tom Nam Ly (*Tommy [age 15]*), Vinh Dang (*Bon*), Mai Le Ho (*Hai*), Mai Le (*Steward*), Phil Neilson (*Marine in Helicopter*), Long Nguyen (*Anh*), Mai Nguyen (*California Wizard*), Term Saefam (*Herbalist*).

Produced by A. Kitman Ho, Robert Kline, Arnon Milchan, Oliver Stone, and Clayton Townsend (Alcor films/Le Studio Canal+/Regency Enterprises) for Warner Brothers. Executive Producer: Mario Kassar. 142 min.

1994 NATURAL BORN KILLERS

Script: Richard Rutowski, Oliver Stone, and David Veloz, from a story by Quentin Tarantino.

Direction: Stone.

Photography (Panavision): Robert Richardson.

Production design: Victor Kempster.

Editing: Brian Berdan and Hank Corwin.

Music: Tom Hajdu, Brent Alewis, Andy Milburn, and Trent Reznor.

Cast: Woody Harrelson (*Mickey Knox*), Juliette Lewis (*Mallory Knox*), Robert Downey, Jr. (*Wayne Gale*), Tommy Lee Jones (*Dwight McClusky*), O-Lan Jones (*Mabel*), Ed White (*Pinball Cowboy*), Richard Lineback (*Sonny*), Lanny Flaherty (*Earl*), Carol-Renee Modrall (*Short Order Cook*), Rodney Dangerfield (*Mallory's Dad*), Edie McClurg (*Mallory's Mom*), Sean Stone (*Kevin*), Jerry Gardner (*Work Boss*), Jack Caffrey (*Work Boss*), Leon Skyhorse Thomas (*Work Boss*), Corinna Everson (*TV Mallory*), Dale Dye (*Dale Wrigley*), Eddy "Doogie" Conna (*Gerald Nash*), Evan Handler (*David*), Kirk Baltz (*Wayne Gale's Cameraman*), Terrylene (*Julie*), Maria Pitillo (*Deborah*), Josh Richman (*Soundman*), Matthew Faber (*Kid*), Jamie Harrold (*Kid*), Jake Beecham (*Kid*), Seiko Yoshida (*Japanese Kid*), Jared Harris (*London Boy*), Katherine McQueen (*London Girl*), Salvator Xuereb (*French Boy*), Emmanuel Xuereb (*French Boy*), Natalie Karp (*French Girl*), Jessie Rutkowski (*Young Girl*), Sally Jackson (*Mickey's Mom*), Phil Neilson (*Mickey's Dad*), Brian Barker (*Young Mickey*), Corinna Laszlo (*Emily*), Balthazar Getty (*Gas Station Attendant*), Tom Sizemore (*Jack Scagnetti*), Red West (*Cowboy Sheriff*), Gerry Runnels (*Indian Cop*), Jeremiah Bitsui (*Young Indian Boy*), Russell Means (*Old Indian*), Lorraine Farris (*Pinky*), Glen Chin (*Druggist*), Saemi Nakamura (*Japanese Reporter*), Pruitt Taylor Vince (*Kavanaugh*), Everett Quinton (*Wurlitzer*), Steven Wright (I) (*Dr. Emil Reingold*), Peter Crombie (*Intense Cop*), John M. Watson Sr. (*Black Inmate*), Joe Grifasi (*Duncan Homolka*), Douglas Crosby (*Mallory's Guard*), Carl Ciarfalio (*Mallory's Guard*), Marshall Bell (*Deputy*), Melinda Renna (*Antonia Chavez*), Jim Carrane (*Smithy*), Bob Swan (*Napalatoni*), Louis Lombardi (*Sparky*), Robert Jordan (*WGN Newscaster*), James Gammon (*Redneck's Buddy in the Diner*), Mark Harmon (*Mickey Knox in Wayne Gale's Reconstruction*), Arliss Howard (*Owen [Diner Patron/Prison Escapee]*), Ashley Judd (*Grace Mulberry*), Denis Leary (*Prison Inmate*), Rachel Ticotin (*Prosecutor Wanda Bisbing*).

Produced by Jane Hamsher, Don Murphy, Clayton Townsend, and Rand Vossler (Regency Enterprises/Le Studio Canal+/Alcor Films) for Warner Brothers. Executive Producers: Arnon Milchan and Thom Mount. 118 min.

1995 NIXON

Script: Stephen J. Rivele, Christopher Wilkinson, and Oliver Stone.
Direction: Stone.
Photography (Panavision): Robert Richardson.
Production design: Victor Kempster.
Editing: Brian Berdan and Hank Corwin.
Music: John Williams.
Cast: Anthony Hopkins (*Richard Nixon*), Joan Allen (*Pat Nixon*), Powers Boothe (*Alexander Haig*), Ed Harris (*Howard Hunt*), Bob Hoskins (*J. Edgar Hoover*), E. G. Marshall (*John Mitchell*), David Paymer (*Ron Ziegler*), David Hyde-Pierce (*John Dean*), Paul Sorvino (*Henry Kissinger*) Mary Steenburgen (*Hannah Nixon*), J. T. Walsh (*John Ehrlichman*), James Woods (*H. R. Haldeman*), Brian Bedford (*Clyde Tolson*), Kevin Dunn (*Charles Colson*), Fyvush Finkel (*Murray Chotiner*), Annabeth Gish (*Julie Nixon*), Tom Bower (*Frank Nixon*), Tony Goldwyn (*Harold Nixon*), Larry Hagman (*"Jack Jones"*), Edward Herrmann (*Nelson Rockefeller*), Madeline Kahn (*Martha Mitchell*), Dan Hedaya (*Trini Cardoza*), Tony Lo Bianco (*Johnny Roselli*), Tony Plana (*Manolo Sanchez*), Saul Rubinek (*Herb Klein*), Robert Beltran (*Frank Sturgis*), John Cunningham (*Bob*), John Diehl (*Gordon Liddy*), John C. McGinley (*Earl*), Michael Chiklis (*TV Director*), David Barry Gray (*Richard Nixon at 19*), Joanna Going (*Young Student*), Lenny Vullo (*Bernard Barker*), George Plimpton (*President's Lawyer*), Corey Carrier (*Richard Nixon at 12*), Ronald von Klaussen (*James McCord*), Kamar De Los Reyes (*Eugenio Martinez*), Ric Young (*Mao-Tse-Tung*), Sean Stone (*Donald Nixon*), Joshua Preston (*Arthur Nixon*), Ian Calip (*Football Player*), Jack Wallace (*Football Coach*), Julie Condra (*Young Pat Nixon*), Annette Helde (*Happy Rockefeller*), Mikey Stone (*Edward Nixon*), Marley Shelton (*Tricia Nixon*), Peter Carlin (*Student #1*), Michelle Krusiec (*Student #2*), Wass W. Stevens (*Protester*), Alex Butterfield (*White House Staffer*), Boris Sichkin (*Leonid Brezhnev*), Fima Noveck (*Andre Gromyko*), Oliver Stone (*Voice-over during credits*).
Produced by Dan Halsted, Eric Hamburg, Richard Rutowski, Oliver Stone, Clayton Townsend, and Andrew G. Vajna (Cinergi/Hollywood Pictures/Illusion Entertainment) for Buena Vista Pictures. 191 min.

1997 U TURN

Script: John Ridley, from his novel *Stray Dogs*.
Direction: Stone.
Photography: Robert Richardson.
Production design: Victor Kempster.
Editing: Hank Corwin and Thomas J. Nordberg.
Music: Ennio Morricone.
Cast: Sean Penn (*Bobby Cooper*), Nick Nolte (*Jake McKenna*), Jennifer Lopez (*Grace McKenna*), Powers Boothe (*Sheriff Potter*), Claire Danes (*Jenny*), Joaquin Phoenix (*Toby N. Tucker*), Billy Bob Thornton (*Darrell*), Jon Voight (*Blind Man*), Abraham Benrubi (*Biker 1*), Julie Hagerty (*Flo*), Bo Hopkins (*Ed*), Valeri Nikolayev (*Mr. Arkady*), Ilia Volokh (*Sergei*), Aida Linares (*Jamilla*), Laurie Metcalf (*Bus Station Clerk*), Liv Tyler (*Girl in Bus Station*), Brent Briscoe (*Boyd*), Annie Tien (*Short Order Cook*), Jeff Flach (*Yes Man*).

431

Produced by Dan Halsted, Richard Rutowski, and Clayton Townsend (Clyde Is Hungry Films/Illusion Entertainment Group/Phoenix Pictures) for Sony Pictures Entertainment. Executive Producer: John Ridley. 125 min.

1999 ANY GIVEN SUNDAY
Script: Stone, John Logan; Rob Huizenga, Pat Toomay, from their novels.
Direction: Stone.
Photography (Panavision): Salvatore Totino.
Production design: Victor Kempster.
Editing: Stuart Levy, Thomas J. Nordberg, Michael Mees, and Keith Salmon.
Music: Richard Horowitz.

Cast: Al Pacino (*Tony D'Amato*), Dennis Quaid (*Jack Rooney*), Jamie Foxx (*Willie Beamen*), Cameron Diaz (*Chrisina Pagniacci*), James Woods (*Dr. Harvey Mandrake*), Matthew Modine (*Dr. Allie Powers*), Ann-Margret (*Margaret Pagniacci*), Jim Brown (*Montezuma Monroe*), LL COOL J (*Julian Washington*), John C. McGinley (*Jack Rose*), Charlton Heston (*Commissioner*).

Produced by Clayton Townsend, Lauren Shuler Donner, Dan Halsted, Oliver Stone for Warner Bros. 162 min.

STANLEY KUBRICK

1953 FEAR AND DESIRE
Script: Howard G. Sackler.
Direction, photography (b&w), editing: Kubrick.

Cast: Frank Silvera (*Mac*), Kenneth Harp (*Corby*), Virginia Leith (*The Girl*), Paul Mazursky (*Sidney*), Steve Coit (*Pletcher*).

Produced by Stanley Kubrick for Joseph Burstyn. 68 min.

1955 KILLER'S KISS
Script: Kubrick, Howard O. Sackler.
Direction, photography (b&w), editing: Kubrick.
Music: Gerald Fried.
Choreography: David Vaughan.

Cast: Frank Silvera (*Vincent Rapallo*), Jamie Smith (*Davy Gordon*), Irene Kane (*Gloria Price*), Jerry Jarret (*Albert*), Ruth Sobotka (*Iris*), Mike Dana, Felice Orlandi, Ralph Roberts, Phil Stevenson (*Hoodlums*), Julius Adelman (*Mannequin Factory Owner*), David Vaughan, Alec Rubin (*Conventioneers*).

Produced by Stanley Kubrick and Morris Bousel (Minotaur) for United Artists. 61 min.

1956 THE KILLING
Script: Kubrick, based on the novel *Clean Break* by Lionel White.
Additional dialogue: Jim Thompson.
Direction: Kubrick.
Photography (b&w): Lucien Ballard.

432

Art direction: Ruth Sobotka Kubrick.
Editing: Betty Steinberg.
Music: Gerald Fried.

Cast: Sterling Hayden (*Johnny Clay*), Jay C. Flippen (*Marvin Unger*), Marie Windsor (*Sherry Peatty*), Elisha Cook (*George Peatty*), Coleen Gray (*Fay*), Vince Edwards (*Val Cannon*), Ted de Corsia (*Randy Kennan*), Joe Sawyer (*Mike O'Reilly*), Tim Carey (*Nikki*), Kola Kwariani (*Maurice*). Produced by James B. Harris (Harris-Kubrick Productions) for United Artists. 83 min.

1957 PATHS OF GLORY

Script: Kubrick, Calder Willingham, and Jim Thompson, based on the novel by Humphrey Cobb.
Direction: Kubrick.
Photography (b&w): George Krause.
Art direction: Ludwig Reiber.
Editing: Eva Kroll.
Music: Gerald Fried.

Cast: Kirk Douglas (*Colonel Dax*), Ralph Meeker (*Corporal Paris*), Adolphe Menjou (*General Broulard*), George Macready (*General Mireau*), Wayne Morris (*Lieutenant Roget*), Richard Anderson (*Major Saint-Auban*), Joseph Turkel (*Private Arnaud*), Timothy Carey (*Private Ferol*), Peter Capell (*Colonel Judge*), Susanne Christian (*German Girl*), Bert Freed (*Sergeant Boulanger*), Emile Meyer (*Priest*), John Stein (*Captain Rousseau*).

Produced by James B. Harris (Harris-Kubrick Productions) for United Artists. 86 min.

1960 SPARTACUS

Script: Dalton Trumbo, based on the novel by Howard Fast.
Direction: Kubrick.
Photography (Super Technirama-70): Russell Metty.
Additional photography: Clifford Stine.
Production design: Alexander Golitzen.
Editing: Robert Lawrence, Robert Schultz, Fred Chulack.
Music: Alex North.

Cast: Kirk Douglas (*Spartacus*), Laurence Olivier (*Marcus Crassus*), Jean Simmons (*Varinia*), Charles Laughton (*Gracchus*), Peter Ustinov (*Batiatus*), John Gavin (*Julius Caesar*), Tony Curtis (*Antoninus*), Nina Foch (*Helena*), Herbert Lom (*Tigranes*), John Ireland (*Crixus*), John Dall (*Glabrus*), Charles McGraw (*Marcellus*), Joanna Barnes (*Claudia*), Harold J. Stone (*David*), Woody Strode (*Draba*).

Produced by Kirk Douglas and Edward Lewis (Bryna) for Universal. 196 min.

1961 LOLITA

Script: Vladimir Nabokov, based on his novel.
Direction: Kubrick.
Photography (b&w): Oswald Morris.
Art direction: William Andrews.
Editing: Anthony Harvey.

Music: Nelson Riddle, Bob Harris.

Cast: James Mason (*Humbert Humbert*), Sue Lyon (*Lolita Haze*), Shelley Winters (*Charlotte Haze*), Peter Sellers (*Clare Quilty*), Diana Decker (*Jean Farlow*), Jerry Stovin (*John Farlow*), Suzanne Gibbs (*Mona Farlow*), Gary Cockrell (*Dick*), Marianne Stone (*Vivian Darkbloom*), Cec Linder (*Physician*), Lois Maxwell (*Nurse Mary Lore*), William Greene (*Swine*).

Produced by James B. Harris (Seven Arts/Anya/Transworld) for MGM. 153 min.

1963 DR. STRANGELOVE,
OR HOW I LEARNED TO STOP WORRYING
AND LOVE THE BOMB

Script: Kubrick, Terry Southern, and Peter George, based on George's novel *Red Alert*.
Direction: Kubrick.
Photography (b&w): Gilbert Taylor.
Production design: Ken Adam.
Editing: Anthony Harvey.
Special Effects: Wally Veevers.
Music: Laurie Johnson.

Cast: Peter Sellers (*Group Captain Lionel Mandrake, President Merkin Muffley, Dr. Strangelove*), George C. Scott (*General Buck Turgidson*), Sterling Hayden (*General Jack D. Ripper*), Keenan Wynn (*Colonel Bat Guano*), Slim Pickens (*Major Kong*), Peter Bull (*Ambassador de Sadesky*), Tracy Reed (*Miss Scott*), James Earl Jones (*Lieutenant Lothar Zogg, Bombardier*), Jack Creley (*Mr. Staines*), Frank Berry (*Lieutenant H. R. Dietrich, D.S.O.*), Glenn Beck (*Lieutenant W. D. Kivel, Navigator*), Shane Rimmer (*Captain Ace Owens, Copilot*), Paul Tamarin (*Lieutenant B. Goldberg, Radio Operator*), Gordon Tanner (*General Faceman*).

Produced by Kubrick (Hawk Films) for Columbia. 94 min.

1968 2001: A SPACE ODYSSEY

Script: Kubrick, Arthur C. Clarke, based on Clarke's story "The Sentinel."
Direction: Kubrick.
Photography (Super Panavision): Geoffrey Unsworth.
Additional photography: John Alcott.
Production design: Tony Masters, Harry Lange, Ernie Archer.
Special photographic effects design and direction: Kubrick.
Special photographic effects supervision: Wally Veevers, Douglas Trumbull, Con Pederson, Tom Howard.
Editing: Ray Lovejoy.
Music: Richard Strauss, Johann Strauss, Aram Khachaturian, György Ligeti.
Costumes: Hardy Amies.

Cast: Keir Dullea (*David Bowman*), Gary Lockwood (*Frank Poole*), William Sylvester (*Dr. Heywood Floyd*), Daniel Richter (*Moonwatcher*), Douglas Rain (*Voice of HAL 9000*), Leonard Rossiter (*Smyslov*), Margaret Tyzack (*Elena*), Robert Beatty (*Halvorsen*), Sean Sullivan (*Michaels*), Frank Miller (*Mission Control*), Penny Brahms (*Stewardess*), Alan Gifford (*Poole's Father*).

Produced by Kubrick for MGM. 141 min.

434

1971 A CLOCKWORK ORANGE

Script: Kubrick, from the novel by Anthony Burgess.
Direction: Kubrick.
Photography: John Alcott.
Production design: John Barry.
Editing: Bill Butler.
Music: Walter Carlos.

Cast: Malcolm McDowell (*Alex*), Patrick Magee (*Mr. Alexander*), Anthony Sharp (*Minister of the Interior*), Godfrey Quigley (*Prison Chaplain*), Warren Clarke (*Dim*), James Marcus (*Georgie*), Aubrey Morris (*Deltoid*), Miriam Karlin (*Cat Lady*), Sheila Raynor (*Mum*), Philip Stone (*Dad*), Carl Duering (*Dr. Brodsky*), Paul Farrell (*Tramp*), Michael Gover (*Prison Governor*), Clive Francis (*Lodger*), Madge Ryan (*Dr. Branom*), Pauline Taylor (*Psychiatrist*), John Clive (*Stage Actor*), Michael Bates (*Chief Guard*).

Produced by Kubrick for Warner Brothers. 137 min.

1975 BARRY LYNDON

Script: Kubrick, from the novel by William Makepeace Thackeray.
Direction: Kubrick.
Photography: John Alcott.
Production design: Ken Adam.
Editing: Tony Lawson.
Music: J. S. Bach, Frederick the Great, Handel, Mozart, Paisiello, Schubert, Vivaldi, The Chieftains.
Music adaptation: Leonard Rosenman.
Costumes: Ulla-Britt Soderlund, Milena Canonero.

Cast: Ryan O'Neal (*Barry Lyndon*), Marisa Berenson (*Lady Lyndon*), Patrick Magee (*The Chevalier*), Hardy Kruger (*Captain Potzdorf*), Marie Kean (*Barry's Mother*), Gay Hamilton (*Nora*), Murray Melvin (*Reverend Runt*), Godfrey Quigley (*Captain Grogan*), Leonard Rossiter (*Captain Quinn*), Leon Vitali (*Lord Bullingdon*), Diana Koerner (*German girl*), Frank Middlemass (*Sir Charles Lyndon*), André Morell (*Lord Wendover*), Arthur O'Sullivan (*Highwayman*), Philip Stone (*Graham*), Michael Hordern (*Narrator*).

Produced by Kubrick and Jan Harlan for Warner Brothers. 185 min.

1980 THE SHINING

Script: Kubrick and Diane Johnson, from the novel by Stephen King.
Direction: Kubrick.
Photography: John Alcott.
Production design: Roy Walker.
Editing: Ray Lovejoy.
Music: Béla Bartók, Wendy Carlos, Rachel Elkin, György Ligeti, Krzysztof Penderecki.

Cast: Jack Nicholson (*Jack Torrance*), Shelley Duvall (*Wendy Torrance*), Danny Lloyd (*Danny Torrance*), Scatman Crothers (*Hallorann*), Barry Nelson (*Stuart Ullman*), Joe Turkel (*Lloyd*), Philip Stone (*Delbert Grady*), Anne Jackson (*Doctor*), Tony Burton (*Larry Durkin*), Lia Beldam (*Young Woman in Bath*), Billie Gibson (*Old Woman in Bath*), Lisa Burns, Louise Burns (*The Grady Girls*).

Produced by Stanley Kubrick (Hawk Films) for Warner Brothers. 145 min.

1987 FULL METAL JACKET

Script: Kubrick, Michael Herr, Gustav Hasford, based on Hasford's novel, *The Short-Timers*.
Direction: Kubrick.
Photography: Douglas Milsome.
Production design: Anton Furst.
Editing: Martin Hunter.
Music: Abigail Mead.

Cast: Matthew Modine (*Private Joker*), Lee Ermey (*Gunnery Sergeant Hartman*), Vincent D'Onofrio (*Private Pyle*), Arliss Howard (*Cowboy*), Adam Baldwin (*Animal Mother*), Dorian Harewood (*Eightball*), Kevyn Major Howard (*Rafterman*), Ed O'Ross (*Lieutenant Touchdown*).

Produced by Kubrick (Puffin Films) for Warner Brothers. 118 min.

1999 EYES WIDE SHUT

Script: Kubrick and Frederic Raphael, based on Arthur Schnitzler's *Traumnovelle*.
Direction: Kubrick.
Photography: Larry Smith.
Production design: Leslie Tomkins and Roy Walker.
Editing: Nigel Galt.
Music: Jocelyn Pock, György Ligeti, Dmitri Shostakovich.

Cast: Tom Cruise (*Dr. William Harford*), Nicole Kidman (*Alice Harford*), Sydney Pollack (*Victor Ziegler*), Marie Richardson (*Marion*), Rade Serbedzija (*Milich*), Leelee Sobieski (*Milich's Daughter*), Todd Field (*Nick Nightingale*), Vinessa Shaw (*Domino*), Alan Cumming (*Desk Clerk*), Carmela Marner (*Waitress at Gillespie's*), Sky Dumont (*Sandor Szavost*), Fay Masterson (*Sally*), Thomas Gibson (*Carl*), Louise J. Taylor (*Gayle*), Stewart Thorndike (*Nuala*), Julienne Davis (*Mandy*), Madison Eginton (*Helena Harford*), Leon Vitali (*Man in Red*).

Produced by Kubrick, Jan Harlan, and Brian W. Cook for Warner Bros. 165 min.

MARTIN SCORSESE

1969 WHO'S THAT KNOCKING AT MY DOOR?

Script and direction: Scorsese (additional dialogue by Betzi Manoogian).
Photography (b&w): Michael Wadleigh, Richard Coll, Max Fisher.
Art direction: Victor Magnotta.
Editing: Thelma Schoonmaker.

Cast: Zina Bethune (*The Young Girl*), Harvey Keitel (*J. R.*), Anne Collette (*Young Girl in Dream*), Lennard Kuras (*Joey*), Michael Scala (*Sally Gaga*), Harry Northup (*Harry*), Bill Minkin (*Iggy*), Phil Carlson (*The Guide*), Wendy Russell (*Gaga's Small Friend*), Robert Uricola (*the Armed Young Man*), Susan Wood (*Susan*), Marissa Joffrey (*Rosie*), Catherine Scorsese (*J. R.'s Mother*), Victor Magnotta, Paul De Bionde (*Waiters*), Saskia Holleman, Tsuai Yu-Lan, Marieka (*Dream Girls*), Martin Scorsese (*Gangster*), Thomas Aiello.

Produced by Joseph Weill, Betzi Manoogian, and Haig Manoogian (Trimrod) for release by Joseph Brenner Associates. 90 min. Earlier versions known as *Bring on the Dancing Girls* (1965) and *I Call First* (1967). Also released as *J. R.*

1972 BOXCAR BERTHA

Script: Joyce H. Corrington, John William Corrington, from the book *Sister of the Road* by Boxcar Bertha Thompson as told to Ben L. Reitman.
Direction: Scorsese.
Photography: John Stephens.
Visual consultant: David Nichols.
Editing: Buzz Feitshans.
Music: Gib Guilbeau, Thad Maxwell.

Cast: Barbara Hershey (*Bertha*), David Carradine (*Bill Shelley*), Barry Primus (*Rake Brown*), Bernie Casey (*Von Morton*), John Carradine (*H. Buckram Sartoris*), Victor Argo, David R. Osterhout (*The McIvers*), "Chicken" Holleman (*Michael Powell*), Grahame Pratt (*Emeric Pressburger*), Harry Northup (*Harvey Hall*), Ann Morell (*Tillie*), Marianne Dole (*Mrs. Mailer*), Joe Reynolds (*Joe*), Gayne Rescher, Martin Scorsese (*Brothel Clients*).

Produced by Roger Corman for American International. 88 min.

1973 MEAN STREETS

Script: Scorsese, Mardik Martin.
Direction: Scorsese.
Photography: Kent Wakeford.
Visual consultant: David Nichols.
Editing: Sid Levin.

Cast: Harvey Keitel (*Charlie*), Robert De Niro (*Johnny Boy*), Amy Robinson (*Teresa*), David Proval (*Tony*), Richard Romanus (*Michael*), Cesare Danova (*Giovanni*), Victor Argo (*Mario*), George Memmoli (*Joey Catucci*), Lenny Scaletta (*Jimmy*), Jeannie Bell (*Diane*), Murray Mosten (*Oscar*), David Carradine (*Drunk*), Robert Carradine (*Young Assassin*), Lois Walden (*Jewish Girl*), Harry Northup (*Vietnam Veteran*), Dino Seragusa (*Old Man*), D'Mitch Davis (*Black Cop*), Peter Fain (*George*), Julie Andelman (*Girl at Party*), Robert Wilder (*Benton*), Ken Sinclair (*Sammy*), Catherine Scorsese (*Woman on the Landing*), Martin Scorsese (*Shorty, The Killer in the Car*).

Produced by Jonathan T. Taplin (Taplin-Perry-Scorsese) for Warner Brothers. 110 min.

1974 ALICE DOESN'T LIVE HERE ANYMORE

Script: Robert Getchell.
Direction: Scorsese.
Photography: Kent Wakeford.
Production design: Toby Carr Rafelson.
Editing: Marcia Lucas.
Original music: Richard LaSalle.

Cast: Ellen Burstyn (*Alice Hyatt*), Kris Kristofferson (*David*), Alfred Lutter (*Tommy*), Billy Green Bush (*Donald*), Diane Ladd (*Flo*), Lelia Goldoni (*Bea*), Lane Bradbury (*Rita*), Vic Tayback (*Mel*), Jodie Foster (*Audrey*), Harvey Keitel (*Ben*), Valerie Curtin (*Vera*), Mur-

437

ray Moston (*Jacobs*), Harry Northup (*Joe and Jim's Bartender*), Mia Bendixsen (*Alice, age 8*), Ola Moore (*Old Woman*), Martin Brinton (*Lenny*), Dean Casper (*Chicken*), Henry M. Kendrick (*Shop Assistant*), Martin Scorsese, Larry Cohen (*Diners at Mel and Ruby's*), Mardik Martin (*Customer in Club During Audition*).

Produced by David Susskind and Audrey Maas for Warner Brothers. 112 min.

1976 TAXI DRIVER
Script: Paul Schrader.
Direction: Scorsese.
Photography: Michael Chapman.
Art direction: Charles Rosen.
Visual consultant: David Nichols.
Editing: Marcia Lucas, Tom Rolf, Melvin Shapiro.
Music: Bernard Herrmann.
Creative consultant: Sandra Weintraub.

Cast: Robert De Niro (*Travis Bickle*), Cybill Shepherd (*Betsy*), Jodie Foster (*Iris*), Harvey Keitel (*Sport*), Peter Boyle (*Wizard*), Albert Brooks (*Tom*), Leonard Harris (*Charles Palantine*), Diahnne Abbott (*Concession Girl*), Frank Adu (*Angry Black Man*), Vic Argo (*Melio*), Gino Ardito (*Policeman at Rally*), Garth Avery (*Iris's Friend*), Harry Cohn (*Cabbie in Belmore*), Copper Cunningham (*Hooker in Cab*), Brenda Dickson (*Soap Opera Woman*), Harry Fischler (*Dispatcher*), Nat Grant (*Stick-Up Man*), Richard Higgs (*Tall Secret Service Man*), Beau Kayser (*Soap Opera Man*), Vic Magnotta (*Secret Service Photographer*), Robert Maroff (*Mafioso*), Norman Matlock (*Charlie T.*), Bill Minkin (*Tom's Assistant*), Murray Moston (*Iris's Timekeeper*), Harry Northup (*Doughboy*), Gene Palma (*Street Drummer*), Carey Poe (*Campaign Worker*), Steven Prince (*Andy, Gun Salesman*), Peter Savage (*The John*), Martin Scorsese (*Passenger Watching Silhouette*), Robert Shields (*Palantine Aide*), Ralph Singleton (*TV Interviewer*), Joe Spinell (*Personnel Officer*), Maria Turner (*Angry Hooker on Street*), Robin Utt (*Campaign Worker*).

Produced by Michael and Julia Phillips (Bill/Phillips production), for Columbia. 112 min.

1977 NEW YORK, NEW YORK
Script: Earl Mac Rauch, Mardik Martin, from a story by Rauch.
Direction: Scorsese.
Photography: Laszlo Kovacs.
Production design: Boris Leven.
Original songs by John Kander and Fred Ebb ("Theme from *New York, New York*," "There Goes the Ball Game," "But the World Goes 'Round," "Happy Endings").
Saxophone solos and technical consultant: Georgie Auld.
Musical supervisor and conductor: Ralph Burns.
Choreography: Ron Field.
Supervising film editors: Irving Lerner, Marcia Lucas.
Editing: Tom Rolf, B. Lovitt.
Costumes: Theadora van Runkle.

Cast: Liza Minnelli (*Francine Evans*), Robert De Niro (*Jimmy Doyle*), Lionel Stander (*Tony Harwell*), Barry Primus (*Paul Wilson*), Mary Kay Place (*Bernice*), Georgie Auld (*Frankie Harte*), George Memmoli (*Nicky*), Dick Miller (*Palm Club Owner*), Murray

Moston (*Horace Morris*), Lenny Gaines (*Artie Kirks*), Clarence Clemons (*Cecil Powell*), Kathi McGinnis (*Ellen Flannery*), Norman Palmer (*Desk Clerk*), Adam David Winkler (*Jimmy Doyle, Jr.*), Dimitri Logothetis (*Desk Clerk*), Frank Sivera (*Eddie di Muzio*), Diahnne Abbott (*Harlem Club Singer*), Margo Winkler (*Argumentative Woman*), Steven Prince (*Record Producer*), Don Calfa (*Gilbert*), Bernie Kuby (*Justice of the Peace*), Selma Archerd (*Wife of Justice of the Peace*), Bill Baldwin (*Announcer in Moonlit Terrace*), Mary Lindsay (*Hatcheck Girl in Meadows*), Jon Cutler (*Musician in Frankie Hart's Band*), Nicky Blair (*Cab Driver*), Casey Kasem (*D. J.*), Jay Salerno (*Bus Driver*), William Tole (*Tommy Dorsey*), Sydney Guilaroff (*Hairdresser*), Peter Savage (*Horace Morris's Assistant*), Gene Castle (*Dancing Sailor*), Louie Guss (*Fowler*), Shera Danese (*Doyle's Girl in Major Chord*), Bill McMillan (*D. J.*), David Nichols (*Arnold Trench*), Harry Northup (*Alabama*), Marty Zagon (*Manager of South Bend Ballroom*), Timothy Blake (*Nurse*), Betty Cole (*Charwoman*), De Forest Covan (*Porter*), Phil Gray (*Trombone Player in Doyle's Band*), Roosevelt Smith (*Bouncer in Major Chord*), Bruce L. Lucoff (*Cab Driver*), Bill Phillips Murry (*Waiter in Harlem Club*), Clint Arnold (*Trombone Player in Palm Club*), Richard Alan Berk (*Drummer in Palm Club*), Jack R. Clinton (*Bartender in Palm Club*), Wilfred R. Middlebrooks (*Bass Player in Palm Club*), Jake Vernon Porter (*Trumpet Player in Palm Club*), Nat Pierce (*Piano Player in Palm Club*), Manuel Escobosa (*Fighter in Moonlit Terrace*), Susan Kay Hunt, Teryn Jenkins (*Girls at Moonlit Terrace*), Mardik Martin (*Well-Wisher at Moonlit Terrace*), Leslie Summers (*Woman in Black at Moonlit Terrace*), Brock Michaels (*Man at Table in Moonlit Terrace*), Washington Rucker, Booty Reed (*Musicians at Hiring Hall*), David Armstrong, Robert Buckingham, Eddie Garrett, Nico Stevens (*Reporters*), Peter Fain (*Greeter in Up Club*), Angelo Lamonea (*Waiter in Up Club*), Charles A. Tamburro, Wallace McClesky (*Bouncers in Up Club*), Ronald Prince (*Dancer in Up Club*), Robert Petersen (*Photographer*), Richard Raymond (*Railroad Conductor*), Hank Robinson (*Francine's Bodyguard*), Harold Ross (*Cab Driver*), Eddie Smith (*Man in Bathroom at Harlem Club*).

Produced by Irwin Winkler and Robert Chartoff for United Artists. 137 min.

1978 THE LAST WALTZ

Direction: Scorsese.

Photography: Michael Chapman, Laszlo Kovacs, Vilmos Zsigmond, David Myers, Bobby Byrne, Michael Watkins, Hiro Narita.

Production design: Boris Leven.

Editing: Yeu-Bun Yee, Jan Roblee.

Concert producer: Bill Graham.

Concert music production: John Simon. (Audio production: Rob Fraboni.)

Music editor: Ken Wannberg.

Treatment and creative consultant: Mardik Martin.

The performers in order of appearance: Ronnie Hawkins, Dr. John, Neil Young, The Staples, Neil Diamond, Joni Mitchell, Paul Butterfield, Muddy Waters, Eric Clapton, Emmylou Harris, Van Morrison, Bob Dylan, Ringo Starr, Ron Wood.

Poems by Michael McClure, Sweet William Fritsch, Lawrence Ferlinghetti.

Interviewer: Scorsese.

The Band: Rick Danko (bass, violin, vocal), Levon Helm (drums, mandolin, vocal), Garth Hudson (organ, accordion, saxophone, synthesizers), Richard Manuel (piano, keyboards, drums, vocal), Robbie Robertson (lead guitar, vocal).

Produced by Robbie Robertson for United Artists. Executive producer: Jonathan

Taplin. Filmed on location at Winterland Arena, San Francisco, November 1976, and MGM Studios, Culver City, and Shangri-La Studios, Malibu, thereafter. 119 min.

1980 RAGING BULL

Script: Paul Schrader and Mardik Martin, based on *Raging Bull* by Jake La Motta, with Joseph Carter and Peter Savage.
Direction: Scorsese.
Photography (b&w): Michael Chapman.
Production design: Gene Rudolph.
Editing: Thelma Schoonmaker.
Music: Pietro Mascagni.

Cast: Robert De Niro (*Jake La Motta*), Joe Pesci (*Joey*), Cathy Moriarity (*Vickie*), Frank Vincent (*Salvy*), Nicholas Colosanto (*Tommy Como*), Mario Gallo (*Mario*), Frank Adonis (*Patsy*), Joseph Bono (*Guido*), Frank Topham (*Toppy*), Theresa Saldano (*Lenore*), Lori Anne Flax (*Irma*), Bill Hanrahan (*Eddie Eagen*), James V. Christy (*Dr. Pinto*), Bernie Allen (*Comedian*), Don Dunphy (*Himself*), Charles Scorsese (*Charlie*), Martin Scorsese (*Man in Dressing Room*), Floyd Anderson (*Jimmy Reeves*), Johnny Barnes (*Sugar Ray Robinson*), Eddie Mustafa Mohammad (*Billy Fox*), Kevin Mahon (*Tony Janiro*), Louis Raftis (*Marcel Cerdan*), Johnny Turner (*Laurent Dauthuille*).

Produced by Robert Chartoff and Irwin Winkler for United Artists. 128 min.

1983 THE KING OF COMEDY

Script: Paul D. Zimmerman.
Direction: Scorsese.
Photography: Fred Schuler.
Production design: Boris Leven.
Editing: Thelma Schoonmaker.
Music production: Robbie Robertson.

Cast: Robert De Niro (*Rupert Pupkin*), Jerry Lewis (*Jerry Langford*), Sandra Bernhard (*Masha*), Diahnne Abbott (*Rita*), Shelley Hack (*Cathy Long*), Margo Winkler (*Receptionist*), Tony Boschetti (*Mr. Gangemi*), Ralph Monaco (*Raymond Wirtz*), Fred De Cordova (*Bert Thomas*), Edgar J. Scherick (*Wilson Crockett*), Thomas M. Tolan (*Gerrity*), Ray Dittrich (*Giardello*), Richard Dioguardi (*Capt. Burke*), Jay Julien (*Langford's Lawyer*), Harry Ufland (*Langford's Agent*), Kim Chan (*Jonno*), Audrey Dummett (*Cook*), Martin Scorsese (*T.V. Director*), Thelma Lee (*Woman in Telephone Booth*), Catherine Scorsese (*Rupert's Mother*), Cathy Scorsese (*Dolores*), Charles Scorsese (*First Man at Bar*), Mardik Martin (*Second Man at Bar*), Ed Herlihy, Victor Borge, Dr. Joyce Brothers, Tony Randall (*Themselves*).

Produced by Arnold Milchan (Embassy International Pictures) for Twentieth Century-Fox. 109 min.

1985 AFTER HOURS

Script: Joseph Minion.
Direction: Scorsese.
Photography: Michael Ballhaus.
Production design: Jeffrey Townsend.

Editing: Thelma Schoonmaker.

Music: Howard Shore.

Cast: Griffin Dunne (*Paul Hackett*), Rosanna Arquette (*Marcy*), Verna Bloom (*June*), Teri Garr (*Julie*), John Heard (*Tom*), Linda Fiorentino (*Kiki*), Catherine O'Hara (*Gail*), Thomas Chong (*Pepe*), Cheech Marin (*Neil*), Will Patton (*Horst*), Robert Plunket (*Mark*), Bronson Pinchot (*Lloyd*).

Produced by Amy Robinson, Griffin Dunne, Robert F. Colesberry (Geffen Company) for Warner Brothers. 97 min.

1986 THE COLOR OF MONEY

Script: Richard Price, based on the novel by Walter Tevis.

Direction: Scorsese.

Photography: Michael Ballhaus.

Production design: Boris Leven.

Editing: Thelma Schoonmaker.

Music: Robbie Robertson.

Cast: Paul Newman (*Eddie*), Tom Cruise (*Vincent*), Mary Elizabeth Mastrantonio (*Carmen*), Helen Shaver (*Janelle*), John Turturro (*Julien*), Bill Cobbs (*Orvis*), Keith McCready (*Grady Seasons*), Forest Whitaker (*Amos*), Bruce A. Young (*Moselle*).

Produced by Irving Axelrad and Barbara De Fina for Touchstone Pictures. 119 min.

1988 THE LAST TEMPTATION OF CHRIST

Script: Paul Schrader, from the novel by Nikos Kazantzakis.

Direction: Scorsese.

Photography: Michael Ballhaus.

Production design: John Beard.

Editing: Thelma Schoonmaker.

Music: Peter Gabriel.

Cast: Tomas Arana (*Lazarus*), Victor Argo (*Apostle Peter*), Gary Basaraba (*Andrew*), Michael Been (*John*), Verna Bloom (*Mary, Mother of Jesus*), Roberts Blossom (*Aged Master*), David Bowie (*Pontius Pilate*), Juliette Caton (*Girl Angel*), Willem Dafoe (*Jesus*), Andre Gregory (*John the Baptist*), Barbara Hershey (*Mary Magdalene*), Harvey Keitel (*Judas*), Irvin Kershner (*Zebedee*), John Lurie (*James*), Leo Marks (*Voice of the Devil*), Barry Miller (*Jerobeam*), Nehemiah Persoff (*Rabbi*), Alan Rosenberg (*Thomas*), Harry Dean Stanton (*Saul/Paul*).

Produced by Barbara De Fina (Cineplex Odeon Films) for Universal Pictures. Executive Producer: Harry J. Ufland. 164 min.

1990 GOODFELLAS

Script: Scorsese, Nicholas Pileggi, from his novel *Wiseguy*.

Direction: Scorsese.

Photography: Michael Ballhaus.

Production design: Krisi Zea.

Editing: Thelma Schoonmaker.

Music: many different artists.

Cast: Robert De Niro (*James Conway*), Ray Liotta (*Henry Hill*), Joe Pesci (*Tommy DeVito*), Lorraine Bracco (*Karen Hill*), Paul Sorvino (*Paul Cicero*), Frank Sivero (*Frankie*

Carbone), Frank Vincent (*Billy Batts*), Frank DiLeo (*Tuddy Cicero*), Catherine Scorsese (*Tommy's Mother*), Charles Scorsese (*Vinnie*), Suzanne Shepherd (*Karen's Mother*), Christopher Serrone (Young Henry), Elaine Kagan (Henry's Mother), Beau Starr (*Henry's Father*), Kevin Corrigan (*Michael Hill*), Michael Imperioli (*Spider*), John Williams (*Johnny Roastbeef*), John Manca (*Nickey Eyes*), Samuel L. Jackson (*Stacks Edwards*), Louis Eppolito (*Fat Andy*). Tony Lip (*Frankie the Wop*), Mikey Black (*Freddy No Nose*), Peter Cicale (*Pete the Killer*), Anthony Powers (*Jimmy Two Times*), Peter Hock (*Mailman*), Chuck Low (*Maurie*).

Produced by Barbara De Fina and Irwin Winkler for Warner Brothers. 146 min.

1991 CAPE FEAR

Script: Wesley Strick, from James R. Webb's 1962 screenplay, from John D. MacDonald's novel *The Executioners*.
Direction: Scorsese.
Photography (Panavision): Freddie Francis.
Production design: Henry Bumstead.
Editing: Thelma Schoonmaker.
Music: Elmer Bernstein and Bernard Herrmann.

Cast: Robert De Niro (*Max Cady*), Nick Nolte (*Sam Bowden*), Jessica Lange (*Leigh Bowden*), Juliette Lewis (*Danielle Bowden*), Joe Don Baker (*Claude Kersek*), Robert Mitchum (*Lieutenant Elgart*), Gregory Peck (*Lee Heller*), Martin Balsam (*Judge*), Illeana Douglas (*Lori Davis*), Fred Dalton Thompson (*Tom Broadbent*), Zully Montero (*Graciella*), Joel Kolker (*Prison Guard*).

Produced by Barbara De Fina (Tribeca Productions) for Universal Pictures. Executive Producers: Kathleen Kennedy, Frank Marshall, Steven Spielberg (uncredited). 128 min.

1993 THE AGE OF INNOCENCE

Script: Jay Cocks and Martin Scorsese, from the novel by Edith Wharton.
Direction: Scorsese.
Photography (Panavision): Michael Ballhaus.
Production design: Dante Ferretti
Music: Elmer Bernstein.

Cast: Daniel Day-Lewis (*Newland Archer*), Michelle Pfeiffer (*Ellen Olenska*), Winona Ryder (*May Welland*), Richard E. Grant (*Larry Lefferts*), Alec McCowen (*Sillerton Jackson*), Geraldine Chaplin (*Mrs. Welland*), Mary Beth Hurt (*Regina Beaubort*), Stuart Wilson (*Julius Beaubort*), Howard Erskine (*Beaubort Guest*), John McLoughlin (*Party Guest*), Christopher Nilsson (*Party Guest*), Miriam Margolyes (*Mrs. Mingott*), Sian Phillips (*Mrs. Archer*), Carolyn Farina (*Janey Archer*), Michael Gough (*Henry Van Der Luyden*), Alexis Smith (*Louisa Van Der Luyden*), Kevin Sanders (*The Duke*), W. B. Brydon (*Mr. Urban Dagonet*), Tracey Ellis (*Gertrude Lefferts*), Christina Pronzati (*Countess Olenska's Maid*), Clement Fowler (*Florist*), Norman Lloyd (*Mr. Letterblair*), Cindy Katz (*Stage Actress*), Thomas Gibson (*Stage Actor*), Jonathan Pryce (*Monsieur Riviere*), June Squibb (*Mingott Maid*), Domenica Scorsese (*Katie Blenker*), Mac Orange (*Archer Maid*), Brian Davies (*Philip*), Thomas Barbour (*Archer Guest*), Henry Fehren (*Bishop*), Patricia Dunnock (*Mary Archer*), Robert Sean Leonard (*Ted Archer*), Joanne Woodward (*Narrator*), Charles Scorsese, Claire Bloom (*uncredited*), Martin Scorsese (*Photographer, uncredited*).

442

Produced by Barbara De Fina, Bruce S. Pustin (Columbia Pictures) for Columbia Pictures Corporation. 139 min.

1995 CASINO

Script: Scorsese, Nicholas Pileggi, from his book *Casino: Love and Honor in Las Vegas*.
Direction: Scorsese.
Photography (Panavision): Robert Richardson.
Production design: Dante Ferretti.
Editing: Thelma Schoonmaker.
Music Consultant: Robbie Robertson.

Cast: Robert De Niro (*Sam "Ace" Rothstein*), Sharon Stone (*Ginger McKenna*), Joe Pesci (*Nicky Santoro*), James Woods (*Lester Diamond*), Don Rickles (*Billy Sherbert*), Alan King (*Andy Stone*), Kevin Pollack (*Phillip Green*), L.Q. Jones (*Pat Webb*), Dick Smothers (*Senator*), Frank Vincent (*Frank Marino*), John I. Bloom (*Slot Machine Manager*), Pasquale Cajano (*Remo Gaggi*), Melissa Prophet (*Jennifer Santoro*), Bill Allison (*John Nance*), Vinny Vella (*Artie Piscano*), Oscar Goodman (*Himself*), Catherine Scorsese (*Piscano's Mother*), Philip Suriano (*Dominick Santoro*), Erika von Tagen (*Older Amy*), Frankie Avalon (*Himself*), Steve Allen (*Himself*), Jayne Meadows (*Herself*), Jerry Vale (*Himself*), Joseph Rigano (*Vincent Borelli*), Gene Ruffini (*Vinny Forlano*), Dominick Grieco (*Americo Capelli*), Richard Amalfitano (*Casino Executive*), Casper Molee (*Counter*), David Leavitt (*Counter*), Peter Conti (*Arthur Capp*), Steve Vignari (*Beeper*), Rick Crachy (*Chastised Dealer*), Larry E. Nadler (*Lucky Larry*), Paul Herman (*Gambler in Phone Booth*), Salvatore Petrillo (*Old Man Capo*), Joey DePinto (*Stabbed Gambler*), Heidi Keller (*Blonde at Bar*), Millicent Sheridan (*Senator's Hooker*), Nobu Matsuhisa (*Ichikawa*), Toru Nagai (*Ichikawa's Associate*), Dom Angelo (*Craps Dealer*), Joe Molinaro (*Shift Manager*), Ali Pirouzkar (*High Roller*), Frankie J. Allison (*Craps Dealer*), Jeff Scott Anderson (*Parking Valet*), Jennifer M. Abbott (*Cashier*), Loren Stevens (*Agent—Piscano Raid*), Gary C. Rainey (*Agent—Piscano Raid*), David Arcerio (*FBI Agent*), Haven Earl Haley (*Judge*), Sam Wilson (*Ambulance Driver*), Michael Toney (*Fat Sally*), Charles Scorsese.

Produced by Barbara De Fina (De Fina-Cappa) for Universal Pictures. 178 min.

1997 KUNDUN

Script: Melissa Mathison.
Direction: Scorsese.
Photography: Roger Deakins.
Production design: Dante Ferretti.
Editing: Thelma Schoonmaker.
Music: Philip Glass.

Cast: Tenzin Thuthob Tsarong (*Dalai Lama, Adult*), Gyurme Tethong (*Dalai Lama, age 10*), Tulku Jamyang Kunga Tenzin (*Dalai Lama, age 5*), Tenzin Yeshi Paichang (*Dalai Lama, age 2*), Tencho Gyalpo (*Dalai Lama's Mother*), Tsewang Migyur Khangsar (*Dalai Lama's Father*), Geshi Yeshi Gyatso (*Lama of Sera*), Sonam Phuntsok (*Reting Rimpoche*), Lobsang Samten (*Master of the Kitchen*), Gyatso Lukhang (*Lord Chamberlain*), Jigme Tsarong (*Taktra Rimpoche*), Tenzin Trinley (*Ling Ripoche*), Robert Lin (*Chairman Mao*).

Produced by Barbara De Fina, and Melissa Mathison (De Fina-Cappa) for Walt Disney Productions. Executive Producer: Laura Fattori. 114 min.

1999 BRINGING OUT THE DEAD
Script: Paul Schrader, from the novel by Joe Comelly.
Direction: Scorsese.
Photography: Robert Richardson.
Production design: Dante Ferretti.
Editing: Thelma Schoomnaker.
Music: Elmer Bernstein.

Cast: Nicolas Cage (*Frank Pierce*), Patricia Arquette (*Mary Burke*), John Goodman (*Larry*), Ving Rhames (*Marcus*), Tom Sizemore (*Tom Wells*), Marc Anthony (*Noel*), Mary Beth Hurt (Nurse Constance), Cliff Curtis (*Cy Coates*), Nestor Serrano (*Dr. Hazmat*), Aida Turturro (*Nurse Crupp*), Cynthia Roman (*Rose*), Afemo Omilami (*Griss*), Cullen O. Johnson (*Mr. Burke*), Arthur J. Nascarella (*Captain Barney*).

Produced by Barbara De Fina and Bruce S. Pustin (DeFina/Cappa) for Paramount. 120 mins.

STEVEN SPIELBERG

Like Robert Altman before him, Spielberg directed a number of television shows before he began making features. In 1985 he returned to television as executive producer and sometime director of *Amazing Stories*. *Duel* was a made-for-television movie shown theatrically abroad and is considered his first major film. I have not included the sequence Spielberg directed for the 1983 film *Twilight Zone: The Movie*.

1971 DUEL
Script: Richard Matheson.
Direction: Spielberg.
Photography: Jack A. Marta.
Production design: Robert S. Smith.
Editing: Frank Morriss.
Music: Billy Goldenberg.

Cast: Dennis Weaver (*David Mann*), Tim Herbert (*Station Attendant*), Charles Seel (*Old Man*), Eddie Firestone (*Café Owner*), Shirley O'Hara (*Waitress*), Gene Dynarski (*Man in Café*), Lucile Benson (*Snakorama Lady*), Alexander Lockwood (*Old Man in Car*), Amy Douglass (*Lady*).

Produced by George Eckstein for Universal Television. 74 min./90 min., theatrical release.

1973 SUGARLAND EXPRESS
Script: Hal Barwood, Matthew Robbins, from a story by Spielberg.
Direction: Spielberg.
Photography (Panavision): Vilmos Zsigmond.
Production design: Joseph Alves.
Editing: Edward M. Abroms, Verna Fields.
Music: John Williams.

Cast: Goldie Hawn (*Lou Jean Poplin*), William Atherton (*Clovis Poplin*), Ben Johnson (*Capt. Tanner*), Michael Sacks (*Officer Slide*), Gregory Walcott (*Officer Mashburn*),

Harrison Zanuck (*Baby Langston*), Steve Kanaly, Louise Latham, K. Hudgins, Buster Danials.

Produced by Richard D. Zanuck and David Brown for Universal. 110 min.

1975 JAWS

Script: Peter Benchley, Carl Gottlieb, from Benchley's novel.
Direction: Spielberg.
Photography (Panavision): Bill Butler.
Underwater photography: Rexford Metz.
Production design: Joseph Alves.
Special effects: Robert A. Mattey.
Editing: Verna Fields.
Music: John Williams.

Cast: Roy Scheider (*Brody*), Richard Dreyfuss (*Hooper*), Robert Shaw (*Quint*), Lorraine Gary (*Ellen Brody*), Murray Hamilton (*Vaughn*), Carl Gottlieb (*Meadows*), Jeffrey C. Kramer (*Hendricks*), Susan Backlinie (*Chrissie*), Jonathan Filley (*Cassidy*), Chris Rebello (*Michael Brody*), Jay Mello (*Sean Brody*), Ted Grossman (*Estuary Victim*), Lee Fierro (*Mrs. Kintner*), Jeffrey Voorhees (*Alex Kintner*), Craig Kingsbury (*Ben Gardner*), Dr. Rober Nevin (*Medical Examiner*), Peter Benchley (*Interviewer*).

Produced by Richard D. Zanuck and David Brown for Universal. 124 min.

1977 CLOSE ENCOUNTERS OF THE THIRD KIND

Script and Direction: Spielberg.
Photography (Panavision): Vilmos Zsigmond.
Additional photography: William A. Fraker, Douglas Slocombe, John Alonzo, Laszlo Kovacs.
Production design: Joe Alves.
Special effects: Douglas Trumbull.
Editing: Michael Kahn.
Music: John Williams.

Cast: Richard Dreyfuss (*Roy Neary*), François Truffaut (*Claude Lacombe*), Teri Garr (*Ronnie Neary*), Melinda Dillon (*Jillian Guiler*), Cary Guffey (*Barry Guiler*), Bob Balaban (*David Laughlin*), J. Patrick McNamara (*Project Leader*), Warren Kemmerling (*Wild Bill*), Roberts Blossom (*Farmer*), Philip Dodds (*Jean Claude*), Shawn Bishop (*Brad Neary*), Adrienne Campbell (*Silvia Neary*), Justin Dreyfuss (*Toby Neary*), Lance Hendricksen (*Robert*), Merrill Connally (*Team Leader*), George Dicenzo (*Major Benchley*).

Produced by Julia Phillips and Michael Phillips for Columbia/EMI. 135 min./"Special Edition" re-release 132 min.

445

1979 1941

Script: Robert Zemeckis, Bob Gale, from a story by Zemeckis, Gale, and John Milius.
Direction: Spielberg.
Photography (Panavision): William A. Fraker.
Production design: Dean Edward Mitzner.
Special effects: A. D. Flowers.
Visual effects supervisor: Larry Robinson.
Editing: Michael Kahn.

Music: John Williams.

Cast: Dan Aykroyd (*Sergeant Tree*), Ned Beatty (*Ward Douglas*), John Belushi (*Wild Bill Kelso*), Lorraine Gary (*Joan Douglas*), Murray Hamilton (*Claude*), Christopher Lee (*Von Kleinschmidt*), Tim Matheson (*Birkhead*), Toshiro Mifune (*Commander Mitamura*), Warren Oates (*Maddox*), Robert Stack (*General Stilwell*), Treat Williams (*Sitarksi*), Nancy Allen (*Donna*), Eddie Deezen (*Herbie*), Bobby DiCicco (*Wally*), Dianne Kay (*Betty*), John Candy (*Foley*), Frank McRae (*Ogden Johnson Jones*), Perry Lang (*Dennis*), Slim Pickens (*Hollis Wood*), Wendie Jo Sperber (*Maxine*), Lionel Stander (*Scioli*), Ignatius Wolfington (*Meyer Mishkin*), Joseph P. Flaherty (*U.S.O. M.C.*)

Produced by Buzz Feitshans (A-Team) for Universal. Executive producer: John Milius. 118 min.

1981 RAIDERS OF THE LOST ARK

Script: Lawrence Kasdan, based on a story by George Lucas and Philip Kaufman.
Direction: Spielberg.
Photography (Panavision): Douglas Slocombe.
Production design: Norman Reynolds and Leslie Dilley.
Visual effects: Richard Edlund, Kit West, Bruce Nicholson, Joe Johnston.
Editing: Michael Kahn.
Music: John Williams.

Cast: Harrison Ford (*Indiana Jones*), Karen Allen (*Marion Ravenwood*), Wolf Kahler (*Dietrich*), Paul Freeman (*Belloq*), Ronald Lacey (*Toht*), John Rhys-Davies (*Sallah*), Denholm Elliott (*Brody*), Anthony Higgins (*Gobler*), Alfred Molina (*Satipo*), Vic Tablian (*Barranca*), George Harris (*Katanga*).

Produced by Frank Marshall (Lucasfilm) for Paramount. Executive producer: George Lucas. 118 min.

1982 E.T. THE EXTRA-TERRESTRIAL

Script: Melissa Mathison.
Direction: Spielberg.
Photography: Allan Daviau.
Effects photography: Mike McAlister.
Special visual effects: Industrial Light and Magic.
Production design: James. D. Bissell.
Editing: Carol Littleton.
Music: John Williams.

Cast: Henry Thomas (*Elliott*), Robert MacNaughton (*Michael*), Drew Barrymore (*Gertie*), Dee Wallace (*Mary*), Peter Coyote ("*Keys*"), K. C. Martel (*Greg*), Sean Frye (*Steve*), Tom Howell (*Tyler*), Erika Eleniak (*Pretty Girl*), David O'Dell (*Schoolboy*), Richard Swingler (*Science Teacher*), Frank Toth (*Policeman*), Carlo Rambaldi, Steve Townsend, Robert Short, Beverly Hoffman, Caprice Rothe, Robert Avila, Eugene Crum, Frank Schepler, Bob Townsend, Steve Willis, Richard Zarro, Ronald Zarro, Pat Billon, Tamara de Treaux, Matthew De Meritt, Tina Palmer, Nancy MacLean, Pam Ybarra (*E.T.*).

Produced by Spielberg and Kathleen Kennedy for Universal. 120 min.

1984 INDIANA JONES AND THE TEMPLE OF DOOM

Script: Willard Huyck and Gloria Katz, based on a story by George Lucas.
Direction: Steven Spielberg.

Photography (Panavision): Douglas Slocombe.
Production design: Elliott Scott.
Visual effects: Dennis Muren.
Editing: Michael Kahn.
Music: John Williams.

Cast: Harrison Ford (*Indiana Jones*), Kate Capshaw (*Willie Scott*), Ke Huy Quan (*Short Round*), Amrish Puri (*Mola Ram*), Roshan Seth (*Chattar Lal*), Philip Stone (*Captain Blumburtt*), Roy Chiao (*Lao Che*), D. R. Nanayakkaru (*Shaman*), Dharmadasa Kuruppu (*Chieftain*), David Yip (*Wu Han*), Ric Young (*Kao Kan*), Raj Singh (*Little Maharaja*), Pat Roach (*Chief Guard*).

Produced by Robert Watts for Paramount. Executive producers: George Lucas and Frank Marshall. 118 min.

1985 THE COLOR PURPLE
Script: Menno Meyjes, based on the novel by Alice Walker.
Direction: Spielberg.
Photography: Allen Daviau.
Production design: J. Michael Riva.
Editing: Michael Kahn.
Music: Quincy Jones.

Cast: Whoopi Goldberg (*Celie*), Danny Glover (*Mr.*), Margaret Avery (*Shug Avery*), Oprah Winfrey (*Sofia*), Willard Pugh (*Harpo*), Akosua Busia (*Nettie*), Adolph Caesar (*Mr.'s Father*), Rae Dawn Chong (*Squeak*), Dana Ivey (*Miss Millie*), Desreta Jackson (*Young Celie*).

Produced by Spielberg, Kathleen Kennedy, Frank Marshall, Quincy Jones (Guber-Peters and Amblin Entertainment) for Warner Brothers. 152 min.

1987 EMPIRE OF THE SUN
Script: Menno Meyjes (uncredited), Tom Stoppard, from a novel by J. G. Ballard.
Direction: Spielberg.
Photography: Allen Daviau.
Production design: Norman Reynolds.
Editing: Michael Kahn.
Music: John Williams.

Cast: Christian Bale (*Jim*), John Malkovich (*Basie*), Miranda Richardson (*Mrs. Victor*), Nigel Havers (*Dr. Rawlins*), Joe Pantoliano (*Frank Demarest*), Leslie Phillips (*Maxton*), Masato Ibu (*Sgt. Nagata*), Emily Richard (*Jim's Mother*), Rupert Frazer (*Jim's Father*), Peter Gale (*Mr. Victor*), Takatoro Kataoka (*Kamikaze Boy Pilot*), Ben Stiller (*Dainty*), David Neidorf (*Tiptree*).

Produced by Kathleen Kennedy, Frank Marshall, and Steven Spielberg (Amblin Entertainment) for Warner Brothers. Executive Producer: Robert Shapiro. 152 min.

1989 ALWAYS
Script: Jerry Belson, Frederick Hazlitt Brennan, from a story by Chandler Sprague and David Boehm and a screenplay by Dalton Trumbo.
Direction: Spielberg.
Photography: Mikael Salomon.

Production design: James D. Bissell.
Editing: Michael Kahn.
Music: John Williams.

Cast: Richard Dreyfuss (*Pete Sandich*), Holly Hunter (*Dorinda Durston*), Brad Johnson (*Ted Baker*), John Goodman (*Al Yackey*), Audrey Hepburn (*Hap*), Roberts Blossom (*Dave*), Keith David (*Powerhouse*), Ed Van Nuys (*Nails*), Marg Helgenberger (*Rachel*), Dale Dye (*Fire Boss*), Brian Haley (*Alex*), James Lashly (*Charlie*), Michael Steve Jones (*Grey*).

Produced by Kathleen Kennedy, Frank Marshall, Steven Spielberg (Amblin Entertainment) for Universal Pictures. 106 min.

1989 INDIANA JONES AND THE LAST CRUSADE

Script: George Lucas, Menno Meyjes, Jeffrey Boam, Tom Stoppard (uncredited).
Direction: Spielberg.
Photography (Panavision): Douglas Slocombe.
Production design: Elliot Scott.
Editing: Michael Kahn.
Music: John Williams.

Cast: Harrison Ford (*Indiana Jones*), Sean Connery (*Professor Henry Jones*), Denholm Elliott (*Marcus Brody*), Alison Doody (*Dr. Elsa Schneider*), John Rhys-Davies (*Sallah*), Julian Glover (*Walter Donovan*), River Phoenix (*Young Indy*), Michael Byrne (*Vogel*), Kevork Malikyan (*Kazim*), Robert Eddison (*Grail Knight*), Richard Young (*Fedora*), Alexei Sayle (*Sultan*), Alex Hyde-White (*Young Henry*), Paul Maxwell (*Panama Hat*), Isla Blair (*Mrs. Donovan*), Vernon Dobtcheff (*Butler*), J. J. Hardy (*Herman*), Bradley Gregg (*Roscoe*), Jeff O'Haco (*Half Breed*), Vince Deadrick (*Rough Rider*), Marc Miles (*Sheriff*), Ted Grossman (*Deputy Sheriff*), Tim Hiser (*Young Panama Hat*), Larry Sanders (*Scout Master*), Will Miles (*Scout #1*), David Murray (*Scout #2*), Frederick Jaeger (*World War One Ace*), Jerry Harte (Professor Stanton), Billy J. Mitchell (*Dr. Mulbrey*), Martin Gordon (*Man at Hitler Rally*), Paul Humpoletz (*German Officer at Rally*), Tom Branch (*Hatay Soldier in Temple*), Graeme Crowther (*Zeppelin Crewman*), Luke Hanson (*Principal SS Officer at Castle*), Chris Jenkinson (*Officer at Castle*), Nicola Scott (*Female Officer at Castle*), Louis Sheldon (*Young Officer at Castle*), Stefan Kalipha (*Hatay Tank Gunner*), Peter Paces (*Hatay Tank Driver*), Pat Roach (*Gestapo*), Suzanne Roquette (*Film Director*), Eugene Lipinski (*G-Man*), George Malpas (*Man on Zeppelin*), Julie Eccles (*Irene*), Nina Almond (*Flower Girl*), Michael Sheard (*Adolf Hitler*).

Produced by Robert Watts (Lucasfilm Ltd.) for Paramount Pictures. Executive Producers: George Lucas, Frank Marshall. 127 min.

1991 HOOK

Script: Jim V. Hart and Malia Scotch Marmo, from a story by Jim V. Hart and Nick Castle, from a play by J. M. Barrie.
Direction: Spielberg.
Photography: Dean Cundey.
Production design: Norman Garwood.
Editing: Michael Kahn.
Music: John Williams.

Cast: Dustin Hoffman (*Captain Hook*), Robin Williams (*Peter Banning/Peter Pan*), Julia Roberts (*Tinkerbell*), Bob Hoskins (*Smee*), Maggie Smith (*Granny Wendy*), Caroline Goodall (*Moira Banning*), Charlie Korsmo (*Jack*), Amber Scott (*Maggie*), Laurel Cronin

(*Liza*), Phil Collins (*Inspector Good*), Arthur Malet (*Tootles*), Isiah Robinson (*Pockets*), Beverly Polcyn (*Prostitute*), Randi Pareira (*Prostitute*), Mary Bond Davis (*Prostitute*), David Crosby (*Tickles*), Nick Tate (*Noodler*), Tony Burton (*Bill Jukes*), Glenn Close (*Gutless*), Nick Ullett (*Pirate Jailer*), Matthew Van Ginkel (*Baby Peter*), Ray Tveden (*Man in Stands*), Kim Robillard (*Toothless Cripple*), Mike Runyard (*Screaming Pirate*), Gary Epper (*Growling Pirate*), Rick Lazzarini (*Puppeteer*), Mark Bryan Wilson (*Puppeteer*).

Produced by Gary Adelson, Craig Baumgarten, and Kathleen Kennedy for TriStar Pictures/Columbia Pictures Corporation/ Amblin Entertainment. Executive Producers: Dodi Fayed and James V. Hart. 144 min.

1993 JURASSIC PARK
Script: Michael Crichton and David Koepp, from a novel by Michael Crichton.
Direction: Spielberg.
Photography: Dean Cundey.
Production design: Rick Carter.
Editing: Michael Kahn and George Lucas.
Digital artists: Eric Armstrong, Joel Aron, Paul Ashdown, Francesca Avilla (among many
  others).
Music: John Williams.

Cast: Sam Neill (*Dr. Alan Grant*), Laura Dern (*Dr. Ellie Sattler*), Jeff Goldblum (*Ian Malcolm*), Richard Attenborough (*John Hammond*), Bob Peck (*Robert Muldoon*), Martin Ferrero (*Donald Gennaro*), B. D. Wong (*Dr. Henry Wu*), Joseph Mazzello (*Tim Murphy*), Ariana Richards (*Lex Murphy*), Samuel L. Jackson (*Ray Arnold*), Wayne Knight (*Dennis Nedry*), Gerald R. Molen (*Dr. Gerry Harding*), Miguel Sandoval (*Rostagno*), Cameron Thor (*Lewis Dodgson*), Christopher John Fields (*Volunteer #1*), Whitby Hertford (*Volunteer Boy*), Dean Cundey (*Mate*), Jophery C. Brown (*Worker in Raptor Pen*), Tom Mishler (*Helicopter Pilot*), Greg Burson (*"Mr. DNA" Voice*), Adrian Escober (*Worker at Amber Mine*), Richard Kiley (*Himself [Tour Voice]*).

Produced by Kathleen Kennedy, Gerald R. Molen, Lata Ryan, Colin Wilson (Amblin Entertainment) for Universal Pictures. 127 min.

1993 SCHINDLER'S LIST
Script: Steven Zaillian, from a novel by Thomas Keneally.
Direction: Spielberg.
Photography (b&w): Janusz Kaminski.
Production design: Allan Starski.
Editing: Michael Kahn.
Digital artist: Joel Aron.
Music: John Williams.

Cast: Liam Neeson (*Oskar Schindler*), Ben Kingsley (*Itzhak Stern*), Ralph Fiennes (*Amon Goeth*), Caroline Goodall (*Emilie Schindler*), Jerzy Sagan (*Ghetto Old Man*), Jonathan Sagall (*Poldek Pfefferberg*), Embeth Davidtz (*Helen Hirsch*), Malgoscha Gebel (*Victoria Klonowska*), Shmulik Levy (*Wilek Chilowicz*), Mark Ivanir (*Marcel*), Béatrice Macola (*Ingrid*), Andrzej Seweryn (*Julian*), Friedrich von Thun (*Rolf Czurda*), Krzysztof Luft (*Herman Toffel*), Harry Nehring (*Leo John*), Norbert Weisser (*Albert Hujar*), Dariusz Szymaniak (*Prisoner at Depot*), Dirk Bender (*Clerk at Depot*), Maciej Winkler (*Black Marketeer*), Radoslaw Krzyzowski (*Black Marketeer*), Jacek Lenczowski (*Black Marketeer*), Hanna Kossowska (*Ghetto Doctor*), Maja Ostaszewska (*Frantic Woman*), Sebastian Skalski (*Stable Boy*), Ryszard Radwanski (*Pankiewicz*), Piotr Kadlcik (*Man in Pharmacy*), Bartek Niebielski (*NCO Plaszow*), Thomas Morris (*Grun*), Sebastian Konrad (*Engineer Man*), Lidia Wyrobiec-Bank (*Clara Sternberg*), Ravit Ferera (*Maria Mischel*), Agnieszka Korzeniowska (*Ghetto Girl*), Dominika Bednarczyk (*Ghetto Girl*), Alicja Kubaszewska (*Ghetto Girl*), Danny Marcu (*Ghetto Man*), Hans Rosner (*Ghetto Man*), Edward Linde Lubaszenko (*Brinnlitz Priest*), Alexander Strobele (*Montelupich Prisoner*), Georges Kern (*Depot Master*), Alexander Buczolich (*Plaszow SS Guard*), Michael Schiller (*Plaszow SS Guard*), Götz Otto (*Plaszow SS Guard*), Wolfgang Seidenberg (*Plaszow SS Guard*), Hubert Kramer (*Plaszow SS Guard*), Razia Israeli (*Plaszow Jewish Girl*), Dorit Seadia (*Plaszow Jewish Girl*), Esti Yerushalmi (*Plaszow Jewish Girl*).

Produced by Branko Lustig, Gerald R. Molen, Lew Rywin, and Steven Spielberg (Amblin Entertainment) for Universal Pictures. Executive Producer: Kathleen Kennedy. 197 min.

1997 THE LOST WORLD: JURASSIC PARK

Script: David Koepp, from a novel by Michael Crichton.
Direction: Spielberg.
Photography: Janusz Kaminski.
Production design: Rick Carter.
Editing: Michael Kahn.
Digital artists: George Aleco-Sima, Jon Alexander, Tim Alexander (among others).
Music: John Williams.

Cast: Jeff Goldblum (*Dr. Ian Malcolm*), Julianne Moore (*Dr. Sarah Harding*), Pete Postlethwaite (*Roland Tembo*), Arliss Howard (*Peter Ludlow*), Richard Attenborough (*John Hammond*), Vince Vaughn (*Nick Van Owen*), Vanessa Lee Chester (*Kelly Malcolm*), Peter Stormare (*Dieter Stark*), Harvey Jason (*Ajay Sidhu*), Richard Schiff (*Eddie Carr*), Thomas F. Duffy (*Dr. Robert Burke*), Joseph Mazzello (*Tim Murphy*), Ariana Richards (*Lex Murphy*), Thomas Rosales (*Carter*), Camilla Belle (*Cathy Bowman*), Cyndi Strittmatter (*Mrs. Bowman*), Robin Sachs (*Mr. Bowman*), Elliot Goldwag (*Senior Board Member*), J. Patrick McCormack (*Board Member*), Ross Partridge (*Curious Man*), Ian Abercrombie (*Butler*), David Sawyer (*Workman*), Geno Silva (*Barge Captain*), Alex Miranda (*Barge Captain's Son*), Ian Zajonc (*Ingen Helicopter Pilot*), Bob Boehm (*Cargo Helicopter Pilot*), Ben Skorstad (*Cargo Helicopter Pilot*), Alan D. Purwin (*Cargo Helicopter Pilot*), Kenyon Williams (*Cargo Helicopter Pilot*), Rick Wheeler (*Cargo Helicopter Pilot*), Bradley Jensen (*Cargo Helicopter Pilot*), Gordon Michaels (*Ingen Worker*), J. Scott Shonka (*Ingen Worker*), Harry Hutchinson (*Ingen Worker*), Bill Brown (*Ingen Worker*), Brian Turk (*Ingen Worker*), Jim Harly (*Harbor Master*), Colton James (*Benjamin*), Carey Eidel (*Benjamin's Dad*), Katy Boyer (*Benjamin's Mom*), David Koepp (*Unlucky Bastard*), Eugene Bass Jr. (*Attorney*), Bernard Shaw (*Himself [CNN Anchor]*), Steven Spielberg (*Popcorn-Eating Man*).

Produced by Gerald R. Molen, Colin Wilson, Bonnie Curtis (Amblin Entertainment) for Universal Pictures. Executive Producer: Kathleen Kennedy. 129 min.

1997 AMISTAD

Script: Steven Zaillian and David H. Franzoni, from a novel by William Owens.
Direction: Spielberg.
Photography: Janusz Kaminski.
Production design: Rick Carter.

450

Editing: Michael Kahn.
Music: John Williams.

Cast: Morgan Freeman (*Theodore Joadson*), Anthony Hopkins (*John Quincy Adams*), Djimon Hounsou (*Cinque*), Razaaq Adoti (*Yamba*), Abu Bakaar Fofanah (*Fala*), Matthew McConaughey (*Baldwin*), Nigel Hawthorne (*Martin Van Buren*), David Paymer (*Secretary Forsyth*), Pete Postlethwaite (*Holabird*), Stellan Skarsaard (*Tappan*), Anna Paquin (*Queen Isabella*), Tomás Milián (*Calderon*), Austin Pendleton (*Professor Gibbs*), Xander Berkeley (*Hammond*), Harry Blackmun (*Supreme Court Justice Joseph Story*), Darren E. Burrows (*British Soldier*), Peter Firth (*Captain Fitzgerald*), Paul Guilfoyle (*Attorney*), Arliss Howard (*John Calhoun*), Jeremy Northam (*Judge Coglin*), León Singer (*Slave Dealer Don Pablo*).

Produced by Debbie Allen, Tim Shriver, Steven Spielberg, Colin Wilson (Amblin Entertainment) for DreamWorks SKG. Executive Producers: Robert M. Cooper, Laurie MacDonald, Walter F. Parkes. 152 min.

1998 SAVING PRIVATE RYAN
Script: Frank Darabont and Robert Rodat.
Direction: Spielberg.
Photography: Janusz Kaminski.
Production design: Tom Sanders.
Editing: Michael Kahn.
Music: John Williams.

Cast: Tom Hanks (*Captain John H. Miller*), Tom Sizemore (*Sarge*), Edward J. Burns (*Reiben*), Matt Damon (*Private Ryan*), Jeremy Davies (*Upham*), Vin Diesel (*Caparzo*), Adam Goldberg (*Mellish*), Barry Pepper (*Jackson*), Giovanni Ribisi (*Wade*), Ted Danson (*Capt. Hamill*), Dennis Farina (*Lt. Col. Anderson*), Harve Presnell (*George Marshall*), Amanda Boxer (*Mrs. Margaret Ryan*), Harrison Young (*Old Ryan*).

Produced by Ian Bryce, Mark Gordon, Gary Levinsohn, Steven Spielberg (Mark Gordon Productions) for Paramount Pictures, DreamWorks SKG, Amblin Entertainment. 170 min.

451

ROBERT ALTMAN

1957 THE DELINQUENTS
Script and direction: Altman.
Photography (b&w): Charles Paddock (or Harry Birch).
Art direction: Chet Allen.
Editing: Helene Turner.
Music: Bill Nolan Quintet Minus Two.
Song: Bill Nolan, Ronnie Norman ("The Dirty Rock Boogie"), sung by Julia Lee.

Cast: Tom Laughlin (*Scotty*), Peter Miller (*Cholly*), Richard Bakalyn (*Eddy*), Rosemary Howard (*Janice*), Helene Hawley (*Mrs. White*), Leonard Belove (*Mr. White*), Lotus Corelli (*Mrs. Wilson*), James Lantz (*Mr. Wilson*), Christine Altman (*Sissy*), George Kuhn (*Jay*), Pat Stedman (*Meg*), Norman Zands (*Chizzy*), James Leria (*Steve*), Jet Pinkston (*Molly*), Kermit Echols (*Barman*), Joe Adleman (*Station Attendant*).

Produced by Altman (Imperial Productions) for United Artists. 72 min.

1957 THE JAMES DEAN STORY

Script: Stewart Stern.

Direction: Altman, George W. George.

Photography (b&w): 29 various cameramen (stills: Camera Eye Pictures).

Production design: Louis Clyde Stoumen.

Music: Leith Stevens.

Song: Jay Livingston, Ray Evans.

Narrator: Martin Gabel.

    Cast: Marcus, Ortense, and Markie Winslow (*Dean's Aunt, Uncle, and Cousin*), Mr. And Mrs. Dean (*His Grandparents*), Adeline Hall (*His Drama Teacher*), Big Traster, Mr. Carter, Jerry Luce, Louis De Liso, Amie Langer, Arline Sax, Chris White, George Ross, Robert Jewett, John Kalin, Lew Bracker, Glenn Kramer, Patsy d'Amore, Billy Karen, Lille Kardell (*His Friends*), Officer Nelson (*Highway Patrolman*).

    Produced by Altman and George W. George for Warner Brothers. 83 min.

1968 COUNTDOWN

Script: Loring Mandel, based on the novel *The Pilgrim Project* by Hank Searls.

Direction: Altman.

Photography (Panavision): William W. Spencer.

Art direction: Jack Poplin.

Editing: Gene Milford.

Music: Leonard Rosenman.

    Cast: James Caan (*Lee*), Robert Duvall (*Chiz*), Joanna Moore (*Mickey*), Barbara Baxley (*Jean*), Charles Aidman (*Gus*), Steve Ihnat (*Ross*), Michael Murphy (*Rick*), Ted Knight (*Larson*), Stephen Coit (*Ehrman*), John Rayner (*Dunc*), Charles Irving (*Seidel*), Bobby Riha Jr. (*Stevie*).

    Produced by William Conrad (Productions) for Warner Brothers. 101 min.

1969 NIGHTMARE IN CHICAGO

Script: Donald Moessinger, from the novel *Killer on the Turnpike* by William P. McGivern.

Direction: Altman.

Photography: Bud Thackery.

Music: Johnny Williams.

    Cast: Charles McGraw (*Georgie Porgie*), Ted Knight (*Reporter*), Robert Ridgely, Philip Abbott, Barbara Turner, Charlene Lee, Arlene Kieta.

    Produced by Altman for Roncom/Universal. 81 min. (Release version of the TV movie *Once Upon a Savage Night*, expanded with outtakes from an original 54 min. to 81 min. Shorter version first televised April 1964.)

1969 THAT COLD DAY IN THE PARK

Script: Gillian Freeman, from the novel by Richard Miles.

Direction: Altman.

Photography: Laszlo Kovacs.

Art direction: Leon Erickson.

Editing: Danford Greene.

Music: Johnny Mandel.

Cast: Sandy Dennis (*Frances Austen*), Michael Burns (*The Boy*), Susanne Benton (*Nina*), Luana Anders (*Sylvie*), John Garfield Jr. (*Nick*), Michael Murphy (*The Rounder*).

Produced by Donald Factor and Leon Mirell (Factor-Altman-Mirell Films) for Commonwealth United Entertainment, Inc. 115 min.

1970 M.A.S.H.

Script: Ring Lardner, Jr., from the novel by Richard Hooker.
Direction: Altman.
Photography (Panavision): Harold E. Stine.
Art direction: Jack Martin Smith, Arthur Lonergan.
Editing: Danford B. Greene.
Music: Johnny Mandel.
Song: Johnny Mandel and Mike Altman ("Suicide Is Painless").

Cast: Donald Sutherland (*Hawkeye Pierce*), Elliott Gould (*Trapper John McIntyre*), Tom Skerritt (*Duke Forrest*), Sally Kellerman (*Major Hot Lips Houlihan*), Robert Duvall (*Major Frank Burns*), Jo Ann Pflug (*Lt. Dish*), René Auberjonois (*Dago Red*), Roger Bowen (*Col. Henry Blake*), Gary Burghoff (*Radar O'Reilly*), David Arkin (*Sgt. Major Vollmer*), Fred Williamson (*Spearchucker*), Michael Murphy (*Me Lay*), Kim Atwood (*Ho-Jon*), Tim Brown (*Corporal Judson*), Indus Arthur (*Lt. Leslie*), John Schuck (*Painless Pole*), Ken Prymus (*Pfc. Seidman*), Dawne Damon (*Capt. Scorch*), Carl Gottlieb (*Ugly John*), Tamara Horrocks (*Capt. Knocko*), G. Wood (*General Hammond*), Bobby Troup (*Sgt. Gorman*), Bud Cort (*Private Boone*), Danny Goldman (*Capt. Murrhardt*), Corey Fischer (*Capt. Bandini*), J. B. Douglas, Yoko Young.

Produced by Ingo Preminger for Aspen/Twentieth Century-Fox. Associate producer: Leon Ericksen. 116 min.

1970 BREWSTER MCCLOUD

Script: Brian McKay (uncredited), Doran William Cannon.
Direction: Altman.
Assistant director: Tommy Thompson.
Photography (Panavision): Lamar Boren, Jordan Cronenweth.
Art direction: Preston Ames, George W. Davis.
Wings designed by Leon Ericksen.
Editing: Lou Lombardo.
Music: Gene Page.
Songs: Francis Scott Key, Rosamund Johnson and James Weldon Johnson, John Phillips, sung by Merry Clayton, John Phillips.

Cast: Bud Cort (*Brewster McCloud*), Sally Kellerman (*Louise*), Michael Murphy (*Frank Shaft*), William Windom (*Haskel Weeks*), Shelley Duvall (*Suzanne Davis*), René Auberjonois (*Lecturer*), Stacy Keach (*Abraham Wright*), John Schuck (*Lt. Alvin Johnson*), Margaret Hamilton (*Daphne Heap*), Jennifer Salt (*Hope*), Corey Fischer (*Lt. Hines*), G. Wood (*Capt. Crandall*), Bert Remsen (*Douglas Breen*), Angelin Johnson (*Mrs. Breen*), William Baldwin (*Bernard*), William Henry Bennet (*Band Conductor*), Gary Wayne Chason (*Camera Shop Clerk*), Ellis Gilbert (*Butler*), Verdie Henshaw (*Feathered Nest Sanatorium Manager*), Robert Warner (*Camera Shop Assistant Manager*), Dean Goss (*Eugene Ledbetter*), Keith V. Erickson (*Prof. Aggnout*), Thomas Danko (*Color Lab Man*), W. E. Terry Jr. (*Police Chaplain*), Ronnie Cammack (*Wendell*), Dixie M. Taylor (*Nursing Home*

453

Manager), Pearl Coffey Chason (*Nursing Home Attendant*), Amelia Parker (*Nursing Home Manageress*), David Welch (*Breen's Son*).

Produced by Lou Adler (Adler-Phillips/Lion's Gate Films) for MGM. Associate producers: Robert Eggenweiler, James Margellos. 105 min.

1971 MCCABE AND MRS. MILLER

Script: Altman, Brian McKay, from the novel *McCabe* by Edmund Naughton.
Direction: Altman.
Assistant director: Tommy Thompson.
Photography (Panavision): Vilmos Zsigmond.
Production design: Leon Ericksen.
Art direction: Phillip Thomas, Al Locatelli.
Editing: Lou Lombardo.
Music: Leonard Cohen.

Cast: Warren Beatty (*John McCabe*), Julie Christie (*Constance Miller*), René Auberjonois (*Sheehan*), Hugh Millais (*Butler*), Shelley Duvall (*Ida Coyle*), Michael Murphy (*Sears*), John Schuck (*Smalley*), Corey Fischer (*Mr. Elliott*), William Devane (*Clement Samuels*), Anthony Holland (*Ernie Hollander*), Bert Remsen (*Bart Coyle*), Keith Carradine (*Cowboy*), Jace Vander Veen (*Breed*), Manfred Shulz (*Kid*), Jackie Crossland (*Lily*), Elizabeth Murphy (*Kate*), Linda Sorenson (*Blanche*), Elizabeth Knight (*Birdie*), Maysie Hoy (*Maysie*), Linda Kupecek (*Ruth*), Janet Wright (*Eunice*), Carey Lee McKenzie (*Alma*), Rodney Gage (*Sumner Washington*), Lili Francks (*Mrs. Washington*).

Produced by David Foster and Mitchell Brower for Warner Brothers. Associate producer: Robert Eggenweiler. 121 min.

1972 IMAGES

Script and direction: Altman (with passages from *In Search of Unicorns* by Susannah York).
Photography (Panavision): Vilmos Zsigmond.
Art direction: Leon Ericksen.
Editing: Graeme Clifford.
Music: John Williams (with sounds by Stomu Yamash'ta).

Cast: Susannah York (*Cathryn*), René Auberjonois (*Hugh*), Marcel Bozzuffi (*René*), Hugh Millais (*Marcel*), Cathryn Harrison (*Susannah*), John Morley (*Old Man*).

Produced by Tommy Thompson for Lion's Gate Films/The Hemdale Group/Columbia. 101 min.

1973 THE LONG GOODBYE

Script: Leigh Brackett, from the novel by Raymond Chandler.
Direction: Altman.
Assistant director: Tommy Thompson.
Photography (Panavision): Vilmos Zsigmond.
Editing: Lou Lombardo.
Music: John Williams.

Cast: Elliott Gould (*Philip Marlowe*), Nina van Pallandt (*Eileen Wade*), Sterling Hayden (*Roger Wade*), Mark Rydell (*Marty Augustine*), Henry Gibson (*Dr. Verringer*), David Arkin (*Harry*), Jim Bouton (*Terry Lennox*), Warren Berlinger (*Morgan*), Jo Ann Brody

454

(*Jo Ann Eggenweiler*), Steve Coit (*Detective Farmer*), Jack Knight (*Mabel*), Pepe Callahan (*Pepe*), Vince Palmieri (*Vince*), Pancho Cordoba (*Doctor*), Enrique Lucero (*Jefe*), Rutanya Alda (*Rutanya Sweet*), Tammy Shaw (*Dancer*), Jack Riley (*Piano Player*), Ken Sansom (*Colony Guard*), Jerry Jones (*Detective Green*), John Davies (*Detective Dayton*), Rodney Moss (*Supermarket Clerk*), Sybil Scotford (*Real Estate Lady*), Herb Kerns (*Herbie*).

Produced by Jerry Bick and Elliot Kastner (Lion's Gate Films) for United Artists. Associate producer: Robert Eggenweiler. 112 min.

1974 THIEVES LIKE US

Script: Calder Willingham, Joan Tewkesbury, Altman, from the novel by Edward Anderson.
Direction: Altman.
Photography: Jean Boffety.
Visual consultants: Jack DeGovia, Scott Bushnell.
Editing: Lou Lombardo.
Radio research: John Dunning.

Cast: Keith Carradine (*Bowie*), Shelley Duvall (*Keechie*), John Schuck (*Chicamaw*), Bert Remsen (*T-Dub*), Louise Fletcher (*Mattie*), Ann Latham (*Lula*), Tom Skerritt (*Dee Mobley*), Al Scott (*Capt. Stammers*), John Roper (*Jasbo*), Mary Waits (*Noel*), Rodney Lee, Jr. (*James Mattingly*), William Watters (*Alvin*), Joan Tewkesbury (*Lady in Train Station*), Eleanor Matthews (*Mrs. Stammers*), Pam Warner (*Woman in Accident*), Suzanne Majure (*Coca-Cola Girl*), Walter Cooper, Lloyd Jones (*Sheriffs*).

Produced by Jerry Bick and George Litto for United Artists. Associate producers: Robert Eggenweiler, Thomas Hal Phillips. 123 min.

1974 CALIFORNIA SPLIT

Script: Joseph Walsh.
Direction: Altman.
Assistant director: Tommy Thompson.
Photography (Panavision): Paul Lohmann.
Production design: Leon Ericksen.
Editing: Lou Lombardo, assisted by Tony Lombardo and Dennis Hill.

Cast: Elliott Gould (*Charlie Waters*), George Segal (*Bill Denny*), Ann Prentiss (*Barbara Miller*), Gwen Welles (*Susan Peters*), Edward Walsh (*Lew*), Joseph Walsh (*Sparkie*), Bert Remsen ("*Helen Brown*"), Barbara London (*Lady on the Bus*), Barbara Ruick (*Reno Barmaid*), Jay Fletcher (*Robber*), Jeff Goldblum (*Lloyd Harris*), Barbara Colby (*Receptionist*), Vince Palmieri (*First Bartender*), Alyce Passman (*Go-Go Girl*), Joanne Strauss (*Mother*), Jack Riley (*Second Bartender*), Sierra Bandit (*Woman at Bar*), John Considine (*Man at Bar*), Eugene Troobnick (*Harvey*), Richard Kennedy (*Used-Car Salesman*), John Winston (*Tenor*), Bill Duffy (*Kenny*), Mike Greene (*Reno Dealer*), Tom Signorelli (*Nugie*), Sharon Compton (*Nugie's Wife*), Arnold Herzstein, Marc Cavell, Alvin Weissman, Mickey Fox, Carolyn Lohmann (*California Club Poker Players*), "Amarillo Slim" Preston, Winston Lee, Harry Drackett, Thomas Hal Phillips, Ted Say, A. J. Hood (*Reno Poker Players*).

Produced by Altman and Joseph Walsh (Won World/Persky Bright/Reno) for Columbia. Associate producer: Robert Eggenweiler. 109 min.

1975 NASHVILLE

Script: Joan Tewkesbury.
Direction: Altman.
Assistant directors: Tommy Thompson, Alan Rudolph.
Photography (Panavision): Paul Lohmann.
Editing: Sidney Levin, Dennis Hill.
Political campaign: Thomas Hal Phillips.
Songs: "200 Years" (lyrics by Henry Gibson, music by Richard Baskin), "Yes, I Do" (lyrics and music by Richard Baskin and Lily Tomlin), "Down to the River" (lyrics and music by Ronee Blakley), "Let Me Be the One" (lyrics and music by Richard Baskin), "Sing a Song" (lyrics and music by Joe Raposo), "The Heart of a Gentle Woman" (lyrics and music by Dave Peel), "Bluebird" (lyrics and music by Ronee Blakley), "The Day I Looked Jesus in the Eye" (lyrics and music by Richard Baskin and Robert Altman), "Memphis" (lyrics and music by Karen Black), "I Don't Know If I Found It in You" (lyrics and music by Karen Black), "For the Sake of the Children" (lyrics and music by Richard Baskin and Richard Reicheg), "Keep a Goin'" (lyrics by Henry Gibson, music by Richard Baskin and Henry Gibson), "Swing Low Sweet Chariot" (arrangements by Millie Clements), "Rolling Stone" (lyrics and music by Karen Black), "Honey" (lyrics and music by Keith Carradine), "Tapedeck in His Tractor (The Cowboy Song)" (lyrics and music by Ronee Blakley), "Dues" (lyrics and music by Ronee Blakley), "I Never Get Enough" (lyrics and music by Richard Baskin and Ben Raleigh), "Rose's Cafe" (lyrics and music by Allan Nicholls), "Old Man Mississippi" (lyrics and music by Juan Grizzle), "My Baby's Cookin' in Another Man's Pan" (lyrics and music by Jonnie Barnett), "One, I Love You" (lyrics and music by Richard Baskin), "I'm Easy" (lyrics and music by Keith Carradine), "It Don't Worry Me" (lyrics and music by Keith Carradine), "Since You've Gone" (lyrics and music by Garry Busey), "Trouble in the U.S.A." (lyrics and music by Arlene Barnett), "My Idaho Home" (lyrics and music by Ronee Blakley).

456

Cast: David Arkin (*Norman*), Barbara Baxley (*Lady Pearl*), Ned Beatty (*Delbert Reese*), Karen Black (*Connie White*), Ronee Blakley (*Barbara Jean*), Timothy Brown (*Tommy Brown*), Keith Carradine (*Tom Frank*), Geraldine Chaplin (*Opal*), Robert Doqui (*Wade*), Shelley Duvall (*L.A. Joan*), Allen Garfield (*Barnett*), Henry Gibson (*Haven Hamilton*), Scott Glenn (*Pfc. Glenn Kelly*), Jeff Goldblum (*Tricycle Man*), Barbara Harris (*Albuquerque*), David Hayward (*Kenny Praiser*), Michael Murphy (*John Triplette*), Allan Nicholls (*Bill*), Dave Peel (*Bud Hamilton*), Cristina Raines (*Mary*), Bert Remsen (*Star*), Lily Tomlin (*Linnea Reese*), Gwen Welles (*Sueleen Gay*), Keenan Wynn (*Mr. Green*), James Dan Calvert (*Jimmy Reese*), Donna Denton (*Donna Reese*), Merle Kilgore (*Trout*), Carol McGinnis (*Jewel*), Sheila Bailey and Patti Bryant (*Smokey Mountain Laurel*), Richard Baskin (*Frog*), Jonnie Barnett, Vassar Clements, Misty Mountain Boys, Sue Barton, Elliott Gould, Julie Christie (*Themselves*).

Produced by Altman (ABC Entertainment) for Paramount. Associate producers: Robert Eggenweiler, Scott Bushnell. 161 min.

1976 BUFFALO BILL AND THE INDIANS,
OR SITTING BULL'S HISTORY LESSON

Story and script: Alan Rudolph, Altman, based on the play *Indians* by Arthur Kopit.
Direction: Altman.
Assistant director: Tommy Thompson.

Photography (Panavision): Paul Lohmnnn.
Production design: Tony Masters.
Music: Richard Baskin.
Editing: Peter Appleton, Dennis Hill.
Costumes: Anthony Powell.

Cast: Paul Newman (*the Star*), Joel Grey (*the Producer*), Kevin McCarthy (*the Publicist*), Harvey Keitel (*the Relative*), Allan Nicholls (*the Journalist*), Geraldine Chaplin (*the Sure Shot*), John Considine (*the Sure Shot's Manager*), Robert Doqui (*the Wrangler*), Mike Kaplan (*the Treasurer*), Bert Remsen (*the Bartender*), Bonnie Leaders (*the Mezzo-Contralto*), Noelle Rogers (*the Lyric Coloratura*), Evelyn Lear (*the Lyric Soprano*), Denver Pyle (*the Indian Agent*), Frank Kaquitts (*the Indian*), Will Sampson (*the Interpreter*), Ken Krossa (*the Arenic Director*), Fred N. Larsen (*the King of the Cowboys*), Jerry and Joy Duce (*the Cowboy Trick Riders*), Alex Green and Gary MacKenzie (*the Mexican Whip and Fast Draw Act*), Humphrey Gratz (*the Old Soldier*), Pat McCormick (*the President of the United States*), Shelley Duvall (*the First Lady*), Burt Lancaster (*the Legend Maker*). With people from the Stoney Indian Reserve.

Produced by Robert Altman for Dino De Laurentiis Corporation-Lion's Gate Films/Talent Associates Norton Simon, Inc./United Artists. Executive producer: David Susskind. Associate producers: Robert Eggenweiler, Scott Bushnell, Jac Cashin. 123 min.

1977 THREE WOMEN
Script and direction: Altman.
Photography (Panavision): Chuck Rosher.
Art direction: James D. Vance.
Visual consultant: J. Allen Highfill.
Murals: Bodhi Wind.
Editing: Dennis Hill.
Music: Gerald Busby.

Cast: Shelley Duvall (*Millie Lammoreaux*), Sissy Spacek (*Pinky Rose*), Janice Rule (*Willie Hart*), Robert Fortier (*Edgar Hart*), Ruth Nelson (*Mrs. Rose*), John Cromwell (*Mr. Rose*), Sierra Pecheur (*Ms. Bunweill*), Craig Richard Nelson (*Dr. Maas*), Maysie Hoy (*Doris*), Belita Moreno (*Alcira*), Leslie Ann Hudson (*Polly*), Patricia Ann Hudson (*Peggy*), Beverly Ross (*Deidre*), John Davey (*Dr. Norton*).

Produced by Robert Altman for Lion's Gate Films. Twentieth Century-Fox. Associate producers: Robert Eggenweiler and Scott Bushnell. 124 min.

1978 A WEDDING
Script: John Considine, Patricia Resnick, Allan Nicholls, Altman, from a story by Considine and Altman.
Direction: Altman.
Assistant director: Tommy Thompson.
Photography (Panavision): Charles Rosher.
Editing: Tony Lombardo.
Music: John Hotchkiss.
Song: "Bird on a Wire" by Leonard Cohen.
Bridal consultant: Carson, Pirie, Scott & Co., Chicago.

Cast: The Groom's Family: Lillian Gish (*Nettie Sloan*), Ruth Nelson (*Beatrice Sloan*

457

Cory), Ann Ryerson (*Victoria Cory*), Desi Arnaz Jr. (*Dino Corelli, the Groom*), Belita Moreno (*Daphne Corelli*), Vittorio Gassman (*Luigi Corelli*), Nina van Pallandt (*Regina Corelli*), Virginia Vestoff (*Clarice Sloan*), Dina Merrill (*Antoinette Sloan Goddard*), Pat McCormick (*Mackenzie Goddard*), Luigi Proietti (*Little Dino*).

The Bride's Family: Carol Burnett (*Tulip Brenner*), Paul Dooley (*Snooks Brenner*), Amy Stryker (*Muffin Brenner, the Bride*), Mia Farrow (*Buffy Brenner*), Dennis Christopher (*Hughie Brenner*), Mary Seibel (*Aunt Marge Spar*), Margaret Ladd (*Ruby Spar*), Gerald Busby (*David Ruteledge*), Peggy Ann Garner (*Candice Ruteledge*), Mark R. Deming (*Matthew Ruteledge*), David Brand, Chris Brand, Amy Brand, Jenny Brand, Jeffrey Jones, Jay D. Jones, Courtney MacArthur, Paul D. Keller III (*the Ruteledge Children*).

The Corelli House Staff: Cedric Scott (*Randolph*), Robert Fortier (*Jim Habor, the Gardener*), Maureen Steindler (*Libby Clinton, the Cook*).

The Wedding Staff: Geraldine Chaplin (*Rita Billingsley*), Mona Abboud (*Melba Lear*), Viveca Lindfors (*Ingrid Hellstrom*), Lauren Hutton (*Flo Farmer*), Allan Nicholls (*Jake Jacobs*), Maysie Hoy (*Casey*), John Considine (*Jeff Kuykendall*), Patricia Resnick (*Redford*), Margery Bond (*Lombardo*), Dennis Franz (*Koons*), Harold C. Johnson (*Oscar Edwards*), Alexander Sopenar (*Victor*).

The Friends and Guests: Howard Duff (*Dr. Jules Meecham*), John Cromwell (*Bishop Martin*), Bert Remsen (*William Williamson*), Pamela Dawber (*Tracy Parrell*), Gavan O'Hirlihy (*Wilson Briggs*), Craig Richard Nelson (*Capt. Reedley Roots*), Jeffry S. Perry (*Bunky Lemay*), Marta Heflin (*Shelby Munker*), Lesley Rogers (*Rosie Bean*), Timothy Thomerson (*Russell Bean*), Beverly Ross (*Nurse Janet Schulman*), David Fitzgerald (*Kevin Clinton*), Susan Kendall Newman (*Chris Clinton*).

The Musicians: Ellie Albers (*Gypsy Violinist*), Tony Llorens (*at the Piano-Bar*), Chuck Banks' Big Band with Chris La Kome (*in the Ballroom*).

Produced by Robert Altman for Lion's Gate Films. Twentieth Century-Fox. Executive producer: Tommy Thompson. Associate producers: Robert Eggenweiler, Scott Bushnell. 124 min.

1979 QUINTET

Script: Altman, Frank Barhydt, Patricia Resnick, from a story by Altman, Resnick, Lionel Chetwynd.
Direction: Altman.
Assistant director: Tommy Thompson.
Photography: Jean Boffety.
Production design: Leon Erickson.
Editing: Dennis Hill.
Music: Tom Pierson.

Cast: Paul Newman (*Essex*), Fernando Rey (*Grigor*), Bibi Anderson (*Ambrosia*), Vittorio Gassman (*St. Christopher*), Nina van Pallandt (*Deuca*), Brigitte Fossey (*Vivia*), David Langton (*Redstone*), Craig Nelson (*Goldstar*), Tom Hill (*Francha*).

Produced by Altman for Lion's Gate Films. Twentieth Century-Fox. Associate producer: Allan Nicholls. 118 min.

1979 A PERFECT COUPLE

Script: Robert Altman and Allan Nicholls.
Direction: Altman.

Assistant director: Tommy Thompson.
Photography: Edmond L. Koons.
Set decoration: Leon Erickson.
Editing: Tony Lombardo.
Music: Allan Nicholls, Tom Pierson.

Cast: Paul Dooley (*Alex Theodopoulos*), Marta Heflin (*Sheila Shea*), Titos Vandis (*Alex's Father*), Belito Moreno (*Eleausa*), Henry Gibson (*Fred Batt*), Dimitra Arliss (*Athena*), Allan Nicholls (*Dana 115*), Ann Ryerson (*Skye 147*), Dennis Franz (*Costa*), Margery Bond (*Wilma*), Ted Neeley (*Teddy*), Fred Bier, Jette Sear (*the Imperfect Couple*).

Produced by Robert Altman, Tommy Thompson, Robert Eggenweiler, Scott Bushnell for Lion's Gate Films. Twentieth Century-Fox. 110 min.

1980 HEALTH

Script: Altman, Frank Barhydt, Paul Dooley.
Direction: Altman.
Assistant director: Tommy Thompson.
Production manager: Robert Eggenweiler.
Photography (Panavision): Edmond L. Koons.
Art direction: Robert Quinn.
Editing: Dennis Hill, Tom Benko.

Cast: Carol Burnett (*Gloria Burbank*), Lauren Bacall (*Esther Brill*), James Garner (*Harry Wolff*), Glenda Jackson (*Isabella Garnell*), Diane Stilwell (*Willow Wertz*), Henry Gibson (*Bobby Hammer*), Paul Dooley (*Dr. Gill Gainey*), Donald Moffat (*Col. Cody*), Alfre Woodard (*Sally Benbow*), Ann Ryerson (*Dr. Ruth Ann Jackie*), Robert Fortier (*Chief of Security*), Allan Nicholls (*Jake Jacobs*), MacIntyre Dixon (*Fred Munson*), Dick Cavett, Dinah Shore (*Themselves*).

Produced by Altman, Tommy Thompson, Scott Bushnell, Wolf Kroeger for Lion's Gate Films. Twentieth Century-Fox. 96 min.

1980 POPEYE

Script: Jules Feiffer, based on the characters by E. C. Segar.
Direction: Altman.
Photography (Panavision): Giuseppe Rotunno.
Production design: Wolf Kroeger.
Location manager: Scott Bushnell.
Editing: John W. Holmes, Davie Simmons.
Supervising editor: Tony Lombardo.
Music and lyrics: Harry Nilsson (additional score by Tom Pierson).

Cast: Robin Williams (*Popeye*), Shelley Duvall (*Olive Oyl*), Ray Walston (*Poopdeck Pappy*), Paul Dooley (*Wimpey*), Paul L. Smith (*Bluto*), Richard Libertini (*Geezil*), Donald Moffat (*Taxman*), MacIntyre Dixon (*Cole Oyl*), Roberta Maxwell (*Nana Oyl*), Donovan Scott (*Caster Oyl*), Allan Nicholls (*Rough House*), Wesley Ivan Hurt (*Swee' Pea*), Bill Irwin (*Ham Gravy*), Robert Fortier (*Bill Barnacle*), Linda Hunt (*Mrs. Oxheart*), Carlo Pellegrini (*Swifty*), Dennis Franz (*Spike*), David Arkin (*Mailman/Policeman*).

Produced by Robert Evans for Paramount Pictures and Walt Disney Productions. Associate producer: Scott Bushnell. 111 min.

459

1982 COME BACK TO THE FIVE AND DIME, JIMMY DEAN, JIMMY DEAN

Script: Ed Graczyk, based on his play.
Direction: Altman.
Photography: Pierre Mignot.
Production design: David Cropman.
Editing: Jason Rosenfield.
Music: Allan Nicholls.

Cast: Sandy Dennis (*Mona*), Cher (*Sissy*), Karen Black (*Joanne*), Sudie Bond (*Juanita*), Marta Heflin (*Edna Louise*), Kathy Bates (*Stella Mae*), Mark Patton (*Joe*).

Produced by Scott Bushnell for Sandcastle 5 Productions/Mark Goodson/Viacom. 102 min.

1983 STREAMERS

Script: David Rabe, from his play.
Direction: Altman.
Assistant director: Allan Nichols.
Photography: Pierre Mignot.
Art direction: Stephen Altman.
Editor: Norman C. Smith.

Cast: Mitchell Lichenstein (*Richie*), Matthew Modine (*Billy*), David Alan Grier (*Roger*), Michael Wright (*Carlyle*), Guy Boyd (*Rooney*), George Dzundza (*Cokes*), Albert Macklin (*Martin*).

Produced by Altman and Nick J. Mileti for Mileti Productions/United Artists. Associate producer: Scott Bushnell. 118 min.

460

1984 O. C. AND STIGGS

Script: Donald Cantrell and Ted Mann.
Direction: Altman.
Photography (Panavision): Pierre Mignot
Production design: Scott Bushnell.
Editing: Elizabeth King
Music: King Sunny Adé and his African Beats

Cast: Daniel H. Jenkins (*O. C.*), Neill Barry (*Stiggs*), Paul Dooly (*Randall Schwab*), Jane Curtin (*Elinore Schwab*), Martin Mull (*Pat Colletti*), Dennis Hopper (*Sponson*), Ray Walston (*Gramps*), Louis Nye (*Garth Sloan*), Melvin Van Peebles (*Wino Bob*), Tina Louise (*Florence Beaugereaux*), Cynthia Nixon (*Michelle*), John Cryer (*Randall Schwab, Jr.*), Donald May (*Jack Stiggs*), Carla Borelli (*Stella Stiggs*)

Produced by Robert Altman and Peter Newman for MGM/UA. Associate Producer: Scott Bushnell. 109 min.

1984 SECRET HONOR

Script: Donald Freed and Arnold M. Stone.
Direction: Altman.
Assistant director: Allan Nicholls.
Photography: Pierre Mignot.
Art direction: Stephen Altman.

Editing: Juliet Weber.
Music: George Burt.
  Cast: Philip Baker Hall (*Richard M. Nixon*).
  Produced by Altman and Scott Bushnell in association with the University of Michigan Department of Communication and the Los Angeles Actors' Studio/Cinecom. 85 min.

1985 FOOL FOR LOVE
Script: Sam Shepard, based on his play.
Direction: Altman.
Photography (Panavision): Pierre Mignot.
Production design: Stephen Altman.
Unit production manager: Allan Nicholls.
Editing: Luce Grunenwaldt and Steve Dunn.
Music: George Burt.
  Cast: Sam Shepard (*Eddie*), Kim Basinger (*May*), Harry Dean Stanton (*Old Man*), Randy Quaid (*Martin*), Martha Crawford (*May's Mother*), Louise Egolf (*Eddie's Mother*), Sura Cox (*Teenage May*), Jonathan Skinner (*Teenage Eddie*), April Russell (*Young May*), Deborah McNaughton (*The Countess*), Lon Hill (*Mr. Valdes*).
  Produced by Menahem Golan and Yoram Globus for Cannon Films. Associate producers: Scott Bushnell and Mati Raz. 105 min.

1987 BEYOND THERAPY
Script: Christopher Durang and Altman, based on the play by Durang.
Direction: Altman.
Photography: Pierre Mignot.
Production design: Stephen Altman.
Editing: Steve Dunn.
Music: Gabriel Yared.
  Cast: Julie Hagerty (*Prudence*), Jeff Goldblum (*Bruce*), Glenda Jackson (*Charlotte*), Tom Conti (*Stuart*), Christopher Guest (*Bob*), Geneviève Page (*Zizi*), Cris Campion (*Andrew*), Sandrine Dumas (*Cindy*), Bertrand Bonvoisin (*Le Gérant*), Nicole Evans (*the Cashier*), Louis-Marie Taillefer (*the Chef*), Matthew Lesniak (*Mr. Bean*), Laure Killing (*Charlie*).
  Produced by Steven M. Haft for New World Pictures. Associate producer: Scott Bushnell. 93 min.

Between 1985 and 1988, Altman made a number of television movies, including *The Laundromat* (1985), *The Dumb Waiter* (1987), *Basements* (1987), *Tanner '88* (1988, multipart series), and *The Caine Mutiny Court-Martial* (1988).

1990 VINCENT AND THEO
Script: Julian Mitchell.
Direction: Altman.
Photography: Jean Lépine.
Production design: Stephen Altman.
Editing: François Coispeau and Geraldine Peroni.
Music: Gabriel Yared.

461

Cast: Tim Roth (*Vincent van Gogh*), Paul Rhys (*Theodore van Gogh*), Jip Wijngaarden (*Sien Hoornik*), Johanna Ter Steege (*Jo Bonger*), Wladimir Yordanoff (*Paul Gauguin*), Jean-Pierre Cassel (*Dr. Paul Gachet*), Bernadette Giraud (*Marguerite Gachet*), Adrian Brine (*Uncle Cent*), Jean-François Perrier (*Leon Bouscod*), Vincent Vallier (*Rene Valadon*), Hans Kesting (*Andries Bonger*), Anne Canovas (*Marie*).

Produced by Ludi Boeken (Belbo Films) for Arena Films. Executive Producer: David Conroy. 138 min (approx).

1992 THE PLAYER

Script: Michael Tolkin from his novel.
Direction: Altman.
Photography: Jean Lépine.
Production design: Stephen Altman.
Editing: Geraldine Peroni.
Music: Thomas Newman.

Cast: Tim Robbins (*Griffin Mill*), Greta Scacchi (*June Gudmundsdottir*), Fred Ward (*Walter Stuckel*), Whoopi Goldberg (*Detective Susan Avery*), Peter Gallagher (*Larry Levy*), Brion James (*Joel Levison*), Cynthia Stevenson (*Bonnie Sherow*), Vincent D'Onofrio (*David Kahane*), Dean Stockwell (*Andy Civella*), Richard E. Grant (*Tom Oakley*), Sydney Pollack (*Dick Mellen*), Vincent D'Onofrio (*David Kahane*), Lyle Lovett (*Detective DeLongpre*), Dina Merrill (*Celia*).

Produced by David Brown, Scott Bushnell, Michael Tolkin, and Nick Wechsler (Guild/Spelling Entertainment) for Avenue Picture Productions. Executive Producers: Cary Brokaw and William S. Gilmore 123 min.

1993 SHORT CUTS

Script: Robert Altman, Frank Barhydt, from short stories by Raymond Carver.
Direction: Altman.
Photography (Panavision): Walt Lloyd.
Production design: Stephen Altman.
Editing: Geraldine Peroni.
Music: Gavin Friday and Mark Isham.

Cast: Andie MacDowell (*Ann Finnigan*), Bruce Davison (*Howard Finnigan*), Jack Lemmon (*Paul Finnigan*), Lane Cassidy (*Casey Finnigan*), Julianne Moore (*Marian Wyman*), Matthew Modine (*Dr. Ralph Wyman*), Anne Archer (*Claire Kane*), Fred Ward (*Stuart Kane*), Jennifer Jason Leigh (*Lois Kaiser*), Chris Penn (*Jerry Kaiser*), Joseph C. Hopkins (*Joe Kaiser*), Josette Maccario (*Josette Kaiser*), Lili Taylor (*Honey Bush*), Robert Downey Jr. (*Bill Bush*), Madeleine Stowe (*Sherri Shepard*), Tim Robbins (*Gene Shepard*), Cassie Friel (*Sandy Shepard*), Dustin Friel (*Will Shepard*), Austin Friel (*Austin Shepard*), Lily Tomlin (*Doreen Piggot*), Tom Waits (*Earl Piggot*), Frances McDormand (*Betty Weathers*), Peter Gallagher (*Stormy Weathers*), Jarrett Lennon (*Chad Weathers*), Annie Ross (*Tess Trainer*), Lori Singer (*Zoe Trainer*), Lyle Lovett (*Andy Bitkower*), Buck Henry (*Gordon Johnson*), Huey Lewis (*Vern Miller*), Danny Darst (*Aubrey Bell*), Margery Bond (*Dora Willis*), Robert DoQui (*Knute Willis*), Darnell Williams (*Joe Robbins*), Michael Beach (*Jim Stone*), Andi Chapman (*Harriet Stone*), Deborah Falconer (*Barbara*), Susie Cusack (*Nancy*), Charles Rocket (*Wally Littleton*), Jane Alden (*Mrs. Schwarzmeier*), Christian Altman (*Jimmy Miller*), Willie Marlett (*Jimmy's Friend*), Dirk Blocker (*Diner Customer*), Alex Trebek (*Himself*), Jerry Dunphy (*Himself*).

Produced by Cary Brokaw, Mike E. Kaplan, David Levy (Fine Line Features/Spelling Entertainment) for Avenue Pictures Productions. Executive Producer: Scott Bushnell. 187 min.

1994 PRÊT-À-PORTER

Script: Robert Altman and Barbara Shulgasser.
Direction: Altman.
Photography (Panavision): Jean Lépine and Pierre Mignot.
Production design: Stephen Altman.
Editing: Suzy Elmige and Geraldine Peroni.
Music: Michael Legrand.

Cast: Marcello Mastroianni (*Sergei [Sergio]*), Sophia Loren (*Isabella de la Fontaine*), Jean-Pierre Cassel (*Olivier de la Fontaine*), Kim Basinger (*Kitty Potter*), Chiara Mastroianni (*Sophie Choiset*), Stephen Rea (*Milo O'Brannigan*) Anouk Aimée (*Simone Lowenthal*), Rupert Everett (*Jack Lowenthal*), Rossy de Palma (*Pilar*), Tara Leon (*Kiki Simpson*), Georgianna Robertson (*Dane Simpson*), Lili Taylor (*Fiona Ulrich*), Ute Lemper (*Albertine*), Forest Whitaker (*Cy Bianco*), Tim Robbins (*Joe Flynn*), Julia Roberts (*Anne Eisenhower*), Lauren Bacall (*Slim Chrysler*), Lyle Lovett (*Clint Lammeraux*), Tracy Ullman (*Nina Scant*), Sally Kellerman (*Sissy Wanamaker*), Linda Hunt (*Regina Krumm*), Danny Aiello (*Major Hamilton*), Teri Garr (*Louise Hamilton*).

Produced by Robert Altman, Scott Bushnell, and Jon Kilik for Miramax Films. Executive Producers: Ian Jessel, Angelo Pastore, Bob Weinstein, and Harvey Weinstein. 133 min.

463

1996 KANSAS CITY

Script: Robert Altman and Frank Barhydt.
Direction: Altman.
Photography: Oliver Stapleton.
Production design: Stephen Altman.
Editing: Geraldine Peroni.
Music: James Carter, Craig Handy, David Murray, Jusha Redman, Jess Davis,
   David Newman, Jr., and many more.

Cast: Jennifer Jason Leigh (*Blondie O'Hara*), Miranda Richardson (*Carolyn Stilton*), Harry Belafonte (*Seldom Seen*), Michael Murphy (*Henry Stilton*), Dermot Mulroney (*Johnny O'Hara*), Steve Buscemi (*Johnny Flynn*), Brooke Smith (*Babe Flynn*), Jane Adams (*Nettie Bolt*), Jeff Feringa (*Addie Parker*), A.C. Tony Smith (*Sheepshan Red*), Martin Martin (*"Blue" Green*), Albert J. Burnes (*Charlie Parker*), Ajia Mignon Johnson (*Pearl Cummings*), Tim Snay (*Rally Speaker*), Tawanna Benbow(*Rose*), Calvin Pritner (*Governor Park*), Jerry Fornelli (*Tom Pendergast*), Michael Omstein (*Jackie Ciro*), Michael Garozzo (*Charlie Gargotta*), Joe Digirolamo (*John Lazia*), John Durbin (*Gas Station Attendant*), Gina Belafonte (*Hey-Hey Club Hostess*), Nancy Marcy (*Telegraph Operator*), Buck Baker (*Train Station Agent*), Dorothy Kemp-Clark (*Mrs. Bruce*), Edward Penninaton (*Governor Park's Butler*), Robert Elliott (*Lazia Man #1*), Marlon Hofflnan (*Lazia Man #2*), Patrick Oldani (*Lazia Man #3*), Philip Trovato (*Lazia Man #4*).

Produced by Robert Altman, Matthew Seig, and David C. Thomas (CiBy 2000) for Sandcastle 5 Productions. Executive Producer: Scott Bushnell. 115 min.

1998 THE GINGERBREAD MAN

Script: Robert Altman from a story by John Grisham.
Direction: Robert Altman.
Photography (Panavision): Changwei Gu.
Production design: Stephen Altman.
Editing: Geraldine Peroni.
Music: Mark Isham.

Cast: Kenneth Branagh (*Rick Magruder*), Embeth Davidtz (*Mallory Doss*), Daryl Hannah (*Lois*), Mae Whitman (*Libby*), Robert Downey, Jr. (*Clyde*), Robert Duvall (*Dixon Doss*), Tom Berenger (*Peter Randall*), Famke Janssen (*Leeanne Magruder*), Mae Whitman (*Libby Magruder*), Jesse James (*Jeff Magruder*), Clyde Hayes (*Carl Alden*).

Produced by Jeremy Tannenbaum and David Levy (Polygram Filmed Entertainment) for Ascot Elite Entertainment Group. Executive Producers: Todd R. Baker, Mark Burg, and Glen Tobias. 114 min.

1999 COOKIE'S FORTUNE

Script: Anne Rapp.
Direction: Altman.
Photography: Toyomichi Kurita.
Production design: Stephen Altman.
Editing: Abraham Lim.
Music: David A. Stewart.

Cast: Glenn Close (*Camille Orcutt*), Julianne Moore (*Cora Duvall*), Chris O'Donnell (*Jason Brown*), Liv Tyler (*Emma Duvall*), Charles Dutton (*Willis Richland*), Patricia Neal (*Jewel Mae "Cookie" Orcutt*), Ned Beatty (*Lester Boyle*), Lyle Lovett (*Manny Hood*), Courtney B. Vance (*Otis Tucker*), Donald Moffat (*Jack Palmer*).

Produced by Robert Altman, David Levy, James McLindon, Ernst Etchie Stroh (Moonstone Entertainment) for October Films. Executive producer: Willi Bär. 117 min.

INDEX

467

469

471

477

480